CENTURY 21

Computer Applications & Keyboarding

SEVENTH EDITION

Jack P. Hoggatt, Ed.D.
Professor of Business Communication and Administrative Management
University of Wisconsin
Eau Claire (WI)

Jon A. Shank, Ed.D.
Professor of Education
Robert Morris College
Moon Township (PA)

Jerry W. Robinson, Ed.D.
Former Keyboarding Instructor
Moeller High School
Cincinnati (OH)

This publication is dedicated to the memory of two Keyboarding pioneers, Dr. T. James Crawford and Dr. Jerry W. Robinson. Dr. Crawford, who passed away on August 15, 2000, was Professor Emeritus at Indiana University, Bloomington, Indiana, and a 50-year author on *Century 21 Keyboarding*. Dr. Robinson, a noted business educator, publisher, and *Century 21* author, passed away in 1997. Both men were visionaries in the field of business education. Their research contributed to the development of learning principles that have guided more than 75 million students and will continue to have an impact on learners for decades to come.

Australia • Canada • Mexico • Singapore • Spain • United Kingdom • United States

Century 21 Computer Applications & Keyboarding
by Hoggatt, Shank, & Robinson

Executive Editor:
Karen Schmohe

Project Manager/ Production Manager:
Jane Congdon

Editor:
Kim Kusnerak

Technology Project Manager:
Gayle Statman

Technology Editor:
Mike Jackson

Consulting Editors:
Penworthy Learning Systems
Becky E. Peveler
Linda Allen, FSCreations

Channel Coordinator:
Nancy Long

Marketing Coordinator:
Cira Brown

Manufacturing Manager:
Carol Chase

Art and Design Coordinator:
Michelle Kunkler

Cover/Internal Design:
Ann Small, a small design studio

Cover/Internal Illustration:
Jeffrey Pelo

Photo Stylist:
Fred M. Middendorf

Compositor:
D&G, Limited, LLC

Printer:
Quebecor World Versailles

ISBN: 0-538-69152-2

Printed in the United States of America
3 4 5 6 7 8 9 10 11 12 13 14
09 08 07 06 05 04 03

For more information, contact
South-Western Educational Publishing
5101 Madison Road
Cincinnati, OH 45227-1490.
Or you can visit our internet site at
www.swep.com

Library of Congress Cataloging-in-Publication Data
Hoggatt, Jack.
Century 21 computer applications & keyboarding/Jack P. Hoggatt, Jon A. Shank; contributing authors, Dorinda Clippinger, Lisa J. Karr.
p. cm.
Includes index.
ISBN 0-538-69152-2 (alk. paper)
1. Keyboarding—Juvenile literature. [1. Keyboarding.] I. Shank, Jon A.

QA76.9.K48 H64 2001 00-041332
652.3—dc21

Additional credits appear on page 528.

CENTURY 21

Computer Applications & Keyboarding 7E

Use the following materials to customize your course and increase your students' skills and knowledge.

KEYBOARDING SOFTWARE

- ***MicroType Multimedia*** Lessons cover alphabetic, numeric, skill building, and keypad instruction. Graphics, games, audio, video, and word processor with timer. Available for Windows and Macintosh.
- ***Quick Check*** Assessment software that checks documents and timed writings from ***Century 21*** keyed in a built-in word processor. Available for Windows and Macintosh.
- ***CheckPro*** New to this edition, this checking software works with commercial word processing software. Available for Windows.
- ***MicroPace Pro*** Diagnoses errors and focuses students on areas that need improvement. Paced and timed writings, drills, and practices. Available for Windows and Macintosh.
- ***KeyChamp*** Develops speed by analyzing students' two-stroke key combinations (digraphs) and recommending speed-building drills. Available for Windows and Macintosh.
- ***Skillbusters*** An interactive mystery game that builds speed and accuracy. Clues surface only after students achieve keyboarding goals. Available for Windows and Macintosh.

WORD PROCESSING SIMULATIONS

- ***The Candidate: Beginning Simulation*** Develop word processing skills while formatting letters, memos, tables, press releases, and reports. Softcover text and CD available together or separately.
- ***SBI: Advanced Simulation*** Reinforce word processing skills using letters, memos, reports, tables, programs, and newsletters. Softcover text and CD available together or separately.
- ***Line Rollering*** Students complete keyboarding, alphabetizing, computation, and proofreading tasks as an assistant for an in-line skating club. Simulation is available with optional data disk.
- ***River Oaks Mall*** Students prepare and format documents in their jobs at River Oaks Mall. Simulation is available with optional data disk.

INTEGRATED APPLICATIONS

- ***Sports Connection Integrated Simulation*** Reinforces essential application skills for the Microsoft Office 2000 suite! Softcover text and CD available together or separately.
- ***Integrated Business Projects*** Fun, applications-oriented text that reinforces the major office applications found in suite software. Hardcover text and data disk available together or separately.
- ***Cyberstop.com*** Work through a sequence of word processing, voice technology, spreadsheet, database, desktop publishing, and telecommunications activities at this cyber business.

SPEECH RECOGNITION

Learn the fundamentals of continuous speech recognition and achieve speech-writing proficiency of 110-150 words per minute with 95-99% accuracy.

- *L&H® VoiceXpress™ for the Office Professional* (download available at www.swep.com/ebooks)
- *IBM® ViaVoice™ for the Office Professional*
- *Dragon® NaturallySpeaking™ for the Office Professional*

SPANISH KEYBOARDING

Designed for the user who wants to learn keyboarding, but is more comfortable reading Spanish. All instructions are written in Spanish, allowing the user to focus on keyboarding rather than language translation. The lessons, skill checks, and assessment exercises themselves are still in English.

- *Digitacion para el dominio de la computadora* (*Keyboarding for Computer Success*)

MOUS CERTIFICATION

Master all of the key functions of Microsoft Word on both the Core and Expert levels.

- *MOUS Certification Review, Microsoft Word 2000* Text/CD Package

CHOICE + COVERAGE = FLEXIBILITY

Arts & Literature

CYCLE 1

Lessons 1-40

- Review Letter Keys
- Build Keyboarding Skill
- Review Figure Keys
- Build Keyboarding Skill
- Learn/Review Symbol Keys
- Build Keyboarding Skill
- Learn to Format Memos and E-mail
- Learn to Format Unbound Reports
- Learn to Format Personal-Business Letters
- Learn to Format Tables
- Prepare for Document Formatting Assessment
- Assessing Document Formatting Skills
- Communication Skills 1-5
- Word Processing 1-4
- Skill Builder 1-2
- Learn Numeric Keypad Operation
- Your Perspective

Social Studies

CYCLE 2

Lessons 41-75

- Building Basic Skill
- Improving E-mail and Memo Formatting Skills
- Improve Report Formatting Skills
- Building Basic Skill
- Improving Letter Formatting Skills
- Improving Table Formatting Skills
- *HPJ Communication Specialists: A Workplace Simulation*
- Preparing for Assessment
- Assessing Document Formatting Skills
- Communication Skills 6-8
- Word Processing 5-8
- Skill Builder 3
- Your Perspective

Science & Math

CYCLE 3

Lessons 76-111

- Enhancing Correspondence Formatting Skill
- Improving Report Formatting Skills
- Improving Table Formatting Skills
- Building Basic Skill
- Creating Employment Documents
- *TSEA: A Science Conference Simulation*
- Preparing for Assessment
- Assessing Document Formatting Skills
- Communication Skills 9-11
- Word Processing 9-11
- Skill Builder 4-6
- Your Perspective

Environment & Health

CYCLE 4

Lessons 112-150

- Processing Business Correspondence
- Building Basic Skill
- Formatting Column Documents
- Processing Worksheets
- Building Basic Skills
- Learn to Create a Business Plan
- *Salk Alumni Association: A Class Reunion Simulation*
- Preparing for Assessment
- Assessing Information Processing Skills
- Communication Skills 12-14
- Word Processing 12-14
- Skill Builder 7-8
- Your Perspective

Technology

COMPUTER APPS

- Using Help
- Database Overview
- Database Applications 1, Developing Database Skills
- Database Applications 2, Expanding Database Skills
- Spreadsheet Applications 1, Extending Spreadsheet Skills
- Spreadsheet Applications 2, Enhancing Spreadsheet Skills
- Creating Electronic Presentations
- *"Hoops": A Workplace Simulation*
- Speech Recognition
- Searching the Web
- Designing Web Pages

WORD PROCESSING 3

ACTIVITY 1

Select

1. Read the copy at the right.
2. Learn how to select text using your wp software.
3. Open file *CD-WP3ACT1*.
4. Select text and italicize, underline, and bold the copy as shown at the right.
5. Select and delete the semicolon and last six words of line 4.

Save as: *WP3ACT1*

Use the mouse and/or various key combinations to **select** (highlight) text, on which various operations may be performed.

Once selected, the text can be bolded, italicized, underlined, deleted, copied, moved, printed, saved, etc.

1. You will need to know how to **bold**, *italicize*, and underline for the exam.
2. Have you read *The Grapes of Wrath* by **John Steinbeck**?
3. Rebecca Smith is employed in the office of **Market & Johnson**.
4. Henry W. Longfellow wrote *Ballads*; Oliver Wendell Holmes wrote *Old Ironsides*.
5. Tanya misspelled *congratulations* and *italicized* on the quiz.

Dedicated Word Processing pages throughout

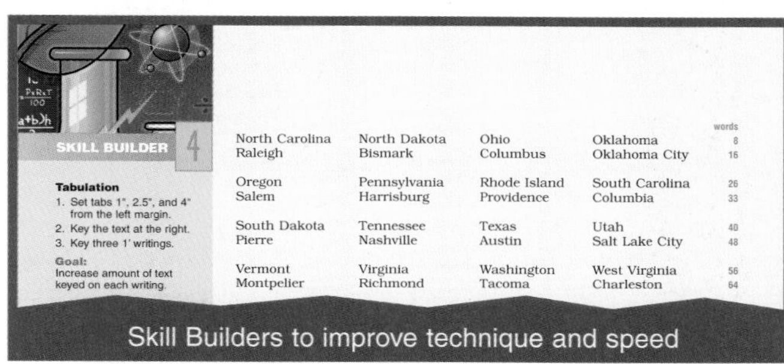
SKILL BUILDER 4

Tabulation

1. Set tabs 1", 2.5", and 4" from the left margin.
2. Key the text at the right.
3. Key three 1' writings.

Goal: Increase amount of text keyed on each writing.

				words
North Carolina Raleigh	North Dakota Bismark	Ohio Columbus	Oklahoma Oklahoma City	8 16
Oregon Salem	Pennsylvania Harrisburg	Rhode Island Providence	South Carolina Columbia	26 33
South Dakota Pierre	Tennessee Nashville	Texas Austin	Utah Salt Lake City	40 48
Vermont Montpelier	Virginia Richmond	Washington Tacoma	West Virginia Charleston	56 64

Skill Builders to improve technique and speed

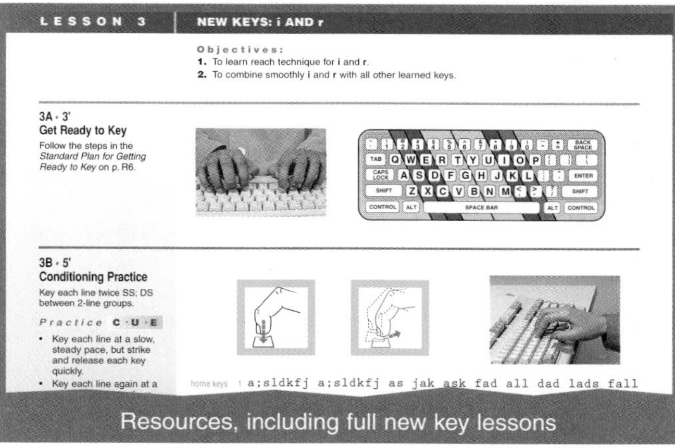
LESSON 3 NEW KEYS: i AND r

Objectives:

1. To learn reach technique for i and r.
2. To combine smoothly i and r with all other learned keys.

3A • 3'
Get Ready to Key
Follow the steps in the *Standard Plan for Getting Ready to Key* on p. R6.

3B • 5'
Conditioning Practice
Key each line twice SS; DS between 2-line groups.

Practice C·U·E

- Key each line at a slow, steady pace, but strike and release each key quickly.
- Key each line again at a

home keys 1 a;sldkfj a;sldkfj as jak ask fad all dad lads fall

Resources, including full new key lessons

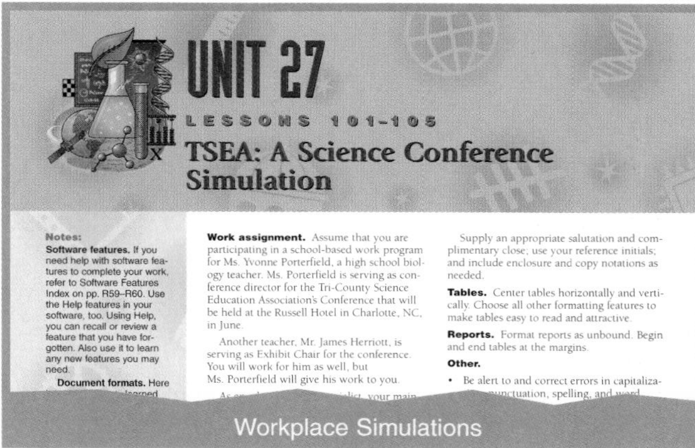
UNIT 27

LESSONS 101-105

TSEA: A Science Conference Simulation

Notes:

Software features. If you need help with software features to complete your work, refer to Software Features Index on pp. R59–R60. Use the Help features in your software, too. Using Help, you can recall or review a feature that you have forgotten. Also use it to learn any new features you may need.

Document formats. Here

Work assignment. Assume that you are participating in a school-based work program for Ms. Yvonne Porterfield, a high school biology teacher. Ms. Porterfield is serving as conference director for the Tri-County Science Education Association's Conference that will be held at the Russell Hotel in Charlotte, NC, in June.

Another teacher, Mr. James Herriott, is serving as Exhibit Chair for the conference. You will work for him as well, but Ms. Porterfield will give his work to you.

Supply an appropriate salutation and complimentary close; use your reference initials; and include enclosure and copy notations as needed.

Tables. Center tables horizontally and vertically. Choose all other formatting features to make tables easy to read and attractive.

Reports. Format reports as unbound. Begin and end tables at the margins.

Other.

- Be alert to and correct errors in capitalization, spelling, and

Workplace Simulations

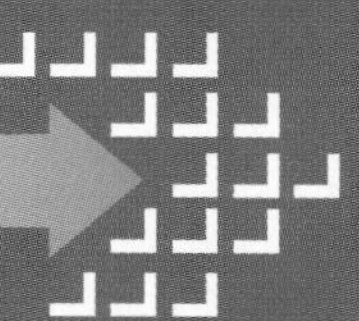

FOUNDATIONS OF INSTRUCTION

Lesson **activities** are labeled.

Icons identify timings checked in ***MicroPace Pro*** and **difficulty** of each timing.

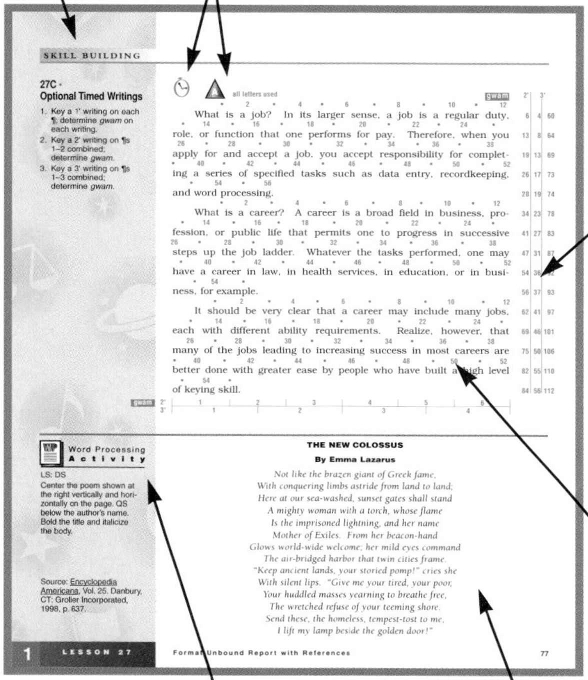

Vertical scales measure gross words a minute for specific timings.

Superior counts help students to calculate characters keyed.

Cycle is identified on every page.

Optional **Word Processing Activities** offer more practice.

Source documents reflect cross-curricular content.

Activities build **proofreading skills**.

Special pages provide opportunities to improve **communication skills**.

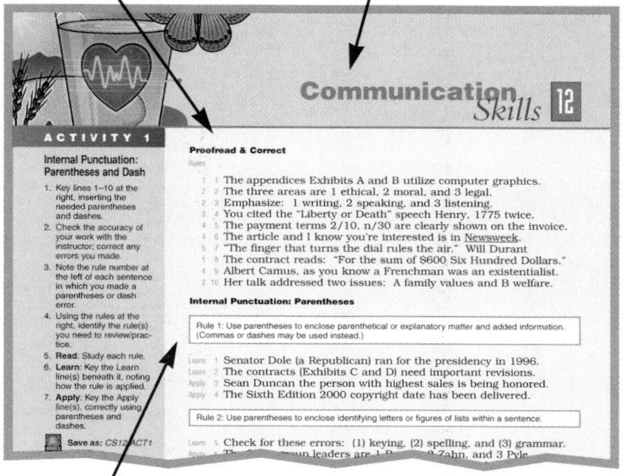

Rules are stated before exercises.

Format Guides give overviews of document formats.

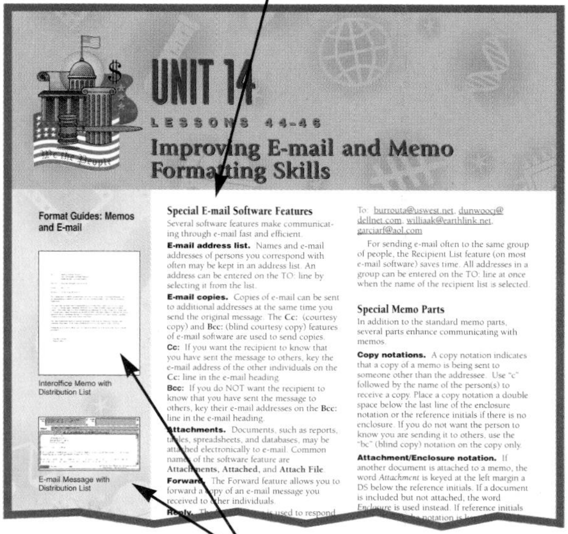

Margin illustrations show correct **document formatting**.

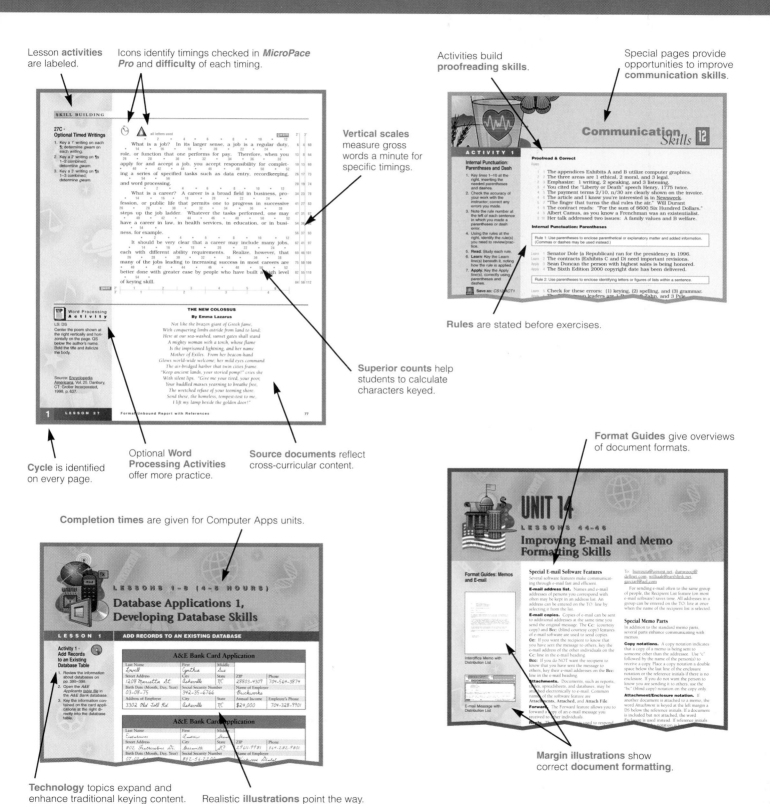

Completion times are given for Computer Apps units.

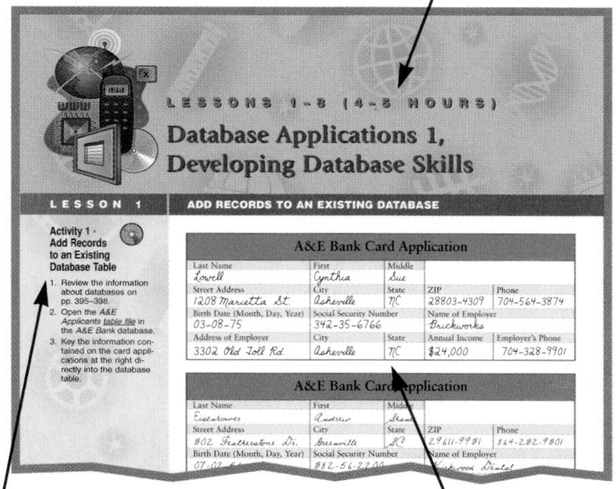

Technology topics expand and enhance traditional keying content.

Realistic **illustrations** point the way.

FOUNDATIONS OF LEARNING

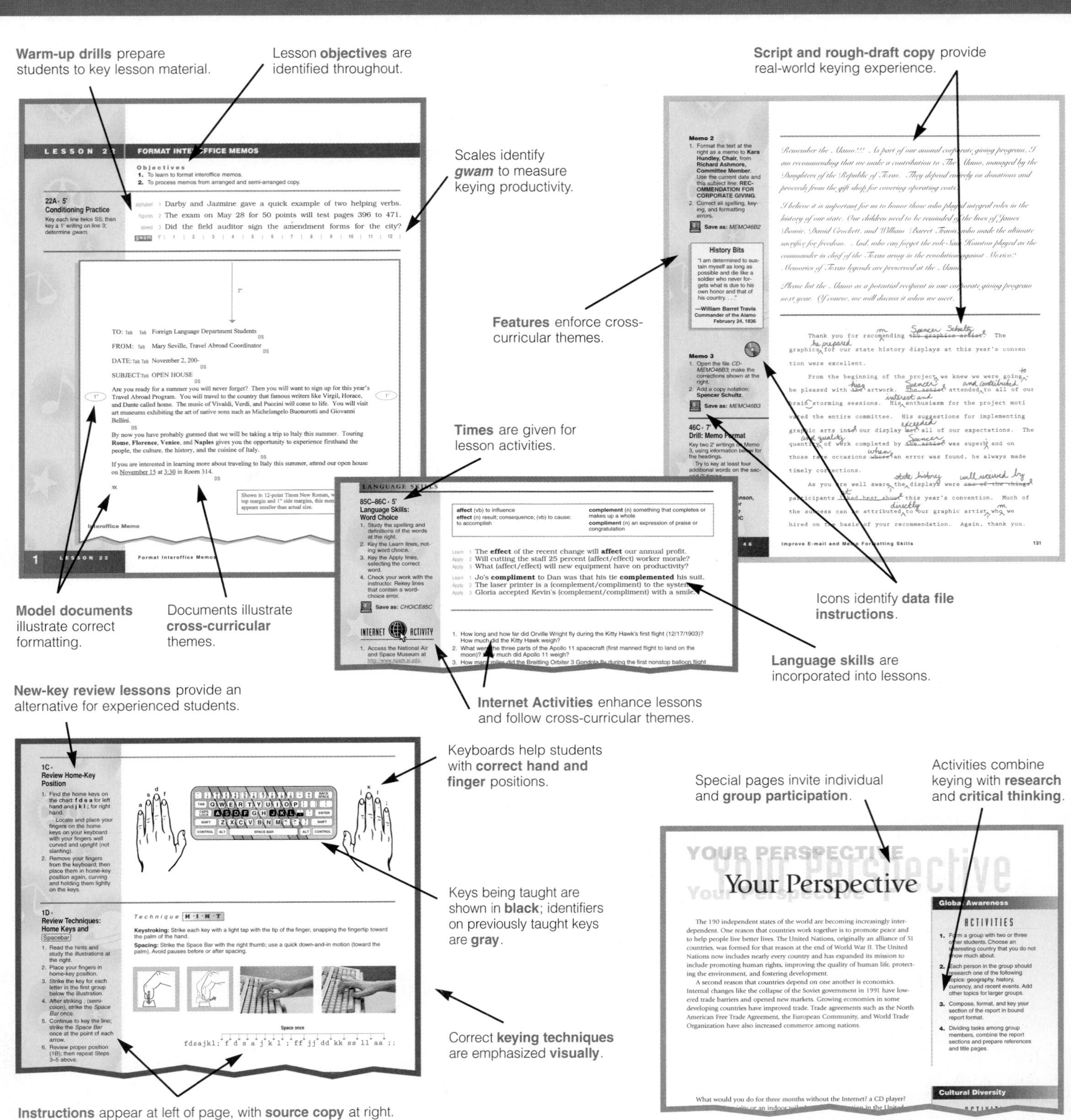

Warm-up drills prepare students to key lesson material.
Lesson **objectives** are identified throughout.
Script and rough-draft copy provide real-world keying experience.
Scales identify ***gwam*** to measure keying productivity.
Features enforce cross-curricular themes.
Times are given for lesson activities.
Model documents illustrate correct formatting.
Documents illustrate **cross-curricular** themes.
Icons identify **data file instructions**.
Language skills are incorporated into lessons.
New-key review lessons provide an alternative for experienced students.
Internet Activities enhance lessons and follow cross-curricular themes.
Keyboards help students with **correct hand and finger** positions.
Activities combine keying with **research** and **critical thinking**.
Special pages invite individual and **group participation**.
Keys being taught are shown in **black**; identifiers on previously taught keys are **gray**.
Correct **keying techniques** are emphasized **visually**.
Instructions appear at left of page, with **source copy** at right.

TECHNOLOGY LEADER TAKES YOU FORWARD

MicroType Multimedia
Lessons cover alphabetic, numeric, skillbuilding, and keypad instruction. Graphics, games, audio, video, and word processor with timer. Available for Windows and Macintosh.

KeyChamp
Develops speed by analyzing students' two-stroke key combinations (digraphs) and recommending speed-building drills. Available for Windows and Macintosh.

Quick Check
Assessment software that checks documents and timed writings from *Century 21,* keyed in a built-in word processor. Available for Windows and Macintosh.

C21 Web Site
Dedicated Web site with materials for students and instructors. Instructor materials include Placement and Performance Tests, Solution Keys, PowerPoint presentations, Activity Pak, Exploring Cultural Diversity, E-Term Dictionary, Certificates, Workplace Enrichment correlations and data files, Formatting Templates, MicroPace Pro Timed Writing Templates, Lesson Plans, and Transparency Masters for Word and Corel.

CENTURY 21
Computer Applications & Keyboarding 7E
goingforward

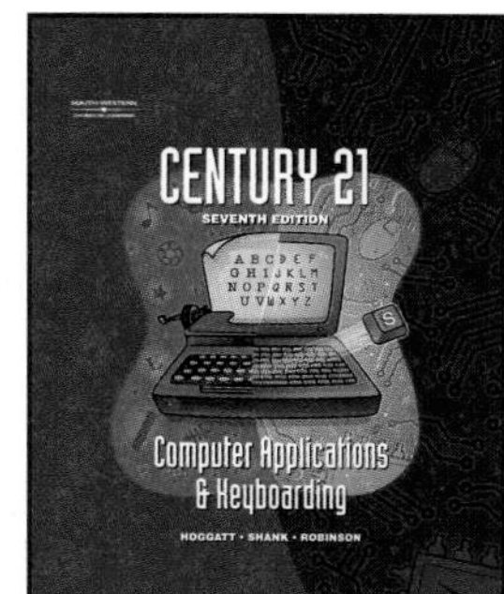

Century 21 Computer Applications & Keyboarding, Seventh Edition

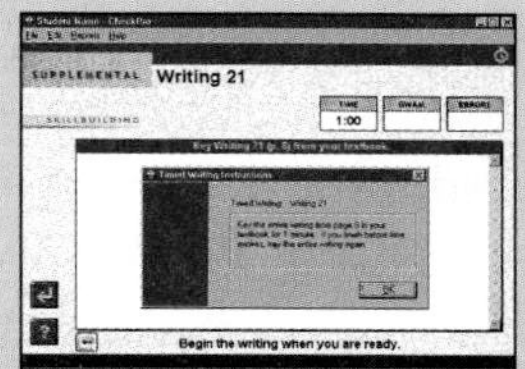

CheckPro
New to this edition, this checking software works with commercial word processing software. Available for Windows.

Skillbusters
An interactive mystery game that builds speed and accuracy. Clues surface only after students achieve keyboarding goals. Available for Windows and Macintosh.

Instructor Resource CD Materials include Placement and Performance Tests, Solution Keys, Exploring Cultural Diversity, Instructor's Manual, Certificates, Workplace Enrichment correlations and data files, Formatting Templates, MicroPace Pro Timed Writing Templates, Lesson Plans, and Transparency Masters for Word and Corel.

MicroPace Pro
Diagnoses errors and focuses students on areas that need improvement. Paced and timed writings, drills, and practices. Available for Windows and Macintosh.

Preface

The *7th Edition of Century 21 Computer Applications & Keyboarding* provides a high degree of flexibility for moving between traditional and new content areas. This flexibility permits the structuring of courses to meet the needs of students, school districts, and the community. Instructors can determine where students will begin—with refresher lessons for those who have had prior touch keyboarding instruction, or with new-key lessons designed for true beginners. A placement test is available.

The 7th Edition presents choices in word processing, database, spreadsheet, electronic presentation, and speech recognition software features. It offers units on "Using Help," "Searching the Web," and "Designing Web Pages," as well as workplace simulations. These units can be incorporated in your course as needed.

For this edition, South-Western/Thomson Learning surveyed business teachers, employed content reviewers, and met with focus groups to determine the needs of today's keyboarding students and instructors. The features of *Century 21 Computer Applications & Keyboarding, 7th Edition*, address those needs.

The *Century 21* family includes a full range of high-quality supplementary items to enhance your courses, including a Web site at www.c21key.swep.com. Thank you for choosing *Century 21*. Whether you are a new instructor, new to *Century 21*, or simply updating your *C21* materials, we know that you will find this edition an exciting solution for your classes.

ABOUT THE AUTHORS

Dr. Jon A. Shank is a Professor of Education at Robert Morris College in Moon Township, Pennsylvania. For more than 20 years, he served as Dean of the School of Applied Sciences and Education at Robert Morris. Dr. Shank retired as Dean in 1998 to return to full-time teaching. He currently teaches methods courses to students who are studying to become business education teachers. Dr. Shank holds memberships in regional, state, and national business education organizations. He has received many honors during his career, including Outstanding Post-Secondary Business Educator in Pennsylvania.

Dr. Jack P. Hoggatt is Department Chair for the Department of Business Communications at the University of Wisconsin-Eau Claire. He has taught courses in Business Writing, Advanced Business Communications, and the communication component of the university's Masters in Business Administration (MBA) program. Dr. Hoggatt has held offices in several professional organizations, including the Wisconsin Business Education Association. He has served as an advisor to local and state business organizations. Dr. Hoggatt is involved with his community and the school activities of his four children.

Dr. Jon Shank (left) and Dr. Jack Hoggatt

Contents

CYCLE 4 ENVIRONMENT & HEALTH

COMPUTER APPS TECHNOLOGY

RESOURCES

Computer Concepts

A **computer** is a machine that processes data and performs tasks according to a set of instructions. To do anything, computers must be given specific directions to follow. They get these directions from software. **Software**, such as that used for word processing, is a set of step-by-step instructions for the computer, written by computer programmers in a programming language like BASIC, Pascal, or C.

Computers also get instructions from you, the user. When you use the mouse (more in a moment about this tool) or the keyboard, you are giving instructions, or *input*, to your computer. That is why the mouse and keyboard are sometimes referred to as **input devices**.

Hardware is computer equipment. It carries out the software instructions. Hardware includes the central processing unit (CPU) as well as the monitor, keyboard, mouse, printer, and other *peripherals*. **Peripheral** is the name used for a piece of hardware that works with the CPU.

USING YOUR COMPUTER SAFELY

Follow these guidelines to use your computer safely:

1. Keep air vents unobstructed to prevent the computer from overheating.
2. Keep food and liquids away from your computer. If something does spill, unplug the computer and notify your instructor immediately.
3. Do not expose disks to excessive heat, cold, or moisture or to magnets, x-ray devices, or direct sunlight.
4. Use a felt-tip marker, not a ballpoint pen or a pencil, to write on disk labels.
5. Do not remove a disk from the drive when the in-use light is on.

STARTING YOUR COMPUTER

Follow these steps to start your computer:

1. Remove any 3.5" disk from that disk drive.
2. Turn on the power. You may need to flip a switch or press a button on the CPU or press a button or key on the keyboard. You may also have to turn on the monitor separately.

Your computer may take a few moments to power up. The computer will execute a series of automatic steps that will load the **operating system**. The operating system—Windows® 98, for example—is the program that manages other programs on the computer.[1] It will prepare the computer to receive your instructions and run software.

GETTING AROUND THE DESKTOP

The screen on your monitor is your **desktop.** Like the desk where you are sitting, your computer desktop is your main work area. It likely contains **icons** (picture symbols) for programs and documents, some resembling file folders that contain programs and documents. You probably have a taskbar or menu bar at the top or bottom of the screen (more about these in a moment). From here, you can start programs, find files, get information about your computer, and shut down the computer when you are finished.

A **mouse** is a tool for getting around the desktop. The same mouse actions are used in any software, though the results may vary depending on the software and version. Here are the basic ways to use a mouse:

- **Point**. Move the mouse (roll it on the work surface) so that the **pointer** (the arrow that represents the mouse's position on the screen) points to an item.
- **Click**. Press the left mouse button once and let go.
- **Double-click**. Press the left mouse button twice quickly and let go.
- **Drag**. Press and hold down the left mouse button and move the pointer to another location.

WHAT IS APPLICATION SOFTWARE?

You have probably heard the terms *application*, *application software*, and *application program*. They all mean the same thing. **Application software** is a computer program designed to perform a specific task directly for the user or for another application. Some common types of application software are word processing, spreadsheet, database, presentation, and Internet software.

[1] Windows® is a registered trademark of Microsoft Corporation in the United States and/or other countries.

STARTING SOFTWARE

Your computer gives you several different ways of starting programs, depending on the operating system and version. Here are two ways:

- If you have the Microsoft® Windows® operating system, click the *Start* button on the taskbar, point to ***Programs***, and click the name of the program you want to open. Your program may be inside a folder. If so, open the folder (by pointing to it) to get to the program.
- With Microsoft® Windows® operating system and Macintosh® computers, double-click the program icon on the desktop. Your program may be inside a folder. If so, open the folder (by double-clicking it) to get to the program.

Application software is displayed in a **window** on the monitor. The features of all windows are the same. At the top is the **title bar.** The title bar displays the name of the file you are working on and, for some programs, the name of the software (such as *Microsoft® Word*). If you haven't yet saved the document with a filename, the title bar will say something like *Document* or *unmodified*, along with the name of the software. Under the title bar, you may see a menu bar and one or more toolbars or button bars. These bars allow you to choose commands in your software. We'll talk more about them in the next section.

The title bar contains boxes that allow you to resize and close the window. At the bottom and right sides of the window are **scroll bars.** You can click or drag these bars with the mouse to navigate (move around in) your document. To learn more about resizing and navigating a window, go to the Windows® Tutorial on pages R37–R39.

CHOOSING COMMANDS

Most software gives you several different ways to choose commands. As you work with a program, you will find the ways that are easiest for you.

Menus. A **menu bar** may appear at the top of your application window, just under the title bar. Like a menu in a restaurant, a menu bar offers you choices. From the menu bar, you can open a document, spell-check it, and so on. To open a menu and see its options, click the menu name in the menu bar. For example, to open the File menu, click *File.* For some software, you have to hold the mouse button down to keep the menu displayed. To choose a command, click it (Windows®) or drag down to it (Macintosh®). In some software, you can also open menus by pressing ALT plus the underlined letter in the menu name. For example, ALT + F opens the File menu. Menu names vary a little but are much the same across application software.

File Edit View Insert Format Tools Window Help

Corel® WordPerfect® 8 Program Menu Bar[2]

Toolbars. **Toolbars** let you choose commands quickly and easily. Most applications have toolbars. They have different names, such as *button bars,* in different software; but all toolbars are similar. They consist of icons or buttons that represent commands; some of the same commands found on menus. The standard toolbar contains icons for basic, often-used commands, such as saving and printing. Toolbars also exist for certain tasks, like formatting text or creating tables. In most software, pointing to a toolbar icon displays the name of the command. Clicking the icon executes the command.

100%

Microsoft® Word 2000 Standard Toolbar[3]

Keyboard shortcuts. Each application has its own set of **keyboard shortcuts** for opening menus and executing commands. Keyboard shortcuts usually consist of pressing a function key (e.g., F1, F2, F3) or pressing the ALT, CTRL, or COMMAND key plus some other key. For example, to open a file in *Microsoft® Word 2000* for PCs, you would key CTRL + O. These shortcuts are often displayed on the menus and can also be found in the software's Help feature.

The following sections tell you how to use menus and toolbars to start, save, print, close, and open documents. The names for menus, commands, and icons in your software may differ slightly from those used here.

[2] Corel® and WordPerfect® are registered trademarks of Corel Corporation or Corel Corporation Limited in Canada, the United States, and/or other countries.
[3] Microsoft® is a registered trademark of Microsoft Corporation.

STARTING A NEW DOCUMENT 

For many applications, starting the program starts a new document automatically. You can simply begin working on the blank screen that is displayed when the program has been loaded. If your software doesn't display a blank screen on starting up, if you want to start a new document later in your working session, or if you want to start a new document with another document already on the screen, do *one* of the following:

- Select the *New* command on the File menu.
- Click the *New* icon, usually the first icon to the left on the standard toolbar.
- Use the keyboard shortcut for the *New* command.

A new document window will display. In some software, you may first see a **dialog box** that gives you setup options for your document. To learn more about dialog boxes, go to the Windows® Tutorial on pages R37–R39. Pressing ENTER or RETURN or clicking *New* or *OK* will take you from the dialog box to a blank document window.

KEYING TEXT

Keying text in a new word processing document is easy. Simply begin keying. Text is entered to the left of the **insertion point** (the flashing line). You will use many features of your word processing software in the special Word Processing pages of this book.

USING HELP

If you need assistance in the form of "how-to" information while working with software, you can get it through the program's Help menu or the Help icon on the toolbar. Help options vary but generally include a table of contents and a searchable index. If you enter the topic or a keyword, the software can search for information about it.

SAVING A DOCUMENT 

Saving a document places a copy of it on a disk in one of the computer's disk drives. This may be the hard (internal) disk of the computer or some kind of removable **medium,** such as a 3.5" disk or Zip disk. This copy will not be erased when your computer is shut down. It is permanent until you delete or modify it.

Save any documents that you think you will need later. You can save a document anytime the document is on the screen—just after starting it, while you are working on it, or when you are done. Save often as you work on a document so that you will not lose your changes in case of a power failure or other problem. Follow these steps to save a document:

1. Select the *Save* command from the File menu, click the *Save* icon on the standard toolbar, or use the keyboard shortcut for the *Save* command.
2. If you did not save the document before, the software will display the Save As dialog box. In this dialog box, look at the *Save in,* ___ *Folder* box, or something similar. If the drive and/or folder where you want to save the file does not show, click the down arrow and double-click drives and folders until the box shows the correct location. The computer's hard drive is most often (C:); the drive that takes 3.5" disks, (A:).
3. If you are saving the file to any kind of removable medium, insert that disk into the disk drive.
4. Key a name for the document in the box that says *File name, Name,* or something similar. Click *Save* or *OK* or press ENTER or RETURN.

If you modify a document after saving it, resave the document by selecting the Save command (Step 1). The Save As dialog box will not appear this time because you already named the file.

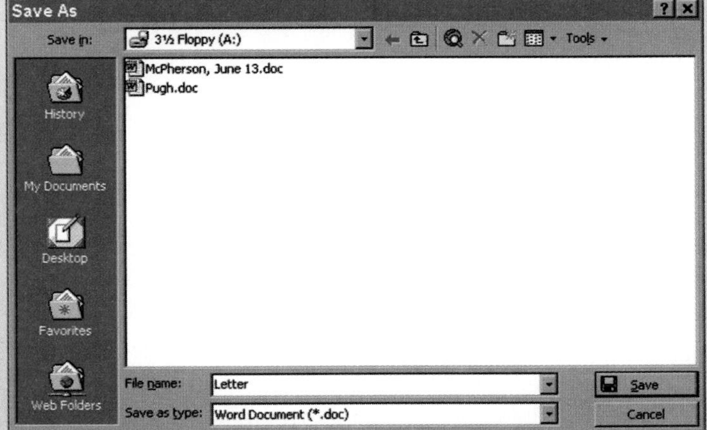

The Microsoft® Word 2000 Save As Dialog Box[4]

PRINTING A DOCUMENT 

Follow these steps to print a document:

1. Turn on the printer. Make sure it is loaded with paper.
2. Display the document on the screen.

---

[4] Microsoft® is a registered trademark of Microsoft Corporation.

3. Select the *Print* command from the File menu, click the *Print* icon on the standard toolbar, or use the keyboard shortcut for the *Print* command.
4. In the Print dialog box, select the print settings you want or use the settings that are already there (the **default settings**). In most software, the default settings print one copy of the document. When you are ready to print, click *OK* or *Print* or press ENTER or RETURN.

CLOSING A DOCUMENT

Closing a document removes it from the window. If you have not yet saved the document, or if you have made changes to it that you haven't saved, you will be asked when you choose the **Close** command whether you first want to save the document. Choosing *No* will erase a document that has not yet been saved. For a document that has been saved, choosing No will erase any changes you have made to the document since last saving it. You can close a document in any of these ways:

- Select the *Close* command from the File menu.
- Click the *Close* icon on the standard toolbar.
- Click the *Close* box or *Close* button. In Macintosh® applications, the Close box is at the top left of the window. The Close button in applications based on the Microsoft® Windows® operating system is the button containing an *x* at the far right of the title or menu bar. Each document window has a Close button, as does the software window. Be sure to choose the Close button for the document, not the software, if you want to continue working in the program.
- Use the keyboard shortcut for the Close command.

OPENING A DOCUMENT

Opening a document means retrieving it from wherever it is stored and displaying it on the screen. Follow these steps to open a document:

1. Select *Open* from the File menu, click the *Open* icon on the standard toolbar, or use the keyboard shortcut for the Open command.
2. Choose or key the filename of the document. If you don't see the filename displayed in the Open dialog box, navigate with the mouse to where the file is stored by choosing the appropriate disk drive (and folder, if any), just as you do when saving a document. If you are retrieving a file from a 3.5" disk, CD-ROM, or Zip disk, you will need to insert that disk into the disk drive to get the file.

CLOSING THE SOFTWARE

Choose one of these options for closing the application software:

- Select the *Exit* or *Quit* command from the File menu.
- Click the *Close* button or *Close* box.

If you still have a file open and have not saved it, or if you have made changes to the file since your last save, you will be *prompted* to save the file. The computer is programmed to remind you of certain steps. These reminders are called **prompts**.

TURNING OFF THE COMPUTER

Follow these steps to turn off your computer:

1. Close all application software.
2. Remove any media from the disk drives.
3. Select *Shut Down* from the Start menu (Microsoft® Windows® operating system), Apple menu (Macintosh® computers), or Special menu (Macintosh® computers). On some Macintosh® computers, you can press the ON/OFF key instead.
4. If you get a prompt asking whether you really want to shut down, click *Yes* or *Shut Down*. On some Macs, you may be prompted to press the ON/OFF key.
5. After the computer has shut down, turn off the power switch on the CPU or keyboard (and monitor, if necessary).

CYCLE 1

UNITS 1-12

Computer Keyboarding: Reinforce & Apply

Computers are not just for business anymore—they are for *every*one, *every*where! In our world of fast-paced communication, almost everything we see on TV and the Internet, hear at rap concerts and Broadway musicals, or read in books and newspapers began as keystrokes entered into a computer by a keyboard operator.

To get the most value from high-speed computers, users must be competent at the input end—the keyboard. A computer processes data and text at the same speed for everyone. But a person who keys 50 words a minute produces twice as much work as a person who keys 25 words a minute for the same amount of time.

Lessons in Cycle 1 *reinforce* your keying skills. E-mail, reports, letters, and tables are some of the ways you then *apply* those skills, using the features of your word processing software. The Internet activities in these lessons represent an increasingly important use of keyboarding. A series of Communication Skills activities can help you do error-free work.

Here you have an opportunity to develop skills for traveling the Information Superhighway. Take it—straightaway!

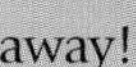

Credits

Photos

Page viii: Photo of authors by Jane Congdon

Pages 2, R2: © Photo by Erik Snobeck/Digital Imaging Group

Pages 3, R3, R7, R8, R9, R10, R12, R14, R16, R17, R18, R20, R21, R22, R24, R26, R28, R29, R30, R33: © Greg Grosse

Pages R5, R34, R40: © Courtesy of PhotoDisc, Inc.

Reviewers

The following reviewed manuscript and provided valuable feedback:

Karen Bean, Harker Heights High School, Harker Heights, TX
Eileen Dittmar, Kent Career/Technical Center, Grand Rapids, MI
Lisa J. Karr, High School Academy, Irving Independent School District, Irving, TX
Janet Knox, Public Schools of North Carolina, Raleigh, NC
Mary Ann Mann, Palestine High School, Palestine, TX
Sue Miller, Shiloh High School, Hume, IL
Carol Mitzner, Reseda High School, Reseda, CA
Barbara Small, Fairfax County Public Schools, Falls Church, VA
James R. Smith, Jr., Public Schools of North Carolina, Raleigh, NC

Additional Credits

Review Coordinator: *Nancy Stamper*
Fee Writers: *Elaine Langlois, Minta Berry, Lisa Karr*
Production Resources: *Diane Bowdler* (page reviewer, solutions coordinator); *Gary Morris* (head copyeditor); *Anne Noschang* (additional copyediting); *Thomas N. Lewis* (counts/controls)

On the Cover

Our first holographic cover shows you the past and future of keyboarding. In 1867 a marvelous invention called the typewriter enabled people to put printed letters onto paper. Touch typing gave us a tool for producing documents rapidly and accurately. Now computer applications are taking keyboarding to exciting new levels, making it more than ever a skill for everyone. This is *KEYBOARDING GOING FORWARD.*

UNIT 1

LESSONS 1–8

Review Letter Keys

LESSON 1 REVIEW HOME KEYS (fdsa jkl;)

Objectives:

1. To review control of home keys (**fdsa jkl;**).

2. To review control of **Space Bar** and **Enter** key.

1A • Review Work Area Arrangement

Arrange work area as shown at the right.

- alphanumeric (main) keyboard directly in front of chair; front edge of keyboard even with edge of table or desk
- monitor placed for easy viewing
- disk drives placed for easy access and disks within easy reach (unless using a network)
- book behind or at side of keyboard; top raised for easy reading

Properly arranged work area

1B • Review Keying Position

The features of proper position are shown at right and listed below:

- fingers curved and upright over home keys
- wrists low, but not touching keyboard
- forearms parallel to slant of keyboard
- body erect, sitting back in chair
- feet on floor for balance

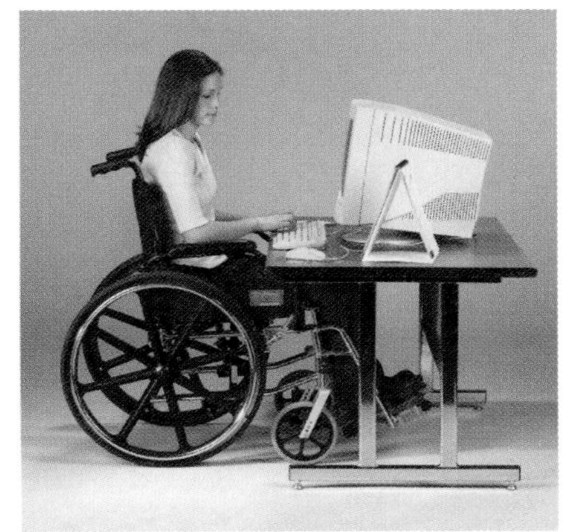

Proper position at computer

Activity 2 • Web Page Design Tips

1. Form groups.
2. Review the Web Page Design Tips at the right.
3. Search the Internet for additional tips on designing Web pages or sites.
4. Summarize the tips you find and present them in a wp document along with the Web address where the tips were located.

Save as: *DWPL4ACT2*

5. Discuss the tips that each member found, and choose the ones that you want to include with those given at the right.
6. Each group should design a Web page that integrates your group's tips with those at the right. Include the Web addresses for the tips you add.
7. Read the copy at the right, and then name and save your Web page.

Save as: *DESIGN_TIPS* (html)

Web Page Design Tips	
Use a background and font color combination that is attractive but easy to read.	Do not use big blocks of text. Users tend to scan text and not read long blocks of text carefully or thoroughly.
Keep pictures and graphics small to avoid long download times.	Use hyperlinks in long Web pages to reduce the need for users to scroll long distances.
Use hyperlinks that enable the user to move from one Web site to another, one Web page to another, and within a Web page easily.	Have a classmate review and critique your Web site, especially the hyperlinks and the readability of the Web pages.
Keep use of scrolling text to a minimum, and avoid using animation because it is annoying to many users.	Use descriptive titles in the title bar and headings at the beginning of each Web page so the user always knows where he/she is.

Use an underline between the words in an HTML filename to make the file more stable. Multiword filenames that have only spaces between the words may not work well with some browsers or Internet programs.

Activity 3 • Web Page Critique

1. Using what you have learned about Web page design in Activity 2, have your group members critique each other's Web pages that were created in Activity 1.
2. Using the suggestions of the group, revise the Web pages you constructed in Activity 1.
3. Submit your revised Web pages to your instructor as required.
4. If permitted, post your Web site to your school's intranet or the Internet.

1C • Review Home-Key Position

1. Find the home keys on the chart: **f d s a** for left hand and **j k l ;** for right hand.

   Locate and place your fingers on the home keys on your keyboard with your fingers well curved and upright (not slanting).
2. Remove your fingers from the keyboard; then place them in home-key position again, curving and holding them lightly on the keys.

1D • Review Techniques: Home Keys and Spacebar

1. Read the hints and study the illustrations at the right.
2. Place your fingers in home-key position.
3. Strike the key for each letter in the first group below the illustration.
4. After striking *;* (semi-colon), strike the *Space Bar* once.
5. Continue to key the line; strike the *Space Bar* once at the point of each arrow.
6. Review proper position (1B); then repeat Steps 3–5 above.

Technique **H • I • N • T**

Keystroking: Strike each key with a light tap with the tip of the finger, snapping the fingertip toward the palm of the hand.

Spacing: Strike the Space Bar with the right thumb; use a quick down-and-in motion (toward the palm). Avoid pauses before or after spacing.

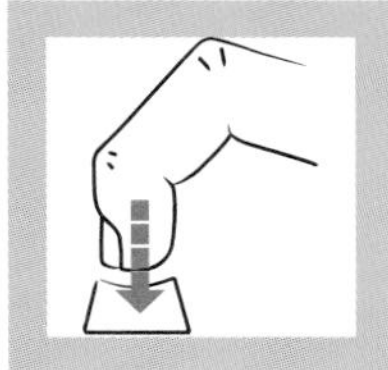

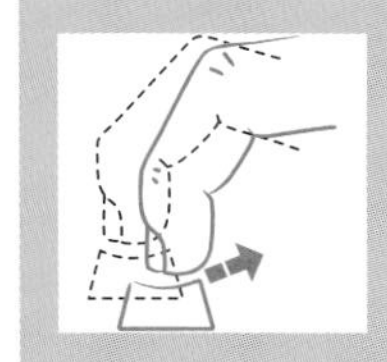

Space once

```
fdsajkl; f d s a j k l ; ff jj dd kk ss ll aa ;;
```

1E • Review Technique: Hard Return at Line Endings

Read the information and study the illustration at the right.

Practice the ENTER key reach several times.

Hard Return
To return the insertion point to the left margin and move it down to the next line, strike ENTER.

This is called a **hard return**. Use a hard return at the end of all drill lines in this unit. Use two hard returns when directed to double-space.

Hard Return Technique
Reach the little finger of the right hand to the ENTER key, tap the key, and return the finger quickly to home-key position.

Activity 6, cont.

2. Select the *Recent Events* heading in the Web page, and insert a bookmark at this point.
3. Select the *Upcoming Events* heading in the Web page, and insert a bookmark at this point.
4. Link *Recent Events* in the top table to the Recent Events bookmark.
5. Link *Upcoming Events* in the top table to the Upcoming Events bookmark.
6. Insert a **Return to the Top** hyperlink with each use of that phrase within the Web page.
7. Verify that the hyperlinks move the user to the correct places within the Web page.
8. Save the revised Web page.

LESSONS 4-6 CONSTRUCT A WEB PAGE

Objectives:

1. To apply skills you have learned to design Web pages.

2. To create and then improve a functional interactive Web site.

Activity 1 • Web Page Design

1. Read the text at the right.
2. Select a purpose for your Web site.
3. Obtain approval of your Web site purpose from your instructor.
4. Read the Web Page Design Tips in the table on the next page.
5. Using wp software, outline the structure and content of each Web page within your site.
6. Create a new folder called *WPDXXX* (*XXX* represents your initials).
7. Create the Web pages, including the hyperlinks, and save the files in your folder.
8. Submit your Web site to your instructor as required.

You are to design Web pages for a Web site that you choose. The Web site must have these elements:

- At least three Web pages that have hyperlinks to each other.
- One or more graphics from the Internet or clip art.
- One or more pictures with descriptive text from the Internet or from files.
- One or more hyperlinks to another Web site.
- Two or more hyperlinks to different locations within the same Web page—"Return to the Top" can be used as one of the hyperlinks.
- One or more hyperlinks to e-mail addresses—may be fictional.
- Tables within each page.
- Scrolling text (used sparingly).
- A background with texture, color, picture, or image.
- Font color that is compatible with the background.

1F • Home-Key and Spacebar Review

Key the lines once; single-spaced (SS) with a double space (DS) between 2-line groups. Do not key line numbers.

Spacing **C • U • E**

Strike the ENTER key twice to insert a DS between 2-line groups.

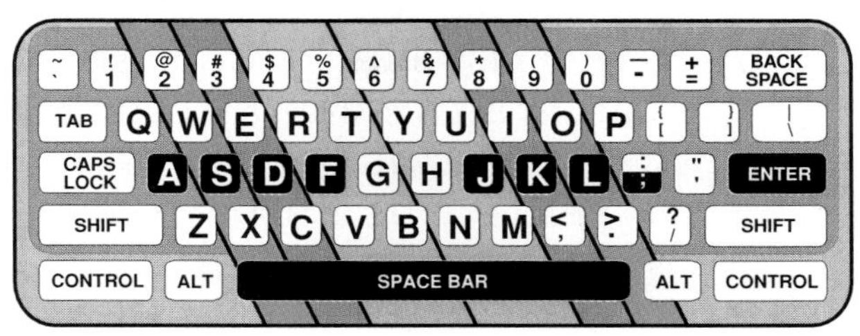


```
1 j jj f ff k kk d dd l ll s ss ; ;; a aa jkl; fdsa
2 j jj f ff k kk d dd l ll s ss ; ;; a aa jkl; fdsa
```
Strike the ENTER key twice to double-space (DS).

```
3 a aa ; ;; s ss l ll d dd k kk f ff j jj fdsa jkl;
4 a aa ; ;; s ss l ll d dd k kk f ff j jj fdsa jkl;
```
DS

```
5 jf jf kd kd ls ls ;a ;a fj fj dk dk sl sl a; a; f
6 jf jf kd kd ls ls ;a ;a fj fj dk dk sl sl a; a; f
```
DS

```
7 a;fj a;sldkfj a;sldkfj a;sldkfj a;sldkfj a;sldkfj
8 a;fj a;sldkfj a;sldkfj a;sldkfj a;sldkfj a;sldkfj
```
Strike the ENTER key 4 times to quadruple-space (QS).

1G • Review Technique: Enter

Key each line twice SS; DS between 2-line groups.

Reach with little finger; tap the ENTER key quickly; return finger to home key.

```
1 a;sldkfj a;sldkfj
2 ff jj dd kk ss ll aa ;;
3 fj fj dk dk sl sl a; a; asdf ;lkj
4 fj dk sl a; jf kd ls ;a fdsa jkl; a;sldkfj
```

1H • Keyboard Reinforcement

Key each line twice SS; DS between 2-line groups.

```
1 a lad; a jak; a lass; all ads; add all; ask a lass
2 as a lad; a fall fad; ask all dads; as a fall fad;
3 as a fall fad; add a jak salad; as a sad lad falls
4 ask a lad; ask a lad; all jaks fall; all jaks fall
5 as a fad; as a dad; ask a lad; as a lass; all lads
6 add a jak; a fall ad; all fall ads; ask a sad lass
7 a sad lad; ask a dad; all jaks; ask a jak; sad dad
8 a sad fall; all fall ads; as a lass asks a sad lad
```

2. Open *BDMBRS* (html) and insert the following hyperlinks in the bottom table:
   - Link **BDMBRS** to **index** by selecting **Home** as the text.
   - Link **BDMBRS** to **EVENTS** by selecting **Events**.
   - Link **BDMBRS** to **HALL** by selecting **Hall of Fame**.
3. Open *EVENTS* (html) and insert the following hyperlinks in the 2nd table:
   - Link **EVENTS** to **index** by selecting **Home** as the text.
   - Link **EVENTS** to **BDMBRS** by selecting **Board Members**.
   - Link **EVENTS** to **HALL** by selecting **Hall of Fame**.
4. Open *HALL* (html) and create the following hyperlinks in the bottom table:
   - Link **HALL** to **index** by selecting **Home** as the text.
   - Link **HALL** to **BDMBRS** by selecting **Board Members**.
   - Link **HALL** to **EVENTS** by selecting **Events**.
5. Verify that the hyperlinks work.
6. Save each revised file.

Activity 6 • Inserting Hyperlinks to Move to Another Place in the Same Web Page

1. Read the text at the right.
2. Learn to create a hyperlink to another place in the same Web page using your software.
3. Complete the activities at the right and on the next page.

Often a Web page is longer than a window and contains multiple sections. Inserting hyperlinks to other places on the Web page helps the user move throughout the page quickly. There is no need to scroll through the Web page's content to find desired information.

These hyperlinks are frequently created by hyperlinking text or graphics to **bookmarks**. The bookmarks are inserted into the Web page text to mark the different locations you want the user to be able to move to quickly.

Also, hyperlinks are frequently inserted at strategic points in a Web page to allow the user to return to the top of the Web page quickly, if desired.

In this activity, you are going to link to specific places within the Web page titled *EVENTS* (html):

(1) You will hyperlink *Recent Events* in the top table to the *Recent Events* heading within the Web page.

(2) You will link *Upcoming Events* in the top table to the *Upcoming Events* heading within the Web page.

(3) You will provide the user with two hyperlinks to return to the top of the Web page—one at the end of the Recent Events section and the other at the end of the Upcoming Events section.

1. Open *EVENTS* (html) and preview this activity by scrolling through the Web page looking for these items:
   a. Locate *Recent Events* and *Upcoming Events* in the top table. You will use these headings as your hyperlinks.
   b. Locate the heading *Recent Events* in the Web page. You will bookmark this text so your hyperlink will move the user to it.
   c. Locate the heading *Upcoming Events* in the Web page. You will bookmark this text so your hyperlink will move the user to it.
   d. Locate the two *Return to the Top* phrases used in the Web page. You will hyperlink these two phrases to the top of the document.

(continued on next page)

LESSON 2 — REVIEW LETTER KEYS (h, e, i, AND r)

Objectives:

1. To review reach technique for **h** and **e**.
2. To review reach technique for **i** and **r**.

2A • 8'* Review [H] and [E]

Key each line twice single-spaced (SS); double-space (DS) between 2-line groups.

*Suggested number of minutes.

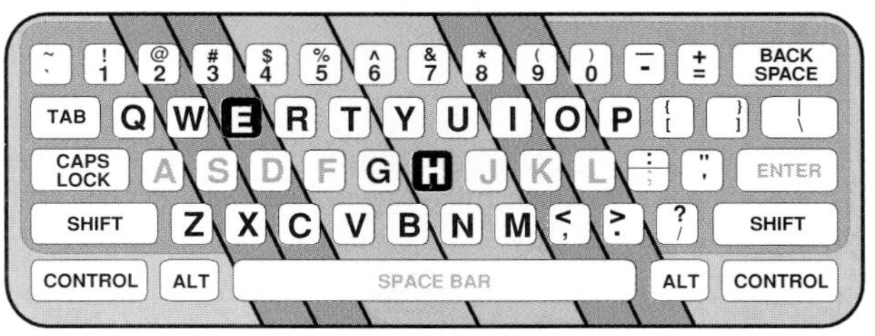

Review h

```
1 j j hj hj ah ah ha ha had had has has ash ash hash
2 hj hj ha ha ah ah hah hah had had ash ash has hash
3 ah ha; had ash; has had; a hall; has a hall; ah ha
```

Review e

```
4 d d ed ed el el led led eel eel eke eke ed fed fed
5 ed ed el el lee lee fed fed eke eke led led ale ed
6 a lake; a leek; a jade; a desk; a jade eel; a deed
```

SKILL BUILDING

2B • 14' Keyboard Reinforcement

Key each line twice SS; DS between 2-line groups.

home row

```
1 ask ask|has has|lad lad|all all|jak jak|fall falls
2 a jak; a lad; a sash; had all; has a jak; all fall
```

h/e

```
3 he he|she she|led led|held held|jell jell|she shed
4 he led; she had; she fell; a jade ad; a desk shelf
```

all keys learned

```
5 elf elf|all all|ask ask|led led|jak jak|hall halls
6 ask dad; he has jell; she has jade; he sells leeks
```

all keys learned

```
7 he led; she has; a jak ad; a jade eel; a sled fell
8 she asked a lad; he led all fall; she has a jak ad
```

all keys learned

```
9 had a jade; she fell; a lake; see dad; he fed dad;
10 she fell|has dad|he had a keel|she has a jade sash
```

Activity 4 • Hyperlinks to a Different Web Site

1. Read the text at the right.
2. Learn to create a hyperlink to a different Web site using a graphic and text.
3. Complete the steps at the right.

As with e-mail, hyperlinks to other Web sites can be inserted by using a graphic, selecting text, or using the site's URL. When the site's URL is used as the hyperlink, the software will usually create the hyperlink.

The three types of hyperlinks are illustrated at the right.

Using a graphic	
Using selected text	Southwestern High School
Using the URL as the text	www.distsw.swep.com

1. Open *index* (html) and create a hyperlink using the text **Southwestern School District**. The URL is http://www.distsw.swep.com. Use the default screen tip. Save the revised file and print a copy.
2. Open *EVENTS* (html) and create a hyperlink to the text **Elite Landscape** (in Recent Events section).The URL is http://www.elite.swep.com. Use the default screen tip. Save the revised file.
3. While still in *EVENTS* (html), create a hyperlink using the text **Class of 1975 Reunion**. Key www.distsw.swep.com as the URL. Use the default screen tip. Save the revised file.
4. Return to *index* (html), create a hyperlink to Southwestern School District (http://www.distsw.swep.com) using the lion mascot. Use **Southwestern School District** as the screen tip. Save the revised file.
5. Return to *EVENTS* (html), create a hyperlink to Southwestern School District using the lion mascot as you did in Step 4. Save the revised file.

Activity 5 • Hyperlinks to Other Web Pages Within the Same Web Site

1. Read the text at the right.
2. Learn to create a hyperlink to a different file within the same Web site.
3. Complete the activities at the right and on the next page.

Tip:
Be sure to identify hyperlinks to Web pages. Key the .htm or .html extension after the filename.

You can hyperlink to other Web pages (files) within a Web site by selecting the text or graphic that the user will click to access the other file. As with other hyperlinks, the hypertext link usually appears in a different font color and underlined. Once the path has been followed, the hypertext link usually changes to another color to indicate that the hyperlink has been used.

In the illustration at the right, the first hyperlink (in blue) has not been followed; the second hyperlink (in purple) has been followed.

In this activity, hyperlinks using text will lead to other files within the SHSAA Web site.

> This text represents a portion of a Web page created using a red font. This first hyperlink is in blue and is underlined. In this example, blue is used as the color for the hyperlink that has not been followed. This second hyperlink uses purple to indicate that this link has been followed.

1. Open *index* (html) and insert the following hyperlinks in the bottom table:
   - Link **index** to **BDMBRS** by selecting **Board Members** as the hyperlink text.
   - Link **index** to **EVENTS** by selecting **Events** as the hyperlink text.
   - Link **index** to **HALL** by selecting **Hall of Fame** as the hyperlink text.

(continued on next page)

2C • 8' Review [I] and [R]

Key each line twice SS; DS between 2-line groups.

Review i

1 k k ik ik if if is is ill ill did did kid kid sail

2 ik ik is is did did his his lie lie side side hail

3 if he; she did; his side; a kid is a; if he is ill

Review r

4 f f rf rf are are jar jar red red ark ark far read

5 rf rf herd herd read read free free rare rare real

6 a jar; a rake; a lark; red jar; hear her; are dark

SKILL BUILDING

2D • 11' Keyboard Reinforcement

1. Key the lines once SS with a DS between 2-line groups.
2. Key the lines again at a faster pace.

Technique Goals:

- fingers deeply curved
- wrists low, but not resting
- hands/arms steady
- eyes on copy as you key

reach review

1 hj ed ik rf hj de ik fr hj ed ik rf jh de ki fr hj

2 he he|if if|all all|fir fir|jar jar|rid rid|as ask

h/e

3 she she|elf elf|her her|hah hah|eel eel|shed shelf

4 he has; had jak; her jar; had a shed; she has fled

i/r

5 fir fir|rid rid|sir sir|kid kid|ire ire|fire fired

6 a fir; is rid; is red; his ire; her kid; has a fir

all keys learned

7 if if|is is|he he|did did|fir fir|jak jak|all fall

8 a jak; he did; ask her; red jar; she fell; he fled

2E • 9' Technique: [Enter]

Key each line twice SS; DS between 2-line groups.

Practice **C • U • E**

Keep up your pace to the end of the line, return quickly, and begin the new line without a pause or stop.

1 if he is;

2 as if she is;

3 he had a fir desk;

4 she has a red jell jar;

5 he has had a lead all fall;

6 she asked if he reads fall ads;

7 she said she reads all ads she sees;

8 his dad has had a sales lead as he said;

Activity 3 • Hyperlinks to an E-mail Address

1. Read the text at the right.
2. Read the Learning Cue below.
3. Learn to create a hyperlink to an e-mail address using a graphic and text.
4. Complete the activities at the right below.

Learning C·U·E

When the user moves the pointer over the hyperlink (graphic or text), a screen tip generally appears in a rectangle above the pointing hand. You can use the default screen tip, or you can insert other text for the screen tip. When the hyperlink is to an e-mail address, the default screen tip is generally *mailto:* followed by the e-mail address.

When a user clicks a hyperlink to an e-mail address, a new e-mail message box is created with the linked e-mail address appearing in the To line. The user then keys the subject line and e-mail message and clicks *send*.

The illustrations at the right show three methods of creating hyperlinks to an e-mail address. The first is to an address that is represented by the mailbox graphic. When the user clicks the mailbox, the e-mail message box will open.

The second is an e-mail address that is used as a hyperlink. It appears in a different font color and is underlined. Most often, the software will recognize the format of an e-mail address and automatically create a hyperlink as soon as the Space Bar is tapped after the last character of the e-mail address is keyed.

The third box also uses text to hyperlink to an e-mail address, but in this example, the text is the person's name rather than the e-mail address.

For additional information, contact:

 Jerry Hernandez

 Rosalind Porter

For additional information, contact:

Jerry Hernandez, hernanj@webgate.com

Rosalind Porter, porter@webgate.com

For additional information, contact:

Jerry Hernandez

Rosalind Porter

1. Open *index* (html) and select *Webmaster* (the last word in the last line of text) to create a hyperlink to this e-mail address: kvarati@swep.com. Use **Kimberly Varati** as the screen tip.

 **Save as:** *index* (html)

2. Open *HALL* (html) and create the same hyperlink from *Webmaster* to kvarati@swep.com as you did in Step 1.

 **Save as:** *HALL* (html)

3. View the document as a Web page, and confirm that the link to the Webmaster is correct by clicking it. If you are able to send e-mail messages, send this message to the Webmaster: **This message is to test the accuracy of the hyperlink to your e-mail address. No response is necessary.** Save the revised Web page.
4. Open *BDMBRS* (html) and key each e-mail address in the last column so that the entire e-mail address is the hyperlink. Use the default screen tip, and key each person's e-mail address in lowercase letters. The e-mail address for each person is the **first initial** of his or her first name plus the **last name**, followed by **@swep.com**. For example, ahess@swep.com and hmalone@swep.com.

 **Save as:** *BDMBRS* (html)

5. Open *EVENTS* (html) and create an e-mail hyperlink to Jack Hyatt (jhyatt@swep.com) by inserting the mailbox graphic file (*mailbox* in *SHSXXX* folder) between **mailbox** and **to** in the Golf Outing section. Use **Jack Hyatt** as the screen tip.

 **Save as:** *EVENTS* (html)

REVIEW LETTER KEYS (o, t, n, AND g)

Objectives:

1. To review reach technique for **o** and **t**.
2. To review reach technique for **n** and **g**.

3A • 5' Conditioning Practice

Key each line twice SS; DS between 2-line groups.

home row 1 a sad fall; had a hall; a jak falls; as a fall ad;

3d row 2 if her aid; all he sees; he irks her; a jade fish;

all keys learned 3 as he fell; he sells fir desks; she had half a jar

3B • 7' Review O and T

Key each line twice SS (slowly, then faster); DS between 2-line groups.

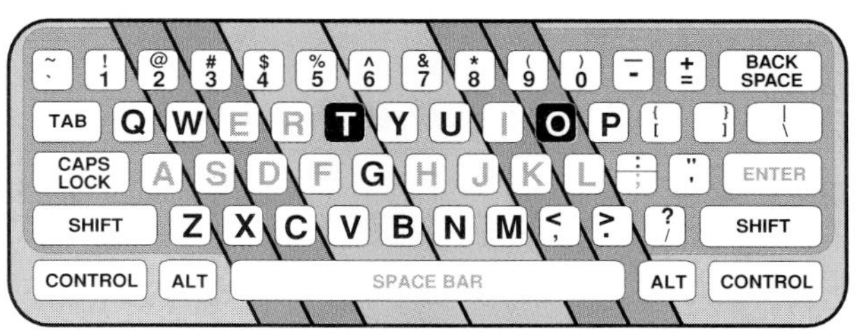

Review o

1 l l ol ol do do of of so so lo lo old old for fore

2 ol ol of of or or for for oak oak off off sol sole

3 do so; a doe; of old; of oak; old foe; of old oak;

Review t

4 f f tf tf it it at at tie tie the the fit fit lift

5 tf tf ft ft it it sit sit fit fit hit hit kit kite

6 if it; a fit; it fit; tie it; the fit; at the site

SKILL BUILDING

3C • 13' Keyboard Reinforcement

1. Key the lines once SS; DS between 2-line groups.
2. Key the lines again at a faster pace.

Technique Goals:

- curved, upright fingers
- wrists low, but not resting
- down-and-in spacing
- eyes on copy as you key

reach review

1 hj ed ik rf ol tf jh de ki fr lo ft hj ed ol rf tf

2 is led fro hit old fit let kit rod kid dot taj sit

h/e

3 he he|she she|led led|had had|see see|has has|seek

4 he led|ask her|she held|has fled|had jade|he leads

i/t

5 it it|fit fit|tie tie|sit sit|kit kit|its its|fits

6 a kit|a fit|a tie|lit it|it fits|it sits|it is fit

o/r

7 or or|for for|ore ore|fro fro|oar oar|roe roe|rode

8 a rod|a door|a rose|or for|her or|he rode|or a rod

space bar

9 of he or it is to if do el odd off too for she the

10 it is|if it|do so|if he|to do|or the|she is|of all

Tip:
Scrolling Text is located in the Web Tools toolbar in *Microsoft Word 2000*.

Note:
Some browsers may not support the scrolling text feature.

1. Open a blank Web page, and use the Scrolling Text feature to key the text below. Select options to scroll it to the left in an infinite loop at a moderate speed.

   This is an example of scrolling text.

2. Using the same text, experiment with other scrolling options in the Scrolling Text dialog box.
3. Open *index* (html) and insert the text below as scrolling text below the mission statement. Save your file.

   Visit the Hall of Fame page to see this year's inductees.

LESSON 3 USE HYPERLINKS IN WEB PAGES

Objective:
To learn to insert a variety of hyperlinks in Web pages.

Activity 1 • Review

1. Open *SHSBKGRD* and save it as a new Web page named *HALL* (html) in the *SHSXXX* folder.
2. Delete existing text and key the text at the right in a table, using 36-pt. font for the Web page title, 24-pt. font for the table title, 18-pt. font for the column headings, and 10-pt. font for the entries. Use a Web design.
3. Using a 12-pt. font, key the two lines of text and bottom table at the right. Use a Web design for the table.
4. You decide all other formatting features, but make this page look like the other three Web pages.
5. Insert **Southwestern High School Alumni Association Hall of Fame** in the title bar.

Save as: *HALL* (html) in the *SHSXXX* folder

Southwestern High School Alumni Association Hall of Fame

Hall of Fame Inductees					
Year	Arts	Business	Education	Medicine	Sports
1998	Paul Adamek '60	Isako Mori '49	Anthony Bauer '67	Wallace Rapp '64	Walter Suchy '48
1999	Robert Rothey '83	Denise Spahr '73	Janice Marks '55	Laura Weigel '72	Victor Ophar '76
2000	Kristine Wood '44	Clarence Booth '79	Roberta Turner '79	Constance Cain '56	Janet Krise '94
2001	Patricia Liley '57	Natalie Mays '61	Harry Heil '82	Africa Cole '83	Stanley Lang '63
2002	Emilio Cruz '91	Eugene Lytle '89	Marlene Kuenzi '91	Michael Wray '68	Jeremy Davis '87

To make reservations for this year's Hall of Fame Banquet, e-mail the Webmaster.

Home	Board Members	Events

Activity 2 • About Hyperlinks

1. Read the text at the right.
2. Consider how hyperlinks can streamline moving between documents.

Web pages can be enriched through the use of **hyperlinks**. Graphics or text hyperlinks usually appear in a different font color and underlined. When hyperlinks are inserted into a Web page, the user can click them to go to a different location.

The location can be a different Web site, a different Web page within the same Web site, another location within the same Web page, or an e-mail address.

In the next four activities, you will insert each of the four kinds of hyperlinks into the Web pages for the Southwestern High School Alumni Association.

3D • 7'
Review (N) and (G)

Key each line twice SS; DS between 2-line groups.

Review n

1 j j nj nj an an and and end end ant ant land lands
2 nj nj an an en en in in on on end end and and hand
3 an en; an end; an ant; no end; on land; a fine end

Review g

4 f f gf gf go go fog fog got got fig figs jogs jogs
5 gf gf go go got got dig dig jog jog logs logs golf
6 to go; he got; to jog; to jig; the fog; is to golf

SKILL BUILDING

3E • 13'
Keyboard Reinforcement

1. Key the lines once SS with a DS between 2-line groups.
2. Key the lines again at a faster pace.

Technique Goals:

- fingers deeply curved
- wrists low, but not resting
- hands/arms steady
- eyes on copy as you key

reach review
1 a;sldkfj ed ol rf jh tf nj gf lo de jh ft nj fr a;
2 he jogs; an old ski; do a log for; she left a jar;

n/g
3 an an | go go | in in | dig dig | and and | got got | end ends
4 go to; is an; log on; sign it; and golf; fine figs

space bar
5 if if | an an | go go | of of | or or | he he | it it | is is | do
6 if it is | is to go | he or she | to do this | of the sign

all keys learned
7 she had an old oak desk; a jell jar is at the side
8 he has left for the lake; she goes there at eight;

all keys learned
9 she said he did it for her; he is to take the oars
10 sign the list on the desk; go right to the old jet

3F • 5'
Technique: (Enter)

Key each line twice SS; DS between 2-line groups.

Practice **C • U • E**

Keep up your pace to the end of the line, return quickly, and begin the new line without a pause or stop.

1 she is gone;
2 she got the dogs;
3 she jogs on the roads;
4 he goes to the lake at one;
5 he has to go get their old dogs;
6 he is a hand on the rig in the north;

Activity 7, cont.

- When the school district decided to renovate the stadium entrance, the SHSAA Board agreed to donate $500 to support this endeavor. The results are definitely an improvement over the "old" entrance many of us remember.

Insert *STADIUM.jpg* here.

Return to the Top

Upcoming Events

Additional information about each of these events can be obtained from the Webmaster.

- The **5th Annual Alumni Golf Outing** will be held at Joplin's Public Golf Course on Saturday, July 15, at 9:30 a.m. Use this mailbox to get more information.

Insert *GOLF.jpg* here.

- The SHSAA Homecoming activities are scheduled for Friday and Saturday, October 6 and 7. A cookout will take place at 6:30 p.m. in Parking Lot A before the football game with Madison High. On Saturday, five new members will be inducted into the **Southwestern High School Alumni Hall of Fame** at the banquet at Lanier Country Club.

Insert *SCHOOL.jpg* here.

- The **Class of 1975 Reunion** is scheduled for August 12 at Lanier Country Club.

Return to the Top

Activity 8 • Scrolling Text

1. Read the text at the right.
2. Learn to scroll text with your software.
3. Complete the steps on the next page.

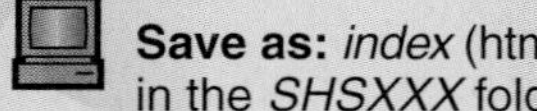

Save as: *index* (html) in the *SHSXXX* folder

Scrolling text, sometimes called **marquee display**, can be used in Web pages. The Scrolling Text feature should be used very infrequently because it annoys many people and it can make the text difficult to read. Scrolling text is useful in some places, for example, on an e-commerce Web site that is advertising a special sale.

The illustration at the right shows the Scrolling Text dialog box. The text to be scrolled is keyed in the top dialog box, and the bottom dialog box shows the effect the selected options have on the text.

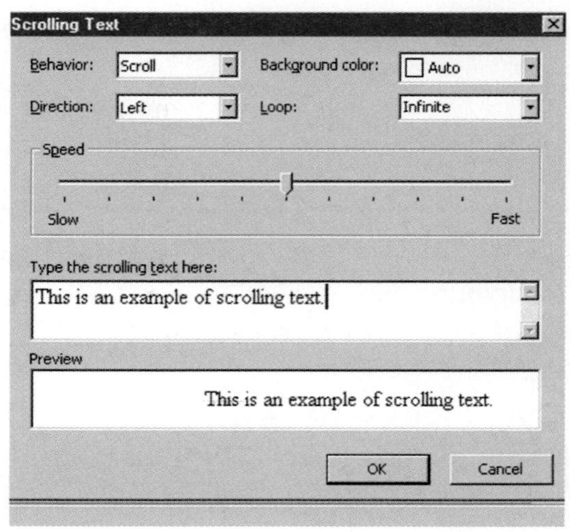

(continued on next page)

LESSON 4 — REVIEW LETTER KEYS (left shift, period, u, AND c)

Objectives:

1. To review reach technique for **left shift** and **.** (period).
2. To review reach technique for **u** and **c**.

4A • 5' Conditioning Practice

Key each line twice SS (slowly, then faster); DS between 2-line groups.

```
reach review        1 ed ik rf ol gf hj tf nj de ki fr lo fg jh ft jn a;
space bar           2 or is to if an of el so it go id he do as in at on
all keys learned    3 he is; if an; or do; to go; a jak; an oak; of all;
```

4B • 7' Review Left Shift and .

Key each line twice SS (slowly, then faster); DS between 2-line groups.

Spacing **C • U • E**

Space once after . following abbreviations and initials. Do not space after . within abbreviations. Space twice after . at end of a sentence* except at line endings. There, return without spacing.

*Although desktop publishing calls for just one space after terminal punctuation, the standard two spaces are specified in this textbook.

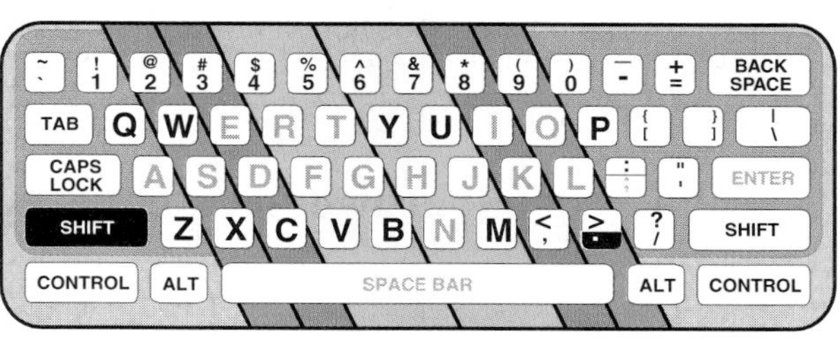

Shifting **C • U • E**

Shift, strike key, and release both in a quick 1-2-3 count.

Review left shift key

```
1 a a Ja Ja Ka Ka La La Hal Hal Kal Kal Jae Jae Lana
2 Kal rode; Kae did it; Hans has jade; Jan ate a fig
3 I see that Jake is to aid Kae at the Oak Lake sale
```

Review . (period)

```
4 l l .l .l fl. fl. ed. ed. ft. ft. rd. rd. hr. hrs.
5 .l .l fl. fl. hr. hr. e.g. e.g. i.e. i.e. in. ins.
6 fl. ft. hr. ed. rd. rt. off. fed. ord. alt. asstd.
```

SKILL BUILDING

4C • 13' Keyboard Reinforcement

1. Key the lines once SS; DS between 2-line groups.
2. Key the lines again at a faster pace.

Technique Goals:

- curved, upright fingers
- wrists low, but not resting
- quick-snap keystrokes
- eyes on copy as you key

```
h/e           1 hj ed jhj ded ha el he she led had eke her ale die
              2 Heidi had a good lead at the end of the first set.

i/r           3 ik rf kik frf is or sir ire ore his risk fire ride
              4 Kier is taking a high risk if he rides that horse.

o/t           5 ol tf lol ftf so it of too oft hot toe lot the old
              6 Ola has lost the list she took to that food store.

n/g           7 nj gf jnj fgf go an got and nag gin hang gone sign
              8 Lang and she are going to sing nine songs at noon.

left shift/.  9 Oak Lake; N. J. Karis; Lt. L. J. Oates; Lara Nador
             10 J. K. Larkin is going to Idaho to see Linda Jakes.
```

Activity 6 • Insert a Picture in a Web Page

1. Read the text at the right.
2. Complete the steps at the right.

Learning **C • U • E**

If you have alignment problems, try placing your graphics or pictures within a centered table on your Web page.

Picture and graphics files, like clip art, can be inserted into Web pages just as they are inserted into wp documents. Once inserted, a picture can be moved, edited, and used as a hyperlink, if desired.

Note: If you use pictures from another Web page, you must give proper credit to that Web page.

1. Open a new Web page and insert *L1PICTURE.jpg*. Size the picture so it is about 3" wide and left-aligned in the upper-left corner.
2. Copy *L1PICTURE* and paste it in the middle of the page.
3. Paste another copy of *L1PICTURE* right-aligned in the lower-right corner.
4. Save this document as a Web page named *DWPL2ACT6* (html), and then view it in a browser to make sure the browser supports the different horizontal positions. **Note:** If your browser does not support center alignment, it will move the picture from the center to a left or right alignment position. If this is the case, you will not be able to center-align pictures.

Activity 7 • Application

1. Open *DWPL1ACT3* (background with font and font color), and save it as a Web page named *EVENTS* (html) in the *SHSXXX* folder.
2. Delete the existing text and key the information at the right and on the next page using the background, font, and font color you chose:
   - Use 36-pt. font for the title and 12 pt. for the table entries.
   - Use the font color for the table borders.
   - Open *index* (html). Copy the mascot (lion) graphic. Close the file. Paste the image centered below the second table.
   - Use bold as shown.
   - Make new pictures 3" wide but keep them in proportion and center-align them, if possible.
3. View *EVENTS* as a Web page and make any needed changes.
4. Insert **Southwestern High School Alumni Association Events** in the title bar.

Save as: *EVENTS* (html) in the *SHSXXX* folder

Southwestern High School Alumni Association Events

Recent Events	**Upcoming Events**

Home	**Board Members**	**Hall of Fame**

Recent Events

➤ Bill Wiles, owner of Elite Landscape, and several other SHSAA members planted and will maintain this flower garden at the intersection near the high school in May. SHSAA donated the flowers.

Insert *FLOWERS.jpg* here. *Make it and all other pictures in this activity 3" wide.*

➤ SHSAA's **2d Annual 5K Run and Walk** was held at the Holt Trail in June. Over 125 alumni participated in this enjoyable event.

Insert *TRAIL.jpg* here.

(continued on next page)

4D • 7' Review [U] and [C]

Key each line twice SS; DS between 2-line groups.

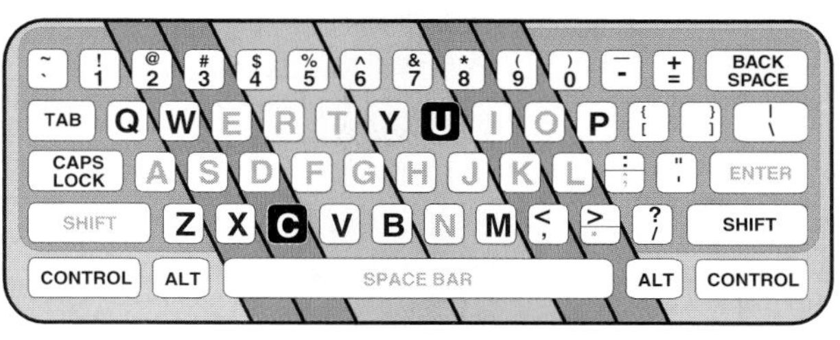

Review u

1 j j uj uj us us us jug jug jut jut due due fur fur
2 uj uj jug jug sue sue lug lug use use lug lug dues
3 a jug; due us; the fur; use it; a fur rug; is just

Review c

4 d d cd cd cod cod cog cog tic tic cot cot can cans
5 cd cd cod cod ice ice can can code code dock docks
6 a cod; a cog; the ice; she can; the dock; the code

SKILL BUILDING

4E • 13' Keyboard Reinforcement

1. Key the lines once SS with a DS between 2-line groups.
2. Key the lines again at a faster pace.

Technique Goals:

- Reach up without moving hands away from your body.
- Reach down without moving hands toward your body.
- Use quick-snap keystrokes.
- Eyes on copy as you key.

3d/1st

1 in cut nut ran cue can cot fun hen car urn den cog
2 Nan is cute; he is curt; turn a cog; he can use it

left shift and .

3 Kae had taken a lead. Jack then cut ahead of her.
4 I said to use Kan. for Kansas and Ore. for Oregon.

key words

5 and cue for jut end kit led old fit just golf coed
6 an due cut such fuss rich lack turn dock turf curl

key phrases

7 an urn|is due|to cut|for us|to use|cut off|such as
8 just in|code it|turn on|cure it|as such|is in|luck

all keys learned

9 Nida is to get the ice; Jacki is to call for cola.
10 Ira is sure that he can go there in an hour or so.

4F • 5' Technique: [Enter]

Key each line twice SS; DS between 2-line groups.

Practice **C • U • E**

Keep up your pace to the end of the line, return quickly, and begin the new line without a pause or stop.

1 Jan has gone to ski;
2 she took a train at nine.
3 Hans lost the three old disks;
4 he needs to find another disk soon.
5 Jack said he left the disks at the lake;
6 Nanci and I can go get the disks at the lake.

Keep eyes on copy as you strike the ENTER key.

5. Have the page title bar read **Southwestern High School Alumni Association Home Page**.

Save as: *index* (html) in the *SHSXXX* folder

Voice Mailbox	535 555-0193

Board Members	Events	Hall of Fame
Southwestern School District		

Activity 4 • Application

1. Open *SHSBKGRD*, delete the text, and save it as a Web page named *BDMBRS* (html) in the *SHSXXX* folder.
2. Key **Southwestern High School Alumni Association Board Members** in 36-pt. font at the top of the page.
3. Key and center the first table at the right, using 24-pt. bold font for the title; 18-pt. bold font for the column headings; and 12-pt. font for the entries. Make the table borders and font color match.
4. Key and center the second table with 1.5" columns, matching border color with font color.
5. Use 12-pt. bold font for the column entries and center them.
6. Insert in title bar **Southwestern High School Alumni Association Board Members**.

Save as: *BDMBRS* (html) in the *SHSXXX* folder

SHSAA BOARD MEMBERS			
Office	Name	Class	E-mail
President	Adrian Hess	1964	
Vice President	Harry Malone	1982	
Corresponding Secretary	William Evans	1976	
Recording Secretary	Amanda Egan	1983	
Treasurer	Barbara Narick	2000	
Historian	Alex Rendulic	1958	
Legal Representative	Gladys Young	1995	
Membership Chair	Paul Lyman	1998	
Special Events Chair	Susan Rhymond	1969	
Webmaster	Kimberly Varati	1994	

Home	Events	Hall of Fame

Activity 5 • Insert Clip Art

1. Read the text at the right.
2. Complete the steps at the right.

Clip art can be inserted into Web pages in the same manner as it is inserted into wp documents. Once inserted, it can be moved, edited, and used as a hyperlink, if desired. (Hyperlinks are presented in Lesson 3.)

Note: If you use clip art from an Internet Web page, first check the copyright policy. If necessary, give proper credit to that Web site.

1. Open a blank Web page and insert images from clip art that you select. Make them about 1.5" wide, and center-align one, right-align the second, and left-align the third.
2. Save this document as a Web page named *DWPL2ACT5* (html), and then view it to make sure the browser supports the different horizontal positions.
3. Find a lion, Southwestern's mascot, in clip art, open *index*, and insert the lion in the horizontal center after the first heading. Size the image so it is about 1.5" wide. Save the revised file.

LESSON 5 | REVIEW LETTER KEYS (w, right shift, b, AND y)

Objectives:

1. To review reach technique for **w** and **right shift**.
2. To review reach technique for **b** and **y**.

5A • 5'
Conditioning Practice

Key each line twice SS (slowly, then faster); DS between 2-line groups.

reach review
1 rf gf de ju jn ki lo cd ik rf .l ed hj tf ol gf ft

u/c
2 us cod use cut sue cot jut cog nut cue con lug ice

all letters learned
3 Hugh has just taken a lead in a race for a record.

5B • 7'
Review W and Right Shift

Key each line twice SS (slowly, then faster); DS between 2-line groups.

Review w

1 s s ws ws sow sow wow wow low low how how cow cows

2 sw sw ws ws ow ow now now row row own own tow tows

3 to sow; is how; so low; to own; too low; is to row

Review right shift key

4 A; A; Al Al; Cal Cal; Ali or Flo; Di and Sol left.

5 Ali lost to Ron; Cal lost to Elsa; Di lost to Del.

6 Tina has left for Tucson; Dori can find her there.

5C • 13'
Keyboard Reinforcement

1. Key the lines once SS; DS between 2-line groups.
2. Key the lines again at a faster pace.

Practice **C • U • E**

Key at a steady pace; space quickly after each word; keep the insertion point moving steadily.

w and right shift
1 Dr. Rowe is in Tulsa now; Dr. Cowan will see Rolf.
2 Gwinn took the gown to Golda Swit on Downs Circle.

n/g
3 to go | go on | no go | an urn | dug in | and got | and a sign
4 He is to sign for the urn to go on the high chest.

key words
5 if ow us or go he an it of own did oak the cut jug
6 do all and for cog odd ant fig rug low cue row end

key phrases
7 we did | for a jar | she is due | cut the oak | he owns it
8 all of us | to own the | she is to go | when he has gone

all keys learned
9 Jan and Chris are gone; Di and Nick get here soon.
10 Doug will work for her at the new store in Newton.

LESSON 2 WEB PAGES WITH TABLES, GRAPHICS, AND PICTURES

Objective:
To create Web pages with tables, graphics, and pictures.

Activity 1 • Web Site for Southwestern High School Alumni Association

In this and the next lesson, you will complete the first few pages of a Web site for the Southwestern High School Alumni Association.

1. Find the folder named *CD-SHSXXX* and change its name by deleting the *CD-* and replacing the *XXX* with your initials.

Note: All files relating to the Southwestern High School Alumni Association Web site must be filed in the *SHSXXX* folder so hyperlinks to your files can be easily inserted in later activities. The Web site then can be uploaded to the Internet or an intranet, if applicable.

2. Southwestern's school colors are brown and yellow. Create a corresponding background and a font color that is readable and attractive. Select a font from Arial, Comic Sans MS, or Verdana. Key your name in the font and font color you chose.
3. Save the background and font selections in a file named *SHSBKGRD* (html). This file will be used for the three SHSAA Web pages in Lessons 2–3.

Activity 2 • Review

1. Open *SHSBKGRD*, delete the text, and save it as a Web page named *index* in the *SHSXXX* folder. *Index.html* is the home page for the SHSAA Web site.
2. Key the text at the right as the home page of a Web site, keying the first line in 36-pt. font; the next two lines in 24-pt. font; the first ¶ in 12-pt. font; and the last ¶ in italicized 10-pt. font.

Save as: *index* (html) in the *SHSXXX* folder

3. View it as a Web page.

Southwestern High School Alumni Association

Proud of Our Past, Building Pride in Our Future

Mission Statement:

SHSAA's mission is to provide a means by which interested alumni of Southwestern High School can maintain an enduring relationship with past and present students, faculty, and staff of the Southwestern School District. By promoting Association membership and alumni activities and providing assistance to the School District and its stakeholders, the SHSAA will accomplish its mission.

This site is maintained by Southwestern High School students and the SHSAA Webmaster. Please e-mail your feedback to the Webmaster.

Activity 3 • Tables

1. Read the text at the right, and learn to create tables for Web pages.
2. Open *index* (html).
3. Insert below the mission statement the two tables found on p. 519. Place each table in the horizontal center; use 12-pt. bold font; and use the font color you selected to color the table borders.

(continued on next page)

Many Web pages use tables to organize information in an attractive manner. The table feature of your word processor can be used to create tables as they are created in wp documents. If you are using *Word*, use one of the Web designs in the Table AutoFormat feature as the table format. The illustration at the right shows the Table AutoFormat dialog box with a Web design selected and displayed.

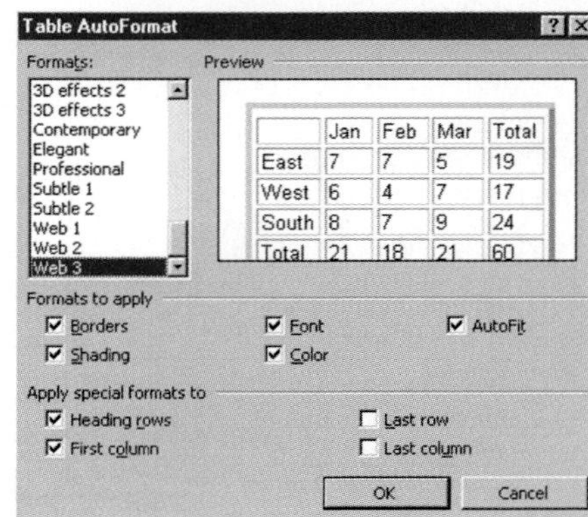

5D • 7' Review (B) and (Y)

Key each line twice SS; DS between 2-line groups.

Review b

1 f f bf bf fib fib rob rob but but big big fib fibs

2 bf bf rob rob lob lob orb orb bid bid bud bud ribs

3 a rib; to fib; rub it; an orb; or rob; but she bid

Review y

4 j j yj yj jay jay lay lay hay hay day day say says

5 yj yj jay jay eye eye dye dye yes yes yet yet jays

6 a jay; to say; an eye; he says; dye it; has an eye

5E • 13' Keyboard Reinforcement

1. Key the lines once SS with a DS between 2-line groups.
2. Key the lines again at a faster pace.

Technique Goals:

- Reach up without moving hands away from your body.
- Reach down without moving hands toward your body.
- Use quick-snap keystrokes.
- Eyes on copy as you key.

reach review

1 fg sw ki gf bf ol ed yj ws ik rf hj cd nj tf .l uj

2 a kit low for jut led sow fob ask sun cud jet grow

3d/1st rows

3 no in bow any tub yen cut sub coy ran bin cow deck

4 Cody wants to buy this baby cub for the young boy.

key words

5 by and for the got all did but cut now say jut ask

6 work just such hand this goal boys held furl eight

key phrases

7 to do | can go | to bow | for all | did jet | ask her | to buy

8 if she | to work | and such | the goal | for this | held the

all letters learned

9 Becky has auburn hair and wide eyes of light jade.

10 Juan left Bobby at the dog show near our ice rink.

gwam 1' | 1 | 2 | 3 | 4 | 5 | 6 | 7 | 8 | 9 | 10 |

5F • 5' Technique: (Enter)

Key each line twice SS; DS between 2-line groups.

Practice **C · U · E**

Keep up your pace to the end of the line, return quickly, and begin the new line without a pause or stop.

Nancy has her coats.

Dan took her to the show.

Jay barely lost the last race.

Becky can go to the dance with Bob.

Jessica said he has brown eyes and hair.

Rebecca was not able to attend the late show.

gwam 1' | 1 | 2 | 3 | 4 | 5 | 6 | 7 | 8 | 9 |

4. Complete the steps at the right to create different backgrounds for this text.

Tip:

Find *L1PICTURE* in the CD-IMAGES folder.

Save as:
DWPL1ACT3 (html)

1. Create backgrounds using solid colors of your choice.
2. Create backgrounds using textures of your choice.
3. Create backgrounds using patterns of your choice.
4. Create a background using the picture with the filename *L1PICTURE*.
5. Choose a background and font color that you believe is very easy to read and attractive. Show your instructor what you have chosen.
6. Save the Web page as an HTML file, preview it, and print. (The background won't print.)

Activity 4 • Title a Web Page

1. Read the text at the right.
2. Learn to create a specific title on a Web page using your software.
3. Open *DWPL1ACT3*.
4. Insert **My Web Page Background** as the title of the Web page.

Save as:
DWPL1ACT4 (html)

Each Web page has a title displayed in the browser title bar at the top of the window. If you do not specify a title for a Web page, the software will create one for you. Since you want the title to accurately describe the content of the Web page, you should specify a title to be displayed.

In *Word*, you specify a Web page title from the Save as Web Page option on the File menu. Click the Change Title button and key the desired title in the Set Page Title dialog box. The Save as Web Page dialog box and the Set Page Title dialog box are illustrated at the right.

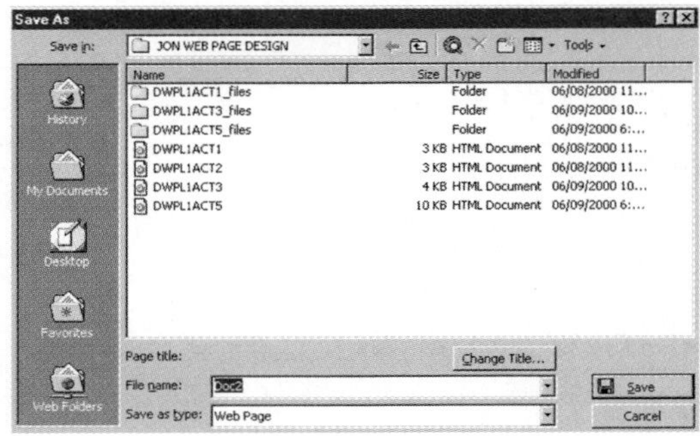

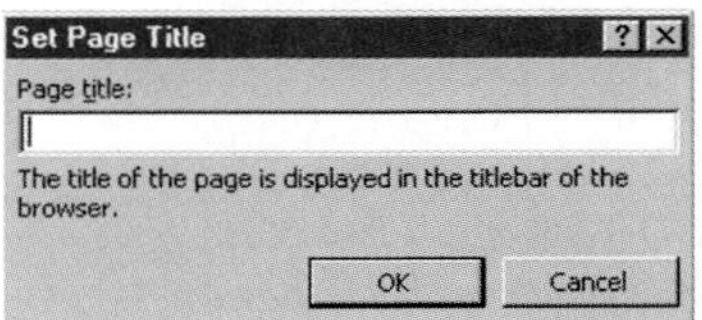

Activity 5 • Application

1. Open *DWPL1ACT4* and delete the existing text. Key the text at the right as a Web page, using the directions given in the text.

Save as:
DWPL1ACT5 (html)

2. Preview the document as a Web page.
3. Compare the Web page text with the text you keyed and directions you followed. Does your browser support all of the wp features used in this activity?

Substitute a sans serif font such as Arial if you don't have the font called for in this activity.

Center-align this text using 36-pt. Verdana font.

Left-align this text using 18-pt. Verdana font.

Right-align this text using 18-pt. Verdana font.

Using left align, 12-pt. Verdana font, and a bullet style you select, list the following lines:

- Bullet 1
- Bullet 2
- Bullet 3

Using 16-pt. Comic Sans MS font, indent the following lines as directed:

Indent this line 0.5" from left margin.

Indent this line 1" from left margin.

Indent this line 1.5" from left margin.

Center a shaded text box with a border. Use 14-pt. Comic Sans MS font for the text. Select a font color.

LESSON 6 REVIEW LETTER KEYS (m, x, p, AND v)

Objectives:

1. To review reach technique for **m** and **x**.
2. To review reach technique for **p** and **v**.

6A • 5' Conditioning Practice

Key each line twice SS (slowly, then faster); DS between 2-line groups.

reach review
1 bf ol rf yj ed nj ws ik tf hj cd uj gf by us if ow

b/y
2 by bye boy buy yes fib dye bit yet but try bet you

all letters learned
3 Robby can win the gold if he just keys a new high.

6B • 7' Review M and X

Key each line twice SS (slowly, then faster); DS between 2-line groups.

Review m

1 j j mj mj am am am me me ma ma jam jam ham ham yam

2 mj mj me me me may may yam yam dam dam men men jam

3 am to; if me; a man; a yam; a ham; he may; the hem

Review x

4 s s xs xs ox ox ax ax six six fix fix fox fox axis

5 xs xs sx sx ox ox six six nix nix fix fix lax flax

6 a fox; an ox; fix it; by six; is lax; to fix an ax

6C • 13' Keyboard Reinforcement

1. Key the lines once SS with a DS between 2-line groups.
2. Key the lines again at a faster pace.

Technique Goals:

- Reach up without moving hands away from your body.
- Reach down without moving hands toward your body.
- Use quick-snap keystrokes.
- Eyes on copy as you key.

3d/1st rows
1 by am end fix men box hem but six now cut gem ribs
2 me ox buy den cub ran own form went oxen fine club

space bar
3 an of me do am if us or is by go ma so ah ox it ow
4 by man buy fan jam can any tan may rob ham fun guy

key words
5 if us me do an sow the cut big jam rub oak lax boy
6 curl work form born name flex just done many right

key phrases
7 or jam|if she|for me|is big|an end|or buy|is to be
8 to fix|and cut|for work|and such|big firm|the call

all letters learned
9 Jacki is now at the gym; Lex is due there by four.
10 Joni saw that she could fix my old bike for Gilda.

Activity 1 • Create, View, and Save a Web Page

1. Read the text at the right.
2. Learn to access the screen in which you will create a Web page.
3. Open a new Web page and key your name, the date, and your school's name on three lines in the upper-left corner of the document.
4. Save the document as an HTML file, and then view the document as a Web page in Web Page Preview.

Save as: *DWPL1ACT1* (html)

Word processors often have various methods of creating Web pages. One method is to use a Web page wizard to create Web pages based on answers you provide to the wizard's questions.

A second method is to use a Web page template that contains text and formatting features that you can customize to create a Web page similar to but slightly different from that in the template.

A third method, and the one suggested for this unit's activities, is to create a Web page using Web Layout View in a word processor. Web Layout View makes it possible to create a Web page, and it simulates the way a document will look when it is viewed as a Web page. Text, graphics, pictures, backgrounds, etc., appear as they would in a Web browser. See the Learning Cue for another way to view a document as a Web page.

Web Layout View can be accessed in different ways. For example, when using *Word*, it can be accessed by opening a new document as a Web page or by opening a document while in another view and then clicking the Web Layout View icon on the toolbar to the left of the horizontal scroll bar.

A wp document that is to be used as a Web page must be saved as an HTML file. When this is done, the word processor will automatically insert HTML code into the document. Without the HTML code a document cannot be posted to the WWW on the Internet or on the company's intranet.

The illustration below shows the Web Page icon that can be selected from File/New to open a blank Web page in *Word*.

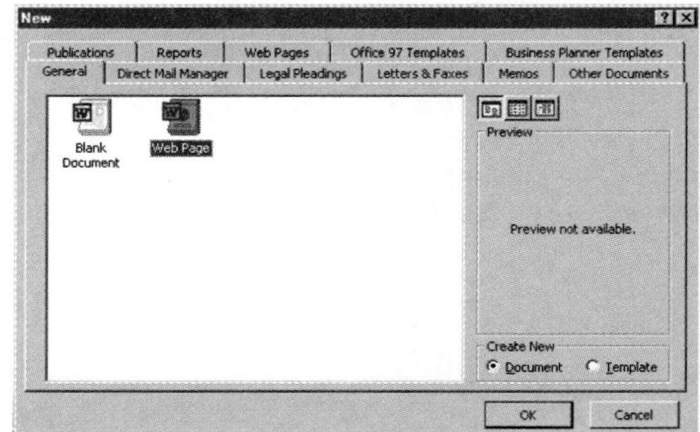

Learning **C • U • E**

When using *Word*, a document can be previewed as a Web page by selecting Web Page Preview from the File menu. This command opens a browser and displays the document as a Web page in the browser.

Activity 2 • View HTML Code

1. Read the text at the right.
2. Learn to view HTML code with your word processor.
3. Open *DWPL1ACT1* and view the HTML code.

When the file in Activity 1 was saved as a Web page, HTML code was automatically inserted into the document. With *Word*, this code can be viewed by selecting *HTML Source* from the View Menu. The illustration at the right shows some of the HTML code that was inserted into the Web page created in Activity 1.

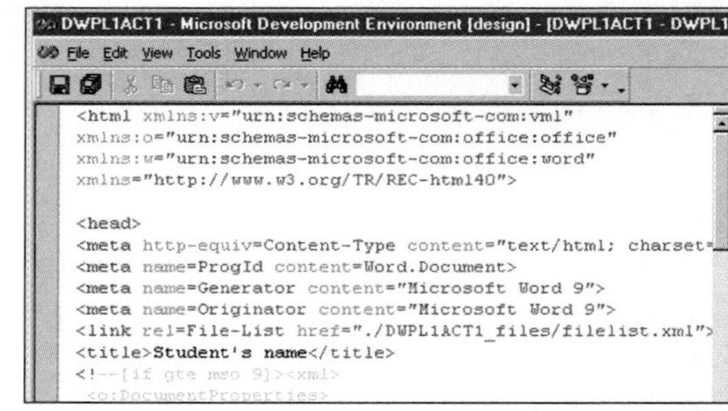

Activity 3 • Backgrounds

1. Read the text at the right.
2. Open a new Web page.
3. On the first three lines, center your name using 48-pt. Arial; your school name using 24-pt. Arial; and today's date using 12-pt. Arial, all in a font color that you select.

(continued on next page)

Backgrounds found on the Format menu can be used to create attractive Web pages. With backgrounds, you can apply various colors and effects: a solid color, a color in a variety of textures or patterns, different gradients that use one or two shaded colors, or a picture.

A good practice is to select the background and the color of the font together so that the combination is easy to read and attractive.

The illustration at the right shows the gradient, texture, pattern, and picture tabs that can be used in *Word*. In addition, 12 textures are displayed.

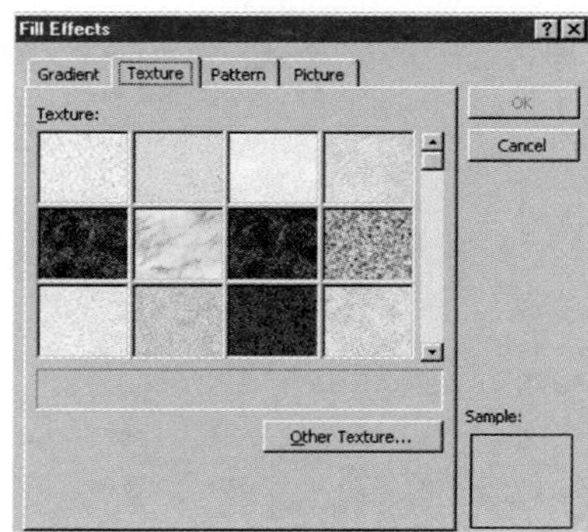

6D • 7' Review P and V

Key each line twice SS; DS between 2-line groups.

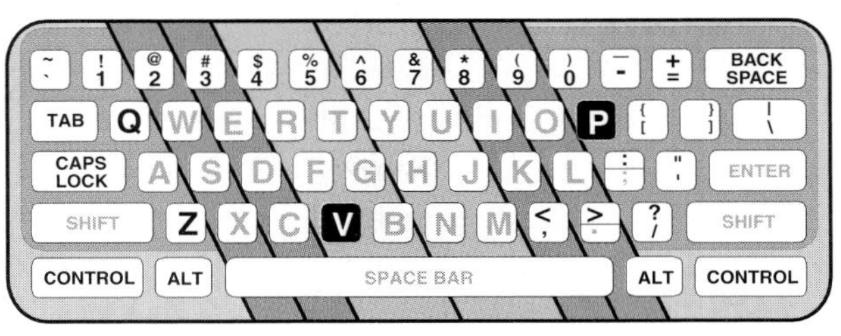

Review p

1 ; ; p; p; pa pa up up apt apt pen pen lap lap kept

2 p; p; pa pa pa pan pan nap nap paw paw gap gap rap

3 a pen; a cap; apt to pay; pick it up; plan to keep

Review v

4 f f vf vf via via vie vie have have five five live

5 vf vf vie vie vie van van view view dive dive jive

6 go via; vie for; has vim; a view; to live; or have

6E • 13' Keyboard Reinforcement

1. Key the lines once SS; DS between 2-line groups.
2. Key the lines again at a faster pace.

Practice **C • U • E**

- Reach up without moving hands away from your body.
- Reach down without moving hands toward your body.
- Use quick-snap keystrokes.
- Eyes on copy as you key.

reach review

1 vf p; xs mj ed yj ws nj rf ik tf ol cd hj gf uj bf

2 if lap jag own may she for but van cub sod six oak

3d/1st rows

3 by vie pen vim cup six but now man nor ton may pan

4 by six but now may cut sent me fine gems five reps

key words

5 with kept turn corn duty curl just have worn plans

6 name burn form when jury glad vote exit came eight

key phrases

7 if they | he kept | with us | of land | burn it | to name it

8 to plan | so sure | is glad | an exit | so much | to view it

all letters learned

9 Kevin does a top job on your flax farm with Craig.

10 Dixon flew blue jets eight times over a city park.

6F • 5' Technique: Spacing with Punctuation

Key each line twice SS; DS between 2-line groups.

Spacing **C • U • E**

Do not space after an internal period in an abbreviation, such as Ed.D.

1 Dr. Kennedy has a Ph.D., not an Ed.D., in physics.

2 Lynn may send a box c.o.d. to Ms. Fox in St. Paul.

3 J. R. and Tim will go by boat to St. Louis in May.

4 Lexi keyed ect. for etc. and lost the match to me.

5 Mr. and Mrs. D. J. Keaton set sail for the island.

6 Ms. Fenton may take her Ed.D. exam early in March.

LESSONS 1–6 (6–8 HOURS)

Designing Web Pages

LESSON 1 LEARNING WEB PAGE BASICS

Objectives:

1. To learn to open a blank Web page.
2. To create a page background.
3. To title and save a Web page file.

Introduction

The overview at the right explains personal and business practices used for creating Web pages. It also introduces you to some basic aspects and features of designing Web pages and Web sites that you will be working with in this unit.

Intranet: a company's internal computer network that allows its employees to access company documents using a Web browser. Internet users outside the company cannot access intranet documents unless they are given special access codes. In other words, an intranet is a company's private Internet.

Designing Web Pages

There are many different ways to create Web pages. Often large companies employ expert programmers who write time-consuming code to create Web pages and maintain complicated Web sites for the Internet or the company's **intranet** (see definition at left).

Other businesses may contract with Web page design companies or consultants to create their Web pages. Some businesses create and maintain their Web sites by using Web page design software that does not require knowledge of HTML.

Many smaller companies, and individuals creating personal Web sites, use word processing, spreadsheet, or electronic presentation software to create Web pages. Pages created with these general application packages can be very effective and can contain many of the features of Web pages designed with more "powerful" software or expert programmers writing code. They are likely, however, to lack some of the "bells and whistles" that the specialized software and expert programmers can provide.

Web Page Activities

Word processing software, such as *Microsoft Word 2000* or an editor such as *Netscape Composer*, can be used to complete the Web page design activities in this unit. Program features, design methods, and Web page appearances may be different if you use a software package other than *Microsoft Word 2000*.

In Lessons 1–3, you will create Web pages for a high school alumni association. The pages include a background and text in various font sizes, styles, and colors. Hyperlinks connect to places within the same Web page, to other Web pages within the same Web site, to different Web sites, and to people with e-mail addresses. Pictures, graphics, and tables are used.

In Lessons 4–6, you have an opportunity to create a Web site of your choice. It can be Web pages for yourself, your family, your school, a business, an organization, etc. You should, therefore, think about the purpose of your Web site and identify the Web pages you will include in your site as you complete the activities in Lessons 1–3.

Viewing Web Pages

You can view your Web page within the word processing software; through a browser; on the school's intranet, if applicable; or on the Internet, if you are permitted to do so.

When viewed on the Internet or intranet, your Web page format may look a little different than it does when viewed with a word processor since browsers do not support all word processing features. For example:

- Character formatting such as shadow, emboss, and engrave is not supported by all browsers.
- Tab settings may not appear when the browser is used.
- Spacing after the punctuation ending a sentence may change from two spaces to one space.
- The alignment of pictures and graphs and the placement of wrapped text may change.
- Headers and footers and page numbers may not appear.
- Row height in tables may change.

LESSON 7 REVIEW LETTER KEYS (q, comma, z, AND colon)

Objectives:

1. To review reach technique for **q** and , (comma).
2. To review reach technique for **z** and : (colon).

7A • 5' Conditioning Practice

Key each line twice SS (slowly, then faster); DS between 2-line groups; if time permits, key the lines again.

all letters learned
1 an dog fix all via own buy for the jam cop ask boy

p/v
2 a pan; a vote; apt to; vie for; her pay; have five

all letters learned
3 Darby will pack sixty pints of guava jam for Beth.

7B • 7' Review Q and ,

Key each line twice SS (slowly, then faster); DS between 2-line groups.

Spacing **C • U • E**

Space once after , used as punctuation.

Learn q

1 a qa qa aq aq quo quo qt. qt. quad quad quit quits
2 qa quo quo qt. qt. quay quay aqua aqua quite quite
3 a qt.; pro quo; a quad; to quit; the quay; a squad

Learn , (comma)

4 k k ,k ,k kit, kit; Rick, Jan, or I will go, also.
5 a ski, a ski; a kit, a kit; a kite, a kite; a bike
6 Tom, I see, is here; Pam, I am told, will be late.

7C • 13' Keyboard Reinforcement

1. Key lines once SS; DS between 2-line groups.
2. Key the lines again at a faster pace.

Technique Goals:

- Reach up without moving hands away from your body.
- Reach down without moving hands toward your body.
- Use quick-snap keystrokes.

reach review
1 qa .l ws ,k ed nj rf mj tf p; xs ol cd ik vf hj bf
2 yj gf hj quo vie pay cut now buy got mix vow forms

3d/1st rows
3 six may sun coy cue mud jar win via pick turn bike
4 to go|to win|for me|a peck|a quay|by then|the vote

key words
5 pa rub sit man for own fix jam via cod oak the got
6 by quo sub lay apt mix irk pay when rope give just

key phrases
7 an ox|of all|is to go|if he is|it is due|to pay us
8 if we pay|is of age|up to you|so we own|she saw me

all letters learned
9 Jevon will fix my pool deck if the big rain quits.
10 Verna did fly quick jets to map the six big towns.

E. In a month, you need to submit a report for your social studies course about one of the U.S. senators from your state. You plan to schedule a meeting with the senator or his/her staff while in Washington, D.C. to get information for your report. To learn more about your senator, search the Web for information about him/her prior to your visit. Find one or more Web sites that provide you with biographical information as well as his/her senatorial activities. Print a page to show what you have found.

F. You know you have time to see only a few attractions on your short visit to Washington, D.C.; therefore, you want to gather as much information as possible about the attractions so you can choose those that are of most interest to you. Search the Internet to find at least three attractions that are of interest to you and print one page from each Web site that describes the attraction. You may want to try to find a visitor's guide to Washington, D.C.

Scenario 2: Find and print the names of the last seven Heisman Trophy winners.

Scenario 3: Find at least three Web sites that permit job applicants to post electronic resumes. Print one page from each of the sites you find.

Scenario 4: You are interested in attending a public college or university in your state to study architecture. Search for Web sites for schools within your state that offer this major. If there are none in your state, expand your search to include a nearby state. Print the page(s) that indicate you found an architecture major at a school.

Scenario 5: You need to write a three- to five-page report on some aspect of recycling or income inequalities, so you search the Web for information. Select and narrow your topic, and then locate Web sites that you can reference in the report. Open a new wp document and do the following:

A. Specify the topic you will use for your report.
B. Copy text or graphics from at least two different Web sites that you can use in the report.
C. Key a reference for each site used.
D. Save as *SWL6ACTS5* and print the wp document and the first page of the home page for each Web site.

Scenario 6: Choose a stock or mutual fund. Find information on its performance for various periods within the last five-year period (or from inception, if less than five years). Print one or more graphs to show its performance.

7D • 7' Review Z and :

Key each line twice SS (slowly, then faster); DS between 2-line groups.

Language Skill **C • U • E**

- Space twice after : used as punctuation.
- Capitalize the first word of a complete sentence following a colon.
- Do not capitalize a sentence fragment following a colon.

Review z

1 a a za za zap zap zap zoo zoo zip zip zag zag zany
2 za za zap zap zed zed oz. oz. zoo zoo zip zip maze
3 zap it, zip it, an adz, to zap, the zoo, eight oz.

Review : (colon)

4 ; ; :; :; Date: Time: Name: Room: From: File:
5 :; :; To: File: Reply to: Dear Al: Shift for :
6 Two spaces follow a colon, thus: Try these steps:

7E • 13' Keyboard Reinforcement

1. Key the lines once SS with a DS between 2-line groups.
2. Key the lines again at a faster pace.

Technique Goals:

- curved, upright fingers
- quiet hands and arms
- steady keystroking pace

q/z
1 zoo qt. zap quo zeal quay zone quit maze quad hazy
2 Zeno amazed us all on the quiz but quit the squad.

p/x
3 apt six rip fix pens flex open flax drop next harp
4 Lex is apt to fix apple pie for the next six days.

v/m
5 vim mam van dim have move vamp more dive time five
6 Riva drove them to the mall in my vivid lemon van.

easy
7 Glen is to aid me with the work at the dog kennel.
8 Dodi is to go with the men to audit the six firms.

alphabet
9 Nigel saw a quick red fox jump over the lazy cubs.
10 Jacky can now give six big tips from the old quiz.

7F • 5' Block Paragraphs

1. Read the note at the right below.
2. Key each paragraph (¶) once SS; DS between them; then key them again faster.
3. If your instructor directs, key a 1' writing on each ¶; determine your *gwam*.

Paragraph 1 — gwam 1'

The space bar is a vital tool, for every fifth or 10
sixth stroke is a space when you key. If you use 20
it with good form, it will aid you to build speed. 30

Paragraph 2

Just keep the thumb low over the space bar. Move 10
the thumb down and in quickly toward your palm to 20
get the prized stroke you need to build top skill. 30

gwam 1' | 1 | 2 | 3 | 4 | 5 | 6 | 7 | 8 | 9 | 10 |

Note: At the end of a full line, the copy and insertion point move to the next line automatically. This is called a **soft return**. Another name for it is **word wrap**. Use word wrap when you key a paragraph. At the end of a paragraph, though, use two hard returns to place a double space between it and the next paragraph.

2. Use the yahoo.com directory to perform a search for sites where you can register the domain name for a Web page you designed. Find the one with the lowest registration fee. Also, select a domain name and see if it is still available. Print the page that states the registration fee and the one that tells you if the domain name is or is not available.

Activity 10 • Other Search Engine Services

1. Read the text at the right.
2. Complete the activities shown by using hyperlinks on either altavista.com or yahoo.com.
3. For each activity step, print one Web page that shows your findings.

Many search engines also provide convenient hyperlinks to other sites that people frequently use to get information from the Web. Some of the links you are likely to encounter can help you shop online, make travel plans and reservations, find people and places, get the latest news, check up-to-the-minute weather forecasts and conditions, and monitor stock market performance.

1. Find the location of your home on a site map.
2. Get driving directions from your home address to your school.
3. Find the telephone number and address of a favorite restaurant in your area.
4. Find the name of a store near your school where a Sony digital camera may be purchased.
5. Find the current index number for the Dow Jones Industrial Average and the NASDAQ stocks.

LESSON 6 APPLY WEB SEARCHING STRATEGIES

Objective:
To apply Internet information retrieval knowledge.

Search Activities

At the right and on the next page are several scenarios that require you to search the Internet for answers or information. You are to decide which search engines you will use and the search query to get the answers or information. Whenever you print a document from the Internet, make sure it has the Web site source, the total page count, and the date and time it was printed.

Scenario 1: You are planning a trip to Washington, D.C., and you decide to use the Internet to gather information that will help you plan and organize your activities.

A. Locate the name, address, telephone number, Web site address, and room prices of two hotels/motels in or near Washington, D.C. Look for lodging that is near a Metrorail subway station. Print page(s) that give the requested lodging information for each of the hotels/motels you find.
B. Since you will drive from your home to Washington, D.C., locate your hotel/motel on an online site map to find driving directions from your home to the hotel/motel. Print the map and directions.
C. Access a Web site that provides information about Smithsonian Institution tours for the public. Print the page(s) that provide the information about the tours.
D. Locate the Smithsonian Institution on an online site map and get driving directions from the hotel/motel. Print the map and directions.

(continued on next page)

REVIEW LETTER KEYS (caps lock, ?, tab, ', -, AND ")

Objectives:

1. To review reach technique for **Caps Lock**, **?** (question mark), **'** (apostrophe), **-** (hyphen), and " (quotation mark).
2. To review reach technique for the **Tab** key.

8A • 5' Conditioning Practice

Key each line twice SS; then key a 1' writing on line 3; determine *gwam* on the scale below line 3.

alphabet 1 Lovak won the squad prize cup for sixty big jumps.

z/: 2 To: Ms. Mazie Pelzer; from: Dr. Eliza J. Piazzo.

easy 3 He is to go with me to the dock to do work for us.

gwam 1' | 1 | 2 | 3 | 4 | 5 | 6 | 7 | 8 | 9 | 10 |

Note: Your **gwam** (gross words a minute) is the figure under the last letter keyed if you key only part of the line. If you key the line and start over, add 10 to that figure.

8B • 7' Review Caps Lock and ?

Key each line twice SS (slowly, then faster); DS between 2-line groups.

Note:
To key a series of capital letters, press CAPS LOCK, using the left little finger. To release CAPS LOCK, tap the CAPS LOCK key again.

Spacing C • U • E

Space twice after a ? at end of a sentence except at line or paragraph endings.

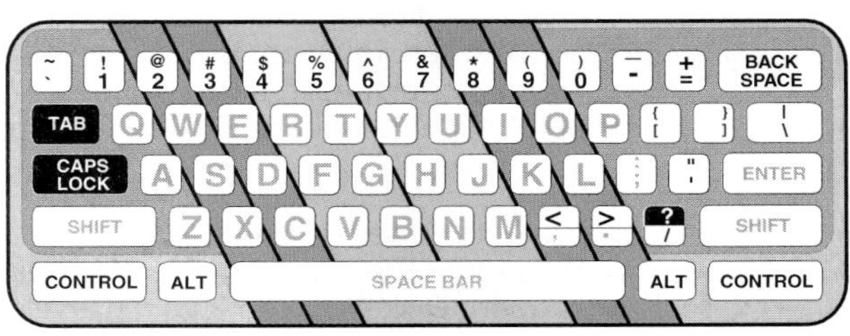

Review caps lock

1 Hal read PENTAGON and ADVISE AND CONSENT by Drury.

2 Oki joined FBLA when her sister joined PBL at OSU.

3 Zoe now belongs to AMS and DPE as well as to NBEA.

Review ? (question mark)

4 ; ; ?; ?; Who? What? When? Where? Why? Is it?

5 Who is it? Is it she? Did he go? Was she there?

6 Is it up to me? When is it? Did he key the line?

8C • 10' Review Tab

Indent and key each ¶ once SS, using word wrap (soft returns); DS between ¶s.

Note:
To indent the first line of a ¶, press TAB, using the left little finger. Usually tabs are set every 0.5" to the right of the left margin.

Tab → The tab key is used to indent blocks of copy such as these.

Tab → It should also be used for tables to arrange data quickly and neatly into columns.

Tab → Learn now to use the tab key by touch; doing so will add to your keying skill.

Tab → Strike the tab key firmly and release it very quickly. Begin the line without a pause.

Tab → If you hold the tab key down, the insertion point will move from tab to tab across the line.

Activity 7 • Natural Language Searches

1. Read the text at the right.
2. Complete the queries at the right and create a table.
3. Complete a table to report the query results and the usefulness of the first two Web sites listed.

 **Save as:** *SWL4ACT7*

With **natural language searching,** you can enter queries the way you would ask another person. For example the query, ***Who was the seventh president of the United States?*** should return information that enables you to answer this question easily and quickly. This method of searching is still relatively new; but it is likely to continue to improve as search engines improve, since it is the easiest method to use.

Using yahoo.com, altavista.com, and ixquick.com, ask the following questions. See if you can find the answer in the first two Web sites listed by each search engine.

1. Who was Abraham Lincoln's wife?
2. Who won the Super Bowl in 1975?

Activity 8 • Wildcard Searches

1. Read the text at the right.
2. Complete the activities at the right.
3. Create a table to record your answers and report the query results.

 **Save as:** *SWL4ACT8*

The asterisk (*) represents a **wildcard**, meaning it is a placeholder for zero or more unknown characters. An asterisk is useful when you don't remember an exact name or phrase, or when you want to retrieve variants on a word. For example, if you want information about automobiles, you can use ***auto**** as the query. This query should return sites referencing meaningful variants such as *auto*, *autos*, *automobile*, and *automotive*; but it will also return information on many other words that begin with *auto*, such as *autopilot*, *automatic*, *autobiography*, etc.

1. Using the queries below, answer the following questions:
   Is query A likely to produce more hits than query B?
   Is query D likely to produce more hits than query C?
   A. ***1998 AND used NEAR automobile***
   B. ***1998 AND used NEAR auto****
   C. ***1998 AND used NEAR auto* AND NOT truck****
   D. ***1998 AND used NEAR (auto* OR car) AND NOT truck****
2. Using altavista.com, make each of the above queries to verify your answers.

Activity 9 • Directory Searches

1. Read the text at the right.
2. Complete the activities shown below and on the next page.
3. Print the Web pages as instructed.

A **Web directory** has topics organized into increasingly specific category names. You start your search by clicking a top-level category name that is most relevant to the topic you are researching. As the topics become more specific, continue to click the one that is most relevant to your search until the path leads you to the information you want. You can move back to a more general category if the path you are following is not leading in the right direction.

Most search engines have the option to search for information via the search box you have used thus far in these lessons and a directory.

You should use the search box and Boolean operators when you know what information you want and just need to find it. Use the directory when you want to see what's out there or what's related to a topic, and when you expect to formulate your thoughts as you explore.

1. Use the altavista.com directory to perform a search on movie reviews. At the moment, you know you want to go to a movie; but you're not sure which one. When you find a review of a movie you want to see, print one page from the Web site.

(continued on next page)

8D • 10'
Review ['], [-], and ["]

Key each line twice SS (slowly, then faster); DS between 2-line groups.

Note:
On your screen, apostrophes and/or quotation marks may look different from those shown in these lines. Whatever their differences in appearance, the marks serve the same purpose.

Review ' (apostrophe)

1 ;; '; '; ;' ;' I've told you it's hers, haven't I?
2 I'm sure it's Jay's. I'll return it if he's home.
3 I've been told it isn't up to us; it's up to them.

Review - (hyphen)

4 ; - -; -; ;- ;- -; -; -;- -;- We use a 2-ply tire.
5 We have 1-, 2-, and 3-bedroom condos for purchase.
6 He rated each as a 1-star, 2-star, or 3-star film.

Review " (quotation mark)

7 ;; "; "; ";" ";" "I believe," she said, "you won."
8 "John Adams," he said, "was the second President."
9 "James Monroe," I said, "was the fifth President."

8E • 18'
Keyboard Reinforcement

1. Key lines once SS; DS between 2-line groups.
2. Key the lines again at a faster pace.
3. Key a 1' writing on lines 10–12.

Reach review (Keep on home keys the fingers not used for reaching.)

1 old led kit six jay oft zap cod big laws five ribs
2 pro quo|is just|my firm|was then|may grow|must try
3 Olga sews aqua and red silk to make six big kites.

Space Bar emphasis (Think, say, and key the words.)

4 en am an by ham fan buy jam pay may form span corn
5 I am|a man|an elm|by any|buy ham|can plan|try them
6 I am to form a plan to buy a firm in the old town.

Shift key emphasis (Reach up and reach down without moving the hands.)

7 Jan and I are to see Ms. Han. May Lana come, too?
8 Bob Epps lives in Rome; Vic Copa is in Rome, also.
9 Oates and Co. has a branch office in Boise, Idaho.

Easy sentence (Think, say, and key the words at a steady pace.)

10 Eight of the girls may go to the social with them.
11 Corla is to work with us to fix the big dock sign.
12 Keith is to pay the six men for the work they did.

gwam 1' | 1 | 2 | 3 | 4 | 5 | 6 | 7 | 8 | 9 | 10 |

Activity 4 • Web Searches with NOT or –

1. Read the text at the right.
2. Complete the queries listed and create a table to report the query results.

 **Save as:** *SWL4ACT4*

The **NOT** or **–** (minus sign) operator is very helpful when you want to exclude documents from your query results. For example, if you wanted information on hurricanes in all states but Florida, your query could be ***hurricanes NOT florida***. This query should return documents referenced to hurricanes but no documents that are referenced to hurricanes in Florida. Some search engines require you to use **AND NOT** (or **ANDNOT**) in the search query to join two terms if the first must be present and the second must **NOT**.

Like other operators, **NOT** or **–** can be combined with other operators to filter a query to return relative files.

1. Using yahoo.com, perform these queries:
   a. Search for **washington**.
   b. Search for **washington +george**.
   c. Search for **washington +george -carver**.
   d. Search for **washington +george -carver -university**.
2. Perform the same queries using altavista.com (AltaVista uses AND and AND NOT).
3. Perform the same queries using ixquick.com (ixquick will recognize AND, + , NOT, AND NOT, ANDNOT, or –).

Activity 5 • Parentheses

1. Read the text at the right.
2. Complete the queries at the right and create a table to report the query results.

 **Save as:** *SWL4ACT5*

Another query option that is very helpful is the use of **parentheses** to group steps together to tell the search engine how to filter information in your query. For example, if you wanted to buy a Ford or Chevrolet car, you could use this query: ***(ford OR chevrolet) NEAR car***. This query would return all documents that reference Ford cars or Chevrolet cars or both cars. If you wanted to restrict your query to used Fords or Chevrolets, you could use this query: ***(ford OR chevrolet) NEAR car NOT new***.

1. Using altavista.com, perform these queries:
   a. Search for **(washington OR jefferson) NEAR president**.
   b. Search for **(george AND washington OR thomas AND jefferson) NEAR president**.
2. Using the same search engine, find information about adopting a Collie or Sheltie breed of dog.

Activity 6 • Phrase Searches

1. Read the text at the right.
2. Complete the queries at the right and create a table to report the query results.

 **Save as:** *SWL4ACT6*

Place quotation marks around a phrase if all the words need to appear together as a phrase, rather than scattered about the Web page. For example, if you are searching for information about George Washington as President, a search for ***"president george washington"*** is likely to result in more relevant hits than a search on ***president AND george AND washington***. **Phrasing** is a very powerful search technique, and it can be made even more powerful if combined with other operators.

1. Using yahoo.com, perform these queries:
   a. Search for **general +colin +powell**.
   b. Search for **"general colin powell"**.
   c. Search for **"general colin powell" +biography**.
2. Using the same search engine, find information about General George Washington at Valley Forge.

UNIT 2

LESSONS 9–12

Build Keyboarding Skill

LESSON 9 SKILL BUILDING

Objectives:

1. To develop proper response patterns to gain speed.
2. To learn to key script copy.

9A • 5' Conditioning Practice

Key each line twice SS; then key a 1' writing on line 3; determine *gwam*.

alphabet	1	Levi Lentz packed my bag with six quarts of juice.
spacing	2	it is|to me|may be|at my|to the|was it|is he|of us
easy	3	A box with the forms is on the mantle by the bowl.

gwam 1' | 1 | 2 | 3 | 4 | 5 | 6 | 7 | 8 | 9 | 10 |

9B • 18' Technique: Response Patterns

1. Key each line twice SS (slowly, then faster); DS between 2-line groups.
2. Key 1' writings on lines 7–9; determine *gwam* (total words keyed) on each writing.

Technique **H·I·N·T**

Word response: Key easy (balanced-hand) words as a word—instead of letter by letter.

Letter response: Key the letters of one-hand words steadily and evenly.

Balanced-hand words (Think and key by word response.)

1 if it to me ox am so do he go is ha an us of to by

2 so men did jam fit pan dog lap fur ham cut own for

3 mend paid city land form they make work it's goals

One-hand words (Think and key by letter response.)

4 in we up as no at on be my ax oh at we no at my as

5 pin was pop tea ink fax imp tax him sad ill car no

6 lump save look were pill rest poll dear jump reads

Balanced-hand phrases (Think and key by word response.)

7 it is|to us|if it|to do|do so|to go|by us|if it is

8 did fit|for the|fix the|may make|paid for|may work

9 for the man|when did she|for the bid|may turn down

One-hand phrases (Think and key by letter response.)

10 as we|be my|in on|my ax|oh no|in my|be sad|was ill

11 car tax|you saw|pink ink|fast car|pin him|were you

12 save my water|saw my|oil taxes|water rates|a fever

gwam 1' | 1 | 2 | 3 | 4 | 5 | 6 | 7 | 8 | 9 | 10 |

Activity 2 • Web Searches with AND, + , and OR Operators

1. Form teams with class members and read the text at the right.
2. Open a blank wp document and recreate the AltaVista table at the right.
3. Complete the eight queries shown in the table by using www.altavista.com. Record the number of hits for each query in the space provided.
4. Study the number of hits. Do they yield numbers that you would expect? Identify those that are puzzling and discuss possible reasons for them.

Save as: *SWL4ACT2A*

To get good results from your search query, you must include certain keywords, exclude certain keywords, and combine certain keywords. Basic searches may require only one or two carefully chosen keywords. On the other hand, complicated searches may require the use of several keywords used in conjunction with **Boolean operators.**

Boolean operators permit you to include, exclude, and combine keywords in your query so the search engine will report hits that are closely related to the information you are seeking. Since all search engines do not recognize the same operators, you should learn how to do an advanced search on each search engine you use. In this activity you will learn to use the operators **AND**, **OR**, and **+** .

The **AND** operator instructs the search engine to search for all documents containing the keyword that precedes and follows **AND**. (Although all search engines do not require the operator to be keyed in ALL CAPS, it is suggested that you do so.)

For example, the query ***tigers AND lions*** will result in files that contain references to **both** of the words. Those that contain only references to tigers or lions will be excluded.

The **+** (plus) symbol performs in the same way as the AND operator.

The **OR** operator instructs the search engine to seach for files containing the keyword before or the keyword after the **OR**.

For example, a query ***horses OR cows*** will return files that contain either or both of the keywords.

Some search engines use **AND** as the default operator if none is entered, while others use **OR**. Therefore, on some engines, ***tigers lions*** would be treated as ***tigers AND lions*** and on others it will be treated as ***tigers OR lions***.

AltaVista SEARCH ENGINE			
Query	**Hits**	**Query**	**Hits**
baseball		lincoln	
baseball AND pittsburgh		abraham	
baseball AND pirates		abraham OR lincoln	
baseball AND pittsburgh AND pirates		abraham AND lincoln	

5. Check your understanding of **AND** and **OR** operators. Read the text box at the right and answer the questions shown below it.
6. Create a table in which to report the team's answers.

Save as: *SWL4ACT2B*

> Assume you have a database of 1,400 documents, of which 400 contain references to A; 300 contain references to B; 200 contain references to both A and B; and 500 contain references to C.

1. How many hits will a query on A yield?
2. How many hits will a query on B yield?
3. How many hits will a query on A OR B yield?
4. How many hits will a query on A AND B yield?
5. How many hits will a query on A AND B OR C yield?
6. How many hits will a query on A OR B OR C yield?

Activity 3 • Web Searches with NEAR

1. Read the text at the right.
2. Complete the activities listed, creating a table to report your findings.

Save as: *SWL4ACT3*

The **NEAR** operator is used by some search engines to look for keywords that are near each other in a document. For example, the query ***lincoln NEAR automobile*** will result in documents that contain these two words near each other, in any order. That is, *lincoln* could come before *automobile* or vice versa. How near the words need to be to each other depends on the default distance used by the search engine.

1. Using AltaVista, search for documents containing **hurricanes**.
2. Using AltaVista, search for documents containing **florida**.
3. Using AltaVista, search for documents containing **hurricanes NEAR florida**.
4. Repeat these searches using yahoo.com and compare the results.

9C • 10' Handwritten Copy (Script)

Key each line twice SS (slowly, then faster); DS between 2-line groups.

1 Now and then the copy you will key is from script.
2 Script is copy that is written with pen or pencil.
3 Copy that is written poorly is often hard to read.
4 Read script a few words "ahead of your fingers."
5 Doing so will help you produce an error-free copy.
6 Leave proper spacing after punctuation marks, too.
7 With practice, you will key script at a good rate.

SKILL BUILDING

9D • 12' Speed Building

1. Key a 1' writing on each ¶; determine *gwam* (the figure/dot above the last letter you keyed).
2. Key two 2' writings on ¶s 1–2 combined; determine *gwam*, using the *gwam* scale at the right (complete lines) and below (partial lines).

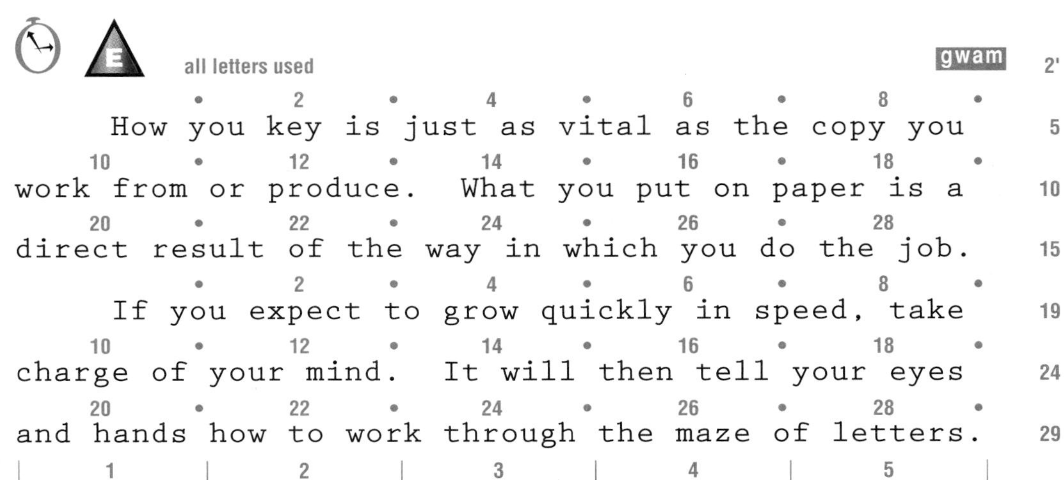

all letters used — gwam 2'

	gwam 2'
How you key is just as vital as the copy you	5
work from or produce. What you put on paper is a	10
direct result of the way in which you do the job.	15
If you expect to grow quickly in speed, take	19
charge of your mind. It will then tell your eyes	24
and hands how to work through the maze of letters.	29

gwam 2' | 1 | 2 | 3 | 4 | 5 |

9E • 5' Technique: Spacebar and Enter

1. Key each line once SS; DS at end of line 6.
2. Key the drill again at a faster pace.

Technique **H • I • N • T**

- Quickly strike the Space Bar immediately after keying last letter in the word.
- Quickly strike ENTER after keying the period at the end of each line.

1 Sue ran to catch the bus.
2 Jan will be ready before noon.
3 Tim will bring his dog to the lake.
4 Mark did not fill the two cars with gas.
5 Don will take the next test when he is ready.
6 Karen is to bring two or three copies of the play.

Speed level of practice
When the purpose of practice is to reach a new speed, use the speed level. Take the brakes off your fingers and experiment with new stroking patterns and new speeds. Do this by:

- reading two or three letters ahead of your keying to foresee stroking patterns;
- getting the fingers ready for the combinations of letters to be keyed;
- keeping your eyes on the copy in the book.

Activity 3 • Print a Graphic from a Web Page

1. Read the text at the right.
2. Learn to save an image, retrieve the image, and print it from your browser.
3. Complete the activities at the right.

There are many graphics on Web pages that you may want to use. You can save a graphic and then print it from your browser; insert it into a wp document, Web page, or electronic presentation; or use it as background for a Web page or wallpaper for your desktop. The graphics are generally saved as images with a .jpg or .gif extension. A lesser-used graphics format is .png.

In this activity, you will save graphics and then print them from a browser and a word processor.

1. Open http://www.pde.psu.edu and save the outline of Pennsylvania at the center top of the Web page as an image file in the folder where you save your current work. Use the default filename: *pdehomenew19.*
2. Open *pdehomenew19* in your browser window (while opening it you may notice that a .gif extension is displayed).
3. Print the image with the Web page source, total page count, and date and time.
4. Open your wp software, insert *pdehomenew19,* and save and print the file.

Save as: *SWL3ACT3A*

5. Find, save with the default filename, and print from your browser one image from each of two different Web sites. Include the Web page source, total page count, and date and time with each image printed.
6. Find, save, and print from your wp software one image from each of two different Web sites.

Save as: *SWL3ACT3B* and *SWL3ACT3C*

LESSONS 4–5 CONDUCT WEB SEARCHES

Objectives:

1. To use various search engines.
2. To develop search strategies to find information on the World Wide Web.

Activity 1 • Search Engines

1. Read the text at the right.
2. Open each search engine listed below and familiarize yourself with its home page. Locate the search box in which the query is keyed. The illustration shows that AltaVista returned more than a million hits when **Lincoln** was keyed in the search box.
3. If desired, bookmark each search engine.
4. Key **Lincoln** in the search box of each search engine and determine how each search engine reports the hits from its database.
www.altavista.com
www.ixquick.com
www.yahoo.com

The WWW contains millions of pages of information on virtually any subject. **Search engines** are used to find the information. A search engine is software that finds Web pages that contain the keyword(s) or phrase you specify. **Queries** (the questions or keywords you specify) and **Boolean logic** (system of logic using operators such as AND, OR, and NOT) are used to focus the search on the relative keywords that will result in the search engine finding Web pages (**hits**) that relate closely to the information you are seeking. Since the databases they use to answer queries differ, search engines will generate different results (hits). Therefore, it is helpful to know how to use various search engines. In these two lessons, you will use AltaVista, ixquick, and Yahoo, unless you are given other instructions.

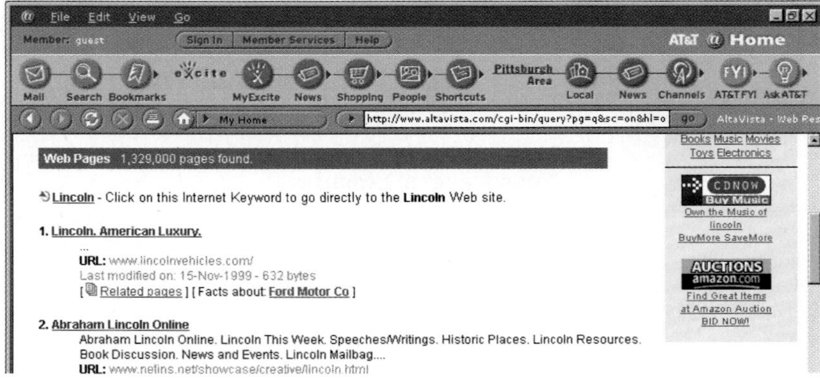

LESSON 10 SKILL BUILDING

Objectives:
1. To build straight-copy speed and control.
2. To improve keying technique.

10A • 5' Conditioning Practice

Key each line twice SS; then key a 1' writing on line 3; determine *gwam.*

alphabet	1	Kevin can fix the unique jade owl as my big prize.
caps lock	2	JAY used the CAPS LOCK key to key CAPITAL letters.
easy	3	The small ornament on their door is an ivory duck.
gwam	1'	| 1 | 2 | 3 | 4 | 5 | 6 | 7 | 8 | 9 | 10 |

Note: To determine *gwam*, see 8A directions if necessary.

10B • 15' Technique: Response Patterns

1. Key each line twice SS (slowly, then faster); DS between 2-line groups.
2. Key a 1' writing on lines 3, 6, 9, and 12.
3. If time permits, take additional timings on lines 3, 6, 9, and 12.

Technique **H • I • N • T**

Combination response: Most copy requires word response for some words and letter response for others. In such copy (lines 7–9), use top speed for easy words, lower speed for words that are harder to key.

letter response	1	In we up be my are pin tar lip car him sad joy set
	2	were you|at my|red kiln|as you see|you are|fat cat
	3	My cat darted up a tree as we sat in Jim's garage.
word response	4	it do am me so men did and lap fit ham pan got hen
	5	to us|by the|it is|to go|she may|for me|to fix the
	6	She may fix the dock if I do the work for the man.
combination response	7	he as is my to in is no am we by on it up do at or
	8	to be|is up|to my|or up|is at|go in|do we|if we go
	9	Steve and Dave may be by my dock; we may see them.
letter	10	Jon was up at noon; Rebecca gave him my red cards.
combination	11	Jay was the man you saw up at the lake in the bus.
word	12	I may go to the lake with the men to fix the door.

10C • 8' Speed Check: Sentences

1. Key a 30" writing on each line. Your rate in *gwam* is shown word-for-word above and below the lines.
2. Key another 30" writing on each line. Try to increase your keying speed.

\| 2 \| 4 \| 6 \| 8 \| 10 \| 12 \| 14 \| 16 \| 18 \| 20 \| 22 \|

1 He may go with us to the city.
2 Pamela may do half the work for us.
3 Ruth may go with us to the city to work.
4 Sign the forms for the firm to pay the girls.
5 Jan may make all the goal if she works with vigor.
6 He may sign the form if they make an audit of the firm.

gwam 30" \| 2 \| 4 \| 6 \| 8 \| 10 \| 12 \| 14 \| 16 \| 18 \| 20 \| 22 \|

Note: If you finish a line before time is called and start over, your *gwam* is the figure at the end of the line PLUS the figure above or below the point at which you stopped.

LESSON 3 WORK WITH WEB PAGES

Objectives:

1. To save and open a Web page.
2. To copy Web page text.
3. To save and print a graphic from a Web page.

Activity 1 • Open Saved Web Pages

1. Read the text at the right.
2. Learn how to save a Web page using your browser.
3. Open http://www.nasa.gov and save the home page as an HTML file (use the default filename—http://www.nasa_gov.html).
4. Open http://www.weather.com to have an unrelated Web site active (this ensures you are viewing nasa.gov from the saved file rather than its active site).
5. Open the saved file from your browser and view it. See which hyperlinks work.
6. Use History to return to the nasa.gov home page and print it.

You can save a Web page so its contents (or HTML code) can be viewed at another time. For example, an interesting Web page from the NASA Web site can be saved so you can share it with your aunt when she visits you next week.

When a Web page is saved, the text, broken image icons, and borders of the image areas will display—the images will not display. The Web page is saved as an HTML file with an .htm or .html extension.

When the saved Web page is opened in a browser connected to the Internet, the hyperlinks may work even though the images on the saved pages are not visible. When the saved page is opened in a browser that is not connected to the Internet, some or all of the hyperlinks on the saved file will not work.

One way to save the Web page so the graphics and text can be viewed at a later time is to send the Web page via e-mail. When the e-mail message is opened, the text and the graphics of the Web page can be viewed on most browsers.

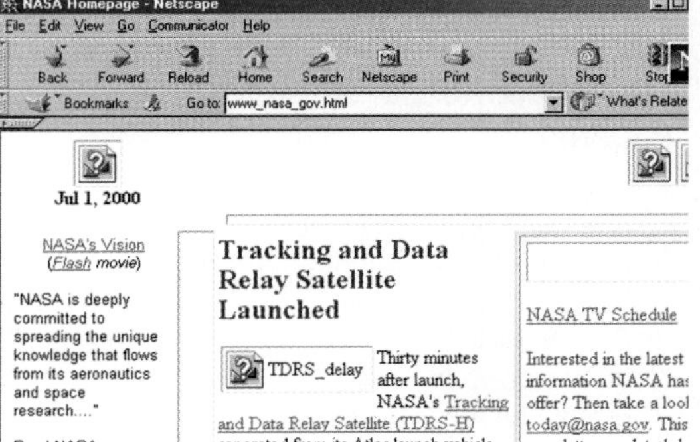

Activity 2 • Copy Text from a Web Page

1. Read the text at the right.
2. Learn to copy and paste selected text from a Web page to a wp document.
3. Complete the activity at the right.

 **Save as:** *SWL3ACT2*

Occasionally you may want to save some of the text from a Web page for use in another document. Being able to do this eliminates the need to use the printer unnecessarily and to rekey text. However, you must properly document the source of the material just as you would for quoted or paraphrased text from printed sources.

To copy text from a Web page:

1. Highlight the text to be copied.
2. Click *Copy*. (You can right-click the mouse and choose *Copy*.)
3. Open a wp software program.
4. Click *Paste*.

Once the text is pasted, you can format it any way you want to in the word processor.

Using the three Web sites given below (or three that you choose), access each site and follow hyperlinks until you locate text you want to copy from each site. Copy the text into a blank wp document, keying a reference for the text copied so the source is known. In general, the reference should contain the same information as a reference from a printed source, followed by the WWW information. Use the following format:

Author's name, if given. "Title of the article in quotation marks." Title of the periodical or electronic text underlined. Date, volume number, and/or page, if any. Complete URL without a period at the end underlined (Date the information was retrieved from the WWW in parentheses in day month year format).

www.nytimes.com www.usatoday.com www.washtimes.com

10D • 15' Speed Check: Paragraphs

1. Key a 1' writing on each paragraph (¶); determine *gwam* on each writing.
2. Using your better *gwam* as a base rate, select a goal rate and key two 1' guided writings on each ¶ as directed below.

Note:

Copy used to build or measure skill is triple-controlled for difficulty: E = easy; LA = low average; A = average

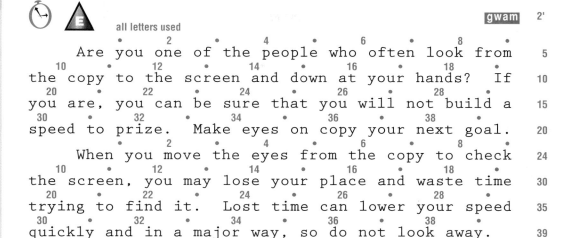

all letters used

	gwam 2'
Are you one of the people who often look from	5
the copy to the screen and down at your hands? If	10
you are, you can be sure that you will not build a	15
speed to prize. Make eyes on copy your next goal.	20
When you move the eyes from the copy to check	24
the screen, you may lose your place and waste time	30
trying to find it. Lost time can lower your speed	35
quickly and in a major way, so do not look away.	39

gwam 2' | 1 | 2 | 3 | 4 | 5 |

Quarter-Minute Checkpoints				
gwam	1/4'	1/2'	3/4'	Time
16	4	8	12	16
20	5	10	15	20
24	6	12	18	24
28	7	14	21	28
32	8	16	24	32
36	9	18	27	36
40	10	20	30	40

Guided (Paced) Writing Procedure

Select a practice goal

1. Key a 1' writing on ¶ 1 of a set of ¶s that contain word-count dots and figures above the lines, as in 10D above.
2. Using the *gwam* as a base, add 4 *gwam* to determine your goal rate.
3. Choose from Column 1 of the table at the left the speed nearest your goal rate. In the quarter-minute columns beside that speed, note the points in the copy you must reach to maintain your goal rate.
4. Determine the checkpoint for each quarter minute from the dots and figures in ¶ 1. (Example: Checkpoints for 24 *gwam* are 6, 12, 18, and 24.)

Practice procedure

1. Key two 1' writings on ¶ 1 at your goal rate, guided by the quarter-minute signals (1/4, 1/2, 3/4, time). Try to reach each of your checkpoints just as the guide is called.
2. Key two 1' writings on ¶ 2 of a set of ¶s in the same way.
3. If time permits, key a 2' writing on the set of ¶s combined, without the guides.

10E • 7' Keying Technique

Key each line twice.

Double letters

1 bill foot berry letter deep pool groom egg balloon
2 Matt will look at a free scanner tomorrow at noon.

Balanced hands

3 risk usual to maid the corn box did pan rifle dish
4 He may go with me to the city by the lake to work.

Shift keys

5 Los Angeles Dodgers|PowerPoint|The Book of Virtues
6 The New York Yankees will play the Boston Red Sox.

Space Bar

7 to do a be box and the or was it see me by ten ask
8 As near as I can tell, it is five or six days old.

Activity 3 • Favorites and Bookmarks

1. Read the text at the right.
2. Learn how to add, use, and delete Web sites to and from a Bookmarks/ Favorites list.
3. Open these sites and bookmark each:
   http://www.weather.com
   http://www.usps.gov
   http://www.nasa.gov
   http://www.time.com
   plus a Web site of your choice
4. Use the Bookmark/ Favorites button to access each site.
5. Print the first page of the Web site you bookmarked with the Web site source, total page count, and time and date.

As you visit many different Web sites, you are likely to find several that you want to revisit frequently. Browsers have a **Bookmark** or **Favorites** feature to keep track of the sites so you will be able to revisit them quickly and easily. You can organize your bookmarked sites in folders.

To add (bookmark) a site to your Bookmark/Favorites list, open the site to be bookmarked, click the Bookmark or Favorites button, and then click *Add.*

To revisit a bookmarked site, click the Bookmark (or Favorites) button, select the desired Web site, and then click the site.

When you no longer want to visit a bookmarked site, you can delete the site from the Bookmarks/Favorites list.

The illustration below left shows the pop-up menu that appears when the Netscape Navigator Bookmark button is clicked. The illustration at the right shows the equivalent menu when the Internet Explorer Favorites button is clicked.

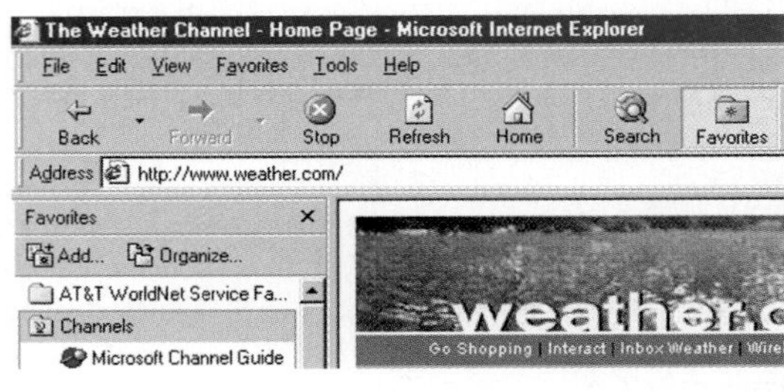

Activity 4 • History

1. Read the text at the right.
2. Learn how to use the History feature on your browser.
3. Open your browser's History file and locate www.usps.gov.
4. Open the usps.gov home page from the History file.
5. Print the first page of usps.gov with the Web site source, total page count, and time and date.

The Back and Forward buttons move you to or from sites you have previously visited during an Internet session. Another way to revisit Web sites is to use the History feature of the browser. One advantage of using History over using the Back or Forward buttons is that you can revisit an unbookmarked site without revisiting all the sites opened between the desired site and the active site.

Another advantage is that the History feature can retain sites from one Internet session to another, even sessions occurring several days apart.

The illustrations below show sample History files in Netscape Navigator (top) and Internet Explorer.

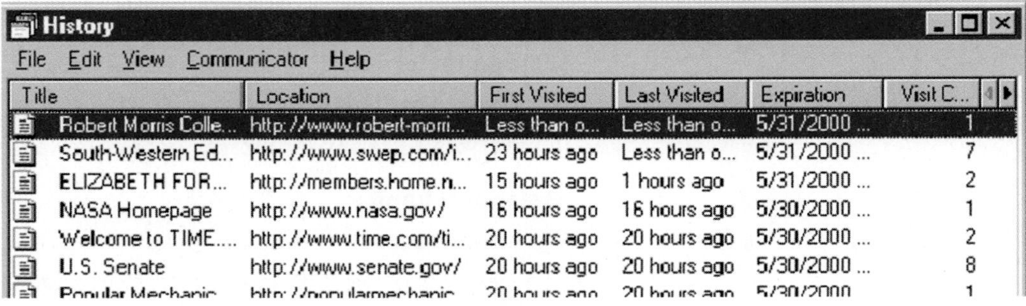
History
File Edit View Communicator Help

Title	Location	First Visited	Last Visited	Expiration	Visit C...
Robert Morris Colle...	http://www.robert-morri...	Less than o...	Less than o...	5/31/2000 ...	1
South-Western Ed...	http://www.swep.com/i...	23 hours ago	Less than o...	5/31/2000 ...	7
ELIZABETH FOR...	http://members.home.n...	15 hours ago	1 hours ago	5/31/2000 ...	2
NASA Homepage	http://www.nasa.gov/	16 hours ago	16 hours ago	5/30/2000 ...	1
Welcome to TIME....	http://www.time.com/ti...	20 hours ago	20 hours ago	5/30/2000 ...	2
U.S. Senate	http://www.senate.gov/	20 hours ago	20 hours ago	5/30/2000 ...	8
Popular Mechanic	http://popularmechanic	20 hours ago	20 hours ago	5/30/2000	1

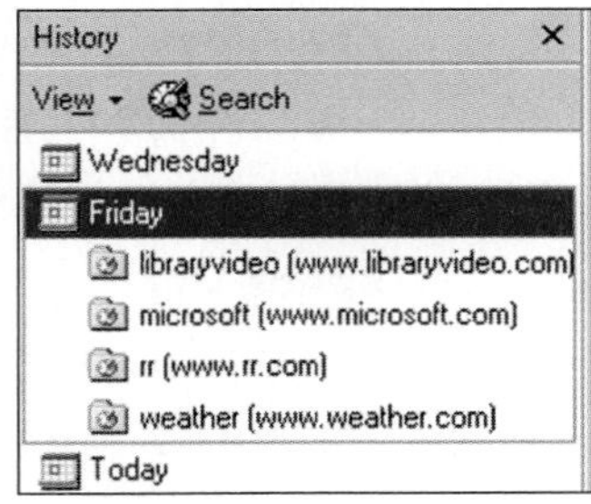

LESSON 11 — SKILL BUILDING

Objectives:

1. To build straight-copy speed and control.
2. To improve keying technique on script and rough-draft copy.

11A • 5' Conditioning Practice

Key each line twice SS; then key a 1' writing on line 3; determine *gwam.*

alphabet	1	Lock may join the squad if we have six big prizes.
?	2	Do I get a locker? Where is it? Do I need a key?
easy	3	Pam may name a tutor to work with the eight girls.

gwam 1' | 1 | 2 | 3 | 4 | 5 | 6 | 7 | 8 | 9 | 10 |

11B • 10' Speed Building

1. Key each line twice SS with a DS between 2-line groups.
2. If time permits, key the lines again to improve keying ease and speed.

Technique Goals:

- Reach up without moving hands away from you.
- Reach down without moving hands toward your body.
- Use quick-snap keystrokes.

za/az	1	zap lazy lizard pizza hazard bazaar frazzle dazzle
	2	Zack and Hazel zapped the lazy lizard in the maze.
ol/lo	3	old load olive look fold lost bold loan allow told
	4	Olympia told the lonely man to load the long logs.
ws/sw	5	swing cows sweet glows swept mows sword knows swap
	6	He swung the sword over the sweaty cows and swine.
ju/ft	7	often jury draft judge left just hefty juice after
	8	Jud, the fifth juror on my left, just wants juice.
ed/de	9	deal need debit edit deed edge deli used dent desk
	10	Jed needed to edit the deed made by the defendant.
ik/ki	11	kick like kind bike kiln hike kids strike king ski
	12	I like the kind of kids who like to hike and bike.

11C • 13' Speed Check: Straight Copy

LS: DS

1. Key one 1' unguided and two 1' guided writings on ¶ 1 and then on ¶ 2, as directed on p. 22.
2. Key two 2' unguided writings on ¶s 1–2 combined; determine *gwam* on each.

E all letters used — gwam 2'

Time and motion are major items in building 4
our keying power. As we make each move through 9
space to a letter or a figure, we use time. So we 14
want to be sure that every move is quick and direct. 20
We cut time and aid speed in this way. 24

A good way to reduce motion and thus save time 28
is just to keep the hands in home position as you 33
make the reach to a letter or figure. Fix your 38
gaze on the copy; then, reach to each key with a 43
direct, low move at your very best speed. 47

gwam 2' | 1 | 2 | 3 | 4 | 5 |

LEARN BROWSER BASICS

Objective:

To use browser features, such as hyperlinks and printing.

Activity 1 • Print a Web Page

1. Read the text at the right and learn to print with your browser.
2. Open http://www.senate.gov and print the home page in portrait orientation, with the Web site source, date and time of printing, and total page count.

Web pages can be printed so you can refer to them when you are not at your computer. There are many options you can select when printing. Among them are: (1) select one or more pages to print; (2) print the Web site source, the date and time the page was printed, and the total page count; (3) set margins or use the default margins; and (4) print in portrait or landscape orientation. Some browsers permit you to preview the Web pages before printing.

This example shows the radio buttons you can click to select the orientation you would like to use.

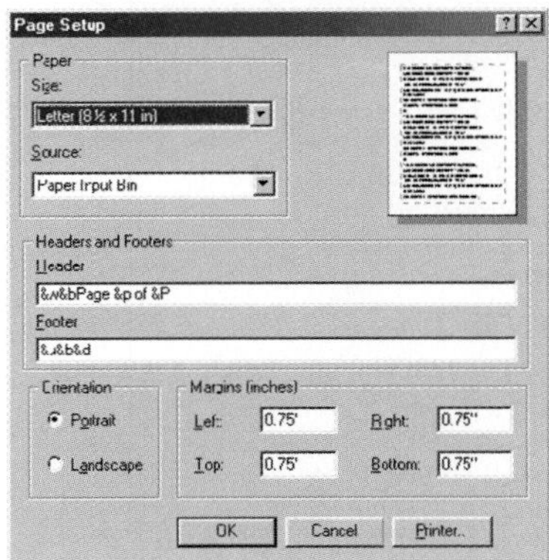

Activity 2 • Hyperlinks

1. Read the text at the right.
2. Complete the activities shown below at the right.
3. Print the Web site source, total page count, and time and date printed for all Web pages you print.

A **hyperlink** is text or a graphic image that links one HTML document to another HTML document. The hyperlink may lead to another place within the same Web site or to a different Web site.

Hyperlinked text is usually displayed in a different color and underlined. When the pointer encounters a hyperlink, it changes to a pointing hand, and the URL of the linked document is displayed in the status bar. Click the hyperlink when the pointer is shaped as a hand, and the browser will open the linked document.

If you go back to the document where you clicked the original hyperlink, the hyperlink will likely be displayed in a different color. This signals that the hyperlink has been previously followed.

The globe in the upper-left corner and the rectangle in the upper-right corner of the Web page below are examples of graphic hyperlinks, called **hypermedia** links. The underscored text phrases are examples of text hyperlinks, called **hypertext** links.

1. Access http://www.nasa.gov.
2. Move your pointer across the text and graphics, noting how frequently the pointer changes to a hand to inform you that a hyperlink to another file exists.
3. Referring to the hyperlink URL in the status bar, click the hyperlink's four files within the www.nasa.gov site and three hyperlinks that will take you to a Web site with a different domain name. Print one page of a linked document with www.nasa.gov as part of the domain name, and print one page of a linked document that does not have www.nasa.gov as part of the domain name.
4. Open http://www.weather.com and follow a hyperlink that leads to a URL that does not have www.weather.com as part of the domain name. Print the first page of the linked document.

Learning Tip:

Hyperlinks often change on a Web page.

11D • 10'
Rough Draft (Edited Copy)

1. Study the proofreaders' marks shown below and in the sentences.
2. Key each sentence DS, making all handwritten (editing) changes.
3. Key the lines again to improve your editing speed.

∧ = insert
= add space
∽ = transpose
ℓ = delete
⁀ = close up
≡ = capitalize

1 A first draft is a preleminary orr tentative one.

2 It is where the creator gets his thoughts on paper.

3 After the draft is created, it will be looked over.

4 Reviewing is the step where a persone refines copy.

5 Proof readers marks are used edit the original copy.

6 The edting changes will be then be made to the copy.

7 After the change have been made read the copy agian.

8 more changes still may need to be made to the copy.

9 Edting proof reading does take a lot time and effort.

10 error free copy is worth the trouble how ever.

11E • 12'
Skill Transfer: Straight Copy to Script and Rough Draft

1. Key each ¶ once SS; DS between ¶s.
2. Key a 1' writing on each ¶; determine *gwam* on each writing; compare the three rates.

Your highest speed should be on ¶ 1 (straight copy); next highest on ¶ 2 (script); lowest on ¶ 3 (rough draft).

3. Key one or two more 1' writings on the two slowest ¶s to improve skill transfer.

Recall

1' *gwam* = total words keyed

A standard word = 5 strokes (characters and spaces).

Straight copy — gwam 1'

Documents free of errors make a good impression. 10
When a document has no errors, readers can focus on 20
the content. Errors distract readers and may cause 31
them to think less of the message. 38

Script

Therefore, it is important to proofread the final 10
copy of a document several times to make sure it 20
contains no errors before it leaves your desk. 29
Readers of error-free documents form a positive image 40
of the person who wrote the message. 47

Rough draft

When a negative image of the per son who wrote the the 10
messge is formed the message is less likely to succeed. 22
remembre you never get a another chance tomake a good 33
impression. 35

Activity 4 • Web Addresses

1. Study the text at the right and on the next page.
2. Open *CD-SWL1ACT4* and complete it as directed.

Save as: *SWL1ACT4*

The Internet uses a multiple-part addressing scheme called a **Uniform Resource Locator (URL)** to define the route to the file being accessed.

To access a specific Internet site, a URL must tell the browser: (1) the **transfer protocol** it is to use to transport a file (HTTP, FTP, and Gopher are examples of protocols), and (2) the **domain name** of the computer where the Internet site is housed (www.swep.com is an example of a domain name).

In addition, a URL can include the pathname of the folder or directory where the file is stored and the name of the file. A slash separates the pathname and filename from the preceding address part.

The Internet address below shows the four parts of a URL.

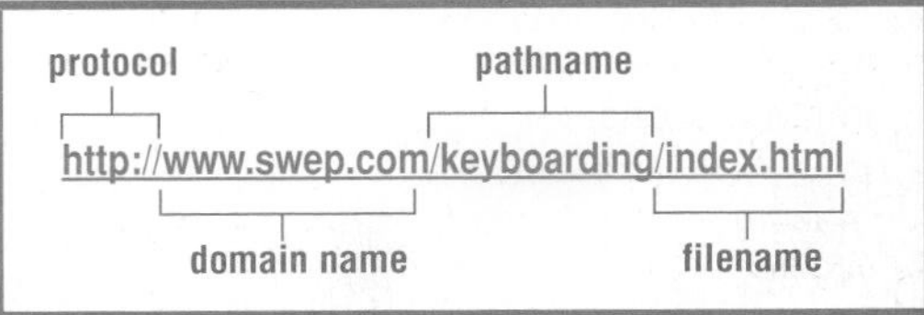

Each domain name is assigned a top-level domain name that is included as the last part of the domain name. The parts of a domain name are separated by periods (dots).

Following is a partial list of top-level domain names and a description of the organizations that use each name:

.com	businesses and other commercial enterprises
.edu	educational institutions
.gov	U.S. governmental agencies
.net	network service providers
.org	charitable and not-for-profit organizations

Activity 5 • Access a Web Site

1. Read the text at the right.
2. Learn how to access (open) a Web site with your browser.
3. Complete the activities at the right.

Learning C • U • E

Some browsers do not require you to key the http://www. portion of a URL. Try to open the three sites in Step 5 using this shortcut.

A quick way to access (open) a Web site is to click inside the Address box, key the URL for the desired Web site, and press ENTER.

Another way to access Web sites is to select the Open or Open Page option on the File pull-down menu, key the URL in the dialog box, and then click OK or Open.

1. Launch your browser. Click in the *Address* box, key http://www.nasa.gov, and press ENTER to open the Web site's home page. Note the information that appears in the title bar and that the Web address is in the Address box.
2. Click the *Home* button to return to your home or start page.
3. Key http://www.nasa.gov/hqpao/welcome.html in the Address box to access the same Web site (NASA) at the Welcome to NASA Web section (*hqpao* is the pathname and *welcome.html* is the filename).
4. Click the *Back* button (this should return you to NASA's home page) and then click the *Forward* button (should return you to NASA's Welcome section).
5. Open the home page for each of the three Web sites listed below, using the Back and Forward buttons frequently to practice moving from one HTML document to another.

   http://www.cnn.com
   http://www.newsweek.com
   http://www.time.com
6. Key http://www.senate.gov in the Address box to open the home page for the U.S. Senate, but use the *Stop* button to quit the search before it is fully loaded.

LESSON 12 SKILL BUILDING

Objectives:

1. To build straight-copy speed and control.
2. To improve keying technique.

12A • 5' Conditioning Practice

Key each line twice SS; then key a 1' writing on line 3; determine *gwam.*

alphabet 1 J. Fox made five quick plays to win the big prize.
spacing 2 It will be fun for us to try to sing the old song.
easy 3 The sorority may do the work for the city auditor.

gwam 1' | 1 | 2 | 3 | 4 | 5 | 6 | 7 | 8 | 9 | 10 |

12B • 12' Difficult-Reach Mastery

1. Key each line twice SS; DS between 2-line groups.
2. Note the lines that caused you difficulty; practice them again to increase rate.

Adjacent (side-by-side) keys (lines 1–4) can be the source of many errors unless the fingers are kept in an upright position and precise motions are used.

Long direct reaches (lines 5–8) reduce speed unless they are made without moving the hands forward and downward.

Reaches with the outside fingers (lines 9–12) are troublesome unless made without twisting the hands in and out at the wrist.

Adjacent keys

1 Jerry and Jason were not ready to buy a newspaper.
2 Polly dropped my green vase on her last trip here.
3 Marty opened the carton to retrieve the power saw.
4 Bert and I were there the week before deer season.

Long direct reaches

5 My niece may bring the bronze trophy back to them.
6 Manny broke his thumb when he spun on the bicycle.
7 Betty is under the gun to excel in the ninth race.
8 They must now face many of the facts I discovered.

Reaches with 3d and 4th fingers

9 A poet told us to zip across the road to get away.
10 Zack saw the sapodilla was almost totally sapless.
11 A poet at our palace said to ask for an allowance.
12 Was it washed when you wore it to our school play?

12C • 13' Script Copy

1. Key the ¶s twice DS (slowly, then faster).
2. Key a 1' writing on ¶ 1.
3. Key a second 1' writing on ¶ 1, trying to key two additional words.
4. Key a 1' writing on ¶ 2.
5. Key a second 1' writing on ¶ 2, trying to key two additional words.
6. To determine *gwam,* count the words in partial lines.

gwam 1'

Thomas Jefferson was a very persuasive writer. Perhaps his most 13
persuasive piece of writing was the Declaration of Independence, which he was 29
asked to prepare with John Adams and Benjamin Franklin to explain the need 44
for independence. 47

We all should recognize parts of that document. For example, "We 13
hold these truths to be self-evident, that all men are created equal, that they are 30
endowed by their Creator with certain unalienable Rights, that among these are 46
Life, Liberty and the pursuit of Happiness." 54

Search the Web button : Takes you to a Web site that provides several search engines that can be used to find information on the Internet.

Web Toolbar button : Removes all toolbars except the Web toolbar from the window. The same button returns the hidden toolbars to the window.

Address box C:\EditTA20\Search the Web\Lessons\SW LESSONS.doc : Displays an active file or Web address and can be used to access an Internet address (site).

Activity 3 • Learn the Browser Window

1. Read the text at the right, learn the key components, and locate them on the illustration and on your browser.
2. Complete the exercise in file *CD-SWL1ACT3*.

Save as: *SWL1ACT3*

A browser window has components similar to those of other software packages. The title bar, menu bar, status bar, and scroll bars serve similar functions to those in other software packages. There are, however, buttons with which you may not be familiar. Study the illustration and key components that are identified and described below.

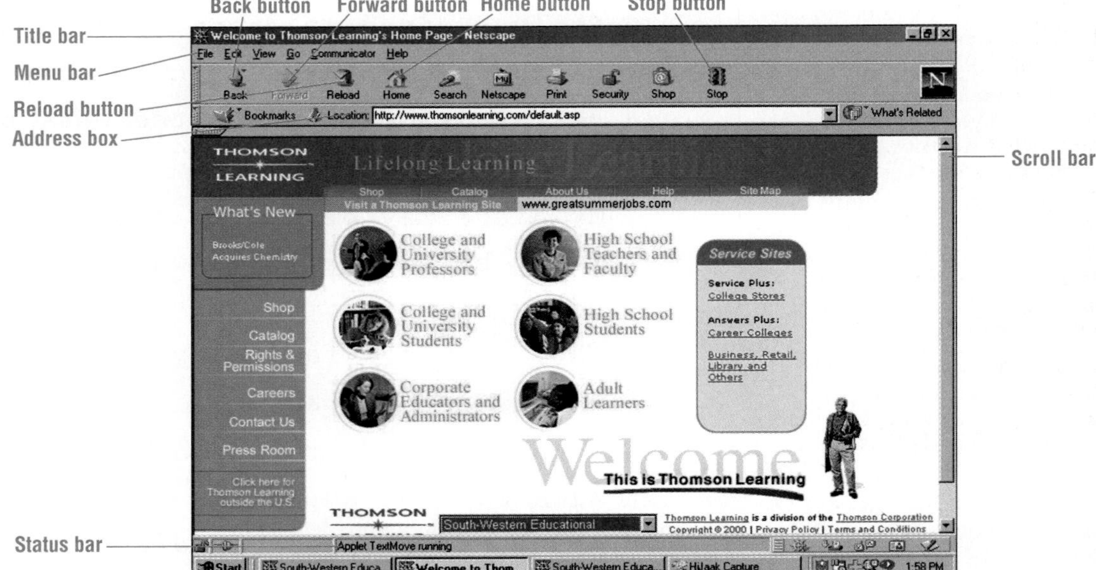

Key Components

Title bar: Shows the name of the browser and the active (open) Web page and contains the Minimize, Restore, and Close buttons.

Menu bar: Contains the pull-down menus used to execute commands.

Back button: When lit, each click takes you back to the last previously viewed Web page.

Forward button: When lit, each click takes you forward to the last previously viewed Web page.

Stop button: Allows you to stop loading a Web page before it is completely loaded.

Refresh or Reload button: Reloads the Web page being viewed.

Home button: Returns you to the home page (or start page) of the browser.

Address, Location, or Netsite box: Displays the active Web address. To use this box to access a Web address, click inside the box, key the Web address, and strike ENTER or click *Go*.

Status bar: Gives the name of the Web page that is loading, the load status, and other important messages.

Scroll bar: Allows you to move up or down (or across) Web pages that are longer or wider than the window.

12D • 12'
Technique: Response Patterns

1. Key each line twice SS; DS between 2-line groups.
2. Key a 1' writing on lines 10–12 to increase speed; find *gwam* on each line.

Technique **H • I • N • T**

Letter response (lines 1–3): Key the letters of these words steadily and evenly.

Word response (lines 4–6): Key these easy words as words—instead of letter by letter.

Combination response (lines 7–9): Key easy words at top speed; key harder words at a lower speed.

	1	milk faced pill cease jump bread join faster jolly
letter response	2	were you|up on|are in fact|my taxes are|star gazed
	3	My cat was in fact up a tree at my estate in Ohio.
	4	oak box land sign make busy kept foal handle gowns
word response	5	go to the|it may work|did he make|she is|he may go
	6	Did he make a big profit for the six formal gowns?
	7	is pin when only their dress forms puppy kept care
combination response	8	when fate|east of|right on|nylon wig|antique cards
	9	Pam was born in a small hill town at the big lake.
letter	10	Edward gave him a minimum rate on state oil taxes.
combination	11	Their eager neighbor may sign up for a tax rebate.
word	12	He may work with the big firms to fix the problem.

gwam 1' | 1 | 2 | 3 | 4 | 5 | 6 | 7 | 8 | 9 | 10 |

12E • 8'
Skill Building

1. Key a 1' writing on each ¶; determine *gwam*.
2. Key two 2' writings on ¶s 1–2 combined; determine *gwam*.

Quarter-Minute Checkpoints				
gwam	1/4'	1/2'	3/4'	Time
16	4	8	12	16
20	5	10	15	20
24	6	12	18	24
28	7	14	21	28
32	8	16	24	32
36	9	18	27	36
40	10	20	30	40

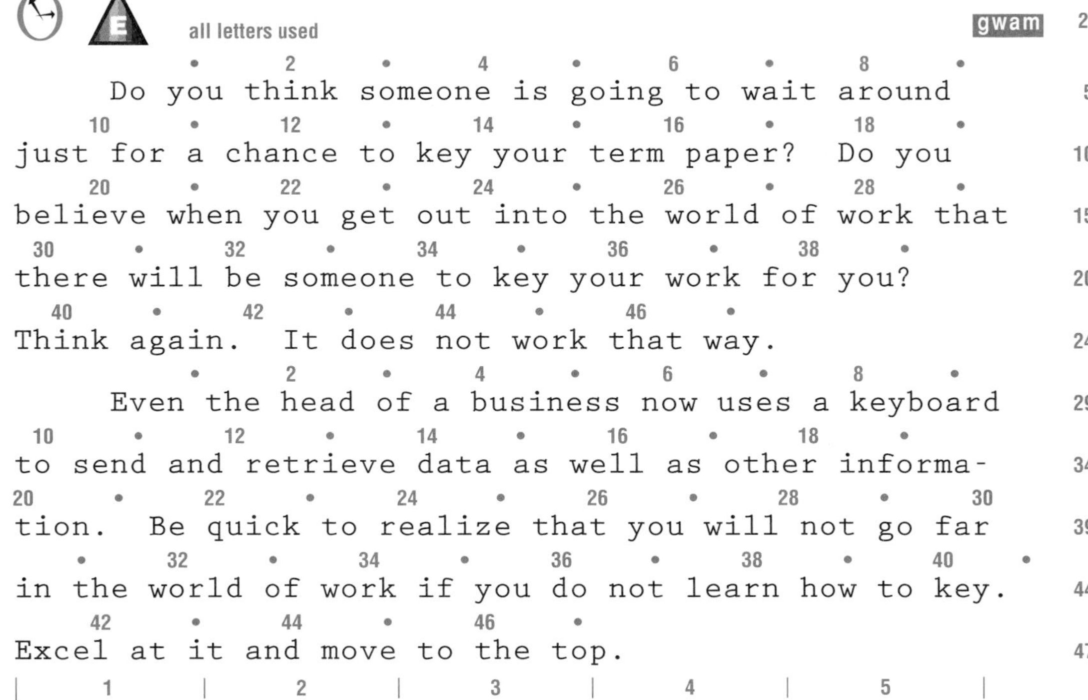

all letters used — gwam 2'

Do you think someone is going to wait around 5
just for a chance to key your term paper? Do you 10
believe when you get out into the world of work that 15
there will be someone to key your work for you? 20
Think again. It does not work that way. 24

Even the head of a business now uses a keyboard 29
to send and retrieve data as well as other informa- 34
tion. Be quick to realize that you will not go far 39
in the world of work if you do not learn how to key. 44
Excel at it and move to the top. 47

gwam 2' | 1 | 2 | 3 | 4 | 5 |

LESSONS 1–6 (4–5 HOURS)

Searching the Web

LESSON 1 KNOW YOUR BROWSER

Objectives:

1. To learn about the Internet and the World Wide Web.
2. To use a browser to access a Web site.

Activity 1 • The Internet

1. Study the text and key terms at the right, referring as needed to the definitions of the key terms given.
2. Open *CD-SWL1ACT1* and complete it as directed.

 **Save as:** *SWL1ACT1*

The **Internet** is a global network of computers that are connected to one another. Any person from any part of the world who has a **browser** connected to the Internet can share information with any other person who is also connected to the Internet. People commonly use the Internet: (1) for e-mail, (2) to research and access information from a variety of resources, (3) to discuss topics or chat with others, (4) for entertainment opportunities and information, (5) to purchase items, and (6) to obtain free software.

Key Terms:

Browser: A special software program used to access information on the Internet. A browser is needed to read HTML files and to move from one HTML document to another on the WWW.

HTML (HyperText Markup Language): A computer language that uses codes to format documents displayed on the WWW.

HTTP (HyperText Transport Protocol): A protocol (or method) that computers use to communicate with each other to move information across the Internet. Addresses of WWW sites using this protocol begin with **http://**.

Home Page: The main page of a Web site to which all other pages within the site are linked. When using a URL without a pathname and filename, it is likely to be the first page displayed.

Internet: A global collection of computers that communicate with each other in various ways.

WWW (World Wide Web): A subset of computers on the Internet that communicate with each other using HTTP.

FTP (File Transfer Protocol) and Gopher: Two subsets that use protocols on the Internet to move files and/or locate, store, or transmit information.

Activity 2 • Open a Browser

1. Read the text at the right, referring to the illustrations.
2. Learn the different ways to open your Internet browser.
3. Open a new wp document, display the Web toolbar, and learn features of the toolbar.
4. Open file *CD-SWL1ACT2* and complete it as directed.

 **Save as:** *SWL1ACT2*

A browser, the gateway to the Internet, can be opened by: (1) clicking a browser icon on the desktop, (2) clicking a browser icon on a toolbar, (3) selecting a browser from the programs accessed via the Start button on the taskbar, and (4) clicking an icon on the Web toolbar in a wp window.

The first two graphics below are icons for two popular browsers—Netscape Navigator and Internet Explorer. The toolbar below the graphics is a Web toolbar that can be used to access and navigate the Internet from wp software.

Toolbar Features

Start Page button : Starts (launches) the browser.

(continued on next page)

Communication Skills 1

ACTIVITY 1

Simple Sentences

1. Study the guides and the simple sentences beneath them.
2. Key the Learn sentences as shown, noting the subjects and predicates.
3. For each sentence 1 through 8, key the sentence number, followed by the subject and predicate.
4. For each line 9 through 11, combine the two sentences into one simple sentence with two nouns as the subject and one verb as the predicate.
5. Revise Sentence 12 by combining the two sentences into one simple sentence with two nouns as the subject and two verbs as the predicate.

 **Save as:** *CS1-ACT1*

A **simple** sentence consists of one independent clause that contains a subject (noun or pronoun) and a predicate (verb).

Learn 1 Pam is president of her class.

Learn 2 Kevin walks to and from school.

Learn 3 Reading mystery novels is my favorite pastime.

Learn 4 The captain of the team is out with a badly sprained ankle.

A **simple** sentence may have as its subject more than one noun or pronoun (compound subject) and as its predicate more than one verb (compound predicate).

Learn 5 She bought a new bicycle. (single subject/single predicate)

Learn 6 Marv and I received new bicycles. (compound subject/single predicate)

Learn 7 Alice washed and waxed her car. (single subject/compound predicate)

Learn 8 He and I cleaned and cooked the fish. (compound subject/compound predicate)

Apply 9 Jorge read AURA by Fuentes. Rosa read it, also.

Apply 10 Hamad cooks his own meals. So does Janelle.

Apply 11 Sara talked with Mona at the concert. Lee talked with her, also.

Apply 12 Mel chooses and buys his own training shoes. Suzy also chooses and buys hers.

ACTIVITY 2

Compound Sentences

1. Study the guides and the sentences beneath them at the right and on the top of p. 28.
2. Key the Learn sentences, noting the words that make up the subjects and predicates of each sentence.
3. For each sentence 13 through 20, key the sentence number, followed by the subjects and predicates.

A **compound** sentence contains two or more independent clauses connected by a coordinating conjunction **(and**, **but**, **for**, **or**, **nor**, **yet**, **so)**.

Learn 13 Jay Sparks likes to hike, and Roy Tubbs likes to swim.

Learn 14 The computer is operative, but the printer does not work.

Learn 15 You may eat in the hotel, or you may choose a café nearby.

Learn 16 The sky is clear, the moon is out, and the sea is very calm.

Each clause of a compound sentence may have as its subject more than one noun/pronoun and as its predicate more than one verb.

Learn 17 Ben and I saw the game, and Bob and Maria went to a movie.

Learn 18 Nick dived and swam, but the others fished off the boat.

Learn 19 You may play solitaire, or you and Joe may play checkers.

(continued on next page)

The Adventures of Huckleberry Finn

The Adventures of Huckleberry Finn was first published in 1885. Many of the characters included in *The Adventures of Tom Sawyer* surface again in this book. Children are able to relate to the fascinating characters and their adventures. In these books, Mark Twain finds a way to express the hopes, fears, joys, and dreams of millions of us.

REFERENCES

Railton, Stephen. "Your Mark Twain." http://etext.lib.virginia.edu/railton/sc_as_mt/yourmt13.html (24 September 1999).

Railton, Stephen. "Sam Clemens as Mark Twain." http://etext.lib.virginia.edu/railton/sc_as_mt/cathompg.html (24 September 1999).

In addition to correcting any errors that have occurred, make the following changes to the report:

Speak . . . ➤

1. Move the first paragraph to make it the second paragraph.
2. Make the sentence that reads *The Adventures of Tom Sawyer was first published in 1876* the first sentence of the paragraph. Make the book title italic.
3. Change *captured generations of readers* to *captured the attention of readers for generations.*
4. Reverse the order of the two references.

4. For lines 21 through 24, combine the two sentences into a compound sentence. Choose carefully from the coordinating conjunctions *and*, *but*, *for*, *or*, *not*, *yet*, and *so*.

 **Save as:** *CS1-ACT2*

Learn 20 Bobby huffed and puffed, but Erin scampered up the hill.

Apply 21 Karen listened to Ravel's BOLERO. Matt read FORREST GUMP.

Apply 22 You may watch STAR TREK. You and Edie may play dominoes.

Apply 23 Ken may play football or basketball. He may not play both.

Apply 24 Linda skated to CABARET music. Jon chose WEST SIDE STORY.

ACTIVITY 3

Complex Sentences

Use the directions in Activity 2 to complete lines 25 through 36. For lines 25 through 32, key the subject and predicate of the independent clause and of the dependent clause for each sentence.

 **Save as:** *CS1-ACT3*

> A **complex** sentence contains only one independent clause and one or more dependent clauses.

Learn 25 The book that you gave Juan for his birthday is lost.

Learn 26 If I were you, I would speak to Paula before I left.

Learn 27 Miss Gomez, who chairs the department, is currently on leave.

Learn 28 Students who use their time wisely usually succeed.

> The subject of a complex sentence may consist of more than one noun or pronoun; the predicate may consist of more than one verb.

Learn 29 All who were invited to the party also attended the game.

Learn 30 If you are to join, you should sign up and pay your dues.

Learn 31 After she and I left, Cliff and Pam sang and danced.

Learn 32 Although they don't know it yet, Fran and Brett were elected.

Apply 33 My PSAT and SAT scores are high. I may not get into Yale.

Apply 34 They attended the symphony. They then had a light supper.

Apply 35 Mindy is to audition for the part. She should apply now.

Apply 36 You are buying a computer. You should also get software.

ACTIVITY 4

Composing

Key each line once SS. In place of the blank line at the end of each sentence, key the word(s) that correctly complete(s) the sentence.

 **Save as:** *CS1-ACT4*

1. A small mass of land surrounded by water is a/an _________.
2. A large mass of land surrounded by water is a/an _________.
3. The earth rotates on what is called its _________.
4. When the sun comes up over the horizon, we say it _________.
5. When the sun goes down over the horizon, we say it _________.
6. A device used to display temperature is a/an _________.
7. A device used to display atmospheric pressure is a/an _________.

5B • 40' Editing a Report

1. Open a new document.
2. Set the margins for an unbound report.
3. Speak the report at the right and on the next page.
4. Format the document.
5. Correct any errors.
6. Make the changes indicated after the report.
7. Print the report.

Save as: *CLEMENS*

Speak . . . ➤

SAMUEL CLEMENS

"Mark Twain"

Sam Clemens was recognized for his fiction as well as for his humor. It has been said, ". . . next to sunshine and fresh air Mark Twain's humor has done more for the welfare of mankind than any other agency." (Railton, "Your Mark Twain," 1999) By cleverly weaving fiction and humor, he developed many literary masterpieces. Some say his greatest masterpiece was "Mark Twain," a pen name (pseudonym) Clemens first used in the Nevada Territory in 1863. This fictitious name became a kind of mythic hero to the American public. (Railton, "Sam Clemens as Mark Twain," 1999) Two of his masterpieces that are among his most widely read books are *The Adventures of Tom Sawyer* and *The Adventures of Huckleberry Finn.*

Samuel Clemens was one of America's most noted authors. The colorful life he led was the basis for his writing. Although his formal education ended when he was 12 years old with the death of his father, his varied career interests provided an informal education that was not unlike many others of his generation. Clemens brought these rich experiences to life in his writing.

<u>The Adventures of Tom Sawyer</u>

Such characters as Tom Sawyer, Aunt Polly, Becky Thatcher, and Huck Finn have captured generations of readers. Boys and girls, young and old, enjoy Tom Sawyer's mischievousness. Who can forget how Tom shared the privilege of whitewashing Aunt Polly's fence? What child isn't fascinated by the episode of Tom and Becky lost in the cave? The Adventures of Tom Sawyer was first published in 1876.

(continued on next page)

UNIT 3

LESSONS 13–14

Review Figure Keys

LESSON 13 — REVIEW FIGURE KEYS (8, 1, 9, 4, AND 0)

Objectives:

1. To review reach technique for **8**, **1**, **9**, **4**, and **0**.
2. To improve skill on script, and rough-draft copy.

13A • 5' Conditioning Practice

Key each line twice SS; then key a 1' writing on line 3; determine *gwam.*

alphabet 1 The exquisite prize, a framed clock, was to be given to Jay.

spacing 2 They may try to be at the dorm in time to eat with the team.

easy 3 The maid was with the dog and six girls by the field of hay.

gwam 1' | 1 | 2 | 3 | 4 | 5 | 6 | 7 | 8 | 9 | 10 | 11 | 12 |

13B • 8' Review 8 and 1

Key each line twice SS (slowly, then faster); DS between 2-line groups.

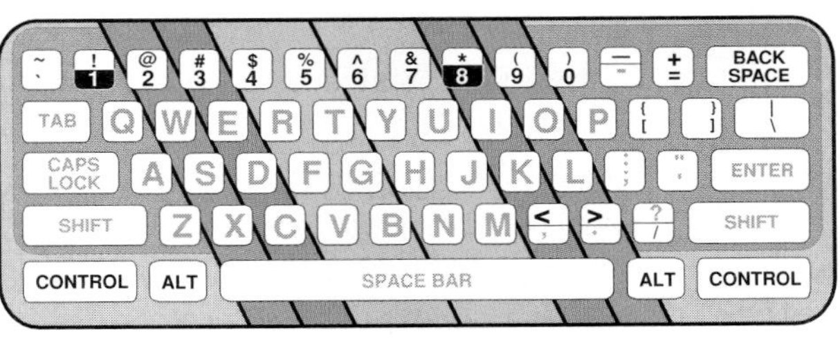

Review 8

1 k k 8k 8k kk 88 k8k k8k 88k 88k Reach up for 8, 88, and 888.

2 Key the figures 8, 88, and 888. Please open Room 88 or 888.

Review 1

3 a a 1a 1a aa 11 a1a a1a 11a 11a Reach up for 1, 11, and 111.

4 Add the figures 1, 11, and 111. Only 1 out of 111 finished.

Combine 8 and 1

5 Key 11, 18, 81, and 88. Just 11 of the 18 skiers have left.

6 Reach with the fingers to key 18 and 188 as well as 1 and 8.

7 The stock person counted 11 coats, 18 slacks, and 88 shirts.

SELECTING AND MOVING TEXT

Objectives:

1. To learn how to move around the document by word, line, and paragraph.
2. To learn how to select text to cut, copy, and paste.

5A • 15' Selecting and Moving Text

1. Read the information at the right.
2. Open a new document.
3. Speak the examples as instructed.
4. Correct any errors.

Save as: *SR5A*

To use speech recognition software to edit a document, you must move the text insertion point using your voice. The insertion point can be moved by character, word, line, or paragraph. You can also move directly to the beginning or end of a document.

Say the sentence below exactly as it appears:

Speak . . . ➤ Since your just completing your college degrees: I knew just where to get the help I need.

Use the move to command to move the text insertion point to a specific character and word as you make the following changes.

Say [Move to. . .]	***Change the word/phrase by saying. . .***
Speak . . . ➤ the first *your*	*you*
completing	*completed*
degrees	*degree*
: (colon)	, (comma)
the second *just*	delete the word
get	*find*
need	*needed*

The edited sentence should look like this:

Since you just completed your college degree, I knew where to find the help I needed.

Note:
All the familiar word processing features are available by voice.

Word processing commands for editing text, including Cut, Copy, and Paste, are also available by voice. For example, to cut selected text, you can say ***[Edit Menu Cut]***. The same technique can be used to copy and paste text.

Say the following paragraph exactly as it appears:

Speak . . . ➤ Your insights into what it takes to make it as a professional musician were also enlightening for your members. It was great learning more about the great composers from you. If we are going to be successful, those of us who want to be professional musicians know we have to dedicate ourselves to that goal.

Use voice commands (***Edit Menu Cut*** and ***Edit Menu Paste***) to edit these sentences:

Speak . . . ➤

1. Cut the second sentence. Move to the beginning of the paragraph and paste the cut sentence.
2. Select the word *also* and cut it.
3. Select *your members* and change it to *our members*.
4. Cut *If we are going to be successful* and paste it at the end of the sentence. Make the change to correct capitalization in the sentence.

13C • 7' Keyboard Reinforcement

Key each line twice SS (slowly, then faster); DS between 2-line groups.

Figures

1 May 1-8, May 11-18, June 1-8, and June 11-18 are open dates.

2 The quiz on the 18th will be on pages 11 to 18 and 81 to 88.

3 He said only 11 of us got No. 81 right; 88 got No. 81 wrong.

Home/1st

4 ax jab gab call man van back band gala calf cabman avalanche

5 small man|can mask|lava gas|hand vase|lack cash|a small vase

6 Ms. Maas can call a cab, and Jan can flag a small black van.

13D • 9' Review 9, 4, and 0

Key each line twice SS (slowly, then faster); DS between 2-line groups.

Note: Use the letter l in line 1. Use the figure 1 in line 2.

Review 9

1 l l 91 91 ll 99 l9l l9l 99l 99l Reach up for 9, 99, and 999.

2 The social security number was 919-99-9191, not 191-99-1919.

Review 4

3 f f 4f 4f ff 44 f4f f4f 44f 44f Reach up for 4, 44, and 444.

4 Add the figures 4, 44, and 444. Please study pages 4 to 44.

Review 0

5 ; ; 0; 0; ;; 00 ;0; ;0; 00; 00; Reach up for 0, 00, and 000.

6 Snap the finger off the 0. I used 0, 00, and 000 sandpaper.

Combine 9, 4, and 0

7 Flights 904 and 490 left after Flights 409A, 400Z, and 940X.

8 My ZIP Code is 40099, not 44099. Is Tanya's 09094 or 90904?

13E • 11' Speed Check

1. Key a 30" writing on each line. Determine *gwam* on each writing.
2. Key another 30" writing on each line—at a faster pace.
3. Key two 2' writings on 12E, p. 26.

| 2 | 4 | 6 | 8 | 10 | 12 | 14 | 16 | 18 | 20 | 22 |

1 Suzy may fish off the dock with us.

2 Pay the girls for all the work they did.

3 Quen is due by six and may then fix the sign.

4 Janie is to vie with six girls for the city title.

5 Duane is to go to the lake to fix the auto for the man.

30" | 2 | 4 | 6 | 8 | 10 | 12 | 14 | 16 | 18 | 20 | 22 |

4A • 35'
Creating a Flyer

1. Open a new document.
2. Set the margins of your document for an unbound report.
3. Create the document shown at the right with your speech recognition software, applying all formatting needed by using voice commands.
4. Print the document.

Save as:
COMPUTERAD

SPECIAL SALE [Arial, 24 pt.]

Multimedia Computer [Arial, 20 pt.]

- Pentium VI/1GHz processor [Arial, 16 pt.]
- 12G hard drive
- 156MB RAM memory
- 17" SVGA noninterlaced color monitor
- 16MB video memory
- 16x CD-RW/DVD drive
- 16-bit stereo sound card and speakers
- 56.6 internal fax/modem
- Preloaded and CD-ROM software
- 3-year computer warranty

Only $2,299 [Times New Roman, 24 pt.]

0% Financing

No payments, no interest for 90 days

[Times New Roman, 16 pt., blue] Computer Source
[Times New Roman, 12 pt.] 605 Toledo Ave.
813-555-0107

13F • 10'
Script and Rough-Draft Copy

1. Key each line once DS (2 hard returns between lines).
2. Key the rough-draft lines again if time permits.

≡ = capitalize

∧ = insert

∼ = transpose

ℓ# = delete space

= add space

/lc = lowercase

⌒ = close up

Script

1 Proofread: Compare copy word for word with the original.
2 Compare all figures digit by digit with your source copy.
3 Be sure to check for spacing and punctuation marks, also.
4 Copy in script or rough draft may not show exact spacing.
5 It is your job to insert correct spacing as you key copy.
6 Soon you will learn how to correct your errors on screen.

Rough draft

7 cap the first word an all proper nouns in every sentence.
8 For example: pablo Mendez is from San juan,Puerto rico.
9 Ami Qwan and parents will return to Taipie this summer.
10 our coffee is from Columbia; tea, fromEngland or china.
11 How many of you have Ethnic origins ina for eign country?
12 did you know which of the states once were part of mexico?

LESSON 14 REVIEW FIGURE KEYS (5, 7, 3, 6, AND 2)

Objectives:

1. To review reach technique for **5**, **7**, **3**, **6**, and **2**.
2. To improve skill transfer and build speed.

14A • 5'
Conditioning Practice

Key each line twice SS; then key a 1' writing on line 3; determine *gwam.*

alphabet 1 Zelda might fix the job growth plans very quickly on Monday.
spacing 2 He will go with me to the city to get the rest of the tapes.
easy 3 The six men with the problems may wish to visit the tax man.

gwam 1' | 1 | 2 | 3 | 4 | 5 | 6 | 7 | 8 | 9 | 10 | 11 | 12 |

14B • 5'
Review 5 and 7

Key each line twice SS (slowly, then faster); DS between 2-line groups.

Review 5

1 f f 5f 5f ff 55 f5f f5f 55f 55f Reach up for 5, 55, and 555.
2 Reach up to 5 and back to f. Did he say to order 55 or 555?

Review 7

3 j j 7j 7j jj 77 j7j j7j 77j 77j Reach up for 7, 77, and 777.
4 Key the figures 7, 77, and 777. She checked Rooms 7 and 77.

FORMATTING TEXT

Objectives:

1. To learn how to apply bold, italic, and underline using speech recognition software.
2. To learn how to control text alignment.
3. To understand how to capitalize letters and words.

Formatting Text

You have already been speaking commands and punctuation. Adding text formatting commands will expand your use of the speech recognition software's tools. Text formatting allows you to place emphasis on selected words, phrases, or sentences. The most common text formats are bold, italic, and underline. Text formatting also involves changing the font or the size of type.

Speech recognition software allows you to change text formats as often as you like. You can:

- Set the formats before you begin speaking. You usually do this when you are choosing the font and type size for your document.
- Format text while you are entering the document. You can turn on and off bold, italic, and underline as you are speaking a document. You simply say the commands like all other commands.
- Format text after you have entered the document. To reduce the number of commands you need to speak, you can wait to add the formatting after you have entered the document. As you are proofreading the document, you can tell the program to select individual words or blocks of text and apply the formatting.

The same formatting rules apply whether you are using speech recognition software or a keyboard.

Aligning Text

The default alignment of your word processor, left alignment, will be used unless you specify otherwise. Just like text formatting, you can:

- Set the alignment before you begin speaking the document. This choice is best when the entire document will not be left-aligned. For example, if your document will be centered, you should tell the software this at the beginning of your document.
- Set the alignment as you are entering the document. You simply tell the software to right-align or center the next paragraph before you speak the paragraph.
- When you proofread the document, you may select lines or paragraphs to be aligned differently. With the text selected, give the software the command to center or right-align the text. With some software, you do not need to select the text first. For example, you can say ***[Center the First Paragraph]***. The software will identify the first paragraph and change the alignment.

You can use the same basic guidelines to indent paragraphs from the right and left margins. If you tell the computer to ***[Indent That]***, it will indent the selected text one tab stop on the left. If the tab stops are set at 0.5", the text will be indented 0.5" from the left margin of the document. You can also direct the software to indent using specific measurements. For example, if you say ***[Right Indent the Last Paragraph One Inch]***, the software will respond by indenting the last paragraph you spoke 1" from the right margin.

Capitalizing

Speech recognition software knows to capitalize the first letter of a sentence and the first letter of a word it recognizes as a proper name. However, you must tell the software if you need other words capitalized. You must also must tell the software when you want every letter in a word to appear in uppercase. For example, the subject of a memo should appear in uppercase. The specific commands for capitalizing and uppercasing copy vary somewhat among the software packages. You will need to practice to find the capitalization and uppercasing techniques that work best for you.

SKILL BUILDING

14C • 8'
Figure-Key Mastery

Key each line twice SS (slowly, then faster); DS between 2-line groups.

Straight copy

1 She moved from 819 Briar Lane to 4057 Park Avenue on May 15.

2 The 50-point quiz on May 17 covers pages 88-94, 97, and 100.

3 The meeting will be held in Room 87 on March 19 at 5:40 p.m.

Script

4 *The 495 representatives met from 7:00 to 8:40 p.m. on May 1.*

5 *Social Security Nos. 519-88-7504 and 798-05-4199 were found.*

6 *My office is at 157 Main, and my home is at 4081 92d Avenue.*

Rough draft

7 Runners 180,90 and 507 were schedule for August 15.

8 her tele phone number was changde to 194-5009 on July 1.

9 Re view Rules 1- on pages 89-90 and rules 15-19 no page 174.

14D • 8'
Review 3, 6, and 2

Key each line twice SS (slowly, then faster); DS between 2-line groups.

Review 3

1 d d 3d 3d dd 33 d3d d3d 33d 33d Reach up for 3, 33, and 333.

2 Add the figures 3, 33, and 333. Read pages 3 to 33 tonight.

Review 6

3 j j 6j 6j jj 66 j6j j6j 66j 66j Reach up for 6, 66, and 666.

4 Key the figures 6, 66, and 666. Did just 6 of 66 finish it?

Review 2

5 s s 2s 2s ss 22 s2s s2s 22s 22s Reach up for 2, 22, and 222.

6 Reach up to 2 and back to s. Ashley reviewed pages 2 to 22.

Combine 3, 6, and 2

7 Only 263 of the 362 flights left on time on Monday, July 26.

8 Read Chapter 26, pages 263 to 326, for the exam on April 23.

Speaking Special Types of Numbers
Special rules apply to speaking the numbers in currency, telephone numbers, dates or times of day.

1. To speak dollar amounts, use the ***Dollar Sign*** command or speak the amount naturally. Use the ***Point*** command instead of the ***Period*** command to indicate *cents*, to avoid a space after the decimal point.

If you say. . .	***The result will be. . .***
[Dollar Sign] 31	$31

2. To speak telephone numbers, say punctuation marks as they should appear.

If you say. . .	***The result will be. . .***
Five five five ***[Dash]*** oh one oh six	555-0106
[Numeral]1 ***[Left Paren]*** 800 ***[Right Paren]*** five five five ***[Dash]*** oh one eighteen	1 (800) 555-0118

3. Speak dates however you want them to appear.

If you say. . .	***The result will be. . .***
Nine ***[Slash]*** eleven ***[Slash]*** oh two	9/11/02
September eleven ***[Comma]*** two thousand two	September 11, 2002

4. To indicate time, always include AM or PM.

If you say. . .	***The result will be. . .***
One o'clock pm	1:00 PM
Six forty-five am	6:45 AM

Note:
You can say *zero* or *oh* to display the numeral 0.

Note:
Some speech recognition software has a date function that allows you to choose one of several date styles. Some programs also have a time format function that allows you to select the time format you prefer.

3B • 20'
Creating a Memo

1. Open a new document.
2. Speak the document at the right.

Save as:
SRMEMO3B

TO: Marshall Sabin | FROM: Tina Hansen | DATE: October 1, 200- | SUBJECT: INFORMATION FOR YOUR REPORT

I found a Web site at http://www.nytheatre-wire.com/PoorR.htm that lists current Broadway plays. Five of the plays opened prior to 1990. These include *Cats* (10/07/82), *Les Miserables* (03/12/87), *The Phantom of the Opera* (01/26/88), and *Tony 'n' Tina's Wedding* (02/06/88). Broadway's longest-running musical, *The Fantasticks*, opened on May 3, 1960.

I scanned this information. You will want to check the Web site and verify the accuracy of the information before you include it in your report. If I find anything else for your report, I will let you know.

3C • 15'
Creating a Table

1. Open a new document.
2. Use your keyboard to set right-aligned tab stops at 3" and 4.5".
3. Use your voice to create the table at the right.

Save as: *SRTBL3C*

Country	**Area (sq. mi.)**	**Life Expectancy**
China	3,705,390	70
India	1,269,340	59
Thailand	198,456	68
Japan	143,749	79
Philippines	115,830	64
North Korea	46,541	69
South Korea	38,023	71
Singapore	224	74

14E • 10'
Skill Transfer

1. Key a 1' writing on each ¶; determine *gwam* on each.
2. Compare rates. On which ¶ did you have highest *gwam*?
3. Key two 1' writings on each of the slower ¶s, trying to equal your highest *gwam* in Step 1.

Note:
Relative speeds on different kinds of copy:

- highest—straight copy
- next highest—script copy
- lowest—statistical copy

To determine *gwam*, use the 1' *gwam* scale for partial lines in ¶s 1 and 2, but count the words in ¶ 3.

all letters/figures used — gwam 1'

You should try now to transfer to other types of copy 11
as much of your straight-copy speed as you can. Handwritten 23
copy and copy in which figures appear tend to slow you down. 35
You can increase speed on these, however, with extra effort. 47

An immediate goal for handwritten copy is at least 90 per- 11
cent of the straight-copy rate; for copy with figures, at 23
least 75 percent. Try to speed up balanced-hand figures such 35
as 26, 84, and 163. Key harder ones such as 452 and 980 more 48
slowly. 49

Copy that is written by hand is often not legible, and 11
the spelling of words may be puzzling. So give major attention 23
to unclear words. Question and correct the spacing used 35
with a comma or period. you can do this even as you key. 47

gwam 1' | 1 | 2 | 3 | 4 | 5 | 6 | 7 | 8 | 9 | 10 | 11 | 12 |

14F • 14'
Speed Building

1. Key a 1' writing on each ¶; determine *gwam* on each writing.
2. Add 2–4 *gwam* to better rate in Step 1 for a new goal.
3. Key three 1' writings on each ¶ trying to achieve new goal.

all letters used — gwam 2'

When you need to adjust to a new situation in which new 6
people are involved, be quick to recognize that at first it 12
is you who must adapt. This is especially true in an office 18
where the roles of workers have already been established. It 24
is your job to fit into the team structure with harmony. 30

Learn the rules of the game and who the key players are; 35
then play according to those rules at first. Do not expect 41
to have the rules modified to fit your concept of what the 47
team structure and your role in it should be. Only after you 53
become a valuable member should you suggest major changes. 59

gwam 2' | 1 | 2 | 3 | 4 | 5 | 6 |

SPEAKING NUMBERS

Objectives:

1. To learn how to make numbers appear as figures and words.
2. To learn to speak numbers in dates, times of day, currency, and telephone numbers.

3A • 15' Speaking Numbers

1. Read the text at the right.
2. Open a new document.
3. Speak the examples below Rule 3 as instructed.
4. Correct any errors.
5. Print the document.
6. Close the document without saving it.

When you speak a number such as *9*, speech recognition software does not know whether you want *nine* or *9* to appear. Use Rules 1–3 below for numbers in your documents.

Rule 1. For numbers 1 through 19, the software will automatically spell out the words. If you want figures, you must speak the command ***Numeral*** before saying the number.

If you say. . .	***The result will be. . .***
11	eleven
[Numeral] 11	11

Rule 2. For numbers 20 and greater, the software will assume you want the figures.

If you say. . .	***The result will be. . .***
Thirty-two	32

Rule 3. For numbers 1,000 and greater, the software adds commas in the correct places. You can say the number the regular way or say each digit in sequence.

If you say. . .	***The result will be. . .***
Three thousand three hundred thirty-two	3,332
Three three three two	3,332

To practice numbers, speak each of the following examples:

Speak . . . ►

Say. . .	***You should see. . .***
7	seven
[Numeral] twelve	12
43	43
One hundred ten	110
Six five four nine	6,549
One hundred ten thousand ninety	110,090
Two million	2,000,000

Now, practice using numbers in sentences. Speak each sentence below so that numbers display as shown. Start each sentence on a new line.

Speak . . . ►

Yesterday, I sold 12 pairs of shoes.
Twelve jurors listened to the evidence.
My friend has 3 cats, 2 dogs, and 14 goldfish.
As a team, we hit 124 home runs and scored 1,457 runs.
When Grandmother turned 100, her nine grandchildren helped her celebrate.
Our office sold 40,200 shares of stock last week.

UNIT 4

LESSONS 15–16

Build Keyboarding Skill

LESSON 15 SKILL BUILDING

Objectives:

1. To improve technique on individual letters.

2. To improve keying speed on 1' and 2' writings.

15A • 5' Conditioning Practice

Key each line twice SS; then key a 1' writing on line 3; determine *gwam.*

alphabet 1 Jack Faber was amazingly quiet during the extensive program.

spacing 2 it has | it will be | to your | by then | in our | it may be | to do the

easy 3 Jan may make a big profit if she owns the title to the land.

gwam 1' | 1 | 2 | 3 | 4 | 5 | 6 | 7 | 8 | 9 | 10 | 11 | 12 |

SKILL BUILDING

15B • 18' Technique: Individual Letters

Key each line twice SS (slowly, then faster); DS between 2-line groups.

Goal:

To keep keystroking action limited to the fingers.

Emphasize continuity and rhythm with curved, upright fingers.

A 1 Anna Haas ate the meal, assuming that her taxi had departed.

B 2 Bobby Barber bribed Bart to buy the baseball, bat, and base.

C 3 Chuck Cusack confiscated a raccoon and a cat from my clinic.

D 4 Donald doubted that Todd could decide on the daily dividend.

E 5 Ellen and Steven designed evening dresses for several years.

F 6 Felicia and her friend split their fifer's fees fifty-fifty.

G 7 Garn Taggart haggled with Dr. Gregg over the geography exam.

H 8 The highest honors for Heath were highlighted on each sheet.

I 9 Heidi Kim is an identical twin who idolizes her twin sister.

J 10 Janet and Jody joined Jay in Jericho in West Jordan in July.

K 11 Karl kept Kay's knickknack in a knapsack in the khaki kayak.

L 12 Molly filled the small holes in the little yellow lunch box.

M 13 Mr. Mark murmured about the minimal number of grammar gains.

gwam 1' | 1 | 2 | 3 | 4 | 5 | 6 | 7 | 8 | 9 | 10 | 11 | 12 |

Speak . . . ➤ George Washington

Abraham Lincoln

Franklin Roosevelt

Winston Churchill

Joseph Stalin

Adolf Hitler

Benito Mussolini

http://www.bls.gov

http://www.noaa.gov

Test the results by speaking the following sentences in any new document. Start all sentences on a new line. Remember to speak punctuation marks as commands.

Speak . . . ➤ George Washington was the first president of the United States.

Abraham Lincoln was president of the United States during the Civil War.

Franklin Roosevelt, Winston Churchill, and Joseph Stalin led their countries in opposing the forces of Adolf Hitler and Benito Mussolini.

Two government Web sites that contain a wealth of information are the sites for the National Oceanic and Atmospheric Administration (http://ww.noaa.gov) and the Bureau of Labor Statistics (http://www.bls.gov).

2C • 30' Proofreading and Editing

1. Read the text at the right.
2. Open a new document.
3. Compose and speak two paragraphs on a topic of your choice.
4. Train any words that the software misunderstands.
5. Proofread and edit your paragraphs.
6. Print the document.
7. Save the document with an appropriate filename.

Proofreading and Editing

Even after you have fully trained your speech recognition software, errors may still occur. Therefore, it is important that you proofread documents carefully. Errors that occur with speech recognition software differ from keyboarding errors. The software will not misspell words that it knows. However, errors that may occur include the following:

- Extra words that the software inserts when it "hears" extraneous noise. Sometimes the sound of your breathing can be interpreted as words by the software. Make sure that your microphone is positioned properly.
- Words and phrases that are different from what you intended. Causes include speaking unclearly or a lack of training of the software. For example, you may have said, "We went to the park," but the words "When top ark" appear. If these errors occur frequently, spend more time training your software or rerecord your voice profile.
- Commands that are misunderstood as words in the document. Remember to pause slightly before and after commands.
- Commands or punctuation marks that are forgotten. For example, you may forget to tell the software to insert a comma. The software does not know where to place punctuation marks, how to break paragraphs, or how to format documents. You must direct the software by speaking all punctuation marks and commands.

Format documents carefully and correct all errors. Spend time training words that the software does not recognize. Then read the document again to make changes. Ask yourself:

- Are the sentences clear? How can they be improved?
- Have I made all the points I intended to make?
- Is the punctuation correct?
- Do the paragraphs contain topic sentences? Do all of the other sentences support the main idea?

15C • 12'
Technique: Tab

1. Key each short story title and opening line shown at the right.
2. Key the copy again at a faster pace.

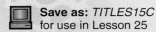

Save as: *TITLES15C* for use in Lesson 25

Technique C • U • E

- Reach up to the TAB key without moving the left hand away from you.
- Strike the TAB key firmly and release it quickly.

Optional Activity

Can you match each short story with its author?

Benjamin Franklin
Helen Keller
Katherine Mansfield
John Steinbeck
James Thurber
Mark Twain

"The Scotty Who Knew Too Much"

Tab → Several summers ago there was a Scotty who went to the country for a visit.

"Roughing It"

Tab → After leaving the Sink, we traveled along the Humboldt River a little way.

"The Autobiography Moral Perfection"

Tab → It was about this time that I conceived the bold and arduous project of arriving at moral perfection.

"The Chrysanthemums"

Tab → The high grey-flannel fog of winter closed off the Salinas Valley from the sky and from all the rest of the world.

"The Story of My Life"

Tab → The most important day I remember in all my life is the one on which my teacher, Anne Mansfield Sullivan, came to me.

"The Doll's House"

Tab → When dear old Mrs. Hay went back to town after staying with the Burnells, she sent the children a doll's house.

15D • 15'
Speed Building: Guided Writing

1. Key one 1' unguided and two 1' guided writings on each ¶, using the procedure on p. 22; determine *gwam*.
2. Key two 2' unguided writings on ¶s 1–2 combined; determine *gwam*.

Quarter-Minute Checkpoints				
gwam	1/4'	1/2'	3/4'	1'
20	5	10	15	20
24	6	12	18	24
28	7	14	21	28
32	8	16	24	32
36	9	18	27	36
40	10	20	30	40
44	11	22	33	44
48	12	24	36	48
52	13	26	39	52
56	14	28	42	56

LA all letters used — *gwam* 2'

When saying hello to someone is the correct thing to do, 6
make direct eye contact and greet the person with vitality 12
in your voice. Do not look down or away or speak only in a 18
whisper. Make the person feel happy for having seen you, and 24
you will feel much better about yourself as a consequence. 30

Similarly, when you shake hands with another person, 35
look that person in the eye and offer a firm but not crushing 41
shake of the hand. Just a firm shake or two will do. Next 47
time you meet a new person, do not puzzle over whether to 53
shake hands. Quickly offer your firm hand with confidence. 59

2' | 1 | 2 | 3 | 4 | 5 | 6 |

LESSON 2 CORRECTING ERRORS

Objectives:

1. To make corrections using your voice.
2. To learn to train unique words and phrases.
3. To understand the importance of proofreading and editing your documents.

2A • 10' Correcting Text

1. Read the text at the right.
2. Open the software to a new document.
3. Practice correcting using the examples shown. (Use the Undo/Scratch command or Select command.)
4. Close the document without saving.

Making Corrections

As you are training software, you should correct errors as soon as they appear on the screen. This process helps the software become more accurate in recognizing your unique speech pattern. After at least 15 to 20 hours of training, the software will understand you well enough that you will be able to correct errors during the proofreading phase of document processing.

The ***Scratch*** or ***Undo*** command will remove the last word or phrase that you spoke. You can repeat this command as needed to continue to erase words, phrases, or commands. Once the word or phrase has been removed, simply speak the words you intended.

You can also correct an error by selecting the error and speaking a correction. When you use the command to ***Select*** text, the selected text appears highlighted on the computer screen. With the text selected, speak a replacement word or phrase; and the new text will replace the highlighted text.

Speak the words . . .	Replace them with these words . . .
Speak . . . ► letter-by-letter order	alphabetic order
map of the United States	United States map
baseball and football	basketball and soccer
green beans and corn	lima beans and corn
reply as soon as possible	reply immediately

2B • 20' Training Words

1. Read the text at the right.
2. Train the names and Web site addresses shown on the next page; then speak the sentences below them.
3. Close the document without saving.

Training Words and Phrases

There are more than 100,000 words in the English language, and new words appear frequently. Speech recognition software has a large vocabulary, but it cannot know all English words. For instance, the software does not know many proper names. You can teach the software any word it does not understand.

To train the software to recognize unfamiliar words, you will need to spell the word letter by letter. Use the software's spelling or training mode. If the word is a proper noun, such as a person's name, you should train the software to capitalize it.

Sometimes the software does not understand each letter you speak. For example, "8" may appear when you say "a." To avoid this problem, you can use the military alphabet below that assigns a word to each letter.

Alpha	**Bravo**	**Charlie**	**Delta**	**Echo**
Foxtrot	**Golf**	**Hotel**	**India**	**Juliet**
Kilo	**Lima**	**Mike**	**November**	**Oscar**
Papa	**Quebec**	**Romeo**	**Sierra**	**Tango**
Uniform	**Victor**	**Whiskey**		
X ray	**Yankee**	**Zulu**		

You can also train Web site addresses. When you train Web site addresses that you use frequently, you don't have to worry about the software misunderstanding you. Most of the software programs recognize the command ***Dot***. If your software does not understand ***Dot***, you will need to say ***Period***.

LESSON 16 SKILL BUILDING

Objectives:

1. To improve technique on individual letters.
2. To improve keying speed on 1'and 2' writings.

16A • 5' Conditioning Practice

Key each line twice SS; then key a 1' writing on line 3; determine *gwam.*

alphabet 1 Jim quickly realized that the beautiful gowns are expensive.

spacing 2 did go | to the | you can go | has been able | if you can | to see the

easy 3 Dick and the girls may go downtown to pay for the six signs.

gwam 1' | 1 | 2 | 3 | 4 | 5 | 6 | 7 | 8 | 9 | 10 | 11 | 12 |

16B • 18' Technique Mastery: Individual Letters

Key each line twice SS (slowly, then faster); DS between 2-line groups.

Goal:

To keep keystroking action in the fingers.

Emphasize continuity and rhythm with curved, upright fingers.

N 1 Neither John nor Ned wanted a no-nonsense lesson on manners.

O 2 One out of four people openly oppose our opening more docks.

P 3 Phillip chomped on apples as the puppy slept by the poppies.

Q 4 Quin quickly questioned the queen about the quarterly quota.

R 5 Ray arrived at four for a carriage ride over the rural road.

S 6 Steve sold six pairs of scissors in East Sussex on Saturday.

T 7 The tot toddled into the store to pet a cat and two kittens.

U 8 Usually you use undue pressure to persuade us to use quotas.

V 9 Vivian survived the vivacious vandal who wore a velvet veil.

W 10 When will the worker be allowed to wash the new west window?

X 11 The tax expert explained the extensive excise tax exemption.

Y 12 You usually yearn to play with Mary day after day after day.

Z 13 Zoro's zippy zigzags dazzled us but puzzled a zealous judge.

gwam 1' | 1 | 2 | 3 | 4 | 5 | 6 | 7 | 8 | 9 | 10 | 11 | 12 |

16C • 5' Skill Building

Key each line twice SS; DS between 2-line groups.

Space Bar

1 is it to go me see was you she pool turn they were next best

2 I will be able to try to fix the computer next week for you.

Word response

3 they did may auto form make both them soap held the ham busy

4 I may make a big sign to hang by the door of the civic hall.

Double letters

5 school butter took sell hood green foot current room stubborn

6 Will was a little foolish at the football assembly this week.

gwam 1' | 1 | 2 | 3 | 4 | 5 | 6 | 7 | 8 | 9 | 10 | 11 | 12 |

Save as: *TRAVELING*

5. Print the document.
6. Turn the microphone off.

Learning to Speak Commands and Punctuation

Commands are used to give directions to the software. You will use commands to do things like the following:

- Turn a microphone on and off.
- Format a document.
- Open, save, print, and close a document.

To speak commands, you should follow all of these basic rules:

- Pause slightly before and after commands. This lets the software identify your words as commands. For example:

  Say <pause> ***[New Line]*** <pause>

- Speak each command as a phrase. For example:

  Say <pause> ***[Select Next Word]*** <pause>, not ***[Select]*** <pause> ***[Next]*** <pause> ***[Word]*** <pause>

- Enunciate each word of a command. For example:

  Say <pause> ***[Move to End of Line]*** <pause>, not ***[MovetoendofLine]*** <pause>

Each software package has its own set of commands that you will have to learn. Some commands, such as those to turn the microphone on and off, are unique to the software. However, many of the commands are known as *natural language commands.* This means that the software understands several different commands for the same operation. For example, the command to delete selected text may be

Delete This

but the software will also delete text if you say

Delete That

Delete It

Speak punctuation much like commands. When writing, you automatically place a period at the end of a sentence. Using speech recognition software, you must tell the software where to place the punctuation. The following list shows the commands to use for common punctuation marks:

Command	Punctuation Mark
Period	.
Comma	,
Colon	:
Semicolon	;
Hyphen (or dash)	-
Question mark	?
Exclamation point	!
Open quote	“
Close quote	”
Apostrophe	’

Speak . . . ►

I attended an open house for our school***[Apostrophe]***s Travel Abroad Program on Friday***[Period]*** This year they will be traveling throughout Italy***[Period]*** From the information I gathered at the open house***[Comma]*** it sounds like a fantastic opportunity***[Period][New Paragraph]***

I mentioned to the coordinator that I had a friend attending another school who might be interested in participating in the program***[Period]*** She encouraged me to invite you***[Period]*** Several students from other schools in the area joined them for last year***[Apostrophe]***s trip and enjoyed traveling with our school***[Period][New Paragraph]***

So***[Comma]*** are you interested in going to Italy this summer***[Question Mark]*** If so***[Comma]*** let me know and I will send the information to you***[Period]***

16D • 10' Handwritten Copy (Script)

Each sentence at the right is from a U.S. president's inaugural address. Key each sentence; then key it again at a faster pace.

Optional Activity

Can you match each quotation at the right with the president who said it?

George Bush
Dwight D. Eisenhower
John F. Kennedy
Franklin D. Roosevelt
Theodore Roosevelt

"How far have we come in man's long pilgrimage from darkness toward light?"

* * * * *

"We must hope to give our children a sense of what it means to be a loyal friend, a loving parent, a citizen who leaves his home, his neighborhood and town better than he found it."

* * * * *

"If we fail, the cause of free self-government throughout the world will rock to its foundations."

* * * * *

"Ask not what your country can do for you—ask what you can do for your country."

* * * * *

"So, first of all, let me assert my firm belief that the only thing we have to fear is fear itself."

16E • 12' Speed Building

1. Key one 1' unguided and two 1' guided writings on ¶ 1.
2. Key ¶ 2 in the same way.
3. Key two 2' unguided writings on ¶s 1–2 combined; determine *gwam*.

Quarter-Minute Checkpoints				
gwam	1/4'	1/2'	3/4'	1'
20	5	10	15	20
24	6	12	18	24
28	7	14	21	28
32	8	16	24	32
36	9	18	27	36
40	10	20	30	40
44	11	22	33	44
48	12	24	36	48
52	13	26	39	52
56	14	28	42	56

LA all letters used — gwam 2'

It is okay to try and try again if your first efforts do 6
not bring the correct results. If you try but fail again and 12
again, however, it is foolish to plug along in the very same 18
manner. Rather, experiment with another way to accomplish the 24
task that may bring the skill or knowledge you seek. 30

If your first attempts do not yield success, do not quit 35
and merely let it go at that. Instead, begin again in a bet- 41
ter way to finish the work or develop more insight into your 47
difficulty. If you recognize why you must do more than just 54
try, try again, you will work with purpose to achieve success. 60

gwam 2' | 1 | 2 | 3 | 4 | 5 | 6 |

BEGINNING SPEECH-WRITING

Objectives:

1. To learn the parts of the software window.
2. To learn to enunciate clearly and speak naturally.
3. To speak commands and punctuation.

1A • 5' Identifying Parts of the Software Window

1. Read the text at the right.
2. Identify the main parts of the speech recognition software window.

The speech recognition software's toolbar appears at the top of your window. To use the software, you can either open its word processing window, or open another type of software such as *Microsoft Word*. Using the illustration below, identify the important parts of the software window.

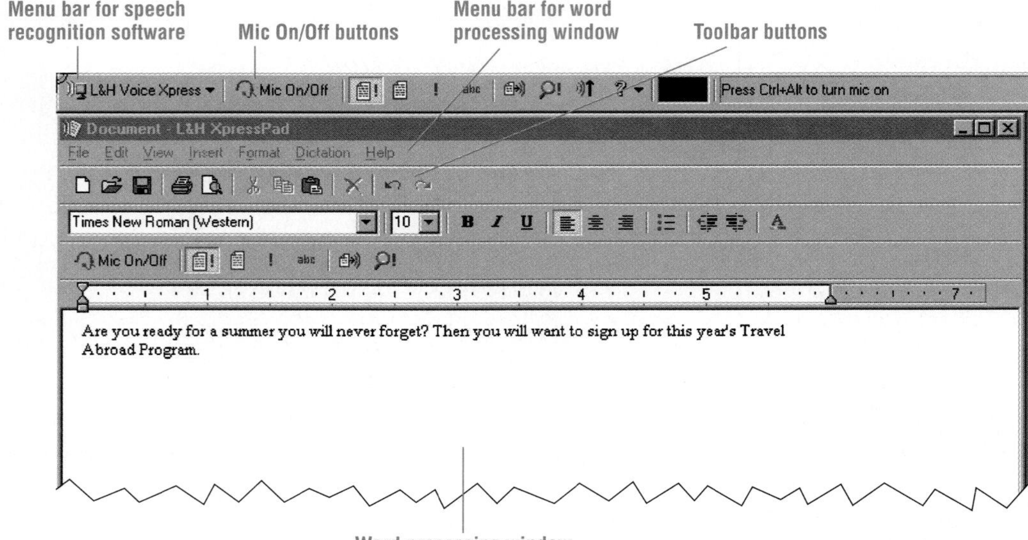

1B • 35' Speaking a Simple Document

1. Read the text at the right and on p. 493.
2. Open your speech recognition software. If necessary, open a word processing window.
3. When you are ready, turn the microphone on and find the arrow marking the beginning of the document on p. 493.
4. Speak the document. All commands and punctuation marks in the documents are shown in bold, italic type and enclosed in brackets. For example: ***[Comma]***

Speaking Clearly and Naturally

Speech recognition software works best when you speak clearly and naturally, taking care to pronounce each word distinctly. The software will "listen" to you, and display the words you speak. The more clearly you speak, the fewer errors will appear. When errors do occur, you should stop and correct them. Correcting errors involves training the software to understand your words. Be patient. It often takes 15 to 20 hours of training to get the software to understand 90 to 98 percent of the words you speak.

The following guidelines will help you:

- Say each word, including commands and punctuation marks, clearly.
- Speak in a normal, conversational tone.
- Find a comfortable speaking pace. Your words may not appear immediately on the screen, but the software is still listening and processing your words.
- Avoid filling pauses with sounds like "uh" or "um." The software will process these sounds also.

(continued on next page)

Communication Skills 2

ACTIVITY 1

Capitalization

1. Key lines 1–10 at the right, supplying capital letters as needed.
2. Check the accuracy of your work with the instructor; correct any errors you made.
3. Note the rule number at the left of each sentence in which you made a capitalization error.
4. Using the rules below the sentences and on p. 39, identify the rule(s) you need to review/practice.
5. **Read**: Study each rule.
6. **Learn**: Key the Learn line(s) beneath it, noting how the rule is applied.
7. **Apply**: Key the Apply line(s), supplying the needed capitalization.

 **Save as:** *CS2-ACT1*

Proofread & Correct

Rules		
1,6	1	has dr. holt moved his offices to hopewell medical center?
1,3,5	2	pam has made plans to spend thanksgiving day in fort wayne.
1,2,8	3	j. c. hauck will receive a d.d.s. degree from usc in june.
1,4,6	4	is tech services, inc., located at fifth street and elm?
1,2,7	5	i heard senator dole make his acceptance speech on thursday.
1,3,6	6	did mrs. alma s. banks apply for a job with butler county?
1,3	7	she knew that albany, not new york city, is the capital.
1,3	8	eldon and cindy marks now live in santa fe, new mexico.
1,6	9	are you going to the marx theater in mount adams tonight?
1,2,6	10	on friday, the first of july, we move to keystone plaza.

Capitalization

Rule 1: Capitalize the first word of a sentence, personal titles, and names of people.

Learn 1 Ask Ms. King if she and Mr. Valdez will sponsor our club.
Apply 2 did you see mrs. watts and gloria at the school play?

Rule 2: Capitalize days of the week and months of the year.

Learn 3 He said that school starts on the first Monday in September.
Apply 4 my birthday is on the third thursday of march this year.

Rule 3: Capitalize cities, states, countries, and specific geographic features.

Learn 5 When you were recently in Nevada, did you visit Lake Tahoe?
Apply 6 when in france, we saw paris from atop the eiffel tower.

Rule 4: Capitalize names of clubs, schools, companies, and other organizations.

Learn 7 The Voices of Harmony will perform at Music Hall next week.
Apply 8 lennox corp. owns the hyde park athletic club in boston.

Rule 5: Capitalize historic periods, holidays, and events.

Learn 9 The Fourth of July celebrates the signing of the Declaration of Independence.
Apply 10 henri asked if memorial day is an american holiday.

(continued on next page)

LESSONS 1–5

Speech Recognition

Introduction

Can you write as fast as you can think? Most people cannot. Whether they are writing with pen and paper or keying the words into a computer, their thoughts race ahead. As technology moves forward, computers are learning to recognize and understand human voices. With training, you can learn to speak your ideas and have them appear on the computer screen.

What Is Speech Recognition Software?

Speech recognition software enables computers to recognize human voices. The software processes the words that the user speaks into a microphone attached to the computer. As the software processes the words, the words appear on the computer screen. The software can understand words, phrases, numbers, and commands.

How Is Speech Recognition Being Used?

The use of speech recognition software is in its infancy. Businesses are encouraging the development of speech recognition software as a way to reduce repetitive stress injuries such as carpal tunnel syndrome. Businesspeople are beginning to use speech recognition software to compose letters, memos, and e-mail messages. Personal use of speech recognition software is also increasing. Although keyboarding will remain an important skill for all computer users, speech recognition provides a useful alternative to long periods of keying. As you work through these exercises, remember that you can always use the keyboard to complete tasks that seem too complicated to accomplish with your voice.

What Do I Need to Get Started?

Speech recognition software requires a computer with a fast processing speed and sufficient memory. The common speech recognition software packages—L&H™ Dragon NaturallySpeaking®, IBM® Via Voice™, and L&H Voice Xpress™—have easy-to-follow directions for installing and setting up the software.

A headset with microphone is also needed. For consistent quality, the microphone should always be positioned in the same place. Most users find that the best position is slightly below the lower lip and 1" to 1.5" from the mouth.

What Is a Voice Profile?

Listen to the voices of people around you. Notice the variations in pitch, tone, accent, and speech patterns. Before you can use speech recognition software, you need to let the software get used to your unique way of speaking. You do this by setting up a **voice profile**. The software will guide you through this process. You will be asked to read several passages that appear on the computer screen. You should read these passages in your normal speaking voice, speaking each word clearly. Although the software can understand individual words, it works better if you speak in phrases and sentences.

The software can store many voice profiles. Each time you start the software, you must select your voice profile. If you experience a large number of errors or if you have a cold that alters your speaking voice, you can have the software rerecord your voice profile. You will also need to create a new voice profile if you change microphones.

Rule 6: Capitalize streets, buildings, and other specific structures.

Learn 11 Jemel lives at Bay Shores near Golden Gate Bridge.
Apply 12 dubois tower is on fountain square at fifth and walnut.

Rule 7: Capitalize an official title when it precedes a name and elsewhere if it is a title of high distinction.

Learn 13 In what year did Juan Carlos become King of Spain?
Learn 14 Masami Chou, our class president, made the scholastic awards.
Apply 15 did the president speak to the nation from the rose garden?
Apply 16 mr. chavez, our company president, chairs two major panels.

Rule 8: Capitalize initials; also, letters in abbreviations if the letters would be capitalized when the words are spelled out.

Learn 17 Does Dr. R. J. Anderson have an Ed.D. or a Ph.D.?
Learn 18 She said that UPS stands for United Parcel Service.
Apply 19 we have a letter from ms. anna m. bucks of washington, d.c.
Apply 20 m.d. means Doctor of Medicine, not medical doctor.

ACTIVITY 2

Listening

Complete the listening activity as directed at the right.

 **Save as:** *CS2-ACT2*

1. Listen carefully to the sounds around you for 3'.
2. As you listen, key a numbered list of every different sound you hear.
3. Identify with asterisks the three loudest sounds you heard.

ACTIVITY 3

Composing

1. Key items 1 and 2 at the right as ¶ 1 of a short composition; supply the information needed to complete each sentence (in parentheses).
2. Key item 3 as ¶ 2, supplying the information noted in the parentheses.
3. Key item 4 as ¶ 3, supplying information noted in the parentheses.
4. Proofread, revise, and correct your composition. Look for improper capitalization, inaccurate information, misspelled words, and weak sentence structure.

 **Save as:** *CS2-ACT3*

1 My name, (first/last), is (African/Asian/European/Hispanic, etc.) in origin.

2 My mother's ancestors originated in (name of country); my father's ancestors originated in (name of country).

3 I know the following facts about the country of my (mother's/father's) ancestors:

1. (enter first fact here)
2. (enter second fact here)
3. (enter third fact here)

4 If I could visit a country of my choice, I would visit (name of country) because (give two or three reasons).

Job 17, cont.

Current "Hoops" Tournaments

- 3-on-3 tournaments
- Males and females
  - 11-12 years old
  - 13-14 years old
  - 15-16 years old
  - 17-18 years old
- Eight tournaments in Fort Collins

Future "Hoops" Tournaments

- 3-on-3 tournaments
- 5-on-5 tournaments
- Same age brackets for males and females
- Sponsor tournaments in:
  - Fort Collins, CO
  - Omaha, NE
  - Casper, WY
  - Ogden, UT

UNIT 5

LESSONS 17–19

Learn/Review Symbol Keys

LESSON 17 — LEARN/REVIEW SYMBOL KEYS (/, $, !, %, <, AND >)

Objectives:

1. To learn or review control of **/**, **$**, **!**, **%**, **<**, and **>**.
2. To combine **/**, **$**, **!**, **%**, **<**, and **>** with other keys.

17A • 5' Conditioning Practice

Key each line twice SS; then key a 1' writing on line 3; determine *gwam*.

alphabet 1 Jackie will budget for the most expensive zoology equipment.

figures 2 I had 50 percent of the responses--3,923 of 7,846--by May 1.

easy 3 The official paid the men for the work they did on the dock.

gwam 1' | 1 | 2 | 3 | 4 | 5 | 6 | 7 | 8 | 9 | 10 | 11 | 12 |

17B • 15' Learn/Review /, $, and !

Key each line twice SS (slowly, then faster); DS between 2-line groups.

Spacing C•U•E

Do not space between a figure and the / or the $ sign.

The / is the shift of the question mark. Strike it with the right little finger.

The $ is the shift of 4. Control it with the left index finger.

The ! is the shift of 1 and is controlled by the left little finger.

Learn/Review / (diagonal or slash) Reach down with the right little finger.

1 ; ; /; /; ;; // ;/; ;/; 2/3 4/5 and/or We keyed 1/2 and 3/4.

2 Space between a whole number and a fraction: 5 2/3, 14 6/9.

3 Do not space before or after the / in a fraction: 2/3, 7/8.

Learn/Review $ (dollar sign) Reach up with the left index finger.

4 f F $f $F fF $$ f$f F$F $4 $4 for $4 Shift for $ and key $4.

5 A period separates dollars and cents: $4.50, $6.25, $19.50.

6 I earned $33.50 on Mon., $23.80 on Tues., and $44.90 on Wed.

Learn/Review ! (exclamation point) Reach up with the left little finger.

7 a A !a !A aA !! a!a A!A 1! 1! I am excited! I won the game!

8 On your mark! Get ready! Get set! Go! Go faster! I won!

9 Great! You made the team! Hurry up! I am late for school!

Job 17—May 10

From the desk of:
Julia Kingsley

Mr. McLemore lost the disk with his slide show for next week's presentation at the Coaches' Conference.

Please create slides similar to those shown at the right and on the next page. Include two additional slides for the coaches about sponsors and information requests. You may have to use different clip art. Use your judgment in applying transitions and animation.

JK

17C • 12' Learn/Review %, <, and >

Key each line twice SS (slowly, then faster); DS between 2-line groups.

Spacing CUE

Do not space between a figure and the % sign.

The % is the shift of 5. Strike it with the left index finger.

The < is the shift of , and is controlled by the right middle finger.

The > is the shift of . and is controlled by the right ring finger.

Learn/Review % (percent sign) Reach up with the left index finger.

1 f F %f fF % % f%F f%F 5%f 5%f Shift for the % in 5% and 15%.

2 Do not space between a number and %: 5%, 75%, 85%, and 95%.

3 Prices fell 10% on May 1, 15% on June 1, and 20% on July 15.

Learn/Review < ("less than" sign) Reach down with the right middle finger.

4 k K <k <K kK << k<K K<K <, <, <k, <k, <K< 10 < 18; 95 , 120.

5 If a < b, and c < d, and e < f, and a < c and e, then a < d.

Learn/Review > ("greater than" sign) Reach down with the right ring finger.

6 l L >l >L lL >> l>L L>L >. >. >l. >l. >L> 20 > 17; 105 > 98.

7 If b > a, and d > c, and f > e, and c and e > a, then f > a.

17D • 10' Skill Building: Symbols

Key each line twice SS (slowly, then faster); DS between 2-line groups.

Combine /, $, and !

1 Only 2/3 of the class remembered to bring the $5 on Tuesday!

2 I was really excited! I received 1/2 of the $50 door prize!

3 Only 1/10 of the sellers earned more than $100! I felt bad!

Combine % and < >

4 Only 25% of the students got the answer to 5x > 10 but < 20.

5 Yes, 90% of the students scored > 75%, and 10% scored < 75%.

6 Only about 15% of the class understood the < and > concepts!

17E • 8' Speed Building

1. Key three 1' writings on the ¶; determine *gwam* on each writing.
2. Key two 2' writings on the ¶; determine *gwam.*

all letters used — gwam 2'

When you key copy that contains both words and numbers, 6
it is best to key numbers using the top row. When the copy 12
consists primarily of figures, however, it may be faster to 18
use the keypad. In any event, keying figures quickly is a 24
major skill to prize. You can expect to key figures often 29
in the future, so learn to key them with very little peeking. 36

gwam 2' | 1 | 2 | 3 | 4 | 5 | 6 |

June - "Hoops" Tournaments

Sun	Mon	Tue	Wed	Thur	Fri	Sat
					1	2
3	4	5	6	7	8	9
10	11	12	13	14	**15** Tournament 1	**16**
17	18	19	20	21	**22** Tournament 2	**23**
24	25	26	27	28	**29** Tournament 3	**30**

200-

LESSON 18 LEARN/REVIEW SYMBOL KEYS (#, &, +, @, AND ( ))

Objectives:

1. To learn or review control of **#**, **&**, **+**, **@**, and **( )**.
2. To combine **#**, **&**, **+**, **@**, and **( )** with other keys.

18A • 5' Conditioning Practice

Key each line twice SS; then key a 1' writing on line 3; determine *gwam.*

alphabet 1 Zack Gappow saved the job requirement list for the six boys.

figures 2 Jay Par's address is 3856 Ash Place, Houston, TX 77007-2491.

easy 3 I may visit the big chapel in the dismal town on the island.

gwam 1' | 1 | 2 | 3 | 4 | 5 | 6 | 7 | 8 | 9 | 10 | 11 | 12 |

18B • 15' Learn/Review #, &, and +

Key each line twice SS (slowly, then faster); DS between 2-line groups.

Spacing 

- Do not space between # and a figure.
- Space once before and after & used to join names.

The # is the shift of 3. The left middle finger controls it.

The & is the shift of 7. Control it with the right index finger.

The + is to the right of the hyphen. Depress the left shift; strike + with the right little finger.

Learn/Review # (number/pounds) Reach up with the left middle finger.

1 d d #d #d dd ## d#d d#d 3# 3# Shift for # as you enter #33d.

2 Do not space between a number and #: 3# of #633 at $9.35/#.

3 Jerry recorded Check #38 as #39, #39 as #40, and #40 as #41.

Learn/Review & (ampersand) Reach up with the right index finger.

4 j j &j &j jj && j&j j&j 7& 7& Have you written to Poe & Son?

5 Do not space before or after & in initials, e.g., CG&E, B&O.

6 She will interview with Johnson & Smith and Jones & Beckett.

Learn/Review + ("plus" sign) Reach up with the right little finger.

7 ; + ; + ;+; ;+; +;+ +;+ 7 + 7, a + b + c < a + b + d, 12 + 3

8 If you add 3 + 4 + 5 + 6 + 7, you will get 25 for an answer.

9 If you add 2 + 3 + 4 + 5 + 6, you will get 20 for an answer.

18C • 15' Skill Building

1. Review the procedure for setting speed goals (Guided Writing Procedure, p. 22).
2. Use this procedure as you key the unguided and guided writings in **15D** (p. 35).
3. Compare your *gwam* today (the better 2' writing) with your previous rate on these paragraphs.

MALES 15-16 YEARS OLD *Blue & Gold Brackets* *June 15-16*				
Blue Bracket *Middle School Gym—Court C*		*Date and Time*	*Gold Bracket* *Middle School Gym—Court D*	
Score	*Teams*		*Teams*	*Score*
	Frontiersmen *Railroaders*	*June 15* *3:00 p.m.*	*Cavaliers* *Miners*	
	Rainmakers *Cowboys*		*Ghost Shooters* *Pikers*	
	Wolves *Shooters*	*June 15* *3:45 p.m.*	*Tetons* *Platters*	
	3-Pointers *Free Stylers*		*Pioneers* *Mustangs*	
	Frontiersmen *Rainmakers*	*June 15* *6:00 p.m.*	*Cavaliers* *Ghost Shooters*	
	Railroaders *Cowboys*		*Miners* *Pikers*	
	Wolves *3-Pointers*	*June 15* *6:45 p.m.*	*Tetons* *Pioneers*	
	Shooters *Free Stylers*		*Platters* *Mustangs*	
	Frontiersmen *Cowboys*	*June 16* *10:00 a.m.*	*Cavaliers* *Pikers*	
	Railroaders *Rainmakers*		*Miners* *Ghost Shooters*	
	Wolves *Free Stylers*	*June 16* *10:45 a.m.*	*Tetons* *Mustangs*	
	Shooters *3-Pointers*		*Platters* *Pioneers*	
	3rd and 4th place games	*June 16* *2:00 p.m.*	*3rd and 4th place games*	
	1st and 2nd place games	*June 16* *2:45 p.m.*	*1st and 2nd place games*	
	Championship game	*June 16* *5:00 p.m.*	*Championship game*	

18D • 15' Learn/Review @, (, and)

Key each line twice SS (slowly, then faster); DS between 2-line groups.

Note:
Use the letter l in lines 4 and 5.

Spacing **C • U • E**

Do not space between a left or right parenthesis and the copy enclosed.

The @ is the shift of 2. Control it with the left ring finger.

The (is the shift of 9 and is controlled by the right ring finger.

The) is the shift of 0; use the right little finger to control it.

Learn/Review @ ("at" sign) Reach up with the left ring finger.

1 s s @s @s ss @@ s@ s@ @ @ The @ is used in e-mail addresses.

2 Change my e-mail address from myers@cs.com to myers@aol.com.

3 I bought 50 shares of F @ $53 1/8 and 100 of USB @ $58 7/16.

Learn/Review ((left parenthesis) Reach up with the right ring finger.

4 l l (l (l ll ((l(l l(l 9(9(Shift for the (as you key (9.

5 As (is the shift of 9, use the l finger to key 9, (, or (9.

Learn/Review) (right parenthesis) Reach up with the right little finger.

6 ; ;);); ;;)) ;); ;); 0) 0) Shift for the) as you key 0).

7 As) is the shift of 0, use the ; finger to key 0,), or 0).

Combine (and)

8 Hints: (1) depress shift; (2) strike key; (3) release both.

9 Tab steps: (1) clear tabs, (2) set stops, and (3) tabulate.

LESSON 19 LEARN/REVIEW SYMBOL KEYS (=, _, *, \, AND [ ])

Objectives:

1. To learn or review control of =, _, \, * , and [ ].
2. To combine =, _, \, * , and [ ] with other keys.

19A • 5' Conditioning Practice

Key each line twice SS; then key a 1' writing on line 3; determine *gwam.*

alphabet 1 Bobby Klun awarded Jayme sixth place for her very high quiz.

figures 2 The rate on May 14 was 12.57 percent; it was 8.96 on May 30.

easy 3 The haughty man was kept busy with a problem with the docks.

gwam 1' | 1 | 2 | 3 | 4 | 5 | 6 | 7 | 8 | 9 | 10 | 11 | 12 |

19B • 15' Skill Building

1. Review the procedure for speed level practice on p. 22 (Guided Writing Procedure).
2. Use this procedure as you key the unguided and guided writings in **16E** (p. 37).
3. Compare your *gwam* today (the better 2' writing) with your previous rate on these paragraphs.

"Hoops" Tournament Application

Division:	Tournament Date:	Age Level of Players:
☐ Males ■ Females	June 15-16	☐ 11-12 year age bracket ☐ 13-14 year age bracket ■ 15-16 year age bracket ☐ 17-18 year age bracket
Name of Your Team:		
Rockies		

Coach or Contact Person (Must be 21 years of age or older):

Last Name	First	Middle Initial	E-mail Address
De Los Santos	Loretta	L.	- - - -

Street Address	City	State	ZIP	Phone
2115 Gaylord Dr.	Loveland	CO	80537	303-776-1375

Player 1:

Last Name	First	Middle Initial	Age as of First Day of Tournament
De Los Santos	Maria	A.	15

Street Address	City	State	ZIP	Phone
2115 Gaylord Dr.	Loveland	CO	80537	303-776-1375

Player 2:

Last Name	First	Middle Initial	Age as of First Day of Tournament
Erstad	Janet	K.	16

Street Address	City	State	ZIP	Phone
3157 Sierra Vista Dr.	Loveland	CO	80537	303-776-2909

Player 3:

Last Name	First	Middle Initial	Age as of First Day of Tournament
Radke	Tabetha	J.	16

Street Address	City	State	ZIP	Phone
80 Mulberry Dr.	Loveland	CO	80538	303-629-4439

Player 4:

Last Name	First	Middle Initial	Age as of First Day of Tournament
Edmonds	Cynthia	S.	16

Street Address	City	State	ZIP	Phone
8880 Snowberry Pl.	Loveland	CO	80537	303-776-1529

Player 5:

Last Name	First	Middle Initial	Age as of First Day of Tournament
Poquette	Paula	B.	15

Street Address	City	State	ZIP	Phone
672 Mustang Dr.	Loveland	CO	80537	303-629-6110

Verification by Coach: To the best of my knowledge the information presented on this form is correct. Please sign below.

Signature:	Loretta L. De Los Santos	Date:	May 5, 200-

19C • 15' Learn/Review [=], [_], and [\]

Key each line twice SS (slowly, then faster); DS between 2-line groups.

The = is the same key as + and is controlled by the right little finger.

The _ is the shift of the - and is controlled by the right little finger.

The \ is above ENTER. Use the right little finger to control it.

Learn/Review = (equals sign) Reach up with the right little finger.

1 ; ; =; =; ;; == ;= ;= += += The = is used in math equations.
2 Solve the following: 3a = 15, 5b = 30, 3c = 9, and 2d = 16.
3 If a = b + c and c = 5 and a = 9, can you determine what b=?

Learn/Review _ (underline) Reach up with the right little finger.

4 ; ; _; _; ;; __ ;_; ;_; -_ -_ Shift for the _ as you key _-.
5 The _ is used in some Internet locations, e.g., http_data_2.
6 My property has _____ parking spaces and _____ storage bins.

Learn/Review \ (backslash) Reach up with the right little finger.

7 ;; \; \; ;; \\ \;\ \;\ \;\; \;\; Do not shift for the \ key.
8 Use the \ key to map the drive to access \\sps25\deptdir556.
9 Map the drive to \\global128\coxjg$, not \\global127\coxjg$.

19D • 15' Learn/Review [*], [[], and []]

Key each line twice SS (slowly, then faster); DS between 2-line groups.

The * is the shift of 8. Control it with the right middle finger.

The [is to the right of p. Strike it with the right little finger.

The] is to the right of [and also is controlled by the right little finger.

Learn/Review * (asterisk) Reach up with the right middle finger.

1 k k *k *k *k* *k* * She used the * for a single source note.
2 Put an * before (*Gary, *Jan, and *Jay) to show high scores.
3 Asterisks (*) can be used to replace unprintable words ****.

Learn/Review [(left bracket) Reach up with the right little finger.

4 ; ; [; [; [;[[;[[[[[[a [B [c [D [e [F [g [H [i [J [k [L.
5 [m [N [o [P [q [R [s [T [u [V [w [X [y [Z [1 [2 [3 [4 [5 [6.

Learn/Review] (right bracket) Reach up with the right little finger.

6 ; ;];];];]];]]]]] A] b] C] d] E] f] G] h] I] j]]K]l.
7 M] n] O] p] Q] r] S] t] U] v] W] x] Y] z] 7] 8] 9] 10] 11]].

Combine [and]

8 Brackets ([]) are used in algebra: x = [5(a+b)] - [2(d-e)].
9 Use [ ] within quotations to indicate alterations [changes].

FEMALES 15-16 YEARS OLD
Yellow & Green Brackets
June 15-16

Yellow Bracket Middle School Gym—Court A		Date and Time	Green Bracket Middle School Gym—Court B	
Score	Teams		Teams	Score
	Columbines Rockies	June 15 3:00 p.m.	Mavericks Gold Nuggets	
	PikesPeakers Bronkettes		River Rafters Rebounders	
	Cowgirls Larks	June 15 3:45 p.m.	Flyers Snow Shooters	
	Jazzettes Aggies		Vailers Huskers	
	Columbines PikesPeakers	June 15 6:00 p.m.	Mavericks River Rafters	
	Rockies Bronkettes		Gold Nuggets Rebounders	
	Cowgirls Jazzettes	June 15 6:45 p.m.	Flyers Vailers	
	Larks Aggies		Snow Shooters Huskers	
	Columbines Bronkettes	June 16 10:00 a.m.	Mavericks Rebounders	
	Rockies PikesPeakers		Gold Nuggets River Rafters	
	Cowgirls Aggies	June 16 10:45 a.m.	Flyers Huskers	
	Larks Jazzettes		Snow Shooters Vailers	
	3rd and 4th place games	June 16 2:00 p.m.	3rd and 4th place games	
	1st and 2nd place games	June 16 2:45 p.m.	1st and 2nd place games	
	Championship game	June 16 5:00 p.m.	Championship game	

UNIT 6

LESSONS 20–21

Build Keyboarding Skill

LESSON 20 SKILL BUILDING

Objectives:

1. To improve technique on individual letters.
2. To improve keying speed on 1' and 2' writings.

20A • 5' Conditioning Practice

Key each line twice SS; then key a 1' writing on line 3; determine *gwam.*

alphabet 1 Jack liked reviewing the problems on the tax quiz on Friday.

figures 2 Check #365 for $98.47, dated May 31, 2001, was not endorsed.

easy 3 The auditor may work with vigor to form the bus audit panel.

gwam 1' | 1 | 2 | 3 | 4 | 5 | 6 | 7 | 8 | 9 | 10 | 11 | 12 |

SKILL BUILDING

20B • 18' Technique Mastery: Individual Letters

Key each line twice SS (slowly, then faster); DS between 2-line groups. Take 30" writings on selected lines.

Technique Goals:

- curved, upright fingers
- quick-snap keystrokes
- quiet hands and arms

Emphasize continuity and rhythm with curved, upright fingers.

A 1 Aaron always ate a pancake at Anna's annual breakfast feast.

B 2 Bobby probably fibbed about being a busboy for the ballroom.

C 3 Cody can check with the conceited concierge about the clock.

D 4 The divided squad disturbed Dan Delgado, who departed today.

E 5 Pete was better after he developed three new feet exercises.

F 6 Jeff Keefer officially failed four of five finals on Friday.

G 7 Her granddaughter, Gwen, gave me eight gold eggs for a gift.

H 8 Hans helped her wash half the cheap dishes when he got home.

I 9 I investigate the significance of insignias to institutions.

J 10 Judge James told Jon to adjourn the jury until June or July.

K 11 Knock, khaki, knickknack, kicks, and kayak have multiple Ks.

L 12 Lillian left her landlord in the village to collect dollars.

M 13 The minimum amount may make the mission impossible for many.

gwam 1' | 1 | 2 | 3 | 4 | 5 | 6 | 7 | 8 | 9 | 10 | 11 | 12 |

Job 11—May 3

From the desk of:
Julia Kingsley

When a "Hoops" Tournament application is returned, send the attached e-mail message to the coach confirming that we have received the application. If the coach didn't list an e-mail address, you will need to send a letter instead.

Two coaches already returned their applications. Matthew Trussoni registered for Tournaments 1, 2, and 3. Brett Perkins registered only for the June 15–16 tournament.

JK

Your "Hoops" Tournament application for the June 15-16, June 22-23, and June 29-30 tournaments has been received. We are looking forward to having the Frontiersmen participate in these tournaments.

As soon as your bracket has been filled and the schedule completed, we will mail the schedule to you. If you have any questions before then, please e-mail me or call the office. Our office hours are 10:30 a.m. to 3:30 p.m. Monday through Friday.

Note: Please revise the message to fit the situation. If someone registers for only one tournament, you will have to modify the message slightly.

Job 12—May 3

From the desk of:
Julia Kingsley

Robert Van Bleek (Park Place Plaza) returned the advertiser form without including a check. Send a letter to him similar to the one sent for Job 6. Get the address for Park Place Plaza from the HoopsAdvertisers *database file. Mr. Van Bleek wants a full-page ad.*

JK

Job 13—May 8

From the desk of:
Julia Kingsley

I found several copies of the blank tournament table we used last year. I've filled in a blank tournament form (p. 485) for the females in the 15–16 years old bracket and attached it. Since I can't find the file, you will have to create the table shell again and input the information. Save the table, as we will be doing similar tables for all age brackets.

JK

Job 14—May 8

From the desk of:
Julia Kingsley

I attached another "Hoops" Tournament application (p. 486). Ms. De Los Santos registered the Rockies for the June 15–16, June 29–30, July 13–14, and July 27–28 tournaments. Please input the information on the form in the database tables for coaches and players. I've already updated the spreadsheet.

After you have completed entering the information in the database tables, send a letter to Ms. De Los Santos confirming receipt of her registration fees and the tournaments that the Rockies are registered for. See Job 11.

JK

Job 15—May 10

From the desk of:
Julia Kingsley

Please key this handwritten tournament schedule (p. 487) for the males in the 15–16 years old age bracket. Use the table you created for Job 13. Change the colors of the shaded cells so we can easily see the difference between the female and male tournament schedules.

JK

Job 16—May 10

From the desk of:
Julia Kingsley

Prepare monthly calendars for July and August similar to the one I prepared for June on p. 488. Use the Help feature for your software if you don't know how to prepare a calendar. Refer to the list of tournament dates I gave you (p. 475). Insert an appropriate graphic on each month.

JK

20C • 12' Handwritten Copy (Script)

Key each quotation twice (slowly, then faster); DS between 2-line groups.

Optional Activity

Can you match the quotation with the writer who is being quoted?

Henry B. Adams
Ralph Waldo Emerson
Thomas Jefferson
John Locke
Katherine Whitehorn
Oscar Wilde

1. "Every man I meet is in some way my superior."
2. "Find out what you like doing best and get someone to pay you for doing it."
3. "I can resist everything except temptation."
4. "I have always thought the actions of men the best interpreters of their thoughts."
5. "A teacher affects eternity; he can never tell, where his influence stops."
6. "I'm a great believer in luck, and I find the harder I work the more I have of it."

SKILL BUILDING

20D • 15' Speed Building: Guided Writing

1. Key one 1' unguided and two 1' guided writings on each ¶; determine *gwam*.
2. Key two 2' unguided writings on ¶s 1–2 combined; determine *gwam*.

Quarter-Minute Checkpoints				
gwam	1/4'	1/2'	3/4'	1'
20	5	10	15	20
24	6	12	18	24
28	7	14	21	28
32	8	16	24	32
36	9	18	27	36
40	10	20	30	40
44	11	22	33	44
48	12	24	36	48
52	13	26	39	52
56	14	28	42	56

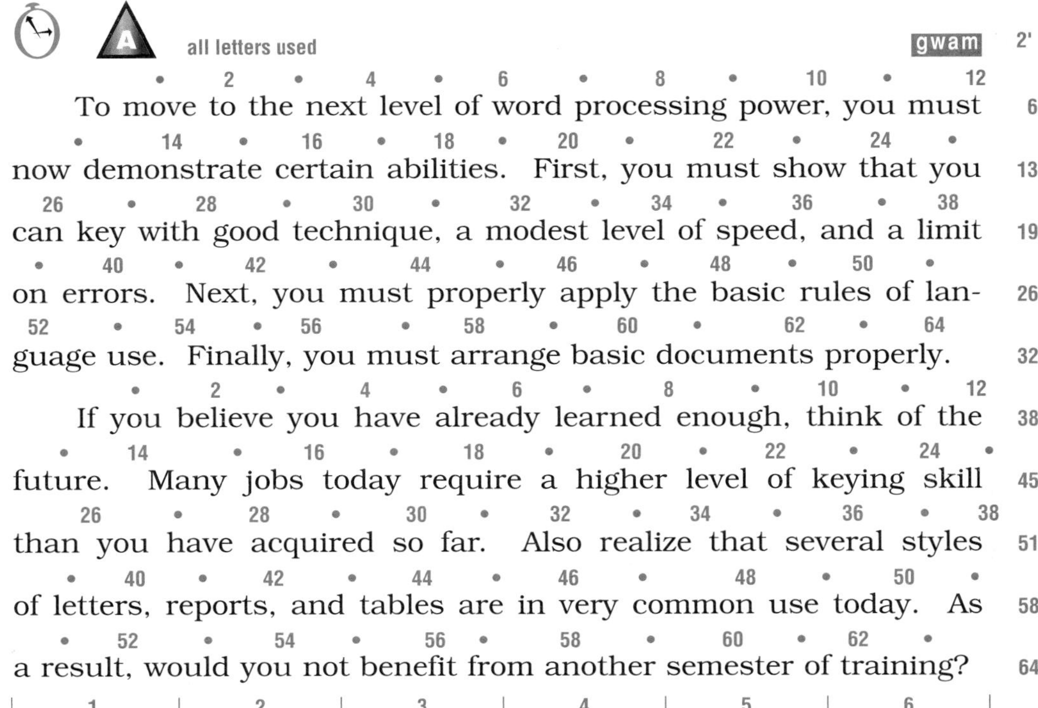

A all letters used — gwam 2'

To move to the next level of word processing power, you must 6
now demonstrate certain abilities. First, you must show that you 13
can key with good technique, a modest level of speed, and a limit 19
on errors. Next, you must properly apply the basic rules of lan- 26
guage use. Finally, you must arrange basic documents properly. 32

If you believe you have already learned enough, think of the 38
future. Many jobs today require a higher level of keying skill 45
than you have acquired so far. Also realize that several styles 51
of letters, reports, and tables are in very common use today. As 58
a result, would you not benefit from another semester of training? 64

gwam 2' | 1 | 2 | 3 | 4 | 5 | 6 |

Job 9—May 1

From the desk of:
Julia Kingsley

I have roughed out what I would like the spreadsheet for the tournament registration revenues to look like. Several other tournament registrations have come in since I did the rough. Prepare a spreadsheet that contains the information shown at the right plus the information below. Update totals.

Team: ***Cowgirls***
Amount Paid: ***$400***
For Tournaments: ***1, 2, 3, 4***
Coach: ***Steve Chi***

Team: ***Aggies***
Amount Paid: ***$300***
For Tournaments: ***1, 3, 8***
Coach: ***Tanya Hanrath***

Team: ***3-Pointers***
Amount Paid: ***$100***
For Tournaments: ***1***
Coach: ***Marge Jenkins***

JK

Registration Revenues

		Tournament 1	Tournament 2	Tournament 3	Tournament 4	Tournament 5	Tournament 6	Tournament 7	Tournament 8
Team Name	Coach	June 15-16	June 22-23	June 29-30	July 6-7	July 13-14	July 20-21	July 27-28	August 3-4
Frontiersmen	*Trussoni M.*	*$100*	*$100*	*$100*					
Boulder "Dashers"	*Perkins B.*	*100*							
Rockies	*De Los Santos L.*	*100*		*100*		*100*		*100*	
Jazzettes	*Woodward D.*	*100*	*100*	*100*	*100*	*100*	*100*	*100*	*100*
Gold Nuggets	*McKinney K.*	*100*							
Cavaliers	*Quaid M.*	*100*	*100*	*100*					
Mustangs	*Brady S.*	*100*			*100*			*100*	
Huskers	*Reed S.*	*100*		*100*	*100*				
	Totals	*$800*	*$300*	*$500*	*$300*	*$200*	*$100*	*$300*	*$100*

Job 10—May 1

From the desk of:
Julia Kingsley

Mr. McLemore is out of the office today. In order for him to stay apprised of the Fort Collins tournament development, he would like you to e-mail him a copy of the registration revenues spreadsheet. His e-mail address is tmclemore@dellnet.com.

JK

LESSON 21 SKILL BUILDING

Objectives:

1. To improve technique on individual letters.
2. To improve keying speed on 1' and 2' writings.

21A • 5' Conditioning Practice

Key each line twice SS; then key a 1' writing on line 3; determine *gwam.*

alphabet 1 Wayne gave Zelda exact requirements for taking the pulp job.

fig/sym 2 Add tax of 5.5% to Sales Slip #86-03 for a total of $142.79.

easy 3 The six girls at the dock may blame the man with their keys.

gwam 1' | 1 | 2 | 3 | 4 | 5 | 6 | 7 | 8 | 9 | 10 | 11 | 12 |

21B • 18' Technique Mastery: Individual Letters

Key each line twice SS (slowly, then faster); DS between 2-line groups. Take 30" writings on selected lines.

Technique Goals:

- curved, upright fingers
- quick-snap keystrokes
- quiet hands and arms

Emphasize continuity and rhythm with curved, upright fingers.

N 1 Ann wants Nathan to know when negotiations begin and finish.

O 2 Robert bought an overcoat to go to the open house on Monday.

P 3 Philippi purchased a pepper plant from that pompous peddler.

Q 4 Quincy quickly questioned the adequacy of the quirky quotes.

R 5 Our receiver tried to recover after arm surgery on Thursday.

S 6 Russ said it seems senseless to suggest this to his sisters.

T 7 Tabetha trusted Tim not to tinker with the next time report.

U 8 She was unusually subdued upon returning to our summerhouse.

V 9 Vivian vacated the vast village with five vivacious vandals.

W 10 Warren will work two weeks on woodwork with the wise owners.

X 11 Six tax experts expect to expand the six extra export taxes.

Y 12 Yes, by year's end Jayme may be ready to pay you your money.

Z 13 Zelda quizzed Zack on the zoology quiz in the sizzling heat.

gwam 1' | 1 | 2 | 3 | 4 | 5 | 6 | 7 | 8 | 9 | 10 | 11 | 12 |

21C • 5' Skill Building

Key each line twice SS; DS between 2-line groups.

Space Bar

1 day son new map cop let kite just the quit year bay vote not

2 She may see me next week to talk about a party for the team.

Word response

3 me dye may bit pen pan cow sir doe form lamb lake busy their

4 The doorman kept the big bushel of corn for the eight girls.

Double letters

5 Neillsville berry dollar trees wheels sheep tomorrow village

6 All three of the village cottonwood trees had green ribbons.

gwam 1' | 1 | 2 | 3 | 4 | 5 | 6 | 7 | 8 | 9 | 10 | 11 | 12 |

"Hoops" Tournament Application

Division:	Tournament Date:	Age Level of Players:
☐ Males ■ Females	June 15-16	☐ 11-12 year age bracket ■ 13-14 year age bracket ☐ 15-16 year age bracket ☐ 17-18 year age bracket
Name of Your Team: Boulder "Dashers"		

Coach or Contact Person (Must be 21 years of age or older):

Last Name	First	Middle Initial	E-mail Address
Perkins	Brett	P.	bpperkins@cs.com

Street Address	City	State	ZIP	Phone
837 Roundtree Ct.	Boulder	CO	80302	303-347-3728

Player 1:

Last Name	First	Middle Initial	Age as of First Day of Tournament
Baxter	Barbara	A.	14

Street Address	City	State	ZIP	Phone
830 Dennison Ln.	Boulder	CO	80303	303-368-2839

Player 2:

Last Name	First	Middle Initial	Age as of First Day of Tournament
Washington	Natasha	K.	13

Street Address	City	State	ZIP	Phone
892 Hazelwood Ct.	Boulder	CO	80302	303-368-1427

Player 3:

Last Name	First	Middle Initial	Age as of First Day of Tournament
Thurston	Jane	M.	14

Street Address	City	State	ZIP	Phone
890 Driftwood Pl.	Boulder	CO	80301	303-347-2225

Player 4:

Last Name	First	Middle Initial	Age as of First Day of Tournament
Santiago	Maria	A.	13

Street Address	City	State	ZIP	Phone
834 Dennison Ln.	Boulder	CO	80303	303-368-7877

Player 5:

Last Name	First	Middle Initial	Age as of First Day of Tournament
Kelley	Rebecca	C.	14

Street Address	City	State	ZIP	Phone
1711 Rockmont Cir.	Boulder	CO	80303	303-368-5678

Verification by Coach: To the best of my knowledge the information presented on this form is correct. Please sign below.

Signature:	*Brett P. Perkins*	Date:	April 16, 200-

21D • 10'
Handwritten Copy (Script)

Key each quotation twice (slowly, then faster); DS between 2-line groups.

Optional Activity

Can you match the quotation with the person who is being quoted?

Helen Keller
Ralph Waldo Emerson
Adlai Stevenson
Henry David Thoreau
Margaret Thatcher
Oscar Wilde

1. "No man is rich enough to buy back his past."

* * * * *

2. "Nothing great was ever achieved without enthusiasm."

* * * * *

3. "Keep your face to the sunshine and you cannot see the shadow."

* * * * *

4. "It is the greatest of all advantages to enjoy no advantage at all."

* * * * *

5. "If you want something said, ask a man; if you want something done, ask a woman."

* * * * *

6. "Man does not live by words alone, despite the fact that sometimes he has to eat them."

SKILL BUILDING

21E • 12'
Speed Building

1. Key one 1' unguided and two 1' guided writings on each ¶.
2. Key two 2' unguided writings on ¶s 1–2 combined; determine *gwam*.

Quarter-Minute Checkpoints				
gwam	1/4'	1/2'	3/4'	1'
20	5	10	15	20
24	6	12	18	24
28	7	14	21	28
32	8	16	24	32
36	9	18	27	36
40	10	20	30	40
44	11	22	33	44
48	12	24	36	48
52	13	26	39	52
56	14	28	42	56

all letters used — **gwam 2'**

As you build your keying power, the number of errors you 6
make is not very important because most of the errors are 12
accidental and incidental. Realize, however, that documents 18
are expected to be without flaw. A letter, report, or table 24
that contains flaws is not usable until it is corrected. So 30
find and correct all errors. 33

The best time to detect and correct errors is immediately 38
after you finish keying the copy. Therefore, just before you 45
print or close a document, proofread and correct any errors you 51
have made. Learn to proofread carefully and to correct all 57
errors quickly. To do the latter, know ways to move the 63
pointer and to select copy. 65

gwam 2' | 1 | 2 | 3 | 4 | 5 | 6 |

"Hoops" Tournament Application

Division:	Tournament Date:	Age Level of Players:
■ Males ☐ Females	June 15-16	☐ 11-12 year age bracket ☐ 13-14 year age bracket ■ 15-16 year age bracket ☐ 17-18 year age bracket
Name of Your Team: Frontiersmen		

Coach or Contact Person (Must be 21 years of age or older):

Last Name	First	Middle Initial	E-mail Address
Trussoni	Matthew	P.	mtrussoni@home.com

Street Address	City	State	ZIP	Phone
732 Bozeman Trl.	Cheyenne	WY	82009	307-376-8756

Player 1:

Last Name	First	Middle Initial	Age as of First Day of Tournament
Sinclair	Mark	A.	16

Street Address	City	State	ZIP	Phone
615 Clark St.	Cheyenne	WY	82009	307-376-7652

Player 2:

Last Name	First	Middle Initial	Age as of First Day of Tournament
Finch	Jeff	R.	15

Street Address	City	State	ZIP	Phone
879 Columbus Dr.	Cheyenne	WY	82007	307-345-7733

Player 3:

Last Name	First	Middle Initial	Age as of First Day of Tournament
Remmington	Jay	M.	16

Street Address	City	State	ZIP	Phone
33 Sagebrush Ave.	Cheyenne	WY	82009	307-376-1090

Player 4:

Last Name	First	Middle Initial	Age as of First Day of Tournament
Martinez	Felipe	J.	16

Street Address	City	State	ZIP	Phone
458 Yellowstone Rd.	Cheyenne	WY	82009	307-345-5648

Player 5:

Last Name	First	Middle Initial	Age as of First Day of Tournament
Roberts	Reece	R.	16

Street Address	City	State	ZIP	Phone
730 Piute Dr.	Cheyenne	WY	82001	307-376-9023

Verification by Coach: To the best of my knowledge the information presented on this form is correct. Please sign below.

Signature:	Matthew P. Trussoni	Date:	April 15, 200-

Communication Skills 3

ACTIVITY 1

Number Expression

1. Key lines 1–10 at the right, expressing numbers correctly (words or figures).
2. Check the accuracy of your work with the instructor; correct any errors you made.
3. Note the rule number at the left of each sentence in which you made a number expression error.
4. Using the rules below the sentences and on p. 50, identify the rule(s) you need to review/practice.
5. **Read**: Study each rule.
6. **Learn**: Key the Learn line(s) beneath it, noting how the rule is applied.
7. **Apply**: Key the Apply line(s), expressing the numbers correctly.

 **Save as:** *CS3-ACT1*

Proofread & Correct

Rules		
1	1	20 members have already voted, but 15 have yet to do so.
2	2	Only twelve of the hikers are here; six have not returned.
3	3	Do you know if the eight fifteen Klondike flight is on time?
3,4	4	We should be at 1 Brooks Road no later than eleven thirty a.m.
5	5	This oriental carpet measures eight ft. by 10 ft.
5	6	The carton is two ft. square and weighs six lbs. eight oz.
6	7	Have you read pages 45 to 62 of Chapter two that he assigned?
7	8	She usually rides the bus from 6th Street to 1st Avenue.
8	9	Nearly 1/2 of the team is here; that is about 15.
8	10	A late fee of over 15 percent is charged after the 30th day.

Number Expression

Rule 1: Spell a number that begins a sentence even when other numbers in the sentence are shown in figures.

Learn 1 Twelve of the new shrubs have died; 48 are doing quite well.
Apply 2 14 members have paid their dues, but 89 have not done so.

Rule 2: Use figures for numbers above ten, and for numbers from one to ten when they are used with numbers above ten.

Learn 3 She ordered 8 word processors, 14 computers, and 4 printers.
Apply 4 Did he say they need ten or 14 sets of Z18 and Z19 diskettes?

Rule 3: Use figures to express date and time (unless followed by o'clock).

Learn 5 He will arrive on Paygo Flight 418 at 9:48 a.m. on March 14.
Apply 6 Candidates must be in Ivy Hall at eight forty a.m. on May one.

Rule 4: Use figures for house numbers except house number One.

Learn 7 My home is at 8 Vernon Drive; my office, at One Weber Plaza.
Apply 8 The Nelsons moved from 4059 Pyle Avenue to 1 Maple Circle.

Rule 5: Use figures to express measures and weights.

Learn 9 Glenda Redford is 5 ft. 4 in. tall and weighs 118 lbs. 9 oz.
Apply 10 This carton measures one ft. by nine in. and weighs five lbs.

(continued on next page)

Job 6—April 24

From the desk of:
Julia Kingsley
Ms. Radeski, manager of The Sub Shoppe, returned the advertisement form to place a half-page ad in the tournament program. She did not include payment for the advertisement. Format and key the letter I've drafted on the attached sheet.
JK

April 24, 200-

Ms. Karin Radeski
The Sub Shoppe
88 Manchester Circle
Fort Collins, CO 80526-1118

Dear Ms. Radeski:

Thank you for returning your form for placing an advertisement in the "Hoops" Tournament Program. In order for your advertisement to appear in the program, we will need to receive your check for $400 for the half-page advertisement before we have the programs printed. Our deadline for submitting the program to the printer is May 28.

If you have any questions or would like to preview your advertisement, you can call or stop by the office between 10:30 a.m. and 3:30 p.m. Monday through Friday.

Sincerely,

Todd McLemore
Tournament Director

xx

Jobs 7 and 8—April 26

From the desk of:
Julia Kingsley
The first "Hoops" Tournament applications for the June 15–16 Tournament arrived. Please create a database for the tournament. Set the database up so there will be two separate tables. The first table will contain the information about the coaches; the second table will include the information about the players. I've listed the fields to be included in each table on the attached sheet. After you create the database, enter the information from the two applications that appear on the next two pages.
JK

Coaches' Table

Fields to be included:

Gender
Age Level
Team
Last Name
First Name
Initial
E-mail Address
Street Address
City
State
ZIP
Phone

Players' Table

Fields to be included:

Gender
Age Level
Team
Last Name
First Name
Initial
Age
Street Address
City
State
ZIP
Phone

Rule 6: Use figures for numbers following nouns.

Learn 11 Review Rules 1 to 18 in Chapter 5, pages 149 and 150, today.
Apply 12 Case 1849 is reviewed in Volume five, pages nine and ten.

Rule 7: Spell (and capitalize) names of small-numbered streets (ten and under).

Learn 13 I walked several blocks along Third Avenue to 54th Street.
Learn 14 At 7th Street she took a taxi to his home on 43d Avenue.

Rule 8: Spell indefinite numbers.

Learn 15 Joe owns one acre of Parcel A; that is almost fifty percent.
Learn 16 Nearly seventy members voted; that is nearly a fourth.
Apply 17 Over 20 percent of the students are out with the flu.
Apply 18 Just under 1/2 of the voters cast ballots for the issue.

ACTIVITY 2

Reading

1. Open the file *CD-CS3READ*.
2. Read the document; close the file.
3. Key answers to the questions at the right.
4. Check the accuracy of your work with the instructor; correct any errors you made.

Save as: *CS3-ACT2*

1. Will at least one member of the cast not return for the next season?
2. Has a studio been contracted to produce the show for next season?
3. Does each cast member earn the same amount per episode?
4. Is the television show a news magazine or comedy?
5. How many seasons has the show been aired, not counting next season?
6. Do all cast members' contracts expire at the same time?
7. What did the cast do three years ago to get raises?

ACTIVITY 3

Composing

1. Read carefully the two creeds (mottos) at the right.
2. Choose one as a topic for a short composition, and make notes of what the creed means to you.
3. Compose/key one or two paragraphs indicating what the creed means to you and why you believe it would be (or would not be) a good motto for your own behavior.

Save as: *CS3-ACT3*

The following creeds were written by Edward Everett Hale:

Harry Wadsworth Club

I am only one,
But still I am one.
I cannot do everything
But I can still do something;
And because I cannot do everything,
I will not refuse to do the something
that I can do.

Lend-a-Hand Society

To look up and not down,
To look forward and not back,
To look out and not in, and
To lend a hand.

Job 5—April 24

From the desk of:
Julia Kingsley
Create a Hotel Information sheet with the information shown on the attached sheet.
JK

HOTEL INFORMATION

Hotel and Address	Price Range	Features
Country Inn 2208 Main St. Fort Collins, CO 80524-1733 Phone: 970-546-6553 E-mail: countryinn@fortcollins.com	*$50-$98* ~~$45-$93~~	Nonsmoking rooms, onsite restaurant, free full breakfast, kitchenettes, whirlpool, indoor pool, fitness center
Cozy Cottage Inn 689 Center Ave. Fort Collins, CO 80526-2210 Phone: 970-546-7752	$30-$55	Cable, pets allowed, nonsmoking rooms, complimentary coffee
Four Season Suites 4817 Main St. Fort Collins, CO 80524-2056 Phone: 970-348-9805	*$89* $59-~~79~~	Suites, nonsmoking rooms, onsite restaurant, free continental breakfast, cable, in-room Jacuzzi, indoor pool, courtesy van, free local calls
The Inn 310 Main St. Fort Collins, CO 80524-1403 Phone: 970-348-7382 *E-mail: mail@theinnfortcollins.com*	*129* $49-$~~119~~	Suites, nonsmoking rooms, onsite restaurant, free continental breakfast, kitchenettes, indoor pool, fitness center ^ *, data port modem hookups*
Red Cedar Inn 453 Cedar St. Fort Collins, CO 80524-1237 Phone: 970-348-5610	$30-$45	Budget motel, nonsmoking rooms, waterbeds, kitchenettes, cable, pets allowed
Royal Motel 1327 Main St. Fort Collins, CO 80524-1620 Phone: 970-546-9230	$50-$79	Suites, nonsmoking rooms, onsite restaurant, cable, indoor pool, children under age 18 free

Insert a row in the table above the Red Cedar Inn for the information given below.

Park Place Plaza
320 Park Place Ct.
Fort Collins, CO 80525-1621
Phone: 970-348-1239
E-mail: mail@parkplaceplaza.com

$60-$140

Nonsmoking rooms, free continental breakfast, kitchenettes, cable, in-room whirlpools, indoor and outdoor pool, sauna, fitness center, Internet connections in rooms

ACTIVITIES 1-3

Learn Numeric Keypad Operation

ACTIVITY 1 NUMERIC KEYPAD KEYS: 4/5/6/0

Objectives:

1. To learn key techniques for **4**, **5**, **6**, and **0**.
2. To key these home-key numbers with speed and ease.

1A • 5' Numeric Keypad Operating Position

1. Position yourself in front of the keyboard—body erect, both feet on floor.
2. Place this book for easy reading—at right of keyboard or directly behind it.

Input copy at right of (or behind) keypad

Proper position at keypad

1B • 5' Home-Key Position

Curve the fingers of the right hand and place them on the keypad:

- index finger on 4
- middle finger on 5
- ring finger on 6
- thumb on 0

Note:
To use the keypad, the Num (number) Lock must be activated.

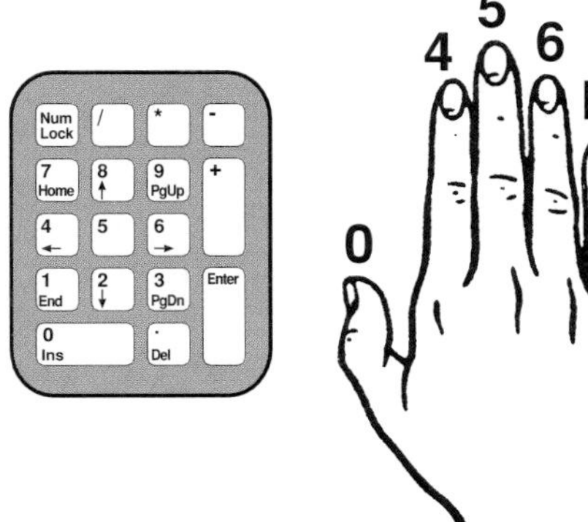

Job 3—April 19

From the desk of:
Julia Kingsley

A tournament packet will be sent to last year's participants and to new inquiries. As part of the packet, we will include "Hoops" Tournament Rules (copy shown at right) and a flyer ("Hoops" Tournament Schedule Flyer). Use your creativity and decision-making skills to create these two documents.

Format and key the copy at the right with the changes shown on the copy.

The tournament flyer should contain relevant tournament information along with the tournament dates (given on p. 475) and appropriate graphics. The Internet has some great basketball graphics that could be imported.

JK

"Hoops" Tournament Rules

- Each team may consist of up to five players; three players will play at one time.
- Teams will be grouped by age level. *There will be a male division and a female division.* Copies of participants' birth certificates must accompany registration materials. Participants may be required to verify their age at the tournament if another team requests verification. *Age is based on first day of tournament.*
- The age-level groupings are as follows:
  - 11-12 years old
  - 13-14 years old
  - 15-16 years old
  - 17-18 years old
  - ~~19 and over~~

Players can play up one age level. For example, an 11-year-old can play on a team of 13- and 14-year-olds. However, players cannot play down; a 17-year-old player cannot play on a team of 15- and 16-year-olds.

- A team is guaranteed at least three games each tournament and may have as many as five games if they advance to the championship game. Each grade level will have a maximum of 16 teams competing. The 16 teams will be divided into two brackets. The first-place winners in each bracket will play each other for the championship of the age level.
- Games will be played on half court and will have a 25-minute time limit.
- Game scoring is as follows:
  - One point for baskets under 20 feet
  - Two points for baskets over 20 feet

Job 4—April 19

From the desk of:
Julia Kingsley

*One of the businesses that advertised in last year's program was missing from the letters signed yesterday. Send a letter to **21st Century Sports**:*

Ms. Glenna McCormack
21st Century Sports
749 Center Ave.
Fort Collins, CO 80526-1394

Update the database to include 21st Century Sports. Also make the change noted on the attached letter to the database and print a copy of the letter.

JK

Todd McLemore, Tournament Director
"Hoops" Tournaments
618 Center Street
Fort Collins, CO 80526-1392

April 17, 200-

Mr. Justin Kummerfeld bought the Pizza Palace. Redo the letter, addressing it to Mr. Kummerfeld. Update the database.

~~Mr. Jason Dixon~~
Pizza Palace
608 Main Street
Fort Collins, CO 80524-1444

Dear Mr. ~~Dixon~~:

"Hoops" will again be sponsoring 3-on-3 basketball tournaments each weekend from June 15-August 4. Over 600 basketball players plus their families and relatives will travel to Fort

1C • 40'
New Keys: [4], [5], [6], and [0] (Home Keys)

Use the calculator accessory on your computer to complete the drills at the right.

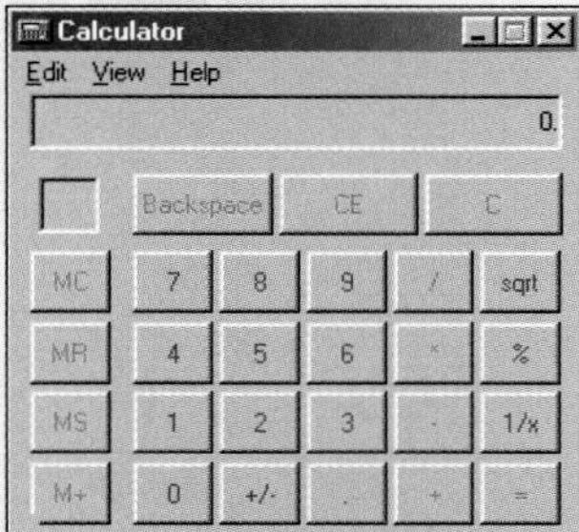

1. Curve the fingers of your right hand; place them upright on the keypad home keys:
   - index finger on 4
   - middle finger on 5
   - ring finger on 6
   - thumb on 0
2. Key/enter each number: Key the number and enter by pressing the + key with the little finger of the right hand.
3. After entering each number in the column, verify your answer with the answer shown below the column.
4. Press *ESC* on the main keyboard to clear the calculator; then enter numbers in the next column.
5. Repeat Steps 2–4 for Drills 1–6 to increase your input rate.

Technique **C • U • E**

Strike each key with a quick, sharp stroke with the *tip* of the finger; release the key quickly. Keep the fingers curved and upright, the wrist low, relaxed, and steady.

Strike *0* with the side of the right thumb, similar to the way you strike the Space Bar.

Drill 1

A	B	C	D	E	F
4	5	6	4	5	6
4	5	6	4	5	6
8	10	12	8	10	12

Drill 2

A	B	C	D	E	F
44	55	66	44	55	66
44	55	66	44	55	66
88	110	132	88	110	132

Drill 3

A	B	C	D	E	F
44	45	54	44	55	66
55	56	46	45	54	65
66	64	65	46	56	64
165	165	165	135	165	195

Drill 4

A	B	C	D	E	F
40	50	60	400	500	600
50	60	40	506	604	405
60	40	50	650	460	504
150	150	150	1,556	1,564	1,509

Drill 5

A	B	C	D	E	F
45	404	404	406	450	650
55	405	505	506	540	560
65	406	606	606	405	605
165	1,215	1,515	1,518	1,395	1,815

Drill 6

A	B	C	D	E	F
40	606	444	554	646	456
50	505	445	555	656	654
60	404	446	556	666	504
150	1,515	1,335	1,665	1,968	1,614

Job 2—April 17

From the desk of: Julia Kingsley

Please format and key the attached as a form letter to last year's advertisers. The advertisers' database file, HoopsAdvertisers, *can be found on your network or Web source. Print a copy of the form letter to Mona Lisa's Cuisine and Park Place Plaza. When our letterhead design is final, you should begin using it.*

JK

April 17, 200-

<Courtesy Title> <First Name> <Last Name>
<Business>
<Address>
<City>, <State> <ZIP>

Dear <Courtesy Title> <Last Name>:

"Hoops" will again be sponsoring 3-on-3 basketball tournaments each weekend from June 15-August 4. Over 600 basketball players plus their families and relatives will travel to Fort Collins for each of the nine weekends. This will have a huge impact on the economy of the Fort Collins area.

We are starting to work on the program that will be distributed at the tournaments to players, coaches, and spectators. Last year you purchased advertising space in the program for <Business>. The advertisement appeared in each of the five tournament programs. This year we have increased the number of tournaments from five to eight.

As you know, we have three different sizes of advertisements. The costs for the different advertisement sizes are as follows:

Quarter-page advertisement	$200
Half-page advertisement	$400
Full-page advertisement	$750

If you are interested in placing an advertisement in this year's tournament programs, please complete the enclosed form and return it by May 15.

Sincerely,

Todd McLemore
Tournament Director

xx

Enclosure

ACTIVITY 2 NUMERIC KEYPAD KEYS: 7/8/9

Objectives:

1. To learn reachstrokes for **7**, **8**, and **9**.
2. To combine the new keys with other keys learned.

2A • 5' Home-Key Review

Review the home keys by calculating totals for the problems at the right.

A	B	C	D	E	F
4	44	400	404	440	450
5	55	500	505	550	560
6	66	600	606	660	456
15	165	1,500	1,515	1,650	1,466

2B • 45' New Keys: [7], [8], and [9]

Learn reach to 7

1. Locate 7 (above 4) on the numeric keypad.
2. Watch your index finger move up to 7 and back to 4 a few times without striking keys.
3. Practice striking *74* a few times as you watch the finger.
4. With eyes on copy, key/enter the data in Drills 1A and 1B. Do not worry about totals.

Learn reach to 8

1. Learn the middle-finger reach to 8 (above 5) as directed in Steps 1–3 above.
2. With eyes on copy, enter the data in Drills 1C and 1D.

Learn reach to 9

1. Learn the ring-finger reach to 9 (above 6) as directed above.
2. With eyes on copy, enter the data in Drills 1E and 1F.

Drills 2–5

1. Calculate the totals for each problem in Drills 2–5. Check your answers with the problem totals shown.
2. Repeat Drills 2–5 to increase your input speed.

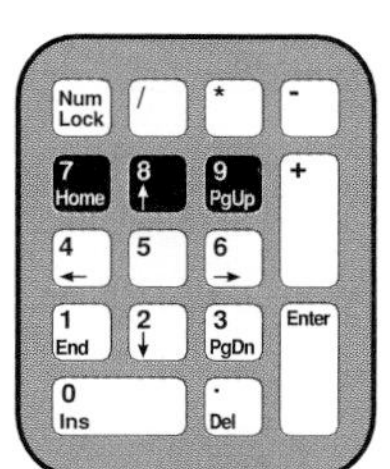

Drill 1

A	B	C	D	E	F
474	747	585	858	696	969
747	477	858	588	969	966
777	474	888	585	999	696
1,998	1,698	2,331	2,031	2,664	2,631

Drill 2

A	B	C	D	E	F
774	885	996	745	475	754
474	585	696	854	584	846
747	858	969	965	695	956
1,995	2,328	2,661	2,564	1,754	2,556

Drill 3

A	B	C	D	E	F
470	580	690	770	707	407
740	850	960	880	808	508
705	805	906	990	909	609
1,915	2,235	2,556	2,640	2,424	1,524

Drill 4

A	B	C	D	E	F
456	407	508	609	804	905
789	408	509	704	805	906
654	409	607	705	806	907
1,899	1,224	1,624	2,018	2,415	2,718

Drill 5

A	B	C	D	E	F
8	69	4	804	76	86
795	575	705	45	556	564
60	4	59	6	5	504
863	648	768	855	637	1,154

Job 1—April 17

From the desk of:
Julia Kingsley

Here is a copy of last year's tournament application. Prepare one for this year with the changes outlined on the application and below.

Merge the Birth Date (Month, Day, Year) cell with the Age cell, and change the name of the merged cell to "Age as of First Day of Tournament" *for each of the five player listings.*

JK

"Hoops" Tournament Application

Division:	Tournament Date:	Age Level of Players:
☐ Males ☐ Females		☐ 11-12 year age bracket ☐ 13-14 year age bracket ☐ 15-16 year age bracket ☐ 17-18 year age bracket ~~☐ 19 and over age bracket~~
Name of Your Team:		

Coach or Contact Person (Must be 21 years of age or older):

Last Name	First	Middle Initial	E-mail Address

Street Address	City	State	ZIP	Phone

Player: 1

Last Name	First	Middle Initial	~~Birth Date (Month, Day, Year)~~ ~~Age~~

Street Address	City	State	ZIP	Phone

Player: 2

Last Name	First	Middle Initial	~~Birth Date (Month, Day, Year)~~ ~~Age~~

Street Address	City	State	ZIP	Phone

Player: 3

Last Name	First	Middle Initial	~~Birth Date (Month, Day, Year)~~ ~~Age~~

Street Address	City	State	ZIP	Phone

Player: 4

Last Name	First	Middle Initial	~~Birth Date (Month, Day, Year)~~ ~~Age~~

Street Address	City	State	ZIP	Phone

Player: 5

Last Name	First	Middle Initial	~~Birth Date (Month, Day, Year)~~ ~~Age~~

Street Address	City	State	ZIP	Phone

Verification by Coach: To the best of my knowledge the information presented on this form is correct. Please sign below.

Signature:		Date:	

Signature: — Shade in gold

Date: — Shade in gold

ACTIVITY 3 NUMERIC KEYPAD KEYS: 1/2/3

Objectives:

1. To learn reachstrokes for **1**, **2**, and **3**.
2. To combine the new keys with other keys learned.

3A • 5' Keypad Review

Review the keypad by calculating the totals for the problems at the right.

A	B	C	D	E	F	G
45	74	740	996	704	990	477
56	85	850	885	805	880	588
67	96	960	774	906	770	699
168	255	2,550	2,655	2,415	2,640	1,764

3B • 45' New Keys: [1], [2], and [3]

Learn reach to 1

1. Locate 1 (below 4) on the numeric keypad.
2. Watch your index finger move down to 1 and back to 4 a few times without striking keys.
3. Practice striking *14* a few times as you watch the finger.
4. With eyes on copy, enter the data in Drills 1A and 1B. Do not worry about totals.

Learn reach to 2

1. Learn the middle-finger reach to 2 (below 5) as in Steps 1–3 above.
2. With eyes on copy, enter data in Drills 1C and 1D.

Learn reach to 3

1. Learn the ring-finger reach to 3 (below 6) as directed above.
2. With eyes on copy, enter data in Drills 1E–1G.

Drills 2–4

Calculate totals for each problem and check your answers.

Learn reach to [.] (decimal point)

1. Learn the ring-finger reach to the decimal point (.) located below the 3.
2. With eyes on copy, calculate the totals for each problem in Drill 5.
3. Repeat Drills 2–5 to increase your input speed.

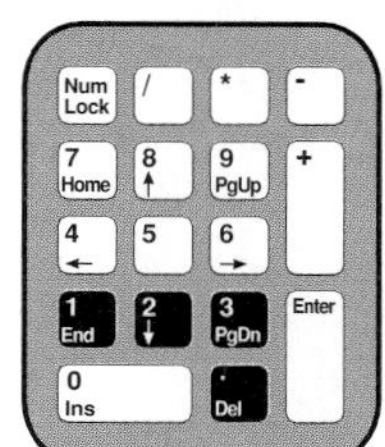

Drill 1

A	B	C	D	E	F	G
144	114	525	252	363	636	120
141	414	252	552	363	366	285
414	141	225	525	336	636	396
699	669	1,002	1,329	1,062	1,638	801

Drill 2

A	B	C	D	E	F	G
411	552	663	571	514	481	963
144	255	366	482	425	672	852
414	525	636	539	563	953	471
969	1,332	1,665	1,592	1,502	2,106	2,286

Drill 3

A	B	C	D	E	F	G
471	582	693	303	939	396	417
41	802	963	220	822	285	508
14	825	936	101	717	174	639
526	2,209	2,592	624	2,478	855	1,564

Drill 4

A	B	C	D	E	F	G
75	128	167	102	853	549	180
189	34	258	368	264	367	475
3	591	349	549	971	102	396
267	753	774	1,019	2,088	1,018	1,051

Drill 5

A	B	C	D	E	F	G
1.30	2.58	23.87	90.37	16.89	47.01	59.28
4.17	6.90	14.65	4.25	3.25	28.36	1.76
5.47	9.48	38.52	94.62	20.14	75.37	61.04

JOBS 1–17 (9–10 HOURS)

"Hoops": A Workplace Simulation

"Hoops" Simulation

Read the copy at the right to familiarize yourself with the workplace simulation you are about to begin. Be prepared to produce standard business documents for a manager and company whose specialty is recreational basketball tournaments.

Work Assignment

You have been hired to work part-time on Tuesday and Thursday afternoons for "Hoops." "Hoops" plans, organizes, and manages 3-on-3 basketball tournaments in Fort Collins, Colorado, throughout the summer. The owner of "Hoops" is Todd McLemore; his administrative assistant is Julia Kingsley.

The position requires the following skills:

- Word processing
- Database
- Spreadsheet
- Electronic presentation
- Interpersonal
- Telephone

You will be assisting Ms. Kingsley in processing all information dealing with the tournaments. The work includes:

- Processing letters and e-mail messages to advertisers, coaches, and players.
- Creating a database for advertisers, coaches, and players.
- Updating a database as registrations and advertising fees are received.
- Formatting tournament forms.
- Preparing tournament information.
- Creating a spreadsheet to keep track of tournament registrations.
- Updating a spreadsheet as registration fees are received.
- Formatting and keying tournament brackets.
- Preparing a slide show for electronic presentation.
- Preparing tournament calendars.

Ms. Kingsley will attach general processing instructions to each task you are given. If a date is not provided on the document, use the date included on the instructions. If the instructions given with the document are not sufficiently detailed, use your decision-making skills to process the document. Since "Hoops" has based its office manual on the *Century 21* textbook, you can also use the text as a reference.

Documents should be attractively formatted. You are expected to produce error-free documents, so proofread and correct your work carefully before presenting it for approval.

Mr. McLemore likes his letters formatted in block format with mixed punctuation. Use the following for the closing lines of his letters:

Sincerely,

Todd McLemore
Tournament Director

Tournament Dates

Tournament	Dates
1	June 15–16
2	June 22–23
3	June 29–30
4	July 6–7
5	July 13–14
6	July 20–21
7	July 27–28
8	August 3–4

WORD PROCESSING 1

ACTIVITY 1

Insert and Typeover, Underline, Italic, and Bold

1. Read the information at the right; learn to use the word processing (wp) features described.
2. Key the lines given below right as shown.
3. Make the following changes in your lines:

line 1
Change "seven" to "eight."

line 2
Change "January" to "October."

line 9
Insert "new" before "car."
Insert "for college" after "left."

line 10
Insert "not" before "know."
Insert "the" after "know."

Save as: *WP1ACT1*

Note:
Do not underline the punctuation after an underlined word, as shown in lines 8 and 10.

Insert
The **Insert** feature is active when you open a software program. Move the insertion point to where you want to insert copy; key the new text. Existing copy will move to the right.

Typeover
Typeover allows you to replace current copy with newly keyed text.

Underline
The **Underline** feature underlines text as it is keyed.

Italic
The **Italic** feature prints letters that slope up toward the right.

Bold
The **Bold** feature prints text darker than other copy as it is keyed.

1 Three of the seven dogs need to have their dog tags renewed.
2 His credit card bill for the month of January was $3,988.76.
3 Rebecca read *Little Women* by Louisa May Alcott for the test.
4 Yes, it is acceptable to *italicize* or underline book titles.
5 Patricia used the **bold** feature to **emphasize** her main points.
6 Their credit card number was **698 388 0054**, not 698 388 9954.
7 I have read both *The Firm* and *The Rainmaker* by John Grisham.
8 She overemphasized by ***underlining***, ***bolding***, and ***italicizing***.
9 I believe James bought a car before he left.
10 Sarah did know difference between affect and effect.

ACTIVITY 2

Alignment: Left, Center, Right

1. Read the copy at the right.
2. Learn the Alignment feature for your wp software.
3. Key the lines at the right. The page number will be right-aligned, the title will be center-aligned, and the last two lines will be left-aligned.

Save as: *WP1ACT2*

Alignment (justification) refers to the horizontal position of a line of text. Use **left** alignment to start text at the left margin. Use **right** alignment to start text at the right margin. Use **center** alignment to center lines of text between the left and right margins.

Page 13

The Final Act

Just before dawn the policeman arrived at the home of Ms. Kennington.

All the lights were shining brightly. . . .

LESSON 7 CAPSTONE ACTIVITY: CREATING YOUR OWN PRESENTATION

Objective:
To create an electronic presentation.

Approx. time: 50 min.

7A • Electronic Presentation Project

Create an electronic presentation using the slides at the right as the first and last slides. For content, use the main points you have learned in Lessons 1–6. Follow the guidelines below:

- Include six bulleted text slides, one for each lesson.
- Insert clip art, sound, and video as appropriate.
- Add a transition to all slides except the first. Add a different transition to that slide.
- Animate the bulleted items so they appear one at a time.
- Prepare a presentation for the class, using the slide show to emphasize key points.

Save as: *PRES-L7*

Preparing an
Electronic Presentation

Your Name
Date
Class

Congratulations!!!

You have
created a dynamic
electronic
presentation!!!

ACTIVITY 3

Undo and Redo

1. Read the copy at the right.
2. Learn how to use the Undo and Redo features of your software.

Use the **Undo** feature to reverse the last change you made in text. Undo restores text to its original location, even if you have moved the insertion point to another position. Use the **Redo** feature to reverse the last Undo action.

3. Key the ¶ below DS using bold as shown.
4. Select and delete "San Francisco" and "Tchaikovsky's."
5. Use the Undo feature to reverse the changes.
6. Use the Redo feature to reverse the last Undo action.

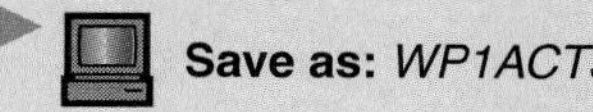
Save as: *WP1ACT3*

The **San Francisco** Symphony Orchestra performed **Tchaikovsky's** 1812 Overture Op. 49 Waltz for their final number.

ACTIVITY 4

Hyphenation

1. Read the copy at the right.
2. Learn how to activate the Hyphenation feature in your wp software.
3. Key the text at the right DS, with hyphenation off. Print the text.
4. With hyphenation on, key the text again. Compare text on screen with the printout.

Save as: *WP1ACT4*

The **Hyphenation** feature automatically divides (hyphenates) words that would normally wrap to the next line.

This evens the right margin, making the text more attractive.

Use the Hyphenation feature to give text a professional look. With the Hyphenation feature on, the software divides long words between syllables at the end of lines. Using hyphenation makes the right margin less ragged. This feature is particularly helpful when keying in narrow columns.

ACTIVITY 5

Speller

1. Read the copy at the right.
2. Learn to use your wp software's Speller.
3. Key the ¶ <u>exactly</u> as it is shown.
4. Use the Speller to identify words spelled incorrectly or not in your Speller's dictionary. Correct all errors by editing or selecting a replacement. Proper names are correct.
5. Proofread after the Speller is used. Correct any errors found.

Save as: *WP1ACT5*

Use the **Speller** to check words, documents, or parts of documents for misspellings. A Speller checks a document by comparing each word in the document to words in its dictio-nary(ies). If the Speller finds a word in your document that is not identical to one in its dic-tionary(ies), the word is displayed in a dialog box. Usually the Speller lists words it "believes" are likely corrections (replacements) for the displayed word. When a word is displayed, you must select one of the following options:

- Retain the spelling displayed in the dialog box.
- Replace a misspelled word that is displayed with a correctly spelled word offered by the Speller.
- Edit a misspelled word that is displayed if the Speller does not list the correctly spelled replacement.
- Delete a word that is incorrectly repeated.

Dr. Lorentz met with the students on Friday to reviiw for for there test. He told the students that their would be three sections to the test. The first secction would be multiplee choice, the second sction would be true/false, and the last section would be short anser. He also said, "If you have spelling errors on you paper, you will have pionts deducted."

Costs

- Complete designs from $150 to $300
- Installation at 15% added to cost of purchased plants
- 30-day, money-back guarantee
- Seasonal promotions

A History of Success

$4,000,000
$3,500,000
$3,000,000
$2,500,000
$2,000,000
$1,500,000
$1,000,000
$500,000
$0
1980 1985 1990 1995

What Should You Do?

- Don't let winter get you down!
- Call or visit our Web site!
- Plan now for a glorious landscape this spring!

We Appreciate You and Your Business!

Call Green Garden Center at
(555)123-4567
or visit our Web site at
www.greengardencenter.com

6B • Printing a Slide Show

1. Read the information at the right.
2. Print the slide show presentation you created in 6A. Choose the print option for black-and-white handouts (6 or 9 slides per page).
3. Create this speaker note for the last slide of your presentation: **Remind audience to pick up brochures and business cards.**

 **Save as:** *PRES-L6*

Slides in your presentation may be used as an on-screen show, 35-mm slides, Web pages, and color or black-and-white overheads or paper **printouts**. You can also print speaker notes, handouts, or an outline of your show.

Most presentation software has a **speaker notes** feature. You can use this feature to enter general notes and additional information about the slides that you want to remember when speaking. Your software will print pages with a reduced version of the slide showing immediately above your notes. Some software prints one slide and its notes per page. Other software lets you choose how many slides (with their notes) to include on each page.

The most important consideration for preparing speaker notes is that you be able to read and use them easily. Use key words and enlarge the type, if necessary, so you can read your notes easily. Organize and write them the way that works best for you.

Presentation software has different options for **handout** preparation. An easy and helpful option is to print reduced versions of your slides with blank lines so the audience can add notes.

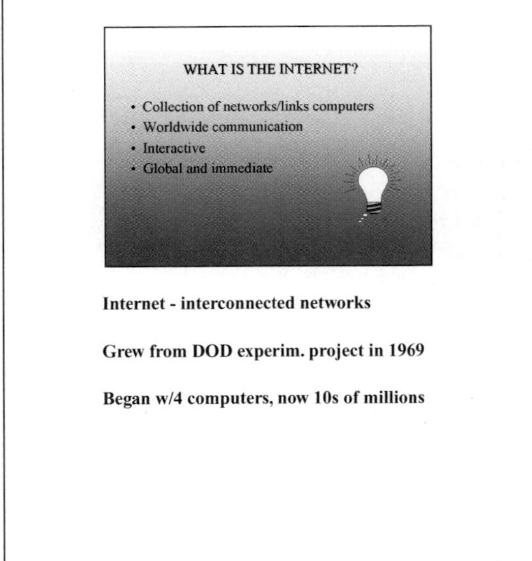

WHAT IS THE INTERNET?

- Collection of networks/links computers
- Worldwide communication
- Interactive
- Global and immediate

Internet - interconnected networks

Grew from DOD experim. project in 1969

Began w/4 computers, now 10s of millions

1

Speaker notes

ACTIVITY 6

View and Zoom

1. Read the copy at right.
2. Learn how to use the View and Zoom features of your software.
3. Open the Activity 1 document (*WP1ACT1*). Follow the steps at the right.

Use the **View** and **Zoom** features to increase or decrease the amount of the page appearing on the screen. As you increase the amount of the page appearing on the screen, the print becomes smaller, but you will see a larger portion of the page. As you decrease the amount of the page appearing on the screen, you will see less of the page; but the print will be larger, making it easier to read.

Reducing the view enough to see the whole page allows you to check the appearance (margins, spacing, graphics, tables, etc.) prior to printing. Enlarging the view makes it easier to see and edit specific portions of the page.

Step 1: View the document as a whole page.
Step 2: View the document at 75 percent.
Step 3: View the document at 200 percent.
Step 4: Close the document (same filename).

ACTIVITY 7

Hard Page Break

1. Read the copy at right.
2. Learn how to insert and delete a hard page break.
3. Key the roster sign-up sheet for the Braves shown at the right. Start at about 2" from the top of the page. DS below the title and between the numbers; 12 players will be signing up for the team.
4. Insert a hard page break at the end of the Braves Roster page and create three more sign-up sheets: one for the Yankees, one for the Angels, and one for the Astros.

Save as: *WP1ACT7*

Word processing software has two types of page breaks: *soft* and *hard*. Both kinds signal the end of a page and the beginning of a new page. The software inserts a soft page break automatically when the current page is full. You insert hard page breaks manually when you want a new page to begin before the current one is full. When a hard page break is inserted, the software adjusts any following soft page breaks so that those pages will be full before a new one is started. Hard page breaks do not move unless you move them. To move a hard page break, you can (1) delete it and let the software insert soft page breaks, or (2) insert a new hard page break where you want it.

BRAVES ROSTER

1.

2.

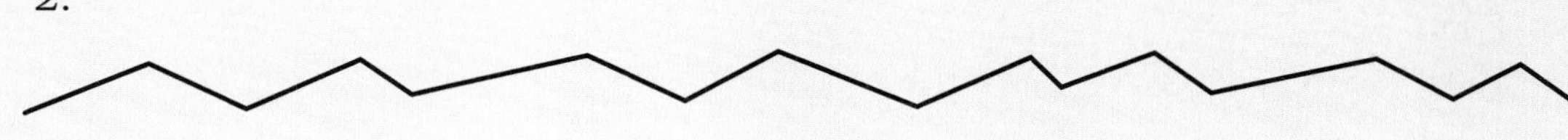

11.

12.

ACTIVITY 8

Tabs

1. Read the copy at the right.
2. Learn how to clear and set tabs (left, right, and decimal tabs) with your wp software.
3. Clear the preset tabs.

(continued on p. 58)

Most wp software has left tabs already set at half-inch (0.5") intervals from the left margin.

These preset tabs can be cleared and reset. Most wp software lets you set **left tabs**, **right tabs**, and **decimal tabs.**

Left tabs
Left tabs align all text evenly at the left by placing the text you key to the right of the tab setting. Left tabs are commonly used to align words.

Right tabs
Right tabs align all text evenly at the right by placing the text you key to the left of the tab setting. Right tabs are commonly used to align whole numbers.

Decimal tabs
Decimal tabs align all text at the decimal point or other character that you specify. If you key numbers in a column at a decimal tab, the decimal points will line up regardless of the number of places before or after the decimal point.

USING SPECIAL EFFECTS, TIMING, AND PRINTING

Objectives:

Approx. time: 100 min.

1. To learn how to use the following features to enhance a slide show: transitions, animation, sound effects, video, and timing.
2. To prepare and print a slide show.

6A • Slide Show Development

1. Read the information at the right.
2. Learn how to add transitions, animation, and sound in your software.
3. Create the slide show at the right and on p. 473.
4. Insert appropriate clip art as shown.
5. In the sorter view, add a transition to all slides except the first. Add a different transition to that slide.
6. Animate the bulleted items so they appear one at a time.
7. Add sound to one slide or add background music to the entire show.
8. Play the slide show for the class.

Save as: *PRES-L6*

Transitions control the way slides move on and off the screen. For instance, slides can dissolve or be replaced by a checkerboard pattern. Some examples of transitions are blinds, box, and fade. Transitions have different names in different software.

Most slide shows use only one or two types of transitions. For example, you could use one transition for the first and last slides and a second transition for some of the remaining slides.

Animation is effective and easy to do. One of the best uses of animation is for bulleted text. You can set bulleted items so that they appear one at a time, which helps the audience to focus on each point as you discuss it. Almost any item on a slide, including clip art and graphs, can be animated.

You can add sounds and movies to your slide shows. **Sounds and videos** can be inserted into individual slides. Sounds can also be set to play as background music for an entire presentation. Examples of sounds are clapping and a track from a CD.

Like other special effects, sound and video can be distracting when overused. Use them for emphasis; use them when it makes sense to do so; and choose sounds and movies that work well for what you want to stress.

Timing controls the speed with which slides replace other slides. Setting times tells the software how long each slide will remain on the screen. If you do not want the presentation to advance automatically, you can move manually from slide to slide. If you plan to use timing, it is important to rehearse your presentation and note how much time you would like each slide to remain on the screen.

Green Garden Landscaping

James Bloom
Green Garden Center

The Obvious Choice

- Environmentally friendly landscaping and maintenance
- Professional landscape architects
- Ongoing expert advice and support
- Seasonal promotions and money-back guarantee

More Strengths

- Outstanding selection of superior trees, shrubs, perennials, and annuals
- In business locally for 20 years
- Consistent record of customer satisfaction

Installation Planning

- **Planning conference** with landscape specialist
- **Analysis** of soil type and existing plantings
- **Design** by experienced landscape architects

4. Set a left tab at 1.5", a right tab at 3.5", and a decimal tab at 4.5".
5. Key the first three lines at the right (DS) using these tab settings. Remember: Strike *Tab* to move to the next column on the same line. Strike ENTER to move to the next line.
6. Reset tabs: left tab at 2", right tab at 5", decimal tab at 6".
7. Key the last three lines (DS) using these tab settings (Step 6).

 **Save as:** *WP1ACT8*

Left tab at 1.5"	**Right tab at 3.5"**	**Decimal tab at 4.5"**
↓	↓	↓
James Hill	6,750	88.395
Mark Johnson	863	1.38
Sue Chen	30	115.31
Left tab at 2"	**Right tab at 5"**	**Decimal tab at 6"**
↓	↓	↓
Juan Ortiz	142,250	0.25
Marsha Black	3,219	13.6
Kay Kent	56,873	297.312

ACTIVITY 9

Apply What You Have Learned

Team members for three teams are shown at the right. Using center alignment, key the information (DS) for each team on a separate page (use hard page breaks), starting at 2" from the top of the page.

The city and state should be bold and italic. The name of the team captain should be underlined.

 **Save as:** *WP1ACT9*

TEAM 1	TEAM 2	TEAM 3
Beaver Meadows, PA	***Chapel Hill, TN***	***Scipio, UT***
Dustin Hedrington (underlined)	Aaron Cain	Bradley Falkner
Keiko Koshuta	Susan Camacho (underlined)	Lisa Friese
Sarah Martin	Nicole Stohlberg	Patric Sammuel (underlined)
Zachary Ostmoe	Karen Xiong	Brent Wroblewski

ACTIVITY 10

Apply What You Have Learned

1. Set a left tab at 1", a right tab at 3.5", and a decimal tab at 5.5".
2. Beginning at about 2", key the text (DS) at the right.

 **Save as:** *WP1ACT10*

Left tab at 1"	**Right tab at 3.5"**	**Decimal tab at 5.5"**
↓	↓	↓
one-eighth	1/8	.125
one-sixth	1/6	.1667
one-fourth	1/4	.25
one-third	1/3	.3333
one-half	1/2	.5
two-thirds	2/3	.6667
three-fourths	3/4	.75
one	1/1	1.0

5E • Pie Charts

Pie Chart 1

1. Read the information at the right.
2. Create the pie chart as shown.

   Chart data:

Freshman	**25**
Sophomore	**40**
Junior	**35**
Senior	**50**

3. Display the legend on the right.

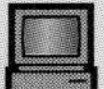 **Save as:** *PIE-L5E1*

Pie charts are best used to display parts of a whole. They show clearly the proportional relationship of only one set of values. Without any numbers displayed, the chart shows only general relationships. In the example shown below, the different colors used for the pie slices are identified in a legend. Colors used on the pie should provide adequate contrast between the slices. Consider, also, the color scheme of your entire presentation so that the pie chart will coordinate with other visuals.

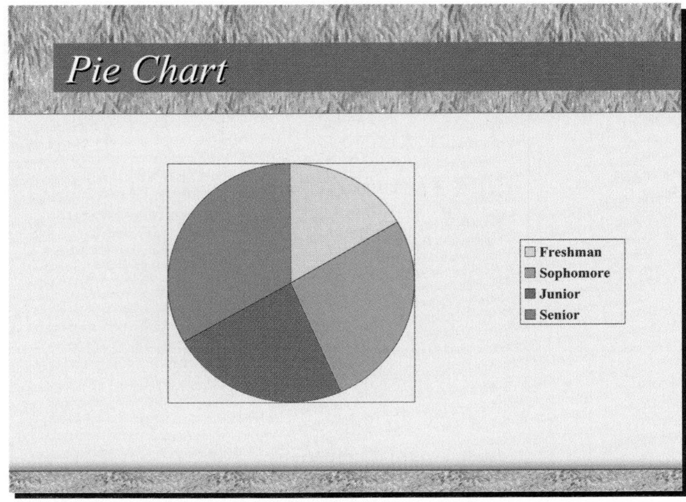

Pie Chart 2

1. Read the information at the right.
2. Change Pie Chart 1 to give it a 3D appearance and to emphasize the pie slices by exploding them.
3. Remove the legend.
4. Display labels and percentages with each slice.

 **Save as:** *PIE-L5E2*

Usually pie charts look attractive with a 3D appearance, as long as the circle does not seem distorted. The pie slice values (shown as actual numbers or percentages) can be displayed beside each of the slices to show relationships exactly. Pie slices can be emphasized by **exploding** (pulling one slice or all slices away from the other slices) and using high-contrast colors for the slices. Pie charts are probably easier to interpret when both the identifying labels and the slice values are positioned beside or on the pie slices. If space on the pie is limited, arrange the labels in a list or use a legend to identify the slices.

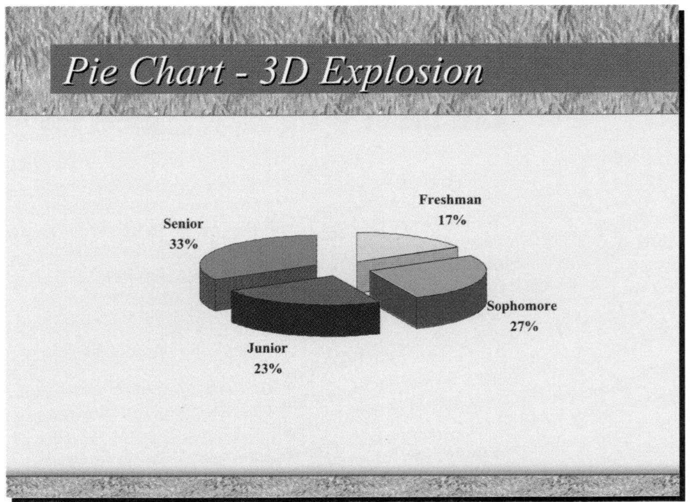

UNIT 7

LESSONS 22–24

Learn to Format Memos and E-mail

Format Guides: Memos and E-mail

Interoffice Memo

Interoffice Memo

Memos (interoffice memorandums) are written messages used by employees within an organization to communicate with one another. A standard format (arrangement) for memos is presented below and illustrated on p. 60.

Memo margins.

Memo margins
Top margin (TM): 2"
Side margins (SM): default or 1"
Bottom margin (BM): about 1"

Memo heading. The memo heading includes who the memo is being sent to (TO:), who the memo is from (FROM:), the date the memo is being sent (DATE:), and what the memo is about (SUBJECT:). Begin all lines of the heading at the left margin and space as shown below.

TO: Tab twice to key name.
DS
FROM: Tab once to key name.
DS
DATE: Tab once to key date.
DS
SUBJECT: Tab once to key subject in ALL CAPS.
DS

Memo body. The paragraphs of the memo all begin at the left margin and are SS with a DS between paragraphs.

Reference initials. If someone other than the originator of the memo keys it, his/her initials are keyed in lowercase letters at the left margin, a DS below the body.

Attachment/Enclosure notations. If another document is attached to a memo, the word "Attachment" is keyed at the left margin a DS below the reference initials (or below the last line of the body if reference initials are not used). If a document accompanies the memo but is not attached to it, key the word "Enclosure."

E-mail

E-mail (electronic mail) is used in most business organizations. Because of the ease of creating and the speed of sending, e-mail messages have partially replaced the memo and the letter. Generally, delivery of an e-mail message takes place within minutes, whether the receiver is in the same building or in a location anywhere in the world.

The format used for e-mail is very similar to that used for memos. It may vary slightly, depending on the program used for creating e-mail. One commonly used format is shown on p. 62.

E-mail heading. The e-mail heading includes the same information as the memo (**To:**, **From:**, **Date:**, **and Subject:**). It may also include a **Cc:** line for sending a copy of the message to additional individuals, a **Bcc:** line for sending a copy of the message to someone without the receiver knowing, and an **Attachment:** line for attaching files to the e-mail message.

E-mail body. The paragraphs of an e-mail message all begin at the left margin and are SS with a DS between paragraphs.

Bar Graph 2

Modify the bar graph created in 5C as follows:

1. Remove the data values from above the bars.
2. Change the chart type to 3D bar graph.

 **Save as:** *GRAPH-L5C2*

Presentation software offers three-dimensional (3D) versions of bar, line, and area graphs and pie charts. A 3D graph or chart often has a more contemporary look than a two-dimensional version.

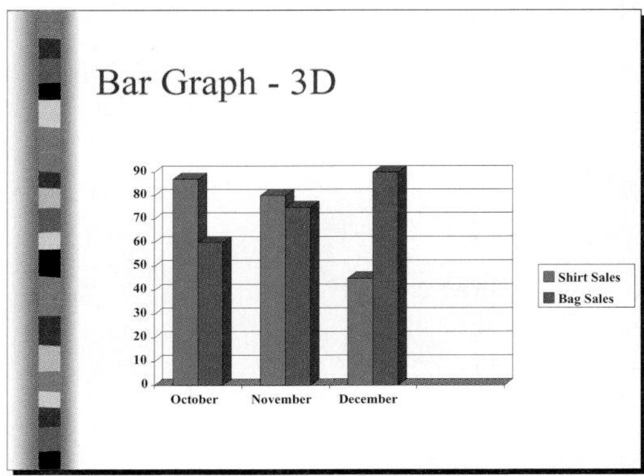

5D • Line and Area Graphs

Line Graph

1. Read the information at the right
2. Start a new presentation and create the line graph as shown.
3. **Graph data:**

1970	**20**
1975	**43**
1980	**30**
1985	**50**
1990	**45**
1995	**60**

4. Include vertical lines in the grid.

 **Save as:** *GRAPH-L5D1*

Line graphs display changes in quantities over time or distance. Usually the X-axis shows a particular period of time or distance. The Y-axis shows measurements of quantity at different times or distances. The baseline of the Y-axis should be zero to provide a consistent reference point when several graphs are used in a presentation. When the numbers for the X-axis are entered, lines appear connecting the values on the graph to reflect the changes in amounts. A grid with vertical lines helps the viewer interpret quantities.

Several sets of data can be displayed by using lines in different colors.

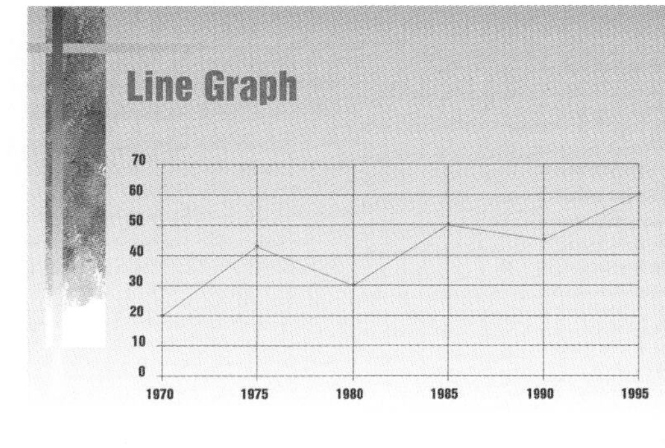

Area Graph

5. Change the line graph to an area graph.
6. Consider the difference in appearance to determine which graph is easier to interpret.

 **Save as:** *GRAPH-L5D2*

If the line needs more emphasis, an **area** graph would be a better choice. The area below the line is filled in with a contrasting color.

If exact data were required, however, a vertical bar graph would be a better choice than an area graph because each bar can be labeled with the appropriate measurement.

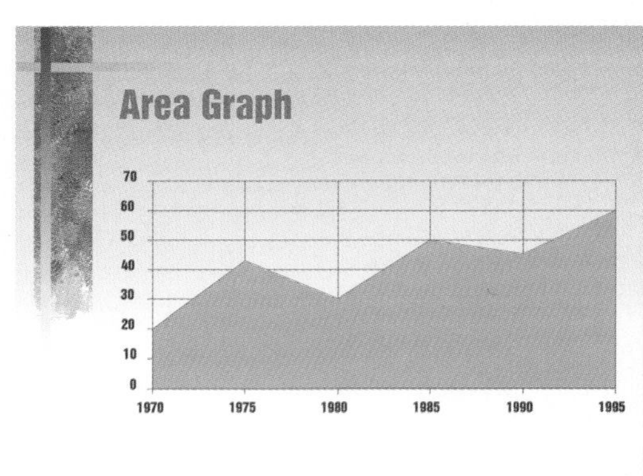

FORMAT INTEROFFICE MEMOS

Objectives

1. To learn to format interoffice memos.
2. To process memos from arranged and semi-arranged copy.

22A • 5'
Conditioning Practice

Key each line twice SS; then key a 1' writing on line 3; determine *gwam*.

alphabet 1 Darby and Jazmine gave a quick example of two helping verbs.

figures 2 The exam on May 28 for 50 points will test pages 396 to 471.

speed 3 Did the field auditor sign the amendment forms for the city?

gwam 1' | 1 | 2 | 3 | 4 | 5 | 6 | 7 | 8 | 9 | 10 | 11 | 12 |

2"

TO: Tab Tab Foreign Language Department Students
DS

FROM: Tab Mary Seville, Travel Abroad Coordinator
DS

DATE: Tab Tab November 2, 200-
DS

SUBJECT: Tab OPEN HOUSE
DS

1" Are you ready for a summer you will never forget? Then you will want to sign up for this year's Travel Abroad Program. You will travel to the country that famous writers like Virgil, Horace, and Dante called home. The music of Vivaldi, Verdi, and Puccini will come to life. You will visit art museums exhibiting the art of native sons such as Michelangelo Buonarotti and Giovanni Bellini. 1"
DS

By now you have probably guessed that we will be taking a trip to Italy this summer. Touring **Rome**, **Florence**, **Venice**, and **Naples** gives you the opportunity to experience firsthand the people, the culture, the history, and the cuisine of Italy.
DS

If you are interested in learning more about traveling to Italy this summer, attend our open house on <u>November 15</u> at <u>3:30</u> in Room 314.
DS

xx

Shown in 12-point Times New Roman, with 2" top margin and 1" side margins, this memo appears smaller than actual size.

Interoffice Memo

LESSON 5 CREATING GRAPHS

Objectives:

1. To learn which graph or chart to use for particular situations.
2. To learn various graph elements.
3. To create graphs.

Approx. time: 100 min.

5A • Graph Overview

Read the information at the right and determine the purpose of each graph type.

Numeric information can be easier to understand when shown as a **graph** rather than in text or a table. The relationship between data sets or trends can be compared with *bar, line,* or *area graphs* or *pie charts.*

Each type of graph or chart is best suited for a particular situation:

- **bar**—comparison of item quantities
- **line, area**—quantity changes over time or distance
- **pie**—parts of a whole

5B • Graph Elements

1. Read the information at the right.
2. Locate the various graph elements in the software you are using.

Elements common to most graphs are identified on the bar graph shown at right. They include:

- **X-axis**—the horizontal axis; usually for categories
- **Y-axis**—the vertical axis; usually for values
- **scale**—numbers on the Y- or X-axis representing quantities
- **tick marks**—coordinate marks on the graph to help guide the reader
- **grids**—lines that extend from tick marks to make it easier to see data values
- **labels**—names used to identify parts of the graph
- **legend**—the key that identifies the shading, coloring, or patterns used for the information shown in the graph

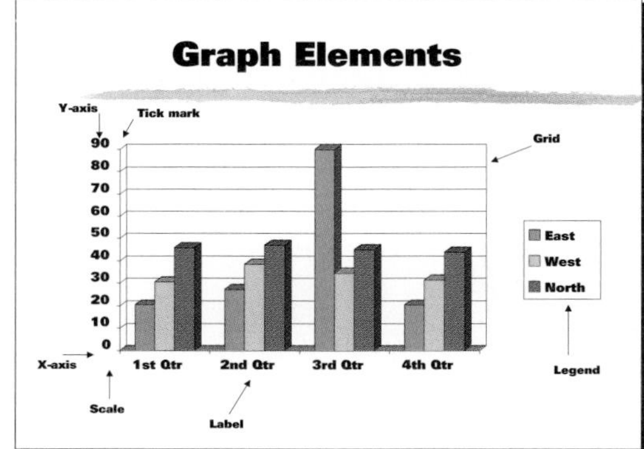

5C • Bar Graphs

Bar Graph 1

1. Read the information at the right.
2. Learn how to create charts and graphs in your software.
3. Create the graph as shown.

Graph data:

	Shirt Sales	Bag Sales
October	87	60
November	80	75
December	45	90

4. Display data values above the bars, labels below the bars, and a legend.

 **Save as:** *GRAPH-L5C1*

Bar graphs (also called **bar charts**) compare one or more sets of data that are plotted on the horizontal X-axis and the vertical Y-axis. The X-axis usually contains category information (such as years or months); the Y-axis usually contains measured quantity values (numbers).

Vertical bars (also called *columns*) are easy to interpret; the baseline on the Y-axis should begin at zero for consistent comparisons when several graphs are used in a presentation. Many special effects can be added, but a simple graph is effective for showing relationships.

A cluster of bars on each point on the X-axis can show multiple data sets. When multiple data sets are used, the colors must provide an adequate contrast to be viewed from a distance, and yet blend with the other colors used in the presentation.

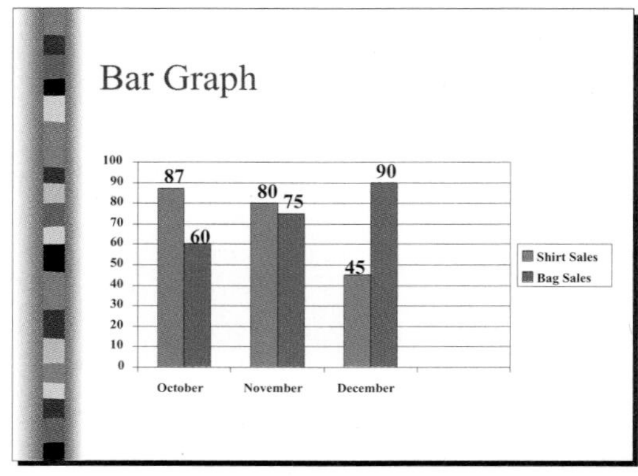

22B • 45' Memos

Study the format guides on p. 59 and the model that shows memo format on p. 60. Note the vertical and horizontal placement of memo parts and the spacing between them.

Memo 1

1. Key the model memo on p. 60.
2. Proofread your copy; correct all keying and formatting errors.

 **Save as:** *MEM022B1*

Memo 2

1. Format and key the text at the right in memo format. Use your initials as the keyboard operator.
2. Proofread your copy; correct all keying and formatting errors.

 **Save as:** *MEMO22B2*

Memo 3

1. Format and key the text at the right in memo format. Use your initials as the keyboard operator.
2. Proofread your copy; correct all keying and formatting errors.

 **Save as:** *MEMO22B3*

TO: Foreign Language Teachers

FROM: Mary Seville, Travel Abroad Coordinator

DATE: November 2, 200-

SUBJECT: OPEN HOUSE

I've enclosed copies of a memo announcing the open house for the Travel Abroad Program. Please distribute the memo to students in your classes.

Last year we had 25 students participate in the trip to England. If you have had the opportunity to talk with them about this experience, you know that the trip was very worthwhile and gave them memories that will last a lifetime. I am confident that the trip to Italy will be just as rewarding to those who participate. As you know, the experiences students gain from traveling abroad cannot be replicated in the classroom.

I appreciate your support of the program and your help in promoting it with your students.

xx

Enclosure

TO: Foreign Language Faculty

FROM: Karla A. Washburn

DATE: December 1, 200-

SUBJECT: TRAVEL ABROAD COORDINATOR

As you may have heard by now, Mary Seville announced her plans to retire at the end of next summer. In addition to hiring a new French teacher, we will need to replace Mary as our Travel Abroad Coordinator. This will be a very difficult task; Mary has done an excellent job.

If you are interested in this position, please let me know before you leave for the winter break. I would like to fill the position early next semester. This will allow the new coordinator to work with Mary as she plans this year's trip. The new coordinator would be expected to travel with Mary and the students to Italy this summer.

We also need to start thinking about a retirement party for Mary. If you are interested in being on a retirement party committee, please let me know.

4E • Cluster Diagram

1. Read the information at the right.
2. Start a new presentation. Select a design template or slide master.
3. Choose or change to an appropriate slide layout.
4. Key the bulleted text.
5. Use the drawing tools to create the cluster diagram. Use the slides at the right as a guide.

Hint:
Copy and paste the Item 1 oval and the first arrow to create the others.

 **Save as:** *PRES-L4E*

The cluster diagram below begins with an oval at the center containing the text for the main topic being explained. Additional ovals with text are positioned around the main topic. For a slide show, these items could be animated to appear one at a time as the discussion progresses.

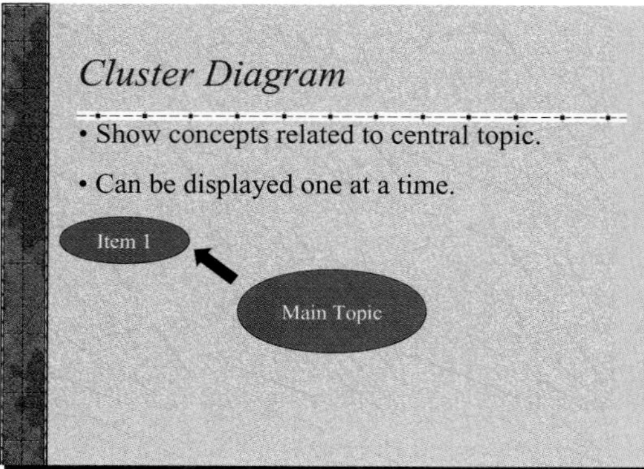

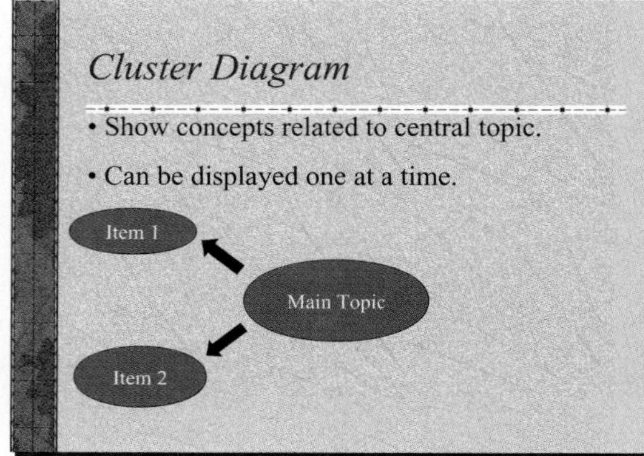

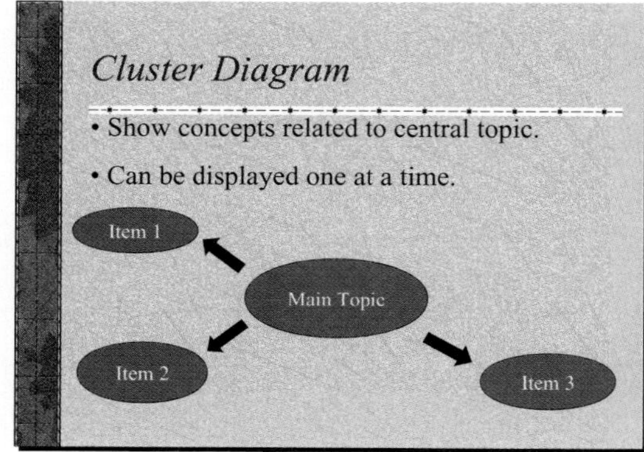

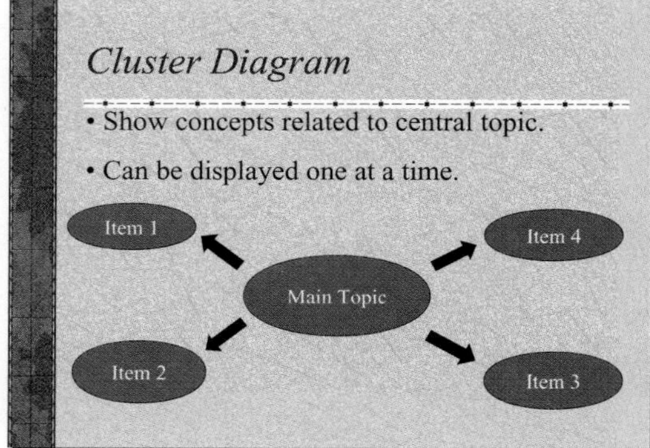

4F • Table

1. Read the information at the right.
2. Start a new presentation. Select a design template or slide master.
3. Insert a table slide. If your software does not have a table layout, learn how to create or import tables in your software.
4. Create the table as shown at the right.

 **Save as:** *TBL-L4F*

Tables can be used in presentations to compare and contrast facts or figures and to list data. Some presentation software includes a table layout slide. In other software, you must create the table in a word processing or spreadsheet program and import it into your presentation.

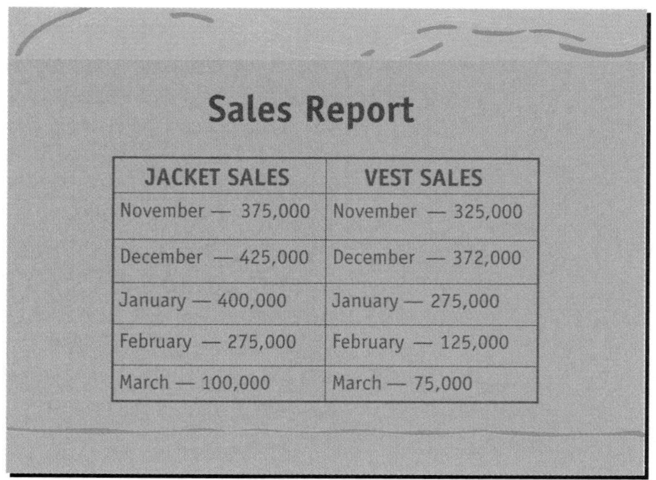

Sales Report

JACKET SALES	VEST SALES
November — 375,000	November — 325,000
December — 425,000	December — 372,000
January — 400,000	January — 275,000
February — 275,000	February — 125,000
March — 100,000	March — 75,000

FORMAT E-MAIL MESSAGES

Objectives:

1. To learn to format e-mail messages.
2. To process e-mail messages from arranged and semi-arranged copy.

23A • 5' Conditioning Practice

Key each line twice SS; then key a 1' writing on line 3; determine *gwam*.

alphabet 1 Jordan placed first by solving the complex quiz in one week.

figures 2 The 389 members met on June 24, 2001, from 6:15 to 7:30 p.m.

speed 3 Jan paid the big man for the fieldwork he did for the firms.

gwam 1' | 1 | 2 | 3 | 4 | 5 | 6 | 7 | 8 | 9 | 10 | 11 | 12 |

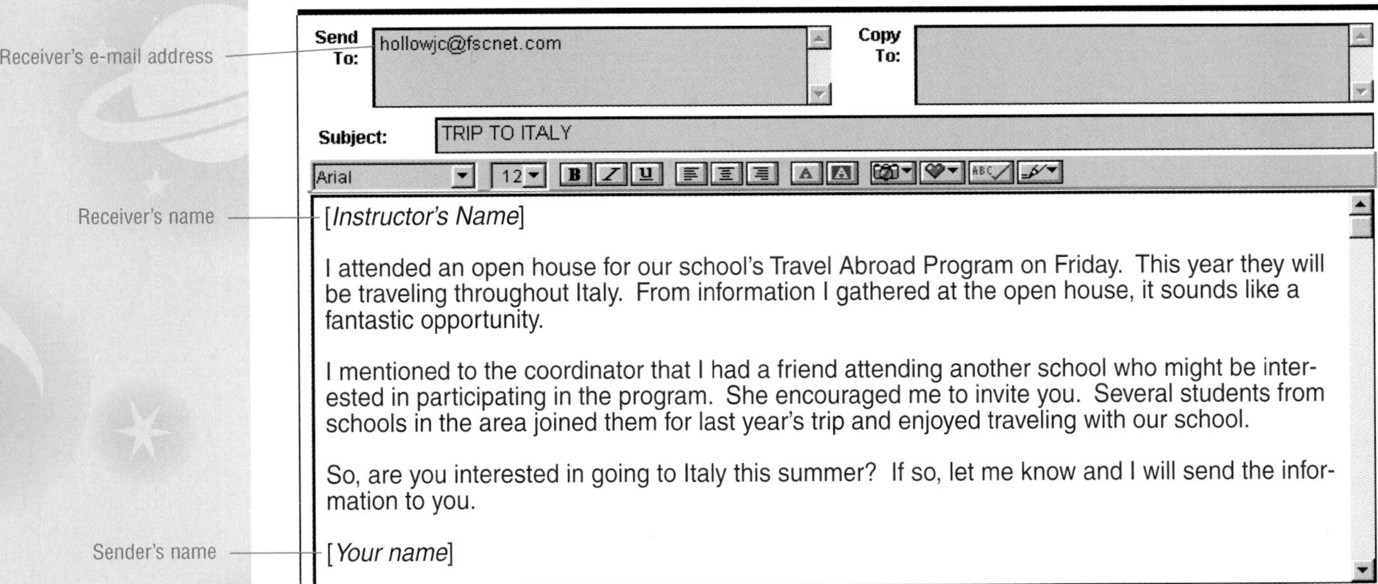

Receiver's e-mail address
Receiver's name
Sender's name
Send To:
hollowjc@fscnet.com
Copy To:
Subject:
TRIP TO ITALY
Arial
12
[Instructor's Name]
I attended an open house for our school's Travel Abroad Program on Friday. This year they will be traveling throughout Italy. From information I gathered at the open house, it sounds like a fantastic opportunity.
I mentioned to the coordinator that I had a friend attending another school who might be interested in participating in the program. She encouraged me to invite you. Several students from schools in the area joined them for last year's trip and enjoyed traveling with our school.
So, are you interested in going to Italy this summer? If so, let me know and I will send the information to you.
[Your name]

E-mail Message

Note:
In some e-mail software, the receiver's name may be keyed in the To: box along with the e-mail address. The date and time the message is sent will appear automatically above or below the message when the receiver gets it. Although no From: box is provided in this example, the sender's e-mail address will appear automatically also.

4C • Stair Steps Diagram

1. Read the information at the right.
2. Insert a slide with the bulleted list layout as the second slide in *PRES-L4*.
3. Key the bulleted text that appears in the fourth slide at the right. Change the type size of this text to 24 point.
4. Use the drawing tools to create the stair steps diagram.

Hint:
Complete the bottom box, copy and paste it to make the remaining steps, and edit the text and color of those boxes.

 **Save as:** *PRES-L4*

This diagram shows a series of ideas. The stair steps diagram begins with a box at the bottom containing the text for the first idea being explained. Additional boxes with text are positioned to look like stairs going up. For a slide

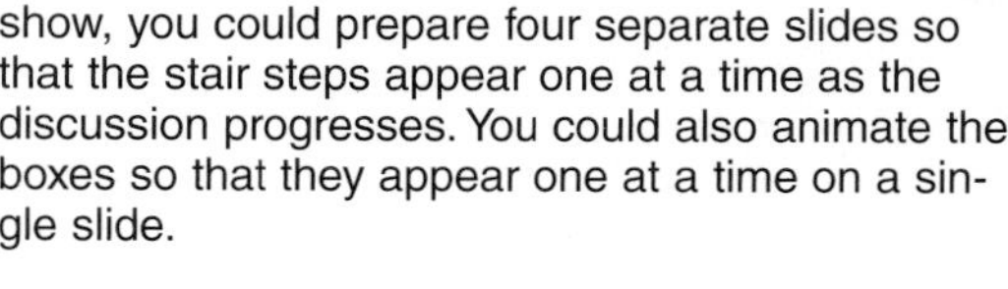
show, you could prepare four separate slides so that the stair steps appear one at a time as the discussion progresses. You could also animate the boxes so that they appear one at a time on a single slide.

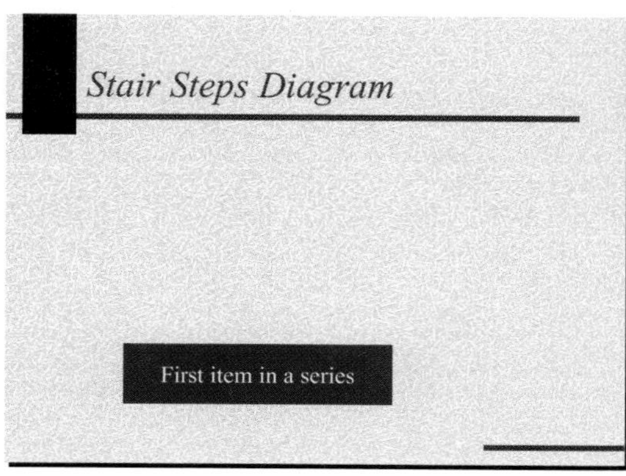

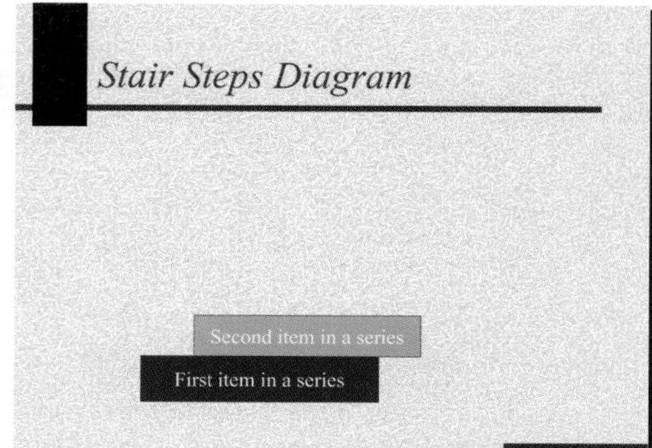

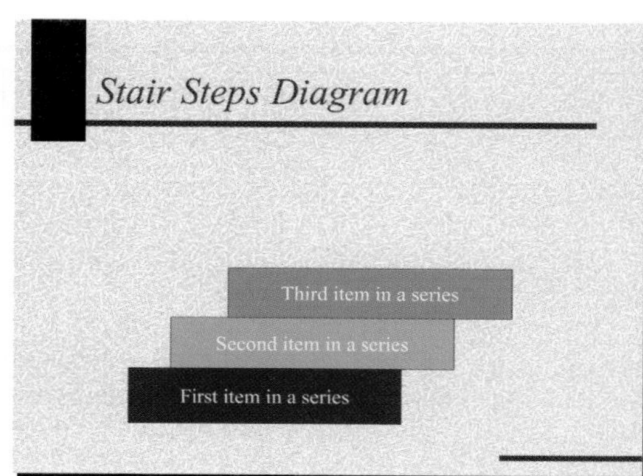

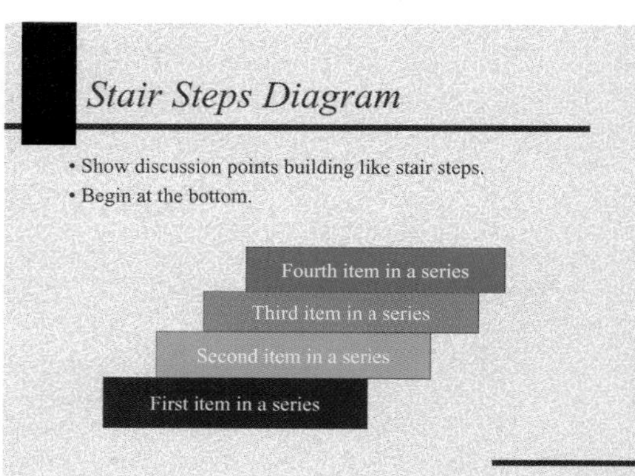

4D • Flowchart

1. Read the information at the right.
2. Insert a slide with an appropriate layout for creating the flowchart as the third slide in the presentation.
3. Use the drawing tools to create the flowchart.

Note:
Flowchart steps are often horizontal or vertical.

 **Save as:** *PRES-L4*

This flowchart shows steps in a process, connected by arrows. Flowcharts can use pictures or shapes. In a flowchart with shapes, each shape has a certain meaning. An oval shows the beginning or end of a process. A parallelogram shows input or output. A diamond shows a decision to be made, worded as a question. Two arrows, one marked "Yes" and one marked "No," extend from the diamond to the flowchart step that results from the decision. A rectangle shows a step that does not require a decision.

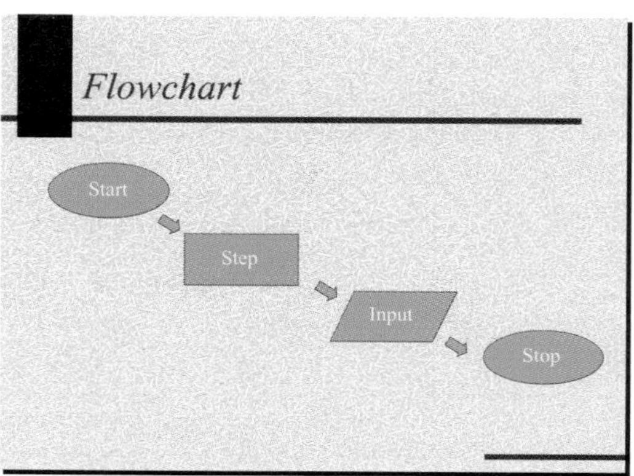

23B • 45' E-mail Messages

Study the format guides on p. 59 and the model that illustrates e-mail on p. 62.

E-mail software users: Use your instructor's e-mail address for the TO: line of each message. Use your e-mail address for the FROM: line.

Word processing software users: Format each message as an interoffice memo, using the names given. Use the current date.

E-mail Message 1

1. Key the model e-mail on p. 62; replace the e-mail address given with your instructor's e-mail address.
2. Proofread your copy; correct all keying and formatting errors.

Save as: *EMAIL23B1**

*E-mail is saved automatically in the e-mail software. Use this filename only if your instructor directs you to save the message on disk.

E-mail Messages 2 and 3

1. Format and key the e-mail messages at the right.
2. Proofread your copy; correct all keying and formatting errors.

Save as: *EMAIL23B2* and *EMAIL23B3*

E-mail Message 2

TO: Margaret Simmons [On e-mail screen, key instructor's e-mail address.]

FROM: Erika Downey [On e-mail screen, use your e-mail address.]

DATE: February 25, 200- [On e-mail screen, date is inserted automatically.]

SUBJECT: HELP!!!

Hopefully, my sister told you that I would be e-mailing you. I'm writing a report on Mark Twain for my English class. Last weekend when Katherine was home, we were talking about this assignment. She mentioned that you were an English major and seemed to think that you had completed a course that focused on Mark Twain. She suggested that I contact you to see if you would be able to suggest some sources that I might use for this assignment.

As part of the report project, we have to read two of his books. I've already started reading *Life on the Mississippi*. Could you offer a suggestion as to what other book I should read for this assignment?

Katherine said that you are planning on coming home with her during spring break. I'll look forward to meeting you.

E-mail Message 3

TO: Marshall Sabin [Or instructor's e-mail address]

FROM: Tina Hansen [Or your e-mail address]

DATE: October 1, 200- [Inserted automatically on e-mail screen]

SUBJECT: INFORMATION FOR YOUR REPORT

I found a site on the World Wide Web at http://www.nytheatre-wire.com/PoorR.htm that lists the plays currently performed in New York City. It appears that there are five plays that were opened prior to 1990. Four of them were opened between 1980-1990. These include *Cats* (10/07/82), *Les Miserables* (03/12/87), *The Phantom of the Opera* (01/26/88), and *Tony n' Tina's Wedding* (02/06/88).

The only other play that I found that had opened prior to 1990 was *The Fantasticks*, which is New York's longest-running musical. It opened on May 3, 1960.

I scanned the information very quickly. You will want to check the Web site and verify the accuracy of the information before you include it in your report. If I find anything else that I think would add to your report, I will let you know.

CREATING DIAGRAMS AND TABLES

Objectives:

Approx. time: 100 min.

1. To learn how diagrams and tables can portray processes and ideas.
2. To create diagrams using the choice, stair steps, flowchart, and cluster designs.
3. To create tables to enhance a presentation.

4A • Diagrams

Read the information at the right.

A **diagram** is a drawing that explains a process or idea. Diagrams can help an audience understand relationships or a sequence of events. Text can be arranged in boxes that are connected with lines or arrows to help the audience visualize the individual steps in a process or the parts of an idea.

While diagrams can become quite complex, the best ones are quite simple. When creating diagrams, be sure to:

- Arrange text in boxes or other appropriate shapes.
- Show connections with lines and directional arrows.
- Use fonts and colors that work well with the rest of the presentation.

4B • Choice Diagram

1. Read the information at the right.
2. Start a new presentation. Select a design template or slide master suitable for creating the slide at the right.
3. Choose the bulleted list layout. If your software starts you with a title layout, learn how to change slide layout in your software and do so.
4. Select the box in which you will key the bulleted text and size or move it so it is at the bottom of the slide.
5. Use the drawing tools to create the choice diagram in the space above the bulleted list.
6. Key the bulleted list.

 **Save as:** *PRES-L4*

This diagram below indicates that a choice must be made between two options. The arrows pointing in opposite directions indicate an either/or situation. This same technique can be used to represent conflict.

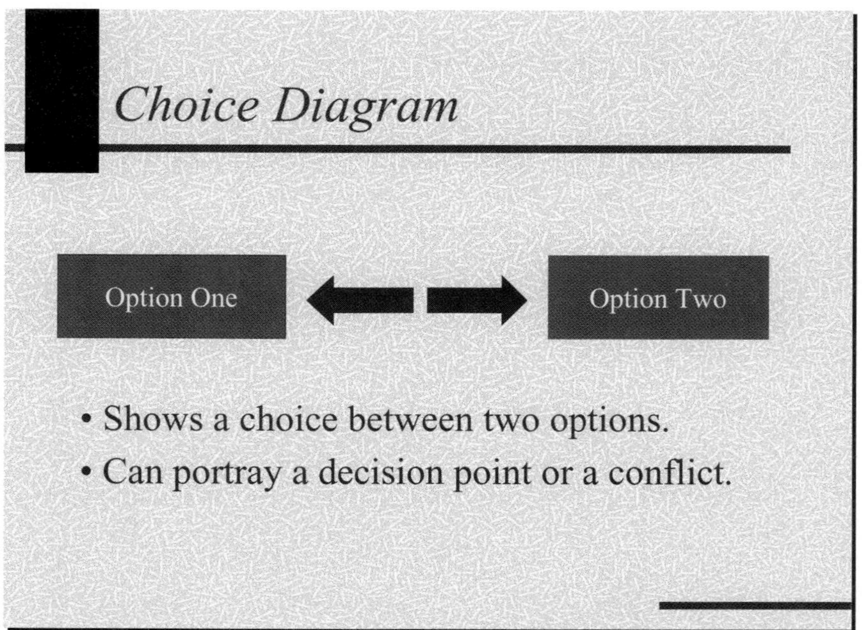

LESSON 24 — FORMAT MEMOS AND E-MAIL

Objectives:

1. To check knowledge of e-mail and memo formats.
2. To check the level of your e-mail and memo processing skill.

24A • 5' Conditioning Practice

Key each line twice SS; then key a 1' writing on line 3; determine *gwam*.

alphabet 1 Dixie quickly gave him two big prizes for completing a jump.

fig/sym 2 I think the textbook (ISBN #0-538-64892-9) sells for $41.70.

speed 3 Helen is to go downtown to do the map work for the auditors.

gwam 1' | 1 | 2 | 3 | 4 | 5 | 6 | 7 | 8 | 9 | 10 | 11 | 12 |

FORMATTING

24B • 45' Memo and E-mail Processing

Memo 1

1. Format and key the memo at the right.
2. Use Speller and proofread your copy; correct all keying and formatting errors.

 **Save as:** *MEMO24B1*

Note:
Use italic instead of underlines for the play titles.

TO: Drama Students

FROM: Ms. Fairbanks

DATE: November 1, 200-

SUBJECT: SELECTION OF SPRING PLAY

There are three plays that I would like you to consider for next semester's performance. They include:

The Importance of Being Earnest, a comedy written by Oscar Wilde. In the play Jack Worthing has a complicated courtship with Lady Bracknell's daughter, Gwendolen. His ward, Cecily, has fallen in love with his friend Algernon.

A Delicate Balance, a comedy written by Edward Albee. The play is a funny look at love, compassion, and the bonds of friendship and family.

A Comedy of Errors, a comedy written by William Shakespeare. The play is about mistaken identities of twins.

I have placed copies of the plays in the library on reserve. Please look them over by November 25 so that we can discuss them in class that day. We will need to make a decision before December 1 so that I can order the playbooks.

3C • Text Boxes

1. Learn how to change fonts and type colors in your software.
2. Insert a slide with a title-only layout (*not* a title slide) as the fourth slide in *PRES-L3*. If you do not have a title-only layout, insert a slide with a chart layout and delete the box for the chart.
3. Use the drawing tools to create the slide at the right. Use the Arial font for the box text. Make the stars yellow. Use a color of your choice for the arrow.

 **Save as:** *PRES-L3*

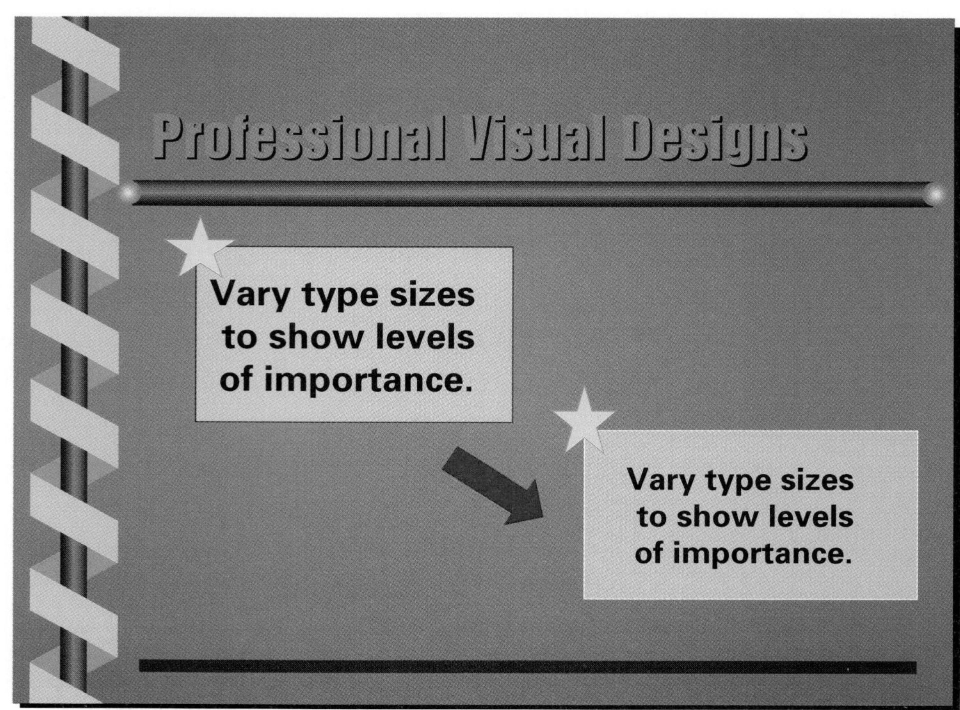

3D • Slides with Clip Art

1. Insert two slides with a text and clip art layout at the end of the presentation. If you do not have a text and clip art layout, insert a slide with a text and chart layout and delete the box for the chart.
2. Create the slides as shown. Insert an appropriate piece of clip art from your software collection in each slide. Size the images as needed and position them properly.

 **Save as:** *PRES-L3*

Memo 2

1. Format and key the memo at the right.
2. Use the Speller and proofread your copy; correct all keying and formatting errors.

 **Save as:** *MEMO24B2*

TO: Office Staff

FROM: Jennifer Green, General Manager

DATE: March 15, 200-

SUBJECT: NEW BOX OFFICE COORDINATOR

Rebecca Dunwoody has been hired to replace DeWayne Hughes as our box office coordinator. DeWayne has decided to return to school to start work on a Master of Business Administration degree. As you are aware, DeWayne has been a valuable asset to our organization for the past five years.

It was not easy finding a person with similar qualifications to replace DeWayne. His enthusiasm and love of music combined with a degree in music as well as a minor in business administration made the job particularly difficult. However, we believe we were successful when we were able to hire Ms. Dunwoody. She is a recent graduate of NYC's music program. While completing her degree, she worked as an assistant for the business manager of one of our competitors.

Please extend your appreciation and best wishes to DeWayne before he leaves on March 30 and welcome Rebecca when she arrives on March 25.

E-mail/Memo 3

1. Key the message at the right. If you are using e-mail software, send the message to your instructor. If you are using wp software, format it as an interoffice memo, using the headings provided.
2. Use the Speller and proofread your copy; correct all keying and formatting errors.

 **Save as:** *MEMO24B3*

TO: Mission Statement Committee

FROM: Jason R. Roberts, Chair

DATE: Current

SUBJECT: MISSION STATEMENT

As we develop our mission statement, we may want to review some of the mission statements of other symphonies. I have already looked at several on the Web. San Francisco's was one that I felt we could model ours after.

They have an overall mission statement followed by specific artistic, community, and organizational goals. I felt their community goals were particularly good, three of them being most appropriate for our organization:

1. Provide musical enrichment to the widest possible audiences.
2. Develop music education for a culturally diverse community.
3. Strengthen orchestra training for young musicians.

To view the complete mission statement, go to http://www.sfsymphony.org/info/mission.htm. I'll look forward to working with you at our next committee meeting.

Gather information about a play or concert you would like to attend. Send e-mail inviting a friend to go with you. Include all the necessary details. Several sites are listed below.

www.sfsymphony.org/
www.nytheatre.com/
www.theatreticket.com/
www.ticketmaster.com/
www.osscs.org/

INSERTING ART AND DRAWING OBJECTS

Objectives:

Approx. time: 50 min.

1. To understand how to use appropriate graphic images, lines, and boxes.
2. To insert, position, and size graphic images, lines, and boxes.
3. To create slides with graphic enhancements.

3A • Clip Art

1. Read the information at the right.
2. Learn how to insert clip art in a slide and how to size and position graphics.
3. Open *PRES-L2*. Insert an appropriate piece of clip art from your software collection in each of the slides you created in 2B. Size and position the clip art attractively.

Save as: *PRES-L3*

Art, or graphics, can enhance a message and help convey ideas. Graphic images might include clip art from your software collection or other sources such as the Internet. Graphic images could also include photo images or even original artwork scanned and converted to a digitized image.

Use graphics only when they are relevant to your topic and contribute to your presentation. Choose graphics that will not distract the audience. Clip art can often be used to add humor. Be creative, but use images in good taste. An image isn't necessary on every slide in a presentation.

3B • Drawing Tools

1. Read the information at the right.
2. Learn how to use the draw feature of your software.
3. Open the title slide of *PRES-L3*. Create a simple logo for Multimedia Design Services. Use a circle, box, or other shape and add a fill to it. Put clip art or text on or around the shape. Place your logo attractively.

Save as: *PRES-L3*

Electronic presentation software has drawing tools that you can use to create lines, arrows, boxes, borders, and other simple shapes. You can add text boxes, color, patterns, and clip art to many of these objects.

- Shapes like arrows or starbursts can focus an audience's attention on important points.
- Lines can be used to separate sections of a visual, to emphasize key words, or to connect elements.
- Boxes, too, can separate elements and provide a distinctive background for text.
- Decorative borders can call attention to the contents of a box.

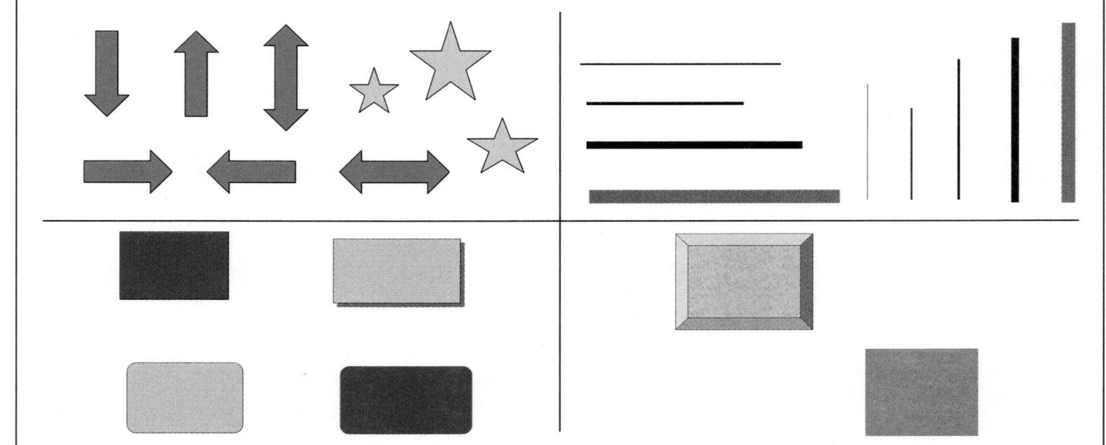

SKILL BUILDER 1

Keyboard Review

1. Key each line twice SS; DS between 2-line groups.
2. If time permits, rekey lines that were awkward or difficult for you.

A/Z 1 Zoe had a pizza at the plaza by the zoo on a lazy, hazy day.
B/Y 2 Abby may be too busy to buy me a book for my long boat trip.
C/X 3 Zeno caught six cod to fix lunch for his six excited scouts.
D/W 4 Wilda would like to own the wild doe she found in the woods.
E/V 5 Evan will give us the van to move the five very heavy boxes.
F/U 6 All four of us bought coats with faux fur collars and cuffs.
G/T 7 Eight guys tugged the big boat into deep water to get going.
H/S 8 Marsha wishes to show us how to make charts on the computer.
I/R 9 Ira will rise above his ire to rid the firm of this problem.
J/Q 10 Quen just quietly quit the squad after a major joint injury.
K/P 11 Kip packed a backpack and put it on an oak box on the porch.
L/O 12 Lola is to wear the royal blue skirt and a gold wool blouse.
M/N 13 Many of the men met in the main hall to see the new manager.
figures 14 I worked from 8:30 to 5 at 1964 Lake Blvd. from May 7 to 26.
fig/sym 15 I quote, "ISBN #0-651-24876-3 was assigned to them in 1995."

Timed Writings

1. Key two 1' writings on each ¶; determine *gwam* on each writing.
2. Key two 2' writings on ¶s 1–2 combined; determine *gwam* on each writing.
3. Key two 3' writings on ¶s 1–2 combined; determine *gwam* and circle errors on each writing.
4. If time permits, key 1' guided writings on each ¶. To set a goal, add 2 to the *gwam* achieved in Step 1.

Quarter-Minute Checkpoints				
gwam	1/4'	1/2'	3/4'	1'
24	6	12	18	24
28	7	14	21	28
32	8	16	24	32
36	9	18	27	36
40	10	20	30	40
44	11	22	33	44
48	12	24	36	48
52	13	26	39	52
56	14	28	42	56

  all letters used

	gwam 2'	3'
As you work for higher skill, remember that how well you	8	4
key fast is just as important as how fast you key. How well	12	8
you key at any speed depends in major ways upon the technique	18	12
or form you use. Bouncing hands and flying fingers lower the	24	16
speed, while quiet hands and low finger reaches increase speed.	31	20
Few of us ever reach what the experts believe is perfect	36	24
technique, but all of us should try to approach it. We must	42	28
realize that good form is the secret to higher speed with	48	32
fewer errors. We can then focus our practice on the improve-	54	36
ment of the features of good form that will bring success.	60	40

2' | 1 | 2 | 3 | 4 | 5 | 6
3' | 1 | 2 | 3 | 4

Bulleted List 1

Presentation Planning

- Consider audience needs carefully.
- Get organized.
- Know your subject well.
- Use visuals appropriate for available equipment and presentation location.
- Prepare materials.

Bulleted List 2

Message Development

- Think about key points.
- Use presentation outline view.
- Develop one idea per visual.
- Proofread and spell-check your presentation.

WORD PROCESSING 2

ACTIVITY 1

Margins

1. Read the copy at the right.
2. Learn how to set margins.
3. Set the left and right margins at 1.5". Key the first paragraph SS.
4. Change the left and right margins to 2". Key the second paragraph SS.

Save as: *WP2ACT1*

Use the **Margins** feature to change the amount of blank space at the top, bottom, right, and left edges of the paper.

The default margin settings are not the same for all software.

A person returning to the office environment after a 25-year absence would have a difficult time coping with the changes that have taken place during that time. Changing technology would best describe the challenges facing today's office worker.

Computers have replaced typewriters. Duplication methods have changed. Shorthand is an endangered skill with fewer and fewer office workers possessing it. And who had heard of the Internet 25 years ago?

ACTIVITY 2

Line Spacing

1. Read the copy at the right.
2. Use 1" right and left margins.
3. Learn how to change the line spacing for your wp software.

Use the **Line Spacing** feature of the software to change the amount of white space left between lines of text. The default setting for most wp software is single space. One-and-a-half spacing and double spacing are also common to most wp software.

4. Key the four lines (include numbers) below using the default line space setting. QS below the last line.
5. Change the line spacing to DS and key the four lines again.

Save as: *WP2ACT2*

1. Click the I-beam where you want the line spacing changed.
2. Select the option to change line spacing.
3. Specify the line spacing.
4. Begin or continue keying.

ACTIVITY 3

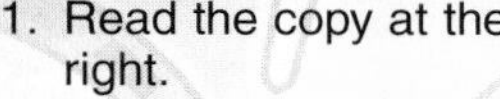

Widow/Orphan

1. Read the copy at the right.
2. Learn the Widow/Orphan feature for your software.
3. Open file *CD-WP2ACT3*. Notice that an orphan line appears at the top of p. 4.
4. Turn on the **Widow/ Orphan** feature at the beginning of that line. Notice how the feature reformats the text to prevent an orphan line.

Save as: *WP2ACT3*

The **Widow/Orphan** feature ensures that the first line of a paragraph does not appear by itself at the bottom of a page (**orphan line**) or that the last line of a paragraph does not appear by itself at the top of a page (**widow line**).

2

well organized, and easy to read.

Finally, support your report with a list of references from which you paraphrased or directly quoted. Quoting or paraphrasing without giving

Example of widow line

CREATING TEXT SLIDES

Objectives:
1. To create a title slide.
2. To create a bulleted list slide.

Approx. time: 50 min.

2A • Title Slide

1. Read the information at the right.
2. Start a new presentation. Select a similar design template or slide master from those available in your software.
3. Select the title slide layout, if necessary.
4. Create the title slide as shown.

 **Save as:** *PRES-L2*

Title slide. A presentation should begin with a title slide. Include the presentation title, presenter name, and other needed information. Titles should be approximately 40–48 points; subtitles, approximately 25–34 points.

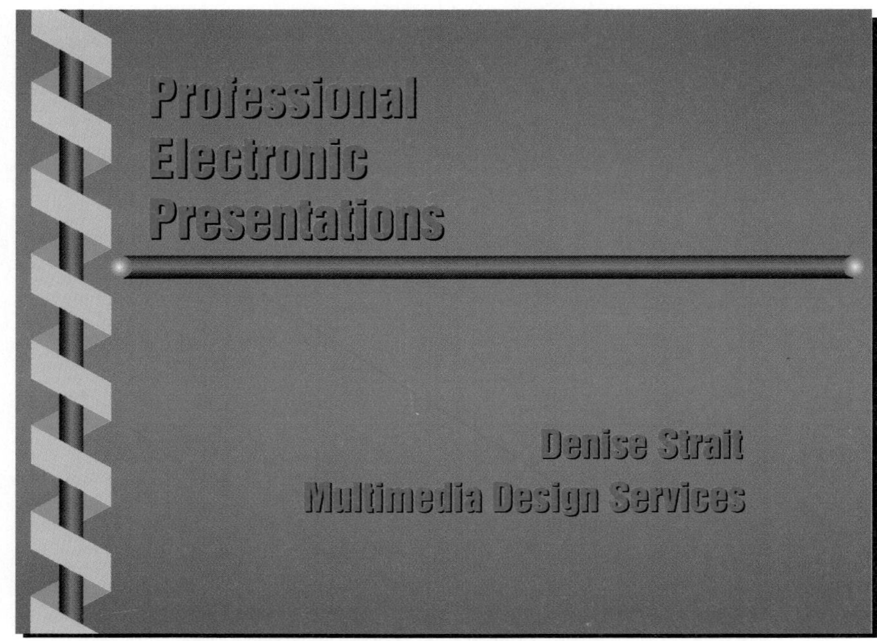

2B • Bulleted List Slides

1. Read the information at the right.
2. Learn how to change font sizes in your software.
3. Insert two slides with the bulleted list layout after the slide you created in 2A.
4. Create the slides as shown on p. 463. Reduce the font size if necessary.

 **Save as:** *PRES-L2*

Bulleted lists. Use lists to guide discussion and to help the audience follow a speaker's ideas. If too much information is placed on a single slide, the text becomes difficult to read. Therefore, keep the information on the slide brief—do not write complete sentences. Be concise.

To make your lists easier to read, use **parallel structure**—word items in the same way. For example, you might begin each bulleted item with a verb in the same tense (*Focus, Add, Limit, Use*).

Use the same case. For example, you might use title case for first-level items and an initial capital letter for the first word for second-level items.

When creating lists, be sure to

- Focus on one main idea.
- Add several supporting items.
- Limit the number of lines in one slide to six.
- Limit long wraparound lines of text.
- Set first-level topics in 30–34 points.
- Set second-level topics in 24–28 points.

ACTIVITY 4

Indentation

1. Read the information at the right.
2. Learn how to change indentations for your wp software.
3. Key the three paragraphs at the right, indenting them as indicated.

Save as: *WP2ACT4*

Use the **Indent** feature to move text away from the margin. A **left indent** (**paragraph indent**) moves the text one tab stop to the right, away from the left margin. A **hanging indent** moves all but the first line of a paragraph one tab stop to the right.

No indent

This example shows text that is not indented from the left margin. All lines begin at the left margin.

Left (paragraph) indent 0.5"

> This example shows text that is indented from the left margin. Notice that each line begins at the indentation point.

Hanging indent 0.5"

This example shows hanging indent. Notice that the first line
> begins at the left margin, but the remaining lines begin at the indentation point.

ACTIVITY 5

Page Numbers

1. Read the copy at the right.
2. Learn how to number pages (and hide page numbers) with your wp software.
3. Open the document created in Activity 3 (*WP2ACT3*).
4. Number all five pages with the page number at bottom center of the page. Hide the number on p. 1.
5. Use View to verify that the page numbers have been added (pp. 2–5) or hidden (p. 1).

Save as: *WP2ACT5*

Use the **Page Numbers** feature to place page numbers in specific locations on the printed page. Most software allows you to select the style of number or letter (Arabic numerals—1, 2, 3; lowercase Roman numerals—i, ii, iii; uppercase Roman numerals—I, II, III; uppercase letters—A, B, C; or lowercase letters—a, b, c). You can place numbers at the top or bottom of the page, aligned at the left margin, center, or right margin. Use the **Hide** or **Suppress** option to keep the page number from appearing on a page.

1 | 2 | 3

4 | 5 | 6

Page numbering positions

1E • Makeover Example

Example 1

1. Examine the slide at the right. Its design does not follow visual design guidelines for font treatments. It is not easy to read.
2. Key a list identifying what is wrong with this visual. Refer to the information on p. 459 and use your own judgment.

Poor Visual Example

PRESENTATION SOFTWARE FEATURES

ELECTRONIC PRESENTATION SOFTWARE HAS MANY SPECIAL FEATURES. WITH ITS DESIGN TEMPLATES AND SLIDE LAYOUTS, YOU CAN CREATE SLIDES QUICKLY AND EASILY. YOU CAN ADD ANIMATION TO SLIDES TO ATTRACT THE INTEREST OF THE AUDIENCE. YOU CAN INSERT CLIP ART FROM YOUR SOFTWARE COLLECTION. MOST SOFTWARE INCLUDES AN APPLICATION FOR CREATING CHARTS AND GRAPHS AND ONE FOR CREATING TABLES.

Example 2

1. Examine the slide at the right. Key a list identifying what makes this design more effective than Example 1. Refer to the information on p. 459 and use your own judgment.
2. How would you present the information that was omitted from Example 1? Key the answer to this question.
3. Create the slide using a similar font. Do not insert clip art.
4. Spell-check this and all slides, if your software does not do so automatically. Proofread your work.

Save as: *PRES-L1E2*

Good Visual Example

Presentation Software Features

- Design Templates and Slide Layouts
- Animation
- Graphics
  - Clip art
  - Charts and graphs
  - Tables

ACTIVITY 6

Apply What You Have Learned

1. Key the text at the right.
2. Center the heading in ALL CAPS 2" from the top; QS below title.
3. DS the first paragraph.
4. SS the second paragraph; indent it from the left margin, using the Paragraph Indent feature.
5. Center and key **REFERENCE** a QS below the second paragraph; QS below REFERENCE and key the reference.
6. Use the Hanging Indent feature to key the reference lines.
7. Use the Speller, then proofread.

 **Save as:** *WP2ACT6*

FAMOUS SPEECHES

Many famous speeches have been delivered over the years. The content of these speeches continues to be used to inspire, motivate, and unify us today. Winston Churchill and Abraham Lincoln delivered two great examples of such speeches.

Winston Churchill served his country as soldier, statesman, historian, and journalist. His military career and work as a reporter took him to India, Cuba, and the Sudan. He was elected to Parliament in 1900, again from 1906-1908, and from 1924-1945. He held dozens of other key posts, including that of Prime Minister. (LaRocco and Johnson, 1997, 49)

REFERENCE

LaRocco, Christine B., and Elaine B. Johnson. British & World Literature for Life and Work. Cincinnati: South-Western Publishing Co., 1997.

ACTIVITY 7

Apply What You Have Learned

1. Set the left and right margins at 2".
2. Center and key each name (bold) and quotation on a separate page, with a QS between the name and quote.
3. Place page numbers at bottom center on each page.

 **Save as:** *WP2ACT7*

Nathan Hale

"I only regret that I have but one life to lose for my country."

Golda Meir

"A leader who doesn't hesitate before he sends his nation into battle is not fit to be a leader."

Jacqueline Kennedy Onassis

"If you bungle raising your kids, I don't think whatever else you do well matters very much."

Oscar Wilde

"Life is too serious to be taken seriously."

ACTIVITY 8

Review Tabs

1. Set a left tab at 1", a right tab at 3.5", and a decimal tab at 4.5".
2. Using these tabs, key lines 2–6 at the right.
3. Clear tabs; reset: left tab, 0.75"; right tab, 3.75"; decimal tab, 5".
4. Key lines 2–6 again.

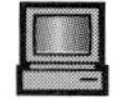 **Save as:** *WP2ACT8*

Player	**Hits**	**Average**
Walker, Colorado	166	.379
Gonzalez, Arizona	206	.336
Abreu, Philadelphia	183	.335
Casey, Cincinnati	197	.332
Cirillo, Milwaukee	198	.326

1C • Design Templates

1. Read the information at the right.
2. Learn to start a new presentation and insert new slides using your software.
3. Examine the various design templates available with your software.
4. Choose one that you like and start a new presentation with it.
5. Insert a new slide for each slide layout available.

 **Save as:** *PRES-L1C1*

Design templates (called **slide masters** or by other names in other software) make designing a presentation easy. They provide a background; preset fonts, sizes, and colors for text; and colors for lines, borders, etc. You select a design template when you create a presentation. You can change to another design template later if you like. You can also override the design template on individual slides.

Presentation software provides **layouts** for different kinds of slides, such as title slides, bulleted text slides, and slides with charts. These layouts are customized for the design template you have chosen.

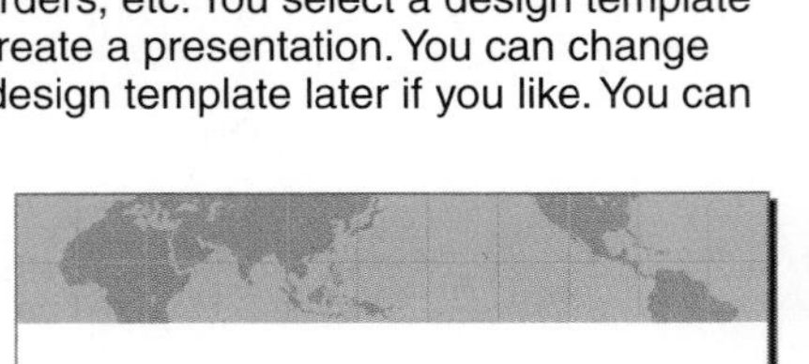

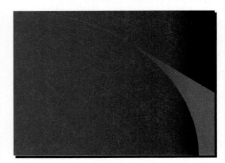

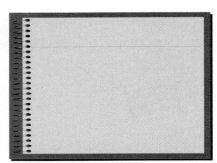

Different templates

1D • Views

1. Read the information at the right.
2. Learn to open a presentation and use the different views in your software.
3. Open *PRES-L1C1*. In outline view, key text of your choice in several slides.
4. In sorter view, change the slide order and delete a slide.
5. In slide show view, watch the slide show. Close without saving.

Like other software, presentation software provides different views, each of which is helpful for different tasks.

- The default **normal** or **slide editor** view lets you create slides individually.
- The **outline** view lets you enter and edit text for all slides at once.
- The **sorter** view shows all the slides in miniature, which is useful for rearranging slides.
- The **slide** show view is used to rehearse and present your slide show.

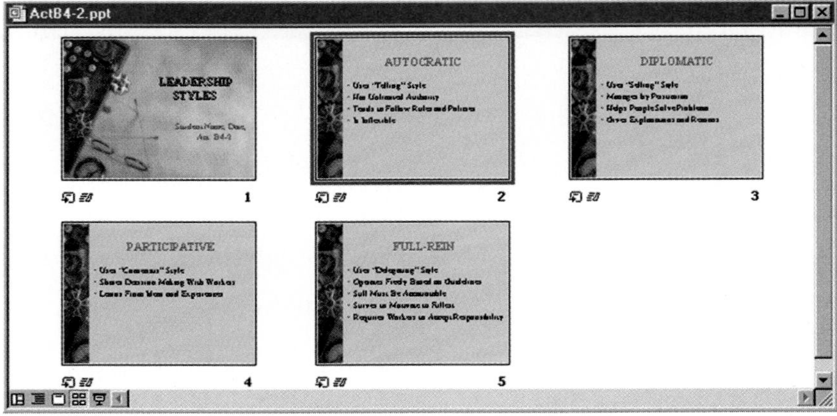

Sorter view

UNIT 8

LESSONS 25–27

Learn to Format Unbound Reports

Format Guides: Unbound Reports

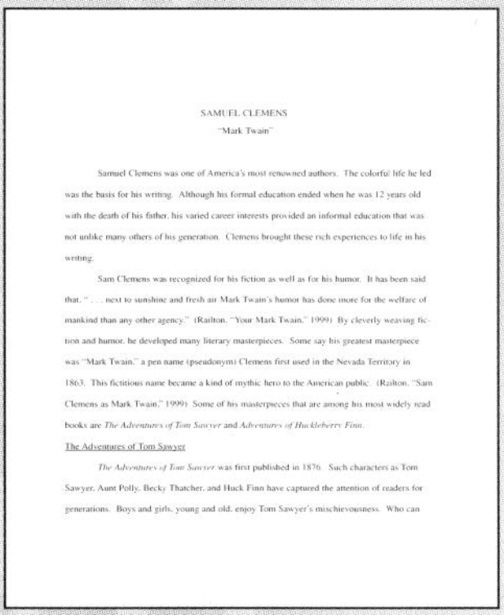

SAMUEL CLEMENS

"Mark Twain"

Samuel Clemens was one of America's most renowned authors. The colorful life he led was the basis for his writing. Although his formal education ended when he was 12 years old with the death of his father, his varied career interests provided an informal education that was not unlike many others of his generation. Clemens brought these rich experiences to life in his writing.

Sam Clemens was recognized for his fiction as well as for his humor. It has been said that, " . . . next to sunshine and fresh air Mark Twain's humor has done more for the welfare of mankind than any other agency." (Railton, "Your Mark Twain," 1999) By cleverly weaving fiction and humor, he developed many literary masterpieces. Some say his greatest masterpiece was "Mark Twain," a pen name (pseudonym) Clemens first used in the Nevada Territory in 1863. This fictitious name became a kind of mythic hero to the American public. (Railton, "Sam Clemens as Mark Twain," 1999) Some of his masterpieces that are among his most widely read books are *The Adventures of Tom Sawyer* and *Adventures of Huckleberry Finn*.

The Adventures of Tom Sawyer

The Adventures of Tom Sawyer was first published in 1876. Such characters as Tom Sawyer, Aunt Polly, Becky Thatcher, and Huck Finn have captured the attention of readers for generations. Boys and girls, young and old, enjoy Tom Sawyer's mischievousness. Who can

Page 1

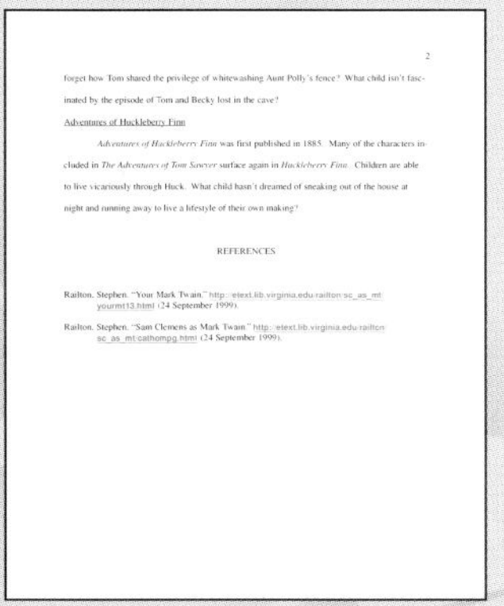

2

forget how Tom shared the privilege of whitewashing Aunt Polly's fence? What child isn't fascinated by the episode of Tom and Becky lost in the cave?

Adventures of Huckleberry Finn

Adventures of Huckleberry Finn was first published in 1885. Many of the characters included in *The Adventures of Tom Sawyer* surface again in *Huckleberry Finn*. Children are able to live vicariously through Huck. What child hasn't dreamed of sneaking out of the house at night and running away to live a lifestyle of their own making?

REFERENCES

Railton, Stephen. "Your Mark Twain." http://etext.lib.virginia.edu/railton/sc_as_mt/yourmt13.html (24 September 1999).

Railton, Stephen. "Sam Clemens as Mark Twain." http://etext.lib.virginia.edu/railton/sc_as_mt/cathompg.html (24 September 1999).

Page 2

Short reports are often prepared without covers or binders. If they consist of more than one page, the pages are usually fastened together in the upper-left corner by a staple or paper clip. Such reports are called **unbound** reports.

Standard Margins

The standard margins for unbound reports are presented below.

First page:	
Side margins:	1"
Top margin:	2"
Bottom margin:	about 1"
Page number:	optional; bottom at center if used
Second and subsequent pages:	
Side margins:	1"
Top margin:	1"
Bottom margin:	about 1"
Page number:	top; right-aligned

Internal Spacing

A QS is left between the report title and the first line of the body. Multiple-line titles are DS.

A DS is left above and below side headings and between paragraphs. Paragraphs may be SS or DS. *The reports you key in this unit will have DS paragraphs.*

Page Numbers

The first page of an unbound report may or may not include a page number. *The reports keyed for this unit will not include a page number on the first page.* On the second and subsequent pages, the page number should be right-aligned at the top of the page. Your software will automatically place the page number in the location you specify.

Textual (Within Text) Citations

References used to give credit for quoted or paraphrased material—called **textual citations**—are keyed in parentheses in the report body. Textual citations include the name(s) of the author(s), year of publication, and page number(s) of the reference material. **Note:** For electronic references (from the Internet), textual citations include the name(s) of the author(s) and the year of publication.

Quotations of up to three keyed lines are enclosed in quotation marks. Long quotations (four lines or more) are left indented (or left and right indented). Paraphrased material is not enclosed in quotation marks, nor is it indented.

An **ellipsis** (. . .) is used to indicate material omitted from a quotation. An ellipsis is three periods, each preceded and followed by a space. If the omitted material occurs at the end of a sentence, include the period or other punctuation before the ellipsis.

```
In ancient Greece, plays were
performed only a few times a
year. . . . The festivals were
held to honor Dionysus in the hope
that he would bless the Greeks. .
. . (Prince and Jackson, 1997, 35)
```

Reference List

All references used in a report are listed at the end under the heading REFERENCES (or BIBLIOGRAPHY or WORKS CITED). QS between the heading and the first reference. References are listed alphabetically by authors' last names. SS each reference; DS between references. Begin first line of each reference at left margin; indent other lines 0.5".

If the reference list appears on the last page of the report body, QS between the last line of text and REFERENCES. If the reference list appears on a separate page, use the same margins as for the first page of the report and include a page number.

1B • Electronic Presentation Software Features

Read and study the information at the right.

Getting Started with Presentation Software

When you start a new presentation, you will choose a **design template**. (This feature may be called a **slide master** or may have some other name, depending on your software.) A design template provides an overall design for a slide show, including a background for the slides and preset fonts, sizes, and colors for text.

For each slide that you create, you will select a **layout**. Presentation software provides layouts for title slides; bulleted text slides; slides with clip art, tables, or charts; and so on. These layouts are customized for the design template you have chosen. Together, design templates and layouts make slide setup quick and easy.

Like other software, presentation software provides several different **views** in which you can work, each of which is helpful for different tasks.

- The default **normal** or **slide editor** view lets you create slides individually.
- The **outline** view (sometimes combined with normal view) lets you enter and edit text for all slides at once.
- The **sorter** view shows all the slides in miniature, which is useful for rearranging slides and for applying features to several slides at a time.
- The **slide show** view is used to rehearse and present your slide show.

In your slide shows, strive for a consistent and uncluttered look. Each slide should have the same background. Each level of text should have the same font, size, case, and color throughout. For the most part, design templates and layouts take care of consistency for you. An attractive appearance is often the result of a simple design.

Design and Delivery of Presentations

Effective presentations require planning and preparation. In addition to creating the slides, the presenter must plan how the slides and his or her words will work together.

As you are planning a presentation, answer the following questions:

- Who is my audience?
- What does my audience already know about the topic?
- What does my audience need to know about the topic?
- What information do I need to gather for the presentation?
- What information should I include on the slides?
- What should I say in my presentation?
- What information should be both spoken and presented on a slide?
- What design features can I use to get and keep my audience's attention?

Design tips.

- Use more slides than you would for a transparency-based presentation and put less on each visual.
- Arrange lists to present concepts one at a time as discussion progresses.
- Use background colors on which text will stand out. Use light text against a dark background or dark text against a light background.
- Use all capital letters only in titles and for occasional emphasis.
- Use key words rather than complete sentences.
- Make sure that the text is large enough to be read from the back of the room.
- Use sound and animation to make a point. Be sure that they do not distract your audience.

Delivery tips.

- Practice your presentation using the slides.
- Show a slide just as you are ready to discuss its content.
- If you are using notes or an outline while speaking, mark the exact points in your presentation to change to the next slide.
- Maintain regular eye contact with the audience.
- Position the computer so that you can easily see it. Avoid turning your back to the audience to look at the screen.
- Do not read from your slides, but do refer to them occasionally.

2" TM

Title

EFFECTIVE COMMUNICATORS

QS

Report body

Communication is the thread that binds our society together. Effective communicators are able to use the thread (communication skills) to shape the future. To be an effective communicator, one must know how to put words together that communicate thoughts, ideas, and feelings. These thoughts, ideas, and feelings are then expressed in writing or delivered orally. Some individuals are immortalized because of their ability to put words together. A few examples of those who have been immortalized are Patrick Henry, Nathan Hale, and Abraham Lincoln.

DS

Side heading

Patrick Henry

DS

1" LM

1" RM

Words move people to action. Patrick Henry's words ("I know not what course others may take; but as for me, give me liberty or give me death!") helped bring about the Revolutionary War in 1775.

DS

Side heading

Nathan Hale

DS

Words show an individual's commitment. Who can question Nathan Hale's commitment when he said, "I only regret that I have but one life to lose for my country."

DS

Side heading

Abraham Lincoln

DS

Words can inspire. The Gettysburg Address (Abraham Lincoln, 1863) inspired the Union to carry on its cause. Today many Americans, still inspired by Lincoln's words, have memorized at least part of his address. "Four score and seven years ago, our fathers brought forth on this continent a new nation, . . . dedicated to the proposition that all men are created equal. . . ."

About 1"

Unbound Report, page 1

LESSONS 1–7

Creating Electronic Presentations

LESSON 1 DESCRIBING AND PLANNING ELECTRONIC PRESENTATIONS

Objectives:

1. To understand the purpose of electronic presentations.
2. To learn about electronic presentation features.
3. To learn basic electronic presentation terminology.
4. To apply presentation templates.

Approx. time: 50 min.

1A • Electronic Presentation Overview

Read and study the information at the right.

What Are Electronic Presentations?

Electronic presentations are computer-generated visual aids (usually slide shows) that you can use to accompany a speech or otherwise provide information to groups of people. Electronic presentations can combine text, graphics, audio, video, and animation to deliver and support key points. With the powerful features of presentation software such as *Microsoft PowerPoint* or *Corel Presentations*, you can create attractive and engaging presentations with ease.

Presentations are an important part of communication in business. Their purpose is to deliver facts or persuade an audience. In either case, the presenter has information to share and hopes the audience will react favorably to it. Typical business situations involving presentations include product introductions, awards, sales promotions, and training sessions.

With presentation software, you can create visuals (slides) that may be projected on a large screen or viewed directly on a computer. You can also produce Web pages, color or black-and-white overheads and paper printouts, audience handouts, and speaker notes.

Key Features of Presentation Software

Presentation software has many of the same features as word processing programs. It is also set up in much the same way as word processing software, with similar menus, commands, toolbars, and Help features. If you have experience with word processing software, you will find that presentation software is easy to use.

Here are some key features of presentation software. You will use many of these features in the following lessons.

- Design templates
- Word processing
- Drawing
- Charts and graphs
- Animation of text, graphic objects, and slide changes (transitions)
- Importing tables, spreadsheets, clip art, sound, and video
- Exporting slides, notes, and handouts to other programs and in other formats

LESSON 25 FORMAT UNBOUND REPORTS

Objectives:

1. To learn format features of unbound reports.
2. To process a one-page unbound report in proper format.

25A • 5' Conditioning Practice

Key each line twice SS; then key a 1' writing on line 3; determine *gwam.*

alphabet 1 Jack will help Mary fix the quaint old stove at the big zoo.

figures 2 Check Numbers 197, 267, 304, and 315 were cashed on June 28.

speed 3 Jan and Sydney may wish to make gowns for the civic socials.

gwam 1' | 1 | 2 | 3 | 4 | 5 | 6 | 7 | 8 | 9 | 10 | 11 | 12 |

FORMATTING

25B • 35' Unbound Report

Save as: *RPT25B*

1. Read the format guides on p. 70; study the model report on p. 71.
2. Key the model report using the spacing guides given on the model; run the Speller, proofread, and correct errors.
3. If time permits, key the report again at rough-draft speed to increase your input speed.

25C • 10' Report Formatting/ Editing

Open *TITLES15C*, which you created in Lesson 15. For each of the six stories, reformat the title, author, and first sentence in report format as shown at the right. Each entry should appear on a separate page.

Save as: *RPTS25C*

2" TM

(Title) THE SCOTTY WHO KNEW TOO MUCH

DS

(Author) by James Thurber

QS

(First sentence) Several summers ago there was a Scotty who went to the country for a visit.

Page number centered at the bottom of the page.

1

LESSON 26 FORMAT UNBOUND REPORT WITH TEXTUAL CITATIONS

Objectives:

1. To process a two-page unbound report in proper format.
2. To format textual citations in a report.
3. To process references.

26A • 5' Conditioning Practice

Key each line twice SS; then key a 1' writing on line 3; determine *gwam.*

alphabet 1 Jessica moved quickly to her left to win the next big prize.

figures 2 Mike used a comma in 3,209 and 4,146 but not in 769 and 805.

speed 3 The key is to name the right six goals and to work for them.

gwam 1' | 1 | 2 | 3 | 4 | 5 | 6 | 7 | 8 | 9 | 10 | 11 | 12 |

Activity 2 • Worksheet with Calculations

1. Create the worksheet at the right, and calculate hours worked by each employee.
2. Write an IF function for calculations in Column H so that all hours worked up to and including 40 are paid at the hourly rate in Cell D17.
3. Write an IF function for Column I to calculate overtime pay that is paid at 1.5 times the hourly rate in D17 for all hours worked over 40.
4. Calculate the average, minimum, and maximum pays and record them in D18–D20, respectively.
5. Use two decimal places for currency, and decide all other formatting features.

Save as: *SS2L12ACT2*

PAYROLL JOURNAL									
FOR WEEK ENDING JUNE 15, 200-									
Employee	Mon	Tue	Wed	Thu	Fri	Hours	Reg Pay	Ovtm Pay	Total
J Abel	8	8	8	8	10				
B Clark	8	8	8	8	10				
C Diaz	9	8	8	10	8				
E Efra	8	8	8	8	8				
F Grant	9	8	7	8	9				
J Jones	7	8	8	8	8				
H Means	9	9	9	9	9				
K Napes	7	8	8	8	10				
K Porto	6	8	8	8	8				
R Silski	8	8	8	8	8				
T Ulia	8	8	8	8	8				
Totals									
The hourly rate is			$10.25						
The average pay is									
The minimum pay is									
The maximum pay is									

Activity 3 • What If

Open *SS2L12ACT2* and answer this question: What are the payroll figures if the hourly rate is increased to $10.75?

Save as: *SS2L12ACT3*

Activity 4 • Letter with Linked Worksheet

1. Create, name, and save the worksheet at right. Format it as desired.
2. Copy the worksheet, with a link, into *CD-SS2L12ACT4* (a wp file) between the first two paragraphs.

Save wp file as: *SS2L12ACT4*

FRAMES BY yourframes.com				
Size	**Quantity**			
	1-6	**7-12**	**13-24**	**24+**
4" X 6"	$ 17.98	$ 16.18	$ 14.56	$ 13.11
5" X 7"	$ 19.98	$ 17.98	$ 16.18	$ 14.57
8" X 10"	$ 21.98	$ 19.78	$ 17.80	$ 16.02

Activity 5 • Update Letter with Link

1. Open your worksheet for *SS2L12ACT4,* and increase each amount by $2.00.
2. Open wp file *SS2L12ACT4,* which will update the letter with the new costs. Use today's date, and address the letter to:

Dr. Patricia Kurtz
1246 Warren Dr.
Denver, CO 80221-7463

3. Save the letter as *SS2L12ACT5.*

2" TM

Title

SAMUEL CLEMENS

DS

"Mark Twain"

QS

Report body

Samuel Clemens was one of America's most renowned authors. The colorful life he led was the basis for his writing. Although his formal education ended when he was 12 years old with the death of his father, his varied career interests provided an informal education that was not unlike many others of his generation. Clemens brought these rich experiences to life in his writing.

1" LM

1" RM

DS

Sam Clemens was recognized for his fiction as well as for his humor. It has been said that, " . . . next to sunshine and fresh air Mark Twain's humor has done more for the welfare of mankind than any other agency." (Railton, "Your Mark Twain," 1999) By cleverly weaving fiction and humor, he developed many literary masterpieces. Some say his greatest masterpiece was "Mark Twain," a pen name (pseudonym) Clemens first used in the Nevada Territory in 1863. This fictitious name became a kind of mythic hero to the American public. (Railton, "Sam Clemens as Mark Twain," 1999) Some of his masterpieces that are among his most widely read books are *The Adventures of Tom Sawyer* and *Adventures of Huckleberry Finn*.

Textual citation

Textual citation

DS

Side heading

The Adventures of Tom Sawyer

DS

The Adventures of Tom Sawyer was first published in 1876. Such characters as Tom Sawyer, Aunt Polly, Becky Thatcher, and Huck Finn have captured the attention of readers for generations. Boys and girls, young and old, enjoy Tom Sawyer's mischievousness. Who can

About 1"

Unbound Report with Textual Citations, page 1

(continued on next page)

3. Open *SS2L11ACT3* and revise the chart as directed in the activities at the right.

Save as:
SS2L11ACT5

1. Add **HOMESTEAD REDS** as a subtitle; change title and subtitle to a bright red 14-pt. font.
2. Change axis titles and legends to bright red.
3. Make victory columns bright red; losses, light green.
4. Change color of walls to light blue.
5. Change the chart to a bar chart, and place the chart on a chart sheet.
6. Print the chart sheet.

Activity 6 • Application

1. Create the worksheet at the right.
2. Create a 3-D column chart with a title and legend, and place it on a chart sheet.
3. Add **For Period Ending December 31, 200-** as a subtitle; make the bars two different shades of green and the background a light brown.
4. Decide other formatting features, and then print the chart sheet.

Save as:
SS2L11ACT6

THE AMERICAN EAGLE FUND		
INVESTMENT	MARKET VALUE	COST
Common stocks	$1,954,983	$1,321,964
Long-term bonds	$945,000	$1,004,351
Short-term bonds	$236,982	$212,956
Preferred stocks	$1,345,925	$1,232,007

LESSON 12 SPREADSHEET APPLICATIONS

Objective:
To apply what you have learned in this and the previous spreadsheet units.

Activity 1 • 3-D Chart for Web Page

1. Create the wp table at the right.

Save as:
SS2L12ACT1A

2. Copy the table into a blank worksheet; make necessary adjustments.

Save as:
SS2L12ACT1B

3. Follow the directions given at the right.

CORRESPONDENCE REPORT					
TYPE	**MON**	**TUE**	**WED**	**THU**	**FRI**
U.S. mail	10	12	8	10	7
E-mail	12	14	11	9	7
Fax	6	4	8	4	2

1. Create a line chart with 3-D effects, and display it as a chart sheet.
2. Make these changes to the chart:
   a. Add **January 5 to 9, 200-** as a subtitle.
   b. Change title and subtitle font to a 14-pt. blue font.
   c. Change axis titles and words in legend to a 12-pt. blue font.
3. Print the chart sheet.
4. Save the worksheet as the Web page *SS2L12ACT1C*.
5. View the worksheet and chart in the browser, and then print only the worksheet.

Page number — 2

forget how Tom shared the privilege of whitewashing Aunt Polly's fence? What child isn't fascinated by the episode of Tom and Becky lost in the cave?

DS

Side heading — Adventures of Huckleberry Finn

DS

1" LM — *Adventures of Huckleberry Finn* was first published in 1885. Many of the characters included in *The Adventures of Tom Sawyer* surface again in *Huckleberry Finn.* Children are able to live vicariously through Huck. What child hasn't dreamed of sneaking out of the house at night and running away to live a lifestyle of their own making? — 1" RM

QS

REFERENCES

QS

List of references

Railton, Stephen. "Your Mark Twain." http://etext.lib.virginia.edu/railton/sc_as_mt/yourmt13.html (24 September 1999).

DS

Railton, Stephen. "Sam Clemens as Mark Twain." http://etext.lib.virginia.edu/railton/sc_as_mt/cathompg.html (24 September 1999).

Unbound Report with Textual Citations, page 2

26B • 37' Unbound Report

Save as: *RPT26B*

1. Review the format guides on p. 70; study the model report on pp. 73–74.
2. Key the model report; follow the spacing guides. Run the Speller, proofread, and correct errors.
3. If time permits, key the report again at rough-draft speed.

LANGUAGE SKILLS

26C • 8' Language Skills: Word Choice

1. Study the spelling/definitions of the words at the right.
2. Key line 1, noting the proper choice of words.
3. Key lines 2–3, choosing the right words.
4. Check your work; correct lines with errors.

Save as: *CHOICE26C*

know (vb) to be aware of the truth of; to have understanding of

no (adv/adj/n) in no respect or degree; not so; indicates denial or refusal

your (adj) of or relating to you or yourself as possessor

you're (contr) you are

Learn 1 Did she **know** that there are **no** exceptions to the rule?
Apply 2 I just (know, no) that this is going to be a great year.
Apply 3 (Know, No), she didn't (know, no) that she was late.

Learn 1 When **you're** on campus, be sure to pick up **your** schedule.
Apply 2 (Your, You're) mother left (your, you're) keys on the table.
Apply 3 When (your, you're) out of the office, (your, you're) supervisor should be informed.

Activity 2 • Line Charts

1. Study the text and illustration at the right.
2. Learn to create a line chart.
3. Open *CD-SS2L11ACT2* and create an embedded line chart with a chart title, axis titles, gridlines, and a legend.

Save as:
SS2L11ACT2

SS software has several chart types in addition to the bar, column, and pie chart. In this activity, you will create a line chart. Line charts are similar to column charts except the columns are replaced by points joined by a line.

The illustration at the right shows a line chart with data series for three persons.

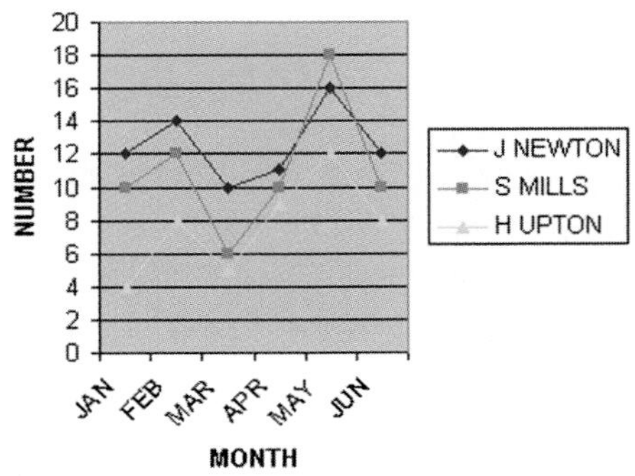

Activity 3 • 3-D Effects

1. Study the text and illustration at the right.
2. Learn to create charts with 3-D effects.
3. Open the file *CD-SS2L11ACT1B* and create an embedded 3-D column chart with a chart title and gridlines.

Save as:
SS2L11ACT3

Many ss charts can be created with 3-D effects. The illustration at the right is a column chart with 3-D effects. You can also select 3-D effects for pie, bar, and line charts.

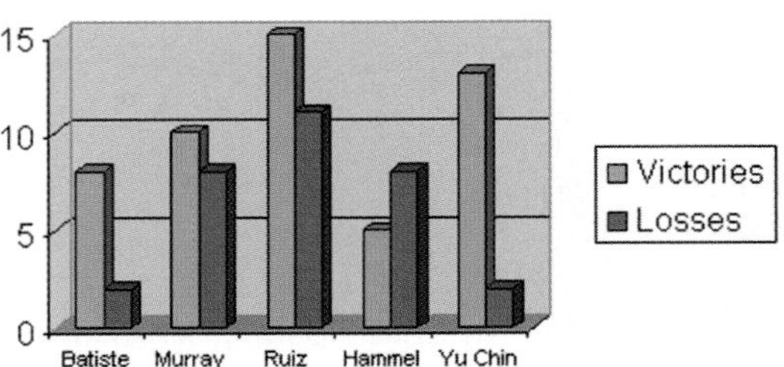

Activity 4 • Chart Sheet

1. Study the text and illustration at the right.
2. Learn to display a chart as a chart sheet.
3. Open the file *CD-SS2L11ACT1C,* create a pie chart with 3-D effects, and display the chart as a chart sheet.

Save as:
SS2L11ACT4

Charts can be created and displayed two ways—as an embedded chart or as a chart sheet. Charts created previously have been created and displayed as embedded charts. That is, the chart is placed within the worksheet so the chart and data can be viewed at the same time.

In this activity, charts will be created and placed on a chart sheet. The chart sheet is a separate sheet in the workbook. You can access the chart sheet by clicking the chart tab to the left of the worksheet tab near the bottom of the worksheet. Chart sheets are saved when the worksheet is saved. You can use the default name(s) assigned or give each chart sheet a specific name. Several charts can be prepared from a worksheet if chart sheets are used.

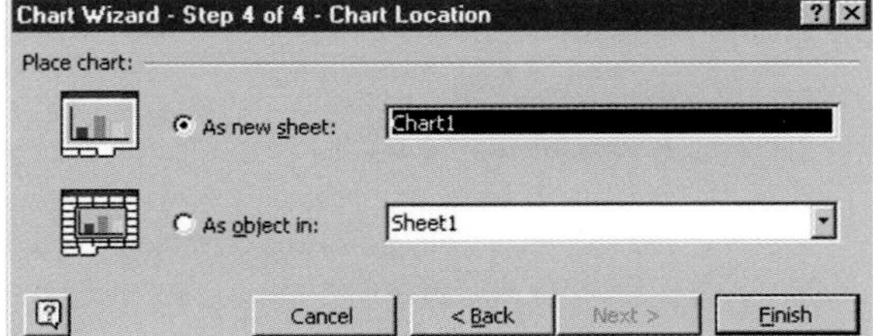

Activity 5 • Edit Charts

1. Study the text at the right.
2. Learn to edit charts.

(continued on next page)

Charts can be edited. For example, subtitles can be added, the font size and style can be changed, and the color of the bars, columns, lines, etc., can be changed. You can even switch from one type of chart to another without beginning again.

LESSON 27 FORMAT UNBOUND REPORT WITH REFERENCES

Objectives:

1. To process a two-page unbound report in proper format.
2. To process a references page.

27A • 5' Conditioning Practice

Key each line twice SS; then key a 1' writing on line 3; determine *gwam.*

alphabet 1 Jacob Lutz made the very quick trip to France six weeks ago.

figures 2 Only 1,359 of the 6,487 members were at the 2001 convention.

speed 3 They may turn down the lane by the shanty to their big lake.

gwam 1' | 1 | 2 | 3 | 4 | 5 | 6 | 7 | 8 | 9 | 10 | 11 | 12 |

FORMATTING

27B • 45' Unbound Reports

Report 1

Format the text at the right as a DS unbound report. Include the references given below on a separate page of the report. Correct errors as you key.

Save as: *RPT27B1*

REFERENCES

***Encyclopedia Americana*, Vol. 25. "Statue of Liberty." Danbury, CT: Grolier Incorporated, 1998.**

Luedtke, Luther S., ed. *Making America*. Chapel Hill: University of North Carolina Press, 1992.

Search the Web for additional information about immigration.

Be prepared to make a few comments to your classmates about what you found.

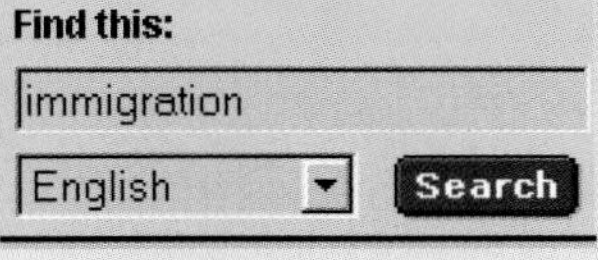

IMMIGRATION TO AMERICA

America has often been called the "melting pot." The name is derived from America's rich tradition of opening its doors to immigrants from all over the world. These immigrants came to the United States looking for something better. Most of them did not possess wealth or power in their home countries. Most were not highly educated. Other than these few commonalities of what they didn't possess, their backgrounds were vastly different. The thread, however, that bound these immigrants together was their vision of improving their current situation.

Emma Lazarus, in a poem entitled "The New Colossus," which is inscribed on the pedestal of the Statue of Liberty, tells of the invitation extended to those wanting to make America their home. ". . . Give me your tired, your poor, your huddled masses yearning to breathe free, ..." (*Encyclopedia Americana*, 1998, Vol. 25, 637)

<u>Immigration Before 1780</u>

Many have accepted the invitation to make America their home. Most of the immigrants before 1780 were from Europe.

The "melting pot" concept can be better understood by the following quote. "I could point out to you a family whose grandfather was an Englishman, whose wife was Dutch, whose son married a French woman, and whose four sons have wives of different nations." (Luedtke, 1992, 3)

<u>Recent Immigration</u>

Recent immigration patterns have changed; the reasons have not. Individuals and families still come to the United States with a vision of improving their lives. The backgrounds of today's immigrants expand beyond the European borders. Today they come from all over the world. At a 1984 oath-taking ceremony in Los Angeles, there were nearly a thousand individuals from the Philippines, 890 from Mexico, 704 from Vietnam, 110 from Lebanon, 126 from the United Kingdom, and 62 from Israel. Although not as large a number, there were also individuals from Lithuania, Zimbabwe, and Tanzania. (Luedtke, 1992, 3)

Activity 3 • View Worksheet on the Web

1. Study the text and illustrations at the right. The illustration on the left shows dialog box options for saving a worksheet in HTML format. The one on the right is the Open dialog box of Internet Explorer.
2. Learn to convert a worksheet to a Web page.
3. Follow the directions at the right.

Save as: *SS2L10ACT3B*

Worksheets can be saved as HTML (HyperText Markup Language) files to be viewed with a Web browser and then posted on the Internet, if desired.

In this activity you will: (1) open a worksheet; (2) use a browser to preview the worksheet; (3) revise the worksheet, if changes are needed; (4) save the worksheet as an HTML file; (5) view the worksheet in a browser; and (6) print it from the browser.

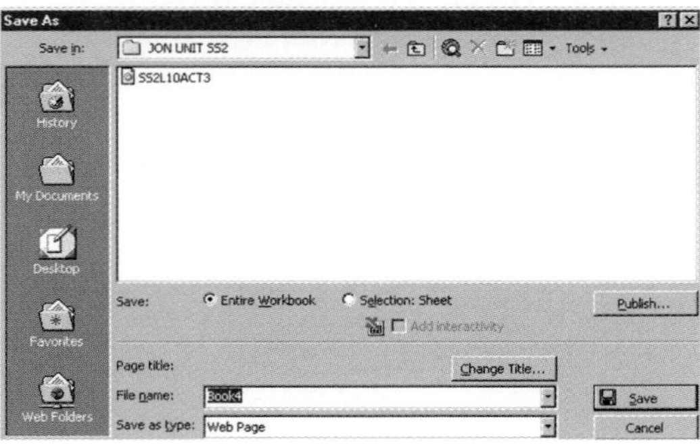

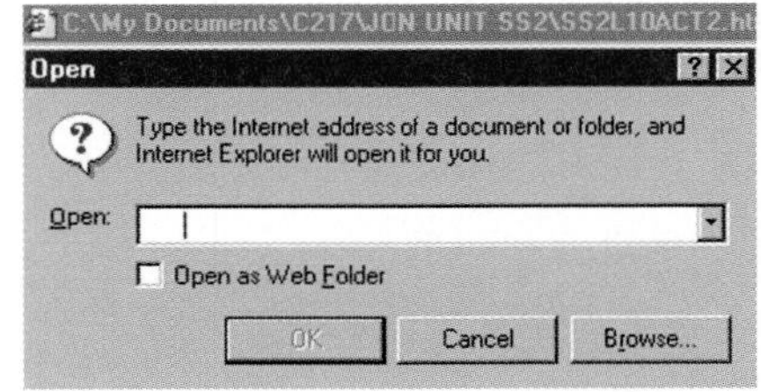

1. Open the worksheet *CD-SS2L9ACT5B,* and save it as *SS2L10ACT3A*.
2. Preview the worksheet in a browser to see if any revisions are needed to improve the worksheet's appearance as a Web page.
3. Close the browser, return to the worksheet, and make the changes, if any.
4. Save the worksheet as a Web page named *SS2L10ACT3B*.
5. Launch your browser and open *SS2L10ACT3B*.
6. From your browser, print *SS2L10ACT3B*.

Activity 4 • Application

1. Open *CD-SS2L9ACT2B*.

Save as: *SS2L10ACT4A*

2. Preview the worksheet as a Web page, and make any needed changes.
3. Save the worksheet as a Web page file named *SS2L10ACT4B*.
4. Launch a browser, open *SS2L10ACT4B* with the browser, view, and then print it from the browser.

LESSON 11 CHARTS

Objective:

To create a line chart and chart sheet, use 3-D effects, and edit charts.

Activity 1 • Charting Review

Create embedded charts as directed at the right.

1. Open *CD-SS2L11ACT1A* and create a bar chart with chart and axis titles and gridlines. Save as *SS2L11ACT1A*.
2. Open *CD-SS2L11ACT1B* and create a column chart with chart and axis titles, gridlines, and legend. Save as *SS2L11ACT1B*.
3. Open *CD-SS2L11ACT1C* and create a pie chart with chart title, legend, and data labels showing %. Save as *SS2L11ACT1C*.

Report 2
Process the play review shown at the right as a DS unbound report. Correct errors as you key.

 **Save as:** *RPT27B2*

PLAY REVIEW

by

Denise Jackson

Carousel, the Rodgers and Hammerstein classic musical, has been revived in a stunning new production at Omnibus University.

Students of Rodgers and Hammerstein's work will note the fresh approach from the opening curtain. Gone is the traditional park scene. In its stead is a cleverly staged "mill" workroom complete with a gigantic loom. The scene rapidly changes to an amusement park with a modern multicolored spinning carousel. Also new in this production are nonspecific ethnic casting, streamlined musical numbers, and updated dialogue.

Carousel is one of the genre's first to use a serious theme. The story recounts the life of Billy Bigelow, a "barker" for the carousel. Billy falls in love with Julie Jordan, a worker at the mill, shunning the advances of the aging carousel owner, Nellie Fowler. Billy then loses his job, marries Julie, and becomes a "worthless bum," in the opinion of Julie's friends. Julie's pregnancy, the turning point in the plot, forces Billy to evaluate his worthiness for parenthood.

Billy decides to turn to thievery rather than to work to get money to support his family. An ill-fated robbery attempt ends with Billy killing himself to avoid being arrested. The next scene finds Billy in heaven, repentant and determined to return to earth to undo some of the harm he has caused. Upon his surrealistic return, he awkwardly but effectively touches the lives of Julie and his daughter.

Critics have called this musical "out of date and out of touch" because of its treatment of women. Most notable is that Billy actually strikes his wife and his daughter. Their reaction to being hit is that "it's only his way of showing affection." In spite of this apparent flaw, Carousel has found new life in this newly staged, artfully performed production.

Activity 5 • Application

Follow the directions at the right.

Save ss file as:
SS2L9ACT5S

Save wp file as:
SS2L9ACT5

1. Open the wp file *CD-SS2L9ACT5A,* and save it as *SS2L9ACT5.*
2. Open the worksheet *CD-SS2L9ACT5B,* and save it as *SS2L9ACT5S.*
3. Delete values in the worksheet file *SS2L9ACT5S* for Last Year; move values for This Year to Last Year; and move the values for Next Year to This Year.
4. Key these new numbers for Next Year from left to right:

   6 $68,217 104 $47,248 15 $49,017
5. Save *SS2L9ACT5S* changes. Open, update, and save *SS2L9ACT5* changes.

LESSON 10 INTEGRATING WORKSHEETS WITH WORD PROCESSING AND THE INTERNET

Objectives:

1. To convert word processing documents to worksheets.
2. To use worksheets as Web pages.

Activity 1 • Convert Word Processing Document to Worksheet

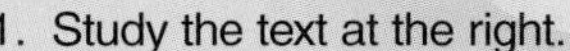

1. Study the text at the right.
2. Learn to convert a wp document to a worksheet.
3. Follow the directions at the right.

Save ss file as:
SS2L10ACT1

Data from a wp document can be converted to a worksheet, and then calculations can be performed on the data. If the wp document is a table or data separated by tabs, it will be copied to separate cells in the worksheet; otherwise, the information will be copied into the highlighted cell of the worksheet.

1. Open the wp document *CD-SS2L10ACT1,* and copy it into a blank worksheet.
2. Add a column at the right with **Total Hits** as the heading; add a row at the bottom with **Totals** as an indented row heading.
3. Perform the calculations in the added column and row.
4. Adjust font size, row height, and column width as needed to improve the appearance.

Activity 2 • Application

1. Create and save this wp table as *SS2L10ACT2A.* Copy the table into a blank worksheet.
2. Add **Bonus** and **Total** columns at the right of the worksheet.
3. Calculate bonuses: Bonuses are 25% of the sales if the sales are more than $1,900. If not, no bonus is earned.
4. Total each salesperson's pay for April.
5. Add an indented **Totals** row at the bottom, and calculate a total for each column.
6. Format the worksheet to make it attractive.

Save ss file as:
SS2L10ACT2B

APRIL PAY SCHEDULE			
Salesperson	**Sales**	**Commission**	**Salary**
Frederick Adams	$1,856	$464	$600
Janice Brown	$2,235	$558	$625
Carlos Cruz	$1,975	$493	$600
Enrico Duarte	$1,857	$464	$575
Lisa Ford	$1,785	$446	$600
Marian Mosley	$2,145	$536	$650
Jerry Roberts	$2,098	$524	$600
Leona Williams	$1,674	$418	$575

27C • Optional Timed Writings

1. Key a 1' writing on each ¶; determine *gwam* on each writing.
2. Key a 2' writing on ¶s 1–2 combined; determine *gwam*.
3. Key a 3' writing on ¶s 1–3 combined; determine *gwam*.

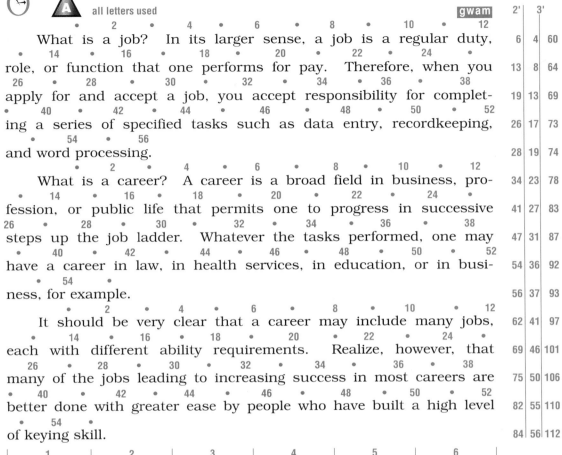

A all letters used

	gwam 2'	3'	
What is a job? In its larger sense, a job is a regular duty,	6	4	60
role, or function that one performs for pay. Therefore, when you	13	8	64
apply for and accept a job, you accept responsibility for complet-	19	13	69
ing a series of specified tasks such as data entry, recordkeeping,	26	17	73
and word processing.	28	19	74
What is a career? A career is a broad field in business, pro-	34	23	78
fession, or public life that permits one to progress in successive	41	27	83
steps up the job ladder. Whatever the tasks performed, one may	47	31	87
have a career in law, in health services, in education, or in busi-	54	36	92
ness, for example.	56	37	93
It should be very clear that a career may include many jobs,	62	41	97
each with different ability requirements. Realize, however, that	69	46	101
many of the jobs leading to increasing success in most careers are	75	50	106
better done with greater ease by people who have built a high level	82	55	110
of keying skill.	84	56	112

gwam 2' 3'

Word Processing Activity

LS: DS

Center the poem shown at the right vertically and horizontally on the page. QS below the author's name. Bold the title and italicize the body.

Source: Encyclopedia Americana, Vol. 25. Danbury, CT: Grolier Incorporated, 1998, p. 637.

THE NEW COLOSSUS

By Emma Lazarus

Not like the brazen giant of Greek fame,
With conquering limbs astride from land to land;
Here at our sea-washed, sunset gates shall stand
A mighty woman with a torch, whose flame
Is the imprisoned lightning, and her name
Mother of Exiles. From her beacon-hand
Glows world-wide welcome; her mild eyes command
The air-bridged harbor that twin cities frame.
"Keep ancient lands, your storied pomp!" cries she
With silent lips. "Give me your tired, your poor,
Your huddled masses yearning to breathe free,
The wretched refuse of your teeming shore.
Send these, the homeless, tempest-tost to me,
I lift my lamp beside the golden door!"

Activity 3 • Update a File

1. Study the text and illustration at the right.
2. Learn to update a link.
3. Follow the directions at the right.

After you make the following changes to the source file (*SS2L9ACT2S*), the destination file (*SS2L9ACT2*) will be updated when you open the latter since the manual update command has not been selected.

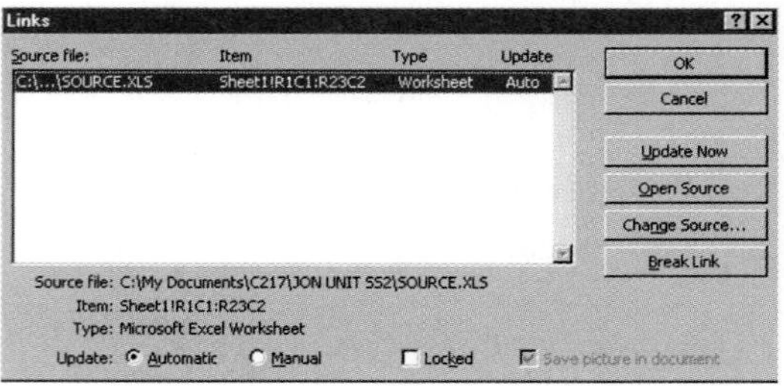

1. Open *SS2L9ACT2S* and change the numbers to those given below:

Increase in net assets	
Operations	
Net investment income	$ 415,676
Net realized gain	$ 3,297,811
Change in net unrealized appreciation (depreciation)	$ 2,877,590
Net increase in net assets resulting from operations	$ 6,591,077
Distributions to shareholders	
From net investment income	$ (399,456)
From net realized gain	$ (2,195,315)
Total distributions	$ (2,594,771)
Share transactions	
Net proceeds from sales of shares	$ 897,120
Reinvestment of distributions	$ 2,987,407
Cost of shares redeemed	$ 10,976,866
Net increase in net assets resulting from share transactions	$ 897,120
Total increase in net assets	$ 10,082,968
Net assets	
Beginning of period	$ 48,595,195
End of period	$ 58,678,163

2. Save the changes to *SS2L9ACT2S*.
3. Open wp file *SS2L9ACT2* and note that the numbers in the financial report have been updated automatically. Save as *SS2L9ACT3*.

Activity 4 • Application

1. Open wp file *CD-SS2L9ACT4* and save it as *SS2L9ACT4*.
2. Create the worksheet (*SS2L9ACT4S*) from the data given, and copy it into wp file *SS2L9ACT4* between the paragraphs.

Save wp file as: *SS2L9ACT4*

Business	Address	Points	Amount
Avenue Deli	309 Franklin Ave.	92	$15,000
Ford's News Stand	302 Franklin Ave.	88	$15,000
Hannon Shoes	415 Shefield Ave.	86	$10,000
Unger Appliances	525 Station St.	83	$10,000
Best Food Market	311 Franklin Ave.	76	$ 5,000
Avenue Restaurant	376 Franklin Ave.	76	$ 5,000

ACTIVITY 1

Pronoun Agreement

1. Key lines 1–10 at the right, using the correct pronouns.
2. Check the accuracy of your work with the instructor; correct any errors you made.
3. Note the rule number at the left of each sentence in which you made a pronoun agreement error.
4. Using the rules below the sentences, identify the rule(s) you need to review/practice.
5. **Read**: Study each rule.
6. **Learn**: Key the Learn line(s) beneath it, noting how the rule is applied.
7. **Apply**: Key the Apply line(s), choosing the correct pronouns.

 **Save as:** *CS4-ACT1*

Proofread & Correct

Rules		
1	1	Suzy knew that (he, she, they) should do her best at all times.
3	2	People who entered the contest say (he, she, they) are confident.
3	3	As soon as class is over, I like to transcribe (our, my) notes.
3	4	Mrs. Kelso gave (her, his, their) lecture in Royce Hall.
2	5	The yacht moved slowly around (her, his, its) anchor.
1	6	As you practice the drills, (his, your) skill increases.
1	7	I played my new clarinet in (my, their, your) last recital.
3	8	The editors planned quickly for (its, their) next luncheon.
4	9	The women's volleyball team won (its, their) tenth game today.
4	10	Our family will take (its, their) annual trip in August.

Pronoun Agreement

Rule 1: A personal pronoun (*I, we, you, he, she, it, their*, etc.) agrees in **person** (first, second, or third) with the noun or other pronoun it represents.

Learn 1 We can win the game if we all give each play our best effort. (1st person)
Learn 2 You may play softball only after you finish all your homework. (2nd person)
Learn 3 Andrea said that she will drive her car to the shopping mall. (3rd person)
Apply 4 Those who saw the exhibit said that (he, she, they) were impressed.
Apply 5 After you run for a few days, (my, your) muscles will be less sore.
Apply 6 Before I take the test, I want to review (our, my) class notes.

Rule 2: A personal pronoun agrees in **gender** (feminine, masculine, or neuter) with the noun or other pronoun it represents.

Learn 7 Miss Kimoto will give her talk after the announcements. (feminine)
Learn 8 The small boat lost its way in the dense fog. (neuter)
Apply 9 Each winner will get a corsage as she receives (her, its) award.
Apply 10 The ball circled the rim before (he, it) dropped through the hoop.

Rule 3: A personal pronoun agrees in **number** (singular or plural) with the noun or other pronoun it represents.

Learn 11 Celine drove her new car to Del Rio, Texas, last week. (singular)
Learn 12 The club officers made careful plans for their next meeting. (plural)
Apply 13 All workers must submit (his, their) vacation requests.
Apply 14 The sloop lost (its, their) headsail in the windstorm.

Rule 4: A personal pronoun that represents a collective noun (*team, committee, family*, etc.) may be singular or plural, depending on the meaning of the collective noun.

Learn 15 Our men's soccer team played its fifth game today. (acting as a unit)
Learn 16 The vice squad took their positions in the square. (acting individually)
Apply 17 The jury will render (its, their) verdict at 1:30 today.
Apply 18 The Finance Committee had presented (its, their) written reports.

LESSON 9

INTEGRATING WORKSHEETS AND WORD PROCESSING DOCUMENTS

Objective:

To learn to copy and link a worksheet to a word processing document.

Activity 1 • Copy a Worksheet into a Word Processing Document

1. Study the text at the right.
2. Open a wp document and learn how to copy/paste a worksheet into it.
3. Complete the directions at the right.

Save wp file as:
SS2L9ACT1

Note:
A file that is to become source copy for an activity will be saved with a filename that ends in "S." For example, the source file for this activity is named *SS2L9ACT1S*.

Frequently, text and numbers are copied from a worksheet into a wp document to avoid rekeying the information. When a worksheet is copied into a wp document, it appears as a table that can then be formatted as needed using the wp table formatting features.

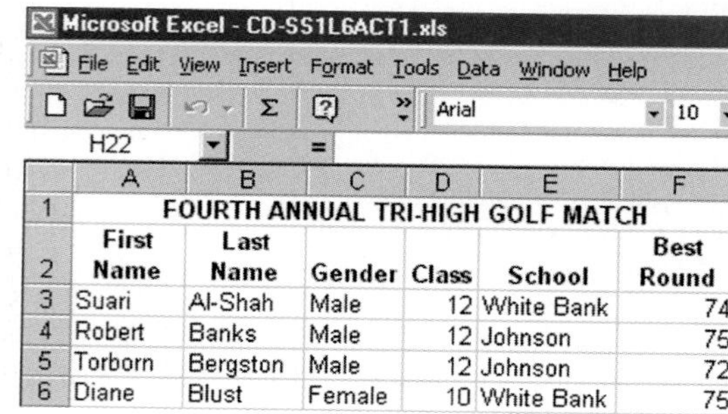

Microsoft Excel - CD-SS1L6ACT1.xls

	A	B	C	D	E	F
1	FOURTH ANNUAL TRI-HIGH GOLF MATCH					
2	First Name	Last Name	Gender	Class	School	Best Round
3	Suari	Al-Shah	Male	12	White Bank	74
4	Robert	Banks	Male	12	Johnson	75
5	Torborn	Bergston	Male	12	Johnson	72
6	Diane	Blust	Female	10	White Bank	75

1. Open the wp document *CD-SS2L9ACT1.*
2. Open the worksheet *CD-SS1L6ACT1* and save it as *SS2L9ACT1S.*
3. Copy the worksheet into the document, placing it about a DS below the last line of the memo body. Leave one blank line below the table, and then key your initials.
4. Format the table so it is centered between the left and right margins with gridlines. You decide other formatting features.

Activity 2 • Link Data

1. Study the text at the right.
2. Learn how to link data between a worksheet and a word processing document.
3. Complete the directions at the right.

Save wp file as:
SS2L9ACT2

Oftentimes, data in a worksheet that has been copied into a wp document is routinely updated. To eliminate the need to rekey the wp document and copy the worksheet each time the data is updated, a link between the wp document and the worksheet can be created.

With linking, data changed on the source file (worksheet) is automatically updated in the destination file (wp document). The **Paste Special** command is used to establish this link.

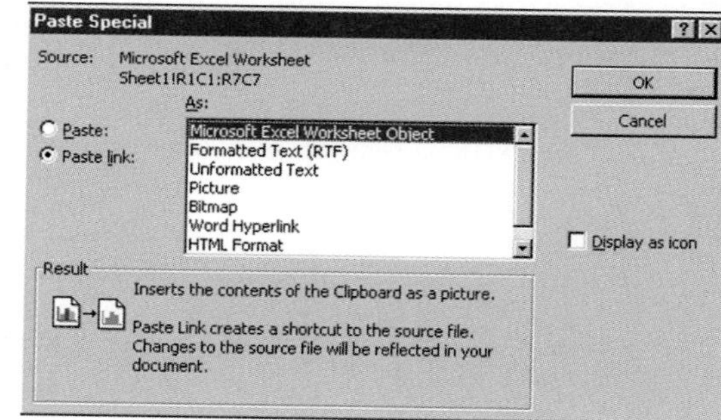

1. Open the wp document *CD-SS2L9ACT2A.*
2. Open the worksheet *CD-SS2L9ACT2B,* and save it as *SS2L9ACT2S.*
3. Use Paste Special to paste the worksheet into the document to link the worksheet and wp document.
4. Place the table a DS below the last line of the memo body. Leave one blank line below the table, and then key your initials.
5. Format the table so it is centered between the left and right margins with gridlines. You decide other formatting features.

ACTIVITY 2

Listening

1. Open the file *CD-CS4LISTN*. This sound file contains a weather forecast.
2. Listen to the forecast; then close the file.
3. Key answers to the questions at the right. Check the accuracy of your work.

Save as: *CS4-ACT2*

1. What were the high and low temperatures for today?
2. What are the predicted high and low temperatures for tomorrow?
3. Is it likely to rain tomorrow?
4. How many days are likely to have rain in the five-day forecast?
5. What is the highest temperature predicted in the five-day forecast?
6. What is the lowest temperature predicted in the five-day forecast?

ACTIVITY 3

Write to Learn

Complete the Write-to-Learn activity as directed at the right.

Save as: *CS4-ACT3*

1. Using word processing or speech recognition software, write a paragraph explaining how to bold and italicize a paragraph after it is keyed.
2. Write a second paragraph explaining how to set the left and right margins of a document in your word processing software.

ACTIVITY 4

Composing

1. Read the paragraph at the right. Was the student's action right or wrong (legally, ethically, or morally)?
2. Can stealing be justified for any reason? Compose a paragraph stating your views and giving your reasons.
3. Revise, proofread, and correct your paragraph.
4. Key the paragraph at the right as ¶ 1; key your corrected paragraph as ¶ 2.

Save as: *CS4-ACT4*

A student sees a designer jacket hanging over the door of a locker. No one seems to be around. The student tries it on; it looks great. He likes it and wants it. He reasons that if the owner can afford an expensive jacket, he can afford another one. So quickly the student puts it in his gym bag and walks away.

3. Complete the activities at the right.
4. Print the worksheet with gridlines and row and column headings.

 **Save as:** *SS2L8ACT3*

1. Key **25** in Cell A1 and **35** in Cell B1. In Cell C1, key an **IF function** that prints EQUAL if A1=B1 or UNEQUAL if A1 and B1 are unequal.
2. In Cell D1, key an **IF function** that prints HELP if the sum of A1+B1 is less than 75 and NO HELP if the sum is 75 or greater.
3. In Cell A3, key **679805**; in Cell B3, **354098**; in C3, **353507**. In Cell D3, key an **IF function** that prints EQUAL if A3-B3=C3 and UNEQUAL if A3-B3 does not equal C3.
4. In Cell A5, key **11**; key **22** in B5; **33** in C5; **44** in D5. In Cell E5, key an **IF function** that prints 1–149 if the sum of A5:D5 is less than 150 and 150+ if the sum of A5:D5 is greater than 150.

Activity 4 • Application

1. Create the worksheet at the right.
2. In Column F, calculate average score to nearest whole number.
3. In Column G, key an IF function that compares the scores in Column F to a score of 75. If the score is less than 75, print **TUTORING** in column G. If it is 75 or more, print nothing.
4. You decide all formatting features.

 **Save as:** *SS2L8ACT4*

GRADE BOOK						
NAME	TEST 1	TEST 2	TEST 3	TEST 4	AVG	NEEDS TUTORING
ABEL	78	85	72	78		
BOGGS	64	66	71	73		
CARR	78	82	86	75		
FRYZ	90	93	88	86		
GOOD	95	82	86	92		
MILLS	71	75	73	76		
POPE	62	71	73	66		
SIA	75	76	81	71		
TODD	66	65	50	61		
WILLS	75	64	75	70		
ZEON	81	74	65	60		

Activity 5 • Application

1. Key the following information into the cells designated.

	A	B
1	1400	1457
2	1548	1632
3	2496	2387
4	4513	4397
5	2835	2854

2. Complete the activities at the right.

1. In Cell A8, key an **IF function** to compare the sum of Column A to the sum of Column B. If A is larger, print the sum of A; if A is not larger, print the sum of B.
2. In Cells A6 and B6, use the **Sum function** to add A1:A5 and B1:B5, respectively, to verify the accuracy of the IF function.
3. Multiply each value in Column B by the value in Cell A1, and print the result in the adjacent cell in Column C.
4. Add the numbers in each row for Rows 1 through 6; divide each row's sum by B5; and print each result in the adjacent cell of Column D.
5. What are the values in A8 and D1:D6 if the value of B5 is increased to 2900?

 **Save as:** *SS2L8ACT5A*

6. What are the values in A8 and D1:D6 if the value of B5 is increased to 3000?

 **Save as:** *SS2L8ACT5B*

WORD PROCESSING 3

ACTIVITY 1

Select

1. Read the copy at the right.
2. Learn how to select text using your wp software.
3. Open file *CD-WP3ACT1*.
4. Select text and italicize, underline, and bold the copy as shown at the right.
5. Select and delete the semicolon and last six words of line 4.

Save as: *WP3ACT1*

Use the mouse and/or various key combinations to **select** (highlight) text, on which various operations may be performed.

Once selected, the text can be bolded, italicized, underlined, deleted, copied, moved, printed, saved, etc.

1. You will need to know how to **bold**, *italicize*, and <u>underline</u> for the exam.
2. Have you read *The Grapes of Wrath* by **John Steinbeck**?
3. <u>Rebecca Smith</u> is employed in the office of **Market & Johnson**.
4. Henry W. Longfellow wrote *Ballads*; Oliver Wendell Holmes wrote *Old Ironsides*.
5. Tanya misspelled *congratulations* and *italicized* on the quiz.

ACTIVITY 2

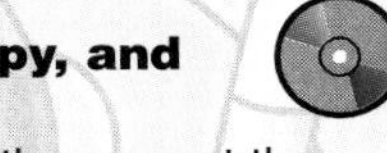

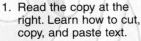

Cut, Copy, and Paste

1. Read the copy at the right. Learn how to cut, copy, and paste text.
2. Open file *CD-WP3ACT2*. Copy the text in this file; paste it a QS below the last line in the file.
3. In the second set of steps, use Cut and Paste to arrange the four steps in order.

Save as: *WP3ACT2*

After you have selected text, you can use the Cut, Copy and Paste features. The **Cut** feature removes selected text from the current location; the **Paste** feature places it at another location. The **Copy** feature copies the selected text so it can be placed in another location (paste), leaving the original text unchanged.

Step 1 Select text to be cut (moved).

Step 2 Click **Cut** to remove text from the current location.

Step 3 Move the insertion point to the desired location.

Step 4 Click **Paste** to place the cut text at the new location.

ACTIVITY 3

Center Page

1. Read the copy at the right. Learn how to center copy vertically.
2. Key the copy DS; center the copy horizontally and vertically.
3. Use the View feature to see how it will look on a printed page.

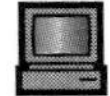

Save as: *WP3ACT3*

Use the **Center Page** feature to center lines of text between the top and bottom margins of the page. This feature leaves an equal (or nearly equal) amount of white space above and below the text. Inserting two hard returns below the last keyed line gives the document a better appearance.

Pot of Gold

by Dianna Vermillion

Together we chased after the rainbow

to find the pot of gold; but in each other,

we found our own treasure to unfold.

[Insert two hard returns]

ANSWERING "WHAT IF" QUESTIONS AND USING THE IF FUNCTION

Objective:
To answer "what if" questions and use the IF function.

Activity 1 • Prepare to Learn

1. Create the worksheet at the right.
2. Calculate next year's quota by multiplying Column B values by Cell A2.
3. You decide all formatting features.

Save as: *SS2L8ACT1*

DETERMINATION OF SALES QUOTA		
1.05	=Company Goal	
Salesperson	Quota This Year	Quota Next Year
Juan Avia	$250,000	
Mary Abelsen	$240,000	
Thomas Willit	$268,000	
Un Chin	$252,000	
Henry Quinez	$220,000	
Marty Merry	$172,000	

Activity 2 • "What If" Questions

1. Study the text at the right.
2. Using *SS2L8ACT1*, answer the "what if" questions at the right.
3. Print the worksheet after each question, unless directed to do otherwise.

Save as: *SS2L8ACT2*

An advantage of ss software is its ability to show the effects on all cells of a change in one cell. For example, in the worksheet in Activity 1, you determined next year's quota for each salesperson if the company were to make the new quota 1.05 (105%) of this year's quota. By changing the 1.05 in Cell A2 to other numbers representing other possible changes, the effect of the change on the quotas for all salespersons can be computed at once.

1. What if the goal is decreased to 95% of this year's quota?
2. What if the goal is increased to 105.5% of this year's quota?
3. Save the worksheet that answers the last "what if" question.

Activity 3 • IF Function

1. Study the text at the right.
2. Learn to write an IF function.

Learning C • U • E

Logical Operators
= (value of two cells are *equal*)
< (value of one cell is *less than* the other)
> (value of one cell is *greater than* the other)
<= (value of one cell is *less than* or *equal* to the other)
>= (value of one cell is *greater than* or *equal* to the other)
<> (values are *unequal*)

(continued on next page)

The IF function compares the contents of two cells. Conditions that contain logical operators (listed at the left) provide the basis for the comparison. For example, an instructor could use the following IF function (see Formula Bar below) to determine whether a student passed or failed a course:

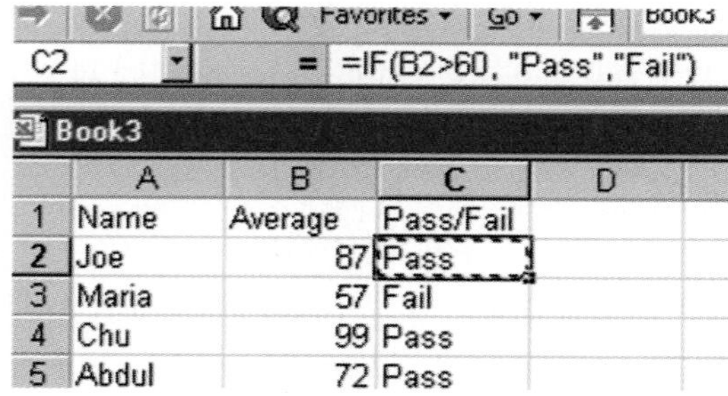

This IF function involves three arguments: The first is the comparison of the scores in Column B to the criteria (a score that is greater than [>] 60 in the example). The second argument is the text or value ("Pass" in the example) that is to be displayed if the comparison is true. The third is the text or value ("Fail") that is to be displayed if the comparison is false.

As illustrated, the arguments of the IF function are keyed inside parentheses and are separated from each other with commas. If text is to be displayed for argument 2 or 3, the text should be keyed inside quotation marks. Quotes are not keyed if values are to be displayed.

ACTIVITY 4

Envelopes

1. Read the copy at the right.
2. Learn how to prepare envelopes using your wp software.
3. Use the Envelopes feature to format a small envelope (No. 6 3/4) for Envelope 1 and a large envelope (No. 10) for Envelope 2.
4. Key the delivery address in ALL CAPS without punctuation, as shown.

 **Save as:** *WP3ACT4*

Use the **Envelopes** feature to format envelopes for the documents you create. This feature allows you to select the size of the envelope, enter the **sender's return address** and the **receiver's delivery (mailing) address**, and print the envelope. Some wp software contains an option for printing the delivery point bar code on the envelope.

Sender's return address:	Receiver's delivery (mailing) address:
Envelope 1 Robert Frederick 1520 Janewood Way Pittsburgh, PA 15220-7623	MS JUANITA LOPEZ 2113 KENMORE TER BROOKLYN NY 11226-9253
Envelope 2 Laura A. Jefferson 76 Livingston Ave. Fort Worth, TX 76110-0021	MR DENNIS BENTON 861 LEDBETTER PL S KENNEWICK WA 99337-6520

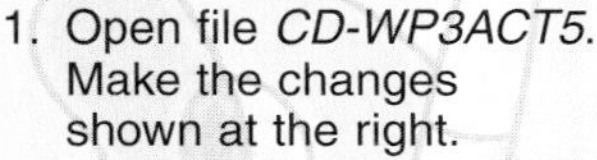

ACTIVITY 5

Apply What You Have Learned

1. Open file *CD-WP3ACT5*. Make the changes shown at the right.
2. At the end of each line, key (bold and italicize) the state nickname.
3. **Bold** the names of the states; *italicize* the state flower.
4. Use the Cut and Paste features to arrange the lines alphabetically by state.
5. Center the text vertically.

 **Save as:** *WP3ACT5*

Vermont, Montpelier - *Red Clover* - ***Green Mountain State***

New Jersey, Trenton - *Purple Violet* - ***Garden State***

Washington, Olympia - *Rhododendron* - ***Evergreen State***

Georgia, Atlanta - *Cherokee Rose* - ***Peach State***

Massachusetts, Boston - *Mayflower* - ***Bay State***

Iowa, Des Moines - *Wild Rose* - ***Hawkeye State***

New York, Albany - *Rose* - ***Empire State***

Missouri, Jefferson City - *Hawthorn* - ***Show Me State***

Texas, Austin - *Bluebonnet* - ***Lone Star State***

Hawaii, Honolulu - *Hibiscus* - ***Aloha State***

ACTIVITY 6

Apply What You Have Learned

Prepare a No. 10 envelope for each address at the right.

 **Save as:** *WP3ACT6-1* and *WP3ACT6-2*

Sender's return address:	Receiver's delivery (mailing) address:
Envelope 1 Roger J. Essex 564 Glencreek Ln. Cleveland, OH 44136-3625	MS LANESSA HOWARD 310 EISENHOWER ST CASPER WY 82604-0032
Envelope 2 Harold Baxter Autumn Forest Dr. Memphis, TN 38125-0013	MR KENT BOZEMAN 382 LOOKOUT MTN RAPID CITY SD 57702-5643

Activity 3 • Application

1. Create the worksheet at the right, supplying the total (TOT), average, and the minimum and maximum values where there is no shading.
2. Calculate the total revenue (REV) by multiplying Column I values by Cell A21.
3. Specify Column A width at 6, B–L at 5, and M at 9.
4. Make all rows .25" high.
5. Print centered on the page with gridlines.

 **Save as:** *SS2L7ACT3*

CANDY BAR SALES BY HOMEROOM												
ROOM	**MON**	**TUE**	**WED**	**THU**	**FRI**	**SAT**	**SUN**	**TOT**	**AVG**	**MIN**	**MAX**	**REV**
101	23	45	32	66	66	72	23					
103	45	65	82	45	45	56	33					
105	45	23	10	75	75	63	77					
107	34	23	15	34	56	45	23					
109	23	35	46	53	53	49	66					
111	22	33	55	88	88	46	23					
113	24	57	80	76	76	62	54					
115	23	56	80	55	55	65	29					
117	78	67	56	46	61	33	60					
119	35	65	73	59	92	47	59					
121	44	56	71	48	98	32	45					
123	35	58	56	59	84	15	38					
TOT												
AVG												
MIN												
MAX												
CANDY BAR PRICE												
$1.25												

Activity 4 • Application

1. Open *SS2L7ACT3* and add a nine-character column at the right with the heading **% of REV**.
2. Calculate each room's percentage of the total revenue and display it in the % of REV column. Format it as a percentage with two decimal places.
3. Shade the AVG, MIN, and MAX rows.
4. Print the worksheet.

 **Save as:** *SS2L7ACT4*

Activity 5 • Application

1. Create the worksheet at the right.
2. Use accounting rules (underlines) as shown.
3. Calculate the % of Net Revenues for each item (use two decimal places).
4. Print centered on the page without gridlines.

 **Save as:** *SS2L7ACT5*

Tip:

% of Net Revenue = *Value in Column B cells/value in Cell B5*

Jones Electric

	12/31/2002	% of Net Revenues
Revenues	$2,257,650	
Returns and Allowances	$ 1,568	
Net Revenues	$2,256,082	
Cost of Goods Sold		
Beginning Inventory	$ 125,612	
Purchases	$ 834,972	
Cost of Goods Available for Sale	$ 960,584	
Ending Inventory	$ 126,829	
Cost of Goods Sold	$ 833,755	
Gross Profit	$1,422,327	
Expenses	$1,165,750	
Net Profit	$ 256,577	

UNIT 9

LESSONS 28–30

Learn to Format Personal-Business Letters

Format Guides: Personal-Business Letter, Block Style

230 Glendale Ct.
Brooklyn, NY 11234-3721
February 15, 200-

Ms. Julie Hutchinson
1825 Melbourne Ave.
Flushing, NY 11367-2351

Dear Julie

It seems like years since we were in Ms. Gerhig's keyboarding class. Now I wish I would have paid more attention. As I indicated on the phone, I am applying for a position as box office co-ordinator for one of the theaters on Broadway. Of course, I know the importance of having my letter of application and resume formatted correctly, but I'm not sure that I remember how to do it.

Since you just completed your business education degree, I knew where to get the help I needed. Thanks for agreeing to look over my application documents; they are enclosed. Also, if you have any suggestions for changes to the content, please share those with me too. This job is so important to me; it's the one I really want.

Thanks again for agreeing to help. If I get the job, I'll take you out to one of New York's finest restaurants.

Sincerely

Rebecca Dunworthy

Enclosures

Personal-Business Letter

A letter written by an individual to deal with business of a personal nature is called a **personal-business letter**. Block format (shown at the left) is commonly used for formatting personal-business letters.

Letters arranged in block format have all parts of the letter beginning at the left margin. The paragraphs are not indented.

Letter Margins

Side margin: 1" (or default)
Top margin: 2"
Bottom margin: about 1"

Instead of a 2" top margin, letters may be centered vertically with the Center Page feature. Inserting two hard returns below the last keyed line places the letter in reading position.

Basic Parts of Personal-Business Letters

The basic parts of the personal-business letter are described below in order of placement.

Return address. The return address consists of a line for the street address and one for the city, state, and ZIP Code.

Date. Key the month, day, and year on the line below the city, state, and ZIP Code.

Letter address. Key the first line of the letter (delivery) address a QS below the date. A personal title (*Miss, Mr., Mrs., Ms.*) or professional title (*Dr., Lt., Senator*) is keyed before the receiver's name.

Salutation. Key the salutation (greeting) a DS below the letter address.

Body. Begin the letter body (message) a DS below the salutation. SS and block the paragraphs with a DS between them.

Complimentary close. Key the complimentary close (farewell) a DS below the last line of the body.

Name of the writer. Key the name of the writer (originator of the message) a QS below the complimentary close. The name may be preceded by a personal title (*Miss, Mrs., Ms.*) to indicate how a female prefers to be addressed in a response. If a male has a name that does not clearly indicate his gender (*Kim, Leslie, Pat,* for example), the title *Mr.* may precede his name.

Special Parts of Letters

In addition to the basic letter parts, letters may include the special letter parts described below.

Reference initials. If someone other than the originator of the letter keys it, key the keyboard operator's initials in lowercase letters at the left margin, a DS below the writer's name.

Attachment/Enclosure notation. If another document is attached to a letter, the word "Attachment" is keyed at the left margin, a DS below the reference initials. If the additional document is not attached, the word "Enclosure" is used. If reference initials are not used, "Attachment" or "Enclosure" is keyed a DS below the writer's name.

3. In Cell F3, key **=A$3+B$3+C3** and then copy to Cells F4:F7. Notice that the formula always added the numbers in Columns A and B, Row 3, to each value in Column C as the formula was copied to each row.
4. Copy Cell F3 to G3 and then copy G3 to G4:G7. In G3:G7, notice that the A changed to B and B changed to C in each cell reference in Column G since the A and B are relative references. The $3 remained the same in each row in Column G since it is an absolute reference. Since C3 is a relative reference, it changed to D3 when copied to G3, and then the number changed each time it was copied to a new row in Column G.

Activity 2 • Minimum and Maximum

1. Study the text at the right.
2. Learn the minimum, maximum, and average functions.
3. Create and then use the MIN, MAX, and/or AVERAGE functions to complete the worksheets at the right.
4. Print both worksheets with gridlines.

Save as: *SS2L7ACT2A* and *SS2L7ACT2B*

The minimum, maximum, and average functions are statistical functions often used with sets of numbers. The **maximum** (MAX) displays the largest number in the set. The **minimum** (MIN) displays the smallest number in the set. The **average** (AVERAGE) calculates the average (mean) number in the set. For example, if the function **=MAX(D1:D12)** were entered in Cell A1, A1 would display the largest number in the range D1:D12. If **=MIN(D1:D12)** were entered in Cell A1, A1 would display the smallest number in the range D1:D12. If **=AVERAGE(D1:D12)** were entered in Cell A1, A1 would display the average of the numbers in the range D1:D12.

SCORES						
PERSON	**A**	**B**	**C**	**D**	**MIN**	**MAX**
JIM	76	88	56	77		
LOIS	79	66	78	89		
JANE	96	99	94	76		
KATE	69	94	82	83		
ELIZA	88	83	75	98		
KIM	65	65	84	94		
PAUL	73	50	98	76		
QUINN	77	76	76	79		
JUAN	95	89	83	89		
ZEB	83	94	75	67		
MIN					XX	XX
MAX					XX	XX

SHOTS							
PLAYER	**GAME 1**	**GAME 2**	**GAME 3**	**GAME 4**	**MIN**	**MAX**	**AVG**
SARA	10	7	12	5			
JUNE	6	12	6	10			
NINA	3	4	8	6			
OPEL	8	4	6	8			
MIN					XX	XX	XX
MAX					XX	XX	XX
AVG					XX	XX	XX

Return address
230 Glendale Ct.
Brooklyn, NY 11234-3721

Date
February 15, 200-

QS

Letter address
Ms. Julie Hutchinson
1825 Melbourne Ave.
Flushing, NY 11367-2351

Salutation
Dear Julie

Body
It seems like years since we were in Ms. Gerhig's keyboarding class. Now I wish I would have paid more attention. As I indicated on the phone, I am applying for a position as box office co-ordinator for one of the theaters on Broadway. Of course, I know the importance of having my letter of application and resume formatted correctly, but I'm not sure that I remember how to do it.

DS

1" LM

Since you just completed your business education degree, I knew where to get the help I needed. Thanks for agreeing to look over my application documents; they are enclosed. Also, if you have any suggestions for changes to the content, please share those with me too. This job is so important to me; it's the one I really want.

1" RM

DS

Thanks again for agreeing to help. If I get the job, I'll take you out to one of New York's finest restaurants.

DS

Complimentary close
Sincerely

QS

Writer
Rebecca Dunworthy

DS

Enclosure notation
Enclosures

Shown in 12-point Times New Roman, with 2" top margin and 1" side margins, this letter appears smaller than actual size.

Personal-Business Letter in Block Format

LESSONS 7–12 (4–5 HOURS)

Spreadsheet Applications 2, Enhancing Spreadsheet Skills

LESSON 7 REFERENCING CELLS AND USING FUNCTIONS

Objectives:

1. To use relative, absolute, and mixed cell references.
2. To apply the minimum, maximum, and average functions.

Activity 1 • Cell References

1. Study the text at the right.
2. Learn to enter relative, absolute, and mixed cell references.
3. Create the seven-row worksheet at the right.
4. Complete the activities that follow.

Save as: *SS2L7ACT1*

You have learned that ss software copies a formula across a row or up or down a column. It also adjusts the formula copied into the new cells to reflect its new address and the address of other cells used in the formula.

When formulas are copied in this manner, the software is using **relative cell referencing**. That is, the copy of the cell is related to its new address. For example, if Cell D1 contains the formula =B1+C1, when this formula is copied to E2, it changes automatically to =C2+D2. Since E2 is down one row and one column over, the cells in the formula are also down one row and one column over from the cells in the original formula.

Sometimes you will not want to change a formula to reflect its new address when copying across a row or up or down a column. In these instances, you will use **absolute cell referencing**. Absolute cell referencing is used by keying a $ sign before the column and row reference in the cell address that is not to change. For example, if you want to divide all the numbers in Column B by a number that is in A1, you would make A1 an absolute cell address by keying a $ before the A and a $ before the 1 ($A$1).

A **mixed cell reference** is one that maintains a reference to a specific row or column but not to both. For example, D$1 is a mixed cell reference. The reference to Column D is relative, and the reference to Row 1 is absolute. When copied to another cell, the reference to Column D will change, but the reference to Row 1 will remain the same.

Cell reference	Example
Relative	=A1+B1+C1
Absolute	=$A$1+$B+$1+$C
Mixed	=$A1+B1+$C$1

	A	B	C	D	E	F	G
1				Cell Referencing			
2	Numbers			Relative	Absolute	Mixed	Mixed
3	1	2	3				
4	4	5	6				
5	7	8	9				
6	10	11	12				
7	13	14	15				

1. In Cell D3, key **=A3+B3+C3** and then copy to Cells D4:D7. Notice that the formula added the numbers in Columns A–C across each row since relative cell referencing was used.
2. In Cell E3, key **=$A$3+$B$3+$C$3** and then copy to Cells E4:E7. Notice that the formula added the numbers in Columns A, B, and C across the same row (Row 3) since absolute cell referencing was used for the row.

(continued on next page)

FORMAT PERSONAL-BUSINESS LETTERS

Objectives:

1. To learn to format personal-business letters in block format.
2. To improve word-choice skills.

28A • 5' Conditioning Practice

Key each line twice SS; then key a 1' writing on line 3; determine *gwam*.

alphabet 1 Before leaving them, Jessie quickly swam a dozen extra laps.
fig/sym 2 Kimberly ordered 37 1/2 yards of #804 linen at $6.59 a yard.
speed 3 Six firms may bid for an authentic map of an ancient island.

gwam 1' | 1 | 2 | 3 | 4 | 5 | 6 | 7 | 8 | 9 | 10 | 11 | 12 |

FORMATTING

28B • 37' Personal-Business Letters in Block Format

Letter 1

Study the format guides on p. 82 and the model letter on p. 83. Note the placement of letter parts and spacing between the parts.

Format/key Letter 1 (the model) on p. 83. Proofread and correct errors.

Save as: *LTR28B1*

Letter 2

Format/key Letter 2 shown at the right. Place letter parts properly and space correctly. Refer to the model on p. 83 as needed. Proofread and correct errors.

Save as: *LTR28B2*

words

2832 Primrose St. 4
Eugene, OR 97402-1716 8
November 20, 200- 12

Mr. Andrew Chaney 15
324 Brookside Ave. NW 20
Salem, OR 97304-9008 24

Dear Mr. Chaney 27

Thank you for taking time out of your busy schedule to speak to our **A**spiring **M**usicians **C**lub. It was great learning more about the "Masters" from you. 57

I particularly enjoyed learning more about the German composers. It is amazing that so many of the great musicians (Johann Sebastian Bach, Ludwig van Beethoven, Robert Schumann, Felix Mendelssohn, and Richard Wagner) are all from Germany. It is my goal to continue my study of music at the **Staatliche Hochschule fur Musik Rheinland** in Germany once I graduate from college. 133

Your insights into what it takes to make it as a professional musician were also enlightening for our members. Those of us who want to become professional musicians know we have to rededicate ourselves to that goal if we are going to be successful. 183

Thank you again for sharing your expertise with our club. 195

Sincerely 197

Stephen R. Knowles 200
AMC Member 202

Activity 1, cont.

2. Format the Social Security and telephone numbers.
3. Insert a column after the In column. Use **Round Score** as the column heading, and then calculate the total score for each golfer.
4. Specify column widths as follows: Columns A and B—9; C and G—12; D, E, H, I, J, and K—8; and F—16.
5. Wrap and center text in all headings.
6. Center-align all columns except A and B—left-align these two.
7. Make all row heights 24 pts. except Row 2—use the default for it.
8. Sort by Gender (ascending), then by Round Score (ascending), and then by Last Name (ascending).
9. Insert a page break so the females print on p. 1 and the males on p. 2.
10. Insert two blank rows at the top of p. 2, and then copy Rows 1 and 2 from p. 1 to these blank rows. Specify Row 2 height at 25.5.
11. Hide the Gender column.
12. Set up the pages so they will print horizontally and vertically centered in landscape orientation with gridlines showing. Include your name as a right-aligned header and today's date as a right-aligned footer.

 **Save as:** *SS1L6ACT1*

Activity 2 • Format Golf Match Information Sheet

1. Open *SS1L6ACT1* and merge cells in Row 1, Columns A–K, and Row 14, Columns A–K.
2. Unwrap the text in the column headings at the top of each page, and then rotate the text in the headings 75°.
3. Sort each page by School (ascending order), then Round Score (ascending), and then Last Name (ascending).
4. Add shading and color as desired.
5. Change font size as desired.
6. Make other formatting changes as desired.

 **Save as:** *SS1L6ACT2*

7. Print p. 1.

Activity 3 • Community Service Record

1. Create a worksheet, indenting and merging cells as shown at the right.
2. Calculate all totals using the most efficient method.
3. Within each team, sort by each person's total (descending) and then by name (ascending).
4. Rotate the months and Totals headings in Row 3.
5. You decide all other formatting features.
6. Center horizontally and vertically in portrait orientation and print the worksheet.

 **Save as:** *SS1L6ACT3*

7. Print cell range A1:K9.

COMMUNITY SERVICE										
TEAM	HOURS SERVED									
	SEP	OCT	NOV	DEC	JAN	FEB	MAR	APR	MAY	TOTALS
Givers										
Young	3	6	2	4	2	4	1	3	5	?
Yarry	2	4	4	3	6	3	5	4	1	?
Estrada	4	4	3	6	2	4	2	4	2	?
Johnson	1	3	5	4	4	3	6	2	2	?
Totals	?	?	?	?	?	?	?	?	?	?
Servers										
Chin	2	4	4	3	6	3	2	5	1	?
Poole	3	3	4	3	6	2	4	2	4	?
Everett	2	3	5	1	2	4	4	3	6	?
Morris	3	6	6	2	5	1	1	2	4	?
Totals	?	?	?	?	?	?	?	?	?	?
V'Teers										
Quinnones	3	3	4	4	4	3	6	1	4	?
Nester	1	2	5	2	3	5	5	2	4	?
Veres	2	4	4	3	5	2	2	4	4	?
Cox	5	2	3	5	5	2	4	3	3	?
Totals	?	?	?	?	?	?	?	?	?	?
Grand Totals	?	?	?	?	?	?	?	?	?	?

LANGUAGE SKILLS

28C • 8'
Language Skills: Word Choice

1. Study the spelling/definitions of the words at the right.
2. Key line 1, noting the proper choice of words.
3. Key lines 2–3, choosing the right words in each line.
4. Check your work; correct lines containing word-choice errors.

Save as: *CHOICE28C*

knew (vb) past tense of know; to have understood; to have recognized the truth or nature of

new (adj) novel; fresh; having existed for a short time; created in recent past

hear (vb) to gain knowledge of by the ear

here (adv) in or at this place; at this point; in this case; on this point

Learn 1 Katie **knew** she needed to buy a **new** computer for college.
Apply 2 Robert (knew, new) a (knew, new) car was out of the question.
Apply 3 All (knew, new) students (knew, new) the orientation schedule.

Learn 1 Did you **hear** the speech President Smith gave when he was **here**?
Apply 2 Liz said she couldn't (hear, here) the jazz singer from (hear, here).
Apply 3 (Hear, Here) is the address you wanted when you were (hear, here).

LESSON 29 FORMAT PERSONAL-BUSINESS LETTERS

Objectives:

1. To review format of personal-business letters in block style.
2. To learn to format/key envelopes.

29A • 5'
Conditioning Practice

Key each line twice SS; then key a 1' writing on line 3; determine *gwam.*

alphabet 1 Six boys quickly removed the juice from a sizzling stew pot.
fig/sym 2 The 2001 profit was $97,658 (up 34% from the previous year).
speed 3 Their neighbor may pay for half the land for the big chapel.

gwam 1' | 1 | 2 | 3 | 4 | 5 | 6 | 7 | 8 | 9 | 10 | 11 | 12 |

FORMATTING

29B • 35'
Personal-Business Letters in Block Format

Letter 1

Review the model personal-business letter on p. 83. Format and key in block style the letter shown at the right.

Save as: *LTR29B1*

Note:
Line endings for opening and closing lines are indicated by color verticals. Insert a hard return at these points.

words

610 Grand Ave. | Laramie, WY 82070-1423 | October 10, 200- | 11
Elegant Treasures | 388 Stonegate Dr. | Longview, TX 75601-0132 | 23
Dear Armani Dealer 27

Last week I noticed that you had Giuseppe Armani figurines in your 40
window. Do you have other figurines? 48

A friend gave me a pamphlet showing three Armani millennium 60
sculptures: **Stardust** (Years 1-999), **Silver Moon** (Years 1000-1999), 74
and **Comet** (Year 2000 and beyond). I want to buy all three sculptures. 88
Do you have them in stock, or could you order them? If not, could you 102
refer me to a nearby dealer? 108

I look forward to adding these exquisite pieces to my collection. 122

Sincerely | Cynthia A. Maustin 127

Activity 6 • Application

Open *SS1L2ACT5* (Lesson 2, Activity 5) and follow the directions at the right.

 **Save as:** *SS1L5ACT6*

1. Sort the information in the range of Cells A4:D9 by Percent Change in descending order.
2. Sort the information in the range of Cells E4:H9 by Percent Change in descending order.
3. Confirm that your name is a right-aligned header and today's date is a left-aligned footer.
4. Center and print the worksheet in landscape orientation.

LESSON 6 SPREADSHEET APPLICATIONS

Objective:

To apply previously learned formatting and formula skills.

Activity 1 • Golf Match Information Sheet

1. Open *CD-SS1L6ACT1.*
2. Complete the activities at the right and on the next page.

1. Key the information given below. Insert the Social Security numbers column after Column B; Telephone Number column after the Class column; and the Out and In columns after Best Round. Continue the steps on the next page.

Social Security	Telephone Number	Out	In
193397298	5355550166	37	36
145876653	5355550189	36	43
256879999	3425550167	37	37
235789099	5355550167	37	38
341842214	3425550199	37	39
536759902	3425550112	36	39
445713201	5355550133	38	35
234619872	3425550103	37	38
345628790	3425550166	38	38
543617864	5355550191	41	42
542759026	3425550143	38	39
453782149	5355550100	36	41
324789235	3425550133	38	36
456326823	5355550199	36	37
725438790	7215550179	37	36
185033002	7215550101	38	36
193547199	5355550165	38	37
248670029	3425550155	40	38
231453671	7215550144	43	41
345127908	3425550130	40	38
345209645	5355550109	40	37
348987086	5355550115	39	36

(continued on next page)

Letter 2
Format and key the text at the right as a personal-business letter in block format.

Save as: *LTR29B2*

	words
117 Whitman Ave. | Hartford, CT 06107-4518 | July 2, 200- | Ms.	12
Geneva Everett | 880 Honeysuckle Dr. | Athens, GA 30606-9231 |	23
Dear Geneva	25
Last week at the Educational Theatre Association National Convention	39
you mentioned that your teaching assignment for next year included	53
an Introduction to Shakespeare class. I find the Internet to be a very	67
useful supplement for creating interest in many of the classes I teach.	82
Here are four Internet locations dealing with Shakespeare that you	95
may find helpful for your new class.	103
http://www.shakespeares-globe.org/Default.htm	112
http://www.wfu.edu/~tedforrl/shakesp.htm	120
http://www.jetlink.net/~massij/shakes/	128
http://www.albemarle-london.com/map-globe.html	137
Another resource that I use is a booklet published by Thomson	150
Learning: *Introducing Shakespeare*. A copy of the title page is	163
attached. It includes scenes from some of Shakespeare's best-known	176
works. Scenes from my favorites (*Romeo and Juliet, A Midsummer*	189
Night's Dream, and *Julius Caesar*) are included.	199
As I come across other resources, I will forward them to you. Enjoy	213
the rest of the summer; another school year will be upon us before we	227
know it.	229
Sincerely | Marshall W. Cline | Attachment	236

FORMATTING

29C • 10' Envelopes

1. Study the guides at the right and the illustrations below. Specific keying details are provided for those choosing to format envelopes without the Envelopes feature because of printer issues.
2. Format a small (No. 6 3/4) envelope for Letter 1 in 29B and a large (No. 10) envelope for Letter 2 in 29B.

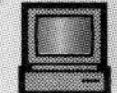

Save as: *ENV29C1* and *ENV29C2*

Sender's return address

Use block style, SS, and Initial Caps or ALL CAPS. If not using the Envelopes feature, begin as near to the top and left edge of the envelope as possible—TM and LM about 0.25".

Receiver's delivery address

Use USPS (postal service) style: block style, SS, ALL CAPS, no punctuation.

Place city name, two-letter state abbreviation, and ZIP Code +4 on last address line. One space precedes the ZIP Code.

If not using the Envelopes feature, tab over 2.5" for the small envelope and 4" for the large envelope. Insert hard returns to place the first line about 2" from the top.

Envelope 1

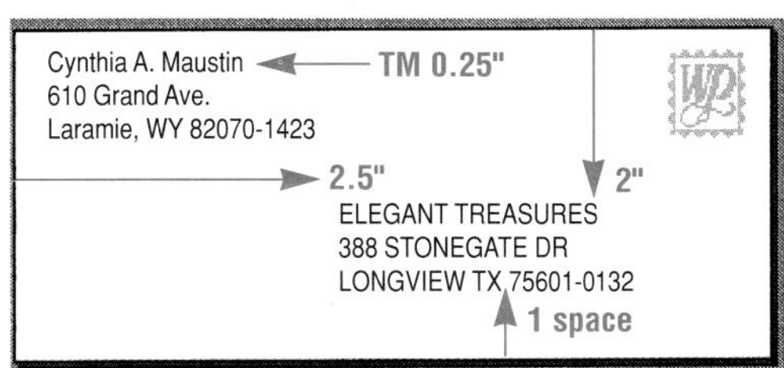

Envelope 2

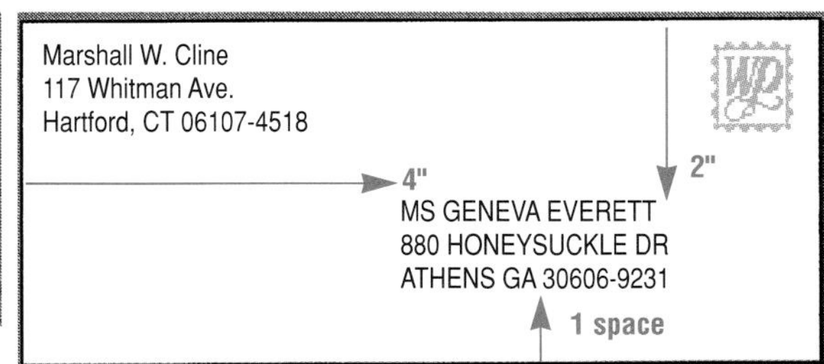

Activity 3 • Sort

1. Study the text and illustration at the right.
2. Learn to sort using your ss software.
3. Open *CD-SS1L5ACT2.*

 **Save as:** *SS1L5ACT3*

4. Complete the steps at the right.
5. Print gridlines and column and row headings in all activities.

Information in a worksheet can be sorted in much the same manner as information in tables was sorted with wp software. Sorting reorganizes data to place it in a more meaningful order. You can sort in ascending order (A–Z or lowest number to highest number) or descending order (the reverse of ascending). You can sort information in one column or two or three columns.

It is always a good idea to rename and save the worksheet before doing the sort, to retain the information in its original order.

1. Open *SS1L5ACT3* and sort by Date Received (earliest first). Print the first 12 rows that include data for 9/10.

 **Save as:** *SS1L5ACT3A*

2. Open *SS1L5ACT3* and sort the information by Last name, then First name, both in ascending alphabetical order. Freeze Row 1 and hide Columns E and G. Print Rows 35–54.

 **Save as:** *SS1L5ACT3B*

3. Open *SS1L5ACT3* and sort by Meal Choice (descending), then Last name (ascending), and then First name (ascending). Hide Column G. Print the last five C meal choices and the first five B meals.

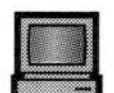 **Save as:** *SS1L5ACT3C*

4. Open *SS1L5ACT3* and sort the information by Ticket No. (descending), then Last and First names (ascending). Hide Columns F and G. Print p. 1 of the worksheet.

 **Save as:** *SS1L5ACT3D*

Activity 4 • Application

1. Open *CD-SS1L2ACT1.*
2. Follow the directions at the right.

 **Save as:** *SS1L5ACT4*

1. Hide Columns B–G.
2. Sort by Gross Pay in ascending order.
3. Key your name as a right-aligned header and today's date as a right-aligned footer.
4. Print the worksheet with gridlines and row and column headings, scaled to fit on one page with 2" side margins and centered vertically.

Activity 5 • Application

1. Open *SS1L1ACT4,* created in Lesson 1, Activity 4.

 **Save as:** *SS1L5ACT5A*

2. Follow the directions at the right.

1. Key this data into the worksheet:

   Morris Towers, 5-story office building, $4.56, $4.86

2. Hide Column C and sort by Present Value (ascending).

 **Save as:** *SS1L5ACT5A*

3. Print the worksheet.
4. Unhide Column C; hide Column D; and sort by Property Cost (descending), then by Property Name (ascending).

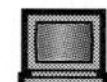 **Save as:** *SS1L5ACT5B*

5. Print the worksheet.
6. Unhide Column D; hide Column B; and sort by Property Name (ascending).

 **Save as:** *SS1L5ACT5C*

7. Print the worksheet.

LESSON 30 FORMAT PERSONAL-BUSINESS LETTERS

Objectives:

1. To format personal-business letters in block format.
2. To format/key envelopes.

30A • 5' Conditioning Practice

Key each line twice SS; then key a 1' writing on line 3; determine *gwam*.

alphabet 1 Jack next placed my winning bid for the prized antique vase.

fig/sym 2 I deposited Lund & Lutz's $937.46 check (#2408) on April 15.

speed 3 Jan is to go to the city hall to sign the land forms for us.

gwam 1' | 1 | 2 | 3 | 4 | 5 | 6 | 7 | 8 | 9 | 10 | 11 | 12 |

FORMATTING

30B • 45' Personal-Business Letters in Block Format

Letter 1

Format and key the letter at the right in block format; check spelling, proofread, and correct the letter before you save it.

Save as: *LTR30B1*

words

1245 Park Ave. 3
New York, NY 10128-2231 8
October 28, 200- 11

Mrs. Tara Cruz 14
4221 Beekman St. 18
New York, NY 10038-8326 22

Dear Mrs. Cruz 25

Mrs. Kenningston's fifth grade class will be attending a production of 40
the Broadway musical *The Lion King* on March 25 to conclude their 53
study of the theater. As you are probably aware, the play is based on 67
the 1994 Disney film about a young lion's coming-of-age struggles. 80

Attending the play will give the fifth graders a real sense of New York 95
theater. The production will be at the New Amsterdam Theatre, built 109
in 1903 and for years considered the most majestic on 42d Street. 122
With its recent renovation, it has been restored almost to its original 136
grandeur. The theatre is best known as the home of the Ziegfeld 149
Follies (1913 through 1927) and George M. Cohan's *Forty-Five Minutes* 163
from Broadway. 166

This will be a great experience for the fifth graders. Mrs. Kenningston 181
would like four parents to help chaperone on the day of the 193
production. Are you interested and willing to assist? I will call you 207
next week to determine your availability and discuss details. 220

Sincerely 222

Marsha Rhodes 224
Parent Volunteer 228

Activity 6 • Application

Create an answer sheet using the following directions.

1. Specify height of Rows 1–27 at 0.25" (18 pts).
2. Specify the following widths:
   Columns A and C: 4
   Columns B and D: 10
   Column E: 2
   Column F: 50
3. Merge Cells A1 to F1, and key **ANSWER SHEET**, centered in 16-pt. font.
4. Key **Item** in Cells A2 and C2 and **Answer** in Cells B2 and D2, centered.
5. In Cell F2, key **SHORT ANSWER RESPONSES**, centered.
6. Merge the following cells: F3 to F10; F11 to F18; F19 to F27; and E2 to E28.
7. Merge Cells A28 to D28 and key **Student Name**, centered horizontally and aligned at the top. Key **Subject and Period** in F28 with the same alignment.
8. Use Fill to enter numbers **1–25** in Column A Cells A3 to A27 and **26–50** in Column C Cells C3 to C27.
9. Center horizontally and top-align **ANSWER 1**, **ANSWER 2**, and **ANSWER 3** in the three large merged cell areas in Column F, with ANSWER 1 being in the first merged cell.
10. Center the worksheet on the page, and print with gridlines.

Save as: *SS1L4ACT6*

LESSON 5 SORT AND FREEZE AND HIDE COLUMNS AND ROWS

Objectives:

1. To sort worksheet information alphabetically and numerically.
2. To freeze and hide columns and rows.

Activity 1 • Freeze

1. Study the text at the right.
2. Learn how to freeze and unfreeze columns and rows.
3. Open *CD-SS1L5ACT1,* freeze Row 1, and then scroll through the worksheet. Notice that the column headings remain visible.
4. Unfreeze Row 1 and close the file.

Often an entire worksheet cannot be seen on the screen because as you scroll through the worksheet, the information in the column and row headings disappears from the screen. You can freeze the column and row headings so they remain visible as you scroll to other parts of the worksheet. In the illustration, Row 1 was frozen and Rows 2–49 disappeared from the screen as the user scrolled to Row 50.

Rows and columns can be unfrozen when the feature is no longer needed.

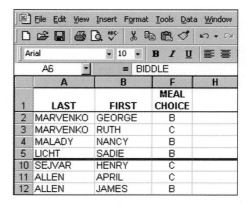

File Edit View Insert Format Tools Data Window Help

Arial 10 B I U

A2 = MARVENKO

	A	B	C	D	E
1	LAST	FIRST	TICKET NO.	DATE RECEIVED	CHECK NO.
50	LOPRESTI	ROSELLA	132	9/15	1442
51	HALL	DORIS	104	9/10	516
52	HALL	WILMA	103	9/10	516
53	DAVIS	LESLIE	116	9/10	1740
54	DAVIS	DAVID	115	9/10	1740
55					

Activity 2 • Hide

1. Study the text at the right.
2. Learn how to hide and unhide columns and rows.
3. Open *CD-SS1L5ACT2.* Hide Columns C, D, E, and G and Rows 8, 9, 10, and 11.
4. Print p. 1 of the worksheet.

Save as: *SS1L5ACT2*

Rows and columns can be temporarily hidden to enable you to view only those parts of a worksheet that you want to see.

Rows and columns can be unhidden when you need to see or print them.

The illustration shows that Columns C, D, E, and G and Rows 6–9 have been temporarily hidden from view.

File Edit View Insert Format Tools Data Window

Arial 10 B I U

A6 = BIDDLE

	A	B	F	H
1	LAST	FIRST	MEAL CHOICE	
2	MARVENKO	GEORGE	B	
3	MARVENKO	RUTH	C	
4	MALADY	NANCY	B	
5	LICHT	SADIE	B	
10	SEJVAR	HENRY	C	
11	ALLEN	APRIL	C	
12	ALLEN	JAMES	B	

Letter 2
Format and key the letter at the right in block format; proofread and correct the letter before you save it.

 **Save as:** *LTR30B2*

Letter 3
Format and key the letter at the right below in block format; proofread and correct the letter before you save it.

 **Save as:** *LTR30B3*

Word Processing **Activity**

Prepare letters for the other three parents who helped chaperone the field trip. Their addresses are shown below.

Mr. Charles Chan
389 Wadsworth Ave.
New York, NY 10040-0025

Ms. Alesha Ramirez
175 Morningside Ave.
New York, NY 10027-8735

Ms. Gwendolyn Maas
1615 Henry Hudson Pky.
New York, NY 10034-6721

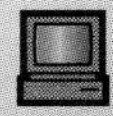 **Save as:**
LTR30B3CHAN
LTR30B3RAMI
LTR30B3MAAS

INTERNET  ACTIVITY

The Web address for Broadway theater information is shown at the right. Visit the site, select **Theatre Listings**, search for **New Amsterdam Theatre**, and find the information about educational discounts and wheelchair accessibility requested by Marsha Rhodes in Letter 2 (30B).

Compose a response to Ms. Rhodes as though you were the New Amsterdam's ticket manager. Prepare a No. 10 envelope.

 **Save as:** *LTR30OPTIONAL*

---

words

1245 Park Ave. | New York, NY 10128-2231 | January 5, 200- | 11
Ticket Manager | New Amsterdam Theatre | Broadway at Eighth Ave. 23
| New York, NY 10036 | Dear Ticket Manager 31

Mrs. Kenningston's fifth grade class from Washington Elementary 44
School will be studying theater during the month of March. To 56
conclude their study, Mrs. Kenningston would like for them to attend 70
a Broadway production of *The Lion King* on March 25. 81

Approximately twenty children would attend the performance along 94
with five chaperones. Does your theatre offer educational discounts 108
for the matinee performance? 114

One of our students needs wheelchair accessibility. What facilities do 128
you have to accommodate this student? 136

The students are very excited about the possibility of attending a live 150
Broadway production. Please provide me with the requested information 164
as soon as possible so that the necessary arrangements can be made. 178

Sincerely | Marsha Rhodes | Parent Volunteer 186

---

words

1245 Park Ave. | New York, NY 10128-2231 | April 1, 200- | Mrs. 12
Tara Cruz | 4221 Beekman St. | New York, NY 10038-8326 | Dear 23
Mrs. Cruz 25

Thank you for helping chaperone the fifth grade class on their field trip 40
to Broadway. When I visited Mrs. Kenningston's classroom yesterday, 53
the children were still excited about having attended the play. Their 68
thank-you note is enclosed. 73

Because of parents like you, educational experiences outside the 86
classroom are possible. These experiences bring to life what the 100
students learn in school. I'm glad our children have this enrichment. 114

Thank you again for accepting the challenge of watching over the fifth 128
graders on their exciting trip to Broadway. I know the task wasn't 142
easy, but I felt it was well worth our time. 151

Sincerely | Marsha Rhodes | Parent Volunteer | Enclosure 161

Web address:
http://www.theatre.com/

Return address (letter):
Broadway at Eighth Ave.
New York, NY 10036

Return address (envelope):
[Your name], Ticket Manager
New Amsterdam Theatre
Broadway at Eighth Ave.
New York, NY 10036

Letter (Delivery) address:
MS MARSHA RHODES
1245 PARK AVE
NEW YORK NY 10128-2231

Activity 3 • Change Row Height

1. Study the text and illustration at the right.
2. Learn to change row height.
3. Complete the steps at the right.

 **Save as:** *SS1L4ACT3*

You can specify the height of rows just as you can specify the width of columns. The height of rows is specified in points (72 points equal 1 inch). You can make the heights larger or smaller than the default setting. The illustration at the right shows rows of varying heights.

12.75 points (the default)
36 points (1/2")
10 points
24 points

1. Specify Row 1 to be 18 points, and key your name in Cell A1.
2. Specify Row 2 to be 36 points, and key your course name in A2.
3. Specify Row 3 to be 54 points, and key your school name in A3.
4. Specify Row 4 to be 72 points, and key today's date in A4.
5. Use AutoFit to adjust the column width to fit the longest entry.
6. Print the worksheet (centered with gridlines). Check the row height—Row 1 = .25"; Row 2 = .5"; Row 3 = .75"; Row 4 = 1".

Activity 4 • Format Numbers

1. Study the text at the right.
2. Learn how to format fractions, dates, times, and Social Security and telephone numbers.
3. Key the worksheet as shown at the right.
4. Format Column A as fractions with up to three digits; B as dates in 00/00/0000 format; C as Social Security numbers; D as phone numbers; and E as military times.
5. Print the worksheet.

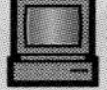 **Save as:** *SS1L4ACT4*

Numbers have been formatted several ways (Currency, Number, Accounting, and Percent) in worksheets you prepared. There are additional options you can select to format numbers. In this activity you will format numbers as fractions, dates, Social Security numbers, telephone numbers, and times.

FORMATTING NUMBERS				
Fractions	**Dates**	**Social Security Numbers**	**Telephone Numbers**	**Times**
0.02	March 3, 2000	256402312	4155550114	11:55 PM
0.2	07/04/1976	192938149	4155550151	1:35 PM
2	31-May-02	238797155	5675550177	1:45 AM
2.2	15-May-99	654893121	5645550121	10:43 AM
0.7456	4/30/76	123009985	8885550110	7:35 PM
3.4937	June 5, 2000	354719930	7175550156	12:15 AM

Activity 5 • Application

1. Create a worksheet with employee data rows 0.5" high.
2. Format dates as Month 00, 0000 and fractions to 1/2.
3. Rotate text in column headings at least 70°.
4. You decide all other formatting features.
5. Print with gridlines.

 **Save as:** *SS1L4ACT5*

Employee	Payroll Number	Social Security	Date Hired	Telephone Number	Personal Days Taken	Vacation Days Taken
Kim Chu	127	256309177	03/23/1997	4135550168	0.5	8
Connor Nesti	128	193408011	12/01/1998	4135550178	1.5	8.5
Helen Jenkins	129	146782351	08/24/1999	7235550199	2	5.5
Kyle Lopes	130	245097543	10/30/1999	7235550161	2	6
Jim Abbott	131	345671976	05/05/2000	7235550144	0	7.5
Larry Kite	132	243660091	09/17/2000	4135550154	0.5	10
Derek Momper	133	675750001	11/23/2001	2485550177	2.5	3.5
Maria Benitiz	134	875239899	07/23/2002	7235550111	1.5	6.5

SKILL BUILDER 2

Speed Building

1. Key each line once SS; DS between 2-line groups.

Goal: No pauses between letters and words.

2. Key a 1' writing on each of lines 4, 6, 8, and 10; determine *gwam* on each.
3. If time permits, rekey the three slowest lines.

space bar
1 city then they form than body them busy sign firm duty turn proxy
2 Jan may do key work for the six men on the audit of the big firm.

shift keys
3 Lake Como | Hawaii or Alaska | Madrid and Bogota | Sparks & Mason, Inc.
4 Karl left for Bora Bora in May; Nan goes to Lake Worth in August.

adjacent keys
5 same wire open tire sure ruin said trim went fire spot lids walks
6 We opened a shop by the stadium to offer the best sporting goods.

long direct reaches
7 vice much many nice once myth lace cents under check juice center
8 Eunice brought a recorder to the music hall to record my recital.

word response
9 their right field world forms visit title chair spent towns usual
10 They wish to go with the girl to the city to make the visual aid.

gwam 1' | 1 | 2 | 3 | 4 | 5 | 6 | 7 | 8 | 9 | 10 | 11 | 12 | 13 |

Timed Writings

1. Key a 1' writing on each ¶; determine *gwam* on each one.
2. Key two 2' writings on ¶s 1–2 combined; determine *gwam* on each writing.
3. Key two 3' writing on ¶s 1–3 combined; determine *gwam* and count errors on each writing.
4. If time permits, key two 1' guided writings on each ¶; one for control and one for speed (add 4 to your rate in Step 1). Set quarter-minute goals using the chart below.

Quarter-Minute Checkpoints

gwam	1/4'	1/2'	3/4'	1'
24	6	12	18	24
28	7	14	21	28
32	8	16	24	32
36	9	18	27	36
40	10	20	30	40
44	11	22	33	44
48	12	24	36	48
52	13	26	39	52
56	14	28	42	56

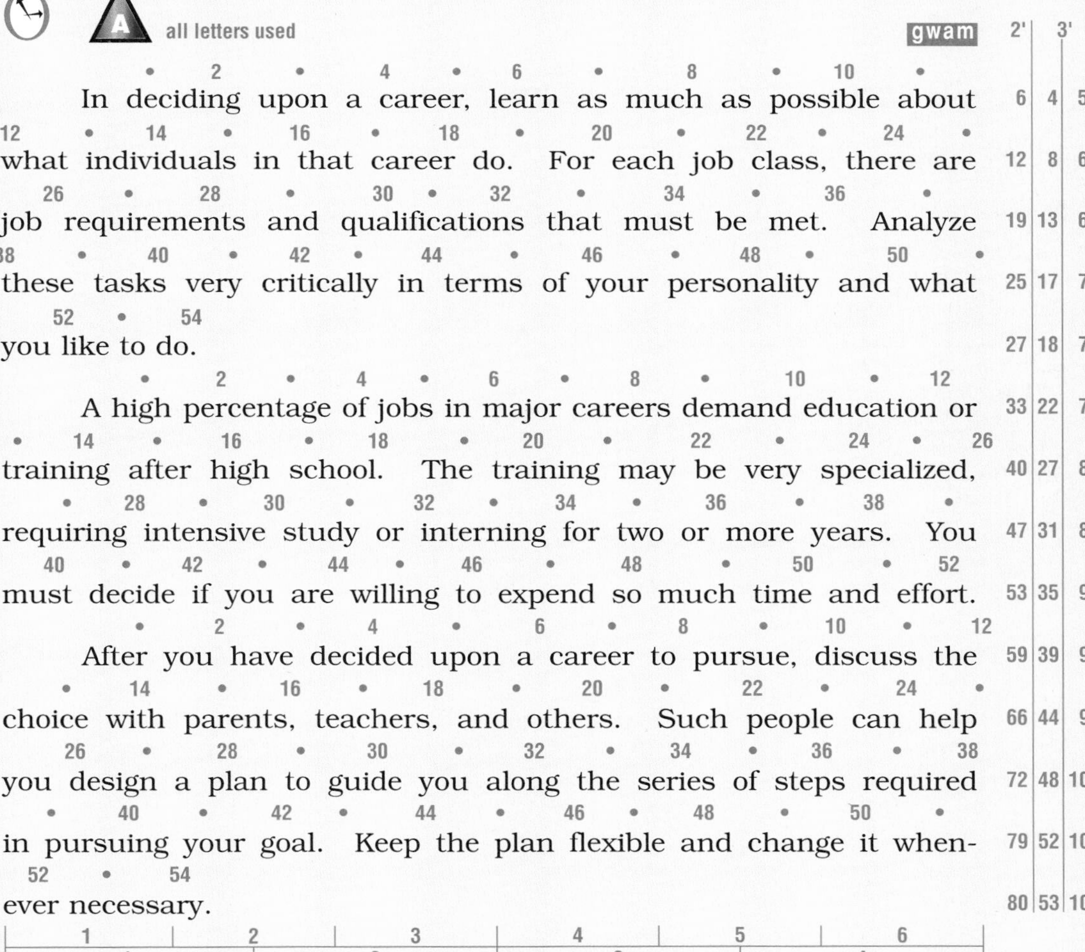

A all letters used

	gwam 2'	3'	
In deciding upon a career, learn as much as possible about	6	4	57
what individuals in that career do. For each job class, there are	12	8	62
job requirements and qualifications that must be met. Analyze	19	13	66
these tasks very critically in terms of your personality and what	25	17	70
you like to do.	27	18	71
A high percentage of jobs in major careers demand education or	33	22	76
training after high school. The training may be very specialized,	40	27	80
requiring intensive study or interning for two or more years. You	47	31	85
must decide if you are willing to expend so much time and effort.	53	35	90
After you have decided upon a career to pursue, discuss the	59	39	93
choice with parents, teachers, and others. Such people can help	66	44	97
you design a plan to guide you along the series of steps required	72	48	102
in pursuing your goal. Keep the plan flexible and change it when-	79	52	106
ever necessary.	80	53	107

gwam 2' | 1 | 2 | 3 | 4 | 5 | 6 |
3' | 1 | 2 | 3 | 4 |

LESSON 4 EXPAND ENTERING AND FORMATTING SKILLS

Objectives:

1. To use Fill and number formats to quickly enter information.

2. To rotate text in column headings and change row heights.

Activity 1 • Fill

1. Study the text at the right.
2. Learn to use Fill with your ss software.
3. Complete the steps at the right.

Save as: *SS1L4ACT1*

Information can be quickly copied to adjacent cells by using the **Fill** feature. This feature can be used to enter a series of days (Monday, Tuesday, Wednesday . . .), months (Jan, Feb, Mar . . .), years (2002, 2003, 2004 . . .), consecutive numbers (100, 102, 103 . . .), or numbers in intervals (2, 4, 6, 8 . . . or 2, 4, 8, 16 . . .) in adjacent cells.

1. Key **FILL** in Cell A1, and then use the Fill feature to copy it to Cells A2:A15.
2. Use Fill Right to copy Cell A5 to Cells B5:J5.
3. Key **Monday** in C7, and use Fill to enter the days in Cells C8:C18.
4. Key **1850** in Cell B1, and use Fill to enter the years through **1858** in the cells to the right of B1.
5. Key **Jan** in E7, and use Fill to enter the months through **Dec** below E7.
6. Key **1** in F7, and use Fill to enter the numbers 2–12 below F7.
7. Key **100** in H7, and use Fill to enter numbers in intervals of 5 to 150 below H7.
8. Use Fill to enter each power of 2 from 2 to 1024 beginning in A19 and moving right.
9. Print the worksheet with gridlines and column and row headings on one page, using left and right margins of 1.25" and a top margin of 3".

Activity 2 • Rotate Text

1. Study the text and illustration at the right.
2. Learn how to rotate text.
3. Create the worksheets at the right, rotating the text in the column headings at 45° in the first worksheet and 60° in the second.

Save as: *SS1L4ACT2A* and *SS1L4ACT2B*

When column headings are considerably longer than the information in the columns, the headings can be rotated to save space.

	A	B	C	D	E	F
1	Student	Monday	Tuesday	Wednesday	Thursday	Friday
2	Jim	Present	Present	Present	Present	Present
3	Harry	Absent	Absent	Absent	Present	Present

Student	Monday	Tuesday	Wednesday	Thursday	Friday
Jim	Present	Present	Present	Present	Present
Harry	Absent	Absent	Absent	Present	Present

Month	Albert	Mary Ann	Roberto	Yin Chi	Zeb
Sep	1	0	0	0	1
Oct	0	0	0	0	0
Nov	1	1	0	2	0
Dec	1	0	0	1	3
Jan	1	0	0	0	0
Feb	0	0	0	0	1

WORD PROCESSING 4

ACTIVITY 1

Insert Table

1. Read the copy at the right.
2. Learn how to create a table with your word processing software.
3. Create and fill in the table shown at the right.

Save as: *WP4ACT1*

Use the **Table** feature to create a grid for arranging information in rows and columns. Tables consist of vertical columns and horizontal rows. Columns are labeled alphabetically from left to right; rows are labeled numerically from top to bottom. The crossing of columns and rows makes **cells**.

When text is keyed in a cell, it wraps around in that cell—instead of wrapping around to the next row. A line space is added to the cell each time the text wraps around.

To fill in cells, use the TAB key or Right arrow key to move from cell to cell in a row and from row to row. (Striking ENTER will simply insert a blank line space in the cell.) To move around in a filled-in table, use the arrow keys, TAB, or the mouse (click the desired cell).

NATIONAL LEAGUE CY YOUNG AWARD WINNNERS

Year	Player	Team
1990	Doug Drabek	Pirates
1991	Tom Glavine	Braves
1992	Greg Maddux	Cubs
1993	Greg Maddux	Braves
1994	Greg Maddux	Braves
1995	Greg Maddux	Braves
1996	John Smoltz	Braves

ACTIVITY 2

Insert and Delete Rows and Columns

1. Read the copy at the right.
2. Open the table you created in Activity 1 (*WP4ACT1*).
3. Insert the information for 1997–1999 and make the other changes shown at the right.

Save as: *WP4ACT2*

The Table feature can be used to edit or modify existing tables. Common modifications include the addition and deletion of rows and columns.

1997	Pedro Martinez	Expos
1998	Tom Glavine	Braves
1999	Randy Johnson	Diamondbacks

1. Delete the 1990–1992 award winners.
2. Delete the column showing the team the award winner played for.
3. Undo the last change made to restore the deleted column.

Activity 3 • Check Spelling

1. Study the text and illustration at the right.
2. Learn to check spelling with your ss software.
3. Open *CD-SS1L3ACT3* and use the spell checker to help proofread the worksheet. Correct errors.

 **Save as:** *SS1L3ACT3*

Spreadsheet software checks spelling in much the same way as wp software does. Words are checked for correct spelling, but not for context. Numbers are not checked at all. It is therefore important that *you proofread* all words and numbers for accuracy and context after the checker has been used. Proper names should be checked carefully, since the spell checker dictionary does not contain many proper names.

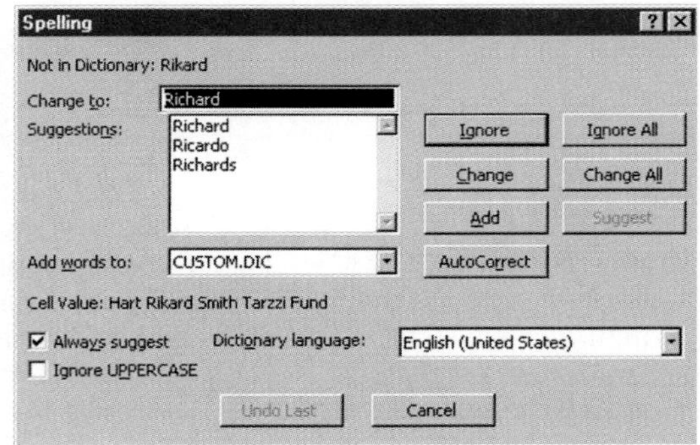

Activity 4 • Application

Create a daily planner for two days as directed at the right.

 **Save as:** *SS1L3ACT4*

1. Specify Column A width at 7; Column B width at 50.
2. Merge Cells A1 and B1 and key **Daily Planner for** ________ (left-aligned) in the merged cell.
3. In Column A, key the time in one-hour intervals in every fourth cell. Start with **8 a.m.** in Cell A2 and end with **7 p.m.** in Cell A46.
4. In Column B, merge every four rows together. The first four cells to be merged are B2:B5 and the last are B46:49.
5. Make a copy of this planner by copying the cells in the range A1:B49 to a new area beginning with cell A50.
6. Key and left-align your name as a header and the page number as a footer.
7. Insert a page break so each copy of the daily planner will print on a separate page.
8. Center the worksheet on the page and then print the second page with gridlines.

Activity 5 • Application

1. Create the worksheet at the right (wrapping text and indenting as shown).
2. Calculate the correct number to be inserted at each set of question marks. The Ending Cash Balance of each quarter becomes the Opening Cash Balance for the next quarter.
3. Key **ROARING SPRINGS GOLF CLUB** as a centered header in 18-pt. font and your name and the date as a left-aligned footer.
4. You decide all other formatting features.
5. Check spelling and preview before printing.

 **Save as:** *SS1L3ACT5*

PROJECTED CASH FLOW FOR 200-

	January to March	April to June	July to September	October to December
Cash Receipts				
Gross Cash Receipts	9500	11000	19000	6550
Returns	445	555	935	305
Net Cash Receipts	???	???	???	???
Cash Disbursements				
Expenses				
Operating Expenses	2335	2357	2390	2240
Other Expenses	150	400	500	300
Total Cash Disbursements	???	???	???	???
Net Cash Flow				
Opening Cash Balance	9606	???	???	???
Net Cash Receipts	???	???	???	???
Cash Disbursements	???	???	???	???
Ending Cash Balance	???	???	???	???

ACTIVITY 3

Join Cells and Change Column Width

1. Read the information at the right.
2. Learn how to join cells.
3. Learn how to adjust column widths.
4. Open the file *CD-WP4ACT3.*
5. Join the cells of Row 1.
6. Adjust the column widths so that the name of each sales representative fits on one line, as shown at the right. Adjust the width of other columns as needed.

Save as: *WP4ACT3*

Use the Table feature to **join** cells (merge two or more cells into one cell). This feature is useful when information in the table spans more than one column or row. The main title, for example, spans all columns.

In a newly created table, all columns are the same width. You can change the width of one or more columns to accommodate entries of unequal widths.

SALES REPORT				
Sales Rep.	Territory	Jan.	Feb.	March
Juan Ramirez	Washington	12,325	13,870	12,005
Shawn Hewitt	Oregon	15,680	17,305	7,950
Maria Hernandez	Idaho	9,480	16,780	14,600
Cheryl Updike	Washington	10,054	8,500	17,085
Tanya Goodman	Washington	19,230	11,230	15,780
Jason Graham	Oregon	15,900	16,730	9,290
Carolyn Plummer	Idaho	20,370	13,558	12,654
Scott Bowe	Idaho	15,750	14,560	16,218
Brandon Olson	Oregon	14,371	11,073	19,301
Laura Chen	Washington	17,320	9,108	18,730

ACTIVITY 4

Change Table Format

1. Read the information at the right.
2. Learn how to make formatting changes in a table.
3. Open *WP4ACT3,* created in Activity 3.
4. Make the formatting changes given below and shown at the right.
   a. Bold and center the main title.
   b. Center-align Column B.
   c. Right-align Columns C, D, and E.
   d. Bold and center the column headings.
   e. Bold and italicize the highest sales figure for each month.

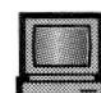

Save as: *WP4ACT4*

The formatting changes (bold, italicize, alignment, etc.) that you have learned to make to text can also be made to the text within a table. You can do this prior to keying the text into the table, or it can be done after the text has been entered. After the table is complete, make changes by selecting the cell (row or column) to be changed and then giving the software command to make the change.

SALES REPORT				
Sales Rep.	**Territory**	**Jan.**	**Feb.**	**March**
Juan Ramirez	Washington	12,325	13,870	12,005
Shawn Hewitt	Oregon	15,680	***17,305***	7,950
Maria Hernandez	Idaho	9,480	16,780	14,600
Cheryl Updike	Washington	10,054	8,500	17,085
Tanya Goodman	Washington	19,230	11,230	15,780
Jason Graham	Oregon	15,900	16,730	9,290
Carolyn Plummer	Idaho	***20,370***	13,558	12,654
Scott Bowe	Idaho	15,750	14,560	16,218
Brandon Olson	Oregon	14,371	11,073	***19,301***
Laura Chen	Washington	17,320	9,108	18,730

Activity 5 • Application

1. Prepare the worksheet at the right, making these changes:
   a. Specify all column widths at 12.
   b. Format numbers as Currency with no cents.
   c. Insert an 8-character column between Columns C and D and a similar column at the right of the last column. (If necessary, use Help to review inserting columns.)
   d. Use **Percent Change** for column headings (wrap the text) and shade appropriately.
   e. Center the Division headings.
2. Calculate totals and percent of change (use Percent and one decimal).
3. Print in landscape orientation, centered on page with your name as a right-aligned header and today's date as a left-aligned footer, both in 18-pt. font.

Save as: *SS1L2ACT5*

JENNCO MONTHLY SALES REPORT					
	Northern Division			Southern Division	
Office	This Month	Same Month Last Year	Office	This Month	Same Month Last Year
Boston	1540000	1444975	Atlanta	1653450	1582625
Baltimore	1562675	1375755	Dallas	1345870	1467050
Cleveland	2143750	2307450	Mobile	1873525	1852840
Chicago	1957500	2010730	Memphis	2769200	2652810
Boise	780560	755050	Omaha	2459550	2234800
Seattle	2289570	2185525	San Diego	3000540	2750750
Totals			Totals		

LESSON 3 PROOFREAD AND MAKE PRINTING ADJUSTMENTS

Objective:
To check spelling, set page breaks, and select print range.

Activity 1 • Set Print Area

1. Study the text at the right, and learn to specify the print area.
2. Open *CD-SS1L3ACT1* and follow the directions at the right.

By default, most ss software prints all the information in a worksheet. If you need to print only a portion (one or more pages, one cell, or a range of cells), you can specify to have only that portion printed.

1. Select cells in the range A1:E9 and print just those cells.
2. Specify and then print only the second page of the worksheet.

Activity 2 • Set Page Breaks

1. Study the text at the right, and learn to adjust page breaks.
2. Open *CD-SS1L3ACT1* and follow the directions at the right.

Save as: *SS1L3ACT2*

When working with multiple-page worksheets, a feature in ss software will insert page breaks the same as wp software inserts breaks in multiple-page documents. The default page breaks can be moved so the worksheet information will appear on the correct page.

1. Verify that *CD-SS1L3ACT1* contains three seating charts.
2. Adjust the page breaks so that one chart is printed per page.
3. Print only the first seating chart. Show gridlines, use portrait orientation, and center horizontally and vertically on the page.

ACTIVITY 5

Center Tables Horizontally and Vertically

1. Read the information at the right.
2. Learn to center tables horizontally and vertically.
3. Open the file you created in Activity 4 (*WP4ACT4*).
4. Center the table vertically.
5. Center the table horizontally.

 **Save as:** *WP4ACT5*

Use the **Center alignment** Table feature to center a table from left to right on a page.

Use the **Vertical alignment**, or **Center Page**, feature to center a table from top to bottom on a page.

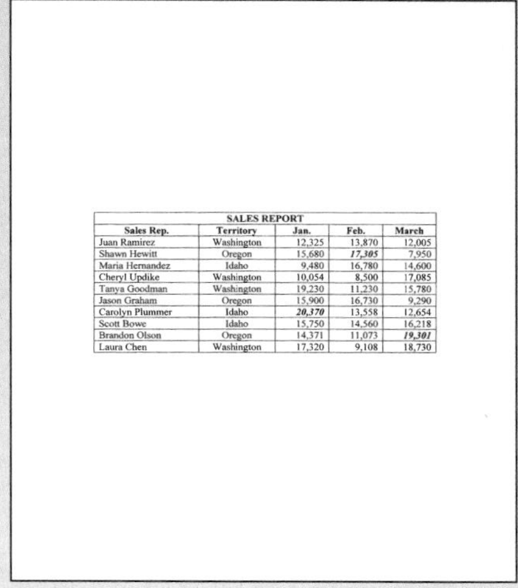

SALES REPORT				
Sales Rep.	**Territory**	**Jan.**	**Feb.**	**March**
Juan Ramirez	Washington	12,325	13,870	12,005
Shawn Hewitt	Oregon	15,680	***17,305***	7,950
Maria Hernandez	Idaho	9,480	16,780	14,600
Cheryl Updike	Washington	10,054	8,500	17,085
Tanya Goodman	Washington	19,230	11,230	15,780
Jason Graham	Oregon	15,900	16,730	9,290
Carolyn Plummer	Idaho	***20,370***	13,558	12,654
Scott Bowe	Idaho	15,750	14,560	16,218
Brandon Olson	Oregon	14,371	11,073	***19,301***
Laura Chen	Washington	17,320	9,108	18,730

ACTIVITY 6

Sort Tables

1. Read the information at the right; learn to use the Sort feature.
2. Open *WP4ACT5*, which you created in Activity 5.
3. Sort the table by Territory (Column B) in descending order as shown.
4. Sort the table by March sales (Column E) in descending order.

 **Save as:** *WP4ACT6*

The **Sort** feature arranges text in a table in a specific order. The feature sorts alphabetic or numeric text in ascending or descending order.

SALES REPORT				
Sales Rep.	**Territory**	**Jan.**	**Feb.**	**March**
Juan Ramirez	Washington	12,325	13,870	12,005
Cheryl Updike	Washington	10,054	8,500	17,085
Tanya Goodman	Washington	19,230	11,230	15,780
Brandon Olson	Oregon	14,371	11,073	***19,301***
Maria Hernandez	Idaho	9,480	16,780	14,600
Carolyn Plummer	Idaho	***20,370***	13,558	12,654
Scott Bowe	Idaho	15,750	14,560	16,218

ACTIVITY 7

Change Row Height and Vertical Alignment

1. Read the copy at the right; learn how to change row height.
2. Open the file created in Activity 6 (*WP4ACT6*). Change row height as follows: main title row, 0.6"; column headings, 0.5"; other rows, 0.4".
3. Change vertical alignment as follows: main title and column headings, **center**; data entry rows, **bottom** alignment.

 **Save as:** *WP4ACT7*

Use the Table feature to change the height of the rows in a table. The height of all the rows of the table can be changed to the same height, or each row can be a different height.

Use the Table feature to change the vertical alignment of text in cells. The text within a cell can be top-aligned, center-aligned, or bottom-aligned.

Top align - 0.3"	Center align - 0.3"	Bottom align - 0.3"
Top align - 0.4"	Center align - 0.4"	Bottom align - 0.4"
Top align - 0.5"	Center align - 0.5"	Bottom align - 0.5"

2. Learn how to set margins and how to center and scale worksheets.
3. Complete the steps at the right.

1. Open *CD-SS1L2ACT1*; change the side margins to 1.125" and the top and bottom margins to 3". Print the worksheet in landscape orientation without gridlines or headings.

 **Save as:** *SS1L2ACT2A*

2. Open *CD-SS1L2ACT1*; center the worksheet vertically and horizontally. Print in landscape orientation with gridlines and headings.

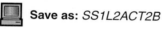

 **Save as:** *SS1L2ACT2B*

3. Open *CD-SS1L2ACT1*; scale the worksheet to fit on one page in portrait orientation. Center it vertically and horizontally and print it.

 **Save as:** *SS1L2ACT2C*

Activity 3 • Print Preview

1. Study the text and illustration at the right.
2. Learn to use Print Preview.
3. Open *CD-SS1L2ACT3* and follow the directions at the right.

 **Save as:** *SS1L2ACT3*

A worksheet should be previewed before it is printed to make sure it is arranged on the page as desired. If it is not, adjustments can be made to the document before it is printed. These adjustments include changing margins, centering the worksheet, or scaling it to the desired size.

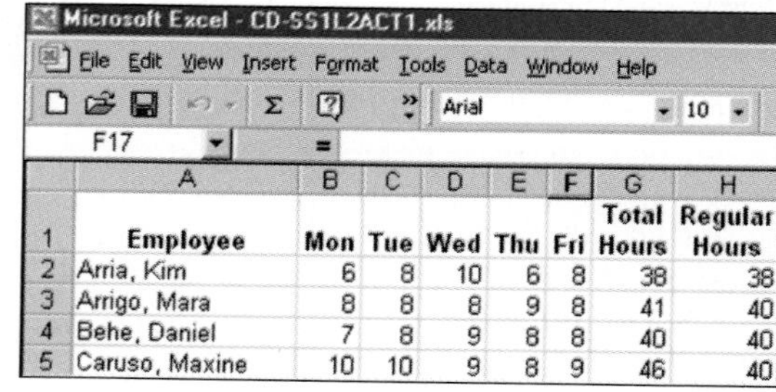

	A	B	C	D	E	F	G	H
1	Employee	Mon	Tue	Wed	Thu	Fri	Total Hours	Regular Hours
2	Arria, Kim	6	8	10	6	8	38	38
3	Arrigo, Mara	8	8	8	9	8	41	40
4	Behe, Daniel	7	8	9	8	8	40	40
5	Caruso, Maxine	10	10	9	8	9	46	40

1. Review the worksheet to see the number of columns it has, paying particular attention to the names of the columns near the right.
2. Select *Print Preview.* If the worksheet doesn't fit on one page in landscape orientation, scale it to one page and then center it horizontally and vertically.
3. Use Print Preview as many times as needed to ensure the entire worksheet is arranged correctly, and then print it with gridlines and column and row headings.

Activity 4 • Headers and Footers

1. Study the text and illustration at the right.
2. Learn to insert headers and footers.
3. Open *CD-SS1L2ACT3* and follow the directions at the right.

 **Save as:** *SS1L2ACT4*

Tip:

The header/footer does not change automatically when font changes are made in the worksheet.

Worksheets can contain headers and footers in much the same way as wp documents can. You can select predefined headers/footers from the ss software, or you can create custom headers/footers. Special codes can be entered in the header/footer to print the date, time, page number, filename, etc. The font, font style, and font size can also be specified. In addition, the header/footer may be left-, center-, or right-aligned.

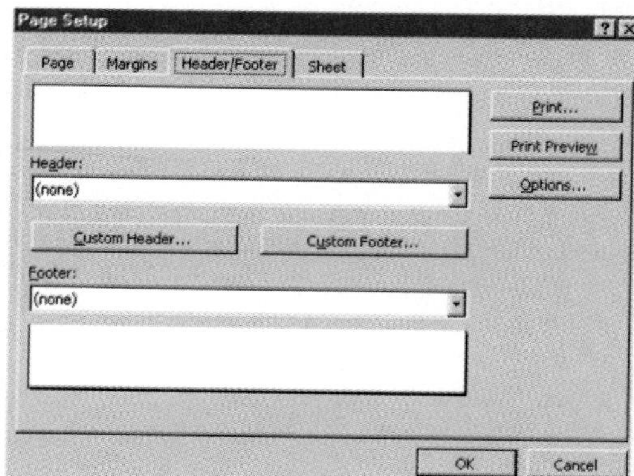

1. Using Arial 14-pt. bold font, insert the filename as a right-aligned header and your name and the date as a centered custom footer.
2. Preview the worksheet. Print it without gridlines or column/row headings when it is arranged attractively on one page.

ACTIVITY 8

Apply What You Have Learned

1. Open the file *CD-WP4ACT8*.
2. Insert a column for the dates, as shown at right.
3. Bold and center column headings.
4. Center the information in the Date column.
5. Adjust column widths to fit the information.
6. Sort the Date column in ascending order.
7. Insert a row for: **1807 - Steamboat - Robert Fulton**.
8. Insert a row above the column headings; merge the cells. Cut and paste the main title in the merged row.
9. Center the table on the page.

Save as: *WP4ACT8*

INVENTIONS

Date	Invention	Inventor
1877	Phonograph	Thomas Edison
1805	Railroad locomotive	Richard Trevithick
1846	Sewing machine	Elias Howe
1867	Revolver	Samuel Colt
1820	Calculating machine	Charles Babbage
1867	Typewriter	Christopher Sholes

ACTIVITY 9

Apply What You Have Learned

1. Open the file CD-*WP4ACT9*. Insert a column for **Sale Price** as shown, and enter the amounts.
2. Insert a row at the end* with the following information in the cells: **Sandager, Rocky Mountain Road, 950**.
3. Adjust column widths to fit the information.
4. Sort the Artist column in ascending order.**
5. Change the row height for the main title to 0.6"; change the row height for the column headings to 0.5"; change the row height for the data rows to 0.4".
6. Change the vertical alignment for the main title and column headings to *center*; change the vertical alignment for the data rows to *bottom*.
7. Center the table on the page.

Save as: *WP4ACT9*

***Note:**
To add a row at the end, place the insertion point in the last existing cell and press TAB.

****Note:**
The $ should precede the first entry in the Sale Price column after the sort ($1,139).

JUNE ART GALLERY SPECIALS		
Artist	**Art Print**	Sale Price
Richmond	*Summer Home*	$9,250
Du Bois	*City Lights*	165
Gennrich	*Brittany's Garden*	425
Sinclair	*Sunday Morning*	1,095
Shoji	*Christmas Morning*	350
Chen	*Coming Home*	1,139
Lindquist	*Dakota Country*	280
Hohenstein	*The Old Mill*	3,325
Debauche	*Campers' Delight*	150

Activity 5 • Application

1. Create and format a worksheet as shown at the right.
2. Calculate the sum in empty shaded Cells D8, D13, D17, and D18. (If necessary, review Formulas using online Help.)
3. Using the Present Value for each industry and the Total Portfolio Value, calculate the percent in empty shaded Cells B8, B13, and B17.
4. Format numbers in Column B as Percents with two decimal places, Column C with a thousands separator, and Column D as Currency with no cents.
5. Right-align all numbers.
6. Print the worksheet.

Save as: *SS1L1ACT5*

MXP COMMON STOCK FUND
December 31, 200-

Industry and Company	**Percent of Portfolio**	**Shares**	**Present Value**
Aerospace			
Fleet Company		4627	205601
Textran		748	37607
Kite Technologies		1312	69459
Total Aerospace			
Energy			
HPNGCO Electric		1701	103855
Gertin Corp		7362	395719
SH Oil		6333	348722
Total Energy			
Real Estate			
The Troyer Company		2151	45324
Suburban Malls, Inc.		6446	164791
Total Real Estate			
Total Portfolio Value			

LESSON 2 PAGE SETUP AND PRINTING

Objectives:

1. To use Print Preview and print in landscape orientation.
2. To change margins, center and scale worksheets, and insert headers and footers.

Activity 1 • Landscape Orientation

1. Study the text and illustration at the right.
2. Learn to print in landscape orientation.
3. Open *CD-SS1L2ACT1* and print the worksheet in landscape orientation.

Save as: *SS1L2ACT1*

Most documents, including letters, memos, reports, tables, and forms, are printed in portrait orientation, or across the width of the paper (the 8.5" side of paper that is 8.5" by 11".) Many worksheets are wider than 8.5"; these can be printed in landscape orientation, which prints across the length of the paper (the 11" side of 8.5" by 11" paper).

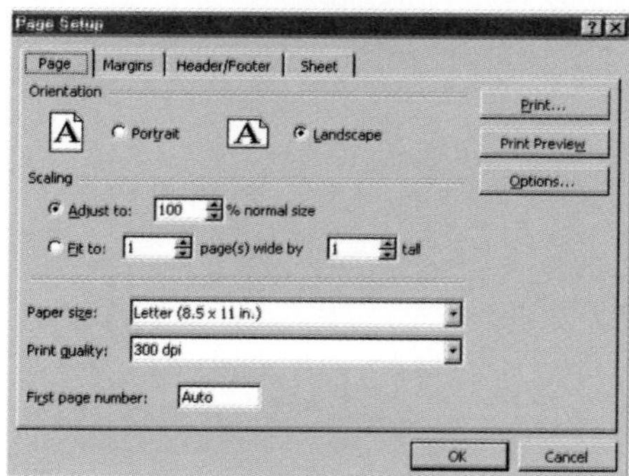

Activity 2 • Change Margins and Center and Scale Worksheets

1. Study the text and illustration at the right.

(continued on next page)

To arrange worksheets attractively on a page, you can: (1) change the top, bottom, and side margins; (2) have the ss software center the worksheet horizontally and/or vertically; and (3) scale the worksheet to print on one page. These changes are made within the Page Setup dialog box.

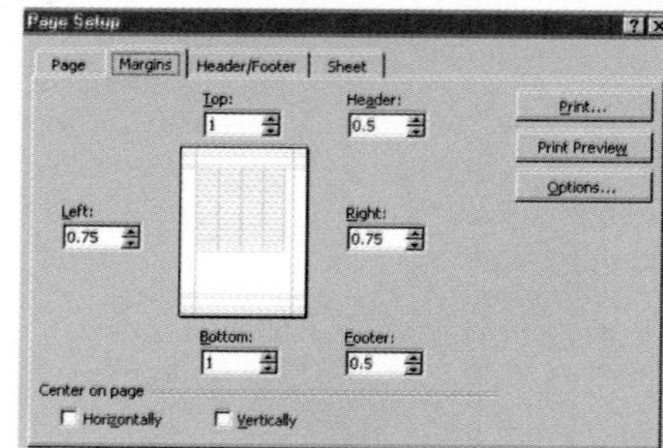

UNIT 10

LESSONS 31–34

Learn to Format Tables

Format Guides: Tables

TOP TEN ANCESTRY GROUPS OF U.S. POPULATION			
1990 Census			
Rank	**Ancestry**	**Number**	**Percent of Population**
1	German	57,947,873	23.3
2	Irish	38,735,539	15.6
3	English	32,651,788	13.1
4	African American	23,777,098	9.6
5	Italian	14,664,550	5.9
6	American	12,395,999	5.0
7	Mexican	11,586,983	4.7
8	French	10,320,935	4.1
9	Polish	9,366,106	3.8
10	Native American	8,708,220	3.5
Source: *The Information Please Almanac*. Boston: Houghton Mifflin Company, 1996.			

Four-Column Table with Source Note

TABLES		
Format Features		
Horizontal Alignment	**Vertical Alignment**	**Row Height**
Left	Top	0.7"
Center	Top	0.7"
Right	Top	0.7"
Left	Center	0.55"
Center	Center	0.55"
Right	Center	0.55"
Left	Bottom	0.4"
Center	Bottom	0.4"
Right	Bottom	0.4"
2"	1.5"	1"

Alignment in Tables

Format Guides: Tables

Although you will use a word processing feature to create tables, you will need these guidelines for making your tables easy to read and attractive.

Parts of a Table

A **table** is an arrangement of data (words and/or numbers) in rows and columns. Columns are labeled alphabetically from left to right; rows are labeled numerically from top to bottom. Tables range in complexity from those with only two columns and a title to those with several columns and special features. The tables in this unit are limited to those with the following parts:

1. Main title usually in ALL CAPS (centered in first row or placed above the table).
2. Secondary title in capital and lowercase letters (centered a DS below the main title).
3. Column heading (centered over the column).
4. Body (data entries).
5. Source note (bottom left).
6. Gridlines (may be hidden).*

---

*Some software prints the gridlines between columns and rows (as shown in the model, p. 95) or allows you to hide all or some of the lines before printing. **Note:** If your software prints gridlines by default, leave the lines in all your tables unless your instructor directs you to hide them. If gridlines do not print, column headings should be underlined. Also, the last entry in an amount column with a total should be underlined.

Table Format Features

The following features (illustrated on p. 95) can be used to make your tables attractive and easy to read.

Vertical placement. A table may be centered vertically (equal top and bottom margins), or it may begin 2" from the top edge of the page.

Horizontal placement. Tables are most attractive when centered horizontally (side to side) on the page.

Column width. Generally, each column should be only slightly wider than the longest data entry in the column. Table columns should be identical widths or markedly different widths. Columns that are only slightly different widths should be avoided.

Row height. All rows, including title rows, may be the same height. To enhance appearance, the main title row height may be slightly more than the secondary title row height, which may be more than the column heading row. The column heading row height may be more than the data entry rows.

Vertical alignment. Within rows, data entries can be aligned at the top, center, or bottom. Most often you will use center vertical alignment for the headings and bottom vertical alignment for data rows beneath the headings. If a source note is included, it should also be bottom-aligned.

Horizontal alignment. Within columns, words may be left-aligned or center-aligned. Whole numbers are right-aligned if a column total is shown; decimal numbers are decimal-aligned. Other figures may be center-aligned.

Activity 3 • Indent Text

1. Study the text and illustration at the right.
2. Learn how to indent text.
3. Create the worksheet at the right:
   a. Indent Rows 2, 5, and 8 once.
   b. Indent Rows 3, 4, 6, 7, 9, and 10 twice.
   c. Indent Row 11 three times.
   d. Format numbers as Accounting with dollar signs and no cents.
   e. Bold as shown.
   f. Use AutoFit to set column widths to widest entry.
4. Print the worksheet with gridlines and row and column headings.

Save as: *SS1L1ACT3*

Use the **Indent Text** feature to help distinguish categories or set text apart within cells. The amount of the indent can be increased or decreased by clicking the proper Indent button on the Formatting toolbar or by changing the indent setting in the Format Cells dialog box.

Microsoft Excel - Book8

File Edit View Insert Format Tools Data Wi

Arial 10 B I U

C5 =

	A	B
1	This is not indented	
2	This is indented once	
3	This is indented twice	
4	This is indented three times	
5	This is indented once	

Distributions to shareholders	**Amount**
From net investment income	
Class A	$ 43,523
Class B	$ 10,325
In excess of net investment income	
Class A	$ 2,354
Class B	$ 574
From return on capital	
Class A	$ 2,765
Class B	$ 750
Total distributions	$ 60,291

Activity 4 • Specify Column Width

1. Read the text at the right and learn to set the column width.
2. Create the worksheet:
   a. Specify Column A width to be 15; Column B, 20; and Columns C and D, 10.
   b. Merge cells in Row 1, then in Row 2, and right-align text.
   c. Wrap text in Cells C3 and D3.
   d. Right-align and vertically center the column headings.
   e. Left-align entries in Columns A and B.
   f. Format numbers in Columns C and D as Currency, right-aligned.
   g. Use bold and shading as desired.
3. Print the worksheet without gridlines or row and column headings.

Save as: *SS1L1ACT4*

By default, column widths typically display about eight spaces. You have used AutoFit to resize a column to the width of the longest entry in a column. Another method is to specify an exact number of spaces in the Column Width dialog box. More than one column can be resized to the same width simultaneously if they are all selected.

The illustration at the right indicates the number of spaces specified in each column.

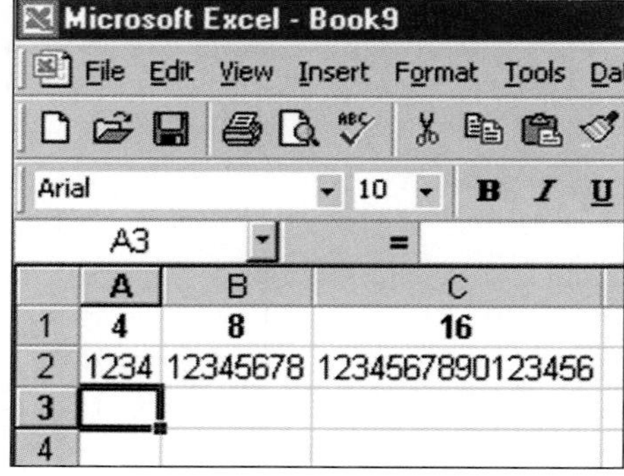

Microsoft Excel - Book9

File Edit View Insert Format Tools Da

Arial 10 B I U

A3 =

	A	B	C
1	**4**	**8**	**16**
2	1234	12345678	1234567890123456
3			
4			

PORTFOLIO SUMMARY
(In Millions of Dollars)

Property Name	Property Description	Property Cost	Present Value
EXS Tower	10-story office building	7.65	8.24
Marion Mall	retail shopping mall	7.54	8.34
Silver Cove	retail shopping center	6.98	7.92
Redbank Plaza	professional building	5.78	6.02
Reisser Building	8-story office building	5.67	5.78
Reading Mill	retail shopping mall	5.58	5.97
Landmark Park	industrial warehouse	4.53	4.91
Market Arena	distribution center	3.31	3.75

Vertical Centering (equal top and bottom margins)

Main title

Secondary title

Column headings

Body

TOP 10 BROADWAY GROSSES		
Week Ending September 12, 1999		
Production	***Gross This Week***	***Gross Last Week***
Annie Get Your Gun	$ 572,885	$ 671,363
Cabaret	466,670	515,787
Chicago	536,852	523,106
Death of a Salesman	351,082	NA
Fosse	566,644	605,993
Les Miserables	375,318	436,915
Miss Saigon	395,522	434,641
Ragtime	420,902	539,158
The Lion King	880,717	875,772
The Phantom of the Opera	601,218	594,636
Totals	$5,167,810	$5,197,371

Horizontal Centering (equal side margins)

Three-Column Table Centered Horizontally and Vertically

LESSONS 1–6 (4–5 HOURS)

Spreadsheet Applications 1, Extending Spreadsheet Skills

LESSON 1 FORMAT CELLS AND COLUMNS

Objective:
To merge cells, wrap and indent text in cells, and specify column widths.

Activity 1 • Merge Cells

1. Study the text and illustration at the right.
2. Learn how to merge cells.
3. Create a worksheet and key the bold text at the right to complete the activity.
4. Print the worksheet with gridlines and row and column headings.

Save as: *SS1L1ACT1*

As with cells in a wp table, cells within a worksheet can be merged with adjacent cells. The text within the merged cells can be center-, left-, or right-aligned horizontally and top-, bottom-, or center-aligned vertically. This is useful for centering worksheet titles and entering column and row entries that span more than one column or row.

The illustration shows a title centered within Cells A1:G1. It also shows column and row headings and entries that span multiple columns or rows.

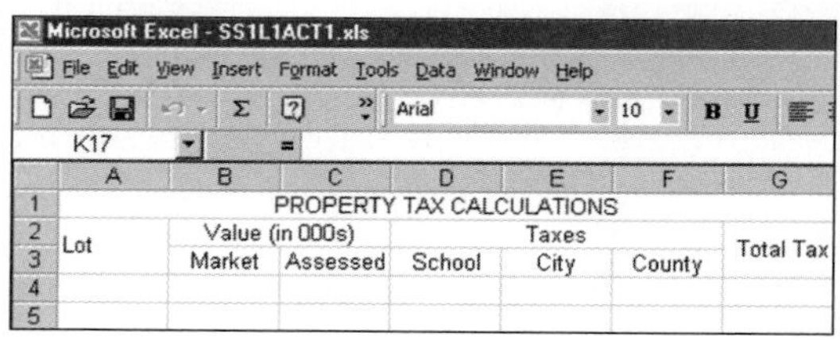

1. Center-align **PROPERTY TAX CALCULATIONS** in Cells A1:G1.
2. Center-align **Value (in 000s)** in Cells B2:C2 and **Taxes** in D2:F2.
3. Left-align and vertically center **Lot** in Cells A2:A3. Right-align and vertically center **Total Tax** in G2:G3.
4. Center-align **Market** in B3; **Assessed** in C3; **School** in D3; **City** in E3; and **County** in F3.

Activity 2 • Wrap Text in Cells

1. Study the text and illustration at the right.
2. Learn how to wrap text.
3. Create a worksheet and key the bold text at the right to complete the activity.
4. Print the worksheet with gridlines and row and column headings.

Save as: *SS1L1ACT2*

Text that is too long for a cell will extend into the adjacent cell if the cell to the right is empty. If the cell to the right is not empty, the text that does not fit will not display. You can choose to have the text wrap within the cell's width in the same way sentences are wrapped in a wp document. The row height will adjust as shown in the illustration at the right.

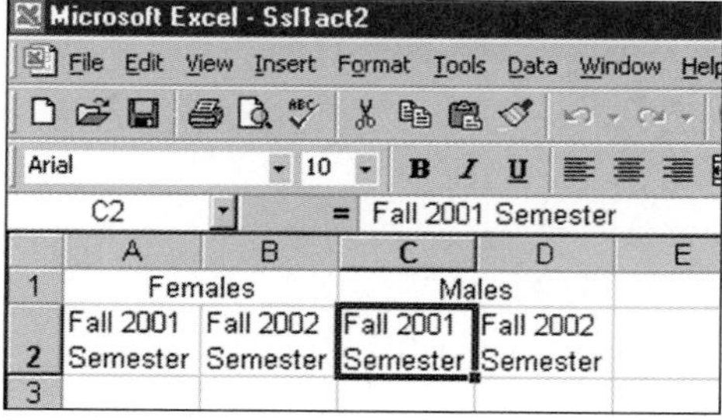

1. Center-align **UNION HIGH SCHOOL ENROLLMENT REPORT** in Cells A1:G1.
2. Center-align **Females** in Cells B2:D2 and **Males** in Cells E2:G2.
3. Center-align and vertically center **Grade** in A2:A3.
4. Using wrap, center-align **Fall 2001 Semester** in Cell B3 and again in Cell E3; **Fall 2002 Semester** in Cell C3 and again in F3; and **Percent Change** in Cells D3 and G3.

LESSON 31 FORMAT TWO-COLUMN TABLES WITH COLUMN HEADINGS

Objectives:

1. To learn placement/arrangement of basic table parts.
2. To format tables using the Table formatting features.

31A • 5' Conditioning Practice

Key each line twice SS; key a 1' writing on line 3; determine *gwam.*

alphabet 1 Meg saw an extra big jet zip quickly over the frozen desert.

fig/sym 2 My income tax for 2001 was $3,875.69--up 4% over 2000's tax.

speed 3 Dick may make a bid on the ivory gowns they got in the city.

gwam 1' | 1 | 2 | 3 | 4 | 5 | 6 | 7 | 8 | 9 | 10 | 11 | 12 |

FORMATTING

31B • 45' Two-Column Tables with Column Headings

1. Study the format guides for tables on p. 94.
2. Study the model on p. 95: vertical and horizontal centering, row height, alignment, and column width.
3. Key Tables 1–3 shown at right and on p. 97.

Table 1

1. Set a top margin of 2".
2. Center and bold the main title; DS.
3. Create a 2 by 9 table (2 columns, 9 rows) and fill in the data shown at the right above.
4. Center and bold the column headings.

Save as: *TBL31B1*

Table 2

1. Center and bold the main title; DS.
2. Create a 2 by 13 table (2 columns, 13 rows) and fill in the data shown at the right.
3. Center and bold the column headings.
4. Center the table horizontally and vertically.

Save as: *TBL31B2*

POEMS TO IMPROVE OUR LIVES

Poem	**Written By**
Great Men	Ralph Waldo Emerson
Success	Henry Wadsworth Longfellow
If	Rudyard Kipling
The Road Not Taken	Robert Frost
Will	Ella Wheeler Wilcox
The Sin of Omission	Margaret E. Sangster
Good and Bad Children	Robert Louis Stevenson
Lady Clare	Alfred Tennyson

THE SOUND OF MUSIC CAST

Character	**Cast Member**
Sister Margaretta	Rebecca Tewksberry
Sister Berthe	Teresa Pohlad
Maria Rainer	Britta Ventura
Captain Georg von Trapp	Mark Stottlemyre
Liesl von Trapp	Brett Hampton
Friedrich von Trapp	Steven Finley
Louisa von Trapp	Nancy Krause
Kurt von Trapp	Joel Lambrecht
Brigitta von Trapp	Laura McDowell
Marta von Trapp	Amy Ross
Gretl von Trapp	Beth Reeves
Admiral von Schreiber	Clayton Perry

Activity 8 • Query and Mail Merge

Prepare the letter shown at the right for *Rockwell Technologies - District 14* sales reps with August sales greater than $70,000.

September 16, 200-

«Title» «First_Name» «Last_Name»
«Address»
«City», «State» «ZIP»

Dear «Title» «Last_Name»

Congratulations! The sales report I received from your district manager lists your name as one of the three sales representatives in District 14 with sales over $70,000 for the month of August.

August was a very good month for District 14 sales representatives. They averaged over $56,104 of sales during August. This was an increase of approximately 4.3 percent over July and an increase of 7.8 percent over last August. This increase is due in large part to your efforts during the month.

We appreciate your hard work to make this the best year ever at Rockwell Technologies.

Sincerely

Leslie R. Fenwick
President

xx

Table 3

1. Center and bold the main title; DS.
2. Create a 2 by 11 table and fill in the data shown at the right.
3. Center and bold the column headings.
4. Center the table horizontally and vertically.

 **Save as:** *TBL31B3*

FAMOUS PAINTINGS

Artist	Painting
Claude Monet	The Boat Studio
Paul Cezanne	Riverbanks
Rembrandt	The Mill
Michelangelo	The Holy Family
Leonardo da Vinci	The Mona Lisa
Vincent van Gogh	The Starry Night
Raphael	The School of Athens
Berthe Morisot	Little Girl Reading
Pierre-Auguste Renoir	Girls at the Piano
Jan Vermeer	The Milkmaid

LESSON 32 FORMAT TWO-COLUMN TABLES WITH MAIN, SECONDARY, AND COLUMN HEADINGS

Objectives:

1. To use Table features to edit existing tables.

2. To format two-column tables with main, secondary, and column headings.

32A • 5' Conditioning Practice

Key each line twice SS; key a 1' writing on line 3; determine *gwam*.

alphabet 1 Jay was amazed at how quickly a proud man fixed the big van.

fig/sym 2 Review reaches: $70, $64, 95%, #20, 5-point, 1/8, B&O 38's.

speed 3 Lane is to fix the big signs by the chapel for the neighbor.

gwam 1' | 1 | 2 | 3 | 4 | 5 | 6 | 7 | 8 | 9 | 10 | 11 | 12 |

FORMATTING

32B • 45' Two-Column Tables

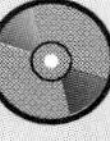

Table 1

1. Open file *CD-TBL32B1.*
2. Make the format changes given at the right.

 **Save as:** *TBL32B1*

1. Join the cells of Row 1; center and bold the main title.
2. Join the cells of Row 2; center the secondary title.
3. Bold and center column headings.
4. Change the row height of main title to 0.5"; secondary title to 0.4"; column headings to 0.35"; and data rows to 0.3".
5. Change the column width of Column A to 3.5", Column B to 2".
6. Change the vertical alignment for the first three rows to **center**; the data rows to **bottom**.
7. Change the horizontal alignment for Column B to **center**.
8. Center the table horizontally and vertically.

Table 2

1. Open file *CD-TBL32B2.*
2. Make the format changes given at the right.

 **Save as:** *TBL32B2*

1. Change the row height for all rows to 0.4".
2. Change the horizontal alignment for Column B to **center**.
3. Change vertical alignment for the column headings to **center**; the data rows to **bottom**.
4. Insert two rows at the end of the table and key the following:

Diego Velazquez — Juan de Pareja

Jean-Auguste-Dominique Ingres — Princess de Broglie

Activity 6 • Report

Create a report similar to the one shown at the right for *Rockwell Technologies - District 14*. Include each sales rep's Last Name, First Name, Territory, and August Sales. Group the reps by Territory and sort by August Sales in ascending order. Select an appropriate layout and style.

Rockwell - District 14

Territory	*August Sales*	*Last Name*	*First Name*
California			
	$34,780.00	Weiss	Daniel
	$39,716.00	Miller	Michelle
	$47,343.00	Keller	Loretta
	$49,655.00	Ryan	Terri
	$49,763.00	Phillips	Lori
	$50,845.00	Taylor	Dean
	$54,900.00	McGraw	Katherine
	$55,428.00	Montessa	Carlos
	$57,381.00	Gonzalez	Renae
	$58,332.00	Zimmer	Albert
	$58,675.00	Winfield	Kevin
	$59,659.00	Chi	Xi
	$59,752.00	Wilkins	Brian
	$60,230.00	Pizarro	Jose
	$62,385.00	Lopez	Juan
	$66,385.00	Rice	Donna
	$82,791.00	Stockton	Greg
Nevada			
	$39,751.00	Hanson	Harriet
	$50,330.00	Bailey	Jamal
	$54,650.00	Chambers	Chad

Activity 7 • Mailing Labels

Prepare a set of mailing labels similar to the ones shown at the right for *District 14* sales reps. Use Avery 5160 labels. Print the labels.

Mr. Justin Hughes 313 Glenwood Dr. NE Vancouver, WA 98662-1148	Ms. Rose Winters 1472 Prescott St. N Porland, OR 97217-8755	Mr. Chad Chambers 2317 Silver Dollar Ave. Las Vegas, NV 89102-9964
Mrs. Harriet Hanson 1890 Rancho Verde Dr. Reno, NV 89511-2221	Mrs. Mai Yang 2187 Klamath St. SE Salem, OR 97306-9031	Mr. Albert Zimmer 330 Van Ness Ave. S Los Angeles, CA 90020-3341
Mr. Mark Aguilera 388 Boston Ln. Eugene, OR 97402-1133	Mr. Kevin Winfield 820 Calle Roca E Palm Springs, CA 92264-0304	Ms. Renae Gonzalez 101 Brookside Ave. Oakland, CA 94618-2212
Ms. Loretta Keller 329 Mountain View Ct. Orange, CA 92669-9911	Mr. Brian Wilkins 40 Beacon St. San Francisco, CA 94131-0167	Mr. Michael Bushlack 2387 Noschka Rd. SW Olympia, WA 98502-1190

Table 3

1. Determine the number of rows and columns needed to create a table for the data shown at the right.
2. Create a table and fill in the data.
3. Center and bold the main title, secondary title, and column headings.
4. Change the row height to 0.4" for all rows.
5. Use **center** vertical alignment for all rows.
6. Center text horizontally in Column B.
7. Center the table horizontally and vertically.

 **Save as:** *TBL32B3*

Table 4

1. Determine the number of rows and columns needed for the data shown at the right.
2. Create a table and fill in the data.
3. Center and bold the main title, secondary title, and column headings.
4. Change the row height to 0.4" for all rows.
5. Use **center** vertical alignment for all title rows; **bottom**-align all data rows.
6. Center text horizontally in Column B.
7. Center the table on the page.

 **Save as:** *TBL32B4*

Table 5

Update Table 4 with the information provided at the right.

 **Save as:** *TBL32B5*

CHILDREN'S STORIES

by Laura Ingalls Wilder

Book	**Year Published**
Little House in the Big Woods	1932
Little House on the Prairie	1935
On the Banks of Plum Creek	1937
By the Shores of Silver Lake	1939
The Long Winter	1940
Little Town on the Prairie	1941
These Happy Golden Years	1943

BROADWAY'S LONGEST RUNS

As of October 3, 1999

Broadway Show	**Number of Performances**
Cats	7,093
A Chorus Line	6,137
Oh! Calcutta (Revival)	5,962
*Les Miserables	5,175
*The Phantom of the Opera	4,905
*Miss Saigon	3,516
42nd Street	3,485
Grease	3,388
Fiddler on the Roof	3,242
Life With Father	3,224

Source: Theatre.com. http://www.BroadwayNow.com/public/longestruns.asp (5 October 1999).

*Shows marked with asterisk (*) were still running at the time of this publication.

As of May 28, 2000

Cats	7,365
Les Miserables	5,431
The Phantom of the Opera	5,181
Miss Saigon	3,788

Go to the News page of the Broadway Web site below. Update Table 5 to reflect Broadway's Longest Runs as of the most recent date listed at the site.

http://www.theatre.com/

Activity 3 • Add Fields to an Existing Database Table

Add the fields shown below to the *Rockwell Technologies - District 14* table.

July Sales
August Sales
Total Sales
Average Monthly Sales

Enter into the table the information shown at the right.

Activity 4 • Query

Run a query on the table to select all the sales reps from California. Include first name, last name, territory, and July and August sales. Sort the query by last name in ascending order. Print a copy of the query.

Activity 5 • Computed Fields

Create a form file of all the sales reps that shows Last Name, First Name, July Sales, August Sales, Total Sales, and Average Monthly Sales. You will need to create computed fields for the Total Sales and Average Monthly Sales using the Expression Builder. Sort the query by last name in ascending order. Print the form in Datasheet View, landscape orientation.

SALES REPRESENTATIVES

Last Name	July Sales	August Sales
Hughes	$55,671	$63,339
Winters	65,882	73,563
Chambers	43,812	54,650
Hanson	50,092	39,751
Yang	27,389	48,762
Zimmer	63,982	58,332
Aguilera	60,010	69,756
Winfield	44,396	58,675
Gonzalez	39,792	57,381
Keller	74,981	47,343
Wilkins	49,201	59,752
Bushlack	70,500	75,306
Lopez	65,730	62,385
Weiss	54,750	34,780
Culver	47,980	58,656
Miller	29,760	39,716
Sherman	80,754	54,354
Bailey	49,753	50,330
Stockton	75,880	82,791
Pizarro	54,900	60,230
Davis, I.	39,763	48,655
Rice	65,830	66,385
Gilmore	40,340	37,381
Chi	52,379	59,659
Phillips	38,751	49,763
Taylor	57,925	50,845
Ryan	42,700	49,655
Backwith	68,524	62,566
Davis, B.	57,247	62,318
Bolling	42,700	47,930
Montessa	59,650	55,428
McGraw	49,831	54,900

LESSON 33 FORMAT THREE-COLUMN TABLES

Objectives:

1. To format three-column tables with main, secondary, and column headings.
2. To improve language skills (word choice).

33A • 5' Conditioning Practice

Key each line twice SS; key a 1' writing on line 3; determine *gwam.*

alphabet 1 Eight extra pizzas will be baked quickly for the jovial men.

fig/sym 2 Kaye said, "Can't you touch-key 45, 935, $608, and 17 1/2%?"

speed 3 Orlando and the girls may do the work for the big city firm.

gwam 1' | 1 | 2 | 3 | 4 | 5 | 6 | 7 | 8 | 9 | 10 | 11 | 12 |

LANGUAGE SKILLS

33B • 8' Language Skills: Word Choice

1. Study the spelling and definitions of the words at the right.
2. Key line 1 (Learn line), noting the proper choice of words.
3. Key lines 2–3 (the Apply lines), choosing the right words to complete the lines correctly.
4. Check your work; correct lines containing word-choice errors.

Save as: *CHOICE 33B*

cite (vb) to quote; to use as support; to commend; to summon

sight (n/vb) ability to see; something seen; a device to improve aim; to observe or focus

site (n) the place something is, was, or will be located or situated

their (pron) belonging to them

there (adv/pron) in or at that place or stage; word used to introduce a sentence or clause

they're (contr) a contracted form of *they are*

Learn 1 He will **cite** the article from the Web **site** about improving your **sight.**

Apply 2 You need to (cite, sight, site) five sources in the report due on Friday.

Apply 3 The (cite, sight, site) he chose for the party was a (cite, sight, site) to be seen.

Learn 1 **There** is the car **they're** going to use in **their** next play production.

Apply 2 (Their, There, They're) making (their, there, they're) school lunches.

Apply 3 (Their, There, They're) is the box of (their, there, they're) tools.

FORMATTING

33C • 37' Three-Column Tables

Table 1

Create and format the table shown at the right, using the information given below.

Main title: row height 0.5"; center vertical alignment

Secondary title: row height 0.45"; center vertical alignment

Column headings: row height 0.4"; center vertical alignment

Data rows: row height 0.3"; bottom vertical alignment

Table: center on page

Save as: *TBL33C1*

TOP 5 BROADWAY GROSSES		
Week Ending *September 12, 1999*		
Production	**Gross This Week**	**Gross Last Week**
Annie Get Your Gun	$ 572,885	*$ 671,363*
Chicago	536,852	*523,106*
Fosse	566,644	*605,993*
The Lion King	880,717	*875,772*
The Phantom of the Opera	601,218	*594,636*
Totals	$3,158,316	*$3,270,870*
Source: Theatre.com. http://www.BroadwayNow.com/public/boxoffice.asp (13 September 1999).		

ASSESSMENT

Activity 1 • Enter Information into Forms

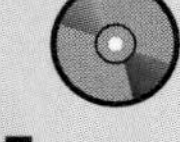

Open the *Rockwell Technologies - District 14* form from your network or Web source. Enter the information shown at the right into the form.

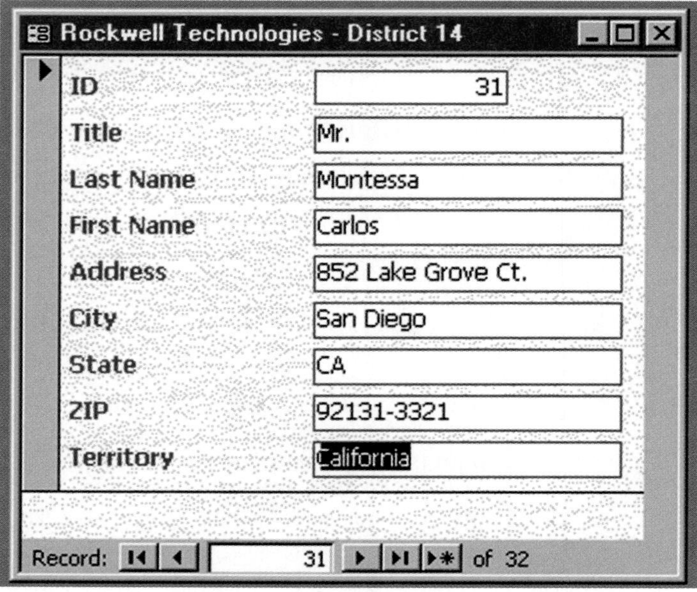

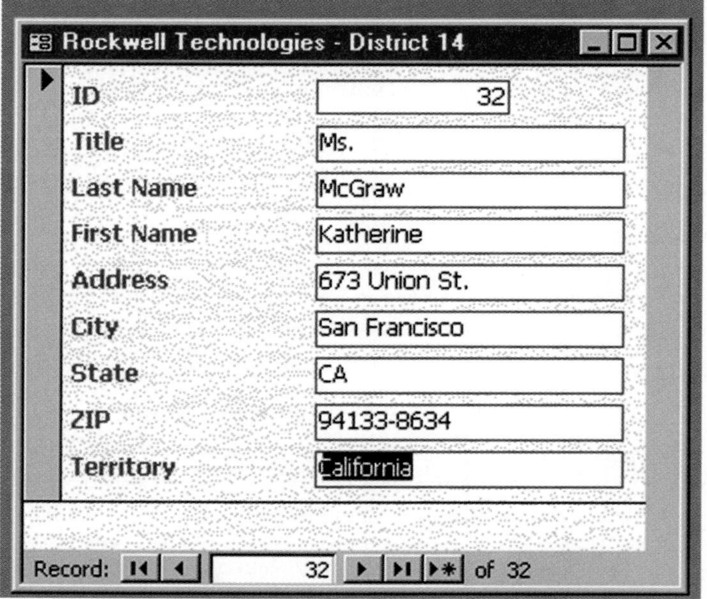

Activity 2 • Edit Records

Make the changes shown at the right to the records in the *Rockwell Technologies - District 14* table.

1. Change **Winters'** address to **1472 Prescott St. N**.
2. Change the ZIP Code for **Culver** to **97301-8824**.
3. Change **Phillips'** address to **387 Ferguson Ave., Modesto, 95354-3210**.

Table 2
Create the table shown at the right using the information given below.

Main title: row height 0.5"; center vertical alignment

Column headings: row height 0.4"; center vertical alignment

Data rows: row height 0.3"; bottom vertical alignment

Table: center on page

Column A: 2" wide

Column B: 1" wide

Column C: 2" wide

Save as: *TBL33C2*

Selected Works by American Authors		
Author	**Life**	**Works**
Robert Lee Forst	1874-1963	West-Running Brook
Henry w. Longfellow	1807-1882	Balleds
Carl Sandburn	1878-1967	Smoke and Steel
Louisa May Ascott	1832-1888	Little Women
William Faulkner	1897-1962	The Sound and the Furry
Samuel L. Clemens	1833-1910	Adventures of Tom Sawyer
Scott F. Fitzgerald	1896-1940	All Sad Young Men

Table 3
Arrange the data at the right as a table. Use **WIMBLEDON SINGLES CHAMPIONS** for the main title; **1995–1999** for the secondary title; and **Women's Champion**, **Year**, **Men's Champion** for the three column headings. Arrange the data attractively on the page.

Save as: *TBL33C3*

1995 Steffi Graf
1998 Jana Novotna
1997 Martina Hingis
1996 Steffi Graf
1999 Lindsay Davenport

1997 Pete Sampras
1999 Pete Sampras
1995 Pete Sampras
1998 Pete Sampras
1996 Richard Krajicek

Table 4
Open Table 2 (*TBL33C2*). Insert data shown at right. Delete the year author died; change column heading to **Year Born**. Sort data by Year Born in ascending order.

Save as: *TBL33C4*

Arthur Miller	*1915*	*Death of a Salesman*
Oliver W. Holmes	*1809*	*Old Ironsides*

LESSON 34 FORMAT FOUR-COLUMN TABLES

Objectives:

1. To format four-column tables with main, secondary, and column headings.
2. To make independent decisions about table formatting features.

34A • 5' Conditioning Practice

Key each line twice SS; key a 1' writing on line 3; determine *gwam*.

alphabet 1 David will buy the six unique jackets from Grady for prizes.
fig/sym 2 Jerry's 2001 tax was $4,875, about 7% ($369) less than 2000.
speed 3 Glen works with vigor to dismantle the downtown city chapel.
gwam 1' | 1 | 2 | 3 | 4 | 5 | 6 | 7 | 8 | 9 | 10 | 11 | 12 |

Activity 4 • Add New Records

1. Update the *Employee Information* file to include the employees shown at the right.
2. Save and print a copy of the table.

First Name	Last Name	Department	Extension	Supervisor
Trevor	Martin	Sales	1521	McKee
Jessica	Van Noy	Finance	6711	Rodriguez
Troy	McMichael	Sales	7220	McKee

Activity 5 • Data Sorts

1. Perform the data sorts shown at the right using the *Employee Information* table.
2. Print copies of the table after each sort has been completed.

1. Sort the table by employee last name in ascending order.
2. Sort the table by supervisor in ascending order.

Activity 6 • Queries

1. Create queries to answer the questions at the right. Include the employee's first and last name, department, and supervisor in each query.
2. Print the results of each query.

1. Which employees have McKee for a supervisor?
2. Which employees have "Jones" for a last name?
3. Which employees work in the Finance Department?

Activity 7

Report 1

1. Generate an entire report similar to the shortened one shown at the right.
2. Complete a primary sort by employee last name in ascending order and a secondary sort by employee first name in ascending order.
3. Title the report **Telephone Directory**.

Report 2

1. Generate another report.
2. Group by department.
3. Sort by employee last name in ascending order.
4. Use **Telephone Directory** for the title of the report.

Additional Review

Review the label and envelope features taught in Lesson 14.

Telephone Directory

Last Name	*First Name*	*Extension*	*Department*
Dombrowski	Michael	5400	Marketing
Harelson	Jason	2289	Finance
Hudson	Connie	5671	Sales
Iwata	Hiroko	2910	Management Information
Jardin	Sarah	3210	Accounting
Jones	Dustin	4093	Sales
Jones	Justin	5560	Finance
Jones	Tim	3208	Accounting
Martin	Trevor	1521	Sales

34B • 45'
Four-Column Tables

Table 1
Format the data at the right as a table. Use **FAMOUS COMPOSERS** for the main title and **1756–1899** for the secondary title. Arrange the data attractively on the page. Use the Sort feature to arrange the composers in alphabetical order.

 **Save as:** *TBL34B1*

Composer	**Nationality**	**Life**	**Music**
Mozart	Austrian	1756-1791	Don Giovanni
Beethoven	German	1770-1827	Ninth Symphony
Berlioz	French	1803-1869	Romeo and Juliet
Mendelssohn	German	1809-1847	Reformation
Chopin	Franco-Polish	1810-1849	Sonata in B Minor
Schumann	German	1810-1856	Rhenish Symphony
Wagner	German	1813-1883	Rienzi
Strauss	Austrian	1825-1899	Blue Danube

Table 2
Format the table at the right, arranging the data attractively.

Use **TOP TEN ANCESTRY GROUPS OF U.S. POPULATION** for the main title and **1990 Census** for the secondary title.

 **Save as:** *TBL34B2*

Rank	Ancestry	Number	Percent of Population
1	German	57,947,873	23.3
2	Irish	38,735,539	15.6
3	English African	32,651,788	13.1
4	~~Afro~~ American	23,777,098	9.6
5	Italain	14,664,550	5.9
6	American	12,395,~~000~~ 999	50
7	Mexican	11,586,983	4.7
8	French	10,320,935	4.1
9	Polish	9,366,106	3.8
10	American ~~Indian~~ Native	8,708,220	3.5
Source: *The Information Please Almanac*. Boston: Houghton Mifflin Company, 1996.			

Table 3
Arrange the data at the right attractively in a table according to Rank (1–10). Use **TOP BASEBALL MOVIES** for the main title; **Fall 1999** for the secondary title; **Rank**, **Movie**, **Year**, and **Percent of Votes** for the column headings.

The tenth movie is **Fear Strikes Out** made in **1957**, **0.6** percent of votes. Include a source note: **Source:** ***USA Today.*** **http://www.usatoday.com/sports/baseball/mlbfs97.htm (17 September 1999).**

Save as: *TBL34B3*

4	Pride of the Yankees	1942	8.0
9	Damn Yankees	1958	1.0
8	Bad News Bears	1976	3.2
2	The Natural	1984	25.1
3	Bull Durham	1988	18.4
6	Eight Men Out	1988	4.4
1	Field of Dreams	1989	29.4%
5	Major League	1989	8.0
7	League of Their Own	1992	4.4

Activity 1 • Create a Database File and Table

1. Create a new database using the filename *Jaeger Enterprises*.
2. Create a table in Design View using the filename *Employee Information*. The table should have the fields shown at the right.

 **Save as:** *Jaeger Enterprises*

First Name
Last Name
Department
Extension

Activity 2 • Add Records to a Database Table

Enter the records given at the right into the *Employee Information* table.

First Name	Last Name	Department	Extension
Julie	Zimmerman	Sales	3107
Dustin	Jones	Sales	4093
Sarah	Jardin	Accounting	3210
Michael	Dombrowski	Marketing	5400
Jason	Harelson	Finance	2289
Hiroko	Iwata	Management Information	2910
Connie	Hudson	Sales	5671
Tim	Jones	Accounting	3208
Rebecca	Miller	Management Information	4932
Adam	Martinez	Sales	1187
Leslie	Scanlon	Marketing	3012
Justin	Jones	Finance	5560
Stacey	Nikolai	Sales	8902
Jack	Nordstrom	Finance	3471

Activity 3 • Add a New Field

1. Add a new field to the *Employee Information* table. Use **Supervisor** for the field name.
2. Key the name of each employee's supervisor (shown at the right) in the table.

Name	Supervisor		Name	Supervisor
J. Zimmerman	McKee		T. Jones	Fuller
D. Jones	McKee		R. Miller	Maddux
S. Jardin	Fuller		A. Martinez	McKee
J. Dombrowski	Chan		L. Scanlon	Chan
J. Harelson	Rodriguez		J. Jones	Rodriguez
H. Iwata	Maddux		S. Nikolai	McKee
C. Hudson	McKee		J. Nordstrom	Rodriguez

Communication Skills 5

ACTIVITY 1

Subject/Verb Agreement

1. Key lines 1–10 at the right, using the correct verb.
2. Check the accuracy of your work with the instructor; correct any errors you made.
3. Note the rule number at the left of each sentence in which you made a verb agreement error.
4. Using the rules below the sentences and on p. 103, identify the rule(s) you need to review/practice.
5. **Read**: Study each rule.
6. **Learn**: Key the Learn line(s) beneath it, noting how the rule is applied.
7. **Apply**: Key the Apply line(s), choosing the correct verb.

 **Save as:** *CS5-ACT1*

Proofread & Correct

Rules		
1	1	Sandra and Rich (is, are) running for class secretary.
1	2	They (has, have) to score high on the SAT to enter that college.
2	3	You (doesn't, don't) think keyboarding is important.
2	4	Why (doesn't, don't) she take the test for advanced placement?
3	5	Neither of the candidates (meet, meets) the leadership criteria.
3	6	One of your art students (is, are) likely to win the prize.
5	7	The number of people against the proposal (is, are) quite small.
4	8	The manager, as well as his assistant, (is, are) to attend.
6	9	Neither the teacher nor her students (is, are) here.
3	10	All the meat (is, are) spoiled, but some items (is, are) okay.

Subject/Verb Agreement

Rule 1: Use a singular verb with a singular subject (noun or pronoun); use a plural verb with a plural subject and with a compound subject (two nouns or pronouns joined by *and*).

Learn 1 The speaker was delayed at the airport for over thirty minutes.
Learn 2 The players are all here, and they are getting restless.
Learn 3 You and your assistant are to join us for lunch.
Apply 4 The treasurer of the class (is, are) to introduce the speaker.
Apply 5 Dr. Cho (was, were) to give the lecture, but he (is, are) ill.
Apply 6 Mrs. Samoa and her son (is, are) to be on a local talk show.

Rule 2: Use the plural verb *do not* or *don't* with pronoun subjects *I, we, you*, and *they* as well as with plural nouns; use the singular verb *does not* or *doesn't* with pronouns *he, she,* and *it* as well as with singular nouns.

Learn 7 I do not find this report believable; you don't either.
Learn 8 If she doesn't accept our offer, we don't have to raise it.
Apply 9 They (doesn't, don't) discount, so I (doesn't, don't) shop there.
Apply 10 Jo and he (doesn't, don't) ski; they (doesn't, don't) plan to go.

Rule 3: Use singular verbs with indefinite pronouns (*each, every, any, either, neither, one*, etc.) and with *all* and *some* used as subjects if their modifiers are singular (but use plural verbs with *all* and *some* if their modifiers are plural).

Learn 11 Each of these girls has an important role in the class play.
Learn 12 Some of the new paint is already cracking and peeling.
Learn 13 All of the workers are to be paid for the special holiday.
Apply 14 Neither of them (is, are) well enough to start the game.
Apply 15 Some of the juice (is, are) sweet; some (is, are) quite tart.
Apply 16 Every girl and boy (is, are) sure to benefit from this decision.

(continued on next page)

Mailing Labels and Envelopes

Mailing labels and envelopes can be created by using the mailing labels and envelopes features of Mail Merge in conjunction with your database file.

Activity 1 • Mailing Labels

1. Create mailing labels (illustrated at the right) for the merge letters generated for *Rockwell Technologies* in Lessons 12–13.
2. Use Avery Product No. 5160 labels.

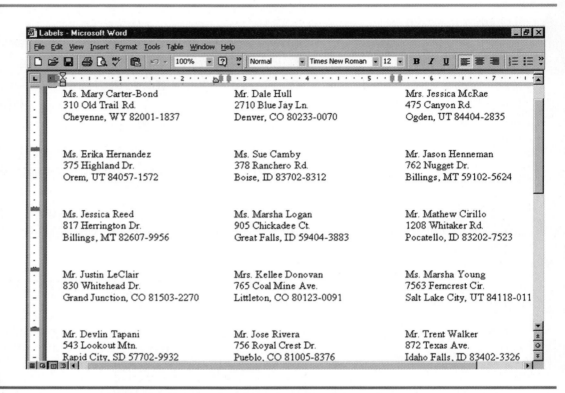

Activity 2 • Mailing Labels

1. Create mailing labels for the merge letters generated for *Eastwick School of Dance* in Lessons 12–13.
2. Use Avery Product No. 5160 labels.

Labels - Microsoft Word

Ms. Mary Carter-Bond 310 Old Trail Rd. Cheyenne, WY 82001-1837	Mr. Dale Hull 2710 Blue Jay Ln. Denver, CO 80233-0070	Mrs. Jessica McRae 475 Canyon Rd. Ogden, UT 84404-2835
Ms. Erika Hernandez 375 Highland Dr. Orem, UT 84057-1572	Ms. Sue Camby 378 Ranchero Rd. Boise, ID 83702-8312	Mr. Jason Henneman 762 Nugget Dr. Billings, MT 59102-5624
Ms. Jessica Reed 817 Herrington Dr. Billings, MT 82607-9956	Ms. Marsha Logan 905 Chickadee Ct. Great Falls, ID 59404-3883	Mr. Mathew Cirillo 1208 Whitaker Rd. Pocatello, ID 83202-7523
Mr. Justin LeClair 830 Whitehead Dr. Grand Junction, CO 81503-2270	Mrs. Kellee Donovan 765 Coal Mine Ave. Littleton, CO 80123-0091	Ms. Marsha Young 7563 Ferncrest Cir. Salt Lake City, UT 84118-011
Mr. Devlin Tapani 543 Lookout Mtn. Rapid City, SD 57702-9932	Mr. Jose Rivera 756 Royal Crest Dr. Pueblo, CO 81005-8376	Mr. Trent Walker 872 Texas Ave. Idaho Falls, ID 83402-3326

Activity 3 • Envelopes

1. Create envelopes as illustrated at the right for the merge letters generated for *A&E Bank* in Lessons 12–13.
2. Use Standard Size 10 envelopes and only print envelopes for Eisenhower and Upshaw.

   The return address for the bank is:

   A&E Bank
   823 Sterling Dr.
   Durham, NC 27712-0231

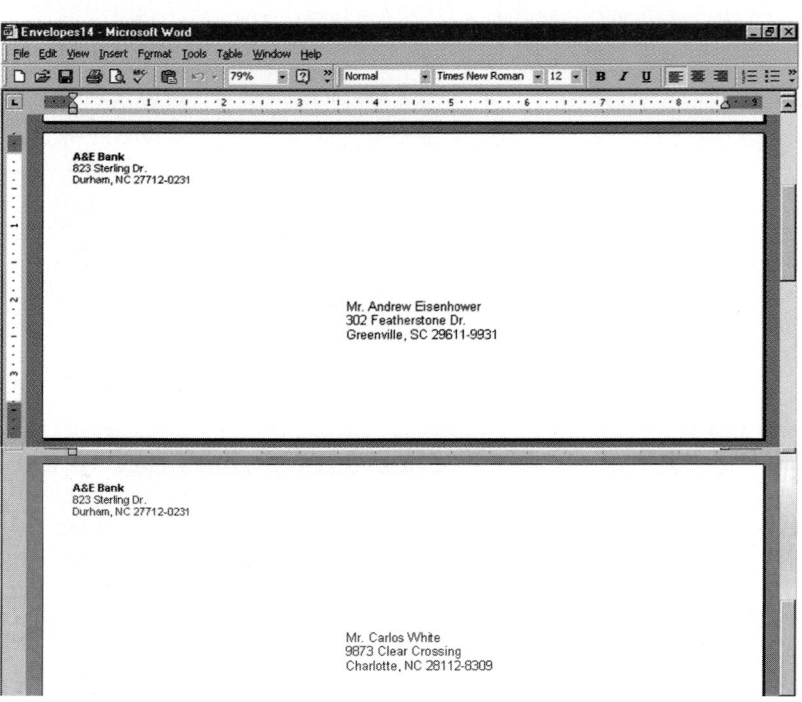

Envelopes14 - Microsoft Word

A&E Bank
823 Sterling Dr.
Durham, NC 27712-0231

Mr. Andrew Eisenhower
302 Featherstone Dr.
Greenville, SC 29611-9931

A&E Bank
823 Sterling Dr.
Durham, NC 27712-0231

Mr. Carlos White
9873 Clear Crossing
Charlotte, NC 28112-8309

Rule 4: Use a singular verb with a singular subject that is separated from the verb by the phrase *as well as* or *in addition to*; use a plural verb with a plural subject so separated.

Learn 17 The letter, in addition to the report, has to be revised.
Learn 18 The shirts, as well as the dress, have to be pressed again.
Apply 19 The driver, as well as the burglar, (was, were) apprehended.
Apply 20 Two managers, in addition to the president, (is, are) to attend.

Rule 5: Use a singular verb if *number* is used as the subject and is preceded by *the*; use a plural verb if *number* is the subject and is preceded by *a*.

Learn 21 A number of them have already voted, but the number is small.
Apply 22 The number of jobs (is, are) low; a number of us (has, have) applied.

Rule 6: Use a singular verb with singular subjects linked by *or* or *nor,* but if one subject is singular and the other is plural, the verb agrees with the nearer subject.

Learn 23 Neither Ms. Moss nor Mr. Katz was invited to speak.
Learn 24 Either the manager or his assistants are to participate.
Apply 25 If neither he nor they (go, goes), either you or she (has, have) to.

ACTIVITY 2

Reading

1. Open the file *CD-CS5READ* and read the document carefully.
2. Close the file.
3. Key the answers to the questions at the right, using complete sentences.
4. Check the accuracy of your work with the instructor; correct any errors you made.

Save as: *CS5-ACT2*

1. What kind of positions are being filled?
2. What is the minimum number of hours each employee must work each week?
3. Is weekend work available?
4. What benefit is offered to employees who have young children to care for?
5. Is the pay based only on performance?
6. When are the position openings available?
7. Do all telemarketing employees work during daytime hours?
8. How can you submit a resume?

ACTIVITY 3

Composing

1. Study the quotations at the right. Consider the relationship between honesty and truth.
2. Compose/key a paragraph to show your understanding of honesty and truth. Describe an incident in which honesty and truth *should* prevail but don't in real life.

Save as: *CS5-ACT3*

Honesty's the best policy.
—Cervantes

Piety requires us to honor truth above our friends.
—Aristotle

To be honest . . . here is a task for all that a man has of fortitude.
—Robert Louis Stevenson

The dignity of truth is lost with protesting.
—Ben Jonson

Activity 2 • Merge Sources

1. Create the form letter shown at the right to send to the parents of students who have not paid their September dance fees.

Save as: *Eastwick Form*

Tip:

Insert necessary fields and data from *Eastwick Fees* into your *Eastwick Address* table. Include a new **Title** field and supply the appropriate courtesy title **Mr.** or **Ms.**

2. Create a query to determine which parents should receive a letter.
3. Merge and print the letters to Finley and Dye.

Save as: *Eastwick Merge*

October 15, 200-

«Title» «First_Name_Guardian» «Last_Name_Guardian»
«Address»
«City», «State» «ZIP»

Dear «Title» «Last_Name_Guardian»:

Please check your records to see if you have paid for «First_Name»'s September dance fees. Our records show that we have not received the fees in the amount of «Monthly_Fees». Let us know if our records are incorrect or send the fees with «First_Name» to her next dance class.

I have enjoyed working with «First_Name» this fall. Observing the students' progress from one skill level to the next is always very satisfying to me. The students are looking forward to performing for you at the December recital.

Sincerely,

Ashley Eastwick
Dance Instructor

xx

Activity 3 • Merge Sources

1. Send the letter at the right to applicants in the *A&E Bank* database with an income greater than $30,000. Be sure to include an enclosure notation.

Save as: *A&E Bank Form*

2. Add a new field, **Courtesy Title**, to the *A&E Bank* database before completing the merge. (Supply the appropriate courtesy title [**Mr.** or **Ms.**] for each applicant.)
3. Merge and print the letters to Eisenhower and Upshaw.

Save as: *A&E Bank Merge*

October 12, 200-

«Courtesy_Title» «First_Name» «Last_Name»
«Street_Address»
«City», «State» «ZIP»

Dear «Courtesy_Title» «Last_Name»:

Your credit card application with A&E Bank has been approved. A copy of our credit card rules and regulations is enclosed. Please contact us at 1-800-563-8800 if you have questions after reviewing the documents.

Your initial line of credit on the card is $5,000. The limit is reviewed on a periodic basis and will be increased as warranted.

We are looking forward to serving your credit needs. When we can be of further service, please contact us.

Sincerely,

Jason R. Rhyer
Credit Card Department

UNIT 11

LESSONS 35–37

Prepare for Document Formatting Assessment

LESSON 35 PREPARE FOR ASSESSMENT: E-MAIL, MEMOS, LETTERS

Objective:

To prepare for assessment of e-mail, memo, and letter formatting skills.

35A • 5' Conditioning Practice

Key each line twice SS; then key a 1' writing on line 3; determine *gwam*.

alphabet 1 Jacques paid a very sizeable sum for the meetings next week.

fig/sym 2 The desk (#539A28) and chair (#61B34) usually sell for $700.

speed 3 Helen did the work for us, but the neighbor will pay for it.

gwam 1' | 1 | 2 | 3 | 4 | 5 | 6 | 7 | 8 | 9 | 10 | 11 | 12 |

FORMATTING

35B • 45' Reinforce E-mail/Memo/Letter Formatting Skills

Document 1 (E-mail)

Format and key the text at the right. If you have e-mail software, format the message as e-mail (from you to your instructor). Format it as an interoffice memo if you do not have e-mail software.

Check your message; correct all errors.

 **Save as:** *EMAIL35B1*

Note: This message contains some *incomplete sentences;* for example, "Tournament started in 1877 at Wimbledon" and "Shakespeare plays in the open air." In an incomplete sentence, a nonessential word or words are missing. Some writers use them to save time when writing informal messages, such as e-mail or memos.

TO: Jessica Holloway

FROM: Barbara Knight

DATE: March 15, 200-

SUBJECT: LONDON EXCURSION

I've listed below several other events, along with a brief description, which are taking place in London while we are there. Please let me know which ones are of interest to you, and I'll get additional information on them.

Lawn Tennis Championship. Tournament started in 1877 at Wimbledon. It is now recognized as one of the premiere Grand Slam events.

Kenwood Lakeside Concerts. Fifty-year tradition of outdoor concerts. Includes fireworks and laser shows.

The Proms. Henry Wood Promenade Concerts started in 1895. Attracts devoted music lovers from around the world.

Outdoor Shakespeare Performances. Shakespeare plays in the open air. Bring a blanket and enjoy!

Royal Academy's Summer Exhibition. Founded in 1768. Over two centuries of summer exhibits of living painters.

Mail Merge Illustration

The illustration at the right shows how the data file was merged with the word processing file to produce the letter at the bottom of the illustration.

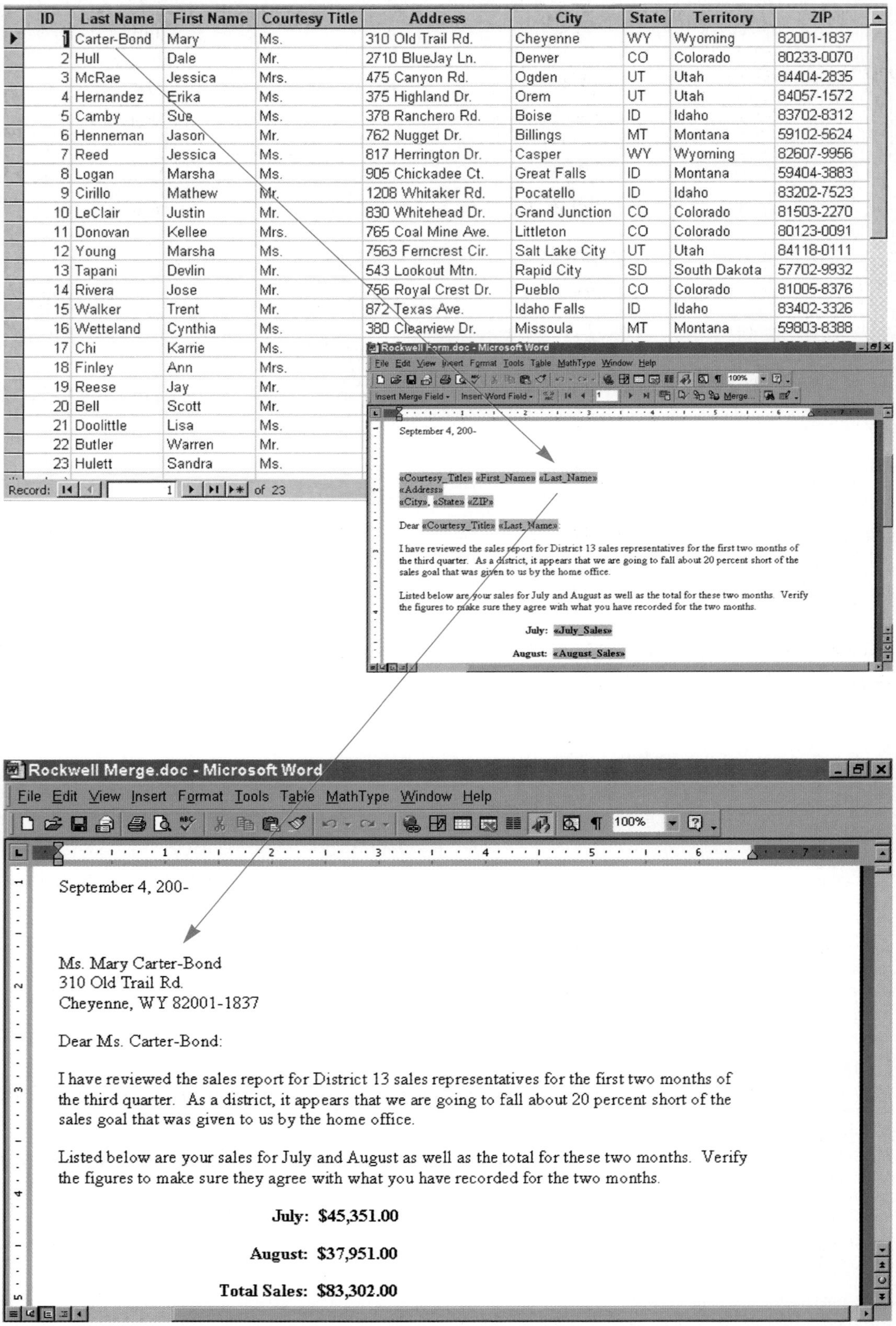

ID | Last Name | First Name | Courtesy Title | Address | City | State | Territory | ZIP
1 Carter-Bond Mary Ms. 310 Old Trail Rd. Cheyenne WY Wyoming 82001-1837
2 Hull Dale Mr. 2710 BlueJay Ln. Denver CO Colorado 80233-0070
3 McRae Jessica Mrs. 475 Canyon Rd. Ogden UT Utah 84404-2835
4 Hernandez Erika Ms. 375 Highland Dr. Orem UT Utah 84057-1572
5 Camby Sue Ms. 378 Ranchero Rd. Boise ID Idaho 83702-8312
6 Henneman Jason Mr. 762 Nugget Dr. Billings MT Montana 59102-5624
7 Reed Jessica Ms. 817 Herrington Dr. Casper WY Wyoming 82607-9956
8 Logan Marsha Ms. 905 Chickadee Ct. Great Falls ID Montana 59404-3883
9 Cirillo Mathew Mr. 1208 Whitaker Rd. Pocatello ID Idaho 83202-7523
10 LeClair Justin Mr. 830 Whitehead Dr. Grand Junction CO Colorado 81503-2270
11 Donovan Kellee Mrs. 765 Coal Mine Ave. Littleton CO Colorado 80123-0091
12 Young Marsha Ms. 7563 Ferncrest Cir. Salt Lake City UT Utah 84118-0111
13 Tapani Devlin Mr. 543 Lookout Mtn. Rapid City SD South Dakota 57702-9932
14 Rivera Jose Mr. 756 Royal Crest Dr. Pueblo CO Colorado 81005-8376
15 Walker Trent Mr. 872 Texas Ave. Idaho Falls ID Idaho 83402-3326
16 Wetteland Cynthia Ms. 380 Clearview Dr. Missoula MT Montana 59803-8388
17 Chi Karrie Ms.
18 Finley Ann Mrs.
19 Reese Jay Mr.
20 Bell Scott Mr.
21 Doolittle Lisa Ms.
22 Butler Warren Mr.
23 Hulett Sandra Ms.
Record: 1 of 23
Rockwell Form.doc - Microsoft Word
File Edit View Insert Format Tools Table MathType Window Help
Insert Merge Field - Insert Word Field - Merge...
September 4, 200-
«Courtesy_Title» «First_Name» «Last_Name»
«Address»
«City», «State» «ZIP»
Dear «Courtesy_Title» «Last_Name»:
I have reviewed the sales report for District 13 sales representatives for the first two months of the third quarter. As a district, it appears that we are going to fall about 20 percent short of the sales goal that was given to us by the home office.
Listed below are your sales for July and August as well as the total for these two months. Verify the figures to make sure they agree with what you have recorded for the two months.
July: «July_Sales»
August: «August_Sales»
Rockwell Merge.doc - Microsoft Word
File Edit View Insert Format Tools Table MathType Window Help
100%
September 4, 200-
Ms. Mary Carter-Bond
310 Old Trail Rd.
Cheyenne, WY 82001-1837
Dear Ms. Carter-Bond:
I have reviewed the sales report for District 13 sales representatives for the first two months of the third quarter. As a district, it appears that we are going to fall about 20 percent short of the sales goal that was given to us by the home office.
Listed below are your sales for July and August as well as the total for these two months. Verify the figures to make sure they agree with what you have recorded for the two months.
July: $45,351.00
August: $37,951.00
Total Sales: $83,302.00

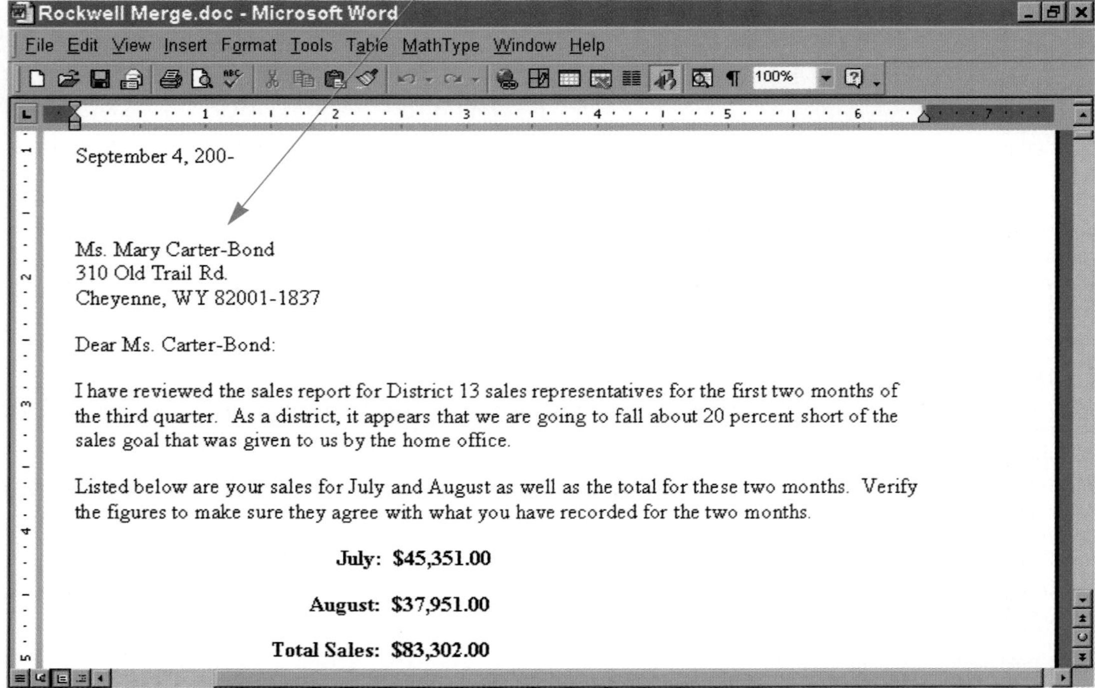

Document 2 (Memo)
Format and key the text at the right as a memo. Check your copy; correct all keying and format errors.

 **Save as:** *MEMO35B2*

TO: Marguerite Mercedes, Director

FROM: Justin Mathews, Administrative Assistant

DATE: March 5, 200-

SUBJECT: BALLET COMPANY ADDRESSES

Attached is the address list for the ballet companies that you requested. I was unable to secure an address for the Bolshoi Ballet in Moscow.

I have seen the Royal Swedish Ballet, the American Ballet Theatre, and the Paris Opera Ballet perform. They were all excellent. The patrons of our Artist Series would be extremely pleased with any of the three performances.

Even though I have not personally seen performances by any of the other groups on the list, I have heard excellent comments by others who have been fortunate enough to see them perform. I don't think we can go wrong by inviting any of those on the list to be a part of next year's Artist Series.

xx

Attachment

Document 3 (Letter)
Format and key the text at the right as a personal-business letter. Replace *xx* with your reference initials. Check your copy; correct all keying and formatting errors.

 **Save as:** *LTR35B3*

Note:
Although the preferred spelling of *theater* (U.S.) ends with *er*, the word ends with *re* for several prominent institutions in this country, as in Britain; notably, American Ballet Theatre, New Amsterdam Theatre, Palace Theatre, and Shubert Theatre.

words

810 Lake Grove Ct. | San Diego, CA 92131-8112 | March 30, 200- 12
Ms. Barbara Knight | 2010 Rosewood Pl. | Riverside, CA 92506-6528 | 24
Dear Barbara 27

Can you believe that we will be in London in less than three months? 41
London is one of my favorite places to visit. 50

I've done some checking on London's theatres. Do any of the three 64
plays I've listed below interest you? If so, let me know, and I'll make the 78
arrangements. 82

Les Miserables: Story revolves around nineteenth-century French 95
Revolution with its struggles, passion, and love. 105

Amadeus: Story about the life of Mozart in eighteenth-century Vienna 119
and his rivalry with composer Sallieri. 127

Starlight Express: Musical by Andrew Lloyd Weber with lyrics by 140
Richard Stilgoe. 144

Les Miserables is being performed at the Palace Theatre, *Amadeus* at 158
the Old Vic, and *Starlight Express* at the Apollo Victoria. The Palace 172
Theatre and The Old Vic were both built in the 1800s. 183

I've confirmed our reservations at the Copthorne Tara. If there is 197
anything else that you would like me to check, let me know. 209

Sincerely | Jessica C. Holloway | xx 215

LESSONS 12-13

COMBINING SOURCES WITH MAIL MERGE

Using Mail Merge

Read the text at the right and study the illustration on p. 425 to learn how information from two sources is combined into one document.

The **Merge** feature is used to combine information from two sources into one document. It is often used for mail merge, which merges a word processing file (form letter) with a database file.

The database file contains a record for each recipient. Each record contains field(s) of information about the person such as first name, last name, address, city, state, ZIP, etc.

The word processing file contains the text of the document (constant information) plus the field codes and field names (variable information). The field codes and names are positioned in the document where the variable information from the database is to appear. A personalized letter to each recipient is the result of merging the two files.

Activity 1 • Merge Sources

1. Create the form letter shown at the right to send to the sales reps in the *Rockwell Technologies* database (*Sales Reps - District 13*).

Save as: *Rockwell Form*

2. Add a new field to the *Sales Reps - District 13* database with a field name **Courtesy Title**.
3. Use **Ms.** for all female reps except McRae, Donovan, and Finley. They prefer to use **Mrs.** for their courtesy title. Use **Mr.** for all male reps.
4. Merge and print the letters to Hernandez, Tapani, and Butler.

Save as: *Rockwell Merge*

September 4, 200-

«Courtesy_Title» «First_Name» «Last_Name»
«Address»
«City», «State» «ZIP»

Dear «Courtesy_Title» «Last_Name»:

I have reviewed the sales report for District 13 sales representatives for the first two months of the third quarter. As a district, it appears that we are going to fall about 20 percent short of the sales goal that was given to us by the home office.

Listed below are your sales for July and August as well as the total for these two months. Verify the figures to make sure they agree with what you have recorded for the two months.

July: «July_Sales»

August: «August_Sales»

Total Sales: «Total_Sales»

Please make every effort possible during September to reach the goal that was set for your territory last May. It is my understanding that most of the other districts are going to meet or exceed the goals that were given to them.

If I can provide additional assistance to you to help you meet your goal, please contact me.

Sincerely,

Paul M. Vermillion
District Sales Manager

PREPARE FOR ASSESSMENT: REPORTS

Objective:
To prepare for assessment of report formatting skills.

36A • 5' Conditioning Practice

Key each line twice SS; then take a 1' writing on line 3; determine *gwam.*

alphabet 1 Quincy just put back five azure gems next to the gold watch.

figures 2 Tim moved from 5142 Troy Lane to 936 - 23d Street on 8/7/01.

speed 3 He lent the field auditor a hand with the work for the firm.

gwam 1' | 1 | 2 | 3 | 4 | 5 | 6 | 7 | 8 | 9 | 10 | 11 | 12 |

FORMATTING

36B • 35' Reinforce Report Formatting Skills

Document 1 (Unbound Report)

Format and key the text at the right as an unbound report. Use **THEATRE** for the title of the report. Check and correct all keying and format errors.

Save as: *RPT36B1*

Tonight the house lights will dim and another performance will begin on Broadway. Perhaps it will be another performance of *Cats*, a play that had accumulated 7,225 performances as of January 23, 2000. Or perhaps it will be the play that replaces *Cats*.

Somewhere, sometime today, another enactment of one of Shakespeare's plays will take place. It may be in a high school auditorium, or it may be at a professional Shakespearean playhouse.

Theatre has enriched the lives of people for many years. No one really knows when the first play production was performed. However, historians say, "Theatre is as old as mankind. There have been primitive forms of it since man's beginnings." (Berthold, 1991, 1) The more commonly recognized form of theatre, the play, dates back to what is referred to as "Greek Theatre" and "Roman Theatre."

Greek Theatre

Greek Theatre started around 500 B.C. Sophocles and Aristophanes are two of the well-known Greek playwrights whose works are still being performed today.

Religious festivals that honored the Greek god of wine and fertility (Dionysus) were part of the culture of Greece around this time. The Greeks felt that if they honored Dionysus, he would in turn bless them with many children, rich land, and abundant crops. Plays were performed as part of these festivals.

To accommodate the large number of people who attended the plays (as many as 14,000 to 17,000 people, according to historians), theatres were built into a hillside. The plays were staged in the morning and lasted until sunset, since there was no electricity for lighting. (Prince and Jackson, 1997, 35)

(continued on next page)

Activities 1 and 2 • Create Reports

1. Open *Software Professionals.*
2. Create reports in the database with the information requested at the right.

Save as: *Software Price List* and *Software Sales*

SOFTWARE PROFESSIONALS		
Report Specifications		
Report 1	Layout: Columnar Style: Bold Title: Software Price List Sort: Ascending by Software	Software Stock Number Name of the Software Price of the Software
Report 2	Layout: Justified Style: Compact Title: Software Sales Sort: Descending by Sales	Software Stock Number Name of the Software Sales

Activities 3 and 4 • Create Reports

1. Open *Eastwick School of Dance.*
2. Create reports in the database with the information requested at the right.

Save as: *Student Address List* and *Student Telephone List*

Eastwick School of Dance		
Report Specifications		
Report 3	Layout: Tabular Style: Formal Title: Student Address List Sort: Ascending by Last Name	Student's Last Name Student's First Name Address City State ZIP
Report 4	Layout: Tabular Style: Soft Gray Title: Student Telephone List Sort: Ascending by Last Name	Student's Last Name Student's First Name Student's Telephone Number

Activities 5 and 6 • Create Reports

1. Open *Rockwell Technologies.*
2. Create reports in the database with the information requested at the right.

Save as: *July/August Sales* and *July/August Sales by Territory*

ROCKWELL TECHNOLOGIES		
Report Specifications		
Report 5	***Layout: Tabular*** ***Style: Corporate*** ***Title: July/August Sales*** ***Sort: Descending by Total Sales***	*Sales Rep's Last Name* *Sales Rep's Territory* *Sales Rep's July Sales* *Sales Rep's August Sales* *Sales Rep's Total Sales*
Report 6	*Prepare a sales report with the same information used in Report 5. Group the sales by territory. Use* ***July/August Sales by Territory*** *for the report title.*	

Document 2 (References List)

Use the information below to create a references list on a separate page. Check and correct all keying and format errors.

REFERENCES

Berthold, Margot. <u>The History of World Theater</u>. New York: The Continuum Publishing Company, 1991.

Prince, Nancy, and Jeanie Jackson. <u>Exploring Theatre</u>. Minneapolis/St. Paul: West Publishing Company, 1997.

Save as: *RPT36B2*

<u>Roman Theatre</u>

The Roman Theatre was the next widely recognized form of the theatre. The first Roman theatrical performance, historians believe, was performed around 365 B.C. Seneca, Plautus, and Terentius are the best known of the early Roman playwrights. Seneca was known for his tragedies, while the other two were known for their comedies.

The Roman plays were similar to those of the Greeks. Unlike the Greeks, however, the Romans did not limit the number of actors in each play. Another major difference between the Greek and Roman theatres was the theatre buildings. *The Romans were great engineers and architects. They built theatres that were unified, freestanding structures several stories high. (Prince and Jackson, 1997, 44)*

SKILL BUILDING

36C • 10' Timed Writings

1. Key a 1' writing on each ¶; determine *gwam*.
2. Key a 2' writing on ¶s 1–2 combined; determine *gwam*.
3. Key a 3' writing on ¶s 1–2 combined; determine *gwam* and count errors.

Quarter-Minute Checkpoints				
gwam	1/4'	1/2'	3/4'	1'
24	6	12	18	24
28	7	14	21	28
32	8	16	24	32
36	9	18	27	36
40	10	20	30	40
44	11	22	33	44
48	12	24	36	48
52	13	26	39	52
56	14	28	42	56
60	15	30	45	60

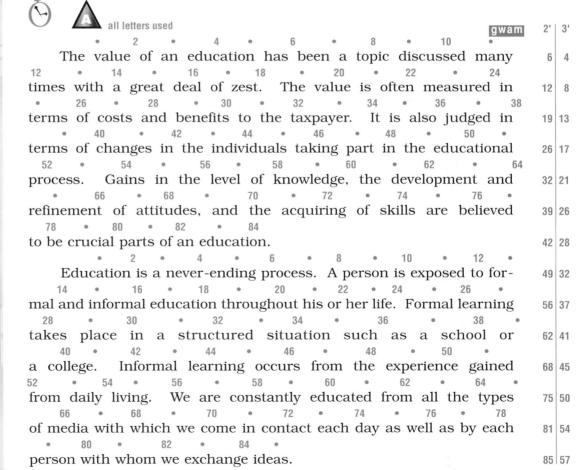

all letters used

	gwam 2'	3'
The value of an education has been a topic discussed many	6	4
times with a great deal of zest. The value is often measured in	12	8
terms of costs and benefits to the taxpayer. It is also judged in	19	13
terms of changes in the individuals taking part in the educational	26	17
process. Gains in the level of knowledge, the development and	32	21
refinement of attitudes, and the acquiring of skills are believed	39	26
to be crucial parts of an education.	42	28
Education is a never-ending process. A person is exposed to for-	49	32
mal and informal education throughout his or her life. Formal learning	56	37
takes place in a structured situation such as a school or	62	41
a college. Informal learning occurs from the experience gained	68	45
from daily living. We are constantly educated from all the types	75	50
of media with which we come in contact each day as well as by each	81	54
person with whom we exchange ideas.	85	57

gwam 2' | 1 | 2 | 3 | 4 | 5 | 6

3' | 1 | 2 | 3 | 4

Report Illustration 2
The report at the right was created using the "Create report by using wizard" feature. The report is in **Portrait** orientation with **Justified** layout in **Formal** style. The report is sorted in **Descending** order by Ending Inventory. Only the first six entries of the report are shown.

Ending Inventory (Justified)

Ending Inventory	Stock Number	Software
4127	B658	Telephone Directory

Ending Inventory	Stock Number	Software
4020	B952	Tax Assistant

Ending Inventory	Stock Number	Software
2247	E758	Keyboard Composition

Ending Inventory	Stock Number	Software
2122	B731	Quick Key WP

Ending Inventory	Stock Number	Software
2121	B794	Your Time Manager

Ending Inventory	Stock Number	Software
2050	E246	Computer Geography

Report Illustration 3
The report at the right was created using the "Create report by using wizard" feature. The report is in **Portrait** orientation with **Columnar** layout in **Bold** style. The report is sorted in **Ascending** order by Ending Inventory. Only the first five entries of the report are shown.

Ending Inventory (Columnar)

Ending Inventory	60
Stock Number	B821
Software	Data Controller
Ending Inventory	325
Stock Number	B833
Software	Office Layout
Ending Inventory	350
Stock Number	E561
Software	Creative Letters
Ending Inventory	463
Stock Number	B586
Software	Graphics Designer
Ending Inventory	600
Stock Number	E320
Software	English Enhancement

PREPARE FOR ASSESSMENT: TABLES

Objective:

To prepare for assessment of table formatting skills.

37A • 5' Conditioning Practice

Key each line twice SS; then key a 1' writing on line 3; determine *gwam.*

alphabet 1 Joyce Savin fixed the big clock that may win a unique prize.

figures 2 Items marked * are out of stock: #785*, #461A*, and #2093*.

speed 3 The firm paid for the rigid sign by the downtown civic hall.

gwam 1' | 1 | 2 | 3 | 4 | 5 | 6 | 7 | 8 | 9 | 10 | 11 | 12 |

FORMATTING

37B • 35' Reinforce Table Formatting Skills

Table 1

Create the table shown at the right using the information given below. Center the table horizontally and vertically.

Main title: row height 0.5"; center vertical alignment

Column headings: row height 0.4"; center vertical alignment

Data rows: row height 0.3"; bottom vertical alignment

Adjust column widths to arrange material attractively on the page.

Save as: *TBL37B1*

Table 2

Create the table shown at the right using the information given for Table 1. Center the table horizontally and vertically.

Adjust column widths to arrange material attractively on the page.

Save as: *TBL37B2*

AMERICAN LITERATURE - 1900s	
Literature	**Author**
A Rose for Emily (1930)	William Faulkner
The Grapes of Wrath (1939)	John Steinbeck
The Scotty Who Knew Too Much (1940)	James Thurber
House Made of Dawn (1968)	N. Scott Momaday
Everyday Use (1973)	Alice Walker
The Wife's Story (1932)	Ursula K. Le Guin
I Ask My Mother to Sing (1986)	Li-Young Lee
The Phone Booth at the Corner (1989)	Juan Delgado

WILLIAM SHAKESPEARE		
Play	**Year Written**	**Category**
The Comedy of Errors	1590	Comedy
Richard II	1595	History
Romeo and Juliet	1595	Tragedy
Much Ado About Nothing	1599	Comedy
Julius Caesar	1599	Tragedy
Hamlet	1601	Tragedy
King Lear	1605	Tragedy
The Tempest	1611	Comedy

Preparing Reports

Read the text at the right to learn about Report features.

The Report features of the database are used for summarizing, formatting, and printing selected data from the database.

Summarizing: Generally, only a portion of the data contained in a database is needed for a particular application. The Summarizing feature allows for the selection of specific data for inclusion in the report.

Formatting: Formatting can be accomplished automatically using the Wizard feature of the software. The form can be modified by using the Design View feature.

Printing: Once the data has been specified and formatted, professional-looking hard copies can be printed and distributed for information and decision-making purposes. Today, electronic distribution of reports is also quite common.

Report Illustration 1
The report at the right was created using the "Create report by using wizard" feature. The report was sorted in **Ascending** order by Ending Inventory. The report was formatted in **Tabular** layout with **Portrait** orientation using **Soft Gray** style.

Ending Inventory

Ending Inventory	Stock Number	Software
60	B821	Data Controller
325	B833	Office Layout
350	E561	Creative Letters
463	B586	Graphics Designer
600	E320	English Enhancement
826	E786	Computerized Reading
827	B839	Art Gallery
1241	B615	Language Skills
1513	B689	Financial Advisors
1622	B929	Basic Spreadsheets
1700	E641	Spelling Mastery
1961	E910	Math Tutor
2050	E246	Computer Geography
2121	B794	Your Time Manager
2122	B731	Quick Key WP
2247	E758	Keyboard Composition
4020	B952	Tax Assistant
4127	B658	Telephone Directory

Tuesday, September 12, 2000 Page 1 of 1

Table 3
Format the data at the right as a table. Use the table formatting features that you have learned to arrange the data attractively on the page.

 **Save as:** *TBL37B3*

NEW YORK PLAYS		
Plays	**Theater**	**Date Opened**
Annie Get Your Gun	Marquis Theater	03/04/99
Beauty and the Beast	Palace Theatre	04/18/94
Cabaret	Studio 54	03/19/98
Cats	Winter Garden Theater	10/07/82
Chicago	Shubert Theatre	11/14/96
Death of a Salesman	Eugene O'Neill Theater	02/10/99
The Lion King	New Amsterdam Theatre	11/13/97
Les Miserables	Imperial Theater	03/12/87
Miss Saigon	Broadway Theater	04/11/91
The Phantom of the Opera	Majestic Theater	01/26/88

Source: Theatre.com. http://www.nytheatre-wire.com/PoorR.htm (1 October 1999).

SKILL BUILDING

37C • 10' Timed Writings

1. Key a 1' writing on each ¶; determine *gwam*.
2. Key a 2' writing on ¶s 1–3 combined; determine *gwam*.
3. Key a 3' writing on ¶s 1–3 combined; determine *gwam* and count errors.

all letters used — gwam 2' | 3'

There is a value in work, value to the worker as well as 6 4
to the employer for whom one works. In spite of the 11 7
stress or pressure under which many people work, gainful work 17 11
provides workers with a feeling of security and self-esteem. 23 15

Some people do not want to work unless they have a job of 29 19
prestige; that is, a job that others admire or envy. To obtain 35 24
such a position, one must be prepared to perform the tasks the 42 28
job requires. Realize this now; prepare yourself. 47 31

School and college courses are designed to help you to 52 35
excel in the basic knowledge and skills the better jobs demand. 59 39
Beyond all of this, special training or work experience may be 65 43
needed for you to move up in your chosen career. 70 47

gwam 2' | 1 | 2 | 3 | 4 | 5 | 6
3' | 1 | 2 | 3 | 4

Activity 2 • Create Forms

1. Open *A&E Bank.*
2. Create a form in the database with the information requested at the right.

Save as: *Applicant's Annual Income*

A&E Bank	
Form Specifications	
Layout: Columnar Style: SandStone Title: Applicant's Annual Income Sort: Descending Order by Annual Income	Last Name First Name Annual Income

Activity 3 • Create Forms

1. Open *Eastwick School of Dance.*
2. Create a form in the database with the information requested at the right.

Save as: *Eastwick Student Enrollment*

Eastwick School of Dance	
Form Specifications	
Layout: Tabular Style: Expedition Title: Eastwick Student Enrollment Sort: Ascending Order by Last Name	Last Name First Name Dance Class 1 Dance Class 2

Activities 4 and 5 • Create Forms

1. Open *Rockwell Technologies.*
2. Create the forms in the database with the information requested at the right.

Save as: *Rockwell Sales for July and August* and *Sales Reps' Territory*

ROCKWELL TECHNOLOGIES	
Form Specifications	
Layout: Tabular *Style: Blends* *Title: Rockwell Sales for July and August* *Sort: Ascending by Last Name*	*Last Name* *First Name* *July Sales* *August Sales*

ROCKWELL TECHNOLOGIES	
Form Specifications	
Layout: Justified *Style: Sumi Painting* *Title: Sales Reps' Territory* *Sort: Ascending by Territory*	*Last Name* *First Name* *Territory*

UNIT 12

LESSONS 38–40

Assessing Document Formatting Skills

LESSON 38 ASSESS E-MAIL, MEMO, AND LETTER FORMATTING SKILLS

Objectives:

1. To assess keying skills.
2. To assess e-mail, memo, and letter formatting skills.

38A • 5' Conditioning Practice

Key each line twice SS; then take a 1' writing on line 3; determine *gwam.*

alphabet 1 Even Jack will be taking part of a history quiz next Monday.

fig/sym 2 Out of stock items (#7850*, #461A*, and #2093*) are in blue.

speed 3 Jana may hang the big sign by the antique door of city hall.

gwam 1' | 1 | 2 | 3 | 4 | 5 | 6 | 7 | 8 | 9 | 10 | 11 | 12 |

38B • 10' Assessment: Keying Skills

1. Key a 1' writing on each ¶; determine *gwam.*
2. Key two 3' writings on ¶s 1–2 combined; determine *gwam* and count errors.

Quarter-Minute Checkpoints				
gwam	1/4'	1/2'	3/4'	1'
24	6	12	18	24
28	7	14	21	28
32	8	16	24	32
36	9	18	27	36
40	10	20	30	40
44	11	22	33	44
48	12	24	36	48
52	13	26	39	52
56	14	28	42	56
60	15	30	45	60

A all letters used — gwam 2' | 3'

As you build your keying skill, the number of errors you 6 4 45
make is not very important because most of the errors are acci- 12 8 49
dental. Realize, however, that documents are expected to be 18 12 53
without flaw. A letter, report, or table that has flaws is not 25 16 58
usable until it is corrected. So find and correct all errors. 31 20 62

The best time to detect and correct your errors is while 36 24 66
the copy is still on a monitor. Therefore, just before removing 43 29 70
the copy from the monitor, proofread it and correct any errors 49 33 74
you have made. Learn to proofread very carefully and to correct 56 37 78
all errors quickly. Improve your production skill in this way. 62 41 83

gwam 2' | 1 | 2 | 3 | 4 | 5 | 6 |
3' | 1 | 2 | 3 | 4 |

Using a Wizard to Create Forms

Read the text at the right to learn about creating forms.

You can use forms to enter or view the information in a database. When using the Forms feature, you have the option of viewing only one record at a time or viewing multiple records at a time. When viewing only one record at a time, it is easy to enter and view data in the clearly labeled fields.

Using the Wizard makes it easy to create well-designed forms. As shown below, the Wizard feature allows you to have all the fields in a database included in the form or only selected fields.

Form Illustration

The forms at the right were created using the "Create form by using wizard" feature. The first form includes every field in the *Software Professionals* database. The second form includes only the Stock Number, Software, and Ending Inventory fields. Both forms are in **Columnar** layout. The third form shows the same fields as the second, but in **Tabular** layout, which allows you to view multiple records on the screen at the same time. The first two forms let you view one record at a time on the screen.

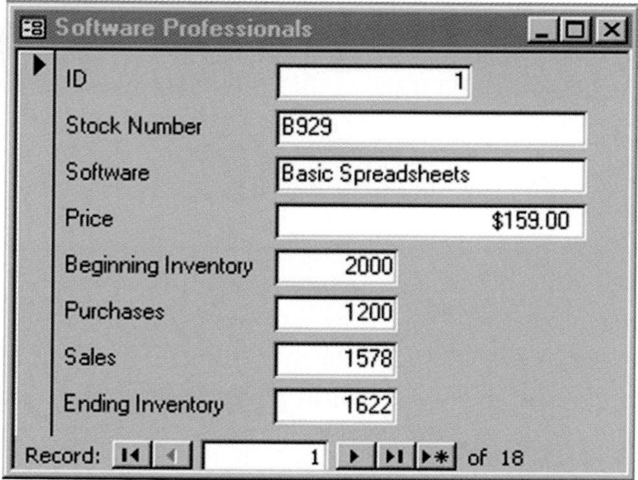

Activity 1 • Create Forms

1. Open *Software Professionals*.
2. Create the three form files shown at the right in the database.
3. Use **Columnar** layout and **Standard** style for the first two forms. Title the first form **Software Professionals** and the second form **Ending Inventory (Columnar)**.
4. Use **Tabular** layout and **Standard** style for the third form and title it **Ending Inventory (Tabular)**.

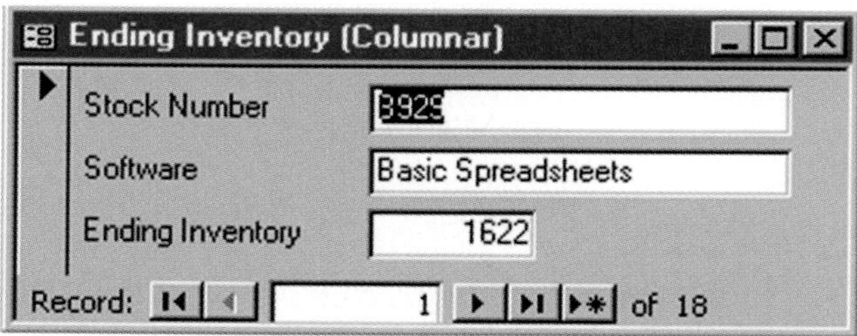

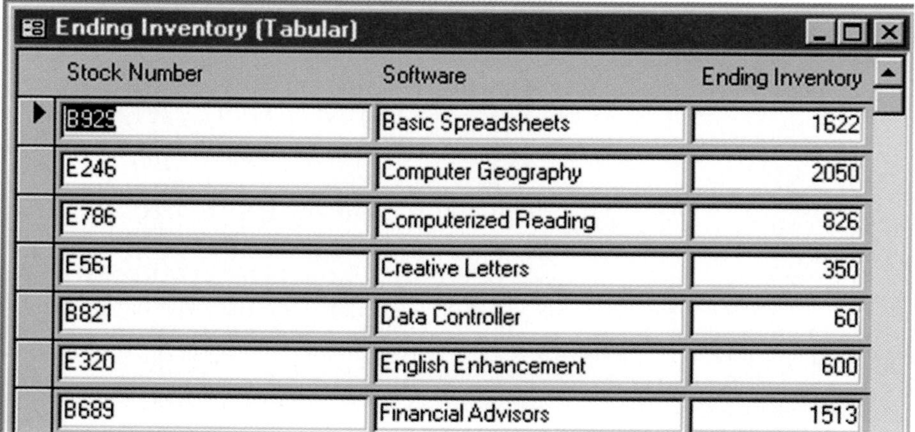

Stock Number	Software	Ending Inventory
B929	Basic Spreadsheets	1622
E246	Computer Geography	2050
E786	Computerized Reading	826
E561	Creative Letters	350
B821	Data Controller	60
E320	English Enhancement	600
B689	Financial Advisors	1513

38C • 35'
Assess Document Formatting Skills

Document 1 (E-mail)
Format and key the text at the right as an e-mail message if you have access to e-mail software. Send the e-mail to your instructor.

If you do not have access to e-mail software, format and key the text as an interoffice memo to **Miguel Martinez** from you.

DATE: **Current Date**
SUBJECT: **MACBETH QUOTE**

Correct all spelling, keying, and formatting errors.

 **Save as:** *EMAIL38C1*

I enjoyed our visit last week at the class reunion. How quickly time passes; it seems like only yesterday that we graduated. Of course, a class reunion is a quick reminder that it **wasn't** yesterday.

I was able to find the quote that we discussed with the group on Friday. Your memory definitely serves you better than mine; it was a quote from George Bernard Shaw. However, he was referring to Shakespeare's *Macbeth*. Here is the exact quote by Shaw: "Life is not a 'brief candle.' It is a splendid torch that I want to make burn as brightly as possible before handing it on to future generations."

I was glad to see that so many of our classmates are living lives as "splendid torches" rather than as "brief candles."

Document 2 (Letter)
Format and key the text at the right as a personal-business letter from **Elizabeth A. Ross**.

Supply an appropriate salutation and complimentary close. Be sure to include your reference initials and an attachment notation.

Return Address and Date:
183 Lennox St.
Portland, ME 04103-5282
May 3, 200-

Letter Address:
Ms. Suzzanne Hamlin, President
Portland Historical Society
1821 Island View Rd.
Portland, ME 04107-3712

Correct all spelling, keying, and formatting errors.

 **Save as:** *LTR38C2*

After doing research on possible historical destinations for our Annual Portland Historical Society trip, I narrowed our choices to the Hildene House in Manchester, Vermont, and The Breakers in Newport, Rhode Island. The Hildene House was built in 1902 for Robert Todd Lincoln, the son of Abraham Lincoln; The Breakers was built for Cornelius Vanderbilt II in 1895.

I met with our planning committee yesterday to share the information I was able to obtain. After discussing the merits of both places, our recommendation is The Breakers for this year's trip. Even though we liked both places, the committee felt that many of our members would have already visited the Hildene House since it is so close to Portland.

I've attached some information on The Breakers. As soon as I receive the additional information I requested about expenses, I will send it to you. You should have it in plenty of time for the June meeting.

Document 3 (Memo)
Format and key the text at the right as a memo to **Suzzanne Hamlin** from **Elizabeth A. Ross**. Date the memo **May 3, 200-**; use **SUMMER TRIP** for the subject line. Correct all spelling, keying, and formatting errors.

 **Save as:** *MEMO38C3*

Here are some of the costs that our group will incur on our trip to The Breakers.

The admission fee for The Breakers is $10. I'll check on group rates this week. Round-trip airfare from Portland to T. F. Green Airport is $235. Of course, you know that rates vary considerably during the summer months. My travel agent will inform me of any summer specials.

I'm still waiting for rates for the hotel accommodations. I've narrowed the list to Castle Hill Inn and Resort, Vanderbilt Hall, and Hotel Viking. Any of the three would provide excellent accommodations. As soon as they send the rates, I'll forward them to you.

Activity 4 • Create Computed Fields

1. Review the example on p. 417.
2. Add fields for **Total Sales** and **Average Monthly Sales** to the *Sales Reps - District 13* table of the *Rockwell Technologies* database.
3. Use the Expression Builder to create formulas to calculate the Total Sales and the Average Monthly Sales.
4. Print a table showing the information requested at the right.

ROCKWELL TECHNOLOGIES	
The printout should include:	
1. 2. 3. 4. 5.	*Sales Reps' Last Names* *July Sales* *August Sales* *Total Sales* *Average Monthly Sales*
Formula for Total Sales	***= [July Sales]+[August Sales]***
Formula for Avg. Monthly Sales	***= ([July Sales]+[August Sales])/2***

Activity 5 • Create Computed Fields

1. Add a field for **Total Fees Paid** to the *Eastwick Fees* table of the *Eastwick School of Dance* database.
2. Use the Expression Builder to create a formula to calculate the Total Fees Paid.
3. Print a table showing the information requested at the right.

Eastwick School of Dance	
The printout should include:	
1. **2.** **3.** **4.** **5.** **6.**	Students' First Names Students' Last Names September Fees October Fees November Fees Total Fees Paid
Formula for Total Fees Paid	**=[Sept. Fees]+[Oct. Fees]+[Nov. Fees]**

Activity 6 • Create Computed Fields

1. Add a field for **Ending Inventory** to the *Software Professionals* table of the *Software Professionals* database.
2. Use the Expression Builder to create a formula to calculate the Ending Inventory.
3. Print a table showing the information requested at the right.

SOFTWARE PROFESSIONALS	
The printout should include:	
1. **2.** **3.** **4.** **5.** **6.**	Stock Number Software Name Beginning Inventory Purchases Sales Ending Inventory
Formula for Ending Inventory	**= [Beginning Inventory]+[Purchases]-[Sales]**

ASSESS REPORT FORMATTING SKILLS

Objectives:

1. To assess keying skills.
2. To assess report formatting skills.

39A • 5' Conditioning Practice

Key each line twice SS; then key a 1' writing on line 3; determine *gwam*.

alphabet 1 Joey was quite amazed by his blocking of seven extra points.

figures 2 In 1990, we had only 345 computers; as of 2000 we owned 876.

speed 3 Diana paid for the antique ornament and the six enamel keys.

gwam 1' | 1 | 2 | 3 | 4 | 5 | 6 | 7 | 8 | 9 | 10 | 11 | 12 |

39B • 35' Assess Report Formatting Skills

Document 1 (Unbound Report)

Format and key the text at the right as an unbound report. Correct all spelling, keying, and formatting errors.

Save as: *RPT39B1*

AMERICA'S CASTLES

The castles listed on A&E's "America's Castles" belonged to the rich and famous. By looking at the history of some of the families that owned these castles, it is easy to see why people say that America is the land of opportunity.

Cornelius Vanderbilt was a man who took advantage of the opportunities America had to offer. He was born on May 27, 1794, to a family of modest means. Cornelius ended his formal schooling by the age of 11. (Encyclopedia Americana, 1998, Vol. 27, 891) He achieved success because he was industrious. He knew how to work, and he knew the value of the money that came from hard work. Other qualities that made him successful were perseverance, enterprise, courage, and trustworthiness. Being trustworthy meant he could command better prices than others doing the same job. (Smith, 528, 1886) Because of these qualities, Cornelius Vanderbilt was able to amass one of the largest fortunes ever made in America from his shipping and railroad enterprises.

Three of America's castles were built by descendants of the man who came out of humble beginnings to amass such a large fortune. The Biltmore House, The Breakers, and Marble House were all built by Cornelius Vanderbilt's descendants.

Biltmore House

The Biltmore House (also known as America's largest home) is located on 8,000 acres near Asheville, North Carolina. It was built for George W. Vanderbilt. The 250-room French

(continued on next page)

Creating Computed Fields

Calculations can be done on existing fields by using the Expression Builder in the Forms feature.

In the illustration at the right, two additional fields were added to the *Sales Reps - District 13* table of the *Rockwell Technologies* database using the Design feature. The values for these two new fields (Total Sales and Average Monthly Sales) were automatically calculated by using the Expression Builder to create formulas.

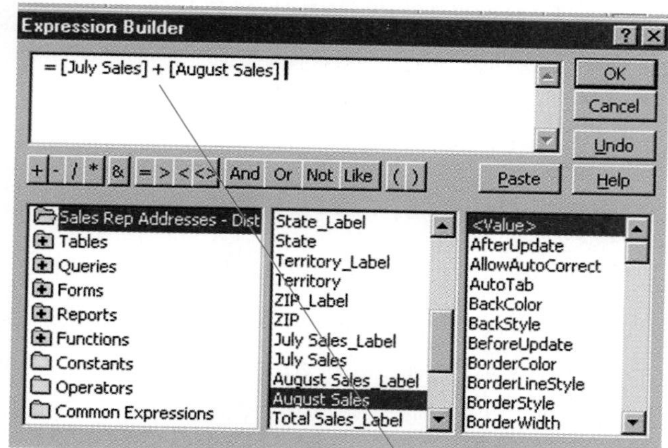

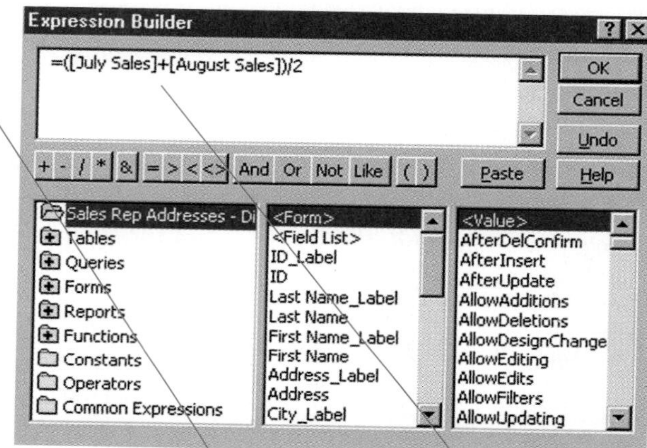

Last Name	July Sales	August Sales	Total Sales	Average Monthly Sales
Carter-Bond	$45,351.00	$37,951.00	$83,302.00	$41,651.00
Hull	$53,739.00	$49,762.00	$103,501.00	$51,750.50
McRae	$33,371.00	$38,978.00	$72,349.00	$36,174.50
Hernandez	$39,371.00	$40,790.00	$80,161.00	$40,080.50
Camby	$42,173.00	$65,386.00	$107,559.00	$53,779.50
Henneman	$17,219.00	$29,737.00	$46,956.00	$23,478.00
Reed	$53,791.00	$59,349.00	$113,140.00	$56,570.00
Logan	$49,712.00	$21,790.00	$71,502.00	$35,751.00
Cirillo	$29,731.00	$37,956.00	$67,687.00	$33,843.50
LeClair	$63,212.00	$40,321.00	$103,533.00	$51,766.50
Donovan	$37,198.00	$45,865.00	$83,063.00	$41,531.50
Young	$44,876.00	$56,791.00	$101,667.00	$50,833.50
Tapani	$49,145.00	$39,645.00	$88,790.00	$44,395.00
Rivera	$55,400.00	$37,751.00	$93,151.00	$46,575.50
Walker	$43,900.00	$44,750.00	$88,650.00	$44,325.00
Wetteland	$33,650.00	$40,765.00	$74,415.00	$37,207.50
Chi	$39,750.00	$48,621.00	$88,371.00	$44,185.50
Finley	$19,765.00	$35,765.00	$55,530.00	$27,765.00
Reese	$67,890.00	$45,780.00	$113,670.00	$56,835.00
Bell	$39,200.00	$43,286.00	$82,486.00	$41,243.00
Doolittle	$64,890.00	$37,102.00	$101,992.00	$50,996.00

Record: 1 of 23

Document 1 (continued)

Renaissance chateau started in 1889 took hundreds of workers five years to build. (A&E, Biltmore, 2000)

The Breakers

The Breakers is located in Newport, Rhode Island. It was built for Cornelius Vanderbilt II. The 70-room castle (Italian Renaissance) was started in 1895. Upon its completion, the castle was filled with antiques from France and Italy. (A&E, Breakers, 2000)

Marble House

Marble House is also located in Newport, Rhode Island. During the 1890s, Newport became the summer colony of New England's wealthiest families. Marble House was built for William K. Vanderbilt, who was a grandson of Cornelius Vanderbilt. Mrs. Vanderbilt intended for the summerhouse to be a "temple to the arts." (A&E, Marble, 2000)

Document 2 (References List)
Use the information at the right to create a references list on a separate page. Correct all spelling, keying, and formatting errors.

 **Save as:** *RPT39B2*

REFERENCES

A&E, "America's Castles--Biltmore House." http://www.aetv.com/tv/shows/castles/biltmore.html (26 January 2000).

A&E, "America's Castles--The Breakers." http://www.aetv.com/tv/shows/castles/breakers.html (26 January 2000).

A&E, "America's Castles--Marble House." http://www.aetv.com/tv/shows/castles/marble.html (26 January 2000).

Encyclopedia Americana, "Cornelius Vanderbilt." Danbury, CT: Grolier Incorporated, 1998.

Smith, Helen Ainslie. *One Hundred Famous Americans*. Reprint of 1886 ed. Freeport, New York: Books for Libraries Press, 1972.

39C • 10'
Assessment: Keying Skills

1. Key a 1' writing on each ¶ of 38B, p. 110; determine *gwam*.
2. Key two 3' writings on ¶s 1–2 combined (38B, p. 110); determine *gwam*, count errors.

Activity 1 • Execute a Query

1. Open *Software Professionals.*
2. Use the Queries feature to answer the questions outlined at the right.
3. Print the results of each query.

SOFTWARE PROFESSIONALS			
No.	**Query**	**Fields to Include**	**Criteria**
1	What are the names of the software packages that were designated as "Educational" (Stock No. starting with **E**)?	Stock Number Software	Like "E*"
2	What software sells for more than $150?	Stock Number Software Price	>150
3	What software sold more than 1,500 units?	Stock Number Software Sales	>1500
4	What software sold less than 500 units?	Stock Number Software Sales	<500

Activity 2 • Execute a Query

1. Open *Eastwick School of Dance.*
2. Use the Queries feature to answer the questions outlined at the right.
3. Print the results of each query.

Eastwick School of Dance			
No.	**Query**	**Fields to Include**	**Criteria**
1	What are the names and addresses of the students living in Minneapolis/St. Paul?	First Name Last Name Address State City ZIP	"Minneapolis" Or "St. Paul"
2	What are the names and addresses of the students living in Wisconsin?		"WI"
3	Which students have not paid their September fees?	Last Name First Name September Fees	Is Null

Activity 3 • Execute a Query

1. Open *Rockwell Technologies.*
2. Use the Queries feature to answer the questions outlined at the right.
3. Print the results of each query.

ROCKWELL TECHNOLOGIES			
No.	***Query***	***Fields to Include***	***Criteria***
1	*What are the names and addresses of our Arizona sales reps?*	*First Name* *Last Name* *Address* *City* *State* *ZIP* *Territory*	*"Arizona"*
2	*What are the names and addresses of our Montana and Wyoming sales reps?*		*"Montana" Or "Wyoming"*
3	*Which sales reps had sales of more than $55,000 during July?*	*First Name* *Last Name* *July Sales*	*>55000*

LESSON 40 ASSESS TABLE FORMATTING SKILLS

Objectives:

1. To assess keying skills.
2. To assess table formatting skills.

40A • 5' Conditioning Practice

Key each line twice SS; then take a 1' writing on line 3; determine *gwam.*

alphabet 1 Peter was amazed at just how quickly you fixed the big vans.
fig/sym 2 Of 34,198 citizens, 25,648 (75%) voted in the 2000 election.
speed 3 Orlando may make a big map to hang by the door of city hall.

gwam 1' | 1 | 2 | 3 | 4 | 5 | 6 | 7 | 8 | 9 | 10 | 11 | 12 |

40B • 10' Assessment: Keying Skills

1. Key a 1' writing on each ¶; determine *gwam.*
2. Key two 3' writings on ¶s 1–2 combined; determine *gwam* and count errors.

Quarter-Minute Checkpoints				
gwam	1/4'	1/2'	3/4'	1'
24	6	12	18	24
28	7	14	21	28
32	8	16	24	32
36	9	18	27	36
40	10	20	30	40
44	11	22	33	44
48	12	24	36	48
52	13	26	39	52
56	14	28	42	56
60	15	30	45	60

all letters used — gwam 3'

Conflict resolution is a practical skill to learn. When 4 72
two people are involved in exchanging ideas, values, or beliefs, 8 76
the possibility for some type of problem exists. Those involved 12 80
with a conflict usually try winning while making the other per- 17 84
son lose. This often leads to winning the battle while losing 21 89
the war. A better way to deal with problems is to realize that 25 93
it is possible to come up with a solution where each person is 29 97
able to win. 30 98

There are quite a number of ideas for dealing with con- 34 102
flict. The next time you are in the middle of a conflict try 38 106
the following approach to solve it. First, step back from the 42 110
situation and try to be objective rather than exchanging per- 46 114
sonal attacks. Try to defuse the situation. Define exactly 50 118
what is causing the problem. Don't view the problem as a win or 55 122
lose situation. After defining the problem, come up with sev- 59 126
eral possible solutions. Discuss the merits of each solution. 63 131
Try to agree on a solution that works for each person who is in- 67 135
volved. 68 135

gwam 3' | 1 | 2 | 3 | 4 |

Creating Queries, cont.

The Queries feature is used to extract and display specific information from a table. The criteria line of the query design box is where instructions are given to the software that tell it which information to display. The basic criteria expressions are:

equal to (=)
greater than (>)
less than (<)

In the illustration at the right, ="CO" was used to extract only those sales reps from Colorado. If the criteria had been = "CO" or "AZ," the sales reps from both Colorado and Arizona would have been displayed.

Query 1—Colorado Sales Reps

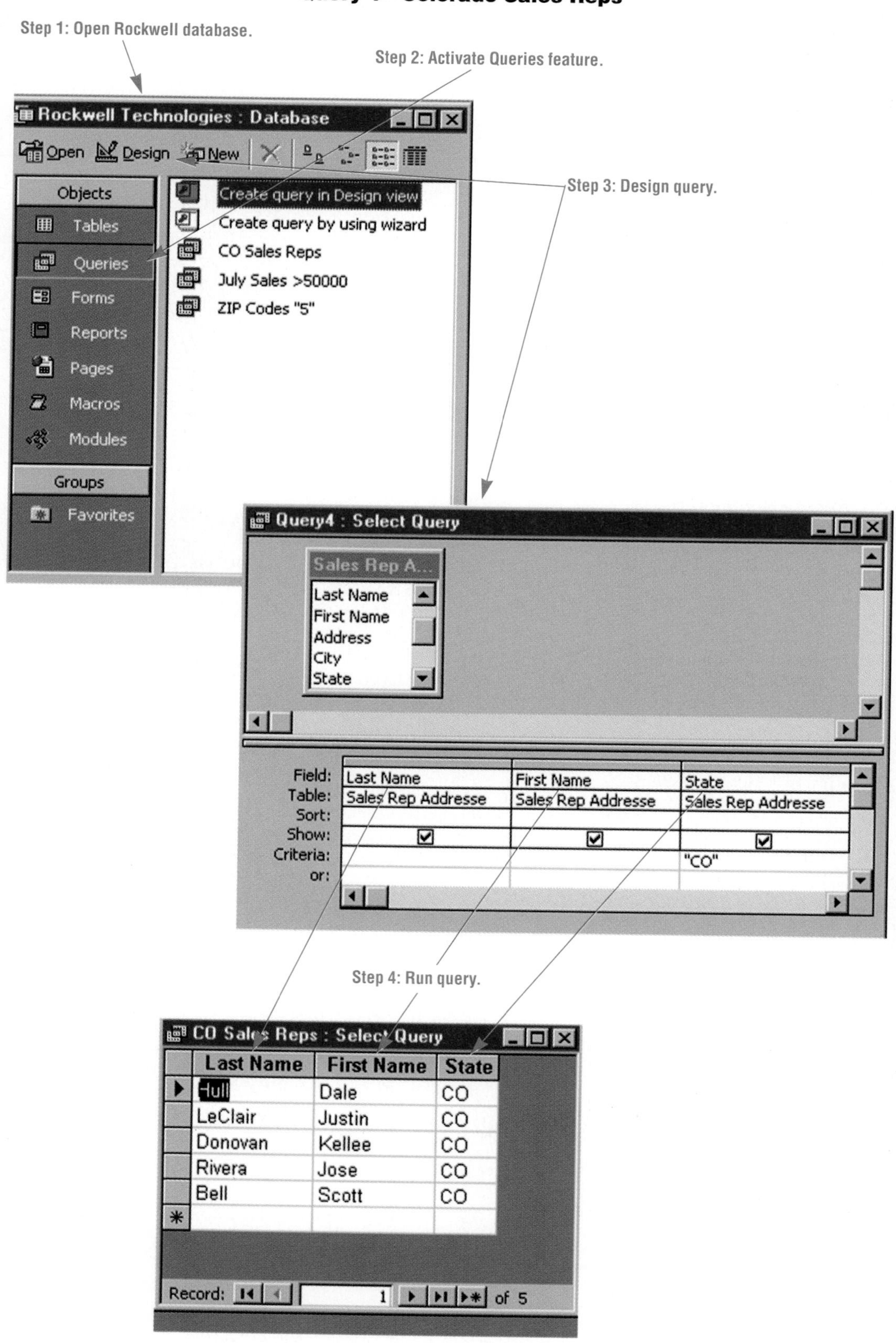

40C • 35' Assess Table Formatting Skills

Table 1
Create the table shown at the right using the information given below. Center the table horizontally and vertically.

Main title: row height 0.7"; center vertically

Column headings: row height 0.4"; center vertically

Data rows: row height 0.3"; bottom vertical alignment

Column widths: Adjust column widths to arrange material attractively on the page.

 **Save as:** *TBL40C1*

Table 2
Create the table shown at the right using the information given for Table 1. Center the table horizontally and vertically. Use **VAN NOY ART GALLERY** for the main title; use **June-August Exhibits** for the secondary title.

Adjust column widths to arrange material attractively on the page.

 **Save as:** *TBL40C2*

Table 3
Using the table formatting features that you have learned to arrange information attractively on a page, format and key the data at the right as a table. Use **THEATER VOCABULARY WORDS** for the main title and **April 7-25** for the secondary title.

 **Save as:** *TBL40C3*

AMERICA'S CASTLES Eastern Region	
Castle	**Location**
The Breakers	Newport, Rhode Island
Chesterwood	Stockbridge, Massachusetts
Drumthwacket	Princeton, New Jersey
George Eastman House	Rochester, New York
Hildene	Manchester, Vermont
Longwood	Kennett Square, Pennsylvania
Lyndhurst Mansion	Tarrytown, New York
Marble House	Newport, Rhode Island
Sunnyside	Tarrytown, New York

Source: A&E, "America's Castles." http://www.aetv.com/tv/shows/castles/index2.html (26 January 2000).

Exhibit	Opening/Closing Dates
Emerging Artists	June 1 - June 10
19th-Century European Paintings	June 11 - June 20
Colonial American Art	June 21 - June 30
Old Masters' Paintings	July 1 - July 15
American Oil Paintings	July 16 - July 31
19th-Century French Prints	August 1 - August 15
American Impressionists	August 16 - 30

Week of April 7	Week of April 14	Week of April 21
blackout	Callbacks	Choreography
Conflict	Critique	Cues
Dialog	Ensemble	Feed back
Floorplan	Illusion	Imagination
Improvisation	intermission	Literary merit
Meladrama	Narrator	Playright
Run-throughs	Screen play	Soliloquy
Theme	Tragedy	Visualization

LESSONS 9–18 (4–5 HOURS)

Database Applications 2, Expanding Database Skills

LESSON 9 CREATING QUERIES AND COMPUTED FIELDS

Creating Queries

Read the text at the right. Next, study the copy below and the illustration to understand how queries can be used to extract information from a database table.

Query 1 was designed to include:

Last Name
First Name
State

The criteria for the state field was set to equal CO, thus extracting only those reps from the state of Colorado.

Query 2 was designed to include:

Last Name
First Name
ZIP

The criteria for the ZIP field was set to be less than 6 (<6), thus extracting only those reps with ZIP codes starting with 5.

Query 3 was designed to include:

Last Name
First Name
July Sales

The criteria for the July Sales field was set for greater than $50,000 (>50000), thus extracting only those sales reps with sales of more than $50,000.

The illustration on the next page shows the steps required to run a query.

(continued on next page)

As discussed earlier, a database is a collection of organized information where answers to many questions can be found. For example, the *Sales Reps - District 13* table of the *Rockwell Technologies* database contains answers to the following questions.

- Who are the sales reps from Colorado?
- Who are the sales reps with ZIP Codes starting with "5"?
- Which sales reps had July sales of more than $50,000?

To generate answers to these questions, a query to the database must be made. A **query** is a question structured in a way that the software (database) can understand.

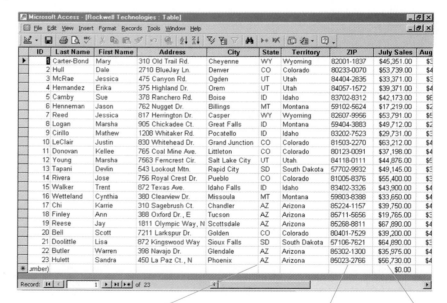

Microsoft Access - [Rockwell Technologies : Table]

ID	Last Name	First Name	Address	City	State	Territory	ZIP	July Sales	Aug
1	Carter-Bond	Mary	310 Old Trail Rd.	Cheyenne	WY	Wyoming	82001-1837	$45,351.00	$3
2	Hull	Dale	2710 BlueJay Ln.	Denver	CO	Colorado	80233-0070	$53,739.00	$4
3	McRae	Jessica	475 Canyon Rd.	Ogden	UT	Utah	84404-2835	$33,371.00	$3
4	Hernandez	Erika	375 Highland Dr.	Orem	UT	Utah	84057-1572	$39,371.00	$4
5	Camby	Sue	378 Ranchero Rd.	Boise	ID	Idaho	83702-8312	$42,173.00	$6
6	Henneman	Jason	762 Nugget Dr.	Billings	MT	Montana	59102-5624	$17,219.00	$2
7	Reed	Jessica	817 Herrington Dr.	Casper	WY	Wyoming	82607-9956	$53,791.00	$5
8	Logan	Marsha	905 Chickadee Ct.	Great Falls	ID	Montana	59404-3883	$49,712.00	$2
9	Cirillo	Mathew	1208 Whitaker Rd.	Pocatello	ID	Idaho	83202-7523	$29,731.00	$3
10	LeClair	Justin	830 Whitehead Dr.	Grand Junction	CO	Colorado	81503-2270	$63,212.00	$4
11	Donovan	Kellee	765 Coal Mine Ave.	Littleton	CO	Colorado	80123-0091	$37,198.00	$4
12	Young	Marsha	7563 Ferncrest Cir.	Salt Lake City	UT	Utah	84118-0111	$44,876.00	$5
13	Tapani	Devlin	543 Lookout Mtn.	Rapid City	SD	South Dakota	57702-9932	$49,145.00	$3
14	Rivera	Jose	756 Royal Crest Dr.	Pueblo	CO	Colorado	81005-8376	$55,400.00	$3
15	Walker	Trent	872 Texas Ave.	Idaho Falls	ID	Idaho	83402-3326	$43,900.00	$4
16	Wetteland	Cynthia	380 Clearview Dr.	Missoula	MT	Montana	59803-8388	$33,650.00	$4
17	Chi	Karrie	310 Sagebrush Ct.	Chandler	AZ	Arizona	85224-1157	$39,750.00	$4
18	Finley	Ann	388 Oxford Dr., E	Tucson	AZ	Arizona	85711-5656	$19,765.00	$3
19	Reese	Jay	1811 Olympic Way, N	Scottsdale	AZ	Arizona	85268-8811	$67,890.00	$4
20	Bell	Scott	7211 Larkspur Dr.	Golden	CO	Colorado	80401-7529	$39,200.00	$4
21	Doolittle	Lisa	872 Kingswood Way	Sioux Falls	SD	South Dakota	57106-7621	$64,890.00	$3
22	Butler	Warren	398 Navajo Dr.	Glendale	AZ	Arizona	85302-1300	$35,975.00	$4
23	Hulett	Sandra	450 La Paz Ct., N	Phoenix	AZ	Arizona	85023-2766	$56,730.00	$4
umber)								$0.00	

Record: 1 of 23

Query1 : Select Query

Last Name	First Name	State
Hull	Dale	CO
LeClair	Justin	CO
Donovan	Kellee	CO
Rivera	Jose	CO
Bell	Scott	CO

Query2 : Select Query

Last Name	First Name	ZIP
Henneman	Jason	59102-5624
Logan	Marsha	59404-3883
Tapani	Devlin	57702-9932
Wetteland	Cynthia	59803-8388
Doolittle	Lisa	57106-7621

Query3 : Select Query

Last Name	First Name	July Sales
Hull	Dale	$53,739.00
Reed	Jessica	$53,791.00
LeClair	Justin	$63,212.00
Rivera	Jose	$55,400.00
Reese	Jay	$67,890.00

Your Perspective

Nel mezzo del cammin di nostra vita
mi ritrovai per una selva oscura,
che la diritta via era smarrita.

Midway in the journey of our life
I found myself in a dark wood,
for the straight way was lost.

An image that you will find in the literature of many times and places is that of a person traveling through a forest. Dante Alighieri used it in the opening lines of *The Divine Comedy*, above (translation by Charles S. Singleton). So did Nathaniel Hawthorne in his short story "Young Goodman Brown" and Robert Frost in his poem "The Road Not Taken." In the late 1980s, Steven Sondheim and James Lapine wrote a successful musical on the theme of traveling through a forest called *Into the Woods*.

Into the Woods begins with wishes, the simple wishes of characters we know from fairy tales. Jack (of "Jack and the Beanstalk") wishes to sell his cow to get money for his mother. Cinderella wishes to go to the ball. Into the woods the characters go, in pursuit of their wishes. And then things start to get complicated.

Into the Woods explores two themes. One is the difficulty of making the right choices; the other is whether the end justifies the means. Is it right for someone to cheat Jack into trading his cow for "magic" beans? What are the risks of stealing a giant's gold to buy back the cow and be rich?

For some of the characters, the woods are where they begin to discover just who they are and who they want to be. Cinderella finds she doesn't want to marry a prince. Neither does she want to be a servant in her stepmother's house. She wants "something in-between."

One way of seeing the woods is as a journey through life, in which the right path can be difficult to find or choose. At the end of the play *Into the Woods*, the remaining characters have learned some lessons about making the right choices. Part of what they have learned is this:

You can't just act,
You have to listen.
You can't just act,
You have to think.

Ethics: The Right Thing to Do

ACTIVITIES

1. Read the material at the left.
2. As a warm-up, key the Italian and then the English lines from *The Divine Comedy*. As you key the English words, think about what they mean.
3. Why do you think woods appear in so many stories? Key a list of adjectives that describe the woods at different times of day.
4. Form a group with some other students. Think of recent movies in which the characters made difficult choices. Why do you think the characters chose as they did? Each person should contribute ideas.
5. Compose and key a paragraph describing a time when you had to make a tough decision. What did you consider in making your choice?

Illustration of a Multiple Sort

The illustration to the right shows a multiple sort on the *Eastwick Address* file. The file was first sorted (*primary sort*) by State in ascending order. This sort placed all the students with a Minnesota address together and all the students with a Wisconsin address together.

The second sort (*secondary sort*) was by City in ascending order. This sort put all the Minnesota cities in alphabetical order and all the Wisconsin cities in alphabetical order.

Learning C·U·E

The **Advanced Filter/Sort** feature was used to do the multiple-level sort. This feature provides a way for entering multiple criteria to display selected records. These records match a specified filter and sort.

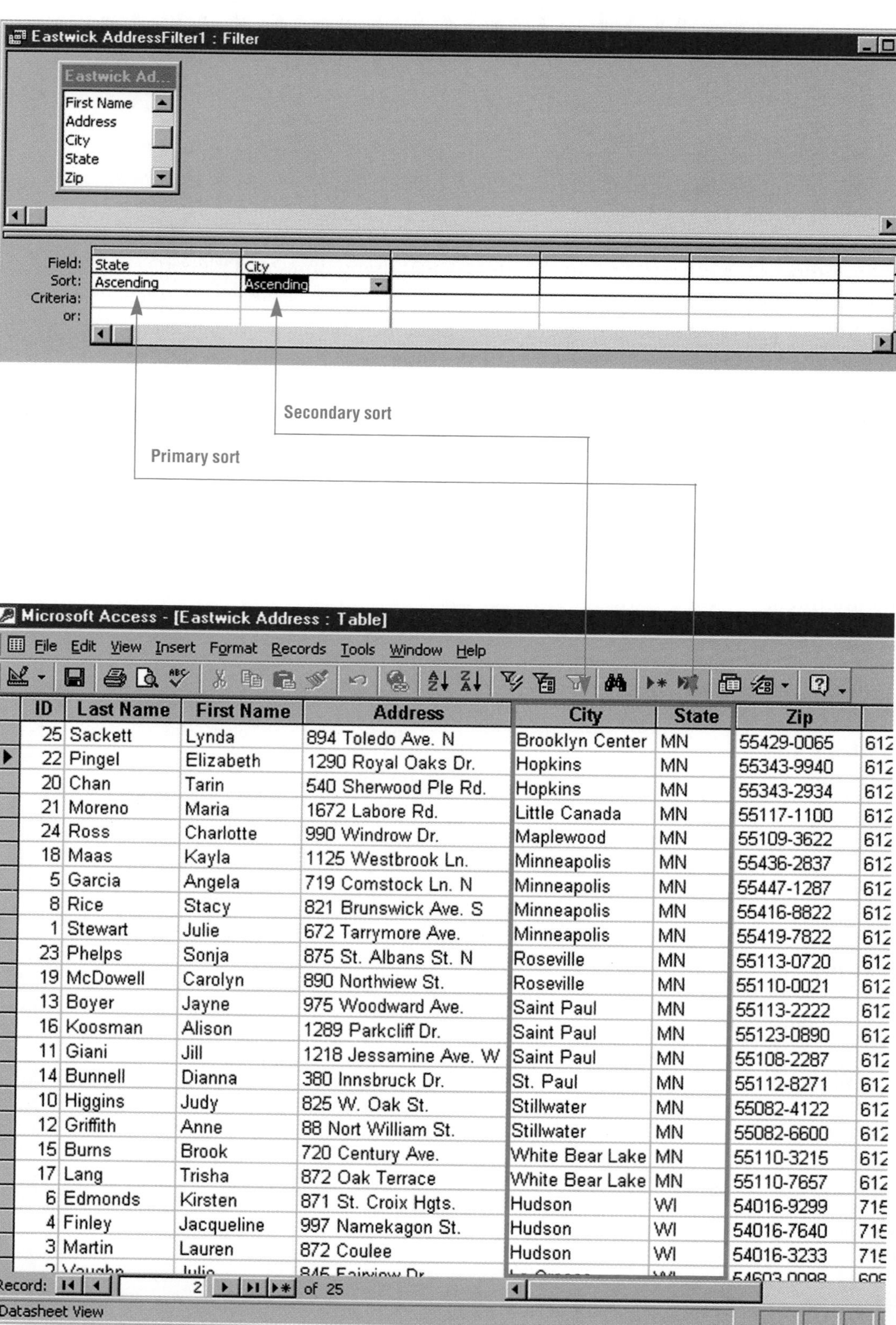

ID	Last Name	First Name	Address	City	State	Zip	
25	Sackett	Lynda	894 Toledo Ave. N	Brooklyn Center	MN	55429-0065	612
22	Pingel	Elizabeth	1290 Royal Oaks Dr.	Hopkins	MN	55343-9940	612
20	Chan	Tarin	540 Sherwood Ple Rd.	Hopkins	MN	55343-2934	612
21	Moreno	Maria	1672 Labore Rd.	Little Canada	MN	55117-1100	612
24	Ross	Charlotte	990 Windrow Dr.	Maplewood	MN	55109-3622	612
18	Maas	Kayla	1125 Westbrook Ln.	Minneapolis	MN	55436-2837	612
5	Garcia	Angela	719 Comstock Ln. N	Minneapolis	MN	55447-1287	612
8	Rice	Stacy	821 Brunswick Ave. S	Minneapolis	MN	55416-8822	612
1	Stewart	Julie	672 Tarrymore Ave.	Minneapolis	MN	55419-7822	612
23	Phelps	Sonja	875 St. Albans St. N	Roseville	MN	55113-0720	612
19	McDowell	Carolyn	890 Northview St.	Roseville	MN	55110-0021	612
13	Boyer	Jayne	975 Woodward Ave.	Saint Paul	MN	55113-2222	612
16	Koosman	Alison	1289 Parkcliff Dr.	Saint Paul	MN	55123-0890	612
11	Giani	Jill	1218 Jessamine Ave. W	Saint Paul	MN	55108-2287	612
14	Bunnell	Dianna	380 Innsbruck Dr.	St. Paul	MN	55112-8271	612
10	Higgins	Judy	825 W. Oak St.	Stillwater	MN	55082-4122	612
12	Griffith	Anne	88 Nort William St.	Stillwater	MN	55082-6600	612
15	Burns	Brook	720 Century Ave.	White Bear Lake	MN	55110-3215	612
17	Lang	Trisha	872 Oak Terrace	White Bear Lake	MN	55110-7657	612
6	Edmonds	Kirsten	871 St. Croix Hgts.	Hudson	WI	54016-9299	715
4	Finley	Jacqueline	997 Namekagon St.	Hudson	WI	54016-7640	715
3	Martin	Lauren	872 Coulee	Hudson	WI	54016-3233	715

Your Perspective

A growing number of "fair trade" organizations provide artists, artisans, and farmers, often from developing countries, with a means of marketing their goods globally at a fair price. One such organization is PEOPLink. PEOPLink works with a network of Trading Partners, mostly nonprofit groups from Latin America, Asia, and Africa, that serve community artisan groups. PEOPLink gives its Trading Partners digital cameras to photograph products and markets those products in its online catalog. The organization also provides online information about the work and lives of the artisans, teaches them to build and maintain their own Web catalogs, gives them online training, and helps them develop their products. The table below shows fair trade products and their countries of origin.

FAIR TRADE ARTS AND CRAFTS

Product	Country
Sculptures	Cameroon
Baskets	Uganda
Molas	Panama
Pitchers	Guatemala
Brooches	Russia

Music has a rich cultural history. From ancient times, different cultures have developed their own styles of music and have invented different instruments with which to express them.

In music, the influence of one culture on another can be clearly seen and can produce exciting results. Take the American composer Aaron Copland, for example. Some of Copland's best-known compositions were based on American folk music, such as the ballets *Billy the Kid* (1938), *Rodeo* (1942), and *Appalachian Spring* (1944). His *El salon Mexico* was inspired by Mexican folk music.

Radio, television, the Internet, and high-quality sound and video recording have made music from many different cultures accessible to listeners worldwide. They have also helped to make music even more multicultural. For example, South Indian *cine*, or motion-picture music, uses both Indian and Western musical instruments and mixes classical Indian music with Western rock and jazz.*

*Source: David Butler, B.SC., M.A., Ph.D. "Music." *Microsoft® Encarta® Online Encyclopedia 2000* http://encarta.msn.com (16 July 2000).

Global Awareness

ACTIVITIES

1. Key and format the table at the left. Use the table formatting features that you have learned to arrange the information attractively on the page.
2. Form a group with some other students. Develop a plan for a school fair in which you could showcase the work of artists from your school and community. Include details such as the date of the fair, where it would be held, how you would invite participants, how many you could invite, and where and how you would advertise the event.

Cultural Diversity

ACTIVITIES

1. Pair up with another student who likes a musician that you also like. Talk about this musician. Address the following questions, taking notes on the answers.
   - **a.** Does this musician's work show the influence of other musicians or other kinds of music? If so, in what way?
   - **b.** Do you think people in another country might form perceptions of this musician's country based on his or her music? If so, what might they be?
   - **c.** Think of the music you like to listen to and the music your parents like. How important is culture to being able to appreciate a particular kind of music?
2. Develop your notes and key them into a one-page essay in unbound report format.

Activity 4 • Sort for Quick Answers

1. Open the *Sales Reps - District 13* table.
2. Run sorts to answer the questions outlined at the right.
3. Create a wp table in which to key your answers.

Save as: *DB1L8ACT4*

4. Print a copy of your table.

ROCKWELL TECHNOLOGIES	
No.	**Question**
1	*How many Arizona sales reps are in District 13?*
2	*How many sales reps sold over $60,000 in July?*
3	*How many sales reps sold over $60,000 in August?*
4	*How many sales reps' last names start with "H"?*
5	*Do any of the sales reps have the same first name?*
6	*Do any of the sales reps have the same last name?*
7	*Which sales reps had less than $30,000 in sales in July?*
8	*Which sales reps had less than $30,000 in sales in August?*

Activity 5 • Sort for Quick Answers

1. Open the *Eastwick School of Dance* database.
2. Run sorts to answer the questions outlined at the right.
3. Create a wp table in which to key your answers.

Save as: *DB1L8ACT5*

4. Print a copy of your table.

Eastwick School of Dance	
No.	
1	How many of the students enrolled in Eastwick School of Dance are from Wisconsin?
2	How many of the students are from Minneapolis?
3	How many students are taking beginning jazz for their first class?
4	How many students are taking beginning jazz for their first or second class?
5	How many students have not paid their September fees?
6	How many students have not paid their October fees?
7	How many students are taking advanced ballet for their first or second class?

CYCLE 2

UNITS 13-21

Computer Keyboarding: Improve & Extend

No matter what career you choose or what jobs you have along the way, a computer—and a computer keyboard—almost certainly will be at the center of your work. You will use new technology to build on existing keying skills.

You may have used, read about, or heard about *speech recognition technology (SRT).* SRT is the ability of computers to understand spoken words and convert them into text. Using SRT, one can enter words and commands by talking to the computer and then watch the document appear on the screen.

Some people believe that SRT will make keyboarding a thing of the past, like the Pony Express or Henry Ford's Model T car. In fact, there is room for many versions of keyboarding technology, including computer keyboards and SRT. So instead of putting your keyboard in a museum, put it to work as you improve and extend your keying skills.

In Cycle 2 you will refine keying techniques, increase communication skills, and learn advanced word processing features. You will process e-mail with attachments, reports with footnotes, and tables with borders and shading, to name a few. And that's not all.

You will go to work in the home office of a growing organization with branches in five cities. Your work for the President/CEO often takes you to the company's Web page.

Let's get started!

LESSON 8 CREATE DATA SORTS

Activity 1 • Use the Sort Feature

1. Read the text at the right.
2. Read and study the example of a multiple sort on p. 413.

The records of tables and forms can be arranged in a specific order by using the **Sort** feature. A sort can be done on one field or on multiple fields.

For example, the Eastwick Address table could be sorted by State in ascending order. A sort using the State field would group all the students from Minnesota first, and all the students from Wisconsin next. It would not, however, arrange the cities in each state alphabetically. A **multiple sort**, first by State and then by City, would be necessary to accomplish this arrangement.

Activity 2 • Create Single and Multiple Sorts

1. Open the *A&E Applicants* table file.
2. Perform the sorts outlined at the right.
3. Print a copy of the multiple sort by State and City.

Single Sorts—Ascending Order

1. Last Name
2. City
3. State
4. ZIP
5. Annual Income

Multiple Sorts—Ascending Order

1. Primary sort by **State**, secondary sort by **City**.
2. Primary sort by **Last Name**, secondary sort by **First Name**.

Activity 3 • Sort for Quick Answers

Learning Tip:
Sorts and queries can be used to arrange information to provide quick answers to questions. (Queries will be taught in a future lesson.)

1. Open the *Software Professionals* table.
2. Run sorts to answer the questions outlined at the right.
3. Create a wp table in which to key your answers.

 **Save as:** *DB1L8ACT3*

4. Print your table.

SOFTWARE PROFESSIONALS	
No.	**Question**
1	What were the top three software packages in terms of number of copies sold?
2	What were the two software packages with the lowest beginning inventory?
3	How many software packages were designed mainly for education? (Software packages designed mainly for education are those with an "E" before the stock number. Software packages designed mainly for business are those with a "B" before the stock number.)
4	How many software packages sell for more than $250?
5	How many software packages sell for less than $100?

UNIT 13

LESSONS 41–43

Building Basic Skill

LESSON 41 IMPROVE KEYING TECHNIQUE

Objectives:

1. To improve keying techniques.
2. To improve keying speed and control.

41A • 5' Conditioning Practice

Key each line twice SS; then take a 1' writing on line 3; determine *gwam*.

alphabet 1 How will Joy pack a dozen big boxes of their expensive equipment?

figures 2 Math 458 had 239 students enrolled in Sections 9, 10, 16, and 17.

speed 3 My sick neighbor did the title work on the bus for the eight men.

gwam 1' | 1 | 2 | 3 | 4 | 5 | 6 | 7 | 8 | 9 | 10 | 11 | 12 | 13 |

SKILL BUILDING

41B • 10' Technique: Letter Keys

1. Key each line twice.
2. Take a 30" timing on each line. If you complete the line, key it again.

Goal:
To keep keystroking action limited to the fingers.

Emphasize continuity and rhythm with curved, upright fingers.

A 1 Alexandra made an appearance at the Alabama and Arkansas parades.

B 2 Bobby babysat both the bubbly Babbit brats at the baseball games.

C 3 Chad, the eccentric character with a classic crew cut, may catch.

D 4 David and Eddie dodged the duck as it waddled down the dark road.

E 5 Eileen elevated her desk eleven inches above all the other desks.

F 6 Before I left, Faye found forty to fifty feet of flowered fabric.

G 7 Greg groggily got up and gazed grudgingly at the haggard old dog.

H 8 She held the hooks for him while he helped her catch the hamster.

gwam 1' | 1 | 2 | 3 | 4 | 5 | 6 | 7 | 8 | 9 | 10 | 11 | 12 | 13 |

SKILL BUILDING

41C • 8' Technique: Number Keys/Tab

1. Key each line twice (key number, depress TAB, key next number).
2. Take three 1' writings, trying to better your rate each time.

Concentrate on figure location; quick tab spacing; eyes on copy.

30	927	565	389	943	828	377	898	901
23	183	279	766	752	109	459	578	623
14	406	180	445	516	207	140	626	354

gwam 1' | 1 | 2 | 3 | 4 | 5 | 6 | 7

4. **Diane Bunnell** is enrolled in **Adv. Ballet**, not Inter. Make the necessary adjustments.
5. **Lynda Sackett** decided not to take **Adv. Tap**. Make the necessary adjustments to reflect this change. The September Fees will stay at $63.00; however, change the Monthly Fee to $30.00 to reflect this change for future months.

Activity 4 • Edit Records

1. Open the *Eastwick Address* database table (*Eastwick School of Dance*).
2. Make the changes given at the right.

1. **Diane Bunnell** has a new address and telephone number.

   380 Innsbruck Dr.
   St. Paul, MN 55112-8271
   612-329-7621
2. **Jackqueline Finley's** name should be spelled **Jacqueline**. Her phone number should be 715-386-67**6**4.
3. Be sure to change the spelling of Brook Byrns (**Burns**) and Tasha Lang (**Trisha**).
4. Change **Judy Higgins'** mother's name to **Ms.** Erin **Schultz**.
5. **Kayla Maas** has a new address and telephone number.

   1125 Westbrook Ln.
   Minneapolis, MN 55436-2837
   612-348-8211

Activity 5 • Edit Records

1. Open the *Sales Reps - District 13* table (*Rockwell Technologies* database).
2. Make the changes given at the right.

1. **Carrie Chi's** first name should be spelled **Karrie**.
2. **Jay Reese** has moved; his new address is:

   1811 Olympic Way, N
   Scottsdale, AZ 85268-8811
3. **Devlin Tapani's** July sales were incorrectly recorded. They should have been **$49,145**.
4. The ZIP Code for **Jason Henneman** should be **59102-5624**.
5. **Mary Carter** would like her name recorded as **Mary Carter-Bond**.

Activity 6 • Edit Records

1. Open the *A&E Applicants* table to correct data entry errors.
2. Make the changes shown at the right to the table.

1. Ms. **Capers'** first name should be spelled **Julie**, not Julia.
2. **Carol Merritt's** address is **121** Delaware St.
3. Ms. **Ford's** name should have been spelled **Glenda**, not Glenna.
4. Mr. **Guidry's** ZIP Code should be **29601-7474**.
5. Ms. **Ford's** income should have been **$41,000**, not $42,000.

SKILL BUILDING

41D • 12'
Speed Forcing Drill

Key each line once at top speed. Then try to complete each sentence on the 15", 12", or 10" call, as directed by your instructor. Force speed to higher levels as you move from line to line.

Emphasis: high-frequency balanced-hand words

	gwam 15"	12"	10"
Diane may go to the dock to visit the eight girls.	40	50	60
She is to go with them to the city to see the dog.	40	50	60
The sorority girls paid for the auto to go to the city.	44	55	66
She is to go to the city with us to sign the six forms.	44	55	66
Dick may go to the big island to fix the auto for the widow.	48	60	72
Glen and the big dog slept by the antique chair on the dock.	48	60	72
Nancy may pay the men for all the work they did down by the lake.	52	65	78
They held the big social for their neighbor downtown at the hall.	52	65	78

SKILL BUILDING

41E • 15'
Skill Check

1. Key a 1' writing on ¶ 1; determine *gwam*.
2. Add 2-4 *gwam* to the rate attained in Step 1, and note quarter-minute checkpoints in the chart below.
3. Key two 1' guided writings on ¶ 1 to increase speed.
4. Practice ¶ 2 in the same way.
5. Key two 3' writings on ¶s 1 and 2 combined; determine *gwam* and find errors.

Quarter-Minute Checkpoints

gwam	1/4'	1/2'	3/4'	1'
24	6	12	18	24
28	7	14	21	28
32	8	16	24	32
36	9	18	27	36
40	10	20	30	40
44	11	22	33	44
48	12	24	36	48
52	13	26	39	52
56	14	28	42	56
60	15	30	45	60

A all letters used — gwam 3'

	3'	
Quite a few of today's consumers buy on credit each day	4	67
without considering the consequences of the costs associated with	8	71
purchases made on credit. A decreased spending capacity in the	12	75
future is one of the main points that needs to be taken into	16	79
account prior to making a major credit purchase. Buyers who	21	83
utilize credit need to remember that earnings going toward the	25	87
repayment of a loan restrict funds that could be used to buy other	29	92
goods or services.	30	93
Buyers must also remember that credit can be expensive; there	35	97
are costs associated with it. One of those costs is interest. In-	39	102
terest is the sum charged for the use of money. Buyers who make	43	106
purchases via credit can also expect to be charged service fees or	48	111
finance charges. Perhaps the biggest cost of credit, however, is	52	115
the opportunity cost. The opportunity cost can be viewed as the	57	119
cost of not acquiring certain goods or services in order to ac-	61	124
quire other goods or services.	63	126

gwam 3' | 1 | 2 | 3 | 4 |

Activity 1 • Move Around in a Database

1. Read the text at the right.
2. Open the *A&E Applicants* table that you worked with in Lesson 1, Activity 1, and practice moving through it.
3. Open the *A&E Applicants* forms file that you worked with in Lesson 1, Activity 2, and practice moving through it.

There are several ways to move to a new location on the screen of a database table or a database form. Some methods take more keystrokes than others. Practicing the fastest methods, those using fewest keystrokes, until they feel automatic makes for efficient database work.

INSERTION POINT MOVES—TABLE

To move:	Keys
One field left	←
One field right	→
One line up	↑
One line down	↓
Leftmost field	HOME
Rightmost field	END
Down one window	**Page Down**
Up one window	**Page Up**
To first record	CTRL + HOME
To last record	CTRL + END

INSERTION POINT MOVES—FORM

To move:	Keys
Next field	↓
Previous field	↑
Top of form	HOME
Bottom of form	END
First record	CTRL + HOME
Last record	CTRL + END
Next record*	**Page Down**
Previous record*	**Page Up**

*In case the record has more than one screen, use CTRL + **Page Up** (**Page Down**).

Activity 2 • Edit Records

1. Read the text at the right.
2. Open the *Software Professionals* database table.
3. Make the changes given at the right.

Editing existing database records is similar to editing word processing documents. Simply move the insertion point to the location where the change is to be made and use the INSERT, DELETE, or BACKSPACE keys to make changes. Larger segments of text may require the use of the Block Text feature to make changes.

1. Change the price of **Computer Geography** to **$279**.
2. Change the name of **Creative Business Letters** to **Creative Letters**.
3. Change the price of **Basic Spreadsheets** to **$159**.
4. Change the beginning inventory of **Data Controller** to **300**.
5. Change the name of **Language Arts Skills** to **Language Skills**.

Activity 3 • Edit Records

1. Open the *Eastwick Fees* database table.
2. Make the changes given at the right.

1. **Stacy Rice** is enrolled in **Inter. Jazz** and **Inter. Ballet**. *(Be sure to change fees.)*
2. **Byrns** should be spelled **Burns**.
3. **Tasha Lang** should be **Trisha Lang**.

(continued on next page)

LESSON 42 IMPROVE KEYING TECHNIQUE

Objectives:

1. To improve keying techniques.
2. To improve keying speed and control.

42A • 5' Conditioning Practice

Key each line twice SS; then key a 1' writing on line 3; determine *gwam*.

alphabet 1 Jake Lopez may give a few more racquetball exhibitions in Dallas.

figures 2 Ray quickly found the total of 8.16, 9.43, and 10.25 to be 27.84.

speed 3 Bob's neighbor may dismantle the ancient shanty in the big field.

gwam 1' | 1 | 2 | 3 | 4 | 5 | 6 | 7 | 8 | 9 | 10 | 11 | 12 | 13 |

SKILL BUILDING

42B • 10' Technique: Letter Keys

1. Key each line twice.
2. Take a 30" writing on each line. If you complete the line, key it again.

Goal:
To keep keystroking action limited to the fingers.

Emphasize continuity and rhythm with curved, upright fingers.

I 1 Michigan, Illinois, Indiana, and Missouri are all in the Midwest.

J 2 Jay juggled plans to join Jane for juice with the judge and jury.

K 3 Katie knocked the knickknacks off the kiosk with her knobby knee.

L 4 Please allow me to be a little late with all legal illustrations.

M 5 Mary is immensely immature; her mannerisms make me extremely mad.

N 6 Nancy knew she would win the nomination at their next convention.

O 7 Roberto opposed opening the store on Monday mornings before noon.

P 8 Pam wrapped the peppermints in purple paper for the photographer.

Q 9 Qwin quietly queried Quincy on the quantity and quality of quail.

gwam 1' | 1 | 2 | 3 | 4 | 5 | 6 | 7 | 8 | 9 | 10 | 11 | 12 | 13 |

SKILL BUILDING

42C • 8' Technique: Number Keys/Tab

1. Set tabs at 2" and at 4".
2. Key the copy at the right.
3. Key three 1' writings, trying to key additional text on each writing.

Concentrate on figure location; quick tab spacing; eyes on copy.

429 Piedmont Ct.	883 Northgate Rd.	801 Montana Ave.
9173 Salem Rd.	554 Taunton Ave.	129 Venturi Rd.
3928 Market St.	885 Kickapoo Trail	820 Scarlett Dr.
890 Richmond St.	910 Plymouth Dr.	856 Lakewood Dr.
830 Manzanita Ave.	819 Oakdale Way	102 Victoria St.
306 Beckett Ter.	282 Curnan Way	823 Brook Ter.

SKILL BUILDING

42D • 15' Skill Check

1. Key three 1' writings on ¶ 1 of 41E. Strive to increase your rate on each writing.
2. Repeat Step 1 using ¶ 2.
3. Key two 3' writings using both ¶s.
4. Determine better 3' *gwam* and record it for later use.

Activity 4 • Add New Table Fields and Data

1. Open the *Eastwick Fees* table (*Eastwick School of Dance* database).
2. Add the fields shown below.

   September Fees
   October Fees
   November Fees
   December Fees
3. Update the records in the database table to include the new information provided at the right.
4. Print a copy of the revised table in landscape orientation.

Eastwick School of Dance

Name	Sept. Fees	Oct. Fees	Nov. Fees	Dec. Fees
Stewart	55	55	55	
Vaughn				
Martin	53	53		
Finley				
Garcia	57	57		
Edmonds	59	59		
Ramirez	58	58		
Rice				
Rizzo				
Higgins	27			
Giani	28	28		
Griffith	59	59		
Boyer	52	52		
Bunnell				
Byrns	57	57	57	
Koosman	66	66		
Lang				
Maas	25	25	25	
McDowell	28	28		
Chan	62	62		
Moreno	29			
Pingel	25	25		
Phelps	62	62	62	
Ross	28	28		
Sackett	63			

SKILL BUILDING

42E • 12'
Speed Forcing Drill

Key each line once at top speed. Then try to complete each sentence on the 15", 12", or 10" call, as directed by your instructor. Force speed to higher levels as you move from line to line.

Emphasis: high-frequency balanced-hand words

	gwam 15"	12"	10"
The sign is on the mantle by the antique ornament.	40	50	60
Pamela kept the food for the fish by the fishbowl.	40	50	60
I paid the man by the dock for the six bushels of corn.	44	55	66
The box with a shamrock and an iris is by the car door.	44	55	66
He owns the chair in the shanty at the end of the cornfield.	48	60	72
Their auditor may work on the problems with the eight firms.	48	60	72
To the right of the lake is the dismal shanty with the six ducks.	52	65	78
The maid may go with them when they go to the city for the gowns.	52	65	78

LESSON 43 IMPROVE KEYING TECHNIQUE

Objectives:

1. To improve keying techniques.
2. To improve keying speed and control.

43A • 5'
Conditioning Practice

Key each line twice SS; then take a 1' writing on line 3; determine *gwam*.

alphabet 1 Jack Lopez will attend the quality frog exhibits over the summer.
figures 2 Tim's score was 79 percent; he missed numbers 18, 26, 30, and 45.
speed 3 Pamela may blame the men for the problem with the neighbor's dog.

gwam 1' | 1 | 2 | 3 | 4 | 5 | 6 | 7 | 8 | 9 | 10 | 11 | 12 | 13 |

SKILL BUILDING

43B • 10'
Technique: Letter Keys

1. Key each line twice.
2. Take a 30" writing on each line. If you complete the line, key it again.

Goals:

- To keep keystroking action limited to the fingers.
- Continuity and rhythm with curved, upright fingers.

R 1 The raindrops bore down on the robbers during the February storm.
S 2 The Mets, Astros, Reds, Twins, Jays, and Cubs sold season passes.
T 3 Trent bought the teal teakettle on the stove in downtown Seattle.
U 4 Ursula usually rushes to the music museum on Tuesday, not Sunday.
V 5 Vivacious Eve viewed seven vivid violets in the vases in the van.
W 6 We swore we would work with the two wonderful kids for two weeks.
X 7 Rex Baxter explained the extra excise tax to excited expatriates.
Y 8 Yes, Ty is very busy trying to justify buying the yellow bicycle.
Z 9 Dazed, Zelda zigzagged to a plaza by the zoo to see a lazy zebra.

gwam 1' | 1 | 2 | 3 | 4 | 5 | 6 | 7 | 8 | 9 | 10 | 11 | 12 | 13 |

SKILL BUILDING

43C • 8'
Technique: Number Keys/Tab

1. Set tabs at 2" and at 4".
2. Key the copy at the right.
3. Key three 1' writings, trying to key additional text on each writing.

313 Richards Rd.	842 Warner Rd.	8634 Pearl Blvd.
67 Simmons St.	7619 Stewart Ave.	129 Silk Oak Dr.
9057 Taurus Ct.	904 Tebbetts Dr.	55 Vineland Ave.
436 Seaton Hall Ln.	802 Mayflower St.	627 Kimball Ave.
4021 Phyllis Way	357 Garvin St.	2004 Huber St.
138 Truman St.	84 Talmadge Pl.	835 Knobloch Ln.

Activity 3 • Add New Table Fields and Data

1. Open the *Sales Reps - District 13* table (*Rockwell Technologies* database).
2. Add the fields shown below.

   Territory
   ZIP
   July Sales
   August Sales

3. Update the records in the database table to include the new information provided at the right.
4. Print a copy of the revised table in landscape orientation.

SALES REPRESENTATIVES

Last Name	Territory	ZIP	July Sales	August Sales
Carter	Wyoming	82001-1837	45,351	37,951
Hull	Colorado	80233-0070	53,739	49,762
McRae	Utah	84404-2835	33,371	38,978
Hernandez	Utah	84057-1572	39,371	40,790
Camby	Idaho	83702-8312	42,173	65,386
Henneman	Montana	59102-6735	17,219	29,737
Reed	Wyoming	82607-9956	53,791	59,349
Logan	Montana	59404-3883	49,712	21,790
Cirillo	Idaho	83202-7523	29,731	37,956
LeClair	Colorado	81503-2270	63,212	40,321
Donovan	Colorado	80123-0091	37,198	45,865
Young	Utah	84118-0111	44,876	56,791
Tapani	South Dakota	57702-9932	59,145	39,645
Rivera	Colorado	81005-8376	55,400	37,751
Walker	Idaho	83402-3326	43,900	44,750
Wetteland	Montana	59803-8388	33,650	40,765
Chi	Arizona	85224-1157	39,750	48,621
Finley	Arizona	85711-5656	19,765	35,765
Reese	Arizona	85268-0012	67,890	45,780
Bell	Colorado	80401-7529	39,200	43,286
Doolittle	South Dakota	57106-7621	64,890	37,102
Butler	Arizona	85302-1300	35,975	46,873
Hulett	Arizona	85023-2766	56,730	46,720

SKILL BUILDING

43D • 12'
Speed Forcing Drill

Key each line once at top speed. Then try to complete each sentence on the 15", 12", or 10" call, as directed by your instructor. Force speed to higher levels as you move from line to line.

Emphasis: high-frequency balanced-hand words

	gwam 15"	12"	10"
Glen and I may key the forms for the city auditor.	40	50	60
He may make a sign to hang by the door of the bus.	40	50	60
They may make a profit if they do all of the busy work.	44	55	66
Six of the boys may bid for the land on the big island.	44	55	66
If he pays for the bus to the social, the girls may go also.	48	60	72
The neighbor paid the maid for the work she did on the dock.	48	60	72
It is their civic duty to handle their problems with proficiency.	52	65	78
Helen is to pay the firm for all the work they do on the autobus.	52	65	78

SKILL BUILDING

43E • 15'
Skill Check

1. Key a 1' writing on ¶ 1; determine *gwam*.
2. Add 2–4 *gwam* to the rate attained in Step 1, and note quarter-minute checkpoints in the chart below.
3. Take two 1' guided writings on ¶ 1 to increase speed.
4. Practice ¶ 2 in the same way.
5. Take two 3' writings on ¶s 1 and 2 combined; determine *gwam* and find errors.

Quarter-Minute Checkpoints				
gwam	1/4'	1/2'	3/4'	1'
24	6	12	18	24
28	7	14	21	28
32	8	16	24	32
36	9	18	27	36
40	10	20	30	40
44	11	22	33	44
48	12	24	36	48
52	13	26	39	52
56	14	28	42	56
60	15	30	45	60

A all letters used

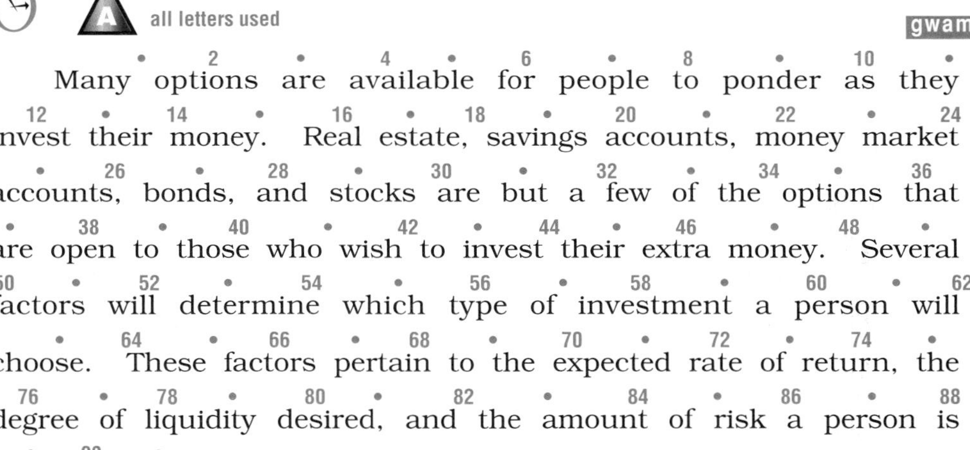

	gwam 3'	
Many options are available for people to ponder as they	4	64
invest their money. Real estate, savings accounts, money market	8	69
accounts, bonds, and stocks are but a few of the options that	12	73
are open to those who wish to invest their extra money. Several	17	77
factors will determine which type of investment a person will	21	81
choose. These factors pertain to the expected rate of return, the	25	86
degree of liquidity desired, and the amount of risk a person is	29	90
willing to take.	30	91
An investor who seeks a high rate of return and who is	34	95
willing to take a high degree of risk often considers the stock	38	99
market. Stock markets or stock exchanges are organizations that	43	103
bring investors together to buy and sell shares of stock. Stock	47	108
represents a share in the ownership of a company. Since more	51	112
risk is associated with an investment that has a high rate of	55	116
return, judgment must be exercised by those thinking about the	60	120
purchase of stock.	61	121

gwam 3' | 1 | 2 | 3 | 4 |

ADD NEW FIELDS

Activity 1 • Add New Fields to an Existing Database Table

1. Read the copy at the right.
2. Add fields shown to the *Software Professionals* database table.

Database software lets you add additional fields to a database table after you have created it. *Software Professionals* would like you to add the fields shown at the right.

Purchases
Sales

Activity 2 • Update Records

1. Update the records in the *Software Professionals* database table to include the new information provided at the right.
2. Print a copy of the revised table in landscape orientation.

	Record 1	Record 2	Record 3
Software:	Basic Spreadsheets	Computer Geography	Computerized Reading
Purchases:	1200	400	500
Sales:	1578	850	674
	Record 4	**Record 5**	**Record 6**
Software:	Creative Bus. Letters	Data Controller	English Enhancement
Purchases:	250	0	1000
Sales:	400	240	1200
	Record 7	**Record 8**	**Record 9**
Software:	Financial Advisors	Graphics Designer	Keyboard Composition
Purchases:	1000	500	1000
Sales:	1987	437	1753
	Record 10	**Record 11**	**Record 12**
Software:	Language Arts Skills	Quick Key WP	Spelling Mastery
Purchases:	500	1000	0
Sales:	759	1378	300
	Record 13	**Record 14**	**Record 15**
Software:	Tax Assistant	Telephone Directory	Art Gallery
Purchases:	0	1000	500
Sales:	980	1873	673
	Record 16	**Record 17**	**Record 18**
Software:	Your Time Manager	Office Layout	Math Tutor
Purchases:	1000	300	0
Sales:	1379	475	39

WORD PROCESSING 5

ACTIVITY 1

Review WP Features

Key sentences 1–5; <u>underline</u>, *italicize*, and **bold** text as you key. Use the Hanging Indent feature to align the second line of text under the first line as shown.

Save as: *WP5ACT1*

1. **Benjamin Britten's** *Four Sea Interludes* include ***Dawn***, ***Sunday Morning***, ***Moonlight***, and ***Storm***.
2. <u>Chris O'Donnell</u>, <u>Renee Zellweger</u>, <u>Brooke Shields</u>, and <u>Mariah Carey</u> star in ***The Bachelor***.
3. The titles of **books** and **movies** should be <u>underlined</u> or *italicized*.
4. <u>Any Given Sunday</u> is a **drama**; <u>Magnolia</u> is a **comedy**; and <u>Supernova</u> is a **sci-fi**.
5. <u>Henry Wadsworth</u> **Longfellow** wrote *Success*; <u>Samuel</u> **Longfellow** wrote *Go Forth to Life*.

ACTIVITY 2

Review WP Features

1. Open the file *CD-WP5ACT2*.
2. <u>Underline</u>, *italicize*, and **bold** text as shown at the right.

Save as: *WP5ACT2*

6. During the first week of February, *The Testament* by **John Grisham** was No. 1 on the <u>Best Sellers</u> list.
7. <u>Time</u> and <u>Newsweek</u> featured articles on the tragic deaths of John F. Kennedy, Jr., and Carolyn Bessette Kennedy.
8. <u>Margins</u> were presented in **WP2**; <u>Cut</u>, <u>Copy</u>, and <u>Paste</u> were presented in **WP3**.
9. Do you know the difference between ***their*** and ***there***?
10. *The Village Blacksmith* (**Longfellow**) and *The Road Not Taken* (**Frost**) were discussed in class on Friday.

ACTIVITY 3

Copy Text to Another File

1. Read the copy at the right.
2. Open the file you created in Activity 2 (*WP5ACT2*); copy Sentences 6–10.
3. Open *WP5ACT1*, the file you created in Activity 1; place the copied text a DS below Sentence 5.

Save as: *WP5ACT3*

Use the **Copy** and **Paste** features to copy text from one file to another.

Use the **Cut** and **Paste** features to move text from one file to another.

Steps to Copy, Cut, and Paste:

1. Select the text.
2. Copy or cut the selected text.
3. Open the document in which you want to place the copied (or cut) text.
4. Place the insertion point where you want to place the text.
5. Paste the text at the insertion point.

Activity 3 • Update a Database Table

1. Open the *Eastwick Fees* table.
2. Key the records information shown at the right in the table.
3. Save and close the database.

Eastwick School of Dance			
Name	Dance Class 1	Dance Class 2	Monthly Fees
Tarin Chan	Inter. Ballet	Adv. Jazz	$62
Marcia Moreno	Inter. Jazz		$29
Elizabeth Pingel	Beg. Tap		$25
Sonja Phelps	Inter. Jazz	Adv. Tap	$62
Charlotte Ross	Beg. Ballet		$28
Lynda Sackett	Inter. Ballet	Adv. Tap	

Activity 4 • Update a Database Table

1. Open the *A&E Applicants* table.
2. Add the two new bank card applicants shown at the right to the table.
3. Save and close the database.

A&E Bank Card Application				
Last Name	First	Middle		
Hutton	Grant	K.		
Street Address	City	State	ZIP	Phone
811 Kirkland Ln.	Charleston	SC	29401-3311	803-129-5501
Birth Date (Month, Day, Year)	Social Security Number		Name of Employer	
09-08-60	181-32-7002		La Crosse Medical Center	
Address of Employer	City	State	Annual Income	Employer's Phone
760 Briarstone Ct.	Charleston	SC	$55,000	803-645-2200

A&E Bank Card Application				
Last Name	First	Middle		
Upshaw	Andrea	Jane		
Street Address	City	State	ZIP	Phone
432 Pennsylvania Ave.	Columbia	SC	29204-6634	803-837-1329
Birth Date (Month, Day, Year)	Social Security Number		Name of Employer	
02-07-63	212-06-8280		Timberdale Insurance	
Address of Employer	City	State	Annual Income	Employer's Phone
671 Wimbledon Ct.	Columbia	SC	$49,500	803-674-1734

ACTIVITY 4

Reinforce Copying Files

Open the files *CD-GETTYS1*, *CD-GETTYS2*, and *CD-GETTYS3*.

Create a copy of the Gettysburg Address as directed at the right.

Save as: *WP5ACT4*

The initial words of each of the three paragraphs of the Gettysburg Address are shown at the right. The names of the files where these paragraphs can be found are shown in parentheses.

Copy the paragraphs from *GETTYS2* and *GETTYS3* and place them in the correct order in *GETTYS1*. Leave a DS between paragraphs.

Paragraph 1: Four score and seven years ago, our fathers brought forth on this continent . . . (*GETTYS1*)

Paragraph 2: Now we are engaged in a great civil war, testing . . . (*GETTYS2*)

Paragraph 3: But in a large sense we cannot dedicate, we cannot consecrate, we cannot hallow this ground. The brave . . . (*GETTYS3*)

ACTIVITY 5

Review WP Features

1. Read line 1 at the right and choose the correct word in parentheses.
2. Key the sentence with the correct word choice underlined and bolded.
3. Repeat Steps 1 and 2 for the remaining sentences.

Save as: *WP5ACT5*

1. I will be (their/there) on Friday.
2. Do you (know/no) the answer?
3. Let me know when (your/you're) available to have (your/you're) picture taken.
4. Which (cite/sight/site) did he choose for the new studio?
5. She (knew/new) his (knew/new) telephone number.

ACTIVITY 6

Review WP Features

1. Open the file *CD-WP5ACT6*.
2. Delete the incorrect word choice and parentheses from each sentence; bold and underline the correct word choice.
3. Copy lines 6–10; open the file created in Activity 5 (*WP5ACT5*); paste copied text a DS below line 5.

Save as: *WP5ACT6*

ACTIVITY 7

Review WP Features

1. Set a left tab at 0.5", a right tab at 3.5", and a decimal tab at 5.5".
2. Key data (DS) at the right; omit column headings.

Save as: *WP5ACT7*

Player/Team	Free Throws	Free Throw %
Hornacek, Utah	109 of 113	.964602
Miller, Indiana	223 of 239	.933054
Armstrong, Orlando	135 of 148	.912162
Brandon, Minnesota	121 of 133	.909774
Allen, Milwaukee	215 of 239	.899582
Cassell, Milwaukee	229 of 260	.880769

ADD NEW RECORDS TO UPDATE A DATABASE

Activity 1 • Add New Records to an Existing Database Table

1. Read the text at the right.
2. Open the *Software Professionals* table.
3. Add the records shown at the right to the table.
4. Save and close the database.

Database software lets you add records to update a database table at any time. Lynda Smoltz provided the information below to be added to the *Software Professionals* database table.

	Record 13	Record 14	Record 15
Stock No.:	B952	B658	B839
Software:	Tax Assistant	Telephone Directory	Art Gallery
Price:	$129	$119	$249
Beg. Invt.:	5000	5000	1000
	Record 16	**Record 17**	**Record 18**
Stock No.:	B794	B833	E910
Software:	Your Time Manager	Office Layout	Math Tutor
Price:	$69	$129	$59
Beg. Invt.:	2500	500	2000

Activity 2 • Update a Database Table

1. Read the text at the right.
2. Open the *Sales Reps - District 13* table (*Rockwell Technologies* database).
3. Add the records shown at the right to the table.
4. Save and close the database.

Mr. Vermillion would like the information about the additional sales reps listed below added to the *Sales Reps - District 13* table.

SALES REPRESENTATIVES

Last Name	First Name	Address	City	State
Walker	Trent	872 Texas Ave.	Idaho Falls	ID
Wetteland	Cynthia	380 Clearview Dr.	Missoula	MT
Chi	Carrie	310 Sagebrush Ct.	Chandler	AZ
Finley	Ann	388 Oxford Dr., E	Tucson	AZ
Reese	Jay	330 Shiloh Way, N	Scottsdale	AZ
Bell	Scott	7211 Larkspur Dr.	Golden	CO
Doolittle	Lisa	872 Kingswood Way	Sioux Falls	SD
Butler	Warren	398 Navajo Dr.	Glendale	AZ
Hulett	Sandra	450 La Paz Ct., N	Phoenix	AZ

UNIT 14

LESSONS 44–46

Improving E-mail and Memo Formatting Skills

Format Guides: Memos and E-mail

TO: Andrew Nelson, Manager
Amy McDonald, Assistant Manager
Judith Smythe, Assistant Manger

FROM: Malcolm McKinley, Travel Agent

DATE: May 3, 200-

SUBJECT: CIVIL WAR BUS TOUR

Yes, I think there would be an interest in a bus tour of some of the Civil War battlefields. My recommendation would be to start with a six-day tour that includes some of the most famous battlefields.

Of course, the one that comes to mind right away is Gettysburg, where over 158,000 Union (George G. Meade) and Confederate (Robert E. Lee) soldiers fought courageously for their causes. This battle (July 1-3, 1863) resulted in an estimated 51,000 lives being lost. Being able to visit the place where President Lincoln delivered the Gettysburg Address would also be of real interest to those considering the trip. I've looked at several Web sites, and evidently something of interest is always going on in or near Gettysburg.

The other battlefields that I recommend including on the tour are Manassas (Virginia) and Antietam (Maryland). Both of these battlefields were key encounters of the Civil War.

Within the next week, I will provide you with more details on a tour such as the one I've briefly presented.

xx

c Timothy Gerrard
Maria Valdez

Interoffice Memo with Distribution List

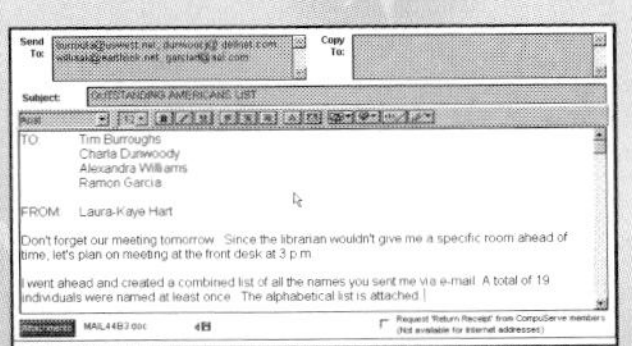

Send To:
Copy To:
Subject: OUTSTANDING AMERICANS LIST

TO: Tim Burroughs
Charla Dunwoody
Alexandra Williams
Ramon Garcia

FROM: Laura-Kaye Hart

Don't forget our meeting tomorrow. Since the librarian wouldn't give me a specific room ahead of time, let's plan on meeting at the front desk at 3 p.m.

I went ahead and created a combined list of all the names you sent me via e-mail. A total of 19 individuals were named at least once. The alphabetical list is attached.

MAIL44B3.doc

Request 'Return Receipt' from CompuServe members (Not available for Internet addresses)

E-mail Message with Distribution List

Special E-mail Software Features

Several software features make communicating through e-mail fast and efficient.

E-mail address list. Names and e-mail addresses of persons you correspond with often may be kept in an address list. An address can be entered on the TO: line by selecting it from the list.

E-mail copies. Copies of e-mail can be sent to additional addresses at the same time you send the original message. The **Cc:** (courtesy copy) and **Bcc:** (blind courtesy copy) features of e-mail software are used to send copies.

Cc: If you want the recipient to know that you have sent the message to others, key the e-mail address of the other individuals on the **Cc:** line in the e-mail heading.

Bcc: If you do NOT want the recipient to know that you have sent the message to others, key their e-mail addresses on the **Bcc:** line in the e-mail heading.

Attachments. Documents, such as reports, tables, spreadsheets, and databases, may be attached electronically to e-mail. Common names of the software feature are **Attachments**, **Attached**, and **Attach File**.

Forward. The Forward feature allows you to forward a copy of an e-mail message you received to other individuals.

Reply. The Reply feature is used to respond quickly to incoming e-mail. The incoming message (unless deleted) and reply are sent to the sender of the original message. The originator's address does not have to be keyed. The original message quickly reminds the originator what the reply is about, so a brief reply is sufficient.

E-mail distribution list. When e-mail is sent to several addresses at once, use a distribution list:

To: burrouta@uswest.net, dunwoocj@dellnet.com, williaak@earthlink.net, garciarf@aol.com

For sending e-mail often to the same group of people, the Recipient List feature (on most e-mail software) saves time. All addresses in a group can be entered on the TO: line at once when the name of the recipient list is selected.

Special Memo Parts

In addition to the standard memo parts, several parts enhance communicating with memos.

Copy notations. A copy notation indicates that a copy of a memo is being sent to someone other than the addressee. Use "c" followed by the name of the person(s) to receive a copy. Place a copy notation a double space below the last line of the enclosure notation or the reference initials if there is no enclosure. If you do not want the person to know you are sending it to others, use the "bc" (blind copy) notation on the copy only.

Attachment/Enclosure notation. If another document is attached to a memo, the word *Attachment* is keyed at the left margin a DS below the reference initials. If a document is included but not attached, the word *Enclosure* is used instead. If reference initials are not used, the notation is keyed a DS below the body of the memo.

Memo distribution list. When a memo is sent to several individuals, a distribution list is used. Format the memo distribution list as shown below:

To: Tim Burroughs
Charla Dunwoody
Alexandra Williams
Ramon Garcia

CREATE A NEW TABLE IN AN EXISTING DATABASE

Activity 1 • Create a New Table in an Existing Database

1. Read the copy at the right.
2. Open the *Eastwick School of Dance* database.
3. Create and save a new table using the filename *Eastwick Fees.*

The owner of Eastwick School of Dance, Ashley Eastwick, would like you to create another table (*Eastwick Fees*) in the *Eastwick School of Dance* database to keep track of the student fees. She would like you to use the field names shown at the right.

Last Name
First Name
Dance Class 1
Dance Class 2
Monthly Fees

Activity 2 • Add Records to a Database File

1. Enter the records information given at the right into the *Eastwick Fees* database table.

   If the monthly fee is not given, use the following Fee Schedule information to calculate the fee.

Fee Schedule	
Beg. Ballet	$28
Beg. Tap	25
Beg. Jazz	27
Inter. Ballet	30
Inter. Tap	29
Inter. Jazz	29
Adv. Ballet	34
Adv. Tap	33
Adv. Jazz	32

2. Save and close the database.

Eastwick School of Dance

Name	Dance Class 1	Dance Class 2	Monthly Fees
Julie Stewart	Beg. Ballet	Beg. Jazz	$55
Julie Vaughn	Adv. Ballet		$34
Lauren Martin	Beg. Ballet	Beg. Tap	$53
Jacqueline Finley	Inter. Ballet		$30
Angela Garcia	Beg. Jazz	Inter. Ballet	
Kirsten Edmonds	Beg. Tap	Adv. Ballet	
Camille Ramirez	Inter. Tap	Inter. Jazz	$58
Stacy Rice	Inter. Jazz		
Loren Rizzo	Beg. Ballet		$28
Judy Higgins	Beg. Jazz		
Jill Giani	Beg. Ballet		$28
Anne Griffith	Inter. Ballet	Inter. Jazz	$59
Jayne Boyer	Beg. Tap	Beg. Jazz	$52
Diane Bunnell	Inter. Ballet		
Brook Byrns	Beg. Jazz	Inter. Ballet	$57
Alison Koosman	Adv. Ballet	Adv. Jazz	$66
Tasha Lang	Beg. Ballet	Inter. Tap	$57
Kayla Maas	Beg. Tap		$25
Carolyn McDowell	Beg. Ballet		

IMPROVE E-MAIL FORMATTING SKILLS

Objectives:

1. To process e-mail messages with attachments and copy notations.
2. To improve language skills.

44A • 5'
Conditioning Practice

Key each line twice SS; then key a 1' writing on line 3; determine *gwam.*

alphabet 1	Tom saw Jo leave quickly for her job after my dog won six prizes.
fig/sym 2	Check No. 203 ($1,486.17) and Check No. 219 ($57.98) are missing.
speed 3	Did their auditor sign the key element of the forms for the firm?
gwam 1'	1 | 2 | 3 | 4 | 5 | 6 | 7 | 8 | 9 | 10 | 11 | 12 | 13

FORMATTING

44B • 37'
Send/Receive E-mail

Document 1 (Attachment)

TM: 2"

LS: SS (Do not indent paragraphs)

1. Format and key the text at the right.
2. Bold all names. DS the heading; QS below the date.
3. Correct all spelling, keying, and formatting errors.

Save as: *MAIL44B1*

History Bits

"If A equals success, then the formula is:

A = X + Y + Z.

X is work. Y is play. Z is keep your mouth shut."

—Albert Einstein

Search the Web to learn more about one of the individuals whose name appears at the right or one of those listed in Document 3 (p. 128).

Compose a paragraph or two about the individual.

AMERICAN HISTORY
your Name
March 18, 200-

Albert Einstein: American physicist whose theory of relativity led to the harnessing of nuclear energy.

Benjamin Franklin: A leading American statesman, inventor, philanthropist, publisher, author, revolutionary, and thinker.

Abraham Lincoln: The sixteenth President of the United States; helped keep the Union together during the Civil War which led to the abolishment of slavery; recognized for his honesty and compassion.

Franklin Roosevelt: Thirty-second President of the United States; led the country during two critical periods in United States history (the Great Depression and World War II).

George Washington: Commander in Chief of the Continental Army during the American Revolution; first President of the United States.

CREATE A DATABASE TABLE

Activity 1 • Create a Database and Personnel Table

1. Read the text at the right.
2. Create a new database using the filename *Rockwell Technologies*.
3. Create and save a table in Design View with the filename *Sales Reps - District 13*.

Paul M. Vermillion, District 13 sales manager, would like you to create a database containing the names and addresses of all sales representatives in his district. He would like you to use the field names shown at the right.

Last Name
First Name
Address
City
State

Activity 2 • Add Records to a Database

1. Enter the records given at the right into the *Sales Reps - District 13* database table.
2. Save and close the database table.

SALES REPRESENTATIVES

Last Name	First Name	Address	City	State
Carter	Mary	310 Old Trail Rd.	Cheyenne	WY
Hull	Dale	2710 BlueJay Ln.	Denver	CO
McRae	Jessica	475 Canyon Rd.	Ogden	UT
Hernandez	Erika	375 Highland Dr.	Orem	UT
Camby	Sue	378 Ranchero Rd.	Boise	ID
Henneman	Jason	762 Nugget Dr.	Billings	MT
Reed	Jessica	817 Herrington Dr.	Casper	WY
Logan	Marsha	905 Chickadee Ct.	Great Falls	ID
Cirillo	Mathew	1208 Whitaker Rd.	Pocatello	ID
LeClair	Justin	830 Whitehead Dr.	Grand Junction	CO
Donovan	Kellee	765 Coal Mine Ave.	Littleton	CO
Young	Marsha	7563 Ferncrest Cir.	Salt Lake City	UT
Tapani	Devlin	543 Lookout Mtn.	Rapid City	SD
Rivera	Jose	756 Royal Crest Dr.	Pueblo	CO

Document 2 (E-mail)

Key the text as e-mail to four classmates. Send a copy to your instructor. Attach Document 1 (*MAIL44B1*). Check your work.

 **Save as:** *MAIL44B2*

SUBJECT: AMERICAN HISTORY | Attached is the list of the five Americans who I feel had the greatest impact on our history. A few notes about the individuals are provided after each name. Narrowing the list to five was very difficult. (¶) I've reserved a room in the library for us to meet on Thursday, March 25, at 3 p.m. By then we should have received and reviewed each other's lists. Be prepared to decide on the final ten individuals to include in the report for Ms. Graham. (¶) I look forward to receiving each of your lists.

Document 3 (Attachment)

TM: 2" **LS:** 1.5

Key the list centered on the page. Center a two-line title in bold: **RECOMMENDATIONS FOR OUTSTANDING AMERICANS REPORT.** Check your work.

 **Save as:** *MAIL44B3*

Susan B. Anthony
Neil Armstrong
Alexander Graham Bell
Thomas Alva Edison
Albert Einstein
Benjamin Franklin
Samuel Gompers
Ulysses S. Grant
Patrick Henry
Thomas Jefferson
Martin Luther King, Jr.
Abraham Lincoln
Douglas MacArthur
Thomas Paine
Sir Walter Raleigh
Eleanor Roosevelt
Franklin Roosevelt
Harriet Beecher Stowe
Henry David Thoreau
George Washington

Document 4 (E-mail)

Key the text as e-mail to the same four classmates as Document 2. Attach Document 3 (*MAIL44B3*). Check your work.

When you receive this e-mail from classmates, forward one message to your instructor.

 **Save as:** *MAIL44B4*

SUBJECT: OUTSTANDING AMERICANS LIST | Don't forget our meeting tomorrow. Since the librarian wouldn't give me a specific room ahead of time, let's plan on meeting at the front desk at 3 p.m. (¶) I went ahead and created a combined list of all the names you sent me via e-mail. A total of 20 individuals were named at least once. The alphabetical list is attached. (¶) See you tomorrow at 3.

LANGUAGE SKILLS

44C • 8' Language Skills: Word Choice

1. Study the spelling/definitions of the words at the right.
2. Key line 1, noting the proper choice of words.
3. Key lines 2–3, choosing the right words to complete the lines correctly.
4. Repeat Steps 2 and 3.
5. Check your work; correct word-choice errors.

 **Save as:** *CHOICE44C*

hole (n) an opening in or through something
whole (adj/n) having all its proper parts; a complete amount or sum

peak (n) pointed end; top of a mountain; highest level
peek (vb) to glance or look at for a brief time

Learn 1 The **whole** group helped dig a **hole** to bury the time capsule.
Apply 2 They ate the (hole, whole) cake before going to the water (hole, whole).
Apply 3 He told us, "The (hole, whole) is greater than the sum of its parts."

Learn 1 If you **peek** out the window, you will see the **peak** of the iceberg.
Apply 2 The (peak, peek) of the mountain came into view as they drove around the curve.
Apply 3 Students were told not to (peak, peek) at the keyboard in order to reach (peek, peak) skill.

CREATE A DATABASE AND TABLE

Activity 1 • Create a Database and Table

1. Study the text at the right.
2. Create a new database using the filename *Software Professionals.*
3. Create a table in Design View.

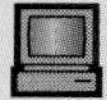
Save as: *Software Professionals*

Learning Tip:

See p. 396 for an example of defining and sequencing fields of a database table.

Information has always been critical to the successful operation of a business. In today's business environment, more and more information is being stored and accessed through the use of databases. As noted earlier, a database is a computerized filing system that is used to organize and maintain a collection of data. The data is stored in tables. A database may contain one table or any number of tables. A few examples of different types of databases include customers' names and addresses, personnel records, sales records, payroll records, telephone numbers, and investment records.

The database you worked with in Lesson 1 was a credit card application file that contained information about each applicant. In the remainder of this unit you will be creating and working with several different databases. The first database you will create is for *Software Professionals*. Lynda Smoltz, the manager, would like you to create a database for the software products they sell. She would like the database table to include the following field information:

Stock Number
Software
Price
Beginning Inventory

Activity 2 • Add Records to a Database

1. Enter the records given at the right into the *Software Professionals* database table.
2. Save and close the database table.

	Record 1	Record 2	Record 3
Stock No.:	B929	E246	E786
Software:	Basic Spreadsheets	Computer Geography	Computerized Reading
Price:	$139	$259	$189
Beg. Invt.:	2000	2500	1000
	Record 4	**Record 5**	**Record 6**
Stock No.:	E561	B821	E320
Software:	Creative Bus. Letters	Data Controller	English Enhancement
Price:	$125	$309	$219
Beg. Invt.:	500	500	800
	Record 7	**Record 8**	**Record 9**
Stock No.:	B689	B586	E758
Software:	Financial Advisors	Graphics Designer	Keyboard Composition
Price:	$99	$165	$155
Beg. Invt.:	2500	400	3000
	Record 10	**Record 11**	**Record 12**
Stock No.:	B615	B731	E641
Software:	Language Arts Skills	Quick Key WP	Spelling Mastery
Price:	$139	$75	$139
Beg. Invt.:	1500	2500	2000

LESSON 45 IMPROVE MEMO FORMATTING SKILLS

Objectives:

1. To increase proficiency in formatting memos.
2. To format memo distribution lists.

45A • 5' Conditioning Practice

Key each line twice SS; then take a 1' writing on line 3; determine *gwam.*

alphabet 1 Rebecca enjoyed explaining her vast knowledge of the zoo marquee.

figures 2 Flight 784 is scheduled to leave at 10:35 from Gate 96 on May 20.

speed 3 The maid may make the usual visit to the dock to work on the map.

gwam 1' | 1 | 2 | 3 | 4 | 5 | 6 | 7 | 8 | 9 | 10 | 11 | 12 | 13 |

FORMATTING

45B • 45' Memos

Memo 1

1. Format and key the copy at the right as an inter-office memo.
2. Check the memo; correct all formatting, spelling, and keying errors.

Save as: *MEMO45B1*

TO: American History Students | FROM: Professor Perry | DATE: January 20, 200- | SUBJECT: NEXT EXAM

Here is the information about next week's exam. It will cover Chapter 22, pp. 702-727, and Chapter 23, pp. 740-769.

The main emphasis of Chapter 22 is the New Deal. You will be expected to explain what the New Deal was, why some people criticized it while others praised it, and the impact of the New Deal on the U.S. economy.

Between 1933 and 1937, many pieces of legislation associated with the New Deal were passed. Make sure you know the purpose of each of the following acts.

* Emergency Banking Act
* Agricultural Adjustment Act
* Federal Emergency Relief Act
* Home Owners Refinancing Act
* National Industrial Recovery Act
* Emergency Relief Appropriation Act
* National Labor Relations Act
* Social Security Act

Chapter 23 covers World War II. We thoroughly discussed this chapter in class. Make sure you review your notes carefully.

If you are knowledgeable about these topics, you should do well on the exam.

Memo 2

1. Format and key the copy at the right as a memo to **Marsha Hanson, Director**. The memo is from **Alison Sadecki**. Use the current date and this subject line: **ANTHONY AND STANTON DISCUSSION**.
2. Include a blind copy notation: **Kevin Hefner**.
3. Check the memo; correct all errors.

Save as: *MEMO45B2*

Even though the Virginia Women's Museum is primarily for recognizing those women who contributed greatly to Virginia's history, I think it appropriate to recognize some early leaders of the women's movement on a national level.

Susan B. Anthony and Elizabeth Cady Stanton are two women who led the struggle for women's suffrage at the national level. They organized the National Woman Suffrage Association. Shouldn't they be recognized for their gallant efforts in our museum as well?

Please include a discussion of this issue on the next agenda.

Activity 2 • Add Records to an Existing Database Form File

1. Open the *A&E Applicants* form file in the *A&E Bank* database.
2. Key the information contained on the card applications at the right into the database form.
3. Print a copy of the *A&E Applicants* table file in landscape orientation after entering the last record.

A&E Bank Card Application

Last Name	First	Middle		
White	Carlos	Benito		
Street Address	**City**	**State**	**ZIP**	**Phone**
9873 Clear Crossing Ln.	Charlotte	NC	28112-8309	704-126-1580
Birth Date (Month, Day, Year)	**Social Security Number**		**Name of Employer**	
06-20-59	829-23-8729		Charlotte Legal Services	
Address of Employer	**City**	**State**	**Annual Income**	**Employer's Phone**
390 Dunbar St.	Charlotte	NC	$55,000	704-140-5554

A&E Bank Card Application

Last Name	First	Middle		
Castillo	Mary	J.		
Street Address	**City**	**State**	**ZIP**	**Phone**
3820 Stonegate Ct.	Greensboro	NC	27406-8631	910-156-2798
Birth Date (Month, Day, Year)	**Social Security Number**		**Name of Employer**	
04-15-57	389-56-9821		Rochelle Gallery	
Address of Employer	**City**	**State**	**Annual Income**	**Employer's Phone**
310 Sherman St.	Greensboro	NC	$25,500	910-190-1200

A&E Bank Card Application

Last Name	First	Middle		
Russell	Reed	Martin		
Street Address	**City**	**State**	**ZIP**	**Phone**
8291 Regency Dr.	Charleston	WV	25341-9938	304-129-8292
Birth Date (Month, Day, Year)	**Social Security Number**		**Name of Employer**	
12-24-57	389-51-8830		Auto Glass Specialists	
Address of Employer	**City**	**State**	**Annual Income**	**Employer's Phone**
8392 White Oak	Charleston	WV	$18,000	304-128-7356

Memo 3

1. Format and key the text at the right as a memo.
2. Send copies to **Timothy Gerrard** and **Maria Valdez**.
3. Check the memo; correct all formatting, spelling, and keying errors.

 **Save as:** *MEMO45B3*

TO: Andrew Nelson, Manager; Amy McDonald, Assistant Manager; Judith Smythe, Assistant Manager | FROM: Malcolm McKinley, Travel Agent | DATE: May 3, 200- | SUBJECT: CIVIL WAR BUS TOUR

Yes, I think there would be an interest in a bus tour of some of the battle campaigns of the Civil War. My recommendation would be to start with a six-day tour that includes some of the most famous battlefields.

Of course, the one that comes to mind right away is Gettysburg, where over 158,000 Union (George G. Meade) and Confederate (Robert E. Lee) soldiers fought courageously for their causes. This battle (July 1-3, 1863) resulted in an estimated 51,000 lives being lost. Being able to visit the place where President Lincoln delivered the Gettysburg Address would also be of real interest to those considering the trip. I've looked at several Web sites, and evidently something of interest is always going on in or near Gettysburg.

The other battlefields that I recommend including on the tour are Manassas (Virginia) and Antietam (Maryland). Both of these battlefields were key encounters of the Civil War.

Within the next week, I will provide you with more details on a tour such as the one I've briefly presented.

LESSON 46 IMPROVE E-MAIL AND MEMO FORMATTING SKILLS

Objectives:

1. To increase proficiency in formatting and keying memos.
2. To increase proficiency in formatting and keying e-mail.

46A • 5' Conditioning Practice

Key each line twice SS; then key a 1' writing on line 3; determine *gwam*.

alphabet 1 Gavin Zahn will buy the exquisite green jacket from the old shop.

figures 2 Check No. 183 was used to pay Invoices 397 and 406 on October 25.

speed 3 Glen may pay the haughty neighbor if the turn signals work right.

gwam 1' | 1 | 2 | 3 | 4 | 5 | 6 | 7 | 8 | 9 | 10 | 11 | 12 | 13 |

FORMATTING

46B • 38' E-mail and Memos

Document 1 (E-mail)

Key the text as e-mail to your instructor and a classmate. (If e-mail software is not available, format/key a memo to **John Ewing**. Use the current date.) Send a blind courtesy copy to a classmate OR key a blind copy notation on the memo: **Sally Enders**. Check your work.

 **Save as:** *MAIL46B1 (or MEMO46B1)*

SUBJECT: FIELD TRIP PROPOSAL | In our American history class, my students are studying the American Revolution. To bring this unit to life, I would like to take the class on a field trip to the Valley Forge Historical Society Museum.

According to their Web site, the museum ". . . offers visitors to Valley Forge the opportunity to understand the value of the sacrifice made by the 12,000 men who camped here during the winter of 1777-78. The spirit of Valley Forge is chronicled through galleries and displays that present the letters, weapons, and personal effects of the great and everyday Continental soldier."

I believe this would be an excellent educational experience for our students. When would you be available to meet with me to discuss a field trip of this nature?

LESSONS 1–8 (4–5 HOURS)

Database Applications 1, Developing Database Skills

LESSON 1 ADD RECORDS TO AN EXISTING DATABASE

Activity 1 • Add Records to an Existing Database Table

1. Review the information about databases on pp. 395–398.
2. Open the *A&E Applicants* table file in the *A&E Bank* database.
3. Key the information contained on the card applications at the right directly into the database table.

A&E Bank Card Application

Last Name	First	Middle		
Lowell	Cynthia	Sue		
Street Address	**City**	**State**	**ZIP**	**Phone**
1208 Marietta St.	Asheville	NC	28803-4309	704-564-3874
Birth Date (Month, Day, Year)	**Social Security Number**		**Name of Employer**	
03-08-75	342-35-6766		Brickworks	
Address of Employer	**City**	**State**	**Annual Income**	**Employer's Phone**
3302 Old Toll Rd.	Asheville	NC	$24,000	704-328-9901

A&E Bank Card Application

Last Name	First	Middle		
Eisenhower	Andrew	Shane		
Street Address	**City**	**State**	**ZIP**	**Phone**
302 Featherstone Dr.	Greenville	SC	29611-9931	864-232-9301
Birth Date (Month, Day, Year)	**Social Security Number**		**Name of Employer**	
07-02-56	382-56-2200		Kirkwood Dental	
Address of Employer	**City**	**State**	**Annual Income**	**Employer's Phone**
380 Lake Shore Dr.	Greenville	SC	$75,000	864-344-8788

A&E Bank Card Application

Last Name	First	Middle		
Johnson	Beth	Anne		
Street Address	**City**	**State**	**ZIP**	**Phone**
3152 Duke St.	Fayetteville	NC	28304-4351	910-188-2211
Birth Date (Month, Day, Year)	**Social Security Number**		**Name of Employer**	
04-15-49	520-66-3820		Fenton Motor, Inc.	
Address of Employer	**City**	**State**	**Annual Income**	**Employer's Phone**
382 Greenbriar Dr.	Fayetteville	NC	$22,000	910-168-8399

Memo 2

1. Format the text at the right as a memo to **Kara Hundley, Chair,** from **Richard Ashmore, Committee Member**. Use the current date and this subject line: **RECOMMENDATION FOR CORPORATE GIVING**.
2. Correct all spelling, keying, and formatting errors.

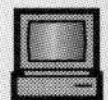

Save as: *MEMO46B2*

History Bits

"I am determined to sustain myself as long as possible and die like a soldier who never forgets what is due to his own honor and that of his country. . . ."

—William Barret Travis
Commander of the Alamo
February 24, 1836

Memo 3

1. Open the file *CD-MEMO46B3*; make the corrections shown at the right.
2. Add a copy notation: **Spencer Schultz**.

Save as: *MEMO46B3*

46C • 7'
Drill: Memo Format

Key two 2' writings on Memo 3, using information below for the headings.

Try to key at least four additional words on the second 2' timing.

TO: Manuel Lopez, Convention Chair

FROM: Marsha Johnson, Display Coordinator

DATE: *Current Date*

SUBJECT: GRAPHIC ARTIST

Remember the Alamo!!! As part of our annual corporate giving program, I am recommending that we make a contribution to The Alamo, managed by the Daughters of the Republic of Texas. They depend entirely on donations and proceeds from the gift shop for covering operating costs.

I believe it is important for us to honor those who played integral roles in the history of our state. Our children need to be reminded of the lives of James Bowie, David Crockett, and William Barret Travis, who made the ultimate sacrifice for freedom. And, who can forget the role Sam Houston played as the commander in chief of the Texan army in the revolution against Mexico? Memories of Texan legends are preserved at the Alamo.

Please list the Alamo as a potential recipient in our corporate giving program next year. Of course, we will discuss it when we meet.

Thank you for recom^m^ending ~~the graphics artist~~ Spencer Schultz. The graphics ^he prepared^ for our state history displays at this year's convention were excellent.

From the beginning of the project^,^ we knew we were going ^to^ be pleased with ~~the~~ his artwork. ~~The artist~~ Spencer^,^ attended ^and contributed^ to all of our brain storming sessions. His ^interest and^ enthusiasm for the project motivated the entire committee. His suggestions for implementing graphic arts int~~o~~ our display ~~met~~ exceeded all of our expectations. The quantity ^and quality^ of work completed by ~~the artist~~ Spencer was superb^;^ and on those rare occasions ~~where~~ when an error was found, he always made timely corrections.

As you are well aware^,^ the ^state history^ displays were ~~one of the things~~ well received by participants ~~liked best about~~ at this year's convention. Much of the success can be attributed ^directly^ to our graphic artist^,^ who^m^ we hired on the basis of your recommendation. Again, thank you.

What Is a Database Report?

Database reports are created from database tables and queries. Reports are used for organizing, summarizing, and printing information. The easiest way to generate a report is by using the Report Wizard. The Report Wizard provides for grouping and sorting the data, as well as for designing various layouts and styles in which to present the data. Notice in the example report shown below that the sales reps are grouped by state and sorted by last name.

Report Illustration

Rockwell Technologies

State	*Last Name*	*First Name*	*Address*	*City*
AZ				
	Butler	Warren	398 Navajo Dr.	Glendale
	Chi	Karrie	310 Sagebrush Ct.	Chandler
	Finley	Ann	388 Oxford Dr., E	Tucson
	Hulett	Sandra	450 La Paz Ct., N	Phoenix
	Reese	Jay	1811 Olympic Way	Scottsdale
CO				
	Bell	Scott	7211 Larkspur Dr.	Golden
	Donovan	Kellee	765 Coal Mine Ave.	Littleton
	Hull	Dale	2710 BlueJay Ln.	Denver
	LeClair	Justin	830 Whitehead Dr.	Grand Junction
	Rivera	Jose	756 Royal Crest Dr.	Pueblo

How Can Database Tables/Forms Be Modified?

When necessary, database tables/forms can be modified. For example, if a new field is needed, it can be added and then the field information for each record can be entered. Also, it is possible to delete a field. When a field is deleted, *all* the information in that field is deleted.

What Is Sorting?

The **Sort** feature is responsible for controlling the sequence, or order, of the records. This feature allows for sorts in ascending or descending order of words (alphabetically) or numbers (numerically). Ascending order is from A to Z and 0 to 9; descending order is from Z to A and 9 to 0.

Preview of Unit

In the two sections of the Database Applications unit, you will have the opportunity to work with databases of several companies. There is **A&E Bank**, whose database contains credit card applicant information. The **Software Professionals** database contains information about its software. **Rockwell Technologies** has a sales rep database; **Eastwick School of Dance** has a student information database. **Jaeger Enterprises** is an employee database you create.

Unit Objectives

Objectives:

1. To create a database.
2. To create database tables.
3. To create database forms.
4. To key information into tables and forms.
5. To create database reports.
6. To conduct queries.
7. To complete a mail merge.
8. To create envelopes and mailing labels.

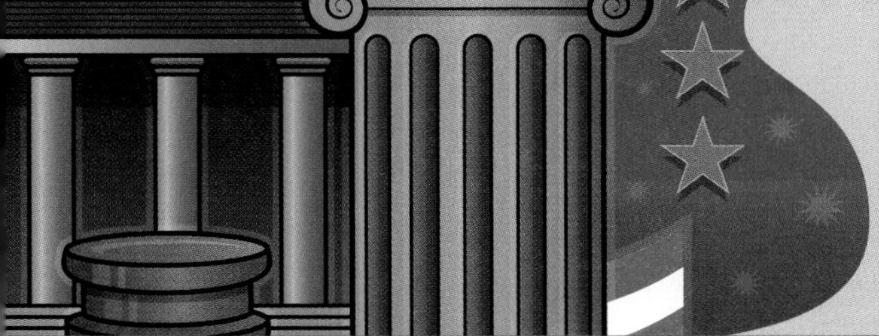

Communication Skills 6

ACTIVITY 1

Terminal Punctuation: Period, Question Mark, Exclamation Point

1. Key the paragraph at the right, using the correct punctuation.
2. Check the accuracy of your work with the instructor; correct any errors you made.
3. Note the rule number at the left of each line in which you made a punctuation error.
4. Using the rules at the right, identify the rule(s) you need to review/practice.
5. **Read**: Study each rule.
6. **Learn**: Key the Learn line(s) beneath it, noting how the rule is applied.
7. **Apply**: Key the Apply line(s), adding the correct terminal punctuation.

 **Save as:** *CS6-ACT1*

Proofread & Correct

Rules

5 "Jump" the fireman shouted to the young boy frozen with
1 fear on the window ledge of the burning building "Will you
3 catch me" the young boy cried to the men and women holding a
1,5,1 safety net forty feet below "Into the net" they yelled
Mustering his courage, the boy jumped safely into the net and
1 then into his mother's outstretched arms

Terminal Punctuation: Period

Rule 1: Use a period at the end of a declarative sentence (a sentence that is not regarded as a question or exclamation).

Learn 1 I wonder why *Phantom of the Opera* has always been so popular.
Apply 2 Fran and I saw *Cats* in London We also saw *Sunset Boulevard*

Rule 2: Use a period at the end of a polite request stated in the form of a question but not intended as one.

Learn 3 Matt, will you please collect the papers at the end of each row.
Apply 4 Will you please call me at 555-0140 to set up an appointment

Terminal Punctuation: Question Mark

Rule 3: Use a question mark at the end of a sentence intended as a question.

Learn 5 Did you go to the annual flower show in Ault Park this year?
Apply 6 How many medals did the U.S.A. win in the 1996 Summer Games

Rule 4: For emphasis, a question mark may be used after each item in a series of interrogative expressions.

Learn 7 Can we count on wins in gymnastics? in diving? in soccer?
Apply 8 What grade did you get for technique for speed for accuracy

Terminal Punctuation: Exclamation Point

Rule 5: Use an exclamation point after emphatic (forceful) exclamations and after phrases and sentences that are clearly exclamatory.

Learn 9 The lady screamed, "Stop that man!"
Learn 10 "Bravo!" many yelled at the end of the Skate America program.
Apply 11 "Yes" her gym coach exclaimed when Kerri stuck the landing.
Apply 12 The burglar stopped when he saw the sign, "Beware, vicious dog"

Form Illustration

What Is a Database Query?

Queries are questions. The Query feature of a database software program allows you to ask for specific information to be retrieved from tables that have been created. For example, the query shown below is based on the table illustration on p. 396. The query answers the question, *"Which sales reps live in Colorado?"*

When the sales rep table is expanded to include sales, a query could be made requesting all sales reps with sales over $45,000 for July or all sales reps with sales less than $45,000. By using the Query feature, you can answer a variety of questions that are based on the information contained in database tables.

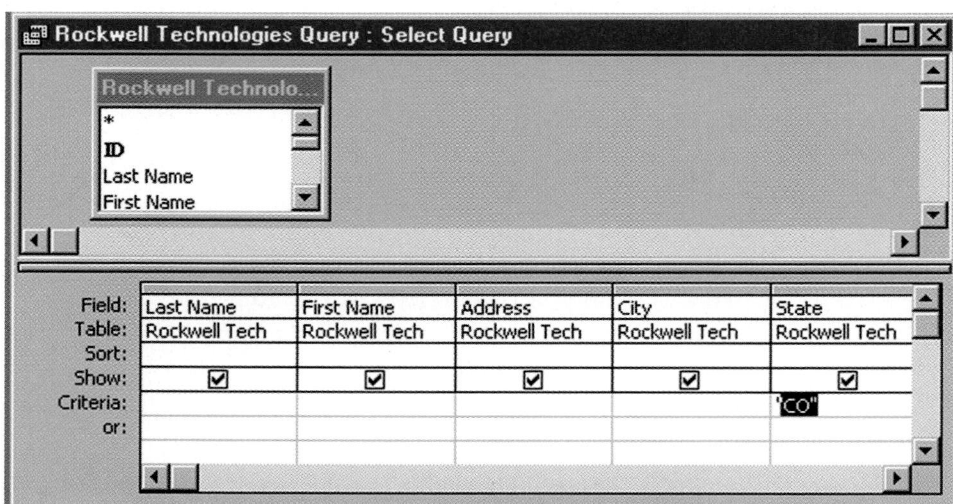

Query Illustration

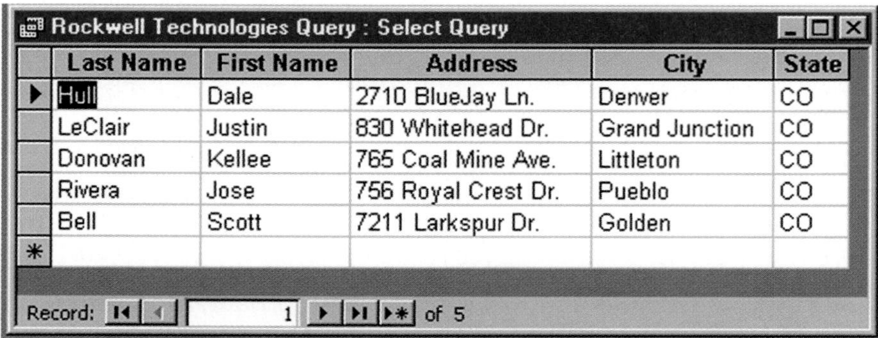
Rockwell Technologies Query : Select Query

Last Name	First Name	Address	City	State
Hull	Dale	2710 BlueJay Ln.	Denver	CO
LeClair	Justin	830 Whitehead Dr.	Grand Junction	CO
Donovan	Kellee	765 Coal Mine Ave.	Littleton	CO
Rivera	Jose	756 Royal Crest Dr.	Pueblo	CO
Bell	Scott	7211 Larkspur Dr.	Golden	CO

Record: 1 of 5

ACTIVITY 2

Listening

Complete the listening activity as directed at the right.

 **Save as:** *CS6-ACT2*

1. Open the sound file (*CD-CS6LISTN*), which contains directions for driving to Mansfield Soccer Field.
2. Take notes as you listen to the directions.
3. Close the file.
4. Using your notes, key the directions in sentence form.
5. Check the accuracy of your work with the instructor.

ACTIVITY 3

Write to Learn

Complete the Write-to-Learn activity as directed at the right.

 **Save as:** *CS6-ACT3*

1. Using word processing or speech recognition software, write a paragraph explaining how you would copy text from one place in a document to another.
2. Write a second paragraph explaining how to merge cells in a table.

ACTIVITY 4

Composing

1. Read the paragraph at the right.*
2. On the basis of your experience in viewing movies and TV, compose a paragraph indicating whether you agree or disagree with the young people who responded to the poll. Give reasons.

 **Save as:** *CS6-ACT4*

*Source: *USA Today*, March 1995.

A poll of young people revealed that U.S. youths thought current TV and movie fare glamorizes violence and sex without portraying the negative consequences of immoral behavior. Over sixty percent of youths surveyed said that such glamorizations on the screen influenced them to engage in such behavior.

Table Illustration

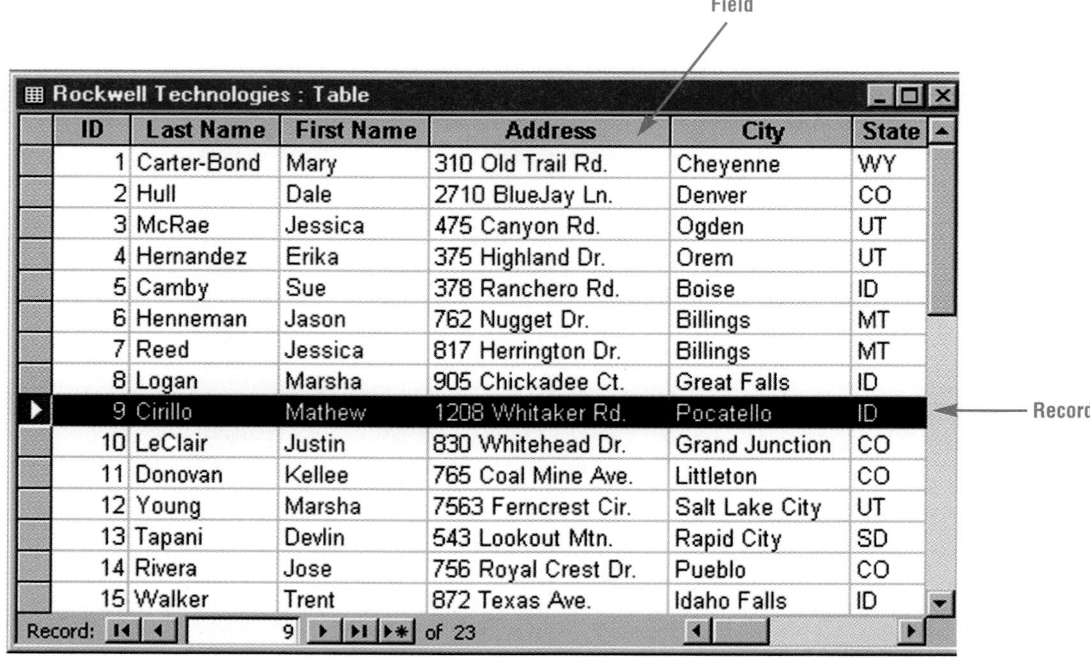

ID	Last Name	First Name	Address	City	State
1	Carter-Bond	Mary	310 Old Trail Rd.	Cheyenne	WY
2	Hull	Dale	2710 BlueJay Ln.	Denver	CO
3	McRae	Jessica	475 Canyon Rd.	Ogden	UT
4	Hernandez	Erika	375 Highland Dr.	Orem	UT
5	Camby	Sue	378 Ranchero Rd.	Boise	ID
6	Henneman	Jason	762 Nugget Dr.	Billings	MT
7	Reed	Jessica	817 Herrington Dr.	Billings	MT
8	Logan	Marsha	905 Chickadee Ct.	Great Falls	ID
9	Cirillo	Mathew	1208 Whitaker Rd.	Pocatello	ID
10	LeClair	Justin	830 Whitehead Dr.	Grand Junction	CO
11	Donovan	Kellee	765 Coal Mine Ave.	Littleton	CO
12	Young	Marsha	7563 Ferncrest Cir.	Salt Lake City	UT
13	Tapani	Devlin	543 Lookout Mtn.	Rapid City	SD
14	Rivera	Jose	756 Royal Crest Dr.	Pueblo	CO
15	Walker	Trent	872 Texas Ave.	Idaho Falls	ID

Defining and Sequencing Fields of Database Tables

Fields should be arranged in the same order as the data in the **source document** (paper form from which data is keyed). This sequence reduces the time needed to enter the field contents and to maintain the records. The illustration below shows the field definition and sequence for the table shown above. The **primary key** shown below is used to identify each record in the table with a number. In this case, a unique ID number would automatically be assigned each sales rep's record.

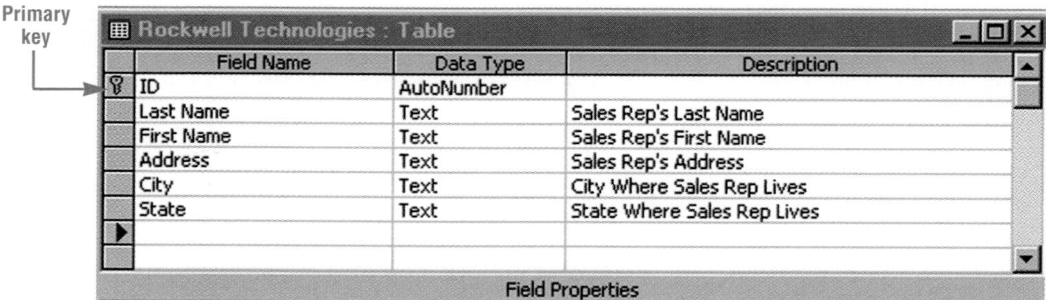

Field Name	Data Type	Description
ID	AutoNumber	
Last Name	Text	Sales Rep's Last Name
First Name	Text	Sales Rep's First Name
Address	Text	Sales Rep's Address
City	Text	City Where Sales Rep Lives
State	Text	State Where Sales Rep Lives

What Is a Database Form?

Database forms are created from database tables and queries. Forms are used for entering, viewing, and editing data.

Database forms are computerized versions of paper forms, such as a job application or a class registration form. On a printed form, you fill in the blanks with the information that is requested, such as your name and address. In a database form, the blanks in which information is entered are called **fields**. In the example above, Last Name, First Name, Address, City, and State are field names. When the blanks are filled in, the form becomes a **record**. The form illustrated on the next page is Record 9 from the above table illustration.

Depending on the software used, a variety of different form formats are available. The form may show only one record (as shown on next page), or it may show multiple records in the database. Forms may be created manually or by using the software Wizard.

WORD PROCESSING 6

ACTIVITY 1

Review WP Features: Margins, Spacing, and Left (Paragraph) Indent

1. Format and key the copy at the right, using a 1.5" left margin and a 1" right margin. DS ¶ 1; SS ¶ 2.
2. Use the Left (Paragraph) Indent feature to indent the long quotation (¶ 2) 0.5" from the left margin.

Save as: *WP6ACT1*

Another speech of significant magnitude was delivered by Winston Churchill. (1940, 572) His words not only lifted the spirits of the British but also were motivational to those committed to the Allied cause.

> We shall go on to the end, we shall fight in France, we shall fight on the seas and oceans, we shall fight with growing confidence and growing strength in the air, we shall defend our island, whatever the cost may be, we shall fight on the beaches, we shall fight on the landing grounds, we. . . .

ACTIVITY 2

Review WP Features: Margins, Alignment, and Hanging Indent

1. Set a 1.5" left margin and a 1" right margin. Use the Align Right feature to place the page number (**6**) 1" from the top at the right margin.
2. Center and key REFERENCES 2" from the top of the paper; QS. Use the Hanging Indent feature to format and key the references shown at the right.

Save as: *WP6ACT2*

6

REFERENCES

Churchill, Winston. "We Shall Fight in the Fields and in the Streets." London, June 4, 1940. Quoted by William J. Bennett, The Book of Virtues. New York: Simon & Schuster, 1993.

Henry, Patrick. "Liberty or Death." Richmond, VA, March 23, 1775. Quoted in North American Biographies, Vol. 6. Danbury, CT: Grolier Education Corporation, 1994.

Lincoln, Abraham. "The Gettysburg Address." Gettysburg, PA, November 19, 1863. Quoted by Joseph Nathan Kane, Facts About the President, 5th ed. New York: The H. W. Wilson Company, 1989.

ACTIVITY 3

Review WP Feature: Copy Text from File to File

The text shown at the right completes the Winston Churchill quote in Activity 1.

1. Open file *CD-CHURCHILL* and copy the text.
2. Open *WP6ACT1* (the file created in Activity 1 above).
3. Paste the copied text at the ellipsis; then delete the ellipsis.

Save as: *WP6ACT3*

shall fight in the fields and in the streets, we shall fight in the hills; we shall never surrender, and even if, which I do not for a moment believe, this island or a large part of it were subjugated and starving, then our Empire beyond the seas, armed and guarded by the British fleet, would carry on the struggle, until in God's good time, the New World, with all its power and might, steps forth to the rescue and the liberation of the old.

Database Overview

What Is a Database?

A **database** is a computerized filing system that is used to organize and maintain a collection of information for future use. Names and addresses, inventory, sales, and client information are but a few examples of types of information that a database may include. See the mail merge illustration on p. 425 for a better understanding of just one of the many applications for the stored data in a database.

What Are the Components of a Database?

A database may include tables for storing information, queries for drawing information from one or more tables, forms for displaying information, and reports for summarizing and presenting information. The illustration below shows the database components that are listed under Objects in *Microsoft Access*.

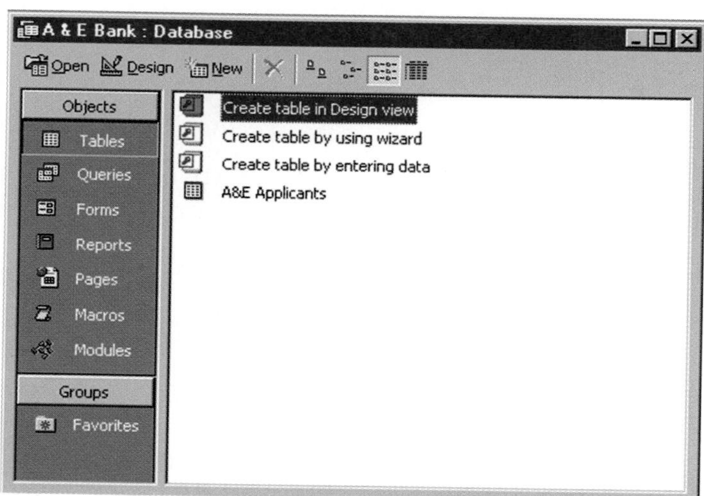

What Is a Database Table?

Database tables are created by the user in software programs such as *Paradox* and *Access* for inputting, organizing, and storing database information. The tables are set up to contain columns and rows of information. In a database table, the columns are called **fields** and rows are called **records**.

The table illustration on the next page shows a table that contains five fields—Last Name, First Name, Address, City, and State (plus the ID number).

Record 9 is highlighted in the illustration and shows the information contained in each of the five fields for Record 9. The database table is the foundation from which forms, queries, and reports are created based on the information in the table.

ACTIVITY 4

Footnotes and Endnotes

1. Read the information at the right; learn to use the Footnote and Endnote feature in your software.
2. Open file *CD-TAXES*. Insert the two footnotes shown at the right where indicated in the file.
3. Delete *(Insert footnote No. x)* from the copy.

 **Save as:** *WP6ACT4*

Use the **Footnote and Endnote** feature to identify sources quoted in your text. WP software automatically positions and prints each footnote at the bottom of the same page as the reference to it. It automatically prints endnotes on a separate page at the end of the report. WP software lets you edit, add, or delete footnotes and endnotes and automatically makes the necessary changes in numbering and formatting.

[1]David J. Rachman and Michael H. Mescon, Business Today (New York: Random House, 1987), p. 529.

[2]Greg Anrig, Jr., "Making the Most of 1988's Low Tax Rate," Money (February 1988), pp. 56-57.

Optional Activity

1. Open *WP6ACT4*.
2. Change both footnotes to endnotes.
3. Print the Endnotes page only.
4. Save the file as *WP6ACT4OP*.

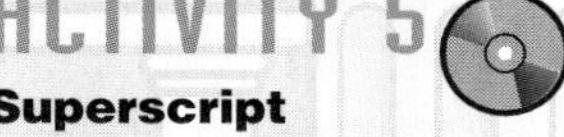

ACTIVITY 5

Superscript

1. Read the information at the right; learn to use the Superscript feature.
2. Open file *CD-VOICEMAIL*. Change the three endnote numbers to superscripts.
3. Delete *(Apply superscript . . .)* from the copy.
4. Format endnotes 2 and 3 (at the right) on page 2 of the file, below endnote 1.

 **Save as:** *WP6ACT5*

Text may be placed slightly higher than other text on a line by using the **Superscript** feature. The superscript is commonly used for footnotes and endnotes not inserted with the Footnote and Endnote feature, and for mathematical formulas and equations.

ENDNOTES

[1]John Grove, "New Media for Your Messages," The Secretary (March 1993), p. 6.

[2]Grove, p. 7.

[3]Amy Gage, "Voice Mail Technology Can Be a Source of Frustration, Irritation," St. Paul Pioneer Press (August 3, 1994), p. 1C.

ACTIVITY 6

Bullets and Numbering

1. Read the information at the right; learn to use the Bullets and Numbering features in your software.
2. Format and key the text at the right using the Bullets and Numbering features. Use bullets of your choice.

 **Save as:** *WP6ACT6*

Bullets (special characters) are used to enhance the appearance of text. Bullets are often used to add visual interest or emphasis. Examples of bullets: ❖ ➢ ✓ •

Numbering is used to show the proper order of a series of steps. Use numbers instead of bullets whenever the order of items is important.

Please contact the following freshmen to determine if they would like to try out for the play next week: (*insert bulleted list*) Anita Rawlins, Roberto Jimanez, Ho Chi.

Then do the following:

1. Check files for names of freshmen in last year's play.
2. Contact them to see if they will participate this year.
3. Contact these sophomores to see if they are still interested: (*insert bulleted list*) Ted Roberts, Marsha Mallory, Clint Hernandez.

Activity 2 • Questions, Answers, and Advice

1. Read the information at the right.
2. Learn how to use the assistant or expert feature in your software.
3. In the assistant or expert feature, key the question **How do I print files?** Read some of the suggestions the feature provides.
4. Ask the assistant or expert two more questions. You can use keywords instead of questions if you like. Read some of the suggestions the feature provides.
5. Try performing a new task in your software with the assistant or expert feature displayed. Was it helpful? Why or why not?
6. Close the assistant or expert feature.

Many software applications and office suites have a Help option that lets you key questions or keywords and get a likely list of Help topics. Topics may include overview or reference information, step-by-step procedures, and visual examples. Depending on the software, you can click or double-click topics to read about them in detail.

You can display the assistant or expert feature all the time or choose it when you need it. If you leave it displayed, the feature will suggest likely commands or offer tips for the task you are doing. It will also walk you through tasks. For example, suppose you are creating a table in *Corel® WordPerfect® 9*.

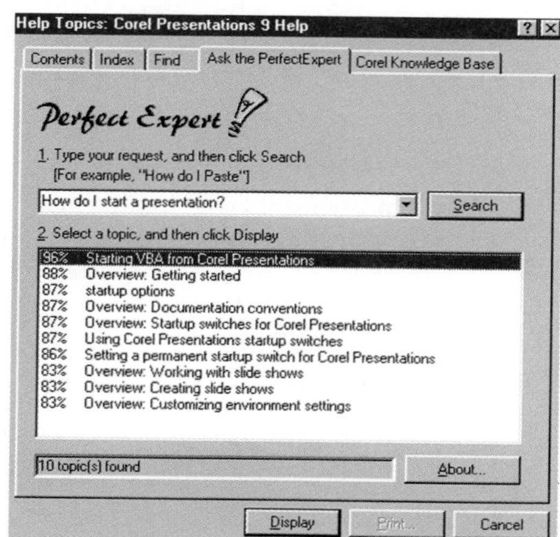

PerfectExpert[5] will suggest the commands and provide the tip at the right below. Some assistant or expert features also offer general tips on how to use the software features more effectively.

The assistant or expert feature may have its own Help menu command (for example, *PerfectExpert*) and/or may be accessible from the first (general) Help menu. You may be able to toggle it on and off through a Help menu command. You may need to click the Close box or button on the assistant or expert to remove it from the screen. *(Microsoft® Office 2000* users, see also Lesson 1, Activity 2.)

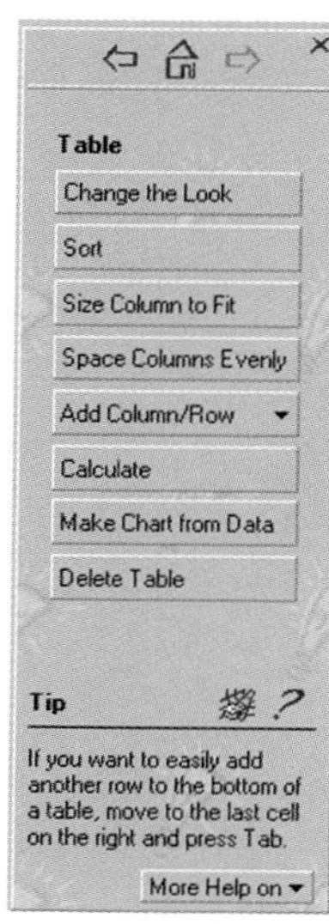

Activity 3 • Web Support

1. Read the information at the right.
2. Learn how to access the software manufacturer's Web site in your software.
3. Go to the software manufacturer's Web site. Spend some time browsing the different options. Take advantage of two or three options. For example, print a helpful article or download clip art or a template (with your instructor's permission).

For many applications, you can get additional help and other resources from the software manufacturer's Web site. For example, you can read background articles on software features and download templates, clip art, and "patch" files to fix problems. Web support often has its own menu command in the Help menu. When you choose this command, you are taken directly to the manufacturer's software page (provided you have Internet access).

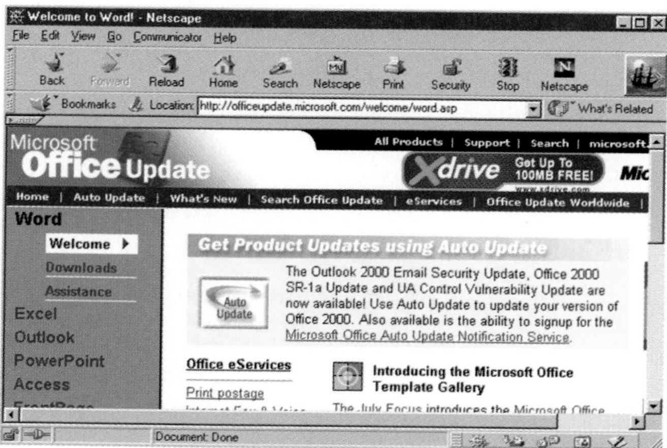

[5]Corel® and Presentations® are registered trademarks of Corel Corporation or Corel Corporation Limited in Canada, the United States, and/or other countries.

ACTIVITY 7

Insert File

1. Read the information at the right; learn to use the Insert File feature for your software.
2. Leaving a 2" top margin, key the copy at the right (except words printed in red).
3. Insert the *CD-EXAM1* and *CD-EXAM2* files where indicated at the right.

Save as: *WP6ACT7*

To insert an existing file into a file that you are currently working on, use the **Insert File** feature.

TABLE EXAMS

Here is a list of the software features you will need to know for the first exam on tables.

Insert ***CD-EXAM1*** file.

For the second exam on tables, you will need to know the following table formatting software features.

Insert ***CD-EXAM2*** file.

ACTIVITY 8

Dot Leader Tab

1. Read the information at the right; learn to use the Dot Leader Tab feature for your software.
2. Format and key the copy at the right, leaving a 2" TM and using the Dot Leader Tab feature. Leave a space before and after inserting the dot leader tab to enhance the appearance of the text.

Save as: *WP6ACT8*

The **Dot Leader Tab** feature automatically places dot leaders (. . . .) between columns of designated text. The leaders lead the eyes from the text in the first column to the text in the second column. A *right* dot leader tab inserts the text to the left of the tab setting; a *left* dot leader tab inserts the text to the right of the tab setting.

TELEPHONE EXTENSIONS

Felix McDowell 1844

Ryan Smith 2915

Maria Sanchez 4895

Rebecca LaFrentz 4817

ACTIVITY 9

Apply What You Have Learned

1. Set a right dot leader tab at the right margin.
2. Key the text, leaving a 2" TM and using dot leaders.
3. Set a left dot leader tab 1.5" to the left of the right margin.
4. QS and key the text again. Notice how the names in the right column are aligned when a left dot leader tab is used versus a right tab.
5. Use the Sort feature to alphabetize by city.

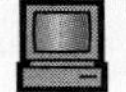

Save as: *WP6ACT9*

BRANCH MANAGERS

Phoenix Manager . . . . Sharon Tietz

Denver Manager . . . . Orlando Perez

Dallas Manager . . . . Karla Kwan

New York Manager . . . . Austin Alexander

Orlando Manager . . . . Chad Nowitzki

Minneapolis Manager . . . . Predrag DeWees

SPECIAL FEATURES

Objectives:

Approx. time: 1 hour

1. To learn to use the pop-up description and assistant or expert features.
2. To access additional software support on the World Wide Web.

Activity 1 • What's *That* Do?

1. Read the information at the right.
2. Learn how to use the pop-up description feature in your software.
3. Take a pop-up description tour of your screen. Use the feature to find out what unfamiliar screen items do. Be sure to include some dialog boxes in your tour.

A valuable Help feature for new users is the pop-up description box. This feature allows you to point to or click items on the screen and get a concise description of their use. This feature may be called ScreenTips, QuickTips, or something similar. The items for which you can get pop-up descriptions vary with the software but may include the following:

- Menus and menu commands
- Toolbars and toolbar buttons
- Scroll bars and other screen areas
- Options in dialog boxes

Here are some methods of getting pop-up descriptions in different software:

- Choose *What's This?* from the Help menu and click the item.
- Point to the item and press SHIFT + F1, or press SHIFT + F1 and click the item.
- Point to the item for a few seconds.
- Right-click the item and select *What's This?* if necessary.
- Click the Question Mark button at the top right of a dialog box; then click the item.

When you are finished reading a description, press ESC or click somewhere else to close the description.

In *Microsoft® Word 2000*, pressing SHIFT + F1 and clicking this button  on the standard toolbar yields this pop-up description:[3]

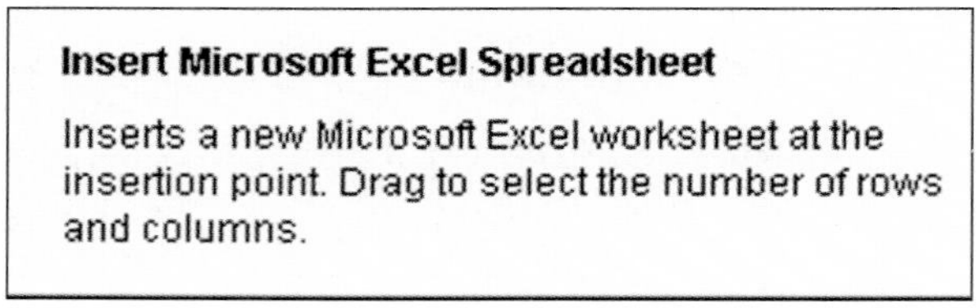

Insert Microsoft Excel Spreadsheet

Inserts a new Microsoft Excel worksheet at the insertion point. Drag to select the number of rows and columns.

In *Corel® WordPerfect® 9*, clicking the Question Mark button in the Columns dialog box and then clicking the Balanced newspaper option yields this pop-up description:[4]

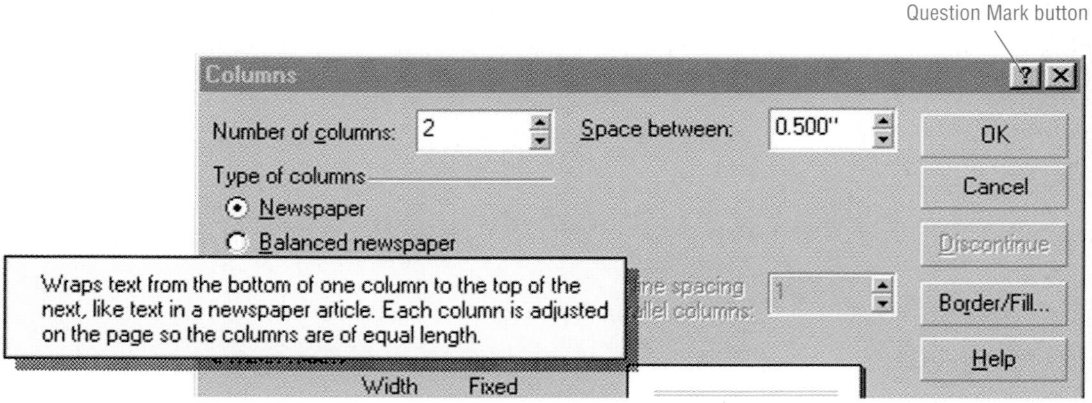

Question Mark button

Columns

Number of columns: 2 | Space between: 0.500" | OK | Cancel | Discontinue | Border/Fill... | Help

Type of columns
- Newspaper
- Balanced newspaper

Wraps text from the bottom of one column to the top of the next, like text in a newspaper article. Each column is adjusted on the page so the columns are of equal length.

Width | Fixed

[3]Microsoft® is a registered trademark of Microsoft Corporation in the United States and/or other countries.

[4]Corel® and WordPerfect® are registered trademarks of Corel Corporation or Corel Corporation Limited in Canada, the United States, and/or other countries.

UNIT 15

LESSONS 47–52

Improve Report Formatting Skills

Format Guides: Bound Reports

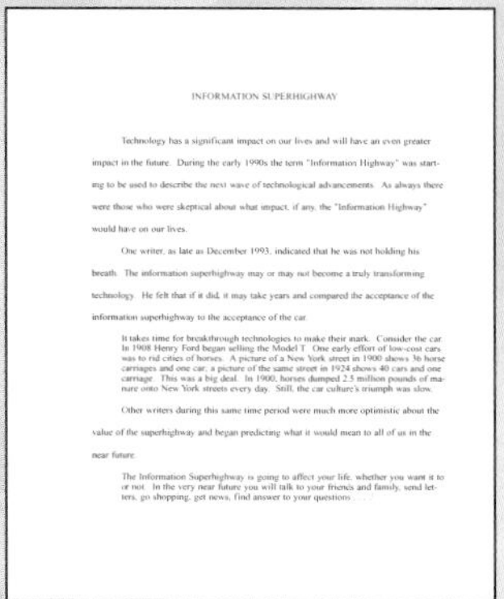

INFORMATION SUPERHIGHWAY

Bound Report with Long Quotations, Endnotes

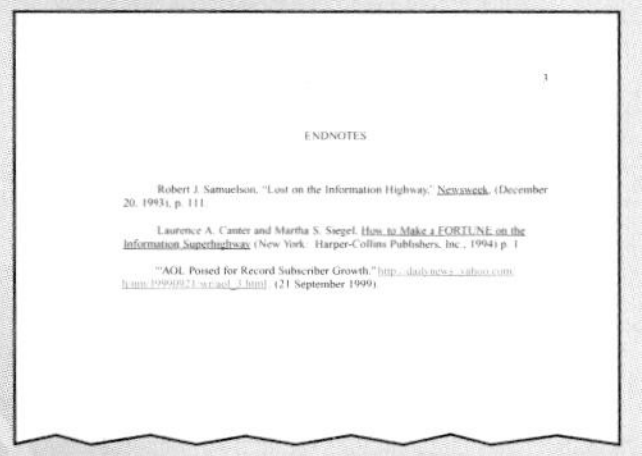

ENDNOTES

Endnotes Page

DELIVERING THE MAIL

Student Name

School Name

Current Date

Bound Report Title Page

In Unit 8 you learned to format short, **unbound** reports using the textual citation method of documentation. In this unit you will learn to format longer **bound** reports. The endnote and footnote methods of documentation are introduced in this unit.

Bound Reports

Longer reports are generally bound at the left margin. The binding takes about one-half inch (0.5") of space. To accommodate the binding, the left margin is increased to 1.5" on all pages.

Standard Margins

Except for the left margin (1" for unbound and 1.5" for bound), all margin settings are the same for unbound and bound reports. The right margin is 1". A top margin of 2" and a bottom margin of about 1" are customarily used on the first page of reports. All remaining pages are keyed with 1" top and bottom margins. Because an exact 1" bottom margin is not always possible, the bottom margin may be adjusted to prevent a side heading or first line of a paragraph from printing as the last line on a page (orphan); or the last line of a paragraph from occurring at the top of a new page (widow). The Widow/Orphan software feature (p. 67) also may be used to prevent these problems.

Page Numbering

The first page of a report usually is not numbered. However, if a page number is used on the first page, position it at the bottom of the page using center alignment. On the second and subsequent pages, position the page number at the top of the page using right alignment.

Internal Spacing

A QS is left between the report title and the first line of the body. Multiple-line titles are DS.

A DS is left above and below side headings and between paragraphs. The reports you key in this unit will have DS paragraphs. However, paragraphs may be SS or DS. The DS paragraphs are indented 0.5".

Long quotes. Quoted material of four or more lines should be SS and indented 0.5" from the left margin. DS above and below the quoted material. The first line is indented an additional 0.5" if the quotation starts at the beginning of a paragraph.

Enumerated items. Indent enumerated items 0.5" from the left margin; block the lines at that point. Single-space individual items; DS between items. Double-space above and below a series of items.

Headings and Subheadings

Main heading. Center the main heading in ALL CAPS.

Side headings. Begin side headings at the left margin. Capitalize the first letter of the first word and all other main words in each heading. Underline side headings.

Paragraph headings. Indent paragraph headings 0.5" from the left margin. Capitalize only the first letter of the first word and any proper nouns; underline the heading; and follow the heading with a period.

Title Page

A cover or title page is prepared for most bound reports. To format a title page, center the title in ALL CAPS 2" from the top. Center the writer's name in capital and lowercase letters 5" from the top. The school name is centered a DS below the writer's name. The date should be centered 9" from the top.

Activity 2 • Index/Find

1. Read the information at the right.
2. Access the Help Index in your software.
3. In the Index keyword box, key **font**. Explore some of the topics that the Index provides.
4. Search for information on three other topics that interest you.
5. Browse the list of topics. Read about two topics that interest you.
6. If your software has a Find feature in Help, learn how to use it. Then use Find to search for two additional topics.

For both new and experienced users, the Index is one of the most useful Help features. Like the index in a book, the Help Index lists topics alphabetically. You key a word in the Index keyword box, such as *italic*, and the Index jumps to the topic. In some software, this will happen before you have even finished keying. You then double-click the item or click a button in the Index dialog box to read about the topic. If your topic isn't included in its list, the Index takes you to the closest topic alphabetically. For instance, keying *ice cream* might take you to *icon*. You can also browse the Index.

When you are reading about a Help topic, you may see underlined text, icons, or text in a different color. Clicking these items will take you to explanations or related topics. You can sometimes use Back or Forward buttons or icons to move through topics.

Depending on the software, the Index may be a separate item in the Help menu, or it may be accessible through the first (general) Help menu command (Help Topics, for example). In *Microsoft® Office 2000* applications, Office Assistant must be turned off to access the Index: In the Office Assistant word balloon, click the Options button and deselect *Use the Office Assistant*.

Some software also offers a Find feature in Help that allows you to do a full-text search of Help or to search for specific words and phrases. Find may be included in the Index dialog box, or it may be separate.

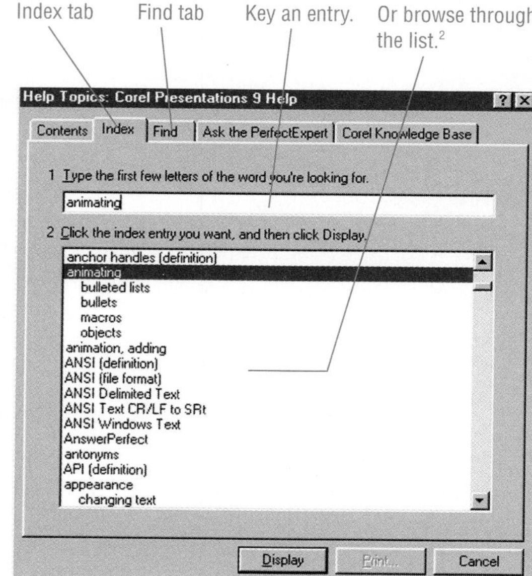

Activity 3 • Contents

1. Read the information at the right.
2. Learn how to access Help Contents in your software.
3. Access Contents and open a category that interests you. Open subcategories if necessary. Read the topic information. Go to related topics, if any.
4. Read two other categories that interest you. Print any information that you think will be helpful in the future.

Like the table of contents in a book, the Contents feature in Help lets you look for information that has been organized by categories.

In *Corel® WordPerfect® 9* Contents shown at the right, a book icon indicates a category. You can see that some categories contain subordinate categories, which are also indicated by book icons. You can "open" one of these books by clicking the book icon or double-clicking the text next to it, and "close" it the same way.

To read about a topic, click the icon (in the example on the right, a question mark) or the text next to it.

Contents may be a separate item in the Help menu, or it may be accessible through the first (general) Help menu command (Help Topics, for example). In *Microsoft® Office 2000* applications, Office Assistant must be turned off to access Contents from the document window.

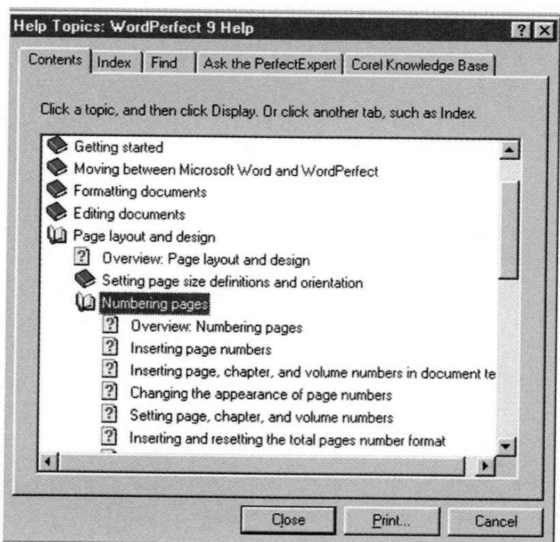

[2]Corel®, Presentations®, and WordPerfect® are registered trademarks of Corel Corporation or Corel Corporation Limited in Canada, the United States, and/or other countries.

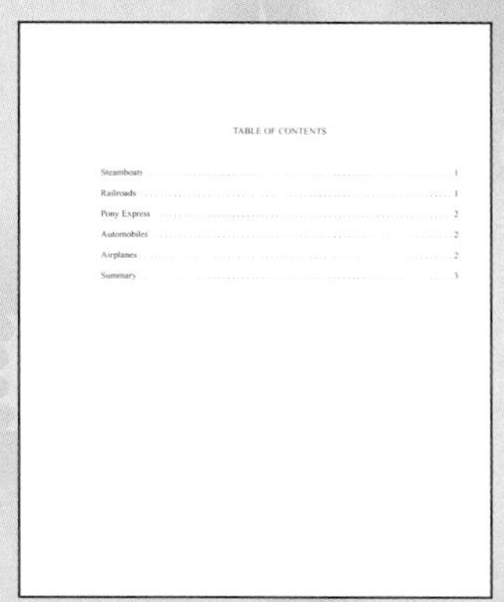
Table of Contents

Table of Contents

A table of contents lists the headings of a report and the page numbers where those headings can be found in the report. The side and top margins for the table of contents are the same as those used for the first page of the report. Include TABLE OF CONTENTS (centered, 2" from top) as a heading. Then QS before listing side and paragraph headings (if included). Side headings are DS beginning at left margin; paragraph headings are indented and SS with a DS above and below them. Page numbers for each entry are keyed at the right margin.

Documentation

Documentation is used to give credit for published material (electronic as well as printed) that is quoted or closely paraphrased (slightly changed). Three types of documentation will be used in this unit: textual citation, endnotes, and footnotes.

Textual citation. The textual citation method of documentation was used in Unit 8. This method includes the name(s) of the author(s), the date of the referenced publication, and the page number(s) of the material cited as part of the report text.

```
(Wagner, 2001, 248)
```

When the author's name is used in the text introducing the quotation, only the year of publication and the page number(s) appear in parentheses.

```
Wagner (2001, 248) said that . . .
```

For electronic references, include the author's name and the year.

Endnotes. The endnotes method of documentation identifies the reference cited by a superscript number. . . .[1]

The complete documentation for the reference is placed at the end of the report in a section titled ENDNOTES. The references listed in the endnotes section are placed in the same order they appear in the report. A corresponding superscript number identifies the reference in the text.

The endnotes page has the same top and side margins as the first page of the report, except that it has a page number 1" from the top at the right margin. Each endnote is SS, with a DS between endnotes. The first line of each endnote is indented 0.5" from the left margin (keyed to a superscript endnote number); all other lines begin at the left margin.

[1]Richard G. Harris, "Globalization, Trade, and Income," Canadian Journal of Economics (November 1993), p. 755.

Footnotes. The footnotes method of documentation also identifies the reference cited by a superscript number. . . .[1]

However, the complete documentation for the reference is placed at the bottom of the same page and is identified with the same superscript number (see model report on p. 142).

Each footnote is indented 0.5" and SS, with a DS between footnotes. Footnotes should be numbered consecutively throughout a report.

References page. Each of these three types of documentation (textual citation, endnotes, and footnotes) requires a references page. All references cited in the report are listed alphabetically by author surnames at the end of a report under the heading REFERENCES (or BIBLIOGRAPHY or WORKS CITED). QS between the heading and the first reference.

Use the same margins as for the first page of the report and include a page number. SS each reference; DS between references. Begin the first line of each reference at the left margin; indent other lines 0.5" (or to the paragraph indentation point).

LESSONS 1–2

Using Help

LESSON 1 HELP BASICS

Objectives:

1. To gain an overview of software Help feaures.

2. To learn to use the Help features Index, Find, and Contents.

Approx. time: 1 hour

Activity 1 • Overview

1. Study the information at the right.
2. Open the Help menu in your software. Examine the menu options. If the menu lists a keyboard shortcut for accessing Help, make a note of it.
3. Press F1 or HELP or use another appropriate keyboard shortcut, if one was listed in your Help menu, for accessing Help features.
4. Compare Help menus in different software. If you have an office suite, compare Help menus in its different applications. Which options are the same? Which are different?

Application software offers a variety of built-in Help features that you can access directly in the software as you work. Help is the equivalent of a print manual on how to use your software. Help also provides interactive functions that a print manual cannot. Depending on your software, Help lets you do the following:

- Search for topics in an alphabetically organized index.
- Browse a table of contents of Help topics organized by categories.
- Do a full-text search. (Search all text, not just keywords.)
- Point to or click screen items for a concise explanation of their use.
- Key questions and get a variety of Help topics to choose from.
- Have Help automatically suggest tips and commands related to what you are doing.
- Get general tips on how to use the features of the program.
- Access Help related to a particular dialog box by clicking the Help button in the dialog box.
- Access technical resources, free downloads, and other options at the software manufacturer's Web site.

In each software application in an office suite, the Help features work the same way.

You can access your software's Help features through the Help menu in the application menu bar. Depending on your software, here are some alternative methods of accessing Help features:

- Press F1 (*Microsoft® Windows®* operating system) or HELP (Macintosh® computer). If your Help menu lists a different keyboard shortcut, use that shortcut.
- Click the appropriate button (often a question mark) on the standard toolbar.

The *Microsoft® Word 2000* Help Menu and Help Button[1]

[1]Microsoft® is a registered trademark of Microsoft Corporation in the United States and/or other countries.

LESSON 47

IMPROVE REPORT FORMATTING SKILLS

Objectives:

1. To format a bound report with textual citations and references.
2. To improve word choice skills.

47A • 5' Conditioning Practice

Key each line twice SS; then key a 1' writing on line 3; determine *gwam*.

alphabet 1 Jack Fitzgerald always competed in the six big equestrian events.

figures 2 Only 6,398 of the 14,652 men scored above 70 percent on the test.

speed 3 Dick is to make a turn to the right at the big sign for downtown.

gwam 1' | 1 | 2 | 3 | 4 | 5 | 6 | 7 | 8 | 9 | 10 | 11 | 12 | 13 |

FORMATTING

47B • 37' Bound Report

Document 1 (Report Body)

1. Review the format guides for bound reports on pp. 137–138 as needed.
2. Format the text at the right and on pp. 140 and 141 as a bound report with textual citations.
3. When you finish, proofread your copy and correct any errors.

Save as: *RPT47B1*

> **History Bits**
>
> "I will return to you in stone."
>
> —**Crazy Horse**
>
> "My fellow chiefs and I would like the white man to know the red man has great heroes, too."
>
> —**Lakota Chief Henry Standing Bear**

PLAINS INDIANS

The American Plains Indians are among the ~~most~~ best known of all Native Americans. These Indians played a significant role in shaping the history of the West. Some of the more noteworthy Plains Indians were big Foot, Black Kettle, Crazy Horse, Red Cloud, Sitting Bull, and Spotted Tail.

Big Foot

Big Foot (?1825-1890) was also known as Spotted Elk. Born in the northern Great Plains, he eventually became a Minneconjou Teton Sioux chief. He was part of a tribal delegation that traveled to Wash ington, D.C., and worke d to establish schools throughout the Sioux territory. He was one of those massacred at Wounded Knee in December 1890. (Bowman, 1995, 63)

Black Kettle

Black Kettle (?1803-1868) was born near the Black Hills in present-day South Dakota. He was recognized as a Southern Cheyenne peace chief for his efforts to bring peace to the region. However, his attempts at accommmodation ~~failed~~ were not successful, and his band was massacred at sand creek in 1864. Even though he continued to seek peace, he was killed with the remainder of his tribe in the Washita Valley of Oklahoma in 1868. (Bowman, 1995, 67)

(Report continued on next page)

COMPUTER APPS

Computer Keyboarding: Explore & Play

It has been noted that students today do not know what life was like before the influence of computers. You have grown up with music CDs, microwave ovens, and telephone answering devices. You use instant messaging and e-mail to stay in touch with family and friends. You might shop on the Internet. Computers control the temperature in your home and the sound in your neighborhood movie theater. As the world becomes increasingly digital, you can expect to solve problems with computers, communicate with computers, and make your living using a computer.

Using computers can be both work and play. The keyboarding skills you are developing will help you make light work of many keying tasks. When your technique and speed are at their best, you can concentrate on the fun aspects of learning. Good keying skills are a tool that you will use for life.

These Computer Apps units let you explore the fascinating world of computers, software, and the Internet. You will use your keying skills to follow the logic of a database and calculate figures instantly with a spreadsheet. You'll learn how to use software Help menus, search the Internet, and design Web pages. You will see how to create exciting electronic presentations and practice capturing information with speech recognition technology. The "Hoops" basketball simulation will show you how much fun you can have bringing your keying and computer skills together on the job.

The activities in this unit will challenge you and teach you to navigate complex software. They will build on the skills you have learned. They will show you how learning and playing can happen at the same time. Finally, you will discover new power to succeed in a digital world.

Crazy Horse

Crazy Horse was also born near the Black Hills. His father was a medicine man;his mother wasthe sister of Spotted Tail. He was recognized as a skilled hunter and fighter. Crazy Horse believed he was imune from battle injury and took part in all the major Sioux battles to protect the Black Hills. He was named war supreme and peace chief of the Oglalas in 1876 and led the Sioux and Cheyenne to victory at the battle of Rosebud in January that year. Perhaps he is remembered most for leading the Sioux and Cheyenne in the battle of the Bighorn where his warriors defeated Custers forces. Crazy Horse is regarded at the greatest leader of the Sioux and a symbol of there heroic resistance.

Red Cloud

Red Cloud (1822-1909) was born near the Platte River in present-day Nebraska. Because of his intelligence, strength, and bravery, he became the the chief of the Oglala Sioux. Red Cloud's War took place between 1865 and 1868. These battles forced the closing of the Bozeman trail and the sining of the Fort Laramie Treaty in 1868. In exchange for peace, the U.S. government accepted the territorial claims of the sioux. (Bowman, 1995, 601)

Sitting Bull (?1831-1890) was born on the Grand River in South Dakota. He was nown among the Sioux as a war rior even during his youth. He was bitterly opposed to white encroachment but made peace in 1868 when the U.S. government gave him a large reservation free of white settlers. When gold was discovered, he joined the Arapaho to fight the invaders. (Bowman, 1995, 673) According to fellow tribesmen, the name Sitting Bull suggested an animal possessed of great endurance that planted immovably on its haunches to fight on to the death. (Utley, 1993, 15)

(Report continued on next page)

Open file *CD-REDCLOUD*. Make the corrections shown at the right. Then copy/paste the text in the PLAINS INDIANS report (Document 1) where indicated.

History Bits

"Impossible!" easterners scoffed. "Herds of bison so immense they stretched as far as the eye could see? Half-mile-deep canyons carved by rivers through solid rock? Winter temperatures so bitter expectorations froze? Preposterous. Unbelievable."

—Bill Vossler

Your Perspective

At the close of the twentieth century, more people were enjoying a better standard of living than ever before. Hundreds of millions had shelter, running water, electricity, a job, even leisure time and extra money to spend.

Yet many people do not enjoy these comforts. Each year, the United Nations (U.N.) publishes a *Human Development Report* that provides, for every country, statistics on quality of life. According to the 2000 report, in the developing world, 1.2 billion people are poor. About 1 billion adults are illiterate. About 1 billion people lack safe water. More than 2.4 billion are without basic sanitation. The total world population at that time was 6 billion.

HUMAN DEVELOPMENT INDEX 2000
Selected Statistics

Countries by Development Level	People Not Expected to Survive to Age 40	Illiterate Adults	People Without Access		Underweight Children Under Age 5
			To Safe Water	To Sanitation	
High	3.3%	..	..	..	..
Medium	11.4%	23.3%	26%	56%	29%
Low	31.9%	50.8%	39%	59%	39%

Source: *U.N. Human Development Report 2000.*

Global Awareness

ACTIVITIES

1. Read the material at the left. Does the information surprise you?
2. Access the most recent U.N. *Human Development Report* at http://www.undp.org. Research one of the countries that ranks lowest in human development. What are some reasons for the ranking?
3. Key your findings in a one-page report. Compare your results with those of other students.
4. Find an organization that assists less developed countries. Think of a school event that would benefit this organization. Write a letter to the organization describing your idea.

When anthropologists set out to learn about a culture, one of their most important clues is food. From the cookbooks, utensils, kitchens, and garbage piles of New World settlements, anthropologists can trace the British colonists' attempts to preserve an English way of life. The colonists initially applied British cooking methods to the food that was available. Then some of the young women learned how Native American women cooked food. The colonists learned, for instance, to roast corn in the fields just after picking, to eat it on the cob, and to mix it with beans and meat in dishes like hominy and succotash.

Recipes for Boston brown bread and Virginia ham are indicators that the colonies were evolving into regions with distinct identities. Foods from different cultures reflect the waves of immigrants that introduced them. The fact that you can buy the same cereal, with the same taste, in Sacramento or St. Louis is one small example of how much of our food is now national in appeal.

Here are some questions we might ask about the food of a country or culture:

- Why are certain foods popular? Can they be grown locally? Are they inexpensive? Do they have cultural meaning?
- Examine the typical diet. Could it be improved to be more nutritional? If so, how?
- Does their diet put people at risk for or protect them from certain diseases? Which diseases are they likely to get, and why?
- Does growing any of these foods affect the environment? If so, how?

Cultural Diversity

ACTIVITIES

1. Read the material at the left.
2. What could someone infer about our society from the fact that we eat "fast foods"? Compose a paragraph at the keyboard to answer this question.
3. Form a group with some other students. Choose a foreign country or culture. Research it, answering the bulleted questions at the left.
4. Create and key a restaurant menu for the country or culture that you chose in Step 3. Use what you have learned in this Cycle to format the menu attractively.
5. As an enrichment activity, prepare one dish from the menu and serve it to your classmates.

Word Processing Activity

Open *CD-SPOTTAIL.* Make the corrections shown at the right, and copy/paste the text to the end of the PLAINS INDIANS report.

Document 2 (References Page)

Prepare a separate references page from the information at the right. Proofread; correct any errors.

Save as: *RPT47B2*

INTERNET ACTIVITY

Use the Internet to learn about a person named in the report. Compose a paragraph about the person.

Spotted Tail

Spotted Tail (?1833-1881) was born along the White River either in present-day South Dakota or near present-day Laramie, Wyoming. He be came the leader of the Brulé Sioux and was one of the signers of the Fort Laramie Treaty of 1868. Eventually, he became the government-appointed chief of the agency Sioux andmade frequent trips to Washington, D.C. in that capacity. (Bowman, 1995, 688) Starting in 1870 spotted Tail became the statesman that made him the greatest chief the Brulés ever new. (Fielder, 1975, p. 29)

Bowman, John S. (ed). The Cambridge Dictionary of American Biography. Cambridge: Cambridge University Press, 1995.

Fielder, Mildred. Sioux Indian Leaders. Seattle: Superior Publishing Company, 1975.

Utley, Robert M. The Lance and the Shield: The Life and Times of Sitting Bull. New York: Henry Holt and Company, 1993.

LANGUAGE SKILLS

47C • 8' Language Skills: Word Choice

1. Study the spelling/definitions of these words.
2. For each set of sentences, key the Learn line; then the Apply lines. Choose the correct word in parentheses.
3. Check your work; correct lines containing word-choice errors.

Save as: *CHOICE47C*

some (n/adv) unknown or unspecified unit or thing; to a degree or extent

sum (n/vb) the whole amount; the total; to find a total; summary of points

hour (n) the 24th part of a day; a particular time

our (adj) of or relating to ourselves as possessors

Learn 1 The large **sum** awarded did not satisfy **some** of the people.
Apply 2 The first grader said, "The (some, sum) of five and two is seven."
Apply 3 (Some, Sum) students were able to find the correct (some, sum) for the problem.

Learn 1 The first **hour** of **our** class will be used for going over the next assignment.
Apply 2 What (hour, our) of the day would you like to have (hour, our) group perform?
Apply 3 Minutes turned into (hours, ours) as we waited for (hour, our) turn to perform.

LESSON 48 FORMAT BOUND REPORT WITH FOOTNOTES

Objectives:

1. To format a bound report with footnotes.
2. To format a references page.

48A • 5' Conditioning Practice

Key each line twice SS; then key a 1' writing on line 3; determine *gwam.*

alphabet 1 Bob Writz quickly thanked them for giving excellent jury reports.
fig/sym 2 The order (No. 3972) for 16 pies and 20 cakes ($385.34) was late.
speed 3 Make the panel suspend the pay of their officials as the penalty.

gwam 1' | 1 | 2 | 3 | 4 | 5 | 6 | 7 | 8 | 9 | 10 | 11 | 12 | 13 |

Your Perspective

Consumption is one of the most important environmental issues of today. As a country grows, it uses more resources. As people move to a higher standard of living, they use more resources. A four-year-old American child has already used more resources and added more waste to the environment than most people in the world will in a lifetime. The question under debate is whether the environment can continue to support the demands placed on it by growing economies and rising populations.

The world population has grown more since 1950 than during the previous four million years. As of September 2000, it was 6 billion. United Nations analysts predict that it will top out at 10 to 11 billion.

The problem isn't so much where to put these people. According to science writer Bill McKibben, everyone in the world today could fit into Texas, each with an area equal to the floor space of a typical U.S. home. It is what it takes to support them—the land to grow the crops that feed them, the timber for making their wood and paper, the mines and oil wells that provide their energy. How many people can the world support?

People on one side of this debate think the question doesn't matter. They argue that past predictions of resource shortages have proven wrong. They say that we can find substitutes for any resources that run low. We can develop technologies to solve environmental problems. We can conserve and become more energy efficient.

On the other side, scientists estimate the earth's carrying capacity—its ability to sustain a population—at between 7.7 and 12 billion people. They point to events like these as signals that that capacity is already under severe strain:

- Since 1950, the burning of fossil fuels has almost quintupled. Use of these fuels produces gases like carbon dioxide that many scientists believe contribute to the greenhouse effect and global warming. The **greenhouse effect** is a process in which certain gases in the atmosphere trap energy from the sun and increase the earth's temperature. **Global warming** is an increase in the earth's temperature that can cause changes in climate.
- Since 1960, the consumption of fresh water has almost doubled. On every continent, water tables are falling; and major rivers like the Colorado run dry before they reach the sea. The United Nations estimates that by 2025, two-thirds of the people on earth will face water shortages.

People on this side of the debate agree that energy efficiency and new inventions will help. But they assert that people will also need to alter their lifestyles so that they consume less of our world's resources.

Ethics: The Right Thing to Do

ACTIVITIES

1. Read the material at the left.
2. In an Earth Day 2000 Gallup poll, Americans reported ways they help the environment. These included recycling (90%), reducing energy usage (83%), trying to use less water (83%), and avoiding environmentally harmful products (83%). Key these topics without the percents in the first column of a three-column table. Under the last item, add three more ways to help the environment. Put a heading at the top of the column.
3. Add two column headings to indicate which items are practiced by (1) you and (2) other members of your family. Add Xs where appropriate in the new columns. Give the table a title.
4. How do you think people would be willing to change their lifestyles further in order to consume fewer resources? Compose a response at the keyboard.
5. Do people need to consume less of the resources they use? Form groups and prepare for a class debate. Key a group paper in unbound report format that states your team's viewpoint and its reasons.

2"

Main heading

GLOBALIZATION

QS

We live in a time of worldwide change. What happens in one part of the world impacts people on the other side of the world. People around the world are influenced by common developments.[1]

Footnote superscript

The term "globalization" is used to describe this phenomenon. According to Harris, the term is being used in a variety of contexts.[2] In a very broad context, media use it almost daily to refer to a wide variety of political, sociological, environmental, and economic trends.

Footnote superscript

1.5" LM

1" RM

The business world, however, uses this term in a much narrower context to refer to the production, distribution, and marketing of goods and services at an international level. Everyone is impacted by the continued increase of globalization in a variety of ways. The types of food we eat, the kinds of clothes we wear, the variety of technologies that we utilize, the modes of transportation that are available to us, and the types of jobs we pursue are directly linked to "globalization." Globalization is changing the world we live in.

<u>Causes of Globalization</u>

Harris indicates that there are three main factors contributing to globalization. These factors include:

Footnotes

---

[1]Robert K. Schaeffer, <u>Understanding Globalization</u> (Lanham, MD: Rowman & Littlefield Publishers, Inc., 1997), p. 1.

[2]Richard G. Harris, "Globalization, Trade, and Income," <u>Canadian Journal of Economics</u> (November 1993), p. 755.

Bound Report with Footnotes

150C • 5' Embedded Charts

Create the charts at the right using the information reported in the worksheets.

Chart 1: Column Chart

1. Open file *CD-L150C1*.
2. Create a column chart to show the amount of trash produced by the six countries. Use **Top Six Trash-Producing Nations** as the title, and show axis titles and gridlines.

 **Save as:** *L150C1*

Chart 2: Pie Chart

1. Open file *CD-L150C2*.
2. Create a pie chart to show the percent of items that are recycled in Banter County. Use **Banter County Recycling Statistics** as the title, show percents as data labels, and show a legend.

 **Save as:** *L150C2*

150D • 15' Timed Writing

Take two 5' writings on the three paragraphs at the right; determine *gwam*; count errors.

A all letters used

	gwam 3'	5'	
Attempts to maximize the standard of living for humans	4	2	41
through the control of nature and the development of new products	8	5	44
have also resulted in the pollution of the environment. In some	12	7	46
parts of the world, the water, air, and soil are so polluted that	17	10	49
it is unsafe for people to live there because of the heightened	21	13	52
risk from disease.	22	13	52
Pollution of the air, land, and water has existed since	26	16	55
people began to live in cities. People living in these early	30	18	57
cities took their garbage to dumps outside the main part of the	34	21	60
city or just put it into the streets or canals. Both of these	39	23	62
disposal methods helped create the pollution process.	42	25	64
Pollution is one of the most serious problems facing people	46	28	67
today. Clean air, water, and land are needed by all living	50	30	69
things. Bad air, water, and soil cause illness and even death	54	33	72
to people and other living things. Bad water quickly kills fish	59	35	74
and ruins drinking water; bad soil reduces the amount of land	63	38	77
that is available for growing food.	65	39	78

gwam 3' | 1 | 2 | 3 | 4
5' | 1 | 2 | 3

48B • 45'
Bound Report

1. Review the report format guides on pp. 137–138; study the model report on p. 142. Note the format of the footnotes.
2. Key the first page of the Globalization report from the model on p. 142; continue keying the report from the rough-draft copy shown at the right. The information for footnotes 3, 4, and 5 is given below.

[3]Harris, p. 763.

[4]Encyclopedia Americana, Vol. 26 (Danbury, CT: Grolier Incorporated, 1993), p. 915.

[5]Louis S. Richman, "Dangerous Times for Trade Treaties," Fortune (September 20, 1993), p. 14.

3. When you finish, proofread your copy and correct any errors.

Save as: *RPT48B*

Note:
You will finish keying the Globalization report in Lesson 49.

- The reduction in trade and investment barriers in the post-world war II period.
- The rapid growth and increase in the size of developing countries' economies.
- Changes in technologies.

Trade Agreements

Originally each nation established its rules governing trade. Regulations and tariffs were often the out come, leading to the tariff wars of the 1930s.

> Nations have found it convenient . . . to agree to rules that limit their own freedom of action in trade matters, and generally to work toward removal of artificial and often arbitrary barriers to trade.[4]

Many trade agreements exist in the world today. There of those agrement (General Agreement on Tariffs and Trade [GATT], the European Community, and the North America Free Trade Agreement [NAFTA]) have had a significant impact on the UnitedStates.

GATT. The first trade agree ment of significance was the General Agreement on Tariffs and Trade. The purpose of GATT was to lower tariff barriers among its members. The success of the organization is evidenced by its members. Originally signed by 22 countrys in 1947, the number of participats countries continues to grow.

> The Uruguay Round of GATT is the most ambitious trade agreement ever attempted. Some 108 nations would lower tariff and other barriers on textiles and agriculture goods; protect one another's intellectual property; and open their borders to banks, insurance companies, and purveyors of other services.[5]

The European Community. The European Community is another example of how trade agreements impact the production, distribution, and marketing of goods and services. The 12 member nations of the European Community have dismantled the internal borders of its members to enhance trade relations.

Dismantling the borders was only the first step toward an even greater purpose—the peaceful union of European countries.

(See Note at left.)

150B • 25' Spreadsheets

Document 1 (Worksheet)

1. Key the worksheet at the right.
2. Do not key commas in the numbers.
3. Calculate the total tons for each year.
4. Calculate the percent of change (no decimal places) from year to year where appropriate.
5. Add a column at the right and calculate the average tons per year for each item (to one decimal place). Include a column heading.
6. Add the main title **Harris County Recycling Statistics (in tons)**.
7. You decide other formatting features, including color and shading.

 **Save as:** *L150B1*

	A	B	C	D	E	F	G	H	I	J
1	Item	1991	1993	% +/-	1995	% +/-	1997	% +/-	1999	% +/-
2	Aluminum cans	206	112		204		285		280	
3	Cardboard	1114	812		923		2054		2229	
4	Steel cans	192	133		338		226		174	
5	Clear glass	466	483		406		222		164	
6	Mixed glass	158	152		11		142		31	
7	Green glass	0	38		88		5		31	
8	Brown glass	0	28		87		2		32	
9	Magazines	0	0		75		169		221	
10	Newsprint	294	376		282		321		389	
11	Mixed paper	0	0		29		20		141	
12	Office paper	30	251		37		88		331	
13	Phone books	0	6		9		31		0	
14	Leaf/yard waste	2152	838		1000		550		663	
15	Total Tons									

Document 2 (Worksheet)

1. Key the worksheet at the right.
2. Calculate the amounts in Columns E, F, and H.
3. Format dollar amounts to include cents.
4. Use the thousands separator when appropriate.
5. Format Column G to one decimal place and Column H to three decimal places.
6. You decide all other formatting features.

 **Save as:** *L150B2*

	A	B	C	D	E	F	G	H
1	Borough of Eastdale Recycling Statistics							
2								Recycled
3								Materials
4					Revenue	Revenue	Recycled	per
5				Recycling	per	per	Materials	Household
6	Year	Population	Households	Revenues	Person	Household	(tons)	(tons)
7	1995	10607	3650	304429			729.6	
8	1996	10738	3703	355678			743.4	
9	1997	10869	3748	355211			869.5	
10	1998	10986	3793	336746			943.1	
11	1999	11102	4041	347891			972.5	

Objectives:

1. To format a bound report with footnotes.
2. To format a references page and title page.

49A • 5' Conditioning Practice

Key each line twice SS; then key a 1' writing on line 3; determine *gwam*.

alphabet 1 Jacques Zhukov played an excellent baseball game for the winners.

figures 2 Since 1987, 450 of our guests were from Maine; 362 from New York.

speed 3 The big city bus was downtown by the signs of the ancient chapel.

gwam 1'	1	2	3	4	5	6	7	8	9	10	11	12	13

FORMATTING

49B • 45' Bound Report

Document 1

Continue the Globalization report begun in Lesson 48. Insert the file *CD-GLOBAL* after the last sentence of the document created in 48B (*RPT48B*). Make the changes shown at the right. The information for footnotes 6–8 is given below.

[6]"Fact Sheet: European Community," Vol. 4, No. 7, Washington, D.C.: U.S. Department of State Dispatch (February 15, 1994), p. 89.

[7]Mario Bognanno and Kathryn J. Ready, eds., North American Free Trade Agreement (Westport, CT: Quorum Books, 1993), p. xiii.

[8]Rahul Jacob, "The Big Rise," Fortune (May 30, 1994), pp. 74-75.

The first step was ~~done~~ accomplished by the Paris and Rome treaties, which established the european community and consequently removed the economic barriers. The treaties called for members to establish a common market; a common customs tariff; and common economic, agricultural, transport, and nuclear policies.[6]

NAFTA. A trade agreement that will have an significant impact on the way business is conducted in the United States is the North American Free Trade Agreement. This trade agreement involves Canada, the United States and Mexico. Proponents of NAFTA claim that the accord will not only increase trade throughout the Americas, but it will also moderate product prices and create jobs in all three of the countries.[7]

Over the years a number of trade agreements have been enacted that promote trade. The result of these agreements has been a ~~better~~ n enhanced quality of life because of the increased access to goods and services produced in other countries.

Growth in Developing Countries' Economies

The growth in developing countries' economies is another major reason for globalizaiton. According to Jacob, the global surge means more consumers who need goods and serviœs.[8] These needs appear because of the increase in percapita incomes of the developing countries.

(Report continued on next page)

Costs of recycling include collection, transportation, and processing fees and equipment, container, and labor expenses.

Recycling saves money!
- ❏ Lowers manufacturing costs for products made from recycled materials
- ❏ Avoids costly landfill and incineration fees
- ❏ Conserves natural resources

5. Balance the columns.
6. You decide all other formatting features.

Save as: *NEWS149B2*

What materials are recycled?

Beginning in January 200-, Marion Township **residents** are required to recycle the following materials:

- ❏ Aluminum, bi-metal, and tin food and beverage cans
- ❏ Clear, brown, and green bottles and jars
- ❏ Newspapers and magazines

Businesses must recycle white paper in addition to the above items.

How do you prepare the recyclables?

Food and beverage cans are to be rinsed and placed in a brown recycling container. The cans may be flattened to save space.

The glass materials are to be separated--clear glass goes in one side of a green recycling container; colored glass goes in the other side. All jars should be rinsed, but labels do not have to be removed. Jar lids or rings are not recycled; they should be discarded in the refuse. Do not recycle window glass, light bulbs, Pyrex, or ceramics.

Newspapers and magazines are to be placed in a red recycling container. Do not tie them in any manner.

White paper (**businesses only**) includes computer paper, bond paper, copier paper, calculator tapes, envelopes without plastic window, etc. These materials are to be placed in the blue container.

What is the recycling schedule?

Place your containers at the curb during the first full week of each month, on the same day as your scheduled garbage collection. Otherwise, you may deposit your recyclables in the appropriate bins behind the Marion Township Municipal Building.

What is the recycling charge?

The annual $12 recycling fee is payable to Marion Township Recycling Fund by January 31 of each year.

LESSON 150 ASSESS SPREADSHEET SOFTWARE AND STRAIGHT-COPY SKILLS

Objective:
To assess ability to prepare worksheets and embedded charts and key straight copy.

150A • 5' Conditioning Practice

Key each line twice SS; then key 30" writings on line 2; determine *gwam*.

alphabet 1 Prexxi just amazed the partial crowd by scoring five quick goals.

figures 2 Call 472-9681 by 11:40 a.m. to arrange the 3:45 p.m. conferences.

speed 3 Nancy laid the ivory memento and oak ornament by the enamel bowl.

gwam 1' | 1 | 2 | 3 | 4 | 5 | 6 | 7 | 8 | 9 | 10 | 11 | 12 | 13 |

Document 1 (cont.)

Complete the Globalization report. Format and key the text at the right at the end of the report (*RPT48B*). The information for footnotes 9 and 10 is given below.

[9]Jacob, p. 74.

[10]Pete Engardio, "Third World Leapfrog," Business Week (May 18, 1994), p. 47.

 **Save as:** *RPT49B1*

Document 2 (Title Page)

Review the "Title Page" section of the format guides, p. 137. Prepare a title page for the Globalization report.

 **Save as:** *RPT49B2*

Document 3 (References Page)

Review the format guides for preparing a references page, p. 138. Using the information from the footnotes and the additional information below, prepare a references page for the Globalization report.

Engardio article, **pp. 47–49**

"Fact Sheet" article, **pp. 87–93**

Harris article, **pp. 755–776**

Jacob article, **pp. 74–90**

Richman article, **p. 14**

 **Save as:** *RPT49B3*

According to the U.S. Department of Commerce, the world's ten biggest emerging markets include:

- Argentina
- Brazil
- China
- India
- Indonesia
- Mexico
- Poland
- South Africa
- South Korea
- Turkey

Of these emerging markets, the most dramatic increase is in the East Asian countries. Estimated per capita incomes rose at an annual rate of 6.5 percent from 1983 to 1993. In China alone, incomes grew 8.5 percent annually.[9]

Recent technological developments have also contributed to globalization. Because of these developments, the world is a smaller place; communication is almost instant to many parts of the world. The extent of the technological developments can be sensed in Engardio's comments:[10]

> Places that until recently were incommunicado are rapidly acquiring state-of-the-art telecommunications that will let them foster both internal and foreign investment. It may take a decade for many countries in Asia, Latin America, and Eastern Europe to unclog bottlenecks in transportation and power supplies. But by installing optical fiber, digital switches, and the latest wireless transmission systems, urban centers and industrial zones from Beijing to Budapest are stepping into the Information Age. Videoconferencing, electronic data interchange, and digital mobile-phone services already are reaching most of Asia and parts of Eastern Europe.
>
> All of these developing regions see advanced communications as a way to leapfrog stages of economic development.

Summary

The world continues to become more globalized. The trend will continue because of three main factors: new and improved trade agreements, rapid growth rates of developing countries' economies, and technological advances. All of these factors foster globalization.

149B • 45'
Column Documents

Document 1 (Flyer)

1. Use the information in the chart at the right to design a one-page flyer. You decide the wording of the various sections.
2. Use word art, 3-D effects, shaded text boxes, and shapes to format the flyer.
3. You decide all other formatting features.

 **Save as:** *FLY149B1*

Event	School Clean Up Day
Sponsor	Student Council
When	Saturday, April 7, 9:30 a.m. to noon
Where	Marion High School and Marion Middle School
Activity	Freshmen and sophomore students will clean the area around the middle school, and juniors and seniors will clean the area around the high school.
Preparation	Safety vests and litterbags will be provided. A box lunch, donated by various local businesses, will be provided in the school cafeteria at noon.
Registration	Sign-up sheet will be in the cafeteria from April 2 to 6.

Document 2 (Newsletter)

1. Format the newsletter at the right and on the next page so the articles are arranged in three columns of equal width, separated by vertical lines. Format the newsletter name so it spans the columns.
2. Use an 11-pt. font for the article text and a 14-pt. font for the article titles.
3. Hyphenate the titles and articles; justify the articles, but not the titles.
4. Insert the text boxes below and on the next page at appropriate places throughout the text.

Recover your containers promptly after collection.

Where do we get our waste?
About 32% of all household waste comes from packaging.

(continued on next page)

Recycling Works!

Marion Township Recycling Guidelines January 200-

Why recycle?

Every day we hear about environmental problems at school, at work, in the newspapers, on television, and on the radio. Garbage is just one of these environmental concerns. It hits the media every time a barge filled with garbage is turned away from port and has no place to go. We hear about it when our taxes are affected by the shipping costs for garbage. We see the impact of it every time we take out the trash.

In the late 1960s and throughout the 1970s, the long-term effect of the loss of our natural resources and pollution became a cause for concern by the public in general. During that time more and more landfills were closed, some because of stricter environmental regulations and others because they were filled.

In the late 1970s and early 1980s, when much recycling was on a "grassroots" volunteer level, "Recycling Pays" was a common slogan used to encourage people to recycle. Recycling projects were often used as fundraisers for community groups such as the Scouts.

Soon, government agencies were asked to formulate long-term plans for trash disposal. Marion Township did such planning before implementing a recycling program that increased, over time, the kinds of materials that residents and businesses are to recycle. The township council recognized that all of us needed to change our habits to help the township maximize its overall waste management efforts.

(continued on next page)

LESSON 50 FORMAT BOUND REPORTS WITH ENDNOTES

Objectives:

1. To format a bound report with endnotes.
2. To format a references page.

50A • 5' Conditioning Practice

Key each line twice SS; then key a 1' writing on line 3; determine *gwam*.

alphabet 1 Completing the five extra job requirements will keep Zelda happy.

figures 2 Check #97 was written for $3,525.16; Check #98 was for $3,785.40.

speed 3 Glen bid on the cornfield by the lake for land for the city hall.

gwam 1' | 1 | 2 | 3 | 4 | 5 | 6 | 7 | 8 | 9 | 10 | 11 | 12 | 13 |

SKILL BUILDING

50B • 12' Straight Copy

1. Key a 3' writing on ¶s 1–3 combined; determine *gwam* and number of errors.
2. Key a 1' writing on each ¶; determine *gwam* and number of errors on each ¶.
3. Take another 3' writing on ¶s 1–3 combined, trying to increase your *gwam* over the writing in Step 1.

all letters used

Text	gwam 3'	5'	
Why are some people so amazingly productive while others are	4	2	47
not? Procrastination is the explanation offered in response to	8	5	49
this query. Productive people do not waste time. They maintain	13	8	52
that you should not put off till the next day what you can do	17	10	54
today. People who are successful tend to be those who manage	21	13	57
time rather than let time manage them.	24	14	59
A number of things can be done to combat procrastination.	28	17	61
First, prepare a listing of each task that needs to be accomplished.	32	19	64
Many of the tasks that appear on the list will take minimal time,	37	22	66
while others on the list may take a substantial amount. As each	41	25	69
task is achieved, it should be deleted from the list. This gives	45	27	72
a person a sense of accomplishment and increases the likelihood	50	30	74
of additional tasks being completed.	52	31	76
The next suggestion is to divide a big job into several smaller	56	34	78
parts. By doing so, the job will not appear so overwhelming. Along	61	37	81
with breaking the job down, set deadlines for completing each	65	39	83
part of the job. The probability of completing a large job is much	70	42	86
greater when it is divided into parts that have assigned deadlines.	74	44	89

gwam 3' | 1 | 2 | 3 | 4 |
5' | 1 | 2 | 3 |

3. Add the titles and company names for the records at the right.
4. Sort by postal code in descending order and then alphabetically by last name, then first name.

 **Save as:** *L148B2*

LastName	Title	Company
Adams	Mrs.	Adams Medical Association
Aitken, Albert	Mr.	Compilers Plus
Aitken, Barbara	Mrs.	Database & More
Gioia	Mr.	Four Springs Golf Course
Harris	Mr.	Brite House Electricians
McClintock	Mr.	Banquets Unlimited
Springer	Mrs.	County Motors

Document 3 (Personalized Form Letters)

1. Use the information at the right to create a main document file.
2. Format the letter in block style with open punctuation.

 **Save as:** *L148B3MD* (main document)

3. Merge *L148B2* and *L148B3MD* and then print the first and last letters.

 **Save as:** *L148BLTRS* (merged letters)

February 15, 200- | <<Title>> <<FirstName>> <<LastName>> | <<Company>> | <<Address1>> | <<City>>, <<State>> <<PostalCode>> | Dear <<Title>> <<LastName>>

This letter is to inform you that your company has been selected to participate in an experimental recycling program for various businesses in Ohio. The program will begin March 1 and is scheduled to end August 31.

<<Title>> <<LastName>>, this recycling program requires you to separate paper products into four categories for recycling purposes. The categories are white paper, newspapers, cardboard boxes, and mixed paper. The enclosed pamphlet describes in detail the kinds of paper that are to go into each of these categories.

Early in September, we will send you a survey to complete. The survey results will provide us with much of the information we need to determine if the paper recycling program will be continued and expanded to other businesses in the state.

Your cooperation and compliance throughout this six-month period is expected and appreciated. If you have any questions that are not answered by the information in the pamphlet, give me a call at (214) 555-0119.

Sincerely | OHIO RECYCLING AUTHORITY | Jeremy Morales | Executive Director | xx | Enclosure |

Document 4 (Mailing Labels)

1. Open file *L148B2* and revise it so the fields are formatted in USPS format (ALL CAPS, no punctuation).

 **Save as:** *L148B4*

2. Create a mailing label for each personalized form letter.

 **Save as:** *L148B4MD* (label main document) and *L148BLBLS* (labels)

LESSON 149 ASSESS COLUMN DOCUMENT FORMATTING SKILLS

Objective:

To assess ability to prepare flyers and newsletters.

149A • 5' Conditioning Practice

Key each line twice SS; then key 30" writings on line 3; determine *gwam*.

alphabet 1 Four expert judges asked how to quickly analyze five board games.

fig/sym 2 He should pay $2,827 on Model #43-60-39 by May 28 to get 15% off.

speed 3 Did a big quake on the island also shake the autobus and cubicle?

gwam 1' | 1 | 2 | 3 | 4 | 5 | 6 | 7 | 8 | 9 | 10 | 11 | 12 | 13 |

50C • 33'
Bound Report

Document 1 (Report Body)

1. Review the format guides for bound reports on pp. 137–138 as needed.
2. Format the copy at the right as a bound report with endnotes.
3. When you finish, use the Speller feature and proofread your copy.

Save as: *RPT50C1*

Document 2 (Endnotes)

Use the information below to prepare the endnotes.

[1]Robert J. Samuelson, "Lost on the Information Highway," Newsweek (December 20, 1993), p. 111.

[2]Laurence A. Canter and Martha S. Siegel, How to Make a FORTUNE on the Information Superhighway (New York: Harper-Collins Publishers, Inc., 1994), p. 1.

[3]"AOL Poised for Record Subscriber Growth," http://dailynews.yahoo.com/h/nm/19990921/wr/aol_3.html (21 September 1999).

Save as: *RPT50C2*

Document 3—Optional (References Page)

Use the endnotes information above to prepare a references page. See R56 for references format.

Note:
The entire Samuelson article is on p. 111 in *Newsweek*.

Save as: *RPT50C3*

INFORMATION SUPERHIGHWAY

Technology has a significant impact on our lives and will have an even greater impact in the future. During the early 1990s, the term "Information Highway" was first used to describe the next wave of technological advancements. As always there were those who were skeptical about what impact, if any, the "Information Highway" (also called the "Information Superhighway") would have on our lives.

One writer, as late as December 1993, indicated that he was not holding his breath. He doubted if the Information Superhighway would become a truly transforming technology; and if so, he felt, it may take decades. This writer went on to compare acceptance of the Information Superhighway to acceptance of the car.

> It takes time for breakthrough technologies to make their mark. Consider the car. In 1908 Henry Ford began selling the Model T. One early effort of low-cost cars was to rid cities of horses. A picture of a New York street in 1900 shows 36 horse carriages and 1 car; a picture of the same street in 1924 shows 40 cars and 1 carriage. This was a big deal. In 1900, horses dumped 2.5 million pounds of manure onto New York streets every day. Still, the car culture's triumph was slow.[1]

Other writers during the early 1990s were much more optimistic about the value of this superhighway and began predicting what it would mean to all of us in the near future.

> The Information Superhighway is going to affect your life, whether you want it to or not. In the very near future you will talk to your friends and family, send letters, go shopping, get news, find answers to your questions . . . .[2]

What is the Information Superhighway?

The Information Superhighway, more commonly called the **Internet**, is a large computer network made up of many smaller networks. By connecting to the Internet, an individual can access and exchange information with anyone else who is connected to the Internet. Currently, millions of individuals are connected; the number increases daily. In the fourth quarter of 1999, America Online Inc., an Internet service provider, added 685,000 new U.S. members.[3]

What has been the Impact of the Superhighway?

The development of the Information Superhighway since 1993 has been much faster than many expected and has even exceeded the visions of those who were predicting its widespread use.

Many individuals use the Information Superhighway daily to send **e-mail** messages and attachments; to participate in **chat groups**; to shop; and to get the latest news, weather, and sports. Taking the Internet away from them would impact them almost as much as taking away the telephone, television, and mail delivery service. The Information Superhighway has been constructed, and "road improvements" will make it even better in the future.

UNIT 38

LESSONS 148–150

Assessing Information Processing Skills

LESSON 148 ASSESS CORRESPONDENCE FORMATTING SKILLS

Objective:
To assess ability to use Mail Merge to process letters and mailing labels.

148A • 5' Conditioning Practice

Key each line twice SS; then key 30" writings on line 1; determine *gwam*.

alphabet 1 Zemjaw caught seven very quiet lions before they exited the park.

figures 2 Order 97-431 for Series 608 storm windows was shipped on June 25.

speed 3 The eight busy men may do the work for the city if she pays them.

gwam 1' | 1 | 2 | 3 | 4 | 5 | 6 | 7 | 8 | 9 | 10 | 11 | 12 | 13 |

148B • 45' Correspondence

Document 1 (Create Data Source File)

1. Using the information at the right, create a data source file for these records. Use initial caps and punctuation as needed in each address.
2. Sort the file in ascending order by postal code, and then alphabetically by last name and then first name.

 **Save as:** *L148B1*

Doris Adams 2405 Grandview Ave. Cincinnati, OH 45206-2220	Roger Harris 4381 Antioch Dr. Enon, OH 45323-6492
Albert Aitken 440 Long Pointe Dr. Avon Lake, OH 44012-2463	Larry McClintock 6821 Burgundy Dr. Canton, OH 44720-4592
Barbara Aitken 440 Long Pointe Dr. Avon Lake, OH 44012-2463	Mary Springer 81 Mayflower Dr. Youngstown, OH 44512-6204
Bruce Gioia Rte. 3, Box 416 Marietta, OH 45750-9057	William Eiber 387 Cranberry Run Youngstown, OH 44512-2504

Document 2 (Change Data Source File)

1. Open file *L148B1*.
2. Add new fields named **Title** and **Company**, and then enter the four records at the right. Delete the Eiber record.

Mr. Gerald Bruni Bruni Auto Parts 11184 Greenhaven Dr. Navarre, OH 44662-9650	Mrs. Mary Phillip Union Cleaning Co. 123 Marrett Farms Union, OH 45322-3412
Ms. Ruth O'Hara Warren Florists 426 Forest St. Warren, OH 44483-3825	Mr. Henry Lewis Lewis Printing 3140 Beaumont St. Massillon, OH 44647-3140

(continued on next page)

LESSON 51 IMPROVE REPORT FORMATTING SKILLS

Objectives:

1. To format a bound report.
2. To format endnotes.

51A • 5' Conditioning Practice

Key each line twice SS; then key a 1' writing on line 3; determine *gwam*.

alphabet 1 Mack Walsh did quite a job to put an extravaganza on before July.

figures 2 Only 386 of the 497 students had completed the exam by 12:50 p.m.

speed 3 The visitor and I may handle all the problems with the amendment.

gwam 1' | 1 | 2 | 3 | 4 | 5 | 6 | 7 | 8 | 9 | 10 | 11 | 12 | 13 |

FORMATTING

51B • 45' Bound Report

Document 1 (Report Body)

1. Review the report format guides on pp. 137–138 as needed.
2. Format the copy at the right as a bound report with endnotes.
3. When you finish, use the Speller feature and proofread your copy.

 **Save as:** *RPT51B1*

Document 2 (Endnotes)

Prepare endnotes from the information below and on p. 149.

[1]Wayne E. Fuller, <u>The American Mail</u> (Chicago: University of Chicago Press, 1972), p. ix.

[2] William M. Leary, <u>Aerial Pioneers</u> (Washington, D.C.: Smithsonian Institution Press, 1985), p. 238.

[3]Richard Wormser, <u>The Iron Horse: How Railroads Changed America</u> (New York: Walker Publishing Company, Inc., 1993), p. 26.

[4]Leary, p. 238.

DELIVERING THE MAIL

For years, people have used written communication as one of their primary means of exchanging information. Those using this form of communicating have depended on the U.S. mail to transport their messages from one place to another.

> For much of American history, the mail was our main form of organized communication. Americans wanting to know the state of the world, the health of a friend, or the fate of their business anxiously awaited the mail. To advise a distant relative, to order goods, to pay a bill, to express views to their congressman or love to their fiancée, they used the mail. No American institution has been more intimately involved in daily hopes and fears.[1]

The history of the U.S. mail is not only interesting but also reflective of changes in American society, specifically transportation. A variety of modes of transporting mail have been used over the years. Speed, of course, was the driving force behind most of the changes.

<u>Steamboats</u>

Congress used inventions to move the mail from place to place. In 1813, five years after Robert Fulton's first experiments on the Hudson River, Congress authorized the Post Office to transport mail by steamboat.[2] Transporting mail to river cities worked very well. However, the efficiency of using steamboats to transport mail between New York and San Francisco was questionable. "The distance was 19,000 miles and the trip could take as long as six to seven months."[3]

<u>Railroads</u>

Although mail was carried by railroads as early as 1834, it was not until 1838 that Congress declared railroads to be post roads.[4] Trains eventually revolutionized mail delivery. The cost of sending a letter decreased substantially, making it more affordable to the public.

(*Report continued on next page*)

147C • 5' Embedded Charts

Create the two charts as instructed at the right.

Chart 1: Bar Chart

1. Open file *CD-L147C1*.
2. Create a bar chart showing the male and female admissions at each hospital. Use **Hospital Admissions** as the title; show gridlines, axis titles, and legend.

 **Save as:** *L147C1*

Chart 2: Pie Chart

1. Open file *CD-L147C2*.
2. Create a pie chart showing the percent of each investment category. Use **Investment Portfolio** as the title; show percents as data labels and show a legend.

 **Save as:** *L147C2*

147D • 15' Timed Writing

Take two 5' writings on the three paragraphs at the right; determine *gwam*; count errors.

all letters used | gwam 3' | 5'

Sleep is a very important element of staying healthy. Many 4 2 45
people who do not get the proper amount of sleep quickly become 8 5 47
edgy, fatigued, and tired. In addition, people who do not get 12 7 50
enough sleep are more likely to be attacked by various diseases. 17 10 52
It is, therefore, important that you get the amount of sleep that 21 13 55
your body needs. 22 13 56

Science knows very little about sleep. There is evidence 26 16 58
that the amount of sleep each individual needs to maintain good 30 18 60
health varies. Some believe that the amount of sleep people need 35 21 63
lessens with age. For example, children below four years of age 39 24 66
frequently need to sleep about half of each day while teenagers 43 26 68
need just eight to ten hours each day to perform adequately. 47 28 71

Most people realize that a good mattress, one that is neither 52 31 73
too hard nor too soft; a quiet room; and darkness are conditions 56 34 76
that help them get enough sleep to restore body power. Also helpful 61 36 78
are covers and electric blankets that are warm but not too heavy. 65 39 81
It is also helpful to avoid excitement and heavy eating before 69 42 84
going to sleep. 70 42 84

gwam 3' | 1 | 2 | 3 | 4
5' | 1 | 2 | 3

Document 2
Endnotes (cont.)

[5]Albro Martin, Railroads Triumphant (New York: Oxford University Press, 1992), p. 94.

[6]Fred Reinfeld, Pony Express (Lincoln: University of Nebraska Press, 1973), p. 55.

[7]Carl H. Scheele, A Short History of the Mail Service (Washington, D.C.: Smithsonian Institution Press, 1970), p. 117.

[8]Fuller, p. 9.

[9]Leary, p. 29.

Save as: *RPT51B2*

> No aspect of American life was untouched by the revolution that the trains brought in bringing mail service almost to the level of a free good. (For many years—ironically enough, until the depression called for an increase in the cost of a first-class letter to three cents—an ordinary first-class letter went for two cents.)[5]

Pony Express

The Pony Express was one of the most colorful means of transporting mail. This method of delivery was used to take mail from St. Joseph, Missouri, westward.

> April 3, 1860, remains a memorable day in the history of the frontier, for that was the day on which the Pony Express began its operations—westward from St. Joseph and eastward from San Francisco. Even in those days San Francisco had already become the most important city in California.[6]

With the East Coast being connected to the West Coast by railroad in 1869, the Pony Express had a relatively short life span.

Automobiles

The invention of the automobile in the late 1800s brought a new means of delivering mail in the United States.

> An automobile was used experimentally for rural delivery as early as 1902 at Adrian, Michigan, and in 1906 the Department gave permission for rural carriers to use their automobiles. The change from horse and wagon to the motor car paralleled improvements in highways and the development of more reliable automotive equipment. . . .[7]

Airplanes

The next major mode of transporting used by the Postal Service was airplanes. Speed was the driving force behind using airplanes. ". . . so closely has speed been associated with the mails that much of the world's postal history can be written around the attempts to send mail faster each day than it went the day before."[8]

The United States was the leader in transporting mail by air. In 1918 when the first air mail route took place (Washington to New York), no other nation in the world operated a scheduled air mail service.[9]

Note:
You will finish keying the report "Delivering the Mail" in Lesson 52.

147B • 25' Spreadsheets

Document 1 (Worksheet)

1. Key the worksheet at the right.
2. Format the numbers with a thousands separator.
3. Calculate the U.S. population for each year.
4. Calculate the percent of increase (to two decimal places) from year to year.
5. Add a column at the right and calculate the average population for each area (no decimal places). Include a column heading.
6. Add the title **U.S. Population (thousands of persons)**.
7. Add a source note: **Bureau of Census, U.S. Department of Commerce, March 1999**.
8. You decide other formatting features, including color and shading.

Save as: *L147B1*

	A	B	C	D	E	F	G	H	I	J
1	**Region**	**1994**	**1995**	**%+**	**1996**	**%+**	**1997**	**%+**	**1998**	**%+**
2	New England	13233	13271		13319		13372		13430	
3	Mideast	44368	44442		44509		44576		44693	
4	Great Lakes	43316	43590		43839		44028		44195	
5	Plains	18235	18369		18478		18587		18695	
6	Southeast	62727	63538		64328		65151		65922	
7	Southwest	27397	27956		28469		28985		29512	
8	Rocky Mountains	8060	8240		8379		8525		8661	
9	Far West	42953	43360		43869		44520		45192	
10	United States									

Document 2 (Worksheet)

1. Key the worksheet at the right.
2. Calculate the overtime pay rate at 1.5 times regular pay rate.
3. Add a column at the right; title it **Gross Pay**; and then calculate gross pay for each employee.
4. Add another column at the right; title it **Net Pay**; and then calculate the net pay for each employee.
5. Calculate appropriate column totals for the entire payroll.
6. Add the title **Jefferson Medical Association Payroll—Week 6**.
7. You decide other formatting features.

Save as: *L147B2*

	A	B	C	D	E	F	G
1		Employee	Regular	Regular	Overtime	Overtime	Total
2	Employee	Number	Hours	Pay Rate	Hours	Pay Rate	Deductions
3	Ronald Alvarez	101	40	$8.87	2		$63.45
4	Barry Barton	103	40	$9.15	0		$67.87
5	Harriet Demonti	106	38	$10.52	0		$59.86
6	Sylvester Everett	108	40	$8.56	6		$64.23
7	Maryanne Gigliotti	110	40	$9.75	4		$54.31
8	Kim Lu	115	36	$8.98	0		$49.78
9	Martin Menendez	123	40	$8.98	0		$64.56
10	John Newton	134	40	$9.65	4		$72.90
11	Susan Tofflin	136	32	$9.45	0		$43.65
12	Beatrice Robertson	145	40	$8.87	6		$68.30
13	William Tellison	152	40	$9.15	2		$65.76
14	Totals						

LESSON 52 EXTEND REPORT FORMATTING SKILLS

Objectives:

1. To complete formatting a bound report.
2. To format a references page, title page, and table of contents.

52A • 5' Conditioning Practice

Key each line twice SS; then key a 1' writing on line 3; determine *gwam*.

alphabet 1 Zack and our equipment manager will exchange jobs for seven days.

figures 2 If you call after 12:30 on Friday, you can reach him at 297-6854.

speed 3 The eight men in the shanty paid for a big bus to go to the city.

gwam 1' | 1 | 2 | 3 | 4 | 5 | 6 | 7 | 8 | 9 | 10 | 11 | 12 | 13 |

FORMATTING

52B • 32' Bound Report

Document 1 (Report Summary)
Complete the report "Delivering the Mail" that you began in Lesson 51.

1. Open the *CD-RPT52B* file. Make the corrections to the text shown at the right.
2. Copy the corrected text and paste at the end of the report keyed in 51B (*RPT51B1*).

Save as: *RPT52B1*

Document 2 (Title Page)
Review the guidelines for formatting a title page on p. 137. Format and key a title page for the report "Delivering the Mail."

Save as: *RPT52B2*

Document 3 (Table of Contents)
Review the guidelines for formatting a table of contents on p. 138. Format and key the information at the right as a table of contents for "Delivering the Mail."

Save as: *RPT52B3*

<u>Summary</u>

(now the U.S. Postal Service)

The Post Office has been the primary means for transporting written messages for many years. As the information age continues to emerge technologies will play a significant roll in getting written messages from the sender to the reciever. Again this change is directly attributable to speed Instead of talking in terms of months required for delivering a message from the east coast to the west coast, ~~it now takes~~ we now talk in terms of seconds. Today, e-mail and faxes ~~as~~ are just as important to a successful business operation as the Post Office.

TABLE OF CONTENTS

> "The efforts of Caroline Darling (RN) were above and beyond the call of duty. She certainly went out of her way to see that all the things I needed were taken care of. I would sincerely hope that she could be officially recognized for her helpfulness and professionalism during a very difficult time for me."
> —a patient of Unit 8

> "Can't thank you enough for being with us during the rough times after the auto accident. You were there when my husband and I arrived and stayed with us until we were discharged. Your service and attention certainly brightened our day and helped to make things better for me and my family."
> —an emergency room patient

5. Balance the columns.
6. You decide all other formatting features.

Save as: *NEWS146B2*

Last year, LAS awarded grants to six students who represented a broad spectrum of interests in the health professions: molecular biology, research, and occupational physical and rehabilitation therapy.

For applications or more information about the LAS Teen Scholarship, call Beth Olszewski, Director, Volunteer and Community Services, at (425) 555-0105.

Staff to Be Recognized for Service Milestones

Jones Memorial Hospital's strength today is due in large part to staff who, over the years, have helped shape the hospital. To celebrate their contributions, Jones will honor staff who this year reached service milestones of 10, 15, 20, 25, 30, 35, and 40 years at its Annual Awards Recognition Event on Tuesday, March 14, from 5:30 to 8 p.m. at Highpoint Center.

Each honoree will receive a gift specially selected for his or her anniversary level and a personal certificate of recognition. Staff who completed five years of service this year also will receive a gift and certificate. The five-year service gifts will be mailed to awardees' homes prior to March 14.

Awardees and their families will receive personal invitations to the event and are encouraged to attend. Supervisors are asked to adjust schedules so that honored staff may take part in this special evening of tribute and celebration.

Jones Memorial Hospital Shines in JCAHO Survey

Jones Memorial Hospital received a preliminary score of 98 with commendations last week following a four-day visit by surveyors from the Joint Commission on Accreditation of Healthcare Organizations (JCAHO).

LESSON 147 PREPARE TO ASSESS SPREADSHEET SOFTWARE AND STRAIGHT-COPY SKILL

Objective:

To prepare for assessment of worksheets, charts, and straight-copy skills.

147A • 5' Conditioning Practice

Key each line twice SS; then key 30" writings on line 2; determine *gwam.*

alphabet 1 If Marge has extra help, the jigsaw puzzle can be solved quickly.

fig/sym 2 A & W Co. used P.O. #708-A to buy 125 chairs (#94-63) @ $25 each.

speed 3 The shamrock ornament is an authentic memento for the busy girls.

gwam 1' | 1 | 2 | 3 | 4 | 5 | 6 | 7 | 8 | 9 | 10 | 11 | 12 | 13 |

FORMATTING

52C • 5'
Table of Contents

In previous lessons, you keyed a report titled "Globalization." The headings in that report are shown at the right. Format and key a table of contents for the report.

Open the file (*RPT49B1*); verify that the page number for each heading is the same in your report. Change the table of contents as needed.

 **Save as:** *RPT52C*

TABLE OF CONTENTS

SKILL BUILDING

52D • 8'
Straight Copy

1. Key a 1' writing on ¶ 1, then on ¶ 2; determine *gwam* and number of errors on each writing.
2. Take a 3' writing on ¶s 1–2 combined; determine *gwam* and number of errors.

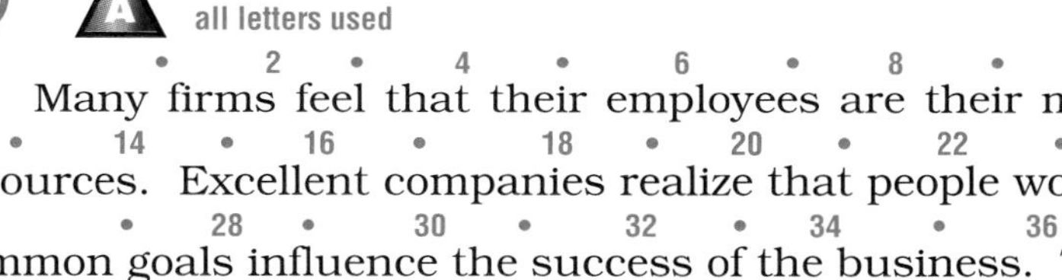

A all letters used

	gwam 3'	5'	
Many firms feel that their employees are their most valuable	4	2	45
resources. Excellent companies realize that people working toward	9	5	47
common goals influence the success of the business. They are also	13	8	50
aware of the need to hire qualified people and then to create a	17	10	53
work environment to allow the people to perform at their highest	22	13	55
potential. Firms that believe that the main job of managers is	26	16	58
to remove obstacles that get in the way of the output of the	30	18	60
workers are the firms that do, in fact, achieve their goals.	34	20	63
Not only do executives and managers in the most successful	38	23	65
firms admit to themselves the value of their employees, but they	42	25	68
also reveal this feeling to their workers. They know that most	46	28	70
people enjoy being given credit for their unique qualities. They	51	31	73
also know that any action on their part that aids the workers in	55	33	75
realizing their own self-worth will lead to a higher return for	59	36	78
the firm, since such people are self-motivated. When leaders do	64	38	81
not have to be occupied with employee motivation, they can devote	68	41	83
their energy to other vital tasks.	70	42	85

gwam 3' | 1 | 2 | 3 | 4
5' | 1 | 2 | 3

146B • 45'
Column Documents

Document 1 (Flyer)

1. Use the information in the chart at the right to design a one-page flyer.
2. Use word art, 3-D effects, shaded text boxes, and shapes to format the flyer.
3. You decide all other formatting features.

 **Save as:** *FLY146B1*

Event	Parenting Skills
Sponsor	Armstrong County Education Association
When	Saturday, March 15
Where	Washington Middle School
	135 Washington Rd., Jefferson City
Focus	The program will focus on facets of parenting ranging from physical and psychological development to educational issues and conflict resolution.
Cost	$10 includes workshops, exhibits, and continental breakfast.
Registration	Call 513.555.0130 or 513.555.0188.

Document 2 (Newsletter)

1. Format the newsletter at the right and on the next page so the articles are arranged in two columns of equal width and the newsletter name spans the width of the columns.
2. Use justification and hyphenation. Use a 16-pt. font for the article titles.
3. Insert the following text box between the first and second articles:

> **Tip of the Week**
> Skiers may injure their thumbs when falling if they're using ski poles with molded plastic grips, which are not flexible. The American Physical Therapy Association recommends using ski poles with soft webbing or leather straps.

4. Insert the text boxes on the next page between the second and third articles and after the last article. Use an 11-pt. font and **Patient Praise** as a title in each text box.

(continued on next page)

Healthscape

Published by Jones Memorial Hospital February 200-

Sports Medicine Offers Physicals for Athletes

The Jones Memorial Hospital Sports Medicine program will offer $15 physical exams and musculoskeletal screenings to local high school athletes participating in spring sports. The Vermont Interscholastic Athletic Association (VIAA) requires all high school athletes to pass a physical exam. The musculoskeletal screenings, which are not required by the VIAA, include tests of muscle strength and flexibility, agility, range of motion in major joints, posture, and body composition.

Sports medicine physicians, physical therapists, and certified athletic trainers will perform the exams and screenings from 8 a.m. to noon Saturday, February 25, in the hospital's Physical Therapy Department, East Wing, fourth floor. For more information or to make an appointment, call (425) 555-0120 between 8:30 a.m. and 5 p.m. Monday through Friday.

Scholarships Available for Teen Volunteers

The Ladies Aid Society (LAS) of Jones Memorial Hospital awards scholarships each year to teenagers who volunteer at Jones. High school seniors who have given 100 or more hours of volunteer service and plan to pursue a career in a health-related field are eligible to apply. LAS Teen Scholarship awards are based on need, volunteer performance, and academic achievement. Applications will be accepted until Wednesday, March 15.

(continued on next page)

UNIT 16

LESSONS 53–54

Building Basic Skill

LESSON 53 — IMPROVE KEYING TECHNIQUE

Objectives:

1. To improve keying techniques.
2. To improve keying speed and control.

53A • 5' Conditioning Practice

Key each line twice SS; then key a 1' writing on line 3; determine *gwam.*

alphabet 1 Next week Zelda Jacks will become a night supervisor for quality.

figures 2 Scores of 94, 83, 72, 65, and 100 gave Rhonda an average of 82.8.

speed 3 Kay paid the maid for the work she did on the shanty by the lake.

gwam 1' | 1 | 2 | 3 | 4 | 5 | 6 | 7 | 8 | 9 | 10 | 11 | 12 | 13 |

SKILL BUILDING

53B • 10' Keying Skill: Speed

1. Key lines 1-6 twice.
2. Take two 30" writings on line 7. If you complete the line, begin again.
3. Repeat Step 2 for lines 8 and 9.

Note: Each word in this drill is among the 600 most-used words in the English language. Increase your keying rate by practicing them frequently.

Balanced-hand words of 2-5 letters

1 or me go am do if so an us by to he it is big the six and but for

2 box did end due for may pay man own make also city with they when

3 them such than city they hand paid sign then form work both their

4 of it | it is | of such | paid them | such as | they work | go to | such a name

5 paid for | go to | pay for | big man | the forms | own them | and then | may go

6 is to go | make it for | pay for it | end to end | by the man | down by the

7 She may wish to go to the city to hand them the work form for us.

8 The city is to pay for the field work both of the men did for us.

9 The man may hand them the six forms when he pays for the big box.

gwam 1' | 1 | 2 | 3 | 4 | 5 | 6 | 7 | 8 | 9 | 10 | 11 | 12 | 13 |

SKILL BUILDING

53C • 8' Technique: Number Keys/Tab

1. Key each line twice (key number, depress TAB, key next number).
2. Take three 1' writings, trying to better your rate each time.

Concentrate on figure location; quick tab spacing; eyes on copy.

930	792	556	938	394	282	737	889	1,901
823	318	927	676	275	910	945	857	2,362
714	640	801	544	651	720	104	262	5,435

gwam 1' 1 2 3 4 5 6 7

Document 3 (Personalized Form Letters)

1. Use the information at the right to create a main document file.
2. Format the letter in modified block style with mixed punctuation and indented ¶s, using an 11-pt. font.

Save as: *L145B3MD* (main document)

3. Merge *L145B2* and *L145B3MD* and then print the first and last letters.

Save as: *L145BLTRS* (merged letters)

Document 4 (Mailing Labels)

1. Open file *L145B2* and revise it so the fields are formatted in USPS format (ALL CAPS, no punctuation) in an 11-pt. font.

Save as: *L145B4*

2. Create and then print a mailing label for each personalized form letter.

Save as: *L145B4MD* (label main document) *L145BLBLS* (labels)

September 15, 200- | <<Title>> <<FirstName>> <<LastName>> | <<Address1>> | <<City>>, <<State>> <<PostalCode>> | Dear <<Title>> <<LastName>>:

Thank you for attending the adult educational series that focused on clinical and emotional disease management issues. It appears that the series was a success from the number of positive comments we have received.

<<FirstName>>, since you have been a strong supporter of the Beakin County United Way during the past several years, we want to be certain that you know about our upcoming events:

- ❑ The Pediatric Educational Program with breakout sessions for teenagers and a lecture/discussion format for parents and guardians on three Monday evenings beginning October 11 at Beakin County Community College.
- ❑ The popular "Evening with Da Vinci" Annual Gala on October 27 at the Beakin Club.
- ❑ The Pace Setter 5K Run/Walk for the Cure of Disease on November 5 at Valley View Park.
- ❑ Funder's Golf Classic on November 8 at Harris Heights Golf Club.
- ❑ "Camp Superkids!" for kids and teens on the weekend of November 13 at Camp Iroquois.

If you want more information about any of these events, please e-mail me at jenko@united-way.org or call me at (713) 555-0144. I have enclosed a form that you can complete and return to register yourself or family members.

Sincerely, | Janice Jenko | Executive Director | xx | Enclosure | <<FirstName>>, Jerry Helco is arranging foursomes for the golf outing, and he wants you to be a part of one of them. He'll call you in a few days to see if you are interested and if you have any preferences for partners.

LESSON 146 PREPARE TO ASSESS COLUMN DOCUMENT SKILL

Objective:

To prepare for assessment of formatting skill on flyers and newsletters.

146A • 5' Conditioning Practice

Key each line twice SS; then key 30" writings on line 3; determine *gwam*.

alphabet 1 Zed quickly explained how my job was lost over internal fighting.

figures 2 The study guides for the exam are on pages 56, 197, 280, and 304.

speed 3 Claudia may pay them to work with us when we dismantle the docks.

gwam 1' | 1 | 2 | 3 | 4 | 5 | 6 | 7 | 8 | 9 | 10 | 11 | 12 | 13 |

SKILL BUILDING

53D • 12' Speed Forcing Drill

1. Key each line once at top speed.
2. Key two 15" timings on each line.

If you finish a line before time is called, start over. Your *gwam* is the figure at the end of the line PLUS the figure above or below the point at which you stopped.

Emphasis: high-frequency balanced-hand words

4 | 8 | 12 | 16 | 20 | 24 | 28 | 32 | 36 | 40 | 44 | 48 | 52

1 Allene is to pay for the six pens for the auditor.
2 Henry is to go with us to the lake to fix the bus.
3 If the pay is right, Jan may make eight gowns for them.
4 They may be paid to fix the six signs down by the lake.
5 Enrique works with vigor to make the gowns for a big profit.
6 Pamela may hang the signs by the antique door of the chapel.
7 Dick and the busy man may work with vigor to fix the eight signs.
8 Did the firm bid for the right to the land downtown by city hall?

gwam 15" | 4 | 8 | 12 | 16 | 20 | 24 | 28 | 32 | 36 | 40 | 44 | 48 | 52

SKILL BUILDING

53E • 15' Skill Check

1. Key a 1' writing on ¶ 1; determine *gwam*.
2. Add 2–4 *gwam* to the rate attained in Step 1, and note quarter-minute checkpoints from the chart below.
3. Take two 1' guided writings on ¶ 1 to increase speed.
4. Practice ¶ 2 in the same way.
5. Take two 3' writings on ¶s 1 and 2 combined; determine *gwam* and count errors.

Quarter-Minute Checkpoints				
gwam	1/4'	1/2'	3/4'	1'
24	6	12	18	24
28	7	14	21	28
32	8	16	24	32
36	9	18	27	36
40	10	20	30	40
44	11	22	33	44
48	12	24	36	48
52	13	26	39	52
56	14	28	42	56
60	15	30	45	60

A all letters used — gwam 3'

An education is becoming more important in our society. More 4 70
jobs will be open to the skilled person with fewer jobs open to 8 74
the unskilled or less educated person. Future jobs will require 13 79
people who can communicate and who have basic math and reading 17 83
skills. It is predicted that there will be a large number of new 21 87
jobs available to those with the appropriate training who want to 26 92
work in an office. These jobs will require the skills listed 30 96
above and an ability to process office documents. 33 99

To quickly process quality office documents will take a great 37 103
deal of training. A person must be able to key rapidly, format a 42 108
variety of documents, make decisions, follow directions, recognize 46 112
all types of errors, and apply language skills. In addition to 50 116
these skills, the best office workers will be willing to put forth 55 121
an extra effort. You should begin to put forth an extra effort 59 125
today to get the training needed to become one of the skilled 63 129
workers in the labor force of the future. 66 132

gwam 3' | 1 | 2 | 3 | 4 |

UNIT 37

LESSONS 145–147

Preparing for Assessment

LESSON 145 PREPARE TO ASSESS CORRESPONDENCE PROCESSING SKILL

Objective:
To prepare for assessment of the use of Mail Merge to process letters and mailing labels.

145A • 5' Conditioning Practice

Key each line twice SS; then key 30" writings on line 1; determine *gwam*.

alphabet 1 Zelda will judge quickly and pay them for excellent book reviews.
fig/sym 2 A loan (#3270-5) was made on 5/14/97 for $68,000 at a rate of 7%.
speed 3 The official paid the men for the handiwork they did on the dock.

gwam 1' | 1 | 2 | 3 | 4 | 5 | 6 | 7 | 8 | 9 | 10 | 11 | 12 | 13 |

145B • 45' Correspondence

Document 1 (Create Data Source File)

1. Create a data source file for the records at the right. Use initial caps and punctuation as needed in each address.
2. Sort alphabetically by last name, then first name.

 **Save as:** *L145B1*

Jodi Duerr Box 1099 Twain Harte, CA 95383-1099	Miguel Rugeirio 18803 S. Alfred St. Cerritos, CA 90701-0230
Scott Letwin 3209 Synder Ave. Modesto, CA 95356-0145	Gina Mysliwiec 28881 Aloma Ave. Laguna Niguel, CA 92677-1406
Denise Ehrhardt 23633 Real Ct. Valencia, CA 91355-2125	William Joyce 6022 Poplar St. Weldon, CA 93283-6022
Beverly Erickson 38-381 Desert Green Dr. Palm Desert, CA 92260-1009	Lori Rugeirio 18803 S. Alfred St. Cerritos, CA 90701-0230

Document 2 (Change Data Source File)

1. Open file *L145B1*.
2. Add a **Title** field, add the four records at the right, and delete the Joyce record.
3. Add the titles for the other records as given at the lower right.
4. Sort alphabetically by last name, then first name.

 **Save as:** *L145B2*

Mrs. Patricia Medich 1640 Fountain Springs Cir. Danville, CA 94526-5635	Mr. Mitchell Lacey 284 Turf Paradise Rancho Mirage, CA 92270-2847
Mrs. Ruth Flynn 6214 Rosalind Ave. El Cerrito, CA 94530-2682	Mr. Charles Oates 9922 Cedar Ave. Bloomington, CA 92316-1850

LastName	Title	LastName	Title
Duerr	Mrs.	Mysliwiec	Mrs.
Ehrhardt	Ms.	Rugeirio, Lori	Mrs.
Erickson	Ms.	Rugeirio, Miguel	Mr.
Letwin	Mr.		

LESSON 54 IMPROVE KEYING TECHNIQUE

Objectives:

1. To improve keying techniques.
2. To improve keying speed and control.

54A • 5' Conditioning Practice

Key each line twice SS; then key a 1' writing on line 3; determine *gwam*.

alphabet 1 Carl asked to be given just a week to reply to the tax quiz form.

figures 2 Rooms 268 and 397 were cleaned for the 10:45 meetings last night.

speed 3 Vivian burns wood and a small bit of coal to make an ample flame.

gwam 1' | 1 | 2 | 3 | 4 | 5 | 6 | 7 | 8 | 9 | 10 | 11 | 12 | 13 |

SKILL BUILDING

54B • 10' Technique: Letter Keys

1. Key lines 1-6 twice.
2. Take two 30" writings on line 7. If you complete the line, begin again.
3. Repeat Step 2 for lines 8 and 9.

Note: Each word in this drill is among the 600 most-used words in the English language. Increase your keying rate by practicing them frequently.

One-hand words of 2-5 letters

1 no you was in we my be him are up as on get you only set see rate

2 few area no free you best date far tax case act fact water act on

3 card upon you few ever only fact after act state great as get see

4 you were | set rate | we are | at no | on you | at my best | get set | you were

5 as few | you set a date | my card | water tax | act on a | tax date | in case

6 my only date | water rate | my tax case | tax fact | my best date | my card

7 No, you are free only after I act on a rate on a state water tax.

8 Get him my extra database only after you set up exact test dates.

9 You set my area tax rate after a great state case on a water tax.

gwam 1' | 1 | 2 | 3 | 4 | 5 | 6 | 7 | 8 | 9 | 10 | 11 | 12 | 13 |

SKILL BUILDING

54C • 8' Technique: Number Keys/Tab

1. Set tabs at 2" and at 4".
2. Key the copy at the right.
3. Key three 1' writings, trying to key additional text on each writing.

Concentrate on figure location; quick tab spacing; eyes on copy.

530 Parkside Ave.	938 Merrimac Dr.	912 Santiago Rd.
4028 Hyde Cr.	665 Harbor Rd.	230 Palmetto St.
4039 Hazelwood Dr.	386 Granville Dr.	931 Columbia St.
901 Doverplum Ter.	216 Eastgate Dr.	856 Somerset St.
941 Scarborough St.	205 Salisbury St.	423 Janeway Ct.
497 Brookview Ln.	930 Ryecroft St.	734 Leemont Ct.
901 Phelps Rd.	283 Berkshire Dr.	925 Lovell Dr.
475 Beaver Rd.	601 Stanford St.	65 Vermont St.

Skill Check

1. Key three 1' writings on each ¶; determine *gwam*. Count errors. If errors are 2 or fewer on any writing, goal is to increase speed by 1 or 2 words on next writing. If errors on any writing are more than 2, goal is control on next writing.
2. Key two 3' writings on ¶s 1–3 combined; determine *gwam* and count errors.
3. Key a 5' writing on ¶s 1–3 combined; determine *gwam* and count errors.

all letters used

	gwam 3'	5'	
You are nearing the end of your keyboarding classes. The	4	2	53
skill level you have attained is much better than that with which	8	5	55
you started when you were given keyboarding instruction for the	13	8	58
very first time. During the early phase of your training, you were	17	10	61
taught to key the letters of the alphabet and the figures by touch.	22	13	64
During the initial period of learning, the primary emphasis was	26	16	66
placed on your keying technique.	28	17	67
After learning to key the alphabet and figures, your next	32	19	70
job was to learn to format documents. The various types of	36	22	72
documents formatted included letters, tables, and manuscripts.	40	24	75
During this time of training, an emphasis also was placed on	44	27	77
increasing the rate at which you were able to key. Parts of the	49	29	80
lessons keyed at this time also were used to help you recognize the	53	32	82
value of and to improve language skills.	56	34	84
The final phase of your training dealt with increasing your	60	36	86
skill at producing documents of high quality at a rapid rate.	64	38	89
Directions were provided for keying special documents; drills	68	41	91
were given to build skill; and problems were provided to assess	72	43	94
your progress. You were also given a number of simulations to	77	46	96
allow you to apply what you had learned. Now you have a skill	81	49	99
that you will be able to use throughout your life.	84	51	101

gwam 3' | 1 | 2 | 3 | 4
5' | 1 | 2 | 3

SKILL BUILDING

54D • 12' Speed Forcing Drill

1. Key each line once at top speed.
2. Key two 15" timings on each line.

If you finish a line before time is called, start over. Your *gwam* is the figure at the end of the line PLUS the figure above or below the point at which you stopped.

Emphasis: high-frequency balanced-hand words

```
1 The man paid the girl to fix the auto turn signal.
2 Ellen bid for the antique chair and antique rifle.
3 Diana may make the title forms for big and small firms.
4 When did the auditor sign the audit forms for the city?
5 They kept the girls busy with the work down by the big lake.
6 Helen may go with us to the city to pay them for their work.
7 The man and I may dismantle the ancient ricksha in the big field.
8 Jay may suspend the men as a penalty for their work on the docks.
```

gwam 15" | 4 | 8 | 12 | 16 | 20 | 24 | 28 | 32 | 36 | 40 | 44 | 48 | 52

SKILL BUILDING

54E • 15' Skill Check

1. Take a 1' writing on ¶ 1; determine *gwam*.
2. Add 2–4 *gwam* to the rate attained in Step 1, and note quarter-minute checkpoints from the chart below.
3. Key two 1' guided writings on ¶ 1 to increase speed.
4. Practice ¶ 2 in the same way.
5. Take two 3' writings on ¶s 1 and 2 combined; determine *gwam* and find errors.

Quarter-Minute Checkpoints				
gwam	1/4'	1/2'	3/4'	1'
24	6	12	18	24
28	7	14	21	28
32	8	16	24	32
36	9	18	27	36
40	10	20	30	40
44	11	22	33	44
48	12	24	36	48
52	13	26	39	52
56	14	28	42	56
60	15	30	45	60

A all letters used

Text	gwam 3'	5'	
Something that you can never escape is your attitude. It	4	2	44
will be with you forever. However, you decide whether your	8	5	47
attitude is an asset or a liability for you. Your attitude	12	7	49
reflects the way you feel about the world you abide in and	16	9	52
everything that is a part of that world. It reflects the way you	20	12	54
feel about yourself, about your environment, and about other peo-	25	15	57
ple who are a part of your environment. Oftentimes, people with	29	17	59
a positive attitude are people who are extremely successful.	33	20	62
At times we all have experiences that cause us to be	36	22	64
negative. The difference between a positive and a negative per-	41	24	66
son is that the positive person rebounds very quickly from a bad	45	27	69
experience; the negative person does not. The positive person is	49	30	72
a person who usually looks to the bright side of things and	53	32	74
recognizes the world as a place of promise, hope, joy, excite-	58	35	77
ment, and purpose. A negative person generally has just the	62	37	79
opposite view of the world. Remember, others want to be around	66	40	82
those who are positive but tend to avoid those who are negative.	70	42	84

gwam 3' | 1 | 2 | 3 | 4
5' | 1 | 2 | 3

Job 15

From the desk of Audry Bates

Use the information at the right to prepare a draft of a program. Format the program on two pages, using 8.5" × 11" paper in landscape orientation. These two pages will be folded into a four-page program, with each page measuring 5½" × 8½".
AB

Save as: *L140JOB15A* (front and back covers) and *L140JOB15B* (inside pages)

Outside Back Cover

- *List names of the Class Officers*--Audry Chomas Bates, President; Blaine Check, Vice President; Gaynell Eastwood, Secretary; Paul Thompson, Treasurer; and Janice Bondi Aberle, Historian.
- *List names of Reunion Committee Members in alpha order*--Janice Bondi Aberle, Audry Chomas Bates, Fred Brydebell, Blaine Check, Gaynell Eastwood, Tom Stark, Helen Linton Ward, and Barbara Staffen Wills.

Outside Front Cover

- 25-Year Reunion
- Salk High School
- Class of 19--
- Saturday, August 15, 200-
- Highlands Country Club, Elizabeth, PA

Inside Left Page

- Insert the following poem

There are no friends like old friends,
And none so good and true;
We greet them when we meet them,
As the roses greet the dew:
No other friends are dearer,
Though born of kindred mold;
And while we prize the new ones,
We treasure more the old.

--David Bank Sickles

Inside Right Page

- Welcome to the 25-Year Reunion, Salk High School Class of 19--
- Program
  - Reception
  - Welcome . . . . Audry Chomas Bates, President
  - Invocation . . . . Louis Moore, Classmate
  - Dinner
  - Remarks . . . . Ronald Pimilo, Class Sponsor
  - Remarks . . . . Janice Bondi Aberle, Historian
  - Special Recognition . . . . Audry Chomas Bates
  - Door Prizes . . . . Barbara Staffen Wills, Classmate
  - Dancing to music provided by Music Selections

Communication Skills 7

ACTIVITY 1

Internal Punctuation: Comma

1. Key lines 1–10 at the right, supplying the needed commas.
2. Check the accuracy of your work with the instructor; correct any errors you made.
3. Note the rule number at the left of each sentence in which you made a comma error.
4. Using the rules below the sentences and on p. 157, identify the rule(s) you need to review/practice.
5. **Read**: Study each rule.
6. **Learn**: Key the Learn line(s) beneath it, noting how the rule is applied.
7. **Apply**: Key the Apply line(s), adding commas as needed.

 **Save as:** *CS7-ACT1*

Proofread & Correct

Rules		
1	1	My favorite sports are college football basketball and soccer.
1	2	If you finish your report before noon please give me a call.
1,2	3	I snacked on milk and cookies granola and some raisins.
3	4	Miss Qwan said "I was born in Taipei, Taiwan."
4	5	Mr. Sheldon the owner will speak to our managers today.
5	6	Why do you persist Kermit in moving your hands to the top row?
6	7	The report which Ted wrote is well organized and informative.
6	8	Only students who use their time wisely are likely to succeed.
3	9	Dr. Sachs said "Take two of these and call me in the morning."
6	10	Yolanda who is from Cuba intends to become a U.S. citizen.

Internal Punctuation: Comma

Rule 1: Use a comma after (a) introductory phrases or clauses and (b) words in a series.

Learn 1 When you finish keying the report, please give it to Mr. Kent.
Learn 2 We will play the Mets, Expos, and Cubs in our next home stand.
Apply 3 If you attend the play take Mary Jack and Tim with you.
Apply 4 The last exam covered memos simple tables and unbound reports.

Rule 2: Do not use a comma to separate two items treated as a single unit within a series.

Learn 5 Her favorite breakfast was bacon and eggs, muffins, and juice.
Apply 6 My choices are peaches and cream brownies or ice cream.
Apply 7 Trays of fresh fruit nuts and cheese and crackers awaited guests.

Rule 3: Use a comma before short direct quotations.

Learn 8 The man asked, "When does Flight 787 depart?"
Apply 9 Mrs. Ramirez replied "No, the report is not finished."
Apply 10 Dr. Feit said "Please make an appointment for next week."

Rule 4: Use a comma before and after a word or words in apposition (words that come together and refer to the same person or thing).

Learn 11 Coleta, the assistant manager, will chair the next meeting.
Apply 12 Greg Mathews a pitcher for the Braves will sign autographs.
Apply 13 The personnel director Marge Wilson will be the presenter.

Rule 5: Use a comma to set off words of direct address (the name of a person spoken to).

Learn 14 I believe, Tom, that you should fly to San Francisco.
Apply 15 Finish this assignment Mary before you start on the next one.
Apply 16 Please call me Erika if I can be of further assistance.

(continued on next page)

Job 14, cont.

From the desk of Audry Bates

At the end of the newsletter, place a reservation form similar to one that we used in the flyer (L140JOB7). Format the form so it spans the width of the page. Add a text box above the form stating the cost per person, how to write the check, and where to send the check.

It doesn't matter where the form ends right now because we'll be moving it later when we add more articles to the newsletter.

AB

Save as: *L140JOB14*

From the desk of Audry Bates

I just received some more information for the newsletter. Open CD-L140JOB14 and insert the text after the paragraph about Ruth Young Todd.

AB

Save as: *L140JOB14*

Want to serve on a committee? Call Janice Bondi Aberle at 412.555.0189 or e-mail her at aberle@starnet.com.

Early Responses from Classmates

Curtis Large and his wife, Becky, have three children--John, Christina, and Harrison. Curtis was graduated from Great Western University after going to Robbins College for two years. He is an environmental engineer, and his primary hobby is restoring vintage cars, especially Corvettes.

Lawanda White Thompson and her husband, Jim, have two daughters--Jamie and Kelly--and one cat (Sir Kidd). She was graduated from the Latrobe School of Nursing and is an RN working in the Pulmonary Disease Department at McKeesport Hospital. She teaches a Mother's Support Group at the local YWCA. Lawanda is an avid gardener who specializes in roses.

Ruth Young Todd is married to Gary. She earned a B.A. degree in Psychology and an M.A. degree in Special Education from Harrison University. She was a special education teacher at Midway Elementary for five years. She retired when the third of her four children (Eric, Donna, George, and Janice) arrived. Her hobbies include nutrition, aerobics, Special Olympics, and gardening.

Check out http://www.salkalumni.org to see who is coming to the reunion and how to get good deals at local hotels.

Lost Classmates

If you know the whereabouts of any of these classmates, please contact Audry Chomas Bates at 412.555.0113 or bates@newlink.net:

Thelma Gillie Cherepko
Delores Miller Martini
Thomas Williams, Jr.
Jim Wythe

Check out http://www.salkalumni.org to find out how you can sign up for the August 14 golf outing, 5K walk, or tennis matches.

Rule 6: Use a comma to set off nonrestrictive clauses (not necessary to the meaning of the sentence); however, do not use commas to set off restrictive clauses (necessary to the meaning of the sentence).

Learn 17 The manuscript, which I prepared, needs to be revised.
Learn 18 The manuscript that presents banking alternatives is complete.
Apply 19 The movie which won top awards dealt with human rights.
Apply 20 The student who scores highest on the exam will win the award.

ACTIVITY 2

Reading

1. Open the file *CD-CS7READ* and read the document carefully.
2. Close the file.
3. Key the answers to the questions at the right.
4. Check the accuracy of your work with the instructor; correct any errors you made.

Save as: *CS7-ACT2*

1. What was the final score of yesterday's soccer match?
2. Was the winning goal scored in the first or second half?
3. Will last year's City League champion be playing in this year's championship match?
4. Will the top-ranked team in the state be playing in this year's championship match?
5. Will the top-ranked team in the city be playing in the championship match?
6. Is the championship game to be played during the day or in the evening?
7. Has one or both of the teams playing in the championship match won a City League championship before?

ACTIVITY 3

Composing

1. Key the paragraph, correcting the word-choice errors it contains. (Every line contains at least one error; some lines contain two or more errors.)
2. Check the accuracy of your work with the instructor; correct any errors you made.
3. Compose a second paragraph to accomplish these goals:
   - Define what *respect* means to you.
   - Identify kinds of behavior that help one earn respect.
   - Identify kinds of behavior that cause the loss of respect.

Save as: *CS7-ACT3*

That all individuals want others too respect them is not surprising. What is surprising is that sum people think their do respect even when there own behavior has been unacceptable or even illegal. Key two the issue is that we respect others *because* of certain behavior, rather then in spite of it. Its vital, than, to no that what people due and say determines the level of respect there given buy others. In that regard, than, respect has to be earned; its not hour unquestioned right to demand it. All of you hear and now should begin to chose behaviors that will led others to respect you. Its you're choice.

Job 12

From the desk of
Audry Bates

Please design a worksheet to record reservations and then enter the ones at the right. Make the worksheet attractive by using different font sizes, colors, and shading. Add an appropriate title. Sort the worksheet alphabetically by last name.

AB

Save as: *L140JOB12*

First	Maiden	Last	Spouse	Guest	Check No.	Amount Paid
Tom		Stange			3275	$30
Janice	Bondi	Aberle	David		2361	$60
Audry	Chomas	Bates	Tom		3571	$60
Blaine		Check	Karen		564	$60
Gaynell		Eastwood		Jerry	116	$60
Louis		Moore			783	$30
Ruth	Young	Todd			2430	$30
Helen	Linton	Ward	Bill		457	$60
Bill		Achtzhen		Mary	587	$60
Guy		Dolata	Jill		7889	$60
Jackie		Thomas		Gary	543	$60

Job 13

From the desk of
Audry Bates

I want to display some charts on a bulletin board at the reunion. Prepare worksheets and then charts for the information at the right. Make a pie chart for WHERE WE LIVE *and a bar chart for the other.*

AB

WHERE WE LIVE

Location	Number
Elizabeth Area	45
Other Pennsylvania	3
Other States	30

Save as: *L140JOB13A*

GROWTH AT SALK HIGH

	Our Seniors	Last Year's Seniors
Boys	33	65
Girls	45	78
Total	78	143

Save as: *L140JOB13B*

Job 14

From the desk of
Audry Bates

I want to begin work on the newsletter that we will send out in May.

Have the title at the right span the width of the page; then key the copy at the right in two equal columns under the title, separated by a vertical line. Design the format, using a default style for the article headings. Then give it to me to proofread. This is a lengthy document, so remember to save your file often.

AB

Save as: *L140JOB14*

SALK HIGH SCHOOL

CLASS OF 19-- NEWSLETTER

Volume 1 May 200-

25th Reunion--An Update

Our 25th reunion will be held on August 15, 200-, at the Highlands Country Club. A "pay-as-you go" reception will begin at 6:30 p.m., and dinner will be served at 7:30 p.m. Music and dancing will be from 8:30 p.m. to 1 a.m.

More than 60 people have already made reservations, and we are expecting to have about a hundred people in attendance. Mr. Ronald Pimilo, our class sponsor at Salk High, and his wife, Carole, will join us for the evening.

If you have not made reservations, please do so soon. Whether you are able to attend or not, be sure to send us information about you and your family that we can include in the directory that will be printed. Let us know about your job, spouse or that someone special in your life, children (and grandchildren), hobbies, vacations, etc.

(continued on next page)

WORD PROCESSING 7

ACTIVITY 1

Insert Date, AutoComplete

1. Read the copy at the right.
2. Learn the Insert Date and Automatic Completion (AutoComplete) features of your wp software.
3. Key the information at the right using the Insert Date and AutoComplete features as indicated. If AutoComplete is not available with your software, use the Insert Date feature in place of it.

Save as: *WP7ACT1*

Use the **Insert Date** feature to enter the date into a document automatically. Some software has an Update Automatically option along with Insert Date. When the Update option is used, the date is inserted as a date *field*. Each time the document is opened or printed, the current date replaces the previous date. The date on your computer must be current to insert the correct date in a document.

Some software provides an **Automatic Completion** (**AutoComplete**) feature, which also inserts the date automatically. When you start keying the month, AutoComplete *recognizes* the word and shows it in a tip box above the insertion point. By pressing the ENTER key, you enter the remainder of the month automatically, without keying it. When you press the Space Bar, the tip box shows the complete date. Striking the ENTER key enters the date.

Part I

<Insert Date>

Mr. Sean McCarthy
633 Country Club Dr.
Largo, FL 34641-5639

<Insert hard page break>

Part II

<Insert Date Field, Update Automatically>

Ms. Brittany Garcia
2130 Mt. Pleasant Dr.
Bridgeport, CT 06611-2301

<Insert hard page break>

Part III

1. Today is <AutoComplete>.
2. Your balance as of <Insert Date Field, Update Automatically> is $42.83.
3. I received your check today, <Insert Date>.
4. You will need to make sure that today's date, <Insert Date Field, Update Automatically>, is included on the form.

ACTIVITY 2

Navigate a Document

1. Read the copy at the right.
2. Learn to move the insertion point using Home, End, PageUp, PageDown, and Ctrl + arrow keys.
3. Key Sentence 1; edit as instructed in Sentences 2, 3, and 4, using *only* the insertion point move keys to navigate.

Save as: *WP7ACT2*

The **Home**, **End**, **PageUp**, and **PageDown** keys can be used to *navigate* (move the insertion point quickly from one location to another) in a document.

The **CTRL** key in combination with the arrow keys can also be used to move the insertion point to various locations.

1. Key the following sentence.

   The basketball game is on Friday.

2. Make the following changes, using the insertion point move keys to navigate.

   The [insert: next] *basketball game is on Friday*[insert: , February 20.]

3. Make these additional changes, using the insertion point move keys to navigate.

   The next [insert: varsity] *basketball game is on Friday, February 20*[insert: , at 7 p.m.]

4. Make these changes.

   The next varsity basketball game is on ~~*Friday,*~~ [insert: Saturday] *February 20, at 7 p.m.* [insert: against Sundance.]

Job 10

From the desk of Audry Bates

Open SALKALUM_DS5 *and convert case to title case in all fields except State and PostalCode. Save this file as* SALKALUM_DS10.

Key the letter at the right and merge it with the addresses of the classmates in file SALKALUM_DS10 *who live in Elizabeth or McKeesport, PA. Save the letter main document as* L140JOB10_MD *and the merged letters as* L140JOB10_LTRS.

Proofread the merged fields in each letter, and make any necessary corrections. Print the first two letters.

Generate a set of mailing labels for these letters. Use the USPS ALL CAPS, *no punctuation style. Save the label main document as* L140JOB10LBLS_MD *and the labels as* L140JOB10_LBLS.

AB

March 5, 200-

<<Title>>. <<Firstname>> <<Lastname>>
<<Address1>>
<<City>>, <<State>> <<PostalCode>>

Dear <<Firstname>>:

As you may have learned, the Salk High School Class of 19-- is having its 25-year reunion on August 15, 200-, at the Highlands Country Club.

Presently, the Class Officers who still live in the area are organizing the event, but your help is needed. Will you serve on a committee? Help is needed with registration, gathering door prizes from neighborhood businesses, and table decorations.

<<Firstname>>, please give Janice Bondi Aberle (412.555.0189), Blaine Check (412.555.0102), Gaynell Eastwood (412.555.0172), or me (412.555.0113) a call to let us know the committee to which you want to be assigned.

Since this is such a major milestone in our lives, we expect a large turnout for the reunion. I hope we can count on you.

Sincerely,

Audry Chomas Bates, Chair
Reunion Committee

xx

Job 11

From the desk of Audry Bates

Mrs. Aberle has found a DJ for the reunion, and I need to send a confirmation letter on our letterhead and a $100 deposit. Address the letter to:

Attention Business Manager
Music Selections
2539 Rose Garden Rd.
Pittsburgh, PA 15220-1880

Add CLASS OF 19-- REUNION COMMITTEE *as a company name in the closing lines.*

AB

Save as: *L140JOB11*

April 5, 200-

Ladies and Gentlemen

CONTRACT FOR SERVICES

This letter confirms that Salk High School's Class of 19-- will employ one of your disc jockeys to play music at our 25th reunion on August 15, 200-.

The reunion will be held at Highlands Country Club, 619 Walker Road, Elizabeth, PA. You are to provide music from 8:30 p.m. until 1 a.m. for $300. The enclosed $100 check is the deposit required to reserve your services. The $200 balance will be paid at the end of the evening's activities.

If you have any questions or need additional information, call me at 412.555.0113. Thank you.

Sincerely
Audry Chomas Bates, Chair

xx
Enclosure

ACTIVITY 3

Macro

1. Read the copy at the right. Learn to use the Macro feature.
2. Define a macro for ***The state capital of***.
3. Key each sentence at the right, inserting the macro for the repeated text.

 **Save as:** *WP7ACT3*

The **Macro** feature of a software package allows the operator to save (record) keystrokes and/or commands for retrieval (playback) later. A macro can be as simple as a few words, such as a company name, or as complex as the commands to create a table that will be used over and over. By eliminating repetitive keying and formatting, a macro saves time.

1. **The state capital of** Alaska is Juneau.
2. **The state capital of** Arizona is Phoenix.
3. **The state capital of** Colorado is Denver.
4. **The state capital of** Delaware is Dover.
5. **The state capital of** Florida is Tallahassee.
6. **The state capital of** Hawaii is Honolulu.

ACTIVITY 4

Reinforce Use of Macro

1. Use the Macro feature to record the table shell at the right.
2. In a new file, use the Macro feature to insert (playback) the table shell. In the shell, key the data shown in Table 1.

Note:

Striking the TAB key after keying the first data row will automatically insert a new row below it.

 **Save as:** *WP7ACT4-1*

3. In a new file, use the Macro feature to insert a table shell. Key the data for Table 2 at the right.

 **Save as:** *WP7ACT4-2*

4. In a new file, use the Macro feature to insert a table shell. Key the data for Table 3 at the right.

 **Save as:** *WP7ACT4-3*

Table Shell

KNOW YOUR STATES		
State	Capital	Flower

Table 1

KNOW YOUR STATES		
State	Capital	Flower
Arkansas	Little Rock	Apple Blossom
Louisiana	Baton Rouge	Magnolia
New Hampshire	Concord	Purple Lilac
New York	Albany	Rose

Table 2

KNOW YOUR STATES		
State	Capital	Flower
California	Sacramento	Golden Poppy
Iowa	Des Moines	Wild Rose
New Jersey	Trenton	Purple Violet
Texas	Austin	Bluebonnet

Table 3

KNOW YOUR STATES		
State	Capital	Flower
Connecticut	Hartford	Mountain Laurel
Georgia	Atlanta	Cherokee Rose
North Carolina	Raleigh	Dogwood
Oregon	Salem	Oregon Grape

Job 7

From the desk of Audry Bates

Here is information to use in a one-page flyer that we are going to mail to our classmates. Please arrange it attractively using appropriate colors and graphics. Add a note for classmates to send information about themselves—their families, work, vacations, etc., to be included in an alumni directory.

AB

Save as: *L140JOB7*

Job 8

From the desk of Audry Bates

Prepare this news release. Use the information at the top of the news release to design a letterhead. Size and position it so it will fit within the 2" top margin. Make sure you keep the letterhead for later use.

AB

Save as: *LETTERHEAD* and *L140JOB8* (news release)

Job 9

From the desk of Audry Bates

Here's the letter inviting the class sponsor. Use our letterhead; use March 1 as the date; and address it to ***Mr. Ronald Pimilo, 780 Peairs Rd., Elizabeth, PA 15037-5779****. Key my name and title as* ***Audry Thomas Bates, Chair, Reunion Committee****.*

AB

Save as: *L140JOB9*

What: 25th Reunion for Salk High School Class of 19--

Who: For classmates and their spouses or guests

When: August 15, 200-; 6:30 p.m. reception; 7:30 p.m. dinner; 8:30 p.m. to 1 a.m. dancing and conversation

Where: Highlands Country Club

Cost: $30 per person (reception on cash basis) payable to 19-- Class Reunion

Reservations: Full payment must be received by June 15

Reply form: Name (First, Last, and Maiden, if applicable)
Address (Street, City, State, and ZIP)
E-mail Address, Telephone Number, and Fax Number
Name of spouse/guest

Reply to: Blaine Check, 922 Grant St., Elizabeth, PA 15037-6390

Additional Information: Visit http://www.salkalumni.org for up-to-date reunion information.

Salk High School Class of 19-- 25th Reunion Committee

3393 Long Hollow Rd. Elizabeth, PA 15037-9823 412.555.0113

News Release For Release: Upon Receipt

Contact: Audry Bates

ELIZABETH, PA, March 1, 200-. The 25th reunion for the Salk High School Class of 19-- will be held August 15, 200-, at the Highlands Country Club at 6:30 p.m. The cost is $30 per person, and all classmates are urged to attend with their spouses or guests. Reservations can be made by sending a check payable to "19-- Class Reunion" to Blaine Check at 922 Grant St., Elizabeth, PA 15037-6390.

For further information, access the Reunion Postings on the Salk High School Alumni Association's Web page at http://www.salkalumni.org. ###

The Salk High School Class of 19-- is holding its 25th reunion on August 15, 200-, at 6:30 p.m. at the Highlands Country Club, and the Reunion Committee wants you and your wife, Carole, to be our guests for the evening.

We expect to have a great turnout of classmates for this major milestone in our lives. As our class sponsor for four years, you have had the opportunity to know us very well as we worked on our various fundraisers and activities like the Junior Prom and Senior Day.

I will telephone you within a few days to see if you will be able to attend and to give you more details.

P.S. Gene Aiken and Fred Brydebell have said that if you don't come, they're not coming! I'm sure others feel the same way!

UNIT 17

LESSONS 55–59

Improving Letter Formatting Skills

Format Guides: Business Letter, Block Style

GREGG G. ELWAY

Business Letter with Attention Line

Business Letter with Address in USPS Style

Business Letter (Page 2) with Second-Page Heading

In Unit 9 you learned to format personal-business letters. In this unit you will learn to format business letters. The only difference between the two is that a business letter is almost always printed on letterhead that includes the return address. Therefore, the return address does not need to be keyed.

Special Parts of Business Letters

In addition to the basic letter parts, business letters may include the special letter parts described below.

Attention line. An attention line should be used only when the writer does not know the name of the person who should receive the letter. For example, if a writer wants a letter to go to the director of special collections of a library but doesn't know the name of that person, *Attention Special Collections Director* or *Attention Director of Special Collections* could be used. When an attention line is used in a letter addressed to a company, key it as the first line of the letter and envelope addresses. When using an attention line, the correct salutation is *Ladies and Gentlemen*.

Subject line. The subject line specifies the topic discussed in the letter. Key the subject line in ALL CAPS, a DS below the salutation.

Reference initials. If someone other than the originator of the letter keys it, key the keyboard operator's initials in lowercase letters at the left margin a DS below the writer's name, title, or department.

Attachment/Enclosure notation. If another document is clipped or stapled to a letter, the word "Attachment" is keyed at the left margin a DS below the reference initials. If another document is included but not attached, the word "Enclosure" is used. If reference initials are not used, *Attachment* or *Enclosure* is keyed a DS below the writer's name.

Copy notation. A copy notation indicates that a copy of a letter is being sent to someone other than the addressee. Use "c" followed by the name of the person(s) to receive a copy. Place a copy notation a DS below the enclosure notation or the reference initials if there is no enclosure:

```
c Hector Ramirez
  Ursula O'Donohue
```

Blind copy notation. When a copy of a letter is to be sent to someone without disclosing to the addressee of the letter, a blind copy (bc) notation is used. When used, *bc* and the name of the person receiving the blind copy are keyed at the left margin a DS below the last letter part on all copies of the letter *except* the original.

```
bc Arlyn Hunter
   Miguel Rodriguez
```

USPS Letter Address Style

The letter address for any letter format may be keyed in uppercase and lowercase letters, or it may be keyed in ALL CAPS with no punctuation (USPS style). See illustration at left.

Second-Page Heading

Occasionally, a letter (or memo) will be longer than one page. Only p. 1 is keyed on letterhead; all additional pages should be keyed on plain paper with a second-page heading. Key the heading 1" from the top of the page SS in block format at the left margin. Include the name of the addressee, the page number, and the date. DS below the date before continuing the letter. See illustration at left.

Job 6

From the desk of Audry Bates

Here are the minutes that Gaynell Eastwood wrote at the 2/23 meeting. Please key and format them.
AB

Save as: *L140JOB6*

CLASS OF 19-- REUNION COMMITTEE MEETING

February 23, 200-

Participants: Audrey Bates, Chair; Janice Aberle; Blaine Check; Gaynell Eastwood

1. The meeting was called to order at 9:10 a.m.
2. The reunion was set for Saturday, August 15, 200-, from 6:30 p.m. to 1 a.m. at the Highlands Country Club.
3. These dates and major activities were established:
   - On February 25, Audrey will place a $100 deposit at Highlands Country Club to reserve the facilities.
   - Audrey and Blaine will prepare and send first mailing by March 31.
   - Janice will select a DJ by April 30.
   - Gaynell will print tickets and order decoration material and supplies by June 30.
   - Audrey and Blaine will prepare and make second mailing by June 30.
4. The budget was approved. It projects revenues of $3,000 from 100 people, each paying $30. (Refreshments at the reception are not included in the $30.) Expenses are projected to be $2,810. If there is an excess of revenue over expenses, the amount will be donated to the Salk High School Alumni Association.
5. The members submitted their updated address lists; and after a lengthy discussion, it was decided that the revised data source table would be used for the first mailing.
6. Mr. Ronald Pimilo, sponsor for the Class of 19--, and his wife will be invited to attend the reunion as our guests.
7. Gaynell Eastwood will gather information and have it posted on the Salk High School Alumni Association's Web page.
8. Blaine Check will provide the copy for the announcement that will be sent as the first mailing. It should refer classmates to the Salk High Alumni Association's Web page for up-to-date reunion information. The reply form should capture e-mail addresses, fax numbers, and maiden names, in addition to the usual information.
9. The next meeting is set for March 28 at 9 a.m. at Mike's Restaurant. Each member is to make an oral progress report.

LESSON 55 REVIEW PERSONAL-BUSINESS LETTER FORMAT

Objectives:

1. To review personal-business letter format.
2. To improve language skills.

55A • 5' Conditioning Practice

Key each line twice SS; then key a 1' writing on line 3; determine *gwam*.

alphabet 1 A man in the park saw a fat lizard quickly devour six juicy bugs.

figures 2 Please revise pages 360, 492, and 578 for the August 21 deadline.

speed 3 Eight girls may sit with the maid in the wheelchair by the docks.

gwam 1' | 1 | 2 | 3 | 4 | 5 | 6 | 7 | 8 | 9 | 10 | 11 | 12 | 13 |

FORMATTING

55B • 37' Personal-Business Letters

Letter 1

Review the model personal-business letter on p. 83. Key in block format the letter shown at the right. Use the return address, date, and letter address shown below. Supply an appropriate salutation and complimentary closing. The letter is from **Suzanne E. Salmon, History Student**. Include a blind copy notation to your instructor.

Return address and date:

1116 Tiffany St.
Bronx, NY 10459-2276
May 3, 200-

Letter address:

Mr. Mitchell R. Clevenger
325 Manhattan Ave.
New York, NY 10025-3827

 **Save as:** *LTR55B1*

For one of the assignments in my U.S. history class, I have to interview a person who is knowledgeable about an event included in our history book. It didn't take long for me to decide whom I was going to contact.

Who better to talk about ***Operation Desert Storm*** than a newsperson assigned to the region to cover the news during this period? Would you be willing to meet with me for about an hour to discuss the Persian Gulf War? I would like to learn more about the following topics:

- The events that led up to the confrontation
- The confrontation
- The impact on the people of Iraq
- The impact on the environment in the region
- The role of General Colin Powell, Chairman of the Joint Chiefs of Staff
- The role of General Norman Schwarzkopf, U.S. Field Commander

Of course, if there are other things you would like to discuss to help me describe this event to the class, I would appreciate your sharing those topics with me also. I will call you next week to see if you will be available to meet with me.

Letter 2

Key in block format the letter shown at the right. Use the return address and date given below. Supply an appropriate complimentary closing for the letter from **Mitchell Clevenger, Reporter**.

Return address and date:

325 Manhattan Ave.
New York, NY 10025-3827
May 7, 200-

 **Save as:** *LTR55B2*

Ms. Suzanne E. Salmon | 1116 Tiffany St. | Bronx, NY 10459-2276 | Dear Ms. Salmon

I would be more than happy to meet with you to discuss my experiences during my assignment in the Persian Gulf region. It was one of the most, if not the most, exciting assignments I've worked on. The night the attack on Baghdad began will be with me for the rest of my life.

Also I will share with you the events in Kuwait that precipitated the war and the war's impact on the Kurd and Shi'ite refugees.

Please call me at 212-183-8211 so we can arrange a time and location to meet. I'm looking forward to meeting you.

Job 3

From the desk of Audry Bates

Here's a budget that I need for the 2/23 meeting. Make it colorful by using different font colors and shading. Make the title larger than the headings and the headings larger than the worksheet entries. Compute the horizontal and vertical totals. Compute the cash on hand by adding the cash on hand at the end of each month to the next month's revenues, and then subtracting the month's expenses.

AB

Save as: *L140JOB3*

CLASS OF 19-- REUNION BUDGET								
	February	**March**	**April**	**May**	**June**	**July**	**August**	**Total**
Revenue								
$30/person	$240	$120	$240	$450	$450	$750	$750	
Expenses								
Food	$100						$1,850	
DJ			$100				$200	
Tickets					$25			
Decorations					$75	$75		
Door Prizes						$100		
Flyers		$40			$40			
Paper	$10				$25			
Labels	$30							
Name Badges							$30	
Postage		$30			$30			
Sponsor							$50	
Total Expenses								
Cash on Hand								

Job 4

From the desk of Audry Bates

Format and key this agenda for the 2/23 meeting.

AB

Save as: *L140JOB4*

Proofreading Alert
The copy contains three errors; find and correct them as you process the agenda.

CLASS OF 19-- REUNION COMMITTEE MEETING

February 23, 200-, 9 a.m.

Third Street Diner

1. *Call meating to order.*
2. *Confirm reunion date, time, and place.*
3. *Establish time line for activities.*
4. *Review and approve budget.*
5. *Finalise data source table.*
6. *Establish next meeting date and ajourn.*

Job 5

From the desk of Audry Bates

Here are the missing addresses, plus a couple that will replace those in our data source table. Update SALKALUM_DS2 *and sort it in alpha order.*

AB

Save as: *SALKALUM_DS5*

Last Name	Address1	City	State	Postal Code
Amos	1374 Foxwood Dr	Monroeville	PA	15146-4522
Brydebell	6229 Smithfield St	Boston	PA	15135-8873
Dale	602 Elizabeth Ave	Elizabeth	PA	15037-1956
Dyer	631 Mildred Ave	Glen Ellyn	IL	60137-2061
Malady	4265 Quick Rd	Holly	MI	48442-4016
Nundini	4513 Orangewood Ln	Bowie	MD	20715-1160
Pascoe	636 Highland Ave	Half Moon Bay	CA	94019-6339
Stange	RD 3 Box 258-A	Monongahela	PA	15063-2593
Tepe	332 Bailey Rd	Lordstown	OH	44481-0635
Todd	734 Holly Hills Dr	Biloxi	MS	39532-7337
Zezeck	5835 Garden Oak	Memphis	TN	38210-1920

55C • 8' Language Skills: Word Choice

1. Study the spelling/definitions of these words.
2. For each set of sentences, key the Learn line; then the Apply lines. Choose the correct word in parentheses.
3. Check your work; rekey lines containing word-choice errors.

Save as: *CHOICE55C*

to (prep/adj) used to indicate action, relation, distance, direction
too (adv) besides; also; to excessive degree
two (pron/adj) one plus one in number

cents (n) specified portion of a dollar
sense (n/vb) meaning intended or conveyed; perceive by sense organs; ability to judge
since (adv/conj) after a definite time in the past; in view of the fact; because

Learn 1 If you are going **to** either of the **two** plays, I would like to go **too**.
Apply 2 (To, Too, Two) of the students are going (to, too, two) play on the team.
Apply 3 (To, Too, Two) much practice made the (to, too, two) players (to, too, two) tired.

Learn 1 **Since** I changed the dollars and **cents** columns, the figures make **sense**.
Apply 2 (Cents, Sense, Since) you bought the stock, it has gone up 77 (cents, sense, since).
Apply 3 The whole thing just doesn't make (cents, sense, since) to me.

LESSON 56 FORMAT BUSINESS LETTERS

Objectives:

1. To learn to format business letters.
2. To increase proficiency in keying opening and closing lines of letters.

56A • 5' Conditioning Practice

Key each line twice SS; then key a 1' writing on line 3; determine *gwam*.

alphabet 1 Zack just saw five prime quail and a big fox by the old railroad.
figures 2 Only 168 of the 573 seniors had voted by 12:40 on Friday, May 29.
speed 3 The heir to the endowment may work on the problems with the firm.

gwam 1'	1	2	3	4	5	6	7	8	9	10	11	12	13

56B • 15' Drill: Personal-Business Letter

1. Take a 3' writing on the letter to determine *gwam*.
2. Key two 1' writings on opening lines through first ¶ of letter. If you finish before time is called, QS and start over. Try to key four more words on the second writing.
3. Key two 1' writings on ¶ 3 through closing lines. If you finish before time is called, QS and start ¶ 3 again. Try to key four more words on the second writing.
4. Key another 3' writing on the letter. Try to increase *gwam* by 4–8 words over your rate in Step 1.

	words
622 Main St. | Moorcroft, WY 82721-7514 | January 5, 200-	11
Ms. Dorothy Shepard | P.O. Box 275 | Moorcroft, WY 82721-2342	22
Dear Ms. Shepard	26
Are you interested in serving on a planning committee for a women's	39
historical museum in Wyoming? The state's nickname (Equality State)	53
stems from the fact that Wyoming women were the first women in the	67
U.S. to achieve voting rights (1869).	74
Since then, many women have played an important part in shaping	87
the history of Wyoming. Are you aware that the first woman governor	101
in the U.S. came from Wyoming? Nellie Tayloe Ross became governor	114
of Wyoming in 1925.	119
Let's build a museum to recognize these women--a place for people to	132
reflect on events of the past and contemplate the future. I will call you	147
next week to see if you are willing to serve on the committee.	160
Sincerely | William P. Shea	165

SALK ALUMNI ASSOCIATION

Objectives:

1. To demonstrate your ability to integrate your knowledge and skills.
2. To demonstrate your ability to solve problems and make correct decisions.

140A–144A • 5' (daily) Conditioning Practice

Key each line twice SS; take 1' writings on lines 1–3 as time permits.

alphabet 1 Mary Jane quickly realized that the beautiful gown was expensive.

figures 2 After a 45-minute delay, Tour 8374 left from Gate 26 at 1:09 p.m.

speed 3 When I visit the man in a wheelchair, we may go to the town mall.

gwam 1' | 1 | 2 | 3 | 4 | 5 | 6 | 7 | 8 | 9 | 10 | 11 | 12 | 13 |

140B–144B • 45' (daily) Work Assignments

Job 1

From the desk of Audry Bates

I started to create a data source table, but I didn't get it finished. Will you add these classmates to it? Use ALL CAPS and no punctuation. The file that I started is named CD-SALKALUM_DS1. After you have added these names to the table, sort the file in alpha order.

AB

Save as: *SALKALUM_DS2*

Mr James Wythe 1401 Second Ave Beaver PA 15009-7667	Ms Mary O'Donnell Box 142 Bunola PA 15020-3210	Ms Louise Moore 6220 Smithfield St Boston PA 15135-1098
Mrs Sue Dainty Lewis 298 Mohawk Dr McKeesport PA 15135-8429	Mrs Janice Horn Juno State Rte 3, Box 280 DeLand FL 32720-2863	Ms Kimberly White 535 Lewis Run Rd Clairton PA 15025-1262
Mrs Jane Resh O'Hare 6320 Holsing St Boston PA 15135-4321	Mr Paul Thompson 813 Sunnydale Dr Streamwood IL 60107-2468	Ms Jackie Thomas 3305 Oakland Ave McKeesport PA 15135-7913
Mrs Tina Smith Gray 810 Golfview Dr McKeesport PA 15135-0641	Mrs Ann Toth Booth 4114 Faith Ct Arlington VA 22311-0934	Mr Harry Zadmik 1930 N Evans St McMinnville OR 97128-4800
Mr Martin Megela 1388 Fayette St Donora PA 15033-3974	Mr Tim Justin 111 Sandro St Indiana PA 15701-4085	Mrs Sandy Lutes May 2540 W Second St Brooklyn NY 11223-2863
Mr Paul Tagliari 600 Amberson Ave Pittsburgh PA 15232-9135	Mrs Ruth Young Todd 115 Ground Oaks Ln Chicora PA 16025-8024	Mrs Freda Rippel Ruby 37 Colonial Dr McKeesport PA 15135-5432

Job 2

From the desk of Audry Bates

E-mail this message to the other committee members. Send SALKALUM_DS2 as an attachment.

AB

Save as: *L140JOB2*

TO: aberle@starnet.com, check@hostnet.com, eastwood@galaxy.net

FROM: bates@newlink.net

Attachment: SALKALUM_DS2

SUBJECT: FEBRUARY 23, 200- MEETING

Please plan to attend the Saturday, 2/23/--, meeting at the Third Street Diner at 9 a.m. Among other things, we need to complete the database so we can send our first mailing soon. I suggest we each do an Internet search to verify that the information is current. Will each of you take about 20 names (Janice--A through C; Blaine--D through L; and Gaynell--M through S). I'll do the rest. If you cannot confirm that the address we have is current, please contact a friend or family member of the classmate to get the current address.

56C • 30' Business Letters

Letter 1

Format and key the text at the right as a business letter in block format. Use the USPS letter address style. Date the letter **February 20, 200-** and supply an appropriate salutation and complimentary closing. The letter is from **William P. Shea**. Don't forget the Enclosure notation.

Letter address:

MR AND MRS ERIC RUSSELL
PO BOX 215
MOORCROFT WY 82721-2152

Save as: *LTR56C1*

Wyoming women were the first women in the United States to have the right to vote (1869). Ester Morris of South Pass City became the first woman judge in 1870. Wyoming was the first state to elect a woman to state office when Estelle Reel was elected State Superintendent of Public Instruction in 1894. Nellie Tayloe Ross became the first female governor in the United States when she was elected governor of Wyoming in 1925.

It is time to honor women such as these for the roles they played in shaping Wyoming and U.S. history. A Wyoming Women's Historical Museum is being planned. With your help, the museum can become a reality.

Our community would benefit from the increased tourist activity. Thousands of tourists visit the nation's first national monument, Devil's Tower, each year. Since Moorcroft is only 30 miles from Devil's Tower, a museum would draw many of them to our city as they travel to and from the Tower.

National and state funds for the project are being solicited; however, additional funding from the private sector will be required. Please look over the enclosed brochure and join the Wyoming Women's Historical Museum Foundation by making a contribution.

Letter 2

Format and key the text at the right as a business letter in block format.

Save as: *LTR56C2*

August 10, 200- | Ms. Dorothy Shepard | P.O. Box 275 | Moorcroft, WY 82721-2342

Dear Ms. Shepard

GROUNDBREAKING CEREMONY

The planning committee is thrilled to announce the groundbreaking ceremony for the **Wyoming Women's Historical Museum:** Saturday, August 25.

As one who played an important role in reaching this milestone, you are invited to a luncheon before the ceremony. The luncheon will be held at the Mead House at 11:30. The groundbreaking will begin at 1:30.

The museum will be a source of great pride for Wyoming residents. Visitors will be reminded of the part Wyoming women played in the history of the state and nation.

Sincerely | William P. Shea | Committee Chair | xx

Letter 3

Format and key the letter in 56B as a personal-business letter in block format.

Save as: *LTR56C3*

LESSON 57 FORMAT BUSINESS LETTERS

Objectives:

1. To format business letters.
2. To increase straight-copy keying skill.

57A • 5' Conditioning Practice

Key each line twice SS; then key a 1' writing on line 3; determine *gwam*.

alphabet 1 A poor joke by the cowardly young boxers left David quite amazed.

figures 2 Pages 386-457 in Chapters 29 and 30 will be reviewed on April 12.

speed 3 I own both the antique bottle and the enamel bottle on the shelf.

gwam 1' | 1 | 2 | 3 | 4 | 5 | 6 | 7 | 8 | 9 | 10 | 11 | 12 | 13 |

UNIT 36

LESSONS 140–144

Salk Alumni Association: A Class Reunion Simulation

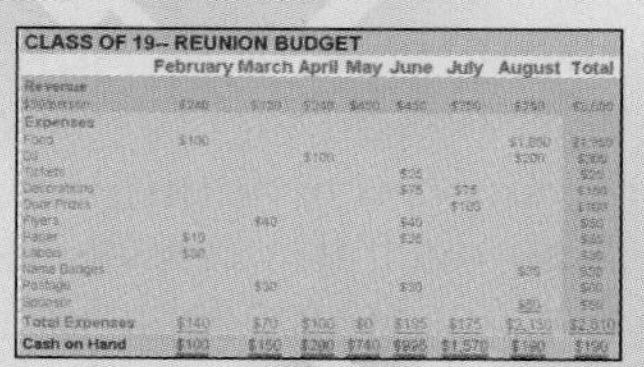

CLASS OF 19-- REUNION BUDGET	February	March	April	May	June	July	August	Total
Revenue								
[illegible]	[illegible]	[illegible]	[illegible]	[illegible]	[illegible]	[illegible]	[illegible]	[illegible]
Expenses								
Food	$100						$1,850	[illegible]
DJ			$100				$200	$300
Tickets					$25			$25
Decorations					$75	$75		$150
Door Prizes						$100		$100
Flyers		$40			$40			$80
Paper	$10				$25			$35
Labels	$30							$30
Name Badges							[illegible]	[illegible]
Postage		$30			$30			$60
[illegible]							[illegible]	[illegible]
Total Expenses	$140	$70	$100	$0	$195	$175	[illegible]	[illegible]
Cash on Hand	$100	$150	$290	$740	[illegible]	$1,570	$190	$190

Budget

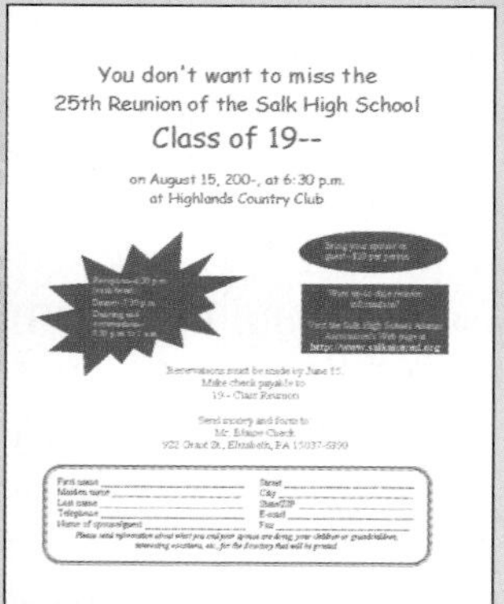

You don't want to miss the
25th Reunion of the Salk High School
Class of 19--

on August 15, 200-, at 6:30 p.m.
at Highlands Country Club

Reservations must be made by June 15.
Make check payable to
19-- Class Reunion

Send money and form to
Mr. Blaine Check

First name
Maiden name
Last name
Telephone
Street
City
State/ZIP
E-mail
Fax

Invitation

SALK HIGH SCHOOL
CLASS OF 19-- NEWSLETTER

25th Reunion—An Update

Early Responses from Classmates

Newsletter

Work Assignment

This unit is designed to give you experiences you likely would have working in an administrative specialist position.

Assume you are a student at Jonas E. Salk High School who is completing a service-learning requirement. You have been assigned to the Salk High School Alumni Association to help a committee organize a 25-year class reunion. You work directly for Mrs. Audry Bates, class president, who is chairing the reunion committee. Three other class officers who still reside in the area also serve on the committee. They are Mr. Blaine Check, Ms. Gaynell Eastwood, and Mrs. Janice Aberle.

As an administrative specialist, your main duty is to process the documents Mrs. Bates and the other committee members need for the reunion.

For the purposes of this simulation, assume that the class having the reunion was graduated 25 years before the current year, and use that year to identify the graduating class. For example, if the current year is 2001, the reunion is for the class of 1976.

You have completed an orientation program that focused on committee activities and goals, the kinds of documents you will prepare, and the hours you will work through the remainder of the school year. To help you further, Mrs. Bates has established the following guidelines for you.

General

1. You are to follow all directions that are given.
2. If a formatting guide or direction is not given, use what you have learned in this class to prepare the documents.
3. Always be alert to and correct errors in punctuation, capitalization, spelling, and word usage.

Correspondence

Prepare all letters in modified block format with mixed punctuation and paragraph indentations. Supply an appropriate salutation and complimentary close and use your reference initials.

Worksheets and Charts

Use spreadsheet software to prepare worksheets and charts. All worksheets and charts should have a title and column headings, and the columns should be as wide as the longest item in each column.

Data Source Table

You will help create a data source table of classmates' names and addresses to use for the mailings. Mrs. Bates will determine the fields that are to be included, and you will use word processing software to work with the table.

Mailing Labels

Use a standard mailing label that is 1" by 2.63", such as Avery 5160.

Filenames

Since Mrs. Bates and others may need to access the files, she will provide filenames for you to use.

57B • 33'
Business Letters

Key in block format the business letters shown at the right.

Letter 1

Date: **May 23, 200-**

Letter address:

Mr. Jamison Cooper
882 Elderberry Dr.
Fayetteville, NC 28311-0065

The letter is from **Susanne J. Warrens**, who is the **Program Chair**. Supply an appropriate salutation and complimentary closing. Send a copy of the letter to **Marsha Edinburgh, President**.

 **Save as:** *LTR57B1*

Letters 2 and 3

Date (Letter 2): **June 4, 200-**

Date (Letter 3): **June 10, 200-**

Letter address:

Ms. Susanne J. Warrens
Program Chair
8367 Brookstone Ct.
Raleigh, NC 27615-1661

The letters are from **Jamison R. Cooper,** who is a **Program Committee Member**. Supply an appropriate salutation and complimentary closing. Be sure to include an Enclosure notation on each letter.

 **Save as:** *LTR57B2* and *LTR57B3*

Last week at our meeting, you mentioned several individuals you thought would be excellent presenters for the opening and closing sessions of next year's convention. I accept your offer to contact them. When you contact them, please share with them the theme of our convention and determine what they would propose as an opening or closing session for our convention. Of course, we need to be concerned with the budget; please determine the fee they would charge.

The information will be needed before June 15 for our meeting. Your willingness to serve on this committee is greatly appreciated. I'll look forward to seeing you in a couple of weeks.

Here is the information you requested. The presenter's name, the title of the presentation, a brief description of the presentation, and the fees charged are included. I've heard Kai Westmoreland and Steve Harmon present; they were excellent.

Kai Westmoreland—*The Great Depression*. Dr. Westmoreland explores the Great Depression in terms of the stock market crash, the economy, income distribution, and international and federal factors. The suffering that millions of American families endured during the depression is brought to life by Dr. Westmoreland's captivating style of presenting. ($500 plus expenses)

Steve Harmon—*World War II*. What better person to speak about World War II than one of the 156,000 Allied soldiers who crossed the English Channel in the D-Day invasion of France in June 1944? Harmon's presentation depicts the grim realities of a world war through the eyes of a young soldier. ($350 plus expenses)

Members who attended this year's convention recommended two other presenters—Tayt McCauley and Judith Earnhardt. McCauley's presentations deal with the Kennedy years; Earnhardt is well known for her presentations on women's suffrage. I have contacted them, but I've not yet heard from them. As soon as I do, I will get the information to you.

Here is the information on Judith Earnhardt and Tayt McCauley that I said I would send to you. Only a brief sketch on each person is given below; their complete resumes (enclosed) are very impressive. Evidently these two as well as the two I previously sent would be excellent choices for our convention. It's just a matter of deciding which two we want to go with and then contacting them to make sure they are available. We will want to do that as quickly as possible, as I'm sure all four are in high demand.

Judith Earnhardt—*Women's Suffrage*. Dr. Earnhardt explores the women's movement and the impact of such organizations as the American Woman Suffrage Association and the National Woman Suffrage Association. The presentation brings to life the early advocates of women's rights—Elizabeth Cady Stanton, Susan B. Anthony, Lucy Stone, and Julia Ward Howe. ($500 plus expenses)

Tayt McCauley—*The Kennedy Years*. Dr. McCauley recounts the events that touched the nation during the years of John F. Kennedy's administration. Included in the presentation are the Bay of Pigs, the Cuban Missile Crisis, the Moon Landing, Civil Rights, and the Kennedy Assassination. ($450 plus expenses)

If you think we need to identify additional presenters, I will be happy to do so. Please let me know if you want me to take care of anything else before our next meeting.

Activity 14
Prepare slides for a presentation using the directions at the right.

Save as:
L134OUTLINE (outline) and *L134PS* (presentation)

1. Use the three levels of headings in the table of contents (Activity 13) to prepare an outline using your word processing software.
2. Send the outline to presentation software to prepare slides for use in an oral presentation.
3. Key **CASA DI ITALIA BUSINESS PLAN** on two lines on a title slide at the beginning of the presentation.
4. Print the slides as a handout, with six slides on a page.

57C • 12'
Timed Writings

1. Key a 3' writing on ¶s 1 and 2 combined; determine *gwam* and number of errors.
2. Key a 1' writing on each ¶; determine *gwam* and number of errors.
3. Key another 3' writing on ¶s 1 and 2 combined; determine *gwam* and number of errors.

all letters used

	gwam 3'	5'	
A college education is one of the best investments a person will	4	3	50
ever make. Acquiring an education takes an investment of time,	9	5	53
effort, and money. As with all investments, the investor must	13	8	55
realize that a definite degree of risk is involved. However, an	17	10	58
investment in a college education does not bear the degree of risk	22	13	61
that you will find with investments in such things as stocks, land,	26	16	63
or precious metals. Even though there is no guaranteed rate of	30	18	66
return on an education, a person will benefit in a variety of ways.	35	21	69
Usually, those with a college degree can expect to earn higher	39	23	71
salaries during their lifetime than those who do not have a college	44	26	74
degree.	44	26	74
What else can a person who has a college degree expect to gain?	49	29	77
One of the most common answers is that they would have more op-	53	31	79
tions than they would have if they did not have the degree. Most	57	34	82
colleges seek to foster the intellectual, social, personal, and	61	37	85
cultural growth of the student. As a result, those who have a	66	39	87
college degree can anticipate greater opportunities with more op-	70	42	90
tions than those who do not have a degree. For example, job, eco-	74	45	92
nomic, social, as well as travel options are all expanded for col-	79	47	95
lege graduates.	80	48	96

gwam 3' | 1 | 2 | 3 | 4
5' | 1 | 2 | 3

LESSON 58 FORMAT LETTERS WITH SPECIAL PARTS

Objectives:

1. To increase skill at formatting business letters.
2. To format business letters with special parts.

58A • 5'
Conditioning Practice

Key each line twice SS; then key a 1' writing on line 3; determine *gwam*.

alphabet 1 Bart can relax if he passed the major quiz with a very high mark.

figures 2 Crowds of 48,216 and 53,079 attended the final games of the year.

speed 3 Dianna and the visitor may handle the problems with the city bus.

gwam 1' | 1 | 2 | 3 | 4 | 5 | 6 | 7 | 8 | 9 | 10 | 11 | 12 | 13 |

Activity 10
Follow the directions at the right.

Save as: *L134BUSPLN*

1. Open *L134BUSPLN* and create a new page at the end for Appendix B.
2. Key **Appendix B** as a Level 1 heading 2" from the top of the page.
3. About 0.5" below the title, insert file *L134ACT9* and center it horizontally on the page.
4. Print Appendix B.

Activity 11
Follow the directions at the right.

Save as: *L134BUSPLN*

1. Open *L134BUSPLN*. Spell-check the entire document.
2. Hyphenate the document.
3. If needed, make adjustments so that ¶s and bullets are divided correctly, headings are kept with text, and tables are not split between pages.
4. Insert a header on all pages except p. 1. Refer to the format guides on p. 358.
5. Print pp. 1, 5, 12, 15, 17, and 19 unless directed otherwise.

Activity 12
Follow the directions at the right to create a title page for the business plan.

Save as: *L134TP*

1. Key **Casa Di Italia** at the top of the title page.
2. Near the center of the page (about 5" from the top), key **Business Plan** on one line and **Michelle Calvini and Rachel Costanzo, Owners** on the next line.
3. About 8" from the top, key **881 McCabe Road, Baldwin Hills, PA 15238-0937, (412) 555-0112**, and **www.casadiitalia.com** on four lines.
4. Use word art, clip art, borders, and shading as desired to make the title page attractive.

Activity 13
1. Use the format guides presented on p. 358 to create a table of contents using the headings at the right and on the next page.
2. If the page numbers given do not agree with those in your document, use your page numbers.

Save as: *L134TC*

Page

58B • 37' Business Letters

Key in block format the business letters shown at the right.

Letter 1

Date: **March 14, 200-**

Letter address:

Ms. Gwen English, President
3801 Wedgewood Rd.
Wilmington, DE 19805-9921

The letter is from **Marsha J. Johnson, Display Coordinator**. Supply an appropriate salutation and complimentary closing.

Save as: *LTR58B1*

Letter 2

Revise Letter 1; address it to the Pennsylvania State President:

Mr. Todd Woodward, President
810 Lexington Cr.
State College, PA 16801-3452

The letter should be changed to reflect the Pennsylvania information given below:

Capital: **Harrisburg**

State Nickname: **The Keystone State**

Admitted to the Union: **No. 2 on December 12, 1787**

Save as: *LTR58B2*

Letter 3

Use the Insert Date feature to insert the current date.

Letter address:

Attention Special Collections Director
University of Virginia Library
Alderman, 2 East
Charlottesville, VA 22903-0011

Supply an appropriate salutation and complimentary closing. The letter is from **Gregg G. Elway, Doctoral Candidate**.

Save as: *LTR58B3*

At last year's national convention, our displays highlighted the U.S. Presidents. This year's exhibits will spotlight the states. Each delegation will have a table to display items relating to their state. Exhibits will be in the order the states were admitted to the Union. State presidents are being asked to coordinate the display for their states. If you are not able to coordinate your state exhibit, please arrange for another state officer to do it.

Each display area will include a backdrop, a table, and two chairs for representatives from your state. The table (2' x 6') will be covered with a white cloth. Your state flag will be displayed in front of the backdrop on the far right. The 10-foot wide backdrop will have a cutout of your state, along with the following information.

Delaware
Capital: Dover
State Nickname: The Diamond State
Admitted to the Union: No. 1 on December 7, 1787

Each delegation can decide what they want to exhibit on the table. We hope you will include something to give to the people attending the convention. You know how attendees like freebies. We anticipate about eight hundred people at the convention.

We are excited about the state exhibits and hope that you and your officers will make **Delaware's** display the best one at the convention.

I'm doing my dissertation on the Civil War generals and their families. Of course, it is easy to gather the needed information on U. S. Grant and Robert E. Lee. So much has been written about these icons of the Civil War that the problem is deciding what to include.

However, I'm not having as much luck with some of the other generals. I'm particularly interested in Galusha Pennypacker, who was claimed to be the youngest general of the Civil War, and in John E. Wool, who was claimed to be the oldest Civil War general. I believe Pennypacker was from Pennsylvania and Wool from New York. From the little I've been able to gather, I believe Pennypacker didn't reach voting age until after the war and Wool was on active duty at the age of 77 when the war began.

I'm going to be in Washington, D.C., next month. Would it be worth my time to drive to Charlottesville to have access to the archives at the University of Virginia? Since I have very limited time on this trip, I want to use it in the best way possible. If you don't feel that your library would be the best place to visit, could you suggest where my time might be better spent?

restaurants take reservations, one has call-ahead seating, and one does not take reservations in any form.

The 6 nearby Italian restaurants and their distance from Casa Di Italia are given below.

The Italian Warehouse--2.5 miles to the east

The Pepper Garden--1.3 miles to the northeast

Mike's Pasta House--1.6 miles to the west

Carbonara Ristorante--5 miles to the north

Calabro's--3.6 miles to the southwest

Sestilli's Restaurant--4.3 miles to the northwest

Activity 8

1. Open *L134BUSPLN.* Format and key the table at the right so it appears after the word *assumptions*: in the *Financials* section.
2. Print the page on which the table appears.

Save as: *L134BUSPLN*

Quarter	Customers Each Day	Revenues per Customer	Total Revenues
September 15 to December 14	140	$20	$252,000
December 15 to March 14	150	$20	$270,000
March 15 to June 14	155	$20	$279,000
June 15 to September 14	130	$20	$234,000

Activity 9

1. Prepare the worksheet at the right.
2. Key the following headings in Column F:
   Cell F1: **YEAR 1**
   Cell F2: **9/15-9/14**
3. Calculate the yearly totals in Cells F3:F16.
4. Print the worksheet and save the file to use as an appendix.

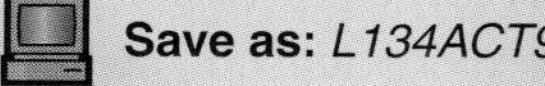

	A	B	C	D	E
1		QTR 1	QTR 2	QTR 3	QTR 4
2		9/15-12/14	12/15-3/14	3/15-6/14	6/15-9/14
3	Revenue	$252,000	$270,000	$279,000	$234,000
4	Cost of sales	$ 93,240	$ 99,900	$103,230	$ 86,580
5	Gross profit	$158,760	$170,100	$175,770	$147,420
6	Expenses				
7	Salaries and wages	$ 68,040	$ 68,040	$ 68,040	$ 68,040
8	Employee benefits	$ 13,860	$ 13,860	$ 13,860	$ 13,860
9	Direct operating expenses	$ 12,600	$ 13,500	$ 13,950	$ 11,700
10	Marketing	$ 6,300	$ 6,750	$ 6,975	$ 5,850
11	Energy and utility service	$ 10,080	$ 10,800	$ 11,160	$ 9,360
12	Administrative and general	$ 9,576	$ 10,260	$ 10,602	$ 8,892
13	Repairs and maintenance	$ 5,040	$ 5,400	$ 5,580	$ 4,680
14	Building costs	$ 15,624	$ 15,624	$ 15,624	$ 15,624
15	Total expenses	$141,120	$144,234	$145,791	$138,006
16	Net income	$ 17,640	$ 25,866	$ 29,979	$ 9,414

58C • 8'
Letter Editing

Open the file *LTR57B1* (Letter 1 of 57B) and make the changes shown at the right. Include a subject line: **KEYNOTE SPEAKERS**. Leave the rest of the letter as it is.

Save as: *LTR58C*

. . . When you contact them, please ~~share with~~ tell them the theme of our convention and determine what they ~~would~~ propose as an opening or closing session ~~for our convention~~. ~~Of course, we need to be concerned with the budget; please determine what they would charge.~~ ¶ As I am sure you are aware, we have a very limited budget. The budget often determines whom we invite. As you discuss fees with them, make sure they are aware that we are an educational institution. Oftentimes, professional presenters are willing to give "educational discounts."

¶ The speaker information will be needed before June 15 for our meeting. . . .

LESSON 59 IMPROVE BUSINESS LETTER FORMATTING

Objectives:

1. To increase proficiency at processing letters.
2. To format two-page business letters.

59A • 5'
Conditioning Practice

Key each line twice SS; then key a 1' writing on line 3; determine *gwam*.

alphabet 1 Vicky acquired a sizable check from the next big jewelry company.

fig/sym 2 Item #4562 will cost Anderson & Sons $639.87 (less 10% for cash).

speed 3 Their big social for their neighbor may also be held in the city.

gwam 1' | 1 | 2 | 3 | 4 | 5 | 6 | 7 | 8 | 9 | 10 | 11 | 12 | 13 |

FORMATTING

59B • 35'
Business Letters

Key in block format the business letter shown at the right.

Letter 1

Date: **May 28, 200-**

Letter address:

Mr. Jon A. Richardson
283 Mount Pleasant Dr.
Oklahoma City, OK 73110-6661

The letter is from **Martin G. Anderson, Professor**. Supply an appropriate salutation and complimentary closing.

Save as: *LTR59B1*

Thank you for your kind letter. I'm glad you enjoyed my presentation at last week's convention. It is always nice to receive positive feedback from colleagues.

As I mentioned in my presentation, integrating the Internet into my class has made learning history more interesting for students. Having students just read about history from a textbook wasn't getting the results I wanted. Students were bored, and quite frankly so was I. Now, after students read the chapters, I integrate Internet activities with my lectures. I further enliven my class with electronic presentations, newspapers, speakers, and field trips. This combination brings to life for the students the events and individuals that have shaped our history. As a result, student motivation has increased and so has mine.

One of the Internet addresses that you will find particularly beneficial is PBS's "The American Experience" (www.pbs.org/wgbh/amex/whoweare.html). It has been active since November 1995 and has received excellent reviews. The 35 feature sites contain stories of people and events that shaped our country. These sites definitely help bring to life some of the incredible men and women who made this country what it is today.

Check out the site and let me know what you think. I'll look forward to seeing you again at next year's convention.

Activity 6

1. Open *L134BUSPLN.* Insert a page break at the end of the business plan.
2. On the new page, key **Appendix A** 2" from the top as a Level 1 heading. QS below the heading.
3. Format and key the comment card at the right so that it will fit on a 4" × 6" card. You decide the layout of the card and the font size, style, color, etc. If desired, use word art and/or other graphics.
4. Print Appendix A.

Save as: *L134BUSPLN*

Dear Customer:

Your opinions are very important to the owners and employees of Casa Di Italia. Will you, therefore, take a moment to complete this card? Thank you.

Michelle Calvini and Rachel Costanzo, Owners

Rate the quality of the food:

Superior		Adequate		Poor
5	4	3	2	1

Rate the quality of the service:

Superior		Adequate		Poor
5	4	3	2	1

Please tell us what we did that pleased or did not please you: ___________

____

____

Activity 7

1. Open *L134BUSPLN* and key the text at the right and on the next page after the *Target Market* section.

Proofreading Alert

The rough-draft copy contains two embedded errors. Proofread your work carefully, checking to make sure all errors have been corrected.

2. Print the page(s) on which this text appears.

Save as: *L134BUSPLN*

<u>Direct Competition</u>

Casa Di Italia will face strong competition from area restaurants, especially Italian restaurants, and specialty food stores. There is won store specializing in Italian foods within 2 (sp) miles of our location. Only on-street parking is available to its customers. There are 6 (sp) Italian restaurants within a 5 (sp)-mile radius of Casa Di Italia. Four of these are well established and two have opened within the past 2 (sp) years. Spot checks during peak dining hours reveal that all but one is attracting customers in adequate or large numbers. Four of the restaurants offer free parking in a restaurant lot, one offers valet parking only, and one has only on ^- street parking available. One restaurants serves high ^- priced meals, four serve moderately priced meals, and one offers low ^- priced meals. None of these restaurants has a specialty food store housed within the restaurant. Four

Letter 2

Key the letter at the right in block format. Remember to include a heading on the second page.

Date: **June 28, 200-**

Letter address:

Ms. Lindsay Grimaldi
3647 Greenpoint Ave.
Long Island City, NY 11101-4534

The letter is from **Jon A. Richardson, Instructor**.

Supply a salutation and complimentary closing.

 **Save as:** *LTR59B2*

Insert List

- The Film & More
- Special Features
- Timelines
- Maps
- People & Events
- Instructor's Guide

INTERNET ACTIVITY

Search the Web to learn more about Lindbergh, Roosevelt, or MacArthur. Key a couple of paragraphs about the individual, including what you learned from the Web search.

History Bits

"She walked in the slums and ghettos of the world, not on a tour of inspection, but as one who could not feel contentment when others were hungry."

—**Adlai Stevenson** about Eleanor Roosevelt

Last month while attending the history convention in Los Angeles, I went to a session titled "How to Bring History to Life." I thoroughly enjoyed the session and have since corresponded with the speaker, Mr. Martin Anderson. He led me to PBS's Web site titled "The American Experience." ¶ Three of the feature sites would integrate nicely into what we have planned for the last nine weeks of the school year. Each site includes:

Insert list here.

I've listed the sites below along with the description provided by PBS. Hopefully, you have access to the Internet at your summer home and will be able to take a quick look at the sites.

Lindbergh www.pbs.org/wgbh/amex/lindbergh/filmmore/index.html *At 25, Charles A. Lindbergh—handsome, talented, and brave—arrived in Paris, the first man to fly across the Atlantic. But the struggle to wear the mantle of legend would be a consuming one. Crowds pursued him; reporters invaded his private life. His marriage, travels with his wife, and the kidnapping and murder of their first child were all fodder for the front page.*

Eleanor Roosevelt www.pbs.org/wgbh/amex/eleanor/filmmore/index.html *Eleanor Roosevelt struggled to overcome an unhappy childhood, betrayal in her marriage, a controlling mother-in-law, and gripping depressions—all the while staying true to her passion for social justice. This biography includes rare home movies, contemporary footage, and . . . brings to vibrant life one of the century's most influential women.*

MacArthur www.pbs.org/wgbh/amex/macarthur/filmmore/index.html *No soldier in modern history has been more admired—or more reviled. Douglas MacArthur, liberator of the Philippines, shogun of occupied Japan, mastermind of the Inchon invasion, was an admired national hero when he was suddenly relieved of his command. A portrait of a complex, imposing, and fascinating American general.*

After reviewing the sites, let me know if you are interested in including them in your American History sections. I will arrange with the media center to have an Internet connection and large monitor available for all our sections on Friday of Weeks 5, 7, and 9. ¶ I enjoyed spending two months back on Utah State's campus. I decided to pursue my Master's degree. After summer school, I made a quick trip to the Grand Canyon and Zion National Park. What beautiful country! ¶ I hope you are enjoying the final days of your summer vacation on Long Island.

59C • 10' Editing Business Letters

Letters 1 and 2

Open 58B Letter 1 (*LTR58B1*); address it to the New Jersey and Georgia state presidents with the information shown at the right.

 **Save as:** *LTR59C1* and *LTR59C2*

Letter address:
Ms. Judith Cruz, President
7632 Stanworth Ln.
Princeton, NJ 08540-0032

New Jersey
Capital: Trenton
State Nickname: The Garden State
Admitted to the Union: No. 3 on December 18, 1787

Letter address:
Mr. Warren Courtier, President
1650 Kensington Dr.
Marietta, GA 30066-1375

Georgia
Capital: Atlanta
State Nickname: The Peach State
Admitted to the Union: No. 4 on January 2, 1788

Activity 4

1. Open *L134BUSPLN* and key the text at the right after ¶ 2 of the *Baldwin Hills Growth* section.
2. Insert **Market Share** as a Level 1 heading, and apply appropriate styles to other headings.
3. Select a character for bulleted items. Apply it to the bullets in this insert and other bulleted items in the business plan.

Proofreading Alert

The rough-draft copy contains one embedded error. Proofread your work carefully, checking to make sure all errors have been corrected.

4. Print the page(s) on which this inserted text appears.

Save as: *L134BUSPLN*

Activity 5

1. Open *L134BUSPLN*. Move the *Management Structure* section to make it the last section in *Management and Organization*.
2. Print the page(s) on which the *Management Structure* section appears.

Save as: *L134BUSPLN*

Casa Di Italia will develop a strong presence in the Baldwin Hills area by serving high-quality, healthy Italian entrees at moderate prices and providing superior service. The competitive advantage will be strengthened by the award-winning chef ~~that~~ who has agreed to work at Casa Di Italia ~~and the specialty retail area that will provide quality products~~.

Target Market

Casa Di Italia target's a variety of people, but for the most part the target customers have these characteristics:

(change to bulleted list)

1. Located in the Baldwin Hills area
2. Make buying decisions based on quality, service, and convenience
3. Part of the middle to upper socioeconomic group
4. Between the ages of 25 and 70
5. Married or dating couples

The census data for ~~the~~ Young County show~~s~~ the following characteristics for the population in ~~our~~ the restaurant's primary service area:

- 57% of the population is between the ages 25 and 69
- 75% or more households have an annual income of $~~4~~35,000 or higher
- 49% of the population is married
- Italian heritage is the third-highest ethnic group in Young County
- 17% of the families are working married couples with children at home
- 13% of the families are working married couples with no children at home
- 20% of the households are single ~~and~~ individuals living ~~at home~~ alone

ACTIVITY 1

Review Table Formatting Features

Open the file *CD-WP8TBL1* and make the following changes to the table to make it look like the table at right.

1. Insert a new column to the right of the first column. Use **Department** for the column heading. Move the department names from Column A to Column B.
2. Merge the cells of the first row (main title).
3. Adjust column widths so the entire ZIP Code fits on one line with the city and state and all column headings fit on one line.
4. Delete the blank row.
5. Change the row height for all rows to 0.5".
6. Change the vertical alignment to *center* for the column heading row and to *bottom* for all entry rows.
7. Center the table horizontally and vertically.

 **Save as:** *WP8ACT1*

DIRECTORY OF DEPARTMENT MANAGERS			
Manager	Department	Address	Home Phone
Michael Ross	Accounting	310 Flagstaff Ave. Saint Paul, MN 55124-3811	555-0102
Tanisha Santana	Finance	4123 Lakeview Rd. Minneapolis, MN 55438-3317	555-0189
Preston Foster	Marketing	376 Norwood Ave. Anoka, MN 55303-7742	555-0156
Natasha Ashford	Personnel	812 Dartmouth Dr. Hopkins, MN 55345-5622	555-0137
Jamal Richards	Purchasing	55 Wyndham Bay Saint Paul, MN 55125-0052	555-0176
Brianne Bostwick	Publications	927 Prestwick Ter. Minneapolis, MN 55443-4747	555-0123

ACTIVITY 2

Review Table Formatting Features

Open the file *CD-WP8TBL2* and change the table format to make it appear as shown at the right. Center the table horizontally and vertically on the page.

 **Save as:** *WP8ACT2*

MAJOR LEAGUE BASEBALL					
National League			American League		
East	West	Central	East	West	Central
Atlanta Florida Montreal New York Philadelphia	Arizona Colorado Los Angeles San Diego San Francisco	Chicago Cincinnati Houston Milwaukee Pittsburgh St. Louis	Baltimore Boston New York Tampa Bay Toronto	Anaheim Oakland Seattle Texas	Chicago Cleveland Detroit Kansas City Minnesota

Activity 3

1. Open *L134BUSPLN* and key the text at the right before the side heading *Baldwin Hills Growth.*
2. Apply appropriate styles to headings.
3. Insert a reference for footnote #1 at the end of the first ¶ and key the following footnote:

   [1] **Unless otherwise noted, national data used in the business plan are from The National Restaurant Association and were obtained at** http://www.restaurant.org/research **in March 2000.**

Note:

Do not be concerned if the footnote "splits" between two pages. You will make adjustments as necessary in Activity 11.

Proofreading Alert

The rough-draft copy contains two embedded errors. Proofread your work carefully, checking to make sure all errors have been corrected.

4. Print the page(s) on which the *Industry Analysis* and *National Growth* sections appear.

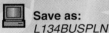

Save as: *L134BUSPLN*

Industry Analysis

Casa Di Italia ~~will be~~ is part of an industry that has established itself as an integral part of an American lifestyle. More than 45% (sp) of today's food dollar is spent away from home, and almost ~~1/2~~ half of all adults are restaurant patrons on a typical day. Children, teenagers, and young adults are more familiar with restaurants and knew cuisines than ever before and are increasing their restaurant ~~visits~~ spending. The same is true for the baby boomers and members of the older generation~~s~~ who have been empowered by strong economic growth and gains in income.

National Growth

The restaurant industry enjoyed 9 (sp) consecutive years of real sales growth as they entered the new century. Sales in 2000 were calculated at $376 billion and are expected to increase steadily to $577 billion by 2010; an increase of 53% (sp) in ten years. ¶ ~~Eat-in~~ Full-service restaurants accounted for ~~more than~~ about two-thirds or $253 billion of the ~~United States~~ 2000 sales. Using the same ratio, full-service restaurants ~~should~~ will account for about $388 billion of the industry sales in 2010.

ACTIVITY 3

Split Cells/ Join Cells

1. Read the copy at the right.
2. Learn/review how to use the Split Cells and Join Cells features for your software.
3. Open the *CD-WP8TBL3* file.
4. Finish keying any columns that are incomplete.
5. Use the Split Cells and Join Cells features to complete the formatting. (You will shade the table as part of Activity 4.)
6. Center the table vertically and horizontally.

Save as: *WP8ACT3*

Use the Split Cells table feature to **split** (divide) cells horizontally or vertically.

Use the Join Cells table feature to **join** (merge) cells horizontally or vertically.

<table>
<tr><td colspan="6">ACCOUNTING MAJOR</td></tr>
<tr><td colspan="4">General Electives
(40 credits)</td><td>Business Core
(32 credits)</td><td>Accounting Requirements
(28 credits)</td></tr>
<tr><td>Category I
(9 Credits)</td><td>Category II
(9 Credits)</td><td>Category III
(11 Credits)</td><td>Category IV
(11 Credits)</td><td rowspan="3">Acct 201
Acct 202
Bcom 206
Bcom 207
MIS 240
Bsad 300
Bsad 305
Fin 320
Mktg 330
Mgmt 340
Mgmt 341
Mgmt 449</td><td rowspan="3">Acct 301
Acct 302
Acct 314
Acct 315
Acct 317
Acct 321
Acct 450
Acct 460
Fin 326
Fin 327</td></tr>
<tr><td>CJ 202
Math 111
Math 245</td><td>Biol 102
Chem 101
Geog 104</td><td>Econ 103
Econ 104
Psyc 100
Soc 101</td><td>No specific courses required.</td></tr>
<tr><td colspan="4">Category I - Communications and Analytical Skills
Category II - Natural Sciences
Category III - Social Sciences
Category IV - Humanities</td></tr>
</table>

ACTIVITY 4A-C

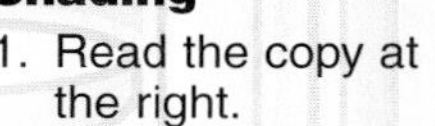

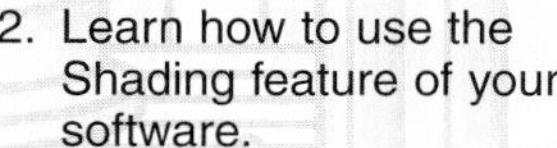

Shading

1. Read the copy at the right.
2. Learn how to use the Shading feature of your software.
3. Open *CD-WP8TBL4*. Shade alternate lines of the table as shown at the right. Use 10% shading except for the last line; use 25% shading on it.

Save as: *WP8ACT4A*

4. Open *WP8ACT2* (Activity 2 file). Shade *National League* with red (or 10% gray). Shade *American League* blue (or 20% gray).
5. For both the National and American Leagues, shade *East* yellow (or 5% gray); *West* green (or 10% gray); and *Central* purple (or 15% gray).

Save as: *WP8ACT4B*

6. Open the Activity 3 file (*WP8ACT3*). Apply 20% shading as shown in Activity 3, above.

Save as: *WP8ACT4C*

Use the **Shading** feature to enhance the appearance of tables to make them easier to read. The Shading feature allows you to fill in areas of the table with varying shades of gray or with color. Shading covers the selected area. It may be the entire table or a single cell, column, or row within a table.

TOP 10 USA BOX OFFICE FILMS*		
Movie	Year of Release	Total Gross
Titanic	1997	$600,743,440
Star Wars	1977	$460,935,655
Star Wars: Episode One—The Phantom Menace	1999	$430,984,033
E.T., the Extra-Terrestrial	1982	$399,804,539
Jurassic Park	1993	$356,763,175
Forrest Gump	1994	$329,452,287
The Lion King	1994	$312,775,367
Return of the Jedi	1983	$309,064,373
Independence Day	1996	$305,400,800
The Empire Strikes Back	1980	$290,158,751
*Box office listing in unadjusted 1999 U.S. dollars.		

Source: "Top 100 All-Time Films at the USA Box Office." Hollywood News. http://www.Hollywood.com (5 February 2000).

LESSONS 134–139

CREATE A BUSINESS PLAN

Objectives:

1. To prepare a business plan with a title page, table of contents, and appendices.
2. To demonstrate your ability to integrate your knowledge and skills.

134A–139A • 5' (daily) Conditioning Practice

Key each line twice; take 30" writings on line 2; determine *gwam.*

alphabet 1 Zeke opened jam jars quickly but avoided ruining the waxed floor.

figures 2 I wrote checks 398-430 and 432-457 in July and 458-461 in August.

speed 3 Jane may work with the girls to make the ritual for the sorority.

gwam 1' | 1 | 2 | 3 | 4 | 5 | 6 | 7 | 8 | 9 | 10 | 11 | 12 |

FORMATTING

134B–139B • 45' (daily) Business Plan

Activity 1

1. Complete the directions at the right to begin the business plan.
2. Print pp. 1 and 9 of the business plan.

Save as: *L134BUSPLN*

1. Open *CD-L134BUSPLN* and preview the business plan to familiarize yourself with its content, organization, and length.
2. Check for inconsistencies in spacing and paragraph indentations, and for spelling errors. Key a list of the errors you find.

Save as: *L134ACT1* (error list)

3. Correct the errors you found.
4. Use the format guides on p. 358 to create styles for Level 1, 2, and 3 headings.
5. Apply the heading styles throughout the report. Headings appear in the draft file as follows:
   Level 1 headings—centered, initial caps
   Level 2 headings—left-aligned with initial caps and underlined
   Level 3 headings—left-aligned with initial caps
6. Double-space the entire report; use a 2" top margin on p. 1.

Activity 2

1. Open *L134BUSPLN* and key the text at the right after the first ¶ of the business plan.
2. Apply an appropriate style to the headings.

Proofreading Alert

The rough-draft copy contains one embedded error; correct it as you process the copy.

3. Print p. 1.

Save as: *L134BUSPLN*

Mission Statement

¶ ~~The~~ mission ~~of~~ Casa Di Italia['s] is to serve and sell hi-quality Italian foods at moderate prices in a friendly, [healthy] ~~family type~~ atmosphere that offers [superior] ~~good~~ service to customers.

Vision Statement

Within 5 [sp] years, Casa Di Italia [will] ~~hopes to~~ be recognized as one of the top 5 [sp] moderately priced Italian restaurants in the Brenthall area.

ACTIVITY 5

Borders

1. Read the copy at the right.
2. Learn how to use the Border feature of your software.
3. Open file CD-*WP8TBL5*. Complete the table so that it appears as shown at the right.

 **Save as:** *WP8ACT5*

Optional Activity 1

Open the Activity 5 file (*WP8ACT5*). Apply a different style border with a *Box* setting.

 **Save as:** *WP8ACT5-1*

Optional Activity 2

Open the Optional Activity 1 file (*WP8ACT5-1*). Apply a border around the cells of the three games Bruce's 6th-grade team plays. Also apply a border around the times they play the games.

 **Save as:** *WP8ACT5-2*

Use the Border feature to enhance the appearance and readability of tables. The **Border** feature allows a border to be added around an entire table or only selected parts of a table.

FIFTH & SIXTH GRADE TOURNAMENT SCHEDULE
Altoona
February 26

Middle School Gym 5th Grade		Time	High School Gym 6th Grade	
Score	Teams		Teams	Score
	Bruce Somerset	9:00	Bruce Somerset	
	St. Croix Central St. Croix Falls		St. Croix Central St. Croix Falls	
	Menomonie Rice Lake	10:10	Menomonie Rice Lake	
	Altoona Eau Claire		Altoona Eau Claire	
	St. Croix Falls Bruce	11:20	St. Croix Falls Bruce	
	St. Croix Central Somerset		St. Croix Central Somerset	
	Rice Lake Eau Claire	12:30	Rice Lake Eau Claire	
	Menomonie Altoona		Menomonie Altoona	
	St. Croix Falls Somerset	1:40	St. Croix Falls Somerset	
	St. Croix Central Bruce		St. Croix Central Bruce	
	Rice Lake Altoona	2:50	Rice Lake Altoona	
	Menomonie Eau Claire		Menomonie Eau Claire	
	3rd and 4th place games	4:00	3rd and 4th place games	
	1st and 2nd place games	5:10	1st and 2nd place games	

ACTIVITY 6

Gridlines

1. Read the copy at the right.

When you remove table borders (*No Border* or *None*), light gray lines, called **gridlines**, replace the borders. These gridlines give you a visual guide as you work with the table; they do not print. The gray gridlines can be turned off by activating the **Hide Gridlines** option. This allows you to see what the table will look like when it is printed.

2. Learn how to use the Gridlines feature of your software.
3. Open the Activity 5 file (*WP8ACT5*). Apply the *None* border setting; then hide the gridlines.

 **Save as:** *WP8ACT6*

UNIT 35

LESSONS 134–139

Learn to Create a Business Plan

Format Guides: Business Plan

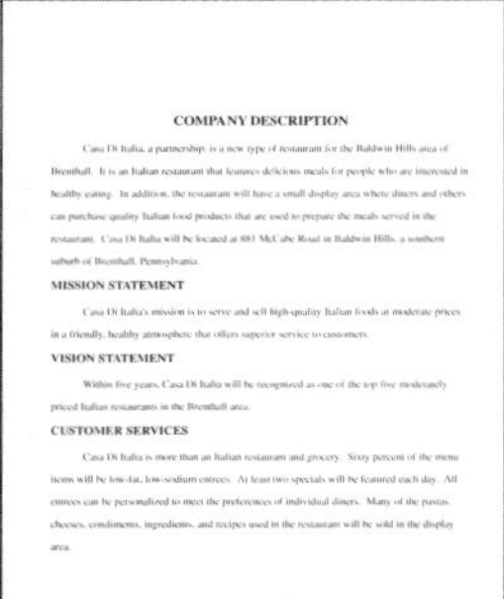

COMPANY DESCRIPTION

MISSION STATEMENT

VISION STATEMENT

CUSTOMER SERVICES

Page 1

TABLE OF CONTENTS

Table of Contents

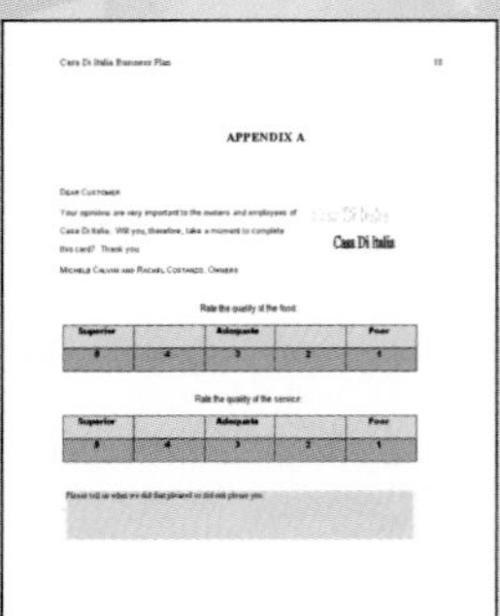

APPENDIX A

Appendix

Business Plan

A business plan is a blueprint for a company. Developing a business plan helps entrepreneurs take an objective, critical look at a business. A well-written plan communicates the company's ideas and message to lenders, investors, and employees. A written business plan also is a management tool that helps measure the performance of the business.

The key elements of a business plan are:

1. A **market analysis** that defines the market and specifies the strategies to be used to achieve the revenues.
2. An **action plan** to guide the implementation of the strategies.
3. **Financial projections** that show the expected results.

Formatting Features

Margins. The margins for an unbound report will be used—1" or default top, bottom, and side margins on all pages except the first (the first page has a 2" top margin).

Page numbering and header. A header with the company name followed by the words "Business Plan" blocked at the LM and the page number flush with the RM is keyed in 12-pt. font on all pages of the report body and appendices except the first page of the report body.

Line spacing and font. The entire report is DS using 12-pt. Times New Roman font unless otherwise directed.

Text. Paragraphs and single-line bulleted lists should have at least two lines (or bullets) at the bottom of the page and carry over at least two lines to the next page. Headings and at least two lines of text should be kept together. Tables should not be split between pages. The report should be hyphenated.

Heading styles

Level 1—centered, ALL CAPS, bold, 16-pt. Times New Roman font, DS

Level 2—left-aligned, ALL CAPS, bold, 14-pt. Times New Roman font, DS

Level 3—left-aligned, small caps, bold, 12-pt. Times New Roman font, DS

Table of contents. Include TABLE OF CONTENTS as a centered heading in ALL CAPS, 2" from top. Then QS before listing Level 1, 2, and 3 headings, including Appendices A and B.

Key Level 1 headings in ALL CAPS, blocked at the LM. Indent Level 2 headings 0.5" and key in initial caps. Indent Level 3 headings 1" and key in initial caps.

DS above and below all Level 1 and 2 headings; SS Level 3 headings.

Key the page number (with leaders) for each heading at the right margin.

Use small Roman numerals (i, ii) centered in a footer to number the table of contents pages.

UNIT 18

LESSONS 60-64

Improving Table Formatting Skills

Format Guides: Tables

WHAT AMERICANS REMEMBER

Top Five Events

Event	Age Group			
	18-35	35-54	55-64	65+
■ Berlin Wall Falls	5	*	*	*
■ Challenger	2	3	4	*
■ Franklin D. Roosevelt Death	*	*	*	5
■ Gulf War Begins	3	5	*	*
■ John F. Kennedy Death	*	2	1	1
■ Martin Luther King, Jr., Death	*	*	5	*
■ Moon Walk	*	4	2	4
■ Oklahoma City Bombing	1	1	3	*
■ Pearl Harbor	*	*	*	2
■ Reagan Shot	4	*	*	*
■ World War II Ends	*	*	*	3
1 = Ranked First, 2 = Ranked Second, etc.; * = Not ranked in top five by this age group.				

Source: The Pew Research Center. "Public Perspectives on the American Century." http://www.people-press.org/mill1sec4.htm (20 August 1999).

Table with Joined and Split Cells

PRESIDENTS 1945 - 2001				
President	Years in Office	Profession	Elected from	Vice President
Harry S. Truman	1945 - 1953	Businessman	Missouri	Alben W. Barkley
Dwight D. Eisenhower	1953 - 1961	Soldier	Kansas	Richard M. Nixon
John F. Kennedy	1961 - 1963	Author	Massachusetts	Lyndon B. Johnson
Lyndon B. Johnson	1963 - 1969	Teacher	Texas	Hubert H. Humphrey
Richard M. Nixon	1969 - 1974	Lawyer	California	Spiro T. Agnew
				Gerald R. Ford
Gerald R. Ford	1974 - 1977	Lawyer	Michigan	Nelson A. Rockefeller
James E. Carter, Jr.	1977 - 1981	Businessman	Georgia	Walter F. Mondale
Ronald W. Reagan	1981 - 1989	Actor	California	George H. W. Bush
George H. W. Bush	1989 - 1993	Businessman	Texas	J. Danforth Quayle
William J. Clinton	1993 - 2001	Lawyer	Arkansas	Albert Gore, Jr.
Blue = Republican Party Affiliation		Red = Democratic Party Affiliation		

Source: Matthew T. Downey, et al. United States History, 1997, pp. 1132–1133.

Table with Shading and Borders

Note:
When you complete a table in this unit, check your work. Correct all spelling, keying, and formatting errors before closing or printing the file.

Format Guides: Tables

Tables are used to organize and present information in a concise, logical way to make it easy for the reader to understand and analyze information. The table format can make information easier or more difficult to understand.

You will be required to use the Table word processing features presented in Word Processing 4 (pp. 90-93) and Word Processing 8 (pp. 169-171) to format the tables in this unit. Most of the tables are already organized; you simply need to create them to look like the examples in the text. However, some of the tables will require you to use your decision-making skills to organize the information before formatting and keying the tables. To complete this unit successfully, you will need to understand the format features given below.

Table Format Features

Vertical placement. Center tables vertically. The top and bottom margins will be equal.

Horizontal placement. Center tables horizontally. The left and right margins will be equal.

Column width and row height. Adjust column width and row height to put more white space around data in the rows and columns. Additional white space makes data easier to read.

Vertical alignment. Within cells, data may be aligned at the top, center, or bottom. Title rows most often use center alignment. Data rows usually are either center- or bottom-aligned.

Horizontal alignment. Within columns, words may be left-aligned or center-aligned. Whole numbers are right-aligned if a column total is shown; decimal numbers are decimal-aligned. Other figures may be center-aligned.

Delete/Insert rows and/or columns. Delete empty rows or columns wherever they occur in a table. Also, insert a row(s) as needed above or below an existing row. Insert a column(s) to the left or right of an existing column as needed.

Join/Split cells. To make a table attractive and easy to read, join two or more cells into one cell for the main title, source note, and other data as needed. Any existing cell can be split (divided) into two or more smaller cells if necessary.

Shading. Use shading to enhance table appearance and to highlight selected columns, rows, or individual cells.

Borders. Borders may be applied around an entire table or around cells, rows, or columns within a table. Borders improve appearance as well as highlight the data within the borders.

Sort. In a table column, text can be sorted alphabetically in ascending (A to Z) or descending (Z to A) order. Also, numbers and dates can be sorted numerically (chronologically), in either ascending or descending order.

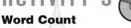

ACTIVITY 5

Word Count

1. Read the text at the right and refer to the illustration.
2. Learn to use Word Count with your wp software.
3. Follow the directions at the right.

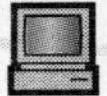 **Save as:** *WP14ACT5*

The **Word Count** feature is used to count the number of words within a document or a specific section of the document. This same command usually provides the number of characters, lines, paragraphs, and pages within the document.

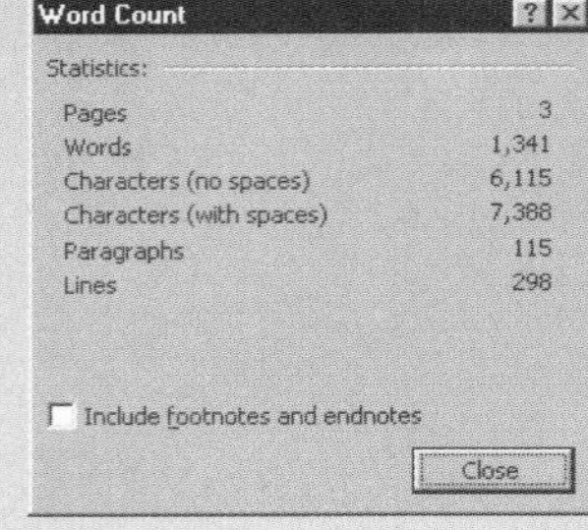

1. Open *CD-WP14ACT1.*
2. Using Word Count, determine and key the answers to these questions:
   a. How many words are in the document?
   b. How many lines are in the document?
   c. How many pages are in the document?
   d. How many words are in the first two paragraphs of the Sports Medicine section?
   e. How many characters (with spaces) are in the second line of the first paragraph?
   f. How many lines are in the first four paragraphs of the Duties and Responsibilities section?

ACTIVITY 6

Send To

1. Read the text at the right and refer to the illustration.
2. Learn to send a wp outline to presentation software.
3. Key the outline at the lower right, using Title and Heading styles appropriately. Use the Outline Numbering feature of your wp software to insert the outline levels (I., A., 1.).

Note:

You can also use Outline View to create the outline.

4. Send the outline to your presentation software.
5. View the outline and slides in the presentation software.
6. Print the slides as handouts with four slides per page.

 **Save as:** *WP14ACT6OUTLN* (wp outline) and *WP14ACT6* (presentation slides)

Outlines created using styles with wp software can be sent to presentation software to make slides that can be used in a presentation.

Text formatted as Title style becomes the opening title slide of the presentation. Text formatted as Heading 1 style becomes a slide title; text formatted as Heading 2 style becomes first-level bullets on a slide; text formatted as Heading 3 style becomes second-level bullets on the slide, etc.

In this activity, default settings will be used to format slides. Later, you will learn how to change the format of the text and the slides.

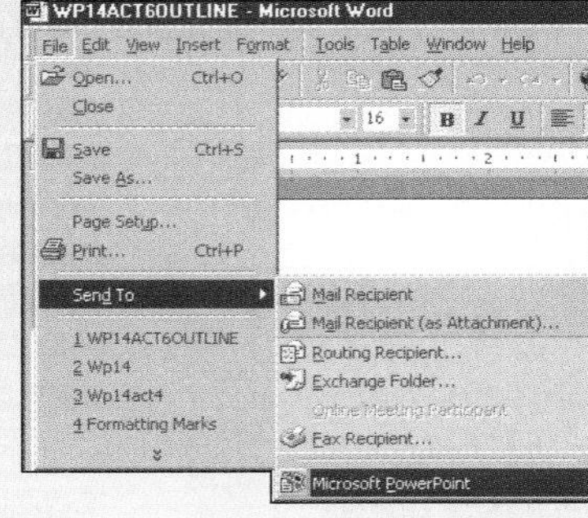

Career Opportunities in Sports Medicine

I. Sports Medicine
  A. Focus
  B. Practitioners
II. Athletic Trainers
  A. Places of Employment
    1. Sports Teams
    2. Clinics
    3. Others
  B. Professional Responsibilities
III. Requirements
  A. Education
  B. Internships
  C. Continuing Education

LESSON 60 — IMPROVE TABLE FORMATTING SKILLS

Objectives:

1. To improve table formatting skills.
2. To improve language skills.

60A • 5' Conditioning Practice

Key each line twice SS; key a 1' writing on line 3; determine *gwam*.

alphabet 1 Zachary enjoyed picking six bouquets of vivid flowers at my home.

figures 2 I bought my first cards on July 25, 1980; I now have 3,467 cards.

speed 3 Dixie owns the six foals and the cow in the neighbor's hay field.

gwam 1' | 1 | 2 | 3 | 4 | 5 | 6 | 7 | 8 | 9 | 10 | 11 | 12 | 13 |

LANGUAGE SKILLS

60B • 8' Language Skills: Word Choice

1. Study the spelling/ definitions of the words at the right.
2. For each set of sentences, key the Learn line, then the Apply lines. Choose the correct word in parentheses.
3. Check your work; correct lines containing word-choice errors.

Save as: *CHOICE60B*

do (vb) to bring about; to carry out

due (adj) owed or owing as a debt; having reached the date for payment

for (prep/conj) used to indicate purpose; on behalf of; because; because of

four (n) the fourth in a set or series

Learn 1 **Do** you know when the three library books are **due**?
Apply 2 The next payment will be (do, due) on Tuesday, March 24.
Apply 3 I (do, due) not know when I will be available to meet again.

Learn 1 The **four** men asked for a salary increase **for** the next **four** years.
Apply 2 The manager left (for, four) an hour just before (for, four) o'clock.
Apply 3 The (for, four) coaches were mad after waiting (for, four) an hour.

FORMATTING

60C • 37' Review Table Formatting

1. Review the format guides for tables on p. 172 and the word processing features on pp. 169–171 as needed.
2. Key Tables 1–3 shown at the right and on p. 174.

Table 1

1. Determine the number of rows and columns needed to create a table for the data at the right. (Key the main title above the table, as shown.)

(continued on next page)

CIVIL WAR PERSONALITIES

Name	Position
Davis, Jefferson	Confederate Commander in Chief
Grant, Ulysses S.	Union Army Commanding General
Jackson, Stonewall	Confederate Army General
Johnston, Joseph E.	Confederate Army General
Lee, Robert E.	Confederate Army Commanding General
Lincoln, Abraham	Union Commander in Chief
Longstreet, James	Confederate Army General
Mead, George	Union Army General
Sheridan, Philip H.	Union Army General
Sherman, William T.	Union Army General
Stuart, J. E. B. (Jeb)	Confederate Army General
Thomas, George H.	Union Army General

Source: Encyclopedia Americana, 1998.

3. Key the text at the right SS, using bullets.
4. Show formatting marks and refer to them to answer these questions below the text you keyed.
   a. How many times was ENTER struck?
   b. How many tabs appear in the copy?
   c. How many times was the Space Bar tapped twice before keying a character?

 **Save as:** *WP14ACT3*

You can incorporate fitness into your daily routine by doing these three activities:

- Walk up stairs for one minute each day instead of taking the elevator. Within a year you should be a pound lighter without changing any other habits.
- Walk the dog; don't just watch the dog walk. In a nutshell--get moving!
- Perform at least 30 minutes of moderate activity each day. If necessary, do the 30 minutes in 10-minute intervals.

ACTIVITY 4

Styles

1. Study the information and illustration at the right.
2. Learn to use styles with your wp software.
3. Key the four headings at the right twice.
4. **Apply existing styles:** Apply Heading 1 style to the first and fifth headings; Heading 2 style to the second and sixth headings; Heading 3 style to the third, fourth, seventh, and eighth headings.
5. **Modify existing styles:** Modify Heading 1 style so it is ALL CAPS, and then apply it to the first heading; modify Heading 2 style so it is bold (not italic), and apply it to the second heading. Read the note at the bottom of the page.
6. **Create new styles:** Key the first ¶ at the right, and then create and apply a style that uses a red, 11-pt. Arial font, right-aligned.

   Key the second ¶ at the right, and apply the style you just created.

 **Save as:** *WP14ACT4*

A **style** is a predefined set of formatting options that has been named and saved so it can be used again to save time and add consistency to a document.

When a style is applied (used), many formatting commands are applied at one time. For example, a style for a report heading may include commands for centering and using a 16-pt. bold Arial font. All four commands would be applied when the style is applied.

Paragraph styles apply to the entire paragraph. Character styles apply only to text selected in the paragraph.

Existing styles can be used, existing styles can be modified and then used, or new styles can be created and then applied.

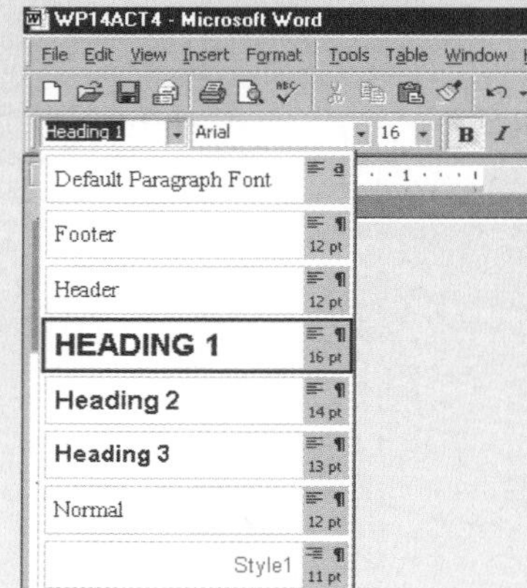

Career Opportunities in Sports Medicine **(Heading 1 style)**

Sports Medicine **(Heading 2 style)**

Focus **(Heading 3 style)**

Practitioners **(Heading 3 style)**

Have you given serious thought to the kind of work you want to do when you are graduated from high school? Do you enjoy helping people with their problems, working on a person-to-person basis?

Athletic trainers must have basic knowledge and competencies in a variety of different specialty areas within the sports medicine field.

Note:
When Heading 1 and 2 styles are modified and applied to lines 1 and 2, the heading style used in lines 5 and 6 is automatically updated.

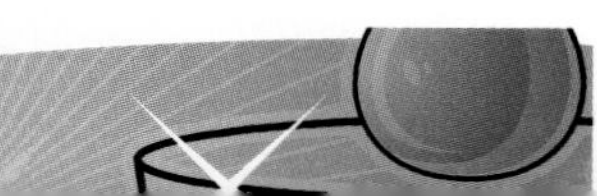

Table 1, cont.

2. Create a table and fill in the information. Adjust column widths as needed.
3. Center and bold the main title and column headings.
4. Change the row height to 0.3" for all rows.
5. Change vertical alignment to *Center* for the column headings and to *Bottom* for all other rows.
6. Center the table horizontally and vertically.

Save as: *TBL60C1*

Table 2

Create the table shown at the right using the information given below.

Main title: row height 0.9"; center vertical alignment; bold text.

Column headings: row height 0.4"; center vertical alignment; bold text.

Data rows: row height 0.3"; bottom vertical alignment; Column B center horizontal alignment.

Table placement: center horizontally and vertically.

Save as: *TBL60C2*

Table 3

Create the table shown at the right using the information given below.

Main title: row height 0.7"; center vertical alignment; bold text.

Column headings: row height 0.4"; center vertical alignment; bold text.

Data rows: row height 0.35"; bottom vertical alignment.

Note:

The source note may be keyed outside the table as shown, or a new row may be inserted for it.

Save as: *TBL60C3*

CIVIL WAR

Eastern Theater Campaigns

Campaign	**Dates**
First Bull Run (Manassas)	July 1861
Peninsular Campaign	April-July 1862
Jackson's Valley Campaign	March-June 1862
Second Bull Run (Manassas)	July-September 1862
Antietam (Sharpsburg) Campaign	September 1862
Fredericksburg Campaign	October-December 1862
Chancellorsville Campaign	April-May 1863
Gettysburg Campaign	June-July 1863
Wilderness Campaign	May 1864
Spotsylvania Campaign	May 1864
Petersburg Campaign	May 1864-April 1865
Grant's Pursuit of Lee	April 3 and 9, 1865
Sherman's March to the Sea	November-December 1864
Sherman's Pursuit of Johnston	December 1864-April 1865

Source: Collier's Encyclopedia, 1991.

THE CONFEDERATE STATES OF AMERICA

State	**Seceded from Union**	**Readmitted to Union**[1]
South Carolina	December 20, 1860	July 9, 1868
Mississippi	January 9, 1861	February 23, 1870
Florida	January 10, 1861	June 25, 1868
Alabama	January 11, 1861	July 13, 1868
Georgia	January 19, 1861	July 15, 1870[2]
Louisiana	January 26, 1861	July 9, 1868
Texas	March 2, 1861	March 30, 1870
Virginia	April 17, 1861	January 26, 1870
Arkansas	May 6, 1861	June 22, 1868
North Carolina	May 20, 1861	July 4, 1868
Tennessee	June 8, 1861	July 24, 1866

[1]Date of readmission to representation in U.S. House of Representatives.
[2]Second readmission date. First date was July 21, 1868, but the representatives were unseated March 5, 1869.

Source: The 1996 Information Please Almanac, pp. 748-781.

WORD PROCESSING 14

ACTIVITY 1

Split Window

1. Read the text at the right and refer to the illustration.
2. Learn to use the Split Window feature with your wp software.
3. Follow the directions at the right.

 **Save as:** *WP14ACT1*

Often it is helpful to be able to see two parts of a document that do not appear in the same window. The **Split Window** feature is used to display a document in two panes, each with its own scroll bars to help you move around in each pane. If needed, the panes can be resized.

This feature can be used when you copy or move text between parts of a long document or when you need to see text that is not visible in the window where you are keying.

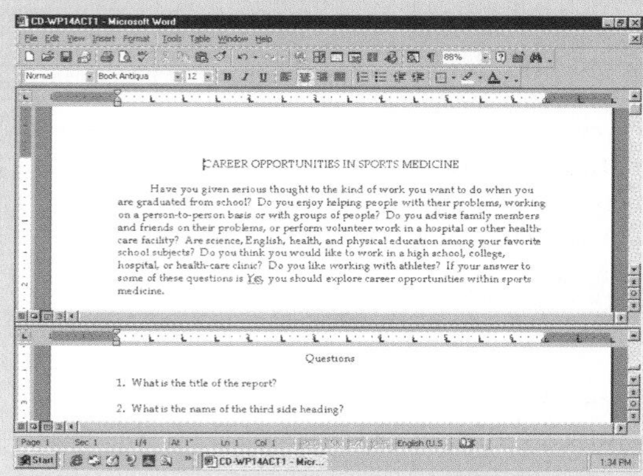

1. Open *CD-WP14ACT1* and split the window.
2. In the lower pane, find *Questions*.
3. Move through the text in the top pane to find the answers to the five questions that appear in the bottom pane, and key your answers in the space between the questions.
4. Move the questions and your answers to the top of p. 1 and print p. 1.

ACTIVITY 2

Go To

1. Read the text at the right and refer to the illustration.
2. Learn to use the Go To command with your wp software.
3. Follow the directions at the right.

 **Save as:** *WP14ACT2*

A quick way to move to a certain page or point in a long document is to use the **Go To** command. This command can be used to go directly to a specific footnote or endnote, for example.

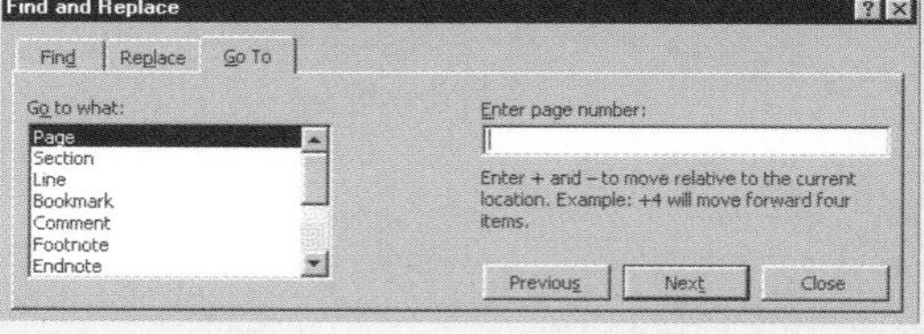

1. Open *CD-WP14ACT2* and split the window.
2. In the lower pane, find *Questions*.
3. Answer the questions by using Go To to find the answers in the text in the top pane.
4. Print the page that contains the questions and your answers.

ACTIVITY 3

Show ¶

1. Read the text and illustration at the right.
2. Learn to reveal formatting marks with your wp software.

(continued on next page)

Word processing documents contain invisible formatting marks that can be displayed. Commonly used marks are:

¶ to show a hard return,
→ to show a tab,
• to show a space between words.

Being able to see the formatting marks is helpful when editing a document or solving formatting problems. The formatting marks do not print.

¶
¶
The·¶·mark·indicates·there·are¶
two·blank·lines·above·this·text¶
and·that·ENTER·was·struck·at·the·¶
end·of·each·line.¶
The·→ indicates·that·the· → tab¶
key·was·struck·after·two·occurrences·¶
of·the·word·THE·in·line·5.¶
The·dots·indicate···the·number·of·¶
spaces·entered.··There·are·three·spaces·¶
between·INDICATE·and·THE·in·line·8.¶

LESSON 61 APPLY SHADING TO TABLES

Objectives:

1. To improve table formatting skills.
2. To enhance tables with shading.
3. To enhance table decision-making skills.

61A • 5' Conditioning Practice

Key each line twice SS; key a 1' writing on line 3; determine *gwam.*

alphabet 1 Hazel saw five or six people jumping quickly over the gray board.

figures 2 They picked up yard waste at 842 Lake, 1073 Park, and 3596 Cedar.

speed 3 The soggy field by the dog kennels was good for a big tug of war.

gwam 1' | 1 | 2 | 3 | 4 | 5 | 6 | 7 | 8 | 9 | 10 | 11 | 12 | 13 |

61B • 8' Table Editing

1. Open *TBL60C1* (60C, Table 1). At the end of the table, include the generals' names shown at the right.
2. Sort the table to arrange the new entries alphabetically with the rest of the entries.

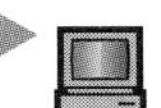

Save as: *TBL61B*

McClellan, George B.	Union Army General
Forrest, Nathan Bedford	Confederate Army General
Johnston, Albert Sidney	Confederate Army General
McDowell, Irvin	Union Army General

FORMATTING

61C • 37' Table Formatting

Table 1

1. Combine the three tables at the right into one. Use **FAMOUS AMERICANS** for the main title.
2. Include the following source note.
   "Black History Innovators." <u>USA Today</u>. http://www.usatoday.com (15 February 2000).
3. Format the table attractively. Adjust row height, column width, alignment, placement, etc. Use 10% shading for the top column headings and 20% shading for the bottom column headings.

Save as: *TBL61C1*

Table 2

With *TBL61C1* (Table 1) open, alphabetize the entries in each column.

Save as: *TBL61C2*

Thinkers and Innovators	
Name	Life
George W. Carver	1864-1943
W. E. B. Du Bois	1868-1963
Madam C. J. Walker	1867-1919
Booker T. Washington	1856-1915
Benjamin Banneker	1731-1806
Mary McLeod Bethune	1875-1955
Charles Drew	1904-1950

Politics	
Name	Life
Frederick Douglass	1817-1895
Rosa Parks	1913-
Harriet Tubman	1823-1913
Thurgood Marshall	1908-1993
Colin Powell	1937-
Shirley Chisholm	1924-
Martin Luther King, Jr.	1929-1968

Arts and Entertainment	
Name	Life
Louis Armstrong	1901-1971
Billie Holiday	1915-1959
Duke Ellington	1899-1974
Ella Fitzgerald	1917-1996
Bill Cosby	1937-
Alex Haley	1921-1992
Oprah Winfrey	1954-

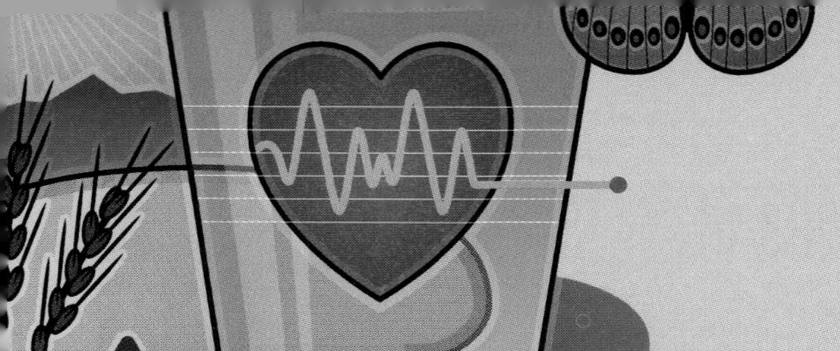

Communication Skills 

ACTIVITY 1

Apply What You Have Learned: Punctuation (Comma)

1. As you key lines 1–10 at the right, insert commas as needed to complete each sentence correctly.
2. Check the accuracy of your work with the instructor; correct any errors you made.
3. Key correctly any sentence in which you made a comma error.

 **Save as:** *CS14-ACT1*

1 When you get to State Street make a right turn at the light.
2 She will ask Ken you and me to serve on the planning committee.
3 They moved to Las Cruces New Mexico on September 15 2002.
4 Elden be sure to turn off all equipment before you leave.
5 Ms. Rogers said "Keep the insertion point moving steadily."
6 Winona who is our class treasurer couldn't attend the meeting.
7 By the middle of 2000 we had 273 employees; in 2002 318.
8 The probability is that only 1 in 280000 have the same DNA.
9 Dr. Woodburn has a strong pleasant personality.
10 The choir director Elena Spitz is planning a special program.

ACTIVITY 2

Apply What You Have Learned: Punctuation

1. As you key lines 1–10 at the right, supply needed punctuation (hyphen, colon, underline, parentheses, and quotation marks).
2. Check the accuracy of your work with the instructor; correct any errors you made.
3. Key correctly any sentence in which you made a punctuation error.

 **Save as:** *CS14-ACT2*

1 Vanessa Williams sang the quite beautiful Colors of the Wind.
2 After you see the film Pocahontas, she said, write a review.
3 Miss Tallchief signed a two year contract as ballet director.
4 Dr. Cho said that "30-second and 1 minute spurts build speed."
5 The dance competition is scheduled for 9 15 a.m. on October 15.
6 My goal is to develop 1 self-confidence and 2 self-esteem.
7 "A textual citation follows the quote." Sanchez, 2002, 273
8 Who, she asked, is your all time favorite country singer?
9 Ms. Ott said: Read Frost's poem The Housekeeper by Monday.
10 Home Improvement was a very popular TV show in the late 1990s.

ACTIVITY 3

Preparing to Speak

Prepare a brief introduction as described at the right.

 **Save as:** *CS14-3OL* and *CS14-3SOUND*

You have been selected to introduce a speaker, Douglas H. Ruckert, to your class. His resume appears on p. 264 of this textbook. The introduction is to be 30" to 1'. The audience is your classmates.

1. Review the resume and decide which points you will include in your introduction.
2. Key an outline of these points.
3. If time and resources permit, record your introduction in a sound file.
4. Submit your outline (and sound file, if made) to your instructor.

Table 3
Key the table at the right and insert the following three names beside the individual's accomplishments.

Albert Einstein
Thomas Alva Edison
Andrew Carnegie

Key the source note outside the table, below the last row. Use the table format features that you have learned to arrange the information attractively on the page.

 **Save as:** *TBL61C3*

History Bits

"I am the better writer, she (Susan B. Anthony) the better critic . . . and together we have made arguments that have stood unshaken by the storms of thirty long years; arguments that no man has answered."
—Elizabeth Cady Stanton

Table 4
Open *TBL60C1* (60C, Table 1). Shade Confederate officer rows in 10% gray shading and Union officer rows in light blue shading (or 5% gray).

 **Save as:** *TBL61C4*

KEY PEOPLE IN
AMERICAN HISTORY

Name	Accomplishment	Life
Alexander Grayam Bell	Invented the telephone in 1976.	1847-1922
John Wilkes Boothe	Actor; Assassin of President Lincoln, April 14, 1865	1838-1865
	Scotish immigrant who built a fortune by building steel mills.	1835-1919
Crazy Horse	Sioux Indian chief who resisted government demands for his tribe to leave the Black Hills.	18421877
Jefferson David	President of the confederate States of America.	1808-1889
	American physicist; theory of relativity led to harnessing nuclear energy.	1879-1955
Thomas Jefferson	Third president of the United States; author of the Declaration of Independence.	1743-1826
Martin Luther King	Civil rights leader; belief in nonviolence was patterned after Mohandas Gandi.	1929-1968
Eleanor Roosevelt	President Franklin D. Roosevelt's wife and a major champoin for civil rights and humanitarian issues.	1884-1962
Elizabeth stanton	American social reformer; led the struggle for women sufferage with Susan B. Anthony.	1815-1902
	American inventor of the incandescent light bulb and the phonograph.	1847-1931

Source: James R. Giese, et al. The American Century, 1999, pp. 929-935.

Select one of the names listed in the table. Use the Internet to find out more about the individual you select. Compose a paragraph or two telling about this person's contribution to American history.

LESSON 62 PRESENT INFORMATION IN TABLES

Objectives:

1. To improve table formatting skills.
2. To use decision-making skills to organize information in a table.

62A • 5' Conditioning Practice

Key each line twice SS; key a 1' writing on line 3; determine *gwam*.

alphabet 1 Jung expects the twelve banks to formalize a few details quickly.
figures 2 The 10 a.m. meeting on May 29 will be in Rooms 360, 247, and 458.
speed 3 Orlando and the neighbor may go downtown to sign the audit forms.

gwam 1' | 1 | 2 | 3 | 4 | 5 | 6 | 7 | 8 | 9 | 10 | 11 | 12 | 13 |

133D • 30'
Skill Check

1. Key three 1' writings on each ¶ for speed; determine *gwam.*
2. Key two 3' writings on all ¶s combined for control; circle errors.
3. Key two 5' writings on all ¶s combined. Record and retain your better 5' *gwam* and error count and compare it to the score you received in 132D.

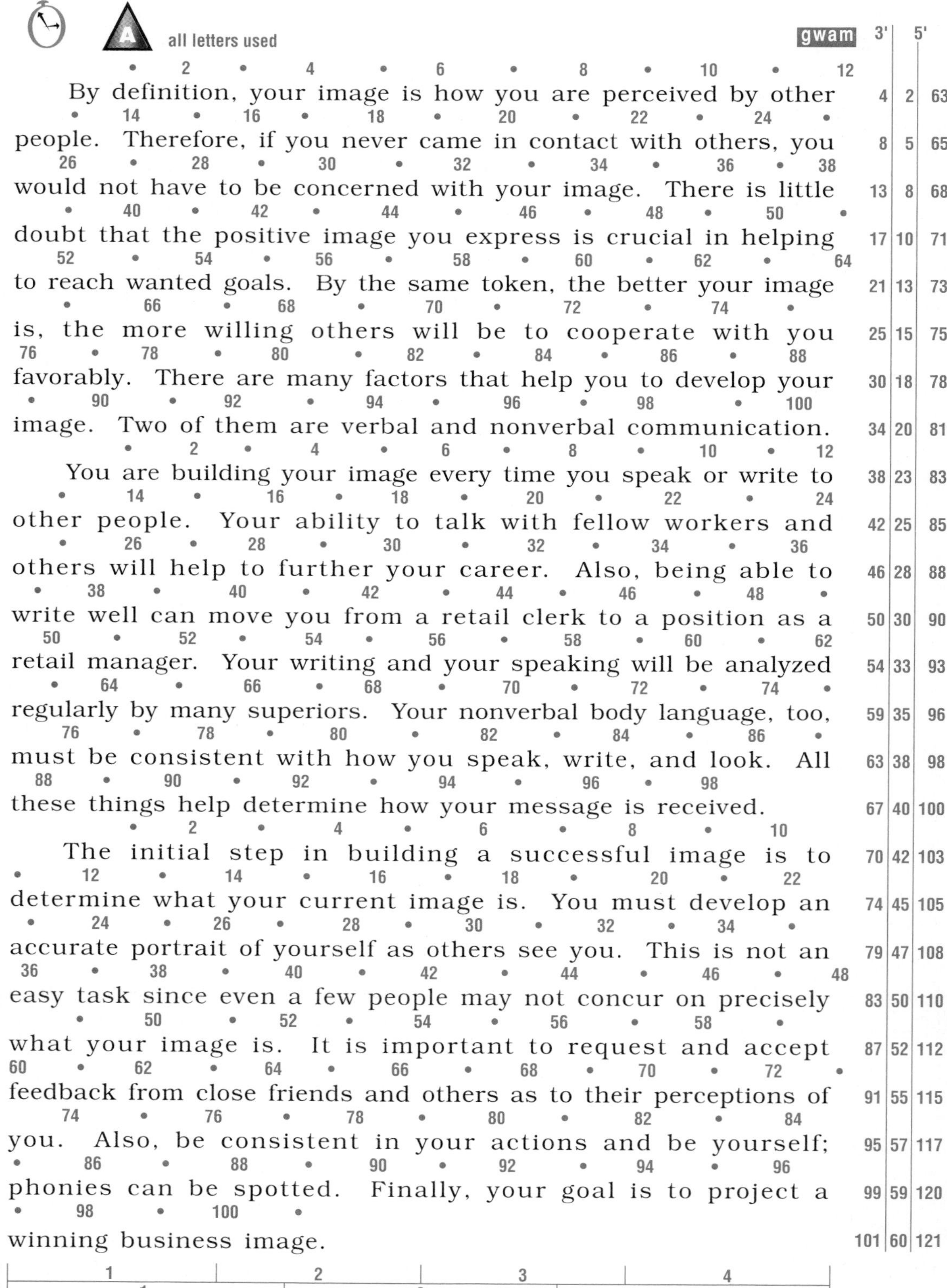

all letters used

	gwam 3'	5'	
By definition, your image is how you are perceived by other	4	2	63
people. Therefore, if you never came in contact with others, you	8	5	65
would not have to be concerned with your image. There is little	13	8	68
doubt that the positive image you express is crucial in helping	17	10	71
to reach wanted goals. By the same token, the better your image	21	13	73
is, the more willing others will be to cooperate with you	25	15	75
favorably. There are many factors that help you to develop your	30	18	78
image. Two of them are verbal and nonverbal communication.	34	20	81
You are building your image every time you speak or write to	38	23	83
other people. Your ability to talk with fellow workers and	42	25	85
others will help to further your career. Also, being able to	46	28	88
write well can move you from a retail clerk to a position as a	50	30	90
retail manager. Your writing and your speaking will be analyzed	54	33	93
regularly by many superiors. Your nonverbal body language, too,	59	35	96
must be consistent with how you speak, write, and look. All	63	38	98
these things help determine how your message is received.	67	40	100
The initial step in building a successful image is to	70	42	103
determine what your current image is. You must develop an	74	45	105
accurate portrait of yourself as others see you. This is not an	79	47	108
easy task since even a few people may not concur on precisely	83	50	110
what your image is. It is important to request and accept	87	52	112
feedback from close friends and others as to their perceptions of	91	55	115
you. Also, be consistent in your actions and be yourself;	95	57	117
phonies can be spotted. Finally, your goal is to project a	99	59	120
winning business image.	101	60	121

gwam 3' | 1 | 2 | 3 | 4
5' | 1 | 2 | 3

SKILL BUILDING

62B • 8' Timed Writings

1. Take two 1' writings for speed; determine *gwam* on each writing.
2. Key one 3' writing for speed; determine *gwam*.

  all letters used

gwam 1' | 3'

Have you ever thought about becoming a teacher? Teachers 12 4
are crucial to our welfare. They are put in charge of one of 24 8
America's most precious resources, students. They are expected to 37 12
assist in developing this resource into a well-rounded person who 51 17
fits in well with other members of our culture. They are also 63 21
expected to produce students who are able to contribute to society 77 26
and make it a better place to live. Our culture hinges on the 89 30
quality of teachers we entrust with our future. 99 33

Being a teacher is quite a challenge. Teachers work with a 111 37
broad range of individuals with a variety of interests, back- 123 41
grounds, and abilities. Teachers try to help all students realize 136 45
their potential and be able to cope with a world that is changing 149 50
very rapidly every day. A teacher's job is to try to equip stu- 162 54
dents with the skills necessary to be lifelong learners, to keep 175 58
pace with changes, and to be productive. In order to be success- 188 63
ful at teaching, a person must like working with people and enjoy 201 67
learning. 203 68

62C • 7' Table Editing

Open *TBL61C3* (61C, Table 3) and make the following changes.

1. Delete *John Wilkes Booth* and *Thomas Jefferson* from the table.
2. Add the three names shown at the right (alphabetical order).
3. Make any adjustments necessary to make the table fit on one page.

 **Save as:** *TBL62C*

Tisquantum	Taught the Pilgrims farming techniques; helped them establish treaties with native tribes.	1580-1622 (approx.)
Sir Walter Raleigh	English adventurer who settled the region from South Carolina north to present-day New York City under a charter from Queen Elizabeth I of England.	1554-1618
John D. Rockefeller	Oil magnate and philanthropist; founded Standard Oil Company in 1870.	1839-1937

LESSON 133 IMPROVE KEYBOARDING SKILLS

Objectives:

1. To improve keyboarding techniques and straight-copy speed and control.
2. To improve language skills.

133A • 5' Conditioning Practice

Key each line twice SS; take 30" writings on line 1; determine *gwam*.

alphabet 1 Freda enjoyed checking the tax problems in the law quiz she gave.

figures 2 Out of 647 seniors and 893 juniors, 1,250 attended the last prom.

speed 3 They may go to the social held at the giant chapel on the island.

gwam 1' | 1 | 2 | 3 | 4 | 5 | 6 | 7 | 8 | 9 | 10 | 11 | 12 | 13 |

LANGUAGE SKILLS

133B • 5' Language Skills: Word Choice

1. Study the spelling and definitions of the words at the right.
2. Key the Learn lines, noting word choice.
3. Key the Apply lines, selecting the correct words.
4. Check the accuracy of your work with the instructor. Rekey lines that contain a word-choice error.

Save as: *CHOICE133B*

desert (n) a region rendered barren by environmental extremes

dessert (n) the last course of a lunch or dinner

miner (n) one who removes minerals/ore from the earth; machine used for that purpose

minor (adj/n) lesser/smaller in amount, extent, or size; under legal age

Learn 1 The diner will keep the **dessert** to eat as a snack in the **desert**.

Apply 2 April is planning to serve apple pie for (desert/dessert) today.

Apply 3 The men filled six water bottles for the (desert/dessert) trip.

Learn 1 The injury to the copper **miner** is no **minor** legal matter.

Apply 2 The law states that a (miner/minor) can't work as a (miner/minor).

Apply 3 This is a (miner/minor) point, but the (miner/minor) will retire soon.

SKILL BUILDING

133C • 10' Technique: Continuity and Rhythm

Key each line three times (slowly, then faster, then in-between rate for control).

Goal:

To keep hands quiet with keystroking action limited to fingers.

Emphasize continuity and rhythm with curved, upright fingers.

p Peppy's playful puppy pulled the papers off the apples and pears.

q Quin quit questioning a requirement for bouquets at the banquet.

r Rory and Larry arrived from a carriage ride over the rural roads.

s Susana sat still as soon as Suno served sushi and sashini dishes.

t Ted took title to two cottages the last time he went to the city.

u Ursula usually rushes to help us unload the sugar from the truck.

v Vera voted to review the vivid videos on my visit to the village.

w Wib was waving wildly when the swimmer was wading into the water.

x Tax experts explain that I am exempt from an existing excise tax.

y Young boys yearn to go yachting each year on my big yellow yacht.

z Zeno puzzled over a zealot who seized a bronze kazoo at a bazaar.

62D • 30'
Table Formatting

Table 1

Key the table at the right using the information given below.

Column headings: row height 0.4"; center vertical alignment; bold text.

Data rows: row height 0.4"; bottom vertical alignment.

Table placement: center horizontally and vertically.

Save as: *TBL62D1*

Table 2

Format the table shown below right using the information below.

Column headings: row height 0.4"; center vertical alignment; bold text; 15% gray shading.

Data rows: row height 0.4"; bottom vertical alignment; 15% gray shading where shown.

Table placement: center horizontally and vertically.

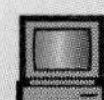
Save as: *TBL62D2*

History Bits

"Under the command of Gen. Eisenhower, Allied naval forces supported by strong air forces began landing Allied armies this morning on the northern coast of France."

—Communiqué No. 1

Table 3

Note that Table 2 contains the same information as Table 1, but arranged in a different way. Use your decision-making skills to create a third table from the information, arranging it in still another way. Insert a row for the source note.

Save as: *TBL62D3*

WHAT AMERICANS REMEMBER

Top Five Events

Rank	Age Group			
	18-35	35-54	55-64	65 and Over
1	Oklahoma City Bombing	Oklahoma City Bombing	JFK Death	JFK Death
2	Challenger	JFK Death	Moon Walk	Pearl Harbor
3	Gulf War Begins	Challenger	Oklahoma City Bombing	WWII Ends
4	Reagan Shot	Moon Walk	Challenger	Moon Walk
5	Berlin Wall Falls	Gulf War Begins	MLK Death	FDR Death

Source: The Pew Research Center, "Public Perspectives on the American Century." http://www.people-press.org/mill1sec4.htm (20 August 1999).

WHAT AMERICANS REMEMBER

Top Five Events

Event	**Age Group**			
	18-35	**35-54**	**55-64**	**65+**
■ Berlin Wall Falls	5	*	*	*
■ Challenger	2	3	4	*
■ Franklin D. Roosevelt Death	*	*	*	5
■ Gulf War Begins	3	5	*	*
■ John F. Kennedy Death	*	2	1	1
■ Martin Luther King, Jr., Death	*	*	5	*
■ Moon Walk	*	4	2	4
■ Oklahoma City Bombing	1	1	3	*
■ Pearl Harbor	*	*	*	2
■ Reagan Shot	4	*	*	*
■ World War II Ends	*	*	*	3
1 = Ranked First, 2 = Ranked Second, etc.; * = Not ranked in top five by this age group.				

Source: The Pew Research Center, "Public Perspectives on the American Century." http://www.people-press.org/mill1sec4.htm (20 August 1999).

132C, cont.

h Healthy habits and high hopes help them through the hockey match.
i Ida will insist on sliding on the big icy path five or six times.
j Jed objected to taking Jim's jeans and jogging jersey on the jet.
k Kit kept Ki's knickknack in a sack in the keel of the knockabout.
l Lolla and Lily will fill all small holes in the left lane early.
m Mia meets my mom most mornings at the mall in the summer months.
n Nora's niece and nephew can be tended by one new nanny on Monday.
o One of four officers opposed opening offshore moorings for boats.

SKILL BUILDING

132D • 25' Skill Check

1. Key three 1' writings on each ¶ for speed; determine *gwam*. Count errors. If the number of errors is two or fewer on any writing, set a goal to increase speed by one or two *gwam* in Step 2. If the number of errors on any writing is more than two, set a goal to increase control (0–2 errors) in Step 2.
2. Key two 3' writings on all ¶s combined; determine *gwam* and count errors.
3. Key two 5' writings on all ¶s combined; determine *gwam* and count errors. Record and retain your better 5' *gwam* and error count for use in 133D.

A all letters used

	gwam 3'	5'	
Character is often described as a person's combined moral or	4	2	43
ethical strength. Most people think it is like integrity, which	8	5	46
is thought to be a person's ability to adhere to a code or a set	13	8	48
standard of values. If a person's values are accepted by society,	17	10	51
others are likely to view her or him as having a somewhat high	21	13	53
degree of integrity.	23	14	54
You need to know that character is a trait that everyone	27	16	57
possesses and that it is formed over time. A person's character	31	19	59
reflects his or her definition of what is good or just. Most	35	21	62
children and teenagers model their character through the words	39	24	64
and deeds of parents, teachers, and other adults with whom they	44	26	67
have regular contact.	45	27	68
Existing character helps mold future character. It is im-	49	29	70
portant to realize that today's actions can have a lasting effect.	53	32	73
For that reason, there is no better time than now to make all	57	34	75
your words and deeds speak favorably. You want them to portray	62	37	78
the things others require of people who are thought to possess a	66	40	80
high degree of character.	68	41	81

gwam 3' 1 2 3 4
5' 1 2 3

LESSON 63 APPLY BORDERS TO TABLES

Objectives:

1. To improve table formatting skills.
2. To format tables with enhanced borders and shading.

63A • 5' Conditioning Practice

Key each line twice SS; key a 1' writing on line 3; determine *gwam*.

alphabet 1 Karla justified a very low quiz score by explaining her problems.

fig/sym 2 My property tax increased by 12.7% ($486); I paid $3,590 in 2001.

speed 3 They may work with us to make a profit for the eighty auto firms.

gwam 1' | 1 | 2 | 3 | 4 | 5 | 6 | 7 | 8 | 9 | 10 | 11 | 12 | 13 |

FORMATTING

63B • 45' Table Formatting

Table 1

Format the table at the right. Use the table formatting features that you have learned to arrange the information attractively on the page. Use a table border and shading similar to the illustration. Adjust column widths so that each data entry fits on a single line.

Save as: *TBL63B1*

PRESIDENTS 1945 - 2001				
President	**Years in Office**	**Profession**	**Elected from**	**Vice President**
Harry S. Truman	1945 - 1953	Businessman	Missouri	Alben W. Barkley
Dwight D. Eisenhower	1953 - 1961	Soldier	Kansas	Richard M. Nixon
John F. Kennedy	1961 - 1963	Author	Massachusetts	Lyndon B. Johnson
Lyndon B. Johnson	1963 - 1969	Teacher	Texas	Hubert H. Humphrey
Richard M. Nixon	1969 - 1974	Lawyer	California	Spiro T. Agnew Gerald R. Ford
Gerald R. Ford	1974 - 1977	Lawyer	Michigan	Nelson A. Rockefeller
James E. Carter, Jr.	1977 - 1981	Businessman	Georgia	Walter F. Mondale
Ronald W. Reagan	1981 - 1989	Actor	California	George H. W. Bush
George H. W. Bush	1989 - 1993	Businessman	Texas	J. Danforth Quayle
William J. Clinton	1993 - 2001	Lawyer	Arkansas	Albert Gore, Jr.
Blue = Republican Party Affiliation		Red = Democratic Party Affiliation		

Source: Matthew T. Downey, et al. United States History, 1997, pp. 1132–1133.

History Bits

"Ask not what your country can do for you—ask what you can do for your country."

—John F. Kennedy

UNIT 34

LESSONS 132–133

Building Basic Skills

LESSON 132 — IMPROVE KEYBOARDING SKILLS

Objectives:

1. To improve keyboarding techniques.
2. To improve straight- and statistical-copy speed and control.

132A • 5' Conditioning Practice

Key each line twice; take 30" writings on line 1; determine *gwam*.

alphabet 1 Tezz quickly indexed jokes for a public performance he will give.

fig/sym 2 Sales discounts (15%) amount to $134,682; an increase of $21,790.

speed 3 The eight busy men may do the work for us if he pays for the ivy.

gwam 1' | 1 | 2 | 3 | 4 | 5 | 6 | 7 | 8 | 9 | 10 | 11 | 12 | 13 |

SKILL BUILDING

132B • 10' Statistical Copy

1. Key one 2' writing. Determine errors and *gwam*.
2. Select a goal: If you have more than four errors in Step 1, select *control* and reduce errors by one on each writing. If you have four or fewer errors, select *speed* and increase *gwam* by 3 on each writing.
3. Key three 2' writings; try to reach your goal on each writing.

	gwam 1'	2'
Let's say that you invested $10,000 in the Clear Horizon	11	6
Fund on January 31, 1990, and reinvested all dividends and capital	24	12
gains. By January 31, 2000, the value of the investment would	37	18
have grown 467.38% to $56,738. This increase on your initial	49	25
investment is even more important because it was earned by a fund	62	31
that invests 85% of its money in companies that do not harm the	75	37
environment. For comparison, the Standard & Poor 500 Index	86	43
increased 442.52% during this same 10-year period.	96	48

gwam 1' | 1 | 2 | 3 | 4 | 5 | 6 | 7 | 8 | 9 | 10 | 11 | 12 | 13 |
2' | 1 | 2 | 3 | 4 | 5 | 6 |

SKILL BUILDING

132C • 10' Technique: Continuity and Rhythm

Key each line three times (slowly, then faster, then in-between rate for control).

Goal:

To keep hands quiet with keystroking action limited to fingers.

Emphasize continuity and rhythm with curved, upright fingers.

a After Al and Ann ate the pancake, each had an apple and a banana.

b Bea became the best batter by being best at batting rubber balls.

c Chris can use pictures of a raccoon and cactus in their calendar.

d Did Red say he was a decoy doing deep runs to defeat the defense?

e Ed, Eve, and Keene were elected to chaperon every evening event.

f Fred figures fifty rafts floated from Fairfax to Fordstaff Falls.

g Greg and Geof glanced at a gaggle of geese going over the garage.

(continued on next page)

Table 2
Format the table at the right. Use the table formatting features that you have learned to arrange the information attractively on the page. Use a border and shading similar to the illustration. Bold all text. DS between data entries.

Save as: *TBL63B2*

THE CONSTITUTION		
The Executive Branch	**The Legislative Branch**	**The Judicial Branch**
• President administers and enforces federal laws • President chosen by electors who have been chosen by the states	• A bicameral or two-house legislature • Each state has equal number of representatives in the Senate • Representation in the House determined by state population • Simple majority required to enact legislation	• National court system directed by the Supreme Court • Courts to hear cases related to national laws, treaties, the Constitution; cases between states, between citizens of different states, or between a state and citizens of another state

Source: Matthew T. Downey, et al. United States History, 1997, p. 158.

Table 3
Format the table at the right. Use the table formatting features that you have learned to arrange the information attractively on the page. Use a border similar to the one shown.

Save as: *TBL63B3*

MOST IMPORTANT PROBLEM		
Question: What do you think is the most important problem facing this country today?		
Year	**Problem**	**Percent**
1961	Unemployment	25
	Threat of war	19
	Threat of Communism	14
	Foreign relations/getting along with other people/nations	10
	Relations with Russia (no mention of war threat)	8
	Domestic economic problems - general	8
	Racial problems	6
1977	Inflation/high cost of living	58
	Unemployment/recession	39
	Energy shortage	23
	International problems/national defense	18
	Crime/courts	18
	Dissatisfaction with government/corruption	7
	Moral decline	6
1989	Economy	35
	Drug abuse	27
	Poverty	10
	Crime	6
	Moral decline	5

Source: Matthew T. Downey, et al. United States History, 1997, pp. 875, 1001, 1050.

131B • 30'
Worksheets

Worksheet 1

1. Key the worksheet at right.
2. Use center alignment; apply Number format (to 1 decimal place); adjust column widths to fit contents.
3. Add title and source note shown at right.

 **Save as:** *L131B1*

Ages	1950	1960	1970	1980	1990	2000	2010	2020
1-18	47.3	64.5	69.8	63.7	64.2	70.8	72.9	77.6
0-5	19.1	24.3	20.9	19.6	22.5	22.9	23.9	26.4
6-11	15.3	21.8	24.6	20.8	21.6	24.6	23.6	25.8
12-18	12.9	18.4	24.3	23.3	20.1	23.6	25.0	25.4

1. In Cell A1, key **MILLIONS OF U.S. CHILDREN UNDER AGE 18** using bold, ALL CAPS.
2. In Cell A7, key **Source: http://www.childstats.gov/ac1999/pop1.htm** in italic.

Worksheet 2

1. Open file *CD-L131B2.*
2. In Column G, calculate a total of all the test scores for each student; in Row 25, calculate a total class score for each test.
3. Make the changes listed at the right.

 **Save as:** *L131B2*

1. In Column H, calculate an average score (to one decimal place) for each student; in Row 26, calculate an average class score (to one decimal place) for each test.
2. Insert these rows in alphabetical order: **MACY | 80 | 75 | 83 | 90 | 95 |** and **WEHNER | 67 | 72 | 85 | 92 | 88 |**.
3. Delete the COMO, ROGERS, and STOEHR rows; center-align all numbers.
4. Shade every other row from Briggs to Zigerell using the same color.
5. Increase the font size to 16 pt. in Cell A1; bold Cell A1 and Row 2.
6. Shade the last two cells in the TOTAL and AVERAGE rows.
7. Copy Row 2 to the row after AVERAGE.
8. Change Gordon's score for Test 2 to **88** and for Test 5 to **78**.
9. Bold all cells in the TOTAL and AVERAGE columns and rows.

131C • 15'
Embedded Charts

Create the charts at the right.

Chart 1: Column Chart

1. Open file *CD-L131C1.*
2. Create a column chart; use **EAGLE FUND** as the title; show gridlines and a legend.

 **Save as:** *L131C1*

Chart 2: Bar Chart

1. Open file *CD-L131C2.*
2. Create a bar chart titled **MAY RECYCLING REPORT**; use **May** and **Soda Cans** as axis titles; and show values as data labels. Show a legend but no gridlines.

 **Save as:** *L131C2*

Chart 3: Pie Chart

1. Open file *CD-L131C3.*
2. Create a pie chart; use **COMMUNITY DAYS SALES** as the title; show values as data labels; and show a legend.

 **Save as:** *L131C3*

1. Read the two ¶s at the right.
2. Access the Mayo Clinic Web site: http://www.mayohealth.org
3. Click the **Nutrition** link and follow a link that interests you.
4. Compose 2-3 ¶s describing what you learned from this site and print 1-2 pages from the site that relate to what you wrote.

Nutrition is the science that pertains to foods and the way our bodies use them. Our bodies use the nutrients in food for energy so all of our bodily functions can be maintained. The energy in food is measured in calories. One food calorie equals the amount of energy required to raise the temperature of 1,000 grams of water one degree Celsius.

The amount of energy needed varies from person to person. Have you ever wondered how much energy you need to maintain your weight, lose weight, or gain weight? How many carbohydrates, fats, proteins, minerals, and vitamins should you have each day to get the energy you need? Perhaps you can get the answers to these or other questions you have at the Mayo Clinic Web site that you will access in this activity.

IMPROVE TABLE FORMATTING SKILLS

Objectives:

1. To improve table formatting skills.
2. To format tables with enhanced borders and shading.

64A • 5'
Conditioning Practice

Key each line twice SS; key a 1' writing on line 3; determine *gwam*.

alphabet 1 Chuck said Dr. Webber plans on requiring just five zoology exams.

fig/sym 2 After deducting the 20% discount, Invoice #14380 totaled $597.60.

speed 3 Orlando may make an official bid for the antique enamel fishbowl.

gwam 1' | 1 | 2 | 3 | 4 | 5 | 6 | 7 | 8 | 9 | 10 | 11 | 12 | 13 |

64B • 45'
Table Editing

Table 1

Key the table at the right; insert each of the following three names next to the individual's accomplishments.

Alex Haley
Thurgood Marshall
Colin Powell

Use the table formatting features that you have learned to arrange the data attractively on the page. Use a border similar to the one shown.

Save as: *TBL64B1*

History Bits

"I have learned that success is to be measured not so much by the position that one has reached in life as by the obstacles which he has overcome while trying to succeed. Out of the hard and unusual struggle through which he is compelled to pass, he gets a strength, a confidence, that one misses whose pathway is comparatively smooth by reason of birth and race."
—Booker T. Washington

FAMOUS AMERICANS

Name	Significant Accomplishments
Charles Drew	Developed a means for preserving blood plasma for transfusion.
	First black officer to hold the highest military post in the U.S., Chairman of the U.S. Joint Chiefs of Staff.
Shirley Chisholm	First black woman to be elected to the U.S. Congress.
	First black member of the U.S. Supreme Court.
Booker T. Washington	Organized a teaching and industrial school for African Americans—Tuskegee Institute.
Benjamin Banneker	First African American to receive a presidential appointment. Famous for his role as a planner for Washington, D.C.
W. E. B. Du Bois	Cofounder of the organization that became the National Association for the Advancement of Colored People (NAACP).
Alice Walker	Pulitzer Prize-winning writer and poet. Novels include *The Color Purple* and *In Love and Trouble*.
	Pulitzer Prize-winning author. Wrote *Roots*, which was made into the highest-rated television miniseries of all time.
Frederick Douglass	Eminent human rights leader of the 19th century; the first black citizen to hold a high rank in the U.S. government.

Source: "Black History Innovators." USA Today. http://www.usatoday.com (15 February 2000).

130C • 25'
Embedded Charts

Chart 1: Column Chart

1. Key the worksheet below.
2. Create a column chart, using **VICTORIES BY PITCHER** as the title.
3. Show data labels and axis titles, but no legend.

 **Save as:** *L130C1*

	A	B
1	PITCHER	VICTORIES
2	Batiste	8
3	Ruiz	15
4	Hammel	5
5	Yu Chin	13

Chart 2: Column Chart

1. Key the worksheet below.
2. Create a column chart, using **PROM ATTENDANCE** as the title.
3. Show axis titles and a legend, but no data labels. Key **Students** for the x axis title, and **Number Attending** for the y axis title.

 **Save as:** *L130C2*

	A	B	C
1		THIS	LAST
2	CLASS	YEAR	YEAR
3	Seniors	132	128
4	Juniors	154	144
5	Sophomores	66	54
6	Freshmen	12	18

Chart 3: Bar Chart

1. Key the worksheet below.
2. Create a bar chart, using **MAY PATIENTS** as the title.
3. Show axis titles but no data labels or legend.

 **Save as:** *L130C3*

	A	B
1	Doctor	Patients
2	Lalli	105
3	Danko	118
4	Lewis	138
5	Harris	97
6	Justi	106
7	Wills	123

Chart 4: Bar Chart

1. Key the worksheet below.
2. Create a bar chart, using **PATIENT REPORT** as the title.
3. Show axis titles, data labels, and a legend. Use **Month** and **Number of Patients** for the axis titles.

 **Save as:** *L130C4*

	A	B	C
1	Month	In Patient	Out Patient
2	APRIL	350	725
3	MAY	365	752
4	JUNE	290	645

Chart 5: Pie Chart

1. Key the worksheet below.
2. Create a pie chart, using **PARTICIPANTS** as the title.
3. Show data labels and a legend.

 **Save as:** *L130C5*

	A	B
1	Area	Number
2	Northeast	155
3	Midwest	145
4	Southeast	175
5	West	135
6	Southwest	75

Chart 6: Pie Chart

1. Key the worksheet below.
2. Create a pie chart, using **BUDGET** as the title.
3. Show data labels and a legend.

 **Save as:** *L130C6*

	A	B
1	CATEGORY	PERCENT
2	Savings	10%
3	Food	20%
4	Clothing	15%
5	Shelter	40%
6	Transportation	15%

LESSON 131 APPLY YOUR KNOWLEDGE

Objective:

To apply what you have learned to prepare worksheets and charts.

131A • 5'
Conditioning Practice

Key each line twice; take 30" writings on line 3; determine *gwam*.

alphabet 1 Hazel fixed the two pairs of jumper cables very quickly for Gwen.

fig/sym 2 Expenses increased $82,965 (5%) and net profit fell $31,470 (6%).

speed 3 Did eighty firms bid on six authentic maps of the ancient island?

gwam 1' | 1 | 2 | 3 | 4 | 5 | 6 | 7 | 8 | 9 | 10 | 11 | 12 | 13 |

Table 2

Information about 12 states is shown at the right. Create and format a table that shows all of the information in one table. Use **INFORMATION ABOUT SELECTED STATES** as a title. Data about each state should make up one row of the table. Include this source note: **James R. Giese, et al. The American Century, 1999, pp. 922-925.**

Place a border around each cell that has a **1** or a **50** to show the states that rank first and last. Shade or color these bordered cells to highlight them even more.

Save as: *TBL64B2*

Alaska Rank Entering Union: 49 Rank Land Area: 1 Rank Population: 49	**Idaho** Rank Entering Union: 43 Rank Land Area: 13 Rank Population: 42	**Montana** Rank Entering Union: 41 Rank Land Area: 4 Rank Population: 44
California Rank Entering Union: 31 Rank Land Area: 3 Rank Population: 1	**Illinois** Rank Entering Union: 21 Rank Land Area: 24 Rank Population: 6	**Nebraska** Rank Entering Union: 37 Rank Land Area: 15 Rank Population: 36
Delaware Rank Entering Union: 1 Rank Land Area: 49 Rank Population: 46	**Kansas** Rank Entering Union: 34 Rank Land Area: 14 Rank Population: 32	**Rhode Island** Rank Entering Union: 13 Rank Land Area: 50 Rank Population: 43
Hawaii Rank Entering Union: 50 Rank Land Area: 47 Rank Population: 41	**Michigan** Rank Entering Union: 26 Rank Land Area: 23 Rank Population: 8	**Wyoming** Rank Entering Union: 44 Rank Land Area: 9 Rank Population: 50

Table 3

Format the table at the right. Use the table formatting features that you have learned to arrange the information attractively on the page. Use a border and shading color similar to the one shown.

Save as: *TBL64B3*

NATIVE AMERICAN NAMES OF PLACES

State: New York

Name of Place	Tribe	Derivation
Adirondacks	Iroquoian	Name of town, park, and mountain range; derived from tribal name, meaning "bark eaters."
Allegheny	Delaware	Name of plateau and reservoir; probably from the name for Allegheny and Ohio rivers.
Manhattan	Algonkian	Name of island and borough; derived from tribal name, probably meaning "island-mountain."
Niagara	Iroquoian	Name of town, county, river, and falls, meaning "point of land cut in two."
Poughkeepsie	Algonkian	Name of town, meaning "little rock at water."
Seneca	Mohegan	Name of county, river, lake, and falls; derived from tribal name, probably meaning "people of the stone."
Susquehanna	Iroquoian	Name of river; derived from tribal name.

Source: The Native North American Almanac, 1994.

Table 4 - Optional Editing Activity

Open *TBL64B2* (64B, Table 2). Insert a column for showing the **Electoral Votes** for each state.

AK 3; CA 54; DE 3; HI 4; ID 4; IL 22; KS 6; MI 18; MT 3; NE 5; RI 4; WY 3

Save as: *TBL64B4*

LESSON 130 — CREATE CHARTS IN WORKSHEETS

Objective:
To prepare embedded column, bar, and pie charts using worksheet information.

130A • 5' Conditioning Practice

Key each line twice; take 30" writings on line 3; determine *gwam*.

alphabet 1 Weber excluded a quick jaunt to the big zoo from my travel plans.

figures 2 My agents will sell 43 tables, 59 beds, 187 chairs, and 206 rugs.

speed 3 Their neighbor may pay the downtown chapel for the ancient ivory.

gwam 1' | 1 | 2 | 3 | 4 | 5 | 6 | 7 | 8 | 9 | 10 | 11 | 12 | 13 |

130B • 20' Charts

1. Read the text at the right.
2. Learn to create charts using your ss software.
3. Create the charts shown below from the information at the right.

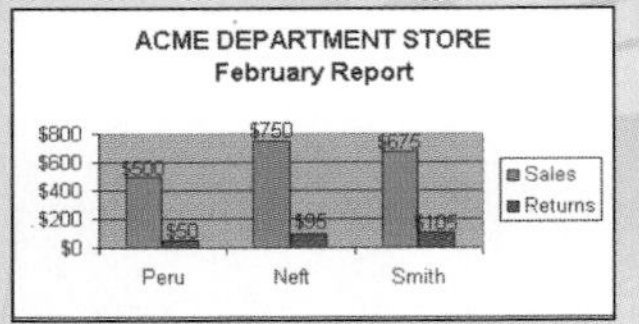

Column Chart

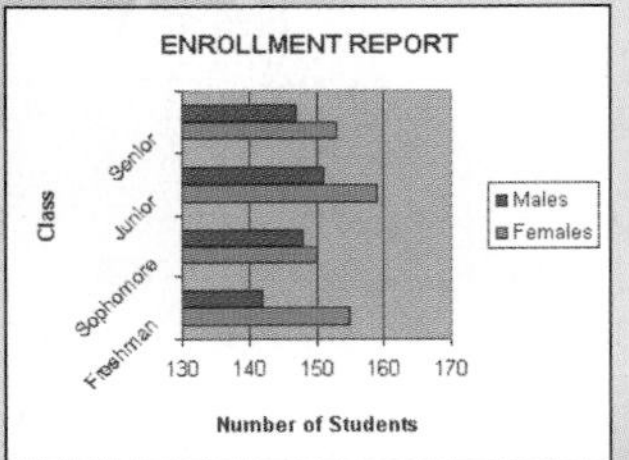

Bar Chart

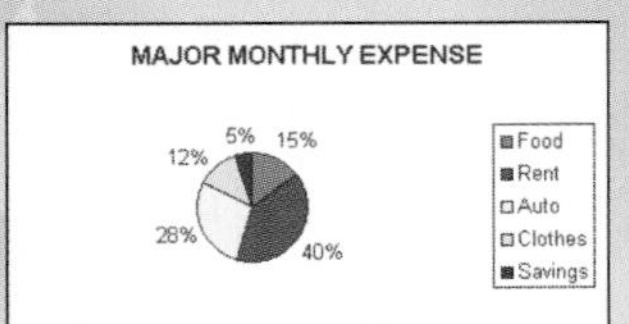

Pie Chart

Spreadsheet software provides options to create a variety of **charts** including **column**, **bar**, **line**, and **pie** charts. Usually, charts can be created as (1) a **chart sheet** that appears as a separate worksheet or (2) an **embedded chart** that appears as an object within a worksheet.

In this activity you will create embedded column, bar, and pie charts using the chart parts described below.

Titles—headings that identify chart contents and axes.

Axes—the **category axis**, sometimes called the *x axis*, is used to plot categories of data.

The **value axis**, usually the *y axis*, is used to plot values associated with the categories of data.

Data points—the bars, columns, or pie slices that represent the numerical data in the chart.

Data labels—numbers or words that identify the values displayed in the chart.

Gridlines—lines through a chart that identify intervals on the axes.

Legend—a key (usually with different colors or patterns) used to identify the chart's data categories.

Chart 1: Column Chart

Open file *CD-L130B1* and create an embedded column chart with gridlines, data labels, and a legend. Use **ACME DEPARTMENT STORE** as the chart title and **February Report** as the chart subtitle.

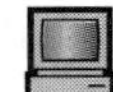

Save as: *L130B1*

Chart 2: Bar Chart

Open file *CD-L130B2* and create an embedded bar chart with gridlines, axis titles, and a legend. Key **Class** for the x axis title and **Number of Students** for the y axis title. Use **ENROLLMENT REPORT** as the chart title.

Save as: *L130B2*

Chart 3: Pie Chart

Open file *CD-L130B3* and create an embedded pie chart displaying a legend and data labels in percents. Use **MAJOR MONTHLY EXPENSE** as the chart title.

Save as: *L130B3*

Communication Skills 8

ACTIVITY 1

Internal Punctuation: Comma and Colon

1. Key lines 1–14 at the right, supplying the needed commas and colons.
2. Check the accuracy of your work with the instructor; correct any errors you made.
3. Note the rule number at the left of each sentence in which you made a comma or colon error.
4. Using the rules below the sentences and on p. 184, identify the rule(s) you need to review/practice.
5. **Read**: Study each rule.
6. **Learn**: Key the Learn line(s) beneath it, noting how the rule is applied.
7. **Apply**: Key the Apply line(s), adding commas and colons as needed.

 **Save as:** *CS8-ACT1*

Proofread & Correct

Rules		
1,3	1	The memorial was dedicated on November 13 1982—not 1,983.
1	2	We played in the Hoosier Dome in Indianapolis Indiana.
1	3	I cited an article in the May 8 1999, *Wall Street Journal.*
2	4	Carl sent Diana a dozen bright red long-stem roses.
2	5	He buys most of his clothes at a store for big tall men.
3	6	Our enrollment for 1999, 1,884; for 2000 2040.
3	7	Where is the request for books and supplies for Room 1,004?
1,3	8	Policy #HP294,873 took effect on September 20 1999.
3	9	Della and Eldon Simms paid $129000 for their new condo.
4	10	Dry cleaning list 1 suit; 2 jackets; 3 pants; 2 sweaters.
5	11	Golden Rule Do unto others as you would have them do unto you.
5	12	I quote Jean Racine "Innocence has nothing to dread."
6	13	Glynda asked me to meet her 2 15 p.m. flight at JFK Airport.
6	14	Ten o'clock in the morning is the same as 10 00 a.m.

Internal Punctuation: Comma

> Rule 1: Use a comma to separate the day from the year and the city from the state.

Learn 1 Lincoln delivered the Gettysburg Address on November 19, 1863.
Learn 2 The convention will be held at Cobo Hall in Detroit, Michigan.
Apply 3 Did you find this table in the March 16 1999, *USA Today*?
Apply 4 Are you entered in the piano competition in Austin Texas?

> Rule 2: Use a comma to separate two or more parallel adjectives (adjectives that could be separated by the word *and* instead of a comma).

Learn 5 The big, loud bully was ejected after he pushed the coach.
Learn 6 Cynthia played a black lacquered grand piano at her concert.
Apply 7 The big powerful car zoomed past the cheering crowd.
Apply 8 A small, red fox squeezed through the fence to avoid the hounds.

> Rule 3: Use a comma to separate (a) unrelated groups of figures that occur together and (b) whole numbers into groups of three digits each. (Policy, year, page, room, telephone, invoice, and most serial numbers are keyed without commas.)

Learn 9 By the year 2000, 1,100 more local students will be enrolled.
Learn 10 The supplies listed on Invoice #274068 are for Room 1953.
Apply 11 During 1999 2050 new graduates entered our job market.
Apply 12 See page 1,069 of *Familiar Quotations*, Cat. Card No. 68-15,664.

(continued on next page)

129D • 25' Worksheets

Worksheet 1

1. Create the worksheet at the right as shown.
2. Enter a formula in Cells F1:F10 to calculate the individual batting averages (Hits/At Bats) to three decimal places.
3. Use the SUM function (or Σ button) to calculate the team totals in Cells B10:E10.
4. Use the AVERAGE function to calculate the team averages with no decimal places in Cells B11:E11.
5. Use color fonts and shading as desired.
6. Adjust Column 1 width to fit cell contents.
7. In Cell A14, key **BASEBALL TEAM STATISTICS**, using a 16-pt. font.

Save as: *L129D1*

	A	B	C	D	E	F
1	PLAYER	AT BATS	HITS	HOMERS	RBI	AVG
2	Roberto Orlando	700	225	23	45	
3	Bill York	423	134	2	14	
4	Ernie Hack	590	176	15	35	
5	Joe Dimperio	805	256	33	102	
6	Jose Carlos	476	175	12	31	
7	Hector Avila	365	75	2	5	
8	George Barnes	402	99	16	45	
9	Harry Bell	575	158	17	55	
10	TOTAL					
11	AVERAGE					

Worksheet 2

Using file *L129D1*, insert the rows at the right after *Harry Bell*. Delete the *Carlos* row.

Save as: *L129D2*

PLAYER	AT BATS	HITS	HOMERS	RBI
Pat Ortega	25	8	1	2
Brett Peterson	45	14	3	7

Worksheet 3

1. Create the worksheet.
2. Use the information below to construct formulas/functions in the column/row indicated:
   - Col E=Col C amount * 2
   - Col F=Col B * Col C amounts
   - Col G=Col D * Col E amounts
   - Col H=Col F + Col G amounts
   - Row 13: SUM(Row 4:Row 12)
   - (Clear the contents in Cells C13 and E13.)
   - Row 14: AVERAGE(Row 4:Row 12); two decimal places.
3. Adjust column widths.
4. In Cell A16, enter **RADIOLOGY PAYROLL**.
5. Use formatting and shading as desired.

Save as: *L129D3*

	A	B	C	D	E	F	G	H
1		**Regular**	**Regular**	**Overtime**	**Overtime**			
2		**Hours**	**Pay**	**Hours**	**Pay**	**Regular**	**Overtime**	**Gross**
3	**Employee**	**Worked**	**Rate**	**Worked**	**Rate**	**Pay**	**Pay**	**Pay**
4	S ABLE	40	$9.50	6				
5	G DILLON	40	$10.00	2				
6	H HUTO	35	$10.15	0				
7	H KATSKI	40	$8.75	3				
8	R MORRIS	40	$11.00	0				
9	P STUTZ	38	$11.25	5				
10	L TIERNO	40	$10.75	2				
11	R WALTER	40	$9.95	0				
12	V ZETZ	40	$10.15	4				
13	**Total**							
14	**Average**							

Internal Punctuation: Colon

Rule 4: Use a colon to introduce an enumeration or a listing.

Learn 13 These students are absent: Adam Bux, Todd Cody, and Sue Ott.
Apply 14 Add to the herb list parsley, rosemary, saffron, and thyme.
Apply 15 We must make these desserts a cake, two pies, and cookies.

Rule 5: Use a colon to introduce a question or a quotation.

Learn 16 Here's the real question: Who will pay for the "free" programs?
Learn 17 Who said: "Freedom is nothing else but a chance to be better"?
Apply 18 My question stands Who are we to pass judgment on them?
Apply 19 He quoted Browning "Good, to forgive; Best, to forget."

Rule 6: Use a colon between hours and minutes expressed in figures.

Learn 20 They give two performances: at 2:00 p.m. and at 8:00 p.m.
Apply 21 You have a choice of an 11 15 a.m. or a 2 30 p.m. appointment.
Apply 22 My workday begins at 8 15 a.m. and ends at 5 00 p.m.

ACTIVITY 2

Listening

Complete the listening activity as directed at the right.

Save as: *CS8-ACT2*

You answered a telephone call from George Steward, your father's business associate. Mr. Steward asked you to take a message for your father.

1. Open the sound file (*CD-CS8LISTN*). As you listen to Mr. Steward's message, take notes as needed.
2. Close the sound file.
3. Key or handwrite the message—in complete sentences—for your father.
4. Check the accuracy of your work with the instructor.

ACTIVITY 3

Composing

1. Key the paragraph, correcting the word-choice errors it contains. (Every line contains at least one error; some lines contain two or more errors.)
2. Check the accuracy of your work with the instructor; correct any errors you made.
3. Compose a second paragraph to meet these two goals:
   - Express your viewpoint about special treatment of "stars."
   - State your view about whether *same offense/same penalty* should apply to everyone alike.

Save as: *CS8-ACT3*

Some people think that because their good at sum sport, music, or other activity, there entitled to respect and forgiveness for anything else they choose to do in the passed. Its not uncommon, than, when such people break the law or violate sum code of conduct, four them to expect such behavior to be overlooked buy those who's job it is to enforce the law or to uphold an established code of conduct. Sum parents, as well as others in hour society, think that a "star's" misbehavior ought too be treated less harshly because of that person's vary impressive "celebrity" status; but all people should be treated equally under and threw the law.

129B • 10' Enter Formulas

1. Read the information at the right.
2. Learn how to enter formulas using your ss software.
3. Complete the activity at the right.

Save as: *L129B*

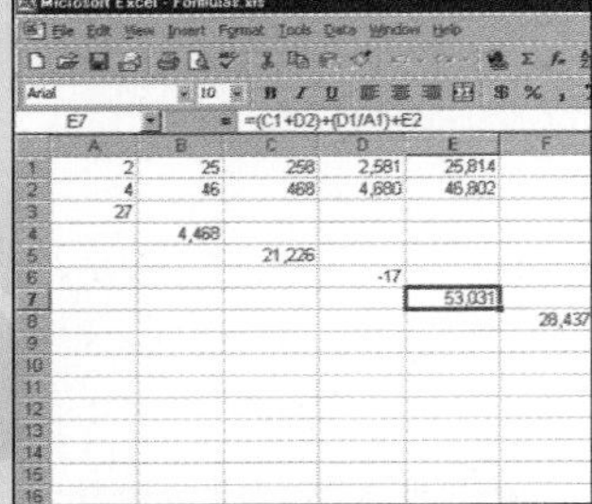

Microsoft Excel - Formulas.xls

E7 = =(C1+D2)+(D1/A1)+E2

	A	B	C	D	E	F
1	2	25	258	2,581	25,814	
2	4	46	468	4,680	46,802	
3	27					
4		4,468				
5			21,226			
6				-17		
7					53,031	
8						28,437
9						
10						
11						
12						
13						
14						
15						
16						

Spreadsheet software can add, subtract, multiply, and divide numbers keyed into the cells. To perform calculations, activate the cell in which the results of the calculation are to appear, and then enter a **formula** in the formula bar. Formulas typically begin with an equals sign (=).

The ss software interprets the formula, following this order of operations: (1) Calculations inside parentheses are performed first before those outside parentheses. (2) Multiplication and division are performed next in the order that they occur in the formula. (3) Addition and subtraction are performed last in their order of occurrence.

1. Open file *CD-L129B* and enter these formulas in the specified cell.
   a. A1+B1 in Cell A3
   b. D2-C1+B2 in Cell B4
   c. A1*B2+E1-D2 in Cell C5
   d. C2*B1/C2+A2-B2 in Cell D6
   e. (C1+D2)+(D1/A1)+E2 in Cell E7
   f. (D1+A1*B2)-(E2/C2-B1*A1)+E1 in Cell F8
   g. In Cell G9, write and enter a formula to add Cells C2, D1, and E2; divide that answer by Cell B1; and then subtract Cell D2.
2. Format the answers for Steps 1a-1g above as *Currency* with two decimal places.

129C • 10' Sum and Average Functions

1. Read the information at the right.
2. Learn how to enter functions using your ss software.
3. Complete the activity at the right.

Save as: *L129C*

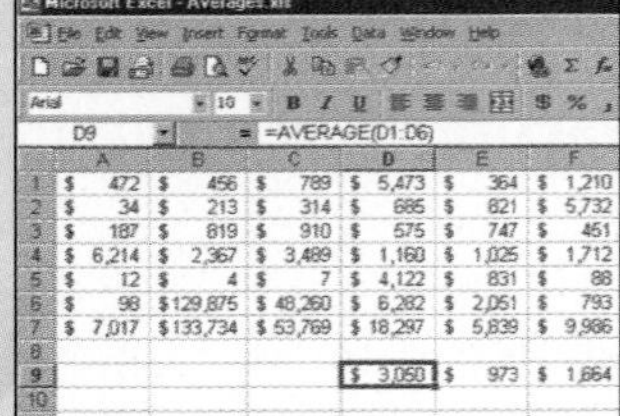

Microsoft Excel - Averages.xls

D9 = =AVERAGE(D1:D6)

	A	B	C	D	E	F
1	$ 472	$ 456	$ 789	$ 5,473	$ 364	$ 1,210
2	$ 34	$ 213	$ 314	$ 686	$ 821	$ 5,732
3	$ 187	$ 819	$ 910	$ 575	$ 747	$ 451
4	$ 6,214	$ 2,367	$ 3,489	$ 1,160	$ 1,025	$ 1,712
5	$ 12	$ 4	$ 7	$ 4,122	$ 831	$ 88
6	$ 98	$129,875	$ 48,260	$ 6,282	$ 2,051	$ 793
7	$ 7,017	$133,734	$ 53,769	$ 18,297	$ 5,839	$ 9,986
8						
9				$ 3,050	$ 973	$ 1,664
10						
11						

Spreadsheet software has built-in or predesigned formulas called **functions**. One of the most commonly used functions is **SUM**. Most ss software has a sum (Σ) button on the toolbar that can be clicked to automatically add the numbers in a column or row without keying the function.

Another frequently used function is **AVERAGE**, which is used to calculate the average of the numbers in a range of cells in a column or row.

Functions have three parts: an equals (=) or plus (+) sign to signal the beginning of a mathematical operation; the function name (SUM or AVERAGE) to identify the operation; and an **argument** (usually the cell range) that defines the numbers to be used in the calculation. Examples of the SUM and AVERAGE functions are: **=SUM(A1:F1)** and **=AVERAGE(A1:F1)**.

1. Open file *CD-L129C*.
2. Use the SUM function to add the numbers in Cells A1:F1, A2:F2, and A3:F3, placing the answers in Column G; add the numbers in Cells A1:A6, B1:B6, and C1:C6, placing the answers in Row 7.
3. Use the Σ button on the toolbar to add the numbers in Cells A4:F4, A5:F5, and A6:F6, placing the answers in Column G; add the numbers in Cells D1:D6, E1:E6, and F1:F6, placing the answers in Row 7.
4. Use the AVERAGE function to average the numbers in Cells A1:F1, A2:F2, and A3:F3, placing the answers in Column I; average the numbers in Cells D1:D6, E1:E6, and F1:F6, placing the answers in Row 9.
5. Format all numbers as *Accounting* with no decimal places, and print gridlines and column/row headings.

SKILL BUILDER 3

Techniques: Figures

1. Set 0.5" side margins.
2. Clear all tabs; then set tabs 2", 4", and 6" from the left margin.
3. Key the lines slowly, tabbing from column to column.
4. Take three 3' writings. Try to key more characters on each writing.

Keep eyes on copy.

				gwam 3'
529-36-2899	12/24/80	(308) 112-2388	$ 628.00	3
358-29-1076	04/30/78	(608) 197-6655	$1,381.00	6
346-50-0190	02/28/81	(520) 130-6754	$5,672.15	9
567-82-8219	10/15/84	(715) 139-2615	$ 56.29	12
628-12-0945	03/27/82	(801) 162-2444	$3,178.87	15
820-67-1029	08/08/79	(308) 138-8567	$9,078.25	18

Reading/Keying Response Patterns

Lines 1–3: each word 3 times (slowly, faster, top speed).

Lines 4–6: each phrase 3 times (slowly, faster, top speed).

Lines 7–9: each sentence 3 times (slowly, faster, top speed).

Goal:
Word-level keying.

Emphasize quick finger reaches, wrists low and relaxed.

balanced-hand words

1 us if he an by is jam fur hen row pay map man sit the and big may
2 dusk dock corn busy both keys firms land rock sign owns mend sick
3 docks bucks eight goals right they shame social towns vivid turns

Emphasize high-speed phrase response.

balanced-hand phrases

4 he owns it | make the signs | paid the man | go to work | if they fix the
5 go to the | they may make | to the problem | with the sign | and the maps
6 with the city | the eighth neighbor | social problem | the big ornament

Emphasize high-speed, word-level response; quick spacing.

balanced-hand sentences

7 Jaynel paid the man by the city dock for the six bushels of corn.
8 Keith may keep the food for the fish by the big antique fishbowl.
9 The haughty girls paid for their own gowns for the island social.

gwam 1' | 1 | 2 | 3 | 4 | 5 | 6 | 7 | 8 | 9 | 10 | 11 | 12 | 13 |

Number Expression Check

Key the sentences at the right; correct number expressions as needed.

1. When you buy 3 cups, they will give you 1 free.
2. 12 of the 26 charter members were at the reunion.
3. If you place your order before two p.m., it will be shipped the next day.
4. Ms. King placed an order for eight copies of The Secretary and 14 copies of Modern Office Technology.
5. Approximately 2/3 of the parents attended the special meeting.
6. The package needs to be delivered to 1 Lakeshore Drive.
7. About 60 students voted for class officers on April seven.
8. The next assignment was Chapter seven, not Chapter eight.
9. Roy is 6 ft. eleven in. tall and weighs 180 lbs.
10. The final flight on July six going to Reno leaves at 8 p.m.

128F • 17' Worksheets

Worksheet 1

1. Create the worksheet at the right as shown.
2. Insert a row between Rows 5 and 6; key **Lunch** in A6, **5** in B6, and **Cafeteria** in C6.
3. Use a red font for Rows 2, 4, 6, and 8, and a green font for Rows 3, 5, 7, and 9.
4. Adjust the column widths to fit the contents.
5. Center-align Cells B2:B9.
6. Insert a row at the top and key **BILL WAVERLY'S SCHEDULE** in Cell A1.
7. Format the worksheet using 14-pt. Arial font for Rows 1 and 2; 12-pt. Arial for all others.

Save as: *L128F1*

	A	B	C
1	COURSE	PERIOD	ROOM
2	Applied Mathematics I	1	134-E
3	Consumer Economics	2	114-S
4	Sophomore English	3	210-E
5	Physical Education	4	Gym-N
6	Computer Applications	6	104-S
7	Principles of Technology	7	101-W
8	World Cultures	8	205-S

Worksheet 2

1. Create the second worksheet at the right as shown.
2. Format the worksheet using 12-pt. Courier New.
3. Adjust column widths.

Save as: *L128F2*

	A	B	C	D	E
1	YEAR	MEDIAN	LOAN	MONTHLY	% OF
2		PRICE	RATE	PAYMENT	INCOME
3	1992	$103,700	8.11%	$615	20.00%
4	1993	$106,800	7.16%	$578	18.80%
5	1994	$109,900	7.47%	$613	19.00%
6	1996	$118,200	7.71%	$675	19.20%
7	1997	$124,100	7.68%	$706	19.30%
8	Source: The World Almanac, 1999.				

Worksheet 3

Open file *L128F2* and make the changes at the right.

Save as: *L128F3*

1. Insert the two rows below in consecutive order by year:

1995	$113,100	7.85%	$654	19.3%
1998	$134,600	7.19%	$730	19.5%

2. Shade each column in a color you select.
3. Change the font to 12-pt. Times New Roman for all the cells that contain data. Bold and center all headings.
4. Adjust column widths.

LESSON 129 PERFORM CALCULATIONS USING FORMULAS AND FUNCTIONS

Objective:

To perform worksheet calculations using formulas and functions.

129A • 5' Conditioning Practice

Key each line twice; take 30" writings on line 3; determine *gwam.*

alphabet 1 Quin, zip that jacket and fix your muffler to brave raging winds.

fig/sym 2 My policy (#312-07-X) paid $26.97 interest and a $47.58 dividend.

speed 3 Pa's neighbor may fish off the dock at the lake by the cornfield.

gwam 1' | 1 | 2 | 3 | 4 | 5 | 6 | 7 | 8 | 9 | 10 | 11 | 12 | 13 |

UNIT 19

LESSONS 65–69

HPJ Communication Specialists: A Workplace Simulation

Work Assignment

HPJ Communication Specialists prepares, organizes, and delivers communication training seminars. Three partners—Stewart **H**errick, Natasha **P**arker, and Spencer **J**orstad—founded the company in 1991. In 1998 Ms. Parker bought out the other two partners. Today the company has five branches located in Dallas, Denver, Minneapolis, New York, and San Francisco.

You have been hired by HPJ to work part-time for the administrative assistant, Helen St. Claire. Ms. St. Claire processes documents for the President and CEO, Natasha S. Parker, as well as for Erika Thomas, the Minneapolis branch manager.

During your training program, you were instructed to use the unbound format for reports and block format for all company letters. Ms. Parker likes all her letters closed as follows:

```
Sincerely



Natasha S. Parker
President & CEO
```

When a document has more than one enclosure, format the enclosure notation as follows:

```
Enclosures: Agenda
            Hotel Confirmation
```

General processing instructions will be attached to each document you are given to process. Use the date included on the instructions for all documents requiring a date.

Use your decision-making skills to arrange documents attractively whenever specific instructions are not provided. Since HPJ has based its word processing manual on the *Century 21* textbook, you can also refer to this text in making formatting decisions. You are expected to produce error-free documents, so check spelling, proofread, and correct your work carefully before presenting it for approval.

If you need help with software features to complete your work, refer to Software Features Index in this text. Use the Help features in your software, too. Using Help, you can recall or review a feature that you have forgotten. Also use it to learn any new features you may need.

HPJ Files and Web Site

Some jobs will require you to use documents stored in HPJ company files. Some documents will require you to gather information from the company's Web site at **http://www.hpj.swep.com**. All files you create should be named with *HPJ*, followed by the job number (*HPJ1*, *HPJ2*, etc.).

Getting Started

Create macros for closing lines of letters and other text, such as *HPJ Communication Specialists*, that you will use often.

3. Complete the activity at the right below.

Save as: *L128D*

Format	*Description*	*Example Value = 2010.503*
General	The default; displays number as keyed	2010.503
Number	Displays numbers with a fixed number of decimal places	2010.50
Currency	Displays numbers with $, two default decimal places, and comma separators	$2,010.50
Accounting	Same as currency except $ and decimal point are aligned vertically in the column	$ 2,010.50
Percentage	Multiplies number keyed by 100 and displays number and two default decimal places with percent sign	201050.30%

1. Open file *CD-L128D*.
2. Format Cells A1:A7 using Number format, two decimal places, and no comma separators.
3. Format Cells B1:B7 using Currency format with two decimal places.
4. Format Cells C1:C7 using Accounting format.
5. Format Cells D1:D7 using Percentage format with two decimal places.
6. Copy D1:D7 to E1:E7 and apply Percentage format with no decimal places.
7. Format Cells A9:D10 using Number format, commas, and no decimal places.
8. Copy A9:D10 to A12:D13 and use Number format with one decimal place.

128E • 7' Format Cell Contents

1. Read the information at the right.
2. Learn how to format text with your ss software.
3. Complete the activity at the right.

Save as: *L128E*

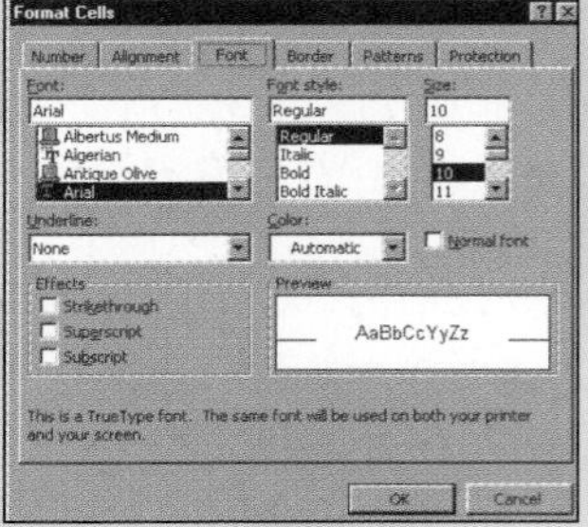

The contents of cells (both numbers and text) can be formatted in much the same way as text is formatted using word processing software. The **font** and **font style**, **size**, **color**, **effect**, and **underline** can be selected and applied to a cell, a cell range, or one or more rows and/or columns.

Cells, rows, and/or columns can be shaded, and information in a cell(s) can be aligned at the left, right, or center.

1. Open file *CD-L127C*.
2. Format Row 1 in 14-pt. Arial font using bold and a green font color.
3. Format Cells A2:F10 in 12-pt. Arial font.
4. Format cell ranges B2:B10, D2:D10, and F2:F10 in a dark brown font color, and shade these same cell ranges with a light brown color.
5. Format Cells A2:A10 in italic and a dark red font color. Shade this range using a light red.
6. Format Cells C2:C10 and E2:E10 in a dark blue font. Shade these cell ranges in a light blue.
7. Key **Wednesday** in Cell D1.
8. Key $^{(1)}$ in superscript position to the right of *Hector* in Cell C10.
9. Double-underline *Bonita* in Cell D7.
10. Adjust column widths to fit contents, and center-align all cells.

HPJ COMMUNICATION SPECIALISTS

Objectives:

1. To use your decision-making skills to process documents.
2. To improve your ability to read and follow directions.

65A-69A • 5' (daily) Conditioning Practice

Key each line twice.

alphabet	1	Seven complete textbooks were required for the new zoology major.
fig/sym	2	Shipping charges ($35.18) were included on the invoice (#426097).
speed	3	A sick dog slept on the oak chair in the dismal hall of the dorm.

gwam 1' | 1 | 2 | 3 | 4 | 5 | 6 | 7 | 8 | 9 | 10 | 11 | 12 | 13 |

65B-69B • 45' (daily) Work Assignments

Job 1

HPJ From the Desk of **Helen St. Claire**

I would like an updated name and address list for the CEO and branch managers. Please get this information from the Web site and create a table similar to the one attached. Addresses are shown at the top of each Web page. Keep a copy of the list. Suggestion: Create a macro for each branch manager's address to use for later jobs.

June 5

HSC

HPJ COMMUNICATION SPECIALISTS

CEO and Branch Manager Address List

June 5, 200-

Ms. Natasha S. Parker, President & CEO HPJ Communication Specialists Address City, State ZIP	Name of Branch Manager, Branch Manager HPJ Communication Specialists Address City, State ZIP
Name of Branch Manager, Branch Manager HPJ Communication Specialists Address City, State ZIP	Name of Branch Manager, Branch Manager HPJ Communication Specialists Address City, State ZIP
Name of Branch Manager, Branch Manager HPJ Communication Specialists Address City, State ZIP	Name of Branch Manager, Branch Manager HPJ Communication Specialists Address City, State ZIP

Job 2

HPJ From the Desk of **Helen St. Claire**

Ms. Parker wants the attached letter sent to each of the branch managers. Find mailing addresses on your address list.

June 5

HSC

Dear

Each of you has indicated a need for additional personnel. I've heard your requests. With this quarter's increase in seminar revenues, I am now in a position to respond to them. Five new communication specialist positions, one for each branch, have been added.

Since training for the positions takes place here at the home office, it is more cost effective to hire communication specialists from this area. I will take care of recruitment and preliminary screening. However, since each of you will work closely with the individual hired, I think you should make the final selection.

When you are here for the annual meeting, I'll schedule time for you to interview eight individuals. If you are not satisfied with any of the eight, we will arrange additional interviews. I should have a job description created within the next week. When it is completed, I'll send it to you for your review.

128B • 7' Changing the Width of Columns

1. Read the text at the right.
2. Learn to size columns using the AutoFit feature.
3. Complete the activity at the right.

Often cells have entries that exceed the default width of a column or have columns that vary greatly in width. To modify the column widths quickly, most ss software programs have an **AutoFit** feature (for example, Excel's AutoFit Selection) that resizes columns to display the longest entry in that column.

1. Open file *CD-L127C* and edit Cell D1 so *Wednesday* is spelled out.
2. Use the AutoFit feature to resize the columns so each column is as wide as its longest entry.

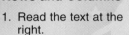

Save as: *L128B1*

3. Open file *CD-L127B* and designate that gridlines and column and row headings should print.
4. Adjust the width of each column so it is as wide as the longest entry in the column.

Save as: *L128B2*

128C • 7' Insert and Delete Rows and Columns

1. Read the text at the right.
2. Learn to insert and delete rows and columns.
3. Complete the activity at the right.

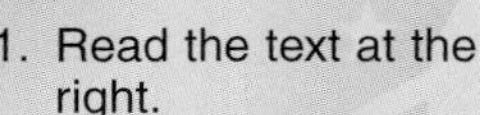

Save as: *L128C*

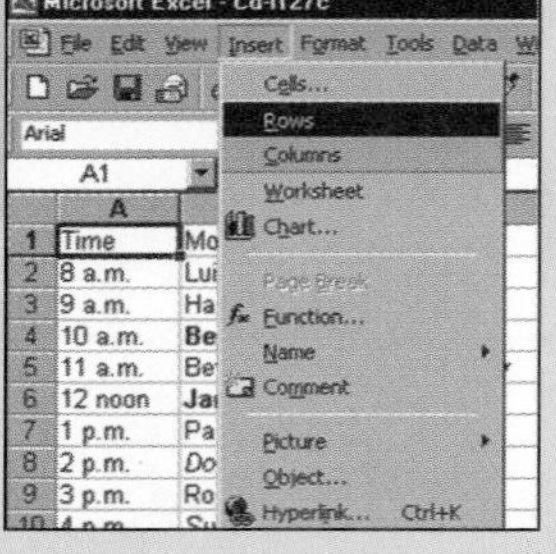

Rows and columns can be **inserted** and **deleted**. One or more rows or columns can be inserted each time this feature is used. Columns may be added at the left or within a worksheet; rows may be added at the top or within a worksheet.

1. Open file *CD-L127C* and insert two rows at the top.
2. Insert one column between Monday and Tuesday, one column between Tuesday and Wednesday, and two columns between Wednesday and Thursday. Delete the Friday column.
3. Key **Murphy** in Cells D2 and I2; **Shandry** in Cells C2, E2, and G2; and **Lawler** in Cell H2.
4. Key **Monday** in C3, **Tuesday** in E3, and **Wednesday** in F3:H3.
5. Insert a row between 2 p.m. and 3 p.m., and key **2:30 p.m.** in Cell A11.
6. Insert three rows between 3 p.m. and 4 p.m.; and key **3:15 p.m.** in A13, **3:30 p.m.** in A14, and **3:45 p.m.** in A15.
7. Clear the contents of Cells B3:I3.
8. Adjust all column widths to fit the cell contents.
9. Key **APPOINTMENT SCHEDULE** in Cell A1.

128D • 7' Format Numbers

1. Read the information at the right and the chart on the next page to learn about number formats.
2. Learn how to format numbers with your ss software.

(continued on next page)

When numbers are keyed into a worksheet, ss software formats them as General, the default format. If another format (Currency, Percentage, numbers with commas or a fixed number of decimal places, Date, etc.) is preferred, the number(s) can be formatted accordingly. The chart on the next page provides information about commonly used number formats.

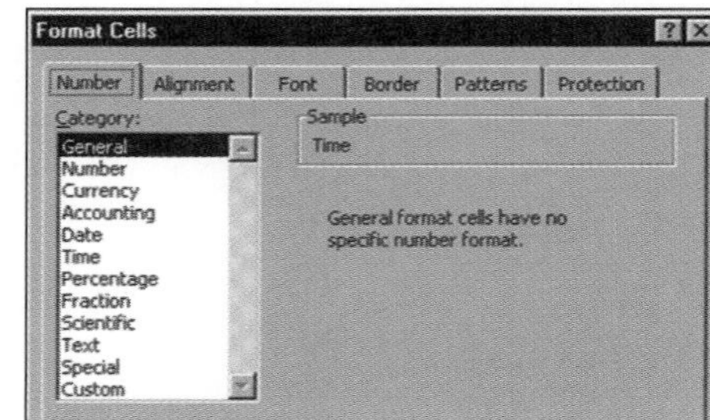

Job 3

HPJ From the Desk of
Helen St. Claire
I've started the attached letter from Ms. Parker to the branch managers. It is saved as CD-HPJJOB3. Please finish the letter.
June 6
HSC

Technology. The changed marketplace is demanding that we explore new ways of delivering our seminars. How can we better use technology to deliver our product? This may include putting selected seminars online, inter- and intra-company communication, etc.

Company growth. What steps can we take to increase company growth? Last year revenues grew by 15 percent; our expenses grew by 8 percent.

Employee incentives. Last year we implemented a branch manager profit sharing plan. Some of you have indicated that we need to expand this profit sharing plan to include our communication specialists.

Regional expansion. Some of the regions have been very successful. How do we capitalize on that success? Is it time to divide the successful regions?

International expansion. **HPJ** has put on several seminars overseas—at a very high cost. Is it time to start thinking about creating a branch of **HPJ** at a strategic overseas location?

I am proud of what we have been able to accomplish this year. The foundation is in place and we are ready to grow. Each of you plays a critical role in the success of **HPJ**. Thank you for your dedication and commitment to making our company the "leader in providing corporate and individual communication training." Best wishes for continued success. I'm looking forward to discussing **HPJ**'s future at this year's annual meeting. If you have additional items that you would like included on the agenda, please get them to me before June 8.

Job 4

HPJ From the Desk of
Helen St. Claire
Format the attached job description. I've included some notes. (Directions for the Outline feature can be found in software Help.)
June 6
HSC

(2" TM) HPJ COMMUNICATION SPECIALIST bf

(DS) Job Description (QS)

bf (HPJ Communication Specialists) work cooperatively with other branch members to develop and deliver communication seminars throughout the United States.

¶ ~~I.~~ II. Duties and Responsibilities

a. Research seminar topics

b. Develop seminars

c. Prepare PowerPoint® presentations for seminars

d. Prepare seminar manual

e. Present seminars

¶ ~~II.~~ I. Position Requirements

a. College degree

b. Excellent oral and written communication skills

c. Excellent interpersonal skills

d. Technology skills

e. Knowledge of business concepts

127F • 13'
Worksheets

Worksheet 1

1. Prepare the worksheet at the right.
2. Print the worksheet with gridlines and row and column headings.

 **Save as:** *L127F1*

	A	B	C	D	E
1	BUDGET				
2	ITEM	BUDGET	JAN	FEB	MAR
3					
4	Rent	400			
5	Electric	44	46	43	42
6	Oil	110	115	90	72
7	Water	20		60	
8	Sewage	22			67
9	Telephone	35	32	38	45
10	Cable TV	35			
11	Insurance	80	120		95
12	Food	315	305	302	325
13	Clothing	75	60	90	55
14	Leisure	75	55	80	60
15	Personal	90	90	85	100
16	Auto Loan	425			
17	Auto Exp.	80	80	95	110
18	Savings	185			

Worksheet 2

Using file *L127F1*, make the following changes:

1. Edit cell A1 to read: **BUDGET AND MONTHLY EXPENSES**.
2. Move Row 18 to Row 3.
3. Copy Column B to Column F.
4. Clear Rows 16 and 17.
5. Edit Cell E15 to 95.
6. Copy B3 to C3:E3 and B4 to C4:E4.
7. Copy B10 to C10:E10.
8. Print the worksheet without gridlines or row and column headings.

 **Save as:** *L127F2*

Worksheet 3

1. Prepare the worksheet at the right, using the Copy feature as much as possible to reduce the amount of keying.
2. Print the worksheet with gridlines and row and column headings.

 **Save as:** *L127F3*

	A	B	C	D	E	F	G
1	NAME	QUIZ 1	QUIZ 2	QUIZ 3	QUIZ 4	QUIZ 5	QUIZ 6
2	JOE	90	90	90	100	90	90
3	MARY	90	90	90	80	90	90
4	PAUL	100	100	100	100	100	100
5	CARL	100	80	90	100	90	90
6	SUE	90	100	100	100	100	80
7	TWILA	90	90	90	80	80	80

LESSON 128 FORMAT WORKSHEETS

Objective:

To format cell contents, adjust column widths, and insert and delete columns and rows.

128A • 5'
Conditioning Practice

Key each line twice; take 30" writings on line 3; determine *gwam*.

alphabet 1 Frank questioned Tim over the jazz saxophone at my new nightclub.

fig/sym 2 The #5346 item will cost Ford & Sons $921.87 (less 10% for cash).

speed 3 If Jen signs the form, I may pay to dismantle the ancient chapel.

gwam 1' | 1 | 2 | 3 | 4 | 5 | 6 | 7 | 8 | 9 | 10 | 11 | 12 | 13 |

Jobs 5 & 6

HPJ From the Desk of
Helen St. Claire

Prepare (don't send) the attached message as e-mail from Ms. Parker to the branch managers. Attach the job description that you created. Get e-mail addresses from the Web site. While you are doing that, please update the address list (Job 1) to include e-mail addresses and phone numbers.

June 7
HSC

SUBJECT: JOB DESCRIPTION FOR COMMUNICATION SPECIALISTS

I've attached a draft of the job description for the communication specialists that we will be hiring for each branch. I wanted to give each of you an opportunity to review it before we advertise for the positions in the newspaper.

If there are additional responsibilities that you would like to see included with the job description before we post it, please let me know by Friday. The advertisement will run in the Star on Sunday and appear on its Job Board Web site next week. I'm confident that we will have an even greater interest in the positions than we had when we hired a couple of communication specialists last January.

Job 7

HPJ From the Desk of
Helen St. Claire

Create the attached seminar description table. You will need to copy seminar descriptions from our Web site. Add color and other enhancements. Your document may be posted on the Web page if NSP approves.

June 8
HSC

NEW SEMINAR DESCRIPTIONS

Seminar Title	Seminar Description	Cost per Person
Business Etiquette: You Cannot Not Communicate!		\$99
Gender Communication: "He Says, She Says"		\$75
International Communication		\$75
Listen Up!		\$99
Technology in the Workplace		\$125

127C • 8' Clear and Delete Cell Contents and Formats

1. Read the text at the right.
2. Learn to clear cell contents and formats with your ss software.
3. Complete the activity at the right.

 **Save as:** *L127C*

Most ss software has a **Clear** command that enables you to clear the contents *or* formats of a cell *or both* without shifting the surrounding cells to replace the cell you cleared.

The **Delete** command (not the DELETE key) deletes the contents *and* formats of a cell, and surrounding cells are shifted to replace the deleted cell.

1. Open file *CD-L127C* and specify that gridlines and row and column headings are to be printed.
2. Make these changes without having surrounding cells shift:
   a. Clear contents in Cells B2, C4, D6, E8, and F10.
   b. Clear format (bold) in Cells B4, B6, D4, D8, F6, and F8.
   c. Clear contents and formats in Cells B8, B10, D2, D5, F2, and F4.
3. Delete Cell B3 and have Cells C3 through F3 shift to the left.
4. Delete Cell C5 and have Cells C6 through C10 shift up.
5. Key **Susan** in Cell F4.

127D • 8' Select a Range of Cells

1. Read the text at the right.
2. Learn to select a range of cells using your ss software.
3. Complete the activity at the right.

 **Save as:** *L127D*

A **range of cells** may be selected to perform an operation (move, copy, cut, clear, format, print, etc.) on more than one cell at a time. A **range** is identified by the cell in the upper-left corner and the cell in the lower-right corner, usually separated by a colon (for example, A5:C10). To select a range of cells, highlight the cell in one corner. Hold down the left mouse button and drag to the cell in the opposite corner. The number of rows and columns in the selected range is typically shown in the ss window.

1. Open file *CD-L127C.*
2. Select the range of Cells B1:F1 and bold the contents of the cells in that range.
3. Select the range of Cells A1:F6 and print the contents of the cells in that range.

127E • 8' Cut, Copy, and Move

1. Read the text at the right.
2. Learn to cut, copy, and move cell contents using your ss software.
3. Complete the activity at the right.

 **Save as:** *L127E*

The contents of a cell or range of cells can be **cut**, **copied**, and **moved** to save time and improve accuracy. Select the cell or range of cells to be cut, copied, or moved; select the operation (*Cut* or *Copy*); select the cell (or first cell in the range) where the information is to be copied or moved; and finally, click *Paste* to copy or move the information.

1. Open file *CD-L127C.*
2. Clear the contents of Cells B6:F6.
3. Move the data in Cells B2:F3 to a range beginning in Cell B11.
4. Copy the data in Cells A2:A10 to a range beginning in Cell A11.
5. Copy the data in Cells A1:F1 to a range beginning in Cell A20.
6. Copy C5 to C6, E5 to E6, B4 to D3, and F4 to F3.
7. Move D12 to B3, C12 to E3, B12 to D6, and F11 to B6.

Job 8

HPJ From the Desk of
Helen St. Claire
Format the attached agenda for the annual meeting in outline format.
June 9
HSC

AGENDA

I. Greetings
II. Overview of past year
III. Seminars
  A. Enhancement
  B. Expansion
  C. Client base
IV. Leadership
V. Company growth
  A. Regional expansion
  B. International expansion
VI. Employee incentives
  A. Branch managers
  B. Communication specialists
VII. Technology
VIII. Miscellaneous
IX. Adjournment

Job 9

HPJ From the Desk of
Helen St. Claire
Ms. Parker would like the attached letter sent to the branch managers. Enclose a copy of the agenda and the hotel confirmation (when it's available) with the letter.
June 9
HSC

Attached is the agenda for the annual meeting. I didn't hear from any of you about additions to the agenda; so if you have items to discuss, we can include them under Miscellaneous.

Your accommodations have been made for the McIntyre Inn. Your confirmation is enclosed. A limousine will pick you up at the Inn at 8:30 a.m. on Monday. Activities have been planned for Monday and Wednesday evenings. Tuesday and Thursday mornings have been left open. You can arrange something on your own, or we can make group arrangements. We'll decide on Monday before adjourning for the day.

I'm looking forward to seeing you on the 26th.

Job 10

HPJ From the Desk of
Helen St. Claire
Create tables for each of the branch managers similar to the attached one for Carter. The information for these tables is saved in the master interview schedule (CD-HPJJOB10). Copy and paste the information from the master to each individual table.
June 9
HSC

HPJ Communication Specialists

Interview Schedule for **Jamal Carter**

June 29, 200-, Room 101

Time	Name of Interviewee
1:00 - 1:15	Joan Langston
1:20 - 1:35	Tim Wohlers
1:40 - 1:55	Mark Enqvist
2:00 - 2:15	Stewart Peters
2:20 - 2:35	Felipe Valdez
2:40 - 2:55	Katarina Dent
3:00 - 3:15	Jennifer Kent
3:20 - 3:35	Sandra Baylor

Worksheet 2

1. Prepare the worksheet at the right.
2. Print without gridlines or column/row headings.

 **Save as:** *L126F2*

	A	B	C	D	E
1	PLAYER	SINGLES	DOUBLES	TRIPLES	HOMERS
2	Bosco	65	13	3	1
3	Elliot	54	14	8	4
4	Horan	58	19	10	5
5	Huang	64	22	9	14
6	Myers	52	21	4	9
7	Pasco	49	14	3	4
8	Cordero	25	7	2	2
9	Paulie	27	2	4	0

LESSON 127 EDIT WORKSHEETS

Objective:

To select a range of cells and edit, clear, copy, and move information in a worksheet.

127A • 5' Conditioning Practice

Key each line twice; take 30" writings on line 3; determine *gwam*.

alphabet 1 Zebb likely will be top judge for the exclusive quarter-mile run.

figures 2 This association has 16,873 members in 290 chapters in 45 states.

speed 3 Jamel is proficient when he roams right field with vigor and pep.

gwam 1' | 1 | 2 | 3 | 4 | 5 | 6 | 7 | 8 | 9 | 10 | 11 | 12 | 13 |

127B • 8' Edit Cell Content

1. Read the text at the right.
2. Learn to edit cell contents using your ss software.
3. Complete the activity at the right.

 **Save as:** *L127B*

The **Edit** feature enables you to change information already entered in a cell. To edit, highlight (activate) the appropriate cell and click in the formula bar to make the needed changes there. Alternatively, you can press the Edit function key (F2) and then make the changes in the active cell.

Either way, cell contents are edited by selecting the text to be changed and then using the **Insert**, **Delete**, **Overtype**, and **Backspace** features as you would with wp software.

If the entire contents of a cell are to be changed, it is more efficient to activate the desired cell and then enter the correct information. The new information will replace the old information.

1. Open file *CD-L127B*.
2. Edit existing cell contents to match what is given below:

   A1: charge　B1: care　C1: butler　D1: compost

   A2: whether　B2: flew　C2: except　D2: personal
3. Change the cell contents to the new contents given below:

   A4: 54321　B4: 20202　C4: four　D4: shirt

   A5: 98765　B5: stars　C5: herd　D5: college
4. Edit or change the cell contents to match what is given below:

   A7: 4567　B7: Jeanne　C7: Kristine　D7: 8614

   A8: Dormont　B8: Sandra　C8: Hutton　D8: Blue

Job 11

HPJ From the Desk of
Helen St. Claire
Prepare the seminar objectives list in final form for Erika Thomas.
June 9
HSC

Seminar Objectives for:
TECHNOLOGY IN THE WORKPLACE
Minneapolis Branch

1. Discuss the role of communication technology in today's business environment and how it has changed over the past ten years.
2. Inform participants of various technological communication tools presently available.
3. Highlight the advantages/disadvantages of these communication technologies.
4. Demonstrate:
   - Videoconferencing
   - Teleconferencing
   - Data conferencing
   - GroupSystems
   - Internet resources
5. Inform participants of various technological communication tools that are in development.
6. Discuss Internet resources available to participants.
7. Discuss how using high-speed communication in today's business environment can give a firm a competitive advantage in the global marketplace.

Job 12

HPJ From the Desk of
Helen St. Claire
Prepare a final draft of the attached memo to Natasha from Erika Thomas. The subject is Monthly Progress Report. Be sure to include the attachment.
June 9
HSC

Here is an update on recent progress of the Minneapolis Branch.

<u>Seminar Bookings</u>

We are fully booked through April and May. Additional communication specialists are desperately needed if we are going to expand into other states in our region. Most of our current bookings are in Minnesota, Iowa, and Wisconsin. We will be presenting in Illinois for the first time in May. I anticipate this will lead to additional bookings that we won't be able to accommodate. This is a problem that I enjoy having. Michigan, Indiana, and Ohio provide ample opportunities for expansion, when resources are made available.

<u>New Seminar</u>

A lot of progress has been made on the new seminar we are developing, "Technology in the Workplace" (see attachment for seminar objectives). Our branch will be ready to preview the seminar at our annual meeting. Not only will the seminar be a great addition to our seminar offerings, but also I believe HPJ can use it to communicate better internally. I will present my ideas when I preview the seminar. The seminar covers:

(Memo continued on next page)

126D • 7'
Enter Text and Numbers

1. Study the information at the right and the illustration below.
2. Learn how to enter information with your ss software.
3. Complete the activity as directed at the right.

Save as: *L126D*

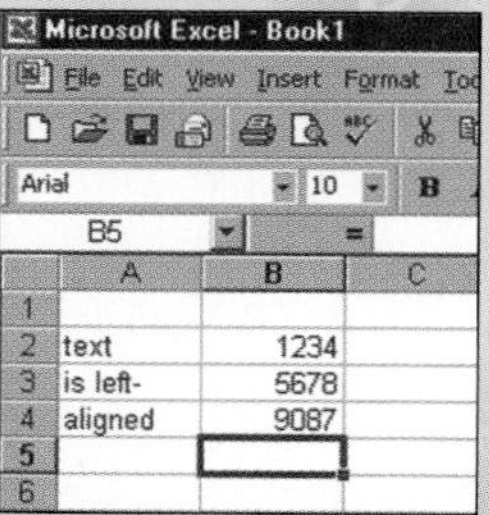

	A	B	C
1			
2	text	1234	
3	is left-	5678	
4	aligned	9087	
5			
6			

Worksheet cells may contain text or numbers. When text is entered in a cell, it is left-aligned in the cell. When numbers are entered, they are right-aligned in the cell. Only numbers can be used in calculations. If a number (such as a date or Social Security number) is to be used as text, it should be formatted as text.

1. Enter the following names, each in a separate cell in Column A, beginning with Row 1: **Mary**, **Henry**, **Pablo**, **Susan**, **Helen**, **John**, **James**, **Paul**, and **Sandy**.
2. Enter the following numbers, each in a separate cell in Row 15, beginning with Column A: **135790**, **673455**, **439021**, **901278**, **569021**, **102938**, **547612**, **102938**, and **601925**.
3. Enter the following invoice numbers as text, each in a separate cell in Column I, beginning with Row 11: **514620**, **687691**, and **432987**.
4. Check that text is left-aligned and numbers are right-aligned.

126E • 6'
Print Gridlines and Column and Row Headings

1. Read the text at the right.
2. Learn how to print (or not print) gridlines and row and column headings on worksheets.
3. Complete the activity at the right.

Save as: *L126E*

Gridlines and **row** and **column headings** may or may not be printed on a worksheet. If the default setting is to *not print* gridlines and/or row and column headings, you must select the desired features if they are to be printed (see illustration at the right below).

If the default setting is to *print* gridlines and/or row and column headings, you must choose not to print any or all of these features if they are not to be printed.

1. Open file *CD-L126E* and use Print Preview to determine if the worksheet will print with gridlines and column/row headings.
2. Change the default setting as follows:
   a. If the worksheet *does not* have gridlines and column/row headings, specify that they print and then print the worksheet.
   b. If the worksheet *has* gridlines and column/row headings, specify that they not print and then print the worksheet.

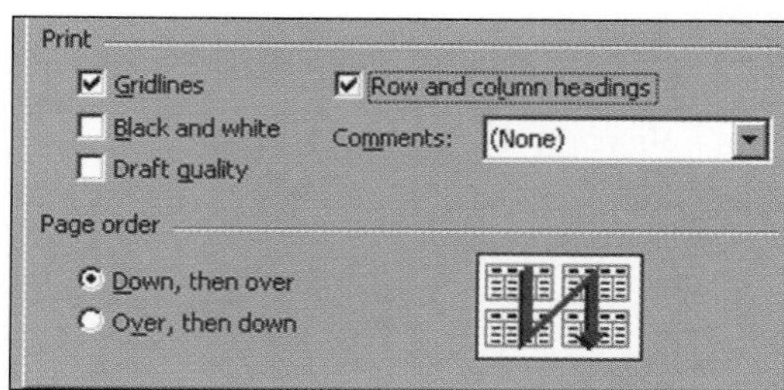

126F • 15'
Worksheets

Worksheet 1

1. Prepare the worksheet at the right.
2. Print the worksheet with gridlines and column and row headings.

Save as: *L126F1*

	A	B	C	D	E	F
1	MONTH	JOHN	MARY	LUIZ	PEDRO	SARA
2	January	5567	6623	7359	4986	6902
3	February	2457	7654	3569	2093	6432
4	March	6930	3096	5792	4607	7908
5	April	4783	6212	4390	5934	5402
6	May	5042	5092	4500	9453	5321
7	June	5430	6098	5781	5009	6023

Job 12, cont.

- Videoconferencing
- Teleconferencing
- Data conferencing
- GroupSystems
- Internet resources

Graphic Designer

A graphic artist has been hired to design all of the materials for the new seminar. He will design promotional items as well as content-related items. Currently he is working on the manual cover and divider pages. These items will be coordinated with the emblems used in the slide show portion of the presentation, along with name tags, promotional paraphernalia, and business cards. This should give our seminar a more professional appearance. If it works as well as I think it is going to, we will have the designer work on materials for our existing seminars to add the "professional" look.

Job 13

HPJ From the Desk of
Helen St. Claire

Format this text as an unbound report with footnotes (shown at bottom of attached copy). The report will be a handout for the "Listen Up!" seminar.
June 12
HSC

LISTEN UP!

According to Raymond McNulty, Everyone who expects to succeed life should realize that success only will come if you give careful consideration to other people. To acomplish this you must be an excellent listener. The most critical skills that an individual acquires is the ability to listen. studies indicate that a person spends 70 percent to 80 percent of their time communicating, of which 45% is spent listening. Nixon and West give the following breakdown for the average individual of time spent communicating.[2]

- Writing
- Reading
- Speaking
- Listening

Since most of the time spent communicating is spent listening, it is important to overcome any obstacles that obstruct our ability to listen and to learn new ways to improve our listening ability.

Barriers to Listening

Anything that interferes with our ability to listen is classified as a barrier to listening. Barriers that obstruct our ability to listen can be divided into two basic categories—external and internal barriers.

(Report continued on next page)

3. Complete the activity at the right to move the active cell to various cells within the worksheet.

1. Use the mouse to make Cell G4 active.
2. Use the mouse to make Cell B24 active.
3. Use the mouse to make Cell A12 active.
4. Use the arrow keys to make Cell D11 active.
5. Use the arrow keys to make Cell F30 active.
6. Use the arrow keys to make Cell P30 active.
7. Use Page Down and arrow keys to make Cell J100 active.
8. Use Page Up and arrow keys to make Cell L40 active.
9. Press CTRL + HOME to make Cell A1 active.

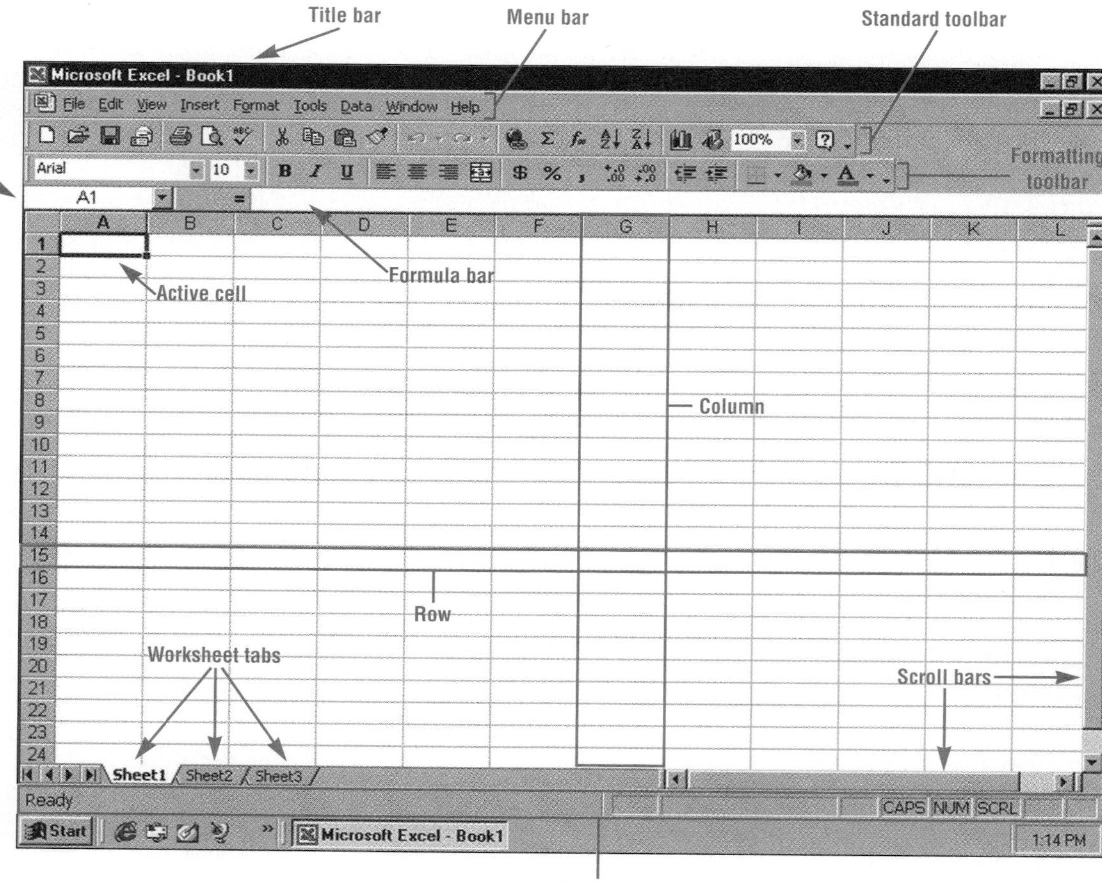

Title bar: displays the application and current worksheet name.

Menu bar: contains the drop-down menu commands.

Standard toolbar and **Formatting toolbar:** provide easy access to frequently used commands.

Cell reference box: identifies the active cell by the letter of the column and the number of the row that it intersects. The cell reference box also identifies a range of cells being selected.

Formula bar: displays the contents of the active cell and is used to create or edit text or values.

Active cell: highlighted with a thick border; stores information that is entered while it is active.

Columns: identified by **letters** that run horizontally.

Rows: identified by **numbers** that run vertically.

Worksheet tabs: identify the active worksheet in the workbook.

Status bar: indicates various items of information such as SCROLL LOCK, NUM LOCK, or CAPS LOCK, when active.

Scroll bars: used to move horizontally or vertically within a worksheet.

Internal barriers. Internal barriers are those that dal with the mental or psychological aspects of listening. The perception of the importance of the message, the emotional state, and the running in and out of the speaker by the listener are examples of internal barriers.

External barriers. External barriers are barriers other than those that deal the mental and psychological makeup of the listner that tend tokeep the listener from devoting attention to what is being said. Telephone interruptions, visitors, noise, and the physical environment are examples of external barriers.

Ways to Improve Listening

Barrier to listening can be over come. However it does take a sincere efort on the part of the speaker. Neher and Waite suggest the following ways to improve listening skills.[3]

- Be aware of the barriers that are especially troublesome for you. Listening difficulties are individualistic. Developing awareness is an important step in overcoming

- Listen as though you will have to paraphrase what is being said. Listen for ideas rather than for facts.

- Expect to work t listening. work at overcoming distractions, such as the speaker's delivery or gestures.

- Concentrate on summarizing the presentation as you listen. If possible, think of additional supporting material that would fit with the point that the speaker is making. Avoid trying to refute the speaker. Try not to be turned off by remarks disagree with.

[1]H. Dan O'Hair, James S. O'Rourke IV, and Mary John O'Hair, _Business Communication: A Framework for Success_ (Cincinnati: South-Western Publishing, 2001), p. 211.

[2]Judy C. Nixon and Judy F. West, "Listening--The New Competency," _The Balance Sheet_ (January/February 1989), pp. 27-29.

[3]William W. Neher and David H. Waite, _The Business and Professional Communicator_ (Needham Heights, MA: Allyn and Bacon, 1993), p. 28.

UNIT 33

LESSONS 126–131

Processing Worksheets

LESSON 126 UNDERSTAND SPREADSHEET SOFTWARE

Objectives:

1. To learn the parts of the spreadsheet (ss) window and worksheet.
2. To enter information, move data, and print a worksheet.

126A • 5' Conditioning Practice

Key each line twice; take 30" writings on line 3; determine *gwam.*

alphabet 1 Many plaques were just the right sizes for various duck exhibits.

fig/sym 2 The blue outfit cost $358.41 (20% off), and she has only $297.60.

speed 3 Karmela did lay the world map and rifle by the end of the mantle.

gwam 1' | 1 | 2 | 3 | 4 | 5 | 6 | 7 | 8 | 9 | 10 | 11 | 12 | 13 |

126B • 10' Spreadsheet Software

1. Study the text at the right and the illustration on the next page.
2. Access your ss software and learn the parts of the program window and worksheet.
3. Open file *CD-L126B* and complete the activity as directed in the file.

 **Save as:** *L126B*

Text and numbers can be keyed into **cells** in **spreadsheet** (ss) software. The cells are arranged in rows and columns on a **worksheet** (like the one on the next page). A group of related worksheets form a file called a **workbook**.

Columns run vertically in a worksheet. Each column has a heading (letters from A to Z, AA to AZ, etc.) running left to right across the top of the worksheet.

Rows run horizontally in a worksheet. Each row has a heading (a number) running down the left side of the worksheet.

Numbers can be added, subtracted, multiplied, and divided in a worksheet, and **formulas** are used to perform calculations quickly and accurately.

One big advantage of ss software is that when a number is changed, all related "answers" are automatically recalculated. Additionally, **charts** can be constructed to present the worksheet information graphically.

126C • 7' Move Around in a Worksheet

1. Read the text at the right and study the illustration on the following page.
2. Learn to move around in a worksheet with your ss software.

(continued on next page)

Information is entered in the **active cell** of a worksheet. The active cell is the cell with the thick border around it (see the illustration on the next page). Cells can be activated with the mouse, the arrow keys, or keyboard shortcuts.

To activate a cell with the mouse, move the pointer to the desired cell and click the left mouse button.

To move the active cell one or more cells to the left, right, up, or down, use the arrow keys.

To move the active cell from one cell to another quickly, use the keyboard shortcuts. For example, to make the first cell in a row active, press HOME; to activate Cell A1, press CTRL + HOME; to move the active cell up one page, press Page Up, etc.

Job 14

HPJ From the Desk of
Helen St. Claire

Here is the company organization chart we have on file (CD-HPJJOB14). Some of the information is missing or outdated. Each branch's Web site contains the most up-to-date information. Print a copy of the file; then verify the information against that on the Web site. Mark the changes on the printed copy; finally, make the changes to the master file.

June 12
HSC

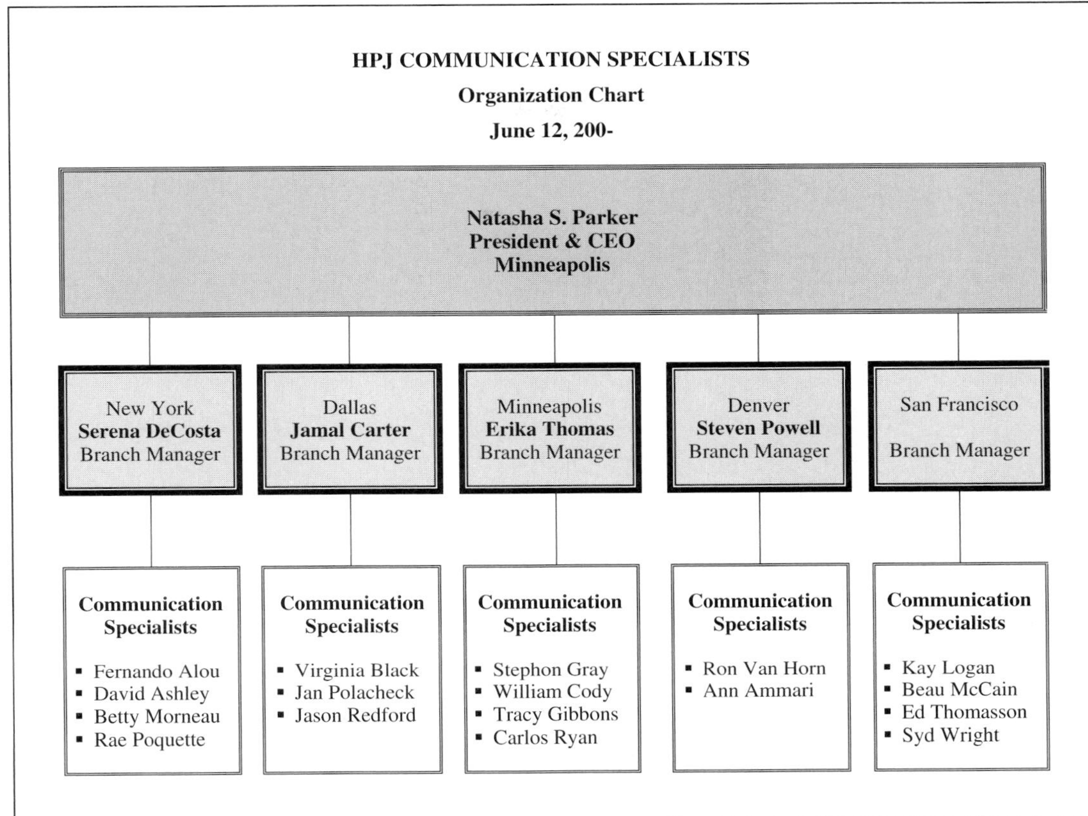

HPJ COMMUNICATION SPECIALISTS
Organization Chart
June 12, 200-

Job 15

HPJ From the Desk of
Helen St. Claire

Prepare (don't send) this message as e-mail to the communication specialists in the Minneapolis branch from Erika Thomas. You will need to get the e-mail addresses from their Web page. New Communication Specialist is the subject.

June 30
HSC

Stewart Peters will join our branch as Communication Specialist on Monday, July 15.

Stewart grew up in New york, where he completed an undergraduate degree in organizational communication at New york University. He recently completed his Master's degree at the University of Minnesota.

Stewart's thesis dealt with interpersonal conflict in the corporate environment. Since we intend to develop a seminar in this area, he will be able to make an immediate contribution.

Please welcome Stewart to HPJ and our branch when he arrives on the 15th.

ACTIVITY 5

Composing

1. Read carefully the material shown at the right.
2. Make your own list of "pet peeves" or violations of good manners (etiquette).
3. Compose/key a ¶ for each item on your list, indicating why it is the wrong thing to do (why it violates good manners and shows lack of consideration and respect for others).

 **Save as:** *CS13-ACT5*

Practicing good manners (etiquette), whether you are at home or in school, with your family or your friends, will help you acquire poise and self-assurance. Being well mannered means following the recognized rules of behavior that help to make your relationships with others more pleasant, whether you are in a private or a public place. The basis of good manners is kindness, thoughtfulness, and a deep concern for others. Good manners are a reflection of your attitude toward others—whether you like people, respect them, are interested in them, and make the effort to get along with them.

Some of the things people (young and old alike) do that show disrespect or a lack of concern for others are listed below:

1. Failure to introduce a companion to an acquaintance with whom you've stopped to chat.
2. Males wearing hats or caps indoors: classrooms, theaters, and restaurants, for example.
3. Loud conversations in the vicinity of others whom you may or may not know.
4. Using off-color or vulgar language to or in the vicinity of people whom you know or may not know.
5. Boisterous behavior in places that are supposed to be relatively quiet and serene (libraries, theaters, and hospitals, for example).
6. Leaning on the car horn while in a slow lane of traffic in an attempt to get slow movers out of the way, or driving well below the speed limit in the fast lane of an expressway.
7. Congregating in a doorway, a hallway, or an aisle, preventing others from passing through.
8. Attacking a sandwich or plate of food with both hands in a gluttonous manner; chewing noisily and talking while your mouth is full.
9. Opening and walking through a door first while a companion trails behind instead of holding the door for your companion (male or female).
10. Calling people unflattering or negative (pejorative) names to get their attention or to minimize their self-esteem.

UNIT 20

LESSONS 70–72

Preparing for Assessment

LESSON 70 PREPARE FOR ASSESSMENT: E-MAILS, MEMOS, LETTERS

Objective:
To prepare for assessment of e-mail, letter, and memo formatting skills.

70A • 5' Conditioning Practice

Key each line twice SS; then key a 1' writing on line 3; determine *gwam*.

alphabet 1 Extensive painting of the gazebo was quickly completed by Jerome.

figures 2 At least 456 of the 3,987 jobs were cut before November 18, 2001.

speed 3 Janel and I may go to the island to dismantle the bicycle shanty.

gwam 1' | 1 | 2 | 3 | 4 | 5 | 6 | 7 | 8 | 9 | 10 | 11 | 12 | 13 |

70B • 45' Reinforce Correspondence Formatting Skills

Document 1 (E-mail)
Format and key the text at the right as e-mail to your instructor. Attach the *CD-SALESRPT* file. Proofread your message; correct all errors.

 **Save as:** *MAIL70B1*

Note: Prepare this message as a memo to your instructor if you do not have e-mail software.

SUBJECT: SALES REPORT

The sales figures you requested are attached. This month's sales figures should be available on Friday. As soon as I receive them, I'll update the file to include those figures and e-mail them to you.

If there is any other information I can provide for the meeting next month, let me know. I'm looking forward to seeing you again in San Francisco.

Document 2 (Memo)
Format and key the text at the right as a memo to **Investment Club Members** from **Gordon Chandler**. Date the memo **April 20, 200-** and use **PORTFOLIO UPDATE** for the subject line.

 **Save as:** *MEMO70B2*

The attached table shows the current value of our portfolio. As you are well aware, market results have been mixed this year. The total value of the portfolio increased 12 percent since January 1. Most of this increase is due to additional contributions by members rather than increases in the value of stocks in the portfolio.

Our cash balance ($23,495.77) is quite large. We should decide at our next meeting what we want to do with this cash. As I recall, we are scheduled to meet on May 6 and will have potential investment opportunity reports from Catherine Cloninger and Mario Fernandez by then.

If you have questions about the report, please call me.

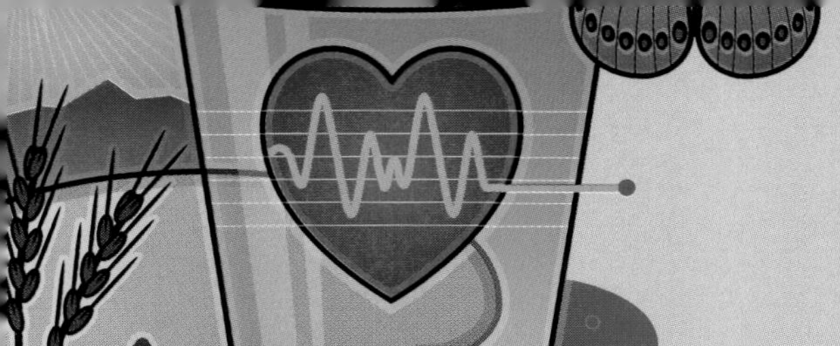

Communication Skills 13

ACTIVITY 1

Application: Subject/Predicate Agreement

1. As you key lines 1–10 at the right, select and key the proper verb shown in parentheses.
2. Check the accuracy of your work with the instructor; correct any errors you made.

 **Save as:** *CS13-ACT1*

1 (Wasn't, Weren't) you aware that the matinee began at 2:30 p.m.?
2 Our senior debate team (has, have) won the city championship.
3 A number of our workers (are, is) to receive proficiency awards.
4 Either the coach or an assistant (are, is) to speak at the assembly.
5 Maria (doesn't, don't) know whether she can attend the beach party.
6 Ms. Yamamoto and her mother (are, is) now American citizens.
7 (Was, Were) the director as well as his assistants at the meeting?
8 The number of applicants for admission (are, is) greater this year.
9 The logic behind their main arguments (elude, eludes) me.
10 It (doesn't, don't) matter to me which of the two is elected.

ACTIVITY 2

Application: Capitalization and Number Expression

1. As you key lines 1–10 at the right, supply the appropriate capitalization and express numbers properly (as words or figures).
2. Check the accuracy of your work with the instructor; correct any errors you made.

 **Save as:** *CS13-ACT2*

1 "the jury," said the judge, "must reach a unanimous decision."
2 for what percentage of total sales is mrs. rhodes responsible?
3 i need a copy of the dictionary of composers and their music.
4 miss valdez told us to go to room eight of corbett hall.
5 the institute of art is at fifth avenue and irving place.
6 "don't you agree," he asked, "that honesty is the best policy?"
7 is the "tony award show" to be shown on tv on april seventeen?
8 dr. robin j. sousa is to address fbla members in orlando.
9 see page 473 of volume one of encyclopedia americana.
10 here is pbc's check 2749 for $83 (less ten percent discount).

ACTIVITY 3

Write to Learn

Complete the Write-to-Learn activity as directed at right.

 **Save as:** *CS13-ACT3*

1. Using word processing or speech recognition software, write a paragraph explaining how to create a heading that spans all columns in a three-column newsletter.
2. Write a second paragraph explaining how to insert a text box behind a short paragraph.

ACTIVITY 4

Preparing to Speak

Prepare a short presentation as described at the right.

 **Save as:** *CS13-4OL* and *CS13-4SOUND*

You will attend a meeting of a club you joined recently. The members likely will ask you to introduce yourself briefly (about 1' to 2').

1. Prepare an outline of the points you want to include. Suggestions follow:
   - State your name and year in school, and mention your hobbies.
   - Describe your aspirations after graduation.
   - Tell the audience about other things you do or like.
2. If time and resources permit, record your speech in a sound file.
3. Submit your outline (and sound file, if made) to your instructor.

Document 3 (Letter)

Format and key the text at the right as a business letter. Include a second-page heading. Place the following inserts in the body where indicated.

Insert 1

- **Depression**
- **Hard times**
- **Better**
- **Depressing/Sad**
- **Recovery**

Insert 2

- **Happy/Peaceful**
- **Rock 'n' Roll**
- **Great/Fun**
- **Getting better**
- **Prosperous**

Insert 3

- **Radio (96%)**
- **Automobile (91%)**
- **Computer (87%)**
- **Highway system (84%)**
- **Airline travel (77%)**

Proofread your copy; correct all keying and format errors.

Save as: *LTR70B3*

Note:
The initials ASAP stand for the words *as soon as possible.*

March 11, 200- | Dr. Haley Morgan | 327 Redwood Dr. | Chattanooga, TN 37421-3619 | Dear Haley

I am excited about researching the "Generation Gap" with you. I have a vested interest in the problem since I have two teenagers who often ask which planet I came from.

The study I mentioned was a 1999 millennium survey entitled *Public Perspectives on the American Century: Technology Triumphs, Morality Falters.* The http: address is www.people-press.org/mill1que.htm. After studying the results, I'm convinced we are products of "Where we were when." For example, note the difference in the top five words used to describe each decade of the twentieth century. First, the 1930s:

Place Insert 1 here.

References to the Great Depression and economic hard times of the thirties were replaced by much happier terms two decades later. The top five terms to describe the 1950s:

Place Insert 2 here.

Who can forget Elvis and Rock 'n' Roll? I've finally achieved a semblance of success in getting my children to appreciate some of the great music of the fifties and sixties—of course, only when none of their friends are around.

Two other parts of that 1999 survey relate to our study: "A Century of Inventions" and "A Century of Social Change." The following list shows the top five inventions of the century and the percentage of respondents who thought the invention represented a change for the better.

Place Insert 3 here.

Television—interestingly—was not rated in the top five; it came in sixth. Seventy-three percent of the respondents said TV was a change for the better, while 27 percent responded "change for the worse," "made no difference," or "I don't know." Nuclear weapons were at the bottom of the list; only 19 percent of those surveyed said nuclear weapons were a change for the better.

Social changes of the century were not viewed as positively as the century's inventions. As shown below, only three categories were viewed as being a change for the better by 50 percent or more of the respondents.

- ✔ Civil rights movement (84%)
- ✔ Women in workplace (83%)
- ✔ Growth of suburbs (52%)
- ✔ Rock 'n' Roll (45%)
- ✔ Legalized abortion (34%)

I will continue to look for materials we can use in the review of related literature. I have cleared my calendar for April 2-3. Let me know ASAP the details for our meeting on those dates.

Cordially | Shawn Spielberg | Associate Professor | xx

125C • 15' Newsletter

1. Using the information at the right, format a newsletter that has two columns of equal width, separated by a vertical line. The newsletter title and publication information should span both columns.
2. Open the file *CD-L125C* and add the articles to the end of the newsletter.
3. You decide all formatting features for the newsletter, including the format of the text boxes.

 **Save as:** *NEWS125C*

ENVIRONMENTAL ALERT!

Volume 12, No. 9 November, 200-

Where to Get Help

Have you ever wondered where to turn for answers to environmental problems? One good place to start is the United States Environmental Protection Agency's (EPA) Web site. The home page contains numerous links to general and specific information that will be of help. You can link to sections for concerned citizens, small businesses, industry, and even get EPA telephone numbers and addresses.

Protection of the environment is a big job. Federal, state, and local agencies across the nation are all involved, employing thousands of citizens who care about their health and natural resources. Every city, county, and state networks with federal groups to share and provide information. If the first person you contact can't answer a question, he or she will know who can.

No longer can we say, "I'm too busy to be concerned with the environment--someone else can take care of it."

LANGUAGE SKILLS

125D • 5' Language Skills: Word Choice

1. Study the spelling and definitions of the words at the right.
2. Key the Learn lines, noting word choice.
3. Key the Apply lines, selecting the correct words.
4. Check the accuracy of your work with the instructor. Rekey lines that contain a word-choice error.

 **Save as:** *CHOICE125D*

choose (vb) to select; to decide on

chose (vb) the past tense of *choose*

than (conj/prep) used in comparisons to show difference between items

then (n/adv) that time; at that time

Learn 1 Jane **chose** a Eureka computer; I may **choose** a Futura.

Apply 2 After he (choose/chose) a red cap, I told him to (choose/chose) blue.

Apply 3 Mae (choose/chose) you as a partner; Janice may (choose/chose) me.

Learn 1 If she is older **than** you, **then** I am older than you.

Apply 2 We (than/then) decided that two hours were more (than/then) enough.

Apply 3 Fewer (than/then) half the workers were (than/then) put on overtime.

1. Access the United States Environmental Protection Agency (EPA) Web site at: http://www.epa.gov.
2. Complete the activity at the right.

1. Click the link that gives basic information **About EPA**; read it; and then write, using keyboard or speech recognition software, a brief paragraph describing what you have learned.
2. Click the home page link **Audience Groups**, select **Students**, and follow at least one link of interest to you. Then key one or more paragraphs describing what you have learned. Print one page from the EPA Web site relating to the paragraph(s) you composed.

LESSON 71 PREPARE FOR ASSESSMENT: REPORTS

Objective:
To prepare for assessment of reports.

71A • 5' Conditioning Practice

Key each line twice SS; then key a 1' writing on line 3; determine *gwam*.

alphabet 1 An exclusive photo of a mosque by Dr. Kjelstad was quite amazing.

figures 2 They were born on May 22, 1964, July 13, 1975, and June 18, 1980.

speed 3 Gus paid the men for the work they did on the shanty by the lake.

gwam 1' | 1 | 2 | 3 | 4 | 5 | 6 | 7 | 8 | 9 | 10 | 11 | 12 | 13 |

71B • 36' Reinforce Report Formatting Skills

Document 1
Format and key the copy below and on p. 198 as an unbound report with footnotes.

Save as: *RPT71B1*

Document 2
Prepare a reference list on a separate page. Insert the page number.

Save as: *RPT71B2*

Document 3
Prepare a title page for the EXPLORERS report.

Save as: *RPT71B3*

EXPLORERS

Explorers are men and women who have the courage to test existing boundaries. Explorers are men and women who aspire for something more out of life than what currently exists. Explorers are men and women who are willing to chart the unknown at a cost to their own comfort and security. It can be argued that explorers possess the ten characteristics of the "achieving" personality type:[1]

- Focus
- Preparedness
- Conviction
- Perseverance
- Creativity
- Curiosity
- Resilience
- Risk taking
- Independence
- A sense of higher purpose

Motivation of Explorers

What motivates explorers? The earliest explorers traveled for the purposes of discovery and adventure. Many of the early explorers mentioned conquest, acquisition of wealth, and territorial acquisition as their reasons for exploring.

Backgrounds of Explorers

Explorers come from all walks of life. Marco Polo was a merchant; Robert Louis Stevenson was a novelist; and Mary Kingsley was a well-born Englishwoman. Noted explorers included conquistadors, lawyers, naturalists, priests, and surgeons. No station in life is immune from the "fever."

> The itch, the fever, the urge—whatever one chooses to call it—is recurrent, if not constant. Once they have gone off, they go again and again. . . . Often the fever manifests itself in childhood . . . and sometimes it stops only with death, violent death.[2]

There are many examples of individuals who had the fever. Three such examples are Christopher Columbus, George Rogers Clark, and Delia Denning Akeley.

Christopher Columbus. Columbus is recognized as one of the earliest noteworthy explorers. On his first voyage Columbus landed on the Bahamas, then Cuba, and Haiti (1492-93). At the time of his explorations, "No other sailor had the persistence, the knowledge and the sheer guts to sail thousands of miles into the unknown ocean until he found land."[3] Columbus' explorations whittled away at the unknown.

George Rogers Clark. Clark was an American frontiersman explorer during the last half of the eighteenth century. Like many frontiersmen who are driven to explore by their need for wide open spaces, Clark explored vast areas of wilderness. According to Havinghurst[4], Clark's name is "synonymous with the settle-

PREPARE AN ADVERTISEMENT AND A NEWSLETTER

Objectives:

1. To prepare an advertisement and a newsletter.
2. To improve language skills.

125A • 5' Conditioning Practice

Key each line twice; take 30" writings on lines 1, 2, and 3; determine *gwam*.

alphabet 1 Max and Jack have the best grades for the two philosophy quizzes.

figures 2 I can call Shirley at 542-0193 on Friday or 542-6807 on Saturday.

speed 3 The neighbor may fix the rifle, bugle, and cycle for the visitor.

gwam 1' | 1 | 2 | 3 | 4 | 5 | 6 | 7 | 8 | 9 | 10 | 11 | 12 | 13 |

125B • 25' Advertisement

Using the information at the right, design a one-page flyer that advertises these two businesses.

Save as: *AD125B*

HUNT RUN RESTAURANT

435-555-0170
Ask for Nancy or Helen

HUNT RUN BED & BREAKFAST

435-555-0175
Ask for Chris or Martha

BANQUET ROOM

IDEAL FOR SHOWERS, RECEPTIONS, REUNIONS, ETC.

SEATING UP TO 120 PEOPLE

NO ROOM CHARGE

BED & BREAKFAST

PERFECT FOR YOUR OUT-OF-TOWN GUESTS

WE CAN ACCOMMODATE UP TO EIGHT PEOPLE IN FOUR ROOMS WITH PRIVATE BATHROOMS

http://www.huntrun.com

Hunt Run Restaurant and Bed & Breakfast are located on Hunt Run Rd., one mile off Rt. 58 between Easton and Huntville at the Hunt Run Golf Course.

ment of the Ohio, adventure in the Kentucky wilderness, conquest of the frontier lands of Illinois and the winning of the West for a new nation." Clark's explorations brought new options for people.

Delia Denning Akeley. Akeley explored Equatorial Africa, collecting specimens of Africa's wild animals for American natural history museums (1905–1929). Armed with little more than courage and an empathetic understanding of the Africans, she proved that a woman could travel in a dangerous country at a dangerous time.[5] Akeley's explorations brought new knowledge to the American people.

Everyone Explores

Not everyone will have the urge to explore as these noted explorers did, but everyone has a little bit of an exploring nature. It may not be the urge to explore for glory or discovery; it may simply be an urge to travel to an area that the individual has not yet visited. The urge may be in the form of exploring a book, museum, or Web site to expand one's knowledge. Or it may be exploring educational and career options. Regardless of the type of exploration done, all explorers are changed by their explorations. Their horizons become much broader.

Footnotes

[1]"A Profile of Greatness: The 10 Characteristics of the Achieving Personality" (April 25, 2000).

In Reference List only, add this Web address in front of date: http://www.4iq.com/great.html

[2]Milton Rugoff, The Great Travelers (New York: Simon and Schuster, 1960), p. xix.

[3]Samuel Eliot Morrison, "Christopher Columbus, Mariner." In Helen Wright and Samuel Rapport (eds.), The Great Explorers (New York: Harper & Row, 1957), pp. 80-81.

[4]Walter Havinghurst, "The Old Frontiersman—George Rogers Clark." In Helen Wright and Samuel Rapport (eds.), The Great Explorers (New York: Harper & Row, 1957), p. 21.

[5]Marion Tinling, Women into the Unknown (New York: Greenwood Press, 1989), p. 10.

71C • 9'
Skill Check

1. Key a 1' writing on each ¶; determine *gwam* and count errors.
2. Take a 3' writing on ¶s 1–3 combined; determine *gwam* and count errors.

all letters used

	gwam 3'	5'	
People in business are concerned about what is communicated	4	2	36
by the written word. As they write memos, letters, and reports,	8	5	38
they may plan for the content but may not plan for the image of	13	8	41
the message. Experts, however, realize that neglecting the way	17	10	43
a document looks can be costly.	19	11	45
Many times a written piece of correspondence is the only	23	14	47
basis on which a person can form an impression of the writer.	27	16	49
Judgments based on a first impression that may be formed by the	31	19	52
reader about the writer should always be considered before mail-	35	21	54
ing a document.	36	22	55
The way a document looks can communicate as much as what it	40	24	57
says. Margins, spacing, and placement are all important features	45	27	60
to consider when you key a document. A quality document is one	49	29	63
that will bring the interest of the reader to the message rather	53	32	65
than to the way it appears.	55	33	66

gwam 3' | 1 | 2 | 3 | 4
5' | 1 | 2 | 3

Document 2 (Four-Page Program Booklet)

1. Prepare a program booklet for the High School Honor Society Induction Ceremony.
2. The booklet will be formatted on *two pages*, using 8.5" × 11" paper in landscape orientation (see illustration at right):
   - **P. 1** will have the text for the outside back and front covers.
   - **P. 2** will have the text for the inside left page and the inside right page.
3. Set left, right, top, and bottom margins on both pages at 0.5".
4. Select landscape orientation and two pages per sheet.
5. Set columns as follows:
   - **Outside Back Cover:** two columns, each 2" wide with 0.5" between them.
   - **Outside Front Cover:** one 4.5" column.
   - **Inside Left Page:** one 4.5" column.
   - **Inside Right Page:** two columns, each 2" wide with 0.5" between them.
6. Insert the information that is given for the covers and pages at the right. You decide all other formatting features and graphics that will be inserted.

Save as: *PROG124B2A* (p. 1) and *PROG124B2B* (p. 2).

Page 1	
Outside Back Cover (5.5" × 8.5")	Outside Front Cover (5.5" × 8.5")
One 8.5" × 11" paper in landscape orientation	

Page 2	
Inside Left Page (5.5" × 8.5")	Inside Right Page (5.5" × 8.5")
One 8.5" × 11" paper in landscape orientation	

Outside Back Cover:

1. Key **SENIOR MEMBERS** as a title that spans both columns.
2. Insert the senior members' names from the file *CD-L124B2* (balance the names in two columns).

Outside Front Cover:

1. Arrange the following information attractively: **High School Honor Society**, **Induction Ceremony**, **Laurel High School**, **December 15, 200-**, **6:30 p.m.**
2. Insert the following text in a shaded text box or shape:

The High School Honor Society inducts students who have achieved academic excellence, displayed good character, demonstrated leadership qualities, and served the school and community.

Inside Left Page:

After keying the title **PROGRAM**, insert this information, including dot leaders:

Welcome . . . . Rob Jansante, President
Opening Remarks. . . . . Dr. Paul Henry, Principal
Speaker. . . . . Dr. Helen Rapp, Laurel Community College
Induction Ceremony
  Scholarship . . . . Matt Roman, Vice President
  Character . . . . Jessica Roman, Treasurer
  Leadership. . . . . Stephanie Davis, Secretary
  Service . . . . Meghan Johnson, Historian
Pledge . . . . Rob Jansante
Presentation of Certificates. . . Rob Jansante and Dr. Paul Henry
Closing. . . . . Rob Jansante

All members and guests are invited to a reception in the Library immediately following the Induction Ceremony.

Inside Right Page:

1. Key **INDUCTEES** as a title that spans both columns.
2. Insert the names of the inductees from the file *CD-L124B2* (balance the names in two columns).

PREPARE FOR ASSESSMENT: TABLES

Objective:
To prepare for assessment of table formatting skills.

72A • 5' Conditioning Practice

Key each line twice SS; then key a 1' writing on line 3; determine *gwam*.

alphabet 1 Zachary James always purchased five or six large antique baskets.

figures 2 Only 1,548 of the 1,967 expected guests had arrived by 12:30 p.m.

speed 3 The neighbor may fix the problem with the turn signal on the bus.

gwam 1' | 1 | 2 | 3 | 4 | 5 | 6 | 7 | 8 | 9 | 10 | 11 | 12 | 13 |

72B • 36' Reinforce Table Formatting Skills

Table 1

Format the table at the right. Use the table formatting features you have learned to arrange the information attractively on the page. Use the following source note.

Source: Fodor's 2000, San Francisco and Fodor's 2000, USA.

Use a border similar to the one shown.

 **Save as:** *TBL72B1*

PLACES TO EXPLORE

San Francisco

Place to Explore	Description	Major Attractions
Union Square	Heart of San Francisco's downtown, major shopping district	• Westin St. Francis Hotel • Old San Francisco Mint
Chinatown	Home to one of the largest Chinese communities outside Asia	• Chinese Culture Center • Old Chinese Telephone Exchange
Nob Hill	Home of the city's elite and some of its finest hotels	• Pacific Union Club • Cable Car Museum • Grace Cathedral • Mark Hopkins Hotel
Civic Center	One of the country's great city, state, and federal building complexes	• City Hall • Civic Center Plaza • Performing Arts Center • War Memorial Opera House
The Embarcadero	Waterfront promenade great for walking and jogging	• Ferry Building • Embarcadero Center • Hyatt Regency Hotel • Justin Herman Plaza
Fisherman's Wharf	Hyde cable-car line, waterfront, Ghirardelli Square, Piers 39 and 41	• Lombard Street • National Maritime Museum • Museum of the City of San Francisco
Financial District	Cluster of steel-and-glass high-rises and older, more decorative architectural monuments to commerce	• Transamerica Pyramid • Bank of America • Pacific Stock Exchange • Stock Exchange Tower

Document 2 (Two-Column Newsletter)

1. Open *NEWS123B1* and insert the text at the right as a third article. Use **Business Ethics** as the article title.
2. Reformat the three columns into two columns.
3. Insert a small graphic relating to people in article 2, and wrap the text around it.
4. Insert the following text box before the last ¶ at the right:

   A code of ethics conveys a company's values and business standards.

5. Reformat all text boxes so they have reverse type and no borders.
6. Use word art and 3-D effects to redesign the newsletter title.
7. Use hyphenation and justification.
8. Balance columns as needed.

 **Save as:** *NEWS123B2*

Ethics is a popular topic today. Many businesses that had written codes for ethical practice years ago set them aside and are now going back to them.

The main purpose of a code of ethics is to convey a company's values and business standards to all its workers. An organization is ethical to the extent that each person in it subscribes to and applies the standards. Far more than a list of do's and don'ts for office employees, ethics cuts across all lines of an organization. It involves how coworkers treat one another as well as how current and future customers, suppliers, and the general public are treated by the business.

Every job has an ethical aspect, and every person has values. When an individual's standards are in sync with the employer's, the situation is generally positive for both. If either of them is inclined to "take shortcuts" or "look the other way" now and then, an unhappy employer-employee relationship is likely to develop.

LESSON 124 CREATE AN ADVERTISEMENT AND A PROGRAM BOOKLET

Objective:

To prepare a one-page advertisement and a four-page program booklet.

124A • 5' Conditioning Practice

Key each line twice; take 30" writings on lines 1, 2, and 3; determine *gwam*.

alphabet 1 A quick check of taxes on the big projects would amaze everybody.

fig/sym 2 Dan said, "Buy #3746 or #1098 at a 25% discount at Stitt & Sons."

speed 3 Eight rich airmen are to endow the chapel on a visit to the town.

gwam 1' | 1 | 2 | 3 | 4 | 5 | 6 | 7 | 8 | 9 | 10 | 11 | 12 | 13 |

124B • 45' Advertisement and Booklet

Document 1 (Advertisement)

1. Create a one-page advertisement for a product of your choice.
2. Name the club or business selling the product.
3. List at least three features or advantages of the product.
4. State where the product can be purchased.
5. Include an object that illustrates the product as much as possible.
6. Use word art, shapes, clip art, 3-D effects, shading, color, borders, and/or text boxes as desired.

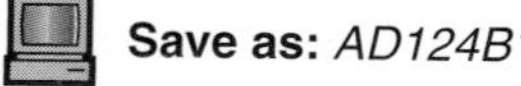

Save as: *AD124B1*

Tables 2 & 3

Format the tables at the right. Use the table formatting features you have learned to arrange the information attractively on the page. Apply a border of your choice.

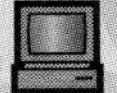

Save as: *TBL72B2* and *TBL72B3*

Determine the current value of this portfolio, using an Internet site such as http://quote.yahoo.com/ to determine the value per share of each stock.

Stock Portfolio

EASTWICK INVESTMENT CLUB

As of April 20, 200-

Stock		Shares Owned	Price per Share	Value of Stock
Company Name	**Symbol**			
Best Buy	BBY	200	78.875	$ 15,775.00
Ford	F	250	55.125	13,781.25
Intel	INTC	150	115.305	17,295.75
Kohls	KSS	200	102.375	20,475.00
McDonald's	MCD	200	35.625	7,125.00
Michael Foods	MIKL	150	20.125	3,018.75
Microsoft	MSFT	100	78.125	7,812.50
Pepsico	PEP	100	37.000	3,700.00
U.S. Airway	U	100	28.125	2,812.50
U.S. Bancorp	USB	200	21.305	4,261.00
Cash				23,495.77
Total Portfolio Value				$119,552.52

MAJOR UNITED STATES RIVERS

River	Length	
	Miles	**Kilometers**
Arkansas	1,459	2,348
Colorado	1,450	2,333
Columbia	1,243	2,000
Mississippi	2,340	3,766
Missouri	2,315	3,726
Red	1,290	2,080
Rio Grande	1,900	3,060
Snake	1,038	1,670
Yukon	1,979	3,185

Source: The 1996 Information Please Almanac. Boston: Houghton-Mifflin.

72C • 9'
Skill Check

1. Key a 1' writing on each ¶ of 71C, p. 198; determine *gwam* and errors.
2. Take a 3' writing on ¶s 1–3 of 71C, p. 198; determine *gwam* and errors.

123B • 45' Newsletters

Document 1 (Three-Column Newsletter from Rough Draft)

1. Format the two articles below as a newsletter with three columns of equal width.
2. The title and publication information should span the three columns and be formatted appropriately.
3. Correct all errors.
4. Format article headings in a large font size. Use 11-pt. font for the article copy. DS above and below article titles and text boxes.
5. Use a 2-line drop cap for the first word in each article.
6. Use shaded text boxes with borders as shown below.
7. Insert vertical lines between columns.
8. Hyphenate and justify the columns.
9. You decide other formatting features.

Save as: *NEWS123B1*

STRATEGIES FOR SUCCESS

Vol. 6, No. 3 Spring, 200-

Reputation and Choice

Reputation is the image people have of your standards of conduct; your ethical and moral principals. Most people think that a good reputation is needed to succeed in any job; and it is therefore one of the most importnat personal assetts you can acquire in your life.

A bad reputation can result from one misdeed.

A good reputation is a valued asset that requires time, effort, and discipline to develop and project. A bad reputation can be a longterm liability established in a short time. It can be a result from just one misdeed and can be a hevay burden to carry throughout life.

It is important to realize, therefore, that most of youhave an opportunity to develope and protect the reputation you want. You have many chioces tomake that will destroy or enhance the image you want to extned. The choices are hard; and honestly, loyalty, and dedicatoin are most often involved.

Choices you make destroy or enhance your reputation.

Learnig About People

Many aspects of a job present challenges to those who strive to do their best in all they do. The most critical challenge all workers face is being able to relate will to the many individuals with whom they have to work. It is common for workers to have daily dealings with bosses, peers, and subordinates. Also, workers will interact with telephone callers and visitors from outside and inside the company.

Relating well to others is a critical challenge.

While it is critical to learn all you can about your job and company, it is often just as cirtical to learn about the people with whom you will work and interact. Frequently, you can rely upon experienced workers for information that will help you analyze the formal and informal structures of the organization. What you learn may help you determine what an employer expects, likes, or dislikes, and will help you make a good adjustment to your workplace.

Learn from experienced workers.

UNIT 21

LESSONS 73–75

Assessing Document Formatting Skills

LESSON 73 ASSESS CORRESPONDENCE FORMATTING

Objectives:

1. To assess e-mail, memo, and letter formatting skills.
2. To assess straight-copy skill.

73A • 5' Conditioning Practice

Key each line twice SS; then take a 1' writing on line 3; determine *gwam* and errors.

alphabet 1 Bugs quickly explained why five of the zoo projects cost so much.
figures 2 Jo's office phone number is 632-0781; her home phone is 832-4859.
speed 3 Pamela may go with us to the city to do the work for the auditor.

gwam 1' | 1 | 2 | 3 | 4 | 5 | 6 | 7 | 8 | 9 | 10 | 11 | 12 | 13 |

73B • 10' Check Keying Skill

Key two 3' writings on ¶s 1–3 combined; determine *gwam* and errors.

 all letters used

	gwam 1'	3'
Attitude is the way people communicate their feelings or	11	4
moods to others. A person is said to have a positive attitude	24	8
when he or she anticipates successful experiences. A person such	37	12
as this is said to be an optimist. The best possible outcomes	50	17
are expected. The world is viewed as a great place. Good is	62	21
found in even the worst situation.	69	23
Individuals are said to have negative attitudes when they	12	27
expect failure. A pessimist is the name given to an individual	24	31
with a bad view of life. Pessimists emphasize the adverse	36	35
aspects of life and expect the worst possible outcome. They	48	39
expect to fail even before they start the day. You can plan on	61	43
them to find gloom even in the best situation.	70	46
Only you can ascertain when you are going to have a good or	12	50
bad attitude. Keep in mind that people are attracted to a	24	54
person with a good attitude and tend to shy away from one with a	37	59
bad attitude. Your attitude quietly determines just how success-	50	63
ful you are in all your personal relationships as well as in	62	67
your professional relationships.	68	69

gwam 1' | 1 | 2 | 3 | 4 | 5 | 6 | 7 | 8 | 9 | 10 | 11 | 12 | 13 |
3' | 1 | 2 | 3 | 4 |

abdominal CT scan was common. However, now it is necessary to specifically order an abdomen and pelvis examination if an image of the pelvic region is deemed necessary.

(¶) For more information about the new requirements, contact Stephen Antoncic, MD, director, Radiology Department, at Extension 3512 or antoncic@upton.com.

What's Up! with Our Colleagues

(¶) Michelle Glatzko, Central Service—at the fall conference of the Tri-County Central Service Association, presented "Isolation Carts and Universal Precautions as Related to Central Service Technicians"; also elected secretary of the chapter.

(¶) Maurice Tarli, volunteer coordinator—elected secretary of the board, Society of Directors of Volunteer Services, Western chapter.

(¶) Two staff members, Larry Szerbin, RN, and Ann Tokar, RN, received degrees. Larry completed a bachelor of science in business administration degree with a major in nursing management from Lynn College. Ann earned a master of science degree in long-term health care from Upton University.

Investment Performance

(¶) If you participate in the Upton Retirement Program or Supplemental Retirement Annuity plans, daily balances of your accounts can be obtained via the Internet. All you need to do is visit http://www.hiaa.com and establish a PIN. With your Social Security number and your PIN, you can obtain end-of-day balances at any time. You no longer need to wait for the quarterly reports to see how your money is growing.

Farewell, Rudy

(¶) A retirement tea will be held for Rudy Beissel, Environmental Support Services, on Thursday, June 24, from 1:30 p.m. to 3 p.m. in the Jones Conference Center. Rudy is retiring after 35 years with Upton.

Career Track

(¶) Lorretta Slobodnick recently was named as an administrative assistant, Medical Records. She reports to Erika Cooper, head, Medical Records. Lorretta earned her associate degree from Upton County Community College and specialized in medical technology. Please welcome her at Extension 1505 or slobodni@upton.com.

Patient Praises

(¶) To Susan Getty, nurse: "Thank you for the compassionate and knowledgeable care." —a stroke patient

(¶) "Thanks to all who helped nurse me back to health!" —a Unit 15D patient

(¶) To Jill Holt, nurse: "Thanks, thanks, thanks! Your skill is appreciated." —a new mom

LESSON 123 PRODUCE THREE-COLUMN NEWSLETTER

Objectives:

1. To prepare a newsletter with three newspaper-style columns.
2. To use shaded text boxes with and without borders, word art, clip art, vertical lines, 3-D effects, and balanced columns.

123A • 5' Conditioning Practice

Key each line twice; take 30" writings on lines 1, 2, and 3; determine *gwam*.

alphabet 1 We realize expert judges may check the value of the unique books.

figures 2 A teacher will have 75 test items from pages 289-306 for Unit 41.

speed 3 The dorm officials may name six sorority girls to go to a social.

gwam 1' | 1 | 2 | 3 | 4 | 5 | 6 | 7 | 8 | 9 | 10 | 11 | 12 | 13 |

73C • 35'
Assess E-mail, Memo, and Letter Formatting Skills

Document 1 (Memo)

Format the text at the right as a memo to **Kathleen Maloney** from **Miguel Gonzalez**. Date: **May 5, 200-**. Subject: **BUDGET REQUEST**.

 **Save as:** *MEMO73C1*

As I searched the Internet for teaching resources, I came across some audiocassettes that would be an excellent addition to my World History course. The audiocassette collection, *The World's 100 Greatest People*, currently sells for $295, plus sales tax and shipping and handling charges of $9.95.

According to the advertisement (http://www.4iq.com/iquest16.html), "The 50 tapes included in this collection represent an audio treasury of 100 biographies detailing the life, time, achievement, and impact of some of history's greatest personalities, including philosophers, explorers, inventors, scientists, writers, artists, composers, religious, political, and military leaders." These tapes could be used in many classes outside the Social Studies Department. Perhaps some of the other departments would be willing to share the cost of the tapes.

When you have a few minutes, I would like to discuss how we should proceed to get these tapes in time for next year.

Document 2 (Letter)

Format the text at the right as a two-page letter to:

Mr. Michael Kent, President
Quote of the Month Club
97 Liberty Sq.
Boston, MA 02109-3625

Use **March 3, 200-** for the date; the letter is from **Patricia Fermanich**, who is the **Program Chair**. Use **Dear Michael** for the salutation and **Sincerely** for the complimentary closing.

Insert these quotations in the letter where indicated:

- **Wendell Lewis Willkie—"Our way of living together in America is a strong but delicate fabric. It is made up of many threads. It has been woven over many centuries by the patience and sacrifice of countless liberty-loving men and women."**
- **Althea Gibson—"No matter what accomplishments you make, somebody helps you."**

 **Save as:** *LTR73C2*

Arrangements for our April **Quote of the Month Club** meeting are progressing nicely. The meeting will be held at Pilgrims' Inn in Plymouth on Saturday, the 15th. The Inn offers excellent accommodations and food. I worked out special pricing with the manager. The cost will be $199.50 per member. This includes a single room, lunch and dinner on Saturday, and a continental breakfast on Sunday. I've asked the Inn to reserve 25 rooms for our members and guests. They will hold them until April 10. I've enclosed the Inn's brochure and list of food options. We can discuss them at the officers' meeting in Boston next week.

Members didn't like the format of our last meeting, so I'm proposing this plan: Each person attending will be assigned to a team, and each team will be given four quotes. The team will select one quote and prepare a five-minute presentation, explaining the meaning of the quote (their opinion). Each team will select a member to present to the entire group. Teams will evaluate each presenter in writing, rather than with oral comments. Some presenters at the last meeting felt uncomfortable being critiqued in front of the entire group.

I selected these four quotations:

- **Walter Elias Disney**—"Our greatest natural resource is the mind of our children."
- **Ayn Rand**—"Throughout the centuries there were men who took first steps down new roads armed with nothing but their own vision."

Insert two bulleted quotations shown at the left.

These topics should provide for excellent discussions leading up to the presentations. When you send the meeting notice, please send the quotes so the members will have time to think about them prior to the meeting.

I'm looking forward to our officers' meeting next week. I may be a few minutes late since I have a 4 p.m. meeting that I must attend.

LESSON 122 PRODUCE TWO-COLUMN NEWSLETTERS

Objective:

To prepare documents with balanced columns, a different number of columns on a page, and a watermark.

122A • 5' Conditioning Practice

Key each line twice; take 30" writings on lines 1, 2, and 3; determine *gwam*.

alphabet 1 Mrs. Gaznox was quite favorably pleased with the market projects.

figures 2 Book prices increased 17% from 05/06/99 to 08/03/02 in 42 stores.

speed 3 The widow may visit the city to see the robot shape an auto body.

gwam 1' | 1 | 2 | 3 | 4 | 5 | 6 | 7 | 8 | 9 | 10 | 11 | 12 | 13 |

122B • 45' Two-Column Newsletter

1. Format the text below and on the next page as a newsletter with two columns of equal width. SS ¶s; DS between ¶s.
2. Place the title and publication information so they span both columns.
3. Use word art to create the title; use a 10-pt. font for the publication information.
4. Justify and hyphenate the text. Change the ¶ indent (tab stop) to 0.25".
5. SS the Patient Praises (p. 328) in an unshaded text box; DS between comments.
6. Place a **DRAFT** watermark behind the columns.
7. Balance the columns on the last page, if needed.

Save as: *NEWS122B*

WHAT'S UP!

Vol. 6, No. 6 June, 200-

Satisfaction Survey Established

(¶) Upton General Hospital has established patient satisfaction as a major organizational goal and is committed to establishing a hospital-wide patient satisfaction survey. Patient satisfaction is recognized as a critical business issue and is a mechanism to demonstrate high-quality care and service to employers, insurers, and the community. "Patient satisfaction surveying is an important tool to help us learn more about our patients' expectations," said Freda Banks, RN, DNS, vice president, Nursing. "By understanding their needs better, we can deliver care in ways that are more satisfying to them."

(¶) The first phase of the patient satisfaction survey process will be implemented in July. Patients in the burn center, in-patient surgery, emergency, and same-day surgery will be surveyed. Preliminary results will be reported to the board of directors and corporate officers at the August board meeting, and then distributed to department heads.

Upton Says Thanks

(¶) Upton says thanks to all the steering committee members for their hard work in preparing for and hosting the on-site review by the Joint Review Committee on Accreditation of Healthcare Providers (JRCAHP). All steering committee and subcommittee members are asked to stop by the Arcadia Dining Room between 11 a.m. and 2 p.m. on Friday, June 25, to enjoy soup and salad and discuss the team's oral exit report. Night-shift staff can enjoy bagels and coffee and a similar discussion in the Main Dining Room from 2 a.m. to 3 a.m. on Saturday, June 26. Watch *What's Up!* for the JRCAHP findings.

New Requirements for Ordering CT Scans

(¶) Due to recent changes in third-party payer requirements, referring physicians are advised to request all necessary imaging studies when placing orders with the Radiology Department. Radiologists cannot extend the examination coverage or add additional studies.

(¶) The abdominal computed tomography (CT) scan is a common order affected by the recent changes. In the past, inclusion of the pelvic region in an

(continued on next page)

Document 3 (E-mail)

Send the text at the right as e-mail to your instructor. (If you do not have e-mail software, prepare the text as a memo to **Sachiko Yang**. DATE: **April 24, 200-**). Use **RESPONSE TO YOUR QUESTION** for the subject.

 **Save as:** *MAIL73C3*

Your question is a good one. Yes, Nellie Tayloe Ross of Wyoming and Miriam (Ma) Ferguson of Texas were elected on the same day, November 4, 1924. However, Ms. Ross took office 16 days before Ms. Ferguson; therefore, Ms. Ross is considered the first woman governor in the United States, and Ms. Ferguson is considered the second. It should also be noted that Ms. Ross completed her husband's term as governor of Wyoming prior to being elected in 1924.

If you have other questions before the exam on Friday, please let me know. I hope you do well on it.

LESSON 74 ASSESS REPORT FORMATTING

Objective:

To assess report formatting skills.

74A • 5' Conditioning Practice

Key each line twice SS; then take a 1' writing on line 3; determine *gwam* and errors.

alphabet 1 Jeff Pizarro saw very quickly how Jason had won the boxing match.

figures 2 Our team average went from .458 on April 17 to .296 on August 30.

speed 3 Nancy may go to the big social at the giant chapel on the island.

gwam 1' | 1 | 2 | 3 | 4 | 5 | 6 | 7 | 8 | 9 | 10 | 11 | 12 | 13 |

74B • 45' Assess Report Formatting Skills

Document 1

Format the text at the right as a *bound* report with footnotes. Use **FOUR OUTSTANDING AMERICANS** for the title.

Footnotes

[1]Susan Clinton, The Story of Susan B. Anthony (Chicago: Children's Press, 1986), p. 5.

[2]Jim Powell, "The Education of Thomas Edison" (April 25, 2000).

[3]"An Overview of Abraham Lincoln's Life" (April 27, 2000).

 **Save as:** *RPT74B1*

Many outstanding Americans have influenced the past, and many more will impact the future. Choosing the "Four Greatest American" does injustice to the hundreds of others who left there mark on our country and diminishes their contributions. This report simply recognizes four great Americans who made America what it is today.

Without these four individuals America perhaps would be quite different than what it is today. The four individuals included in this report are: Susan B. Anthony, Thomas A. Edison, Benjamin Franklin, and Abraham Lincoln.

Susan B. Anthony is noted for her advancement of womens rights. She and Elizabeth Cady Stanton organized the national woman suffrage association. The following quote shows her commitment to the cause.

> At 7 a.m. on November 5, 1872, Susan B. Anthony broke the law by doing something she had never done before. After twenty years of working to win the vote for women, she marched to the polls in Rochester, New York, and voted. Her vote—for Ulysses S. Grant for president—was illegal. In New York state, only men were allowed to vote.[1]

Health Resources on the Web (Repeat from Wednesday)
3:30-5 p.m., Room 610
Provides an overview of quality health resources on the Internet and how to locate them using Westbrook Hospital's Library System Web page.

Document 2 (Three-Column Newsletter Articles)

1. Format the two articles at the right using three columns of equal width.
2. Use 16-pt. bold font for titles.
3. Using a light gray, shade the second ¶ in the first article.
4. Between the two articles, insert the tip below in a text box that has no border, using reverse type.
5. Justify and hyphenate the text.

 **Save as:** *ART121B2*

This Issue's Tip
If you've asked for a doggie bag to take home from a restaurant, you should refrigerate it within two hours. Reheat leftovers to 165 degrees Fahrenheit until warmed throughout.

Basic Life Support Renewal Courses

(¶) The School of Nursing at North Hills Hospital will hold its annual basic life support (BLS) renewal courses in March. The courses are open to all staff.

(¶) Staff members whose jobs require them to hold a valid BLS completion card must attend a renewal course every two years, according to American Heart Association guidelines. Heart Saver Plus (adult) and Health Care Provider (adult, infant, and child) BLS renewal courses will be offered.

(¶) Renewal courses will be held Monday through Friday, March 15 through March 19, and March 22 through March 26, from 7 a.m. to 8 p.m. Renewal courses also will be held Saturday, March 20, from 7 a.m. to 2 p.m. All courses will be held in Wilkins Hall, Room 135.

(¶) Staff should allow 60 to 90 minutes to complete the renewal course exam. To receive a BLS renewal, staff will be required to complete a written test and demonstrate their BLS skills. The renewal course is open to anyone who is due to take a renewal course, even if it is not required for his or her job.

Science Judges Sought

(¶) An additional 25 judges with expertise in science and an interest in children are needed for the 61st annual North Hills Science and Engineering Fair. The competition will be held from 8 a.m. to 1 p.m. March 31 at the North Hills Science Center.

(¶) Jeffrey Sidora, science fair coordinator, said 60 judges are needed to examine exhibits created by 150 students from 6 area schools. The judges should have technical backgrounds, such as master's degrees in biology, chemistry, physics, computer science, mathematics, engineering, robotics, medicine, microbiology, earth science, or environment.

(¶) The judges have to be willing to make a time commitment from 8 a.m. to 1 p.m. Lunch will be provided. At the fair, students in grades 6 through 12 compete for the best science and engineering projects in their age brackets.

Document 2 (References Page)
Format a references page from the information below.

Clinton, Susan. The Story of Susan B. Anthony. Chicago: Children's Press, 1986.

"An Overview of Abraham Lincoln's Life." http://www.home.att.net/~rjnorton/Lincoln77.html (27 April 2000).

Powell, Jim. "The Education of Thomas Edison." http://www.self-gov.org/freeman/9502powe.htm (25 April 2000).

Save as: *RPT74B2*

Document 3 (Title Page)
Format a title page for the report.

Save as: *RPT74B3*

Anthony continued to fight for women's rights, however, for the next 33 years of her life. Even though hse died in 1906 and the amendment granting women the right to vote (nineteenth amendment) was not passed until 1920, that amendment is often called the Susan B. Anthony Amendment in honor of Anthony's eforts to advance women's rights.

Thomas Alva Edison

Imagine life without the incandescent light bulb, phonograph, kinetoscope (a small box for viewing moving films), or any of the other 1,090 inventions patiented by Edison. Life certainly would be different without these inventions or later inventions that came as a result of Edison's ~~his~~ work.

Interestingly enough, most of Edison's learning took place at home under the guidance of his mother. "Nancy Edison's secret: she was more dedicated than any teacher was likely to be, and she had the flexibility to experiment with various ways of nurturing her son's live for learning."[2]

Benjamin Franklin

Benjamin Franklin was a man of many talents. He was an inventor, printer, diplomat, philosopher, author, postmaster, and leader. A few of his more noteworthy accomplishments included serving on the committee that created the Declaration of Independence; publishing Poor Richard's Almanac; and inventing the lightning rod, ~~the~~ Franklin stove, ~~the~~ odometer, and bifocal glasses.

Abraham Lincoln

For many Americans the impact of Abraham Lincoln is as great today as it was during his life time.

> Abraham Lincoln is remembered for his vital role as the leader in preserving the Union and beginning the process that led to the end of slavery in the United States. He is also remembered for his character, his speeches and letters, and as a man of humble origins whose determination and perseverance led him to the nation's highest office.[3]

DS Lincoln is a great example of one who dealt positively with adversity in his personal and professional life. His contributions towards the shaping of America will be long remembered.

121B • 45' Newspaper-Style Columns

Document 1 (Two-Column Announcement)

1. Key the text at the right and on the next page.
2. Format the text in two columns of equal width.
3. Insert appropriate clip art at the top of the first column. Make it about 1" high and surround it with a border.
4. Center the title and sub-title in the first column using a 20-pt. font, bold.
5. Using a light gray, shade each day and date.
6. Format the name of events as shown (small caps, bold). SS them and DS between events and above and below the dates.
7. Use a 2-line drop cap for the first word in each course description.
8. Justify and hyphenate text.

 **Save as:** *ANN121B1*

Calendar of Events
Week of February 2

Monday, February 2

FUNDAMENTALS OF PRESENTATION SOFTWARE (Repeated on Wednesday)
9-10 a.m., Room 609
Teaches participants how to make overhead transparencies, speaker's notes, and handouts using Adam Pro View.

RECRUITING TOP-NOTCH TALENT
12 noon-3:30 p.m., Room 1543
Recruiting strategy session covers the hospital's latest methods for attracting top-notch applicants.

WESTBROOK CHAMBER OF COMMERCE MEETING
1-2:30 p.m., Executive Dining Room, 6th Floor
Westbrook Hospital is hosting this luncheon to announce the renovation project and explain its impact on local business and industry.

Tuesday, February 3

INTRANET TECHNOLOGY
4:30-5:30 p.m., Room 610
Gives employees hands-on training in using Westbrook's intranet to improve communications and work flow.

FUNDAMENTALS OF ADAM WORD EZE
5-7 p.m., Room 609
Teaches participants how to prepare documents that include graphics, clip art, text boxes, and shading, using Adam Word Eze.

Wednesday, February 4

FUNDAMENTALS OF PRESENTATION SOFTWARE (Repeat from Monday)
9-10 a.m., Room 609
Teaches participants how to make overhead transparencies, speaker's notes, and handouts using Adam Pro View.

HEALTH RESOURCES ON THE WEB (Repeated on Thursday)
3:30-5 p.m., Room 610
Provides an overview of quality health resources on the Internet and how to locate them using Westbrook Hospital's Library System Web page.

Thursday, February 5

CALCULATING AND CHARTING WITH SPREADSHEET SOFTWARE
1-3 p.m., Room 609
Teaches participants how to use formulas and charts using Adam Data Pro software.

ASSESS TABLE FORMATTING

Objective:
To assess table formatting skills.

75A • 5' Conditioning Practice

Key each line twice SS; then take a 1' writing on line 3; determine *gwam* and errors.

alphabet 1 Hazel Jackson reported quite extensive damage to the big freeway.

fig/sym 2 Model #80-93 sells for $425 plus 6% sales tax and 17% excise tax.

speed 3 He may pay us to work for the men when they dismantle the chapel.

gwam 1' | 1 | 2 | 3 | 4 | 5 | 6 | 7 | 8 | 9 | 10 | 11 | 12 | 13 |

75B • 45' Assess Table Formatting Skills

Table 1

Format the table at the right. Adjust column widths: Columns A and B, 2"; Column C, 1.75". Adjust row height: 0.3" (all rows). Use the horizontal and vertical alignment in cells as shown. Apply bold and shading (gray–5%) and a double-line border around every cell (as shown). Center the table horizontally and vertically.

 **Save as:** *TBL75B1*

Fan Balloting

MAJOR LEAGUE ALL-CENTURY TEAM

Position	**Player**	**No. of Votes**
Catcher	Johnny Bench	1,010,403
	Yogi Berra	704,208
Pitcher	Nolan Ryan	992,040
	Sandy Koufax	970,434
First Baseman	Lou Gehrig	1,207,992
	Mark McGwire	517,181
Second Baseman	Jackie Robinson	788,116
	Rogers Hornsby	630,761
Shortstop	Cal Ripken Jr.	669,033
	Ernie Banks	598,168
Third Baseman	Mike Schmidt	855,654
	Brooks Robinson	761,700
Outfield	Babe Ruth	1,158,044
	Hank Aaron	1,156,782
	Ted Williams	1,125,583
	Willie Mays	1,115,896
	Joe DiMaggio	1,054,423
	Mickey Mantle	988,168

Source: USA Today. http://www.usatoday.com/sports/baseballmlbfs28.htm (25 October 1999).

Flyer 2

1. Use the information beside the guide words at the right to design a flyer.
2. Include word art, 3-D effects, shaded text boxes, and shapes when formatting the flyer.
3. You decide all other formatting features.

 **Save as:** *FLY120B2*

Event:	The Dangers of Drinking and Driving
Sponsored by:	Students Against DUI
When:	Friday, May 3, at 3:30 p.m.
Where:	Gymnasium B, Welton High School
Cost:	Free admission with school ID card
Guest speaker:	Sgt. Terry Hollinsworth State Trooper Welton South Barracks
Main feature:	Students will use a simulator to observe the effects of DUI.

Flyer 3

1. Use the information beside the guide words at the right to design a flyer.
2. Design and include an excuse/permission form as part of the flyer.
3. You decide all formatting features.

 **Save as:** *FLY120B3*

Sponsoring teacher:	Mrs. Porterfield
When:	Wednesday, October 3, Periods 1, 2, 5, 6, and 7
Where:	Classroom 222
Guest speaker:	Dr. Ida Meinert Nutritionist, Blair Hospital
Topic:	Recognizing Eating Disorders
Excuse form:	Space for student's name, name and period of the class to be missed, name of teacher whose class will be missed, and signature of teacher granting permission.

Flyer 4

Using the instructions at the right as a guide, design a flyer your teacher can use to inform others of the value of the course in which you are using this textbook.

 **Save as:** *FLY120B4*

1. Key the name of the course.
2. Identify some course activities you enjoy.
3. Describe the important things you have learned.
4. Specify reasons why others should take this course.
5. Identify the hardware and software that you use.
6. Explain how this course helps you in other classes or at work.

LESSON 121 PREPARE NEWSPAPER-STYLE COLUMNS

Objective:

To prepare documents using preset newspaper-style columns, text boxes, shaded paragraphs, justified lines, and drop caps.

121A • 5' Conditioning Practice

Key each line twice; take 30" writings on lines 1, 2, and 3; determine *gwam*.

alphabet 1 Waj and Zogy are quick at solving complex problems with formulas.

figures 2 William's 169 stores in 48 states served over 320,750 last month.

speed 3 The men may focus on their work if they are apt to make a profit.

gwam 1' | 1 | 2 | 3 | 4 | 5 | 6 | 7 | 8 | 9 | 10 | 11 | 12 | 13 |

Table 2

Format the table at the right. Adjust column widths: Columns A and B, 1"; Columns C and D, 0.75"; Columns E and F, 1.25". Adjust row height: 0.25" (all rows). In cells, use *bottom* vertical alignment and the horizontal alignment shown. Apply bold and shading (gray-5%, gray-10%, red, and light blue) and a triple-line border around every cell (as shown). Center the table horizontally and vertically.

Save as: *TBL75B2*

UNITED STATES WOMEN GOVERNORS

Name		**Party Affiliation**		**State**	**Years Served**
Last	**First**	**Dem.**	**Rep.**		
Collins	Martha	X		Kentucky	1984-1987
Ferguson	Miriam	X		Texas	1925-1927
Finney	Joan	X		Kansas	1991-1995
Grasso	Ella	X		Connecticut	1975-1980
Hollister	Nancy		X	Ohio	1998-1999
Hull	Jane		X	Arizona	1997-present
Kunin	Madeleine	X		Vermont	1985-1991
Mofford	Rose	X		Arizona	1988-1991
Orr	Kay		X	Nebraska	1987-1991
Ray	Dixy	X		Washington	1977-1981
Richards	Ann	X		Texas	1991-1995
Roberts	Barbara	X		Oregon	1991-1995
Ross	Nellie	X		Wyoming	1925-1927
Shaheen	Jeanne	X		New Hampshire	1997-present
Wallace	Lurleen	X		Alabama	1967-1968
Whitman	Christine		X	New Jersey	1994-present

Source: "GenderGap in Government." http://www.gendergap.com/government/governor.htm (21 March 2000).

Table 3

Format the table at the right. Use a 2" top margin. Adjust column width: Column A, 1.5"; Columns B-E, 0.5". Adjust row height: 0.3" (all rows). In cells, use *bottom* vertical alignment and the horizontal alignment shown. Apply bold and shading (gray-5%) as shown. Remove the outside table border. Center the table horizontally.

Save as: *TBL75B3*

SALARY COMPARISON

Employee	**Proposed Salary**		**Current Salary**	
	Salary	**Rank**	**Salary**	**Rank**
Douglas, Jason	$39,790	8	$39,000	7
Hazelkorn, Rebecca	41,230	7	38,500	8
Jackson, Charla	37,952	9	37,000	9
Loomis, Scott	25,796	10	23,000	10
Market, Michael	47,682	5	45,500	4
Nelson, Tim	62,265	1	59,725	1
Reed, Maja	52,980	3	51,900	2
Sutherland, Tara	54,769	2	51,695	3
Tekulve, Jaycee	49,780	4	44,500	6
Welsch, Gary	47,290	6	45,000	5

UNIT 32

LESSONS 120–125

Formatting Column Documents

LESSON 120 CREATE ONE-COLUMN FLYERS

Objective:

To prepare one-column flyers using shapes, word art, 3-D effects, and text boxes.

120A • 5' Conditioning Practice

Key each line twice; take 30" writings on lines 1, 2, and 3; determine *gwam*.

alphabet 1 Zack told Peg to be quiet and enjoy the first extra cowboy movie.

fig/sym 2 Ho's expenses are cab--$59; airline--$260; auto--$37 (148 miles).

speed 3 Claudia is to land the giant dirigible by the busy downtown mall.

gwam 1' | 1 | 2 | 3 | 4 | 5 | 6 | 7 | 8 | 9 | 10 | 11 | 12 | 13 |

120B • 45' Flyers

Flyer 1

1. Prepare a one-page flyer using all the information at the right.
2. Use word art, 3-D effects, small caps, shaded text boxes, and shapes when formatting the flyer.
3. You decide the size, shape, color, and placement of all information on the flyer.

Save as: *FLY120B1*

5K Run or Walk

Join RT Alumni
on
Saturday, August 14, 200-
at 9 a.m.
in East Park

$12 ENTRANCE FEE INCLUDES T-SHIRT, PRIZES, AND REFRESHMENTS
CALL (422) 555-0192 TO REGISTER

PRIZES WILL BE AWARDED TO TOP THREE MEN AND WOMEN FINISHERS IN THREE AGE GROUPS

Visit our Web site at http://www.pphs.org/5k

Your Perspective

Ethical issues confront us every day. They occur in our community, nation, and world. They also arise in our personal and professional lives.

- A stadium promises money and jobs, but some taxpayers would rather see the public funds to be expended on it spent on schools instead.
- A hydroelectric dam would provide a reservoir as well as electricity, but it would also destroy a wildlife habitat.
- In a grocery store, you see a student you know putting items under her coat.

Deciding what to do in situations like this isn't easy. What is a good way to think them through? What is a good way to make an ethical decision?

1. **Get the facts.** You can read about the new stadium and listen to what people on both sides of the issue have to say about it. You can learn more about reservoirs and how they affect the environment. You can try to find out more about the student from other people at school.
2. **Don't let assumptions get in the way of the facts.** As the actor and comedian Will Rogers said, "It isn't what we don't know that gives us trouble[;] it's what we know that ain't so." You don't like it when people make assumptions about you. Make sure your judgment isn't colored by preconceptions or stereotypes.
3. **Consider the consequences for everyone.** Try to see the situation from the point of view of each party involved. What is each person or group likely to lose or gain as a result of your decision?
4. **Consider your personal values.** Apply your own beliefs and standards to the problem.
5. **Make your decision.**

Ethics: The Right Thing to Do

ACTIVITIES

1. Read the material at the left.
2. Key a paragraph telling how you would use the five-step process to make a decision about the student in the grocery store.
3. Form a group with some other students. Discuss an ethical issue in your community. Make sure everyone contributes. Did everyone in the group agree?
4. Compose, format, and key a one-page personal-business letter to the editor of your local or school newspaper. Briefly explain the issue chosen in Step 3 and state your point of view. Include your reasons. Always present your viewpoint in a professional and respectful manner.

ACTIVITY 10

Changing the Number and Width of Columns

1. Read the information at the right.
2. Learn how to change the width and number of columns using your wp software.
3. Follow the directions at the right to change the number and width of columns.

The number and width of columns can be changed when newspaper-style columns are used. The change can be made before or after keying the text, and both the number and width of columns can vary on a page. Typically, you can select from several preset formats, or you can design a specific format you need.

1. Open *WP13ACT9* and reformat the text into two columns of equal width.

 **Save as:** *WP13ACT10A*

2. Reformat *WP13ACT10A* by deleting the last sentence, centering the title in a single column, and formatting the text into three columns of equal width below the title.

 **Save as:** *WP13ACT10B*

ACTIVITY 11

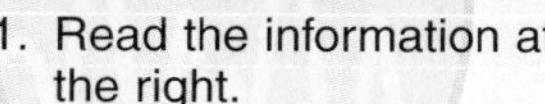

Balanced Column Lengths

1. Read the information at the right.
2. Learn how to balance column lengths using your wp software.
3. Follow the directions at the right.

Oftentimes, newspaper-style columns need to be **balanced** (equal or nearly equal in length). The desired balance can be achieved by inserting column breaks as needed.

1. Open *CD-WP13ACT11* and reformat the document into two newspaper-style columns of equal width.
2. Balance the columns so they are equal in length.

 **Save as:** *WP13ACT11A*

3. Reformat *WP13ACT11A* into a three-column document with balanced length, making certain to leave no widow/orphan lines.

 **Save as:** *WP13ACT11B*

ACTIVITY 12

Vertical Lines Between Columns

1. Read the text at the right.
2. Learn to insert vertical lines with your wp software.
3. Follow the directions at the right.

If desired, vertical lines can be placed between newspaper-style columns to enhance the appearance of the document. The lines can be inserted before or after keying the document.

1. Open *WP13ACT10B* and add vertical lines between the columns.

 **Save as:** *WP13ACT12A*

2. Open *WP13ACT10B* and reformat using two columns of unequal width with a vertical line between the columns.

 **Save as:** *WP13ACT12B*

ACTIVITY 13

Watermarks

1. Read the text at the right.
2. Learn to insert a watermark using your wp software.
3. Follow the directions at right.

A **watermark** is any text or graphic that, when printed, appears either on top of or behind the document's text. For example, your school's mascot may appear as a watermark on the school newspaper or stationery. A watermark stating "draft" or "confidential" is often added to letters or memos.

Open *WP13ACT12A* and add the word **DRAFT** as a watermark behind the text.

 **Save as:** *WP13ACT13*

Your Perspective

The 190 independent states of the world are becoming increasingly interdependent. One reason that countries work together is to promote peace and to help people live better lives. The United Nations, originally an alliance of 51 countries, was formed for that reason at the end of World War II. The United Nations now includes nearly every country and has expanded its mission to include promoting human rights, improving the quality of human life, protecting the environment, and fostering development.

A second reason that countries depend on one another is economics. Internal changes like the collapse of the Soviet government in 1991 have lowered trade barriers and opened new markets. Growing economies in some developing countries have improved trade. Trade agreements such as the North American Free Trade Agreement, the European Community, and World Trade Organization have also increased commerce among nations.

Global Awareness

ACTIVITIES

1. Form a group with two or three other students. Choose an interesting country that you do not know much about.
2. Each person in the group should research one of the following topics: geography, history, currency, and recent events. Add other topics for larger groups.
3. Compose, format, and key your section of the report in bound report format.
4. Dividing tasks among group members, combine the report sections and prepare references and title pages.

What would you do for three months without the Internet? a CD player? How about electricity or an indoor toilet? A television station in the United Kingdom took a suburban London row house—and a modern British family—back in time 100 years to answer questions like these.

The house was stripped of modern conveniences and restored to what it would have been like at the end of the nineteenth century. The Bowler family lived, for three months, exactly like a London family in 1900, and their experiences were the subject of a TV series.

Each person in the family—two parents and four children—had three outfits and three sets of underwear, all that a middle-class Victorian family could have afforded. Washing clothes took 12 hours, with the two younger girls staying home from school to help. No pizza or fast-food burgers were allowed. The family ate food that would have been served in Victorian England and brushed their teeth with hog-bristle brushes dipped in bicarbonate of soda. They had no telephones, but the mail arrived three times a day.

The Bowlers could ride bikes and swim. The children played cards, took old-time photographs, wrote and acted a play, and read. The pace of life slowed down. When the series was over, the Bowlers returned to modern life with a new appreciation of some of their things—and the knowledge that they could do fine without some things.

Cultural Diversity

ACTIVITIES

1. Read the material at the left.
2. Key a list of items invented in the last 100 years that you use daily.
3. Compare lists as a class activity. Make a list that represents the best thinking of the group.
4. Try to spend one day without some of the items on your list. What was most difficult to live without? What was the easiest? Key a paragraph about your experiences. Be prepared to share them with the class.

ACTIVITY 7

Justify

1. Read the text at the right.
2. Learn to justify text with your wp software.
3. Follow the directions at the right.

Throughout earlier activities, you have center-, left-, and right-aligned text. Another way to align text is to **justify** (or **full justify**) it. When text is justified, the left and right margins are aligned evenly. The word processor inserts extra spaces between words so that each line ends evenly at the right margin.

This and the preceding paragraph are justified—the text is aligned at both the left and right margins (except for the last line of the paragraph). Justify is used with newspaper-style columns to make reading easier.

1. Open *CD-WP13ACT5* again.
2. Justify the text in each of the three ¶s.

Save as: *WP13ACT7*

ACTIVITY 8

Drop Cap

1. Read the text at the right.
2. Learn to drop an initial cap with your wp software.
3. Follow the directions at the right using drop caps.

You can format paragraphs to begin with a large initial capital letter that takes up two or more vertical lines of regular text. **Drop caps** are objects that can be formatted and sized. Two drop cap formats are usually available. One capitalizes the first letter of the first word in the paragraph with a large dropped capital letter and then wraps the text around the drop cap. The second creates a dropped capital letter, but places it in the margin beginning at the first line.

1. Open *CD-WP13ACT8.*
2. Format ¶ 1 with a drop cap with text wrapped around it.
3. Format ¶ 2 with a drop cap that is placed in the left margin.
4. Format ¶ 3 the same as ¶ 1, but drop the cap only two lines and change the cap to Arial font.

Save as: *WP13ACT8*

ACTIVITY 9

Newspaper-Style Columns

1. Read the information at the right.
2. Learn how to format newspaper-style columns with your wp software.
3. Key the text at the right and on the next page using a 4" top margin, 4" bottom margin, 1" side margins, and three newspaper-style columns of equal width.

Save as: *WP13ACT9*

Except for tables, the documents you have created have had a single column of text that extended from the left margin to the right margin.

Multiple-column documents, such as pamphlets, leaflets, brochures, and newsletters, use **newspaper-style columns** to divide a document into two or more vertical columns that are placed side by side on a page. The columns may be of equal or unequal width.

As you key, text fills the length of a column before moving to the next column to the right.

CAREER FAIR

The Annual Career Fair will be held May 15 from 9 a.m. to 12:30 p.m. in Gymnasium A. A list of the 20 employers who will attend will be published next week. The employers represent many different areas that hire scientists, technicians, and engineers within the environmental field. Therefore, there will be a variety of career opportunities for our students to explore.

All junior and senior students are urged to attend and speak to as many of the employers as possible. To ensure that students speak to many employers, they will need to obtain signatures of the employers they visit and give the signatures to the Career Fair Coordinator when they leave the gymnasium.

It is important that students dress and act appropriately during the Career Fair. Standard or casual business dress is suggested. Students should have up-to-date resumes to distribute. Also, students should use correct grammar and speak clearly without using slang to improve their chances of making a favorable first impression.

CYCLE 3

UNITS 22-29

Computer Keyboarding: Expand & Integrate

You see it on an Internet job board: *WANTED—full-time administrative specialist. Competence with latest Office Suite software. Keying 50* wam, *plus effective interpersonal and communication skills. . . .*

The best part, you suddenly realize, is that you probably qualify for the position described. You (and your skills) are ready—but how do you go about landing this kind of job? Answers to that question are at the center of Cycle 3.

First you'll need a resume (summary) of your qualifications. In fact, two versions of it. You'll need an employment application letter to go with those resumes. And don't forget a reference list. Be sure you're familiar with items found on employment application forms, too.

Employment interviews are also basic to job hunting. Cycle 3 tells how to take advantage of these opportunities for you and the interviewer to give *and* get information—disclosing whether you're right for the job and whether it's right for you. Following up an interview with a thank-you letter is a good idea, and you'll see how here.

Performance tests on job-related tasks are common among employers. Lesson 100 is your chance to take an employment test.

In addition, all the other units in Cycle 3—plus special pages between units—can make you more marketable in any line of work.

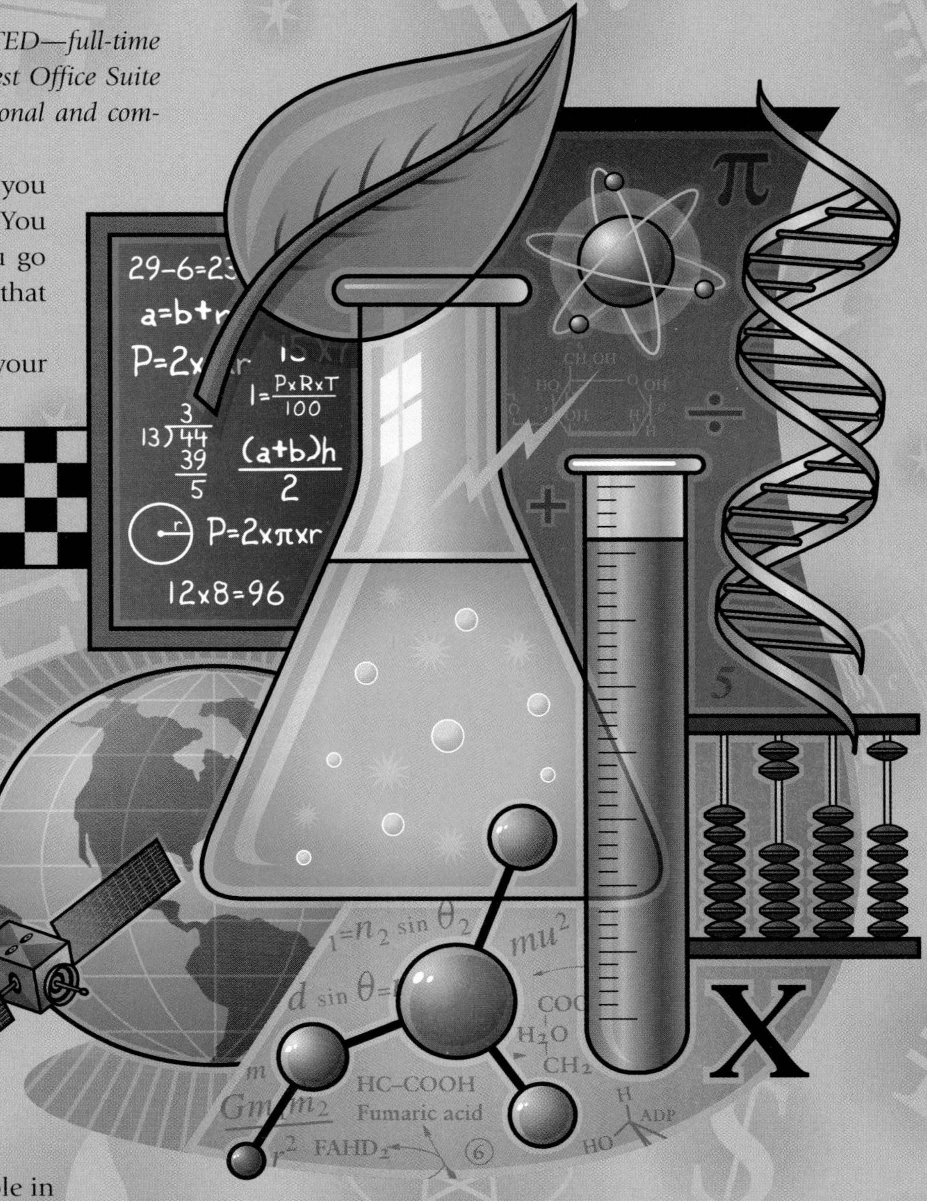

3. Near the bottom of the page, insert a text box and key your first and last name, your school name, and the date inside the box on three lines. Format the text box and text as you choose.

 **Save as:** *WP13ACT3*

ACTIVITY 4

Shapes

1. Read the text at the right and study the illustration below.

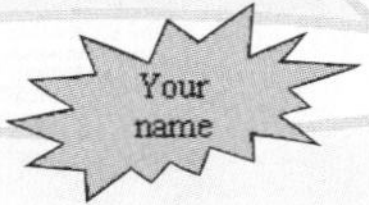

2. Learn to insert shapes with your wp software.
3. Follow the directions at the right.

Word processors have a variety of **shapes** (stars, banners, callouts, arrows, circles, boxes, flowchart symbols, etc.) that you can add to a document. Once added, these shapes can be manipulated and formatted similar to other graphic objects. The illustration at the left shows a star that has been inserted, sized, shaped, and shaded. Text has been added, and the outside border and text have been colored blue.

1. Select a star shape from those available with your software. Make the star approximately 4" wide, center it on the page, and insert your name using a large, bold font for the text.

 **Save as:** *WP13ACT4A*

2. Select a shape of your choice from those available with your software. Size it appropriately, enter your school name as text, shade the object, remove its border, and make other formatting changes you think appropriate.

 **Save as:** *WP13ACT4B*

ACTIVITY 5

Shaded Paragraphs

1. Read the text at the right.
2. Learn to shade ¶s using your wp software.
3. Follow the directions at the right to shade ¶s.

Like objects, paragraphs can be **shaded** to focus the reader's attention on their contents. The illustration at the right shows a shaded paragraph.

> This is an example of a paragraph that has been shaded. Readers are more apt to pay attention to its contents.

1. Open *CD-WP13ACT5*.
2. Using light colors, shade each ¶ differently.

 **Save as:** *WP13ACT5*

ACTIVITY 6

Wrap Text Around Graphics

1. Read the text at the right.
2. Learn to wrap text around a graphic using your wp software.
3. Follow the directions at the right.

You can choose how text is to appear near a graphic. Text near a graphic object can be **wrapped** (positioned) so it is above and below the object only, surrounds the object, or appears to be keyed behind or in front of the object.

In this example, the word processing operator has selected the option that places the text around the object. Other options are available and can be tried to give the desired result.

1. Open *CD-WP13ACT5* again.
2. Choose a shape or clip art image (approx. 1" high) to insert in the middle of each ¶. Wrap the text tightly around the object in the first ¶; above and below the object in the second ¶; and squarely around the object in the third ¶.

 **Save as:** *WP13ACT6*

SKILL BUILDER 4

Tabulation

1. Set tabs 1", 2.5", and 4" from the left margin.
2. Key the text at the right.
3. Key three 1' writings.

Goal:
Increase amount of text keyed on each writing.

				words
North Carolina	North Dakota	Ohio	Oklahoma	8
Raleigh	Bismark	Columbus	Oklahoma City	16
Oregon	Pennsylvania	Rhode Island	South Carolina	26
Salem	Harrisburg	Providence	Columbia	33
South Dakota	Tennessee	Texas	Utah	40
Pierre	Nashville	Austin	Salt Lake City	48
Vermont	Virginia	Washington	West Virginia	56
Montpelier	Richmond	Tacoma	Charleston	64
Wisconsin	Wyoming			67
Madison	Cheyenne			71

Keying Technique

1. Key each line once.
2. Key a 1' writing on each even-numbered line.

Alphabet

1 zebra extra vicious dozen happen just quick forgot way limp exact
2 Everyone except Meg and Joe passed the final weekly biology quiz.

Fig/Sym

3 Account #2849 | 10% down | for $6,435.70 | Lots #8 & #9 | $250 deductible
4 The fax machine (#387-291) is on sale for $364.50 until March 21.

Bottom row

5 modem zebra extinct moving backbone moon vacate exam computerized
6 Zeno's vaccine injection for smallpox can be given in six months.

Third row

7 you tip rip terror yet peer quit were pet tire terrier pepper out
8 Our two terrier puppies were too little to take to your pet show.

Double letters

9 footnote scanner less process letters office cell suppress footer
10 Jill, my office assistant, will process the four letters by noon.

Balanced hands

11 wish then turn us auto big eight down city busy end firm it goals
12 If the firm pays for the social, the eight officials may also go.

Shift keys

13 The New York Times | Gone with the Wind | Chicago Tribune | WordPerfect
14 Alan L. Martin finished writing "Planning for Changing Technology."

Adjacent keys

15 were open top ask rest twenty point tree master merge option asks
16 The sort option was well received by all three new group members.

Space Bar

17 it is fix and fox go key do by box men pen six so the to when big
18 Did they use the right audit form to check the city busline?

gwam 1' | 1 | 2 | 3 | 4 | 5 | 6 | 7 | 8 | 9 | 10 | 11 | 12 | 13 |

WORD PROCESSING 13

ACTIVITY 1

Word Art

1. Study the text at the right and the illustration below.

2. Learn how to use word art with your wp software.
3. Follow the directions at the right using word art.

You can change text into a graphic object by using **word art**. Most word processors have a **word art gallery** that contains predefined styles such as curved and stretched text as shown in the illustration at the left. After you choose a style, the word art is inserted into your document as an object that you can edit by using a drawing toolbar. Use the toolbar to change the object's color, size, alignment, shape, direction, or spacing. You can also select how text is to be wrapped around the object or select another style.

1. Open a new document and use word art to insert your first and last name across the top of the page. Center your name; size, shape, and format it as you want.
2. In the same document, use word art to insert the name of your school or school mascot across the bottom of the page. Center the text; size, shape, and format it as you want, using one or more of your school colors.

 **Save as:** *WP13ACT1*

ACTIVITY 2

3-D Effects

1. Read the text at the right.
2. Learn to use 3-D effects with your wp software.
3. Follow the directions at the right.

You can also enhance an object by applying **3-D effects** to it. See the illustration of word art with 3-D effects at the right.

1. Open a new document. Use word art to insert your first and last name near the center of the page.
2. Use the Word Art toolbar to format your name as you desire.
3. Choose a 3-D effect and apply it to your name.

 **Save as:** *WP13ACT2*

ACTIVITY 3

Text Boxes

1. Study the information at the right and the illustration of a text box below.

This is a shaded text box that illustrates reverse type (white letters on dark background).

2. Learn how to insert and format a text box with your wp software.
3. Complete the activities as directed at the right and on the next page.

Text boxes are frequently used for labels or callouts in a document. Once a text box is inserted in a document, you can format, resize, and move it as you would a graphic object. You can change the border style or delete the border. Text that is keyed within the text box can be formatted just as regular text is formatted.

1. Open a new document. Insert a text box that is about 1" high × 2" wide and is horizontally centered near the top margin of the page. Key the following copy in the text box, using 12-pt. Arial italicized font, and then resize the text box to fit the text.

This text box uses 12-pt. Arial italicized font for the letters.

2. Near the vertical center of the page, horizontally center a second text box that is about 1" high × 2" wide. Shade the text box with a dark color and remove the border. Using center alignment and white 12-pt. Arial font, key the following copy in the text box. Resize the text box as needed.

This is centered text in a shaded text box that has no border.

(continued on next page)

WORD PROCESSING 9

ACTIVITY 1

Change Fonts

1. Read the copy at the right.
2. Learn to use the Font features on your wp software.
3. Format the five lines at the right as directed in each line.

 **Save as:** *WP9ACT1*

Note:
A point (pt.) is about 1/72 of an inch.

The **font** is the type, or letters, in which a document is printed. A font consists of the *typeface, style, size,* and *effect.* The **typeface** is the design of the letters. Examples include Times New Roman, Courier New, and Arial. Font **styles** include bold and italic, with which you are familiar. Font **size** is measured in *points* (such as 10 pt. and 16 pt.). Fonts measured in points are *scalable*; that is, they can be printed in almost any size. An effect may be added to give text a special look. **Effects**, such as shadow, emboss, small caps, and outline, are best when used infrequently.

The Font features may be used before or after text is keyed to change font, size, and/or effect. The number and size of fonts available depend on the software and printer used.

1. Key this line using a Courier font, size 10 pt. Use bold style on the last word.
2. Key this line using Times New Roman, size 12 pt. Use italic style on the font name.
3. Key this line using Arial, 14 pt. Apply bold and italic to the font name.
4. Key this line in Comic Sans MS, 18 pt. Apply bold style and outline effect to the font name.
5. Key this line using the font, size, style, and effect of your choice.

ACTIVITY 2

Change Case

1. Read the copy at the right.
2. Learn to use the Change Case feature in your wp software.
3. Key each line at right exactly as shown.
4. Select and change each line as directed in the line.

 **Save as:** *WP9ACT2*

Use the **Change Case** feature to change capitalization. For example, the Sentence Case option capitalizes the first letter of the first word. The lowercase option changes all selected text to lowercase; the UPPERCASE option changes selected text to all capitals. The Title Case option capitalizes the first letter in each word of the selected text. The Toggle Case option reverses the case of selected text.

1. CHANGE THIS LINE OF TEXT TO SENTENCE CASE.
2. CHANGE THIS LINE OF TEXT TO LOWERCASE.
3. Change this line of text to uppercase.
4. Change this line of text to title case.
5. CHANGE THIS LINE OF TEXT WITH TOGGLE CASE.

ACTIVITY 3

Find and Replace Text

1. Read the copy at the right.
2. Learn to find and replace text using your wp software.
3. Key the paragraph at the right.
4. Find and count each occurrence of *are* and *each month.*
5. Replace all occurrences of these words: *assessments* with *taxes, subtracted* with *deducted, month* with *pay period.*

Save as: *WP9ACT3*

The **Find** feature is used to locate a specified keystroke, word, or phrase in a document. You can refine this feature to find only occurrences that match the specified case; to find only whole words containing the specified text; to find all forms of a specified word; and to find specified text involving the asterisk (*) and question mark (?) as wildcard (unspecified) characters. The **Replace** feature also finds a specified keystroke, word, or phrase and then replaces it with another keystroke, word, or phrase. All occurrences of the specified text can be replaced at one time, or replacements can be made individually (selectively).

An individual has to pay a number of assessments. FICA assessments are the assessments that support the Social Security system and are subtracted from your pay each month. Federal income assessments are also subtracted from your check each month. Assessments that are not subtracted from your check each month include property assessments and sales assessments.

119D • 25'
Skill Check

1. Key three 1' writings on each ¶ for speed; determine *gwam*.
2. Key two 3' writings on all ¶s combined for control; circle errors.
3. Key two 5' writings on all ¶s combined. Record and retain your better 5' *gwam* and error count and compare to score received in 118C.

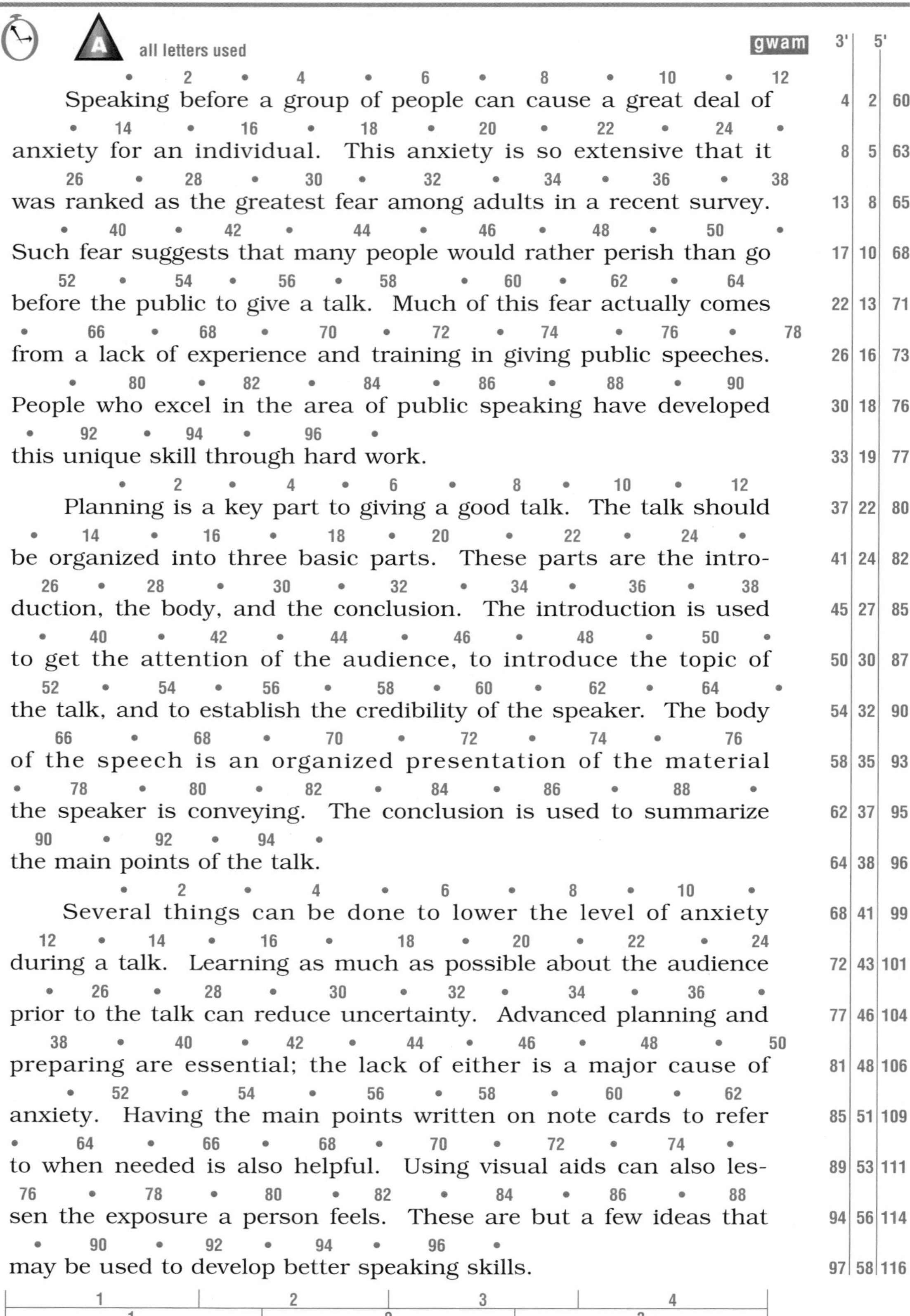

all letters used

Text	gwam 3'	5'	
Speaking before a group of people can cause a great deal of	4	2	60
anxiety for an individual. This anxiety is so extensive that it	8	5	63
was ranked as the greatest fear among adults in a recent survey.	13	8	65
Such fear suggests that many people would rather perish than go	17	10	68
before the public to give a talk. Much of this fear actually comes	22	13	71
from a lack of experience and training in giving public speeches.	26	16	73
People who excel in the area of public speaking have developed	30	18	76
this unique skill through hard work.	33	19	77
Planning is a key part to giving a good talk. The talk should	37	22	80
be organized into three basic parts. These parts are the intro-	41	24	82
duction, the body, and the conclusion. The introduction is used	45	27	85
to get the attention of the audience, to introduce the topic of	50	30	87
the talk, and to establish the credibility of the speaker. The body	54	32	90
of the speech is an organized presentation of the material	58	35	93
the speaker is conveying. The conclusion is used to summarize	62	37	95
the main points of the talk.	64	38	96
Several things can be done to lower the level of anxiety	68	41	99
during a talk. Learning as much as possible about the audience	72	43	101
prior to the talk can reduce uncertainty. Advanced planning and	77	46	104
preparing are essential; the lack of either is a major cause of	81	48	106
anxiety. Having the main points written on note cards to refer	85	51	109
to when needed is also helpful. Using visual aids can also les-	89	53	111
sen the exposure a person feels. These are but a few ideas that	94	56	114
may be used to develop better speaking skills.	97	58	116

gwam 3' | 1 | 2 | 3 | 4
5' | 1 | 2 | 3

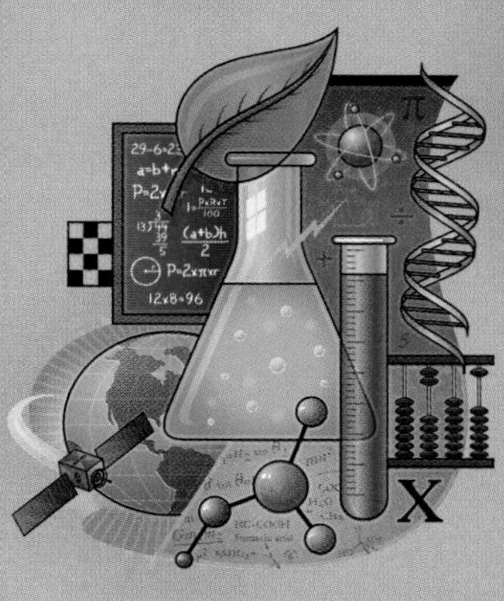

UNIT 22

LESSONS 76–80

Enhancing Correspondence Formatting Skills

Format Guides: Business Letters

April 15, 200-

Attention Science Department Chair
East Tulsa High School
10916 N. Garnett Rd.
Tulsa, OK 74116-1016

Ladies and Gentlemen

PHYSICS LABORATORY EQUIPMENT DONATION

AnTech Laboratories has up-to-date physics laboratory furniture and equipment that it can donate to your high school. We feel certain that your physics teacher and students will derive great benefits from what we are offering.

A list of the major items we can donate is enclosed. All items will be available before the end of July so they can be delivered and installed before school starts in late August.

Please call me at (918) 138-5000, and we will arrange a meeting for your personnel to see the furniture and equipment.

Sincerely,

Jose L. Domingo
Public Relations

xx

Enclosure

Our CEO, Mrs. Donna Scanlon, is a graduate of East Tulsa High (Class of 1983), and she hopes this donation will enable you to expand your science education program.

Letter in Modified Block Format with Indented Paragraphs

Ms. Valerie E. Lopez
Page 2
October 28, 200-

Please tell me if these two days are good for you. If you have e-mail, you can send your message to alaron@brighton.com.

Sincerely

Justin A. Alaron
Senior Actuary

xx

Enclosures

Letter (p. 2) in Modified Block Format with Blocked Paragraphs, and Second-Page Heading

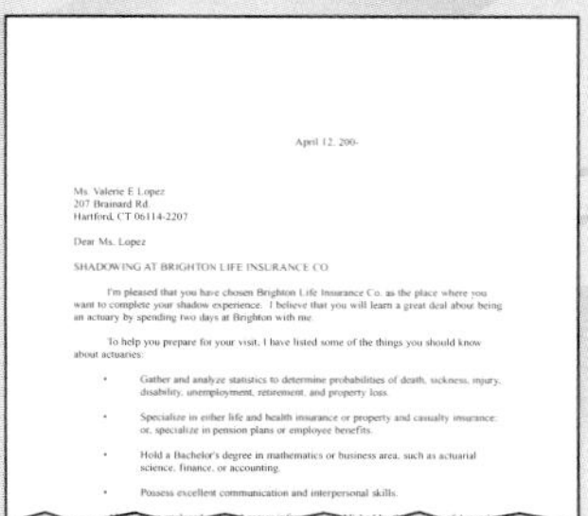

April 12, 200-

Ms. Valerie E Lopez
207 Brainard Rd.
Hartford, CT 06114-2207

Dear Ms. Lopez

SHADOWING AT BRIGHTON LIFE INSURANCE CO

I'm pleased that you have chosen Brighton Life Insurance Co. as the place where you want to complete your shadow experience. I believe that you will learn a great deal about being an actuary by spending two days at Brighton with me.

To help you prepare for your visit, I have listed some of the things you should know about actuaries:

- Gather and analyze statistics to determine probabilities of death, sickness, injury, disability, unemployment, retirement, and property loss.
- Specialize in either life and health insurance or property and casualty insurance; or, specialize in pension plans or employee benefits.
- Hold a Bachelor's degree in mathematics or business area, such as actuarial science, finance, or accounting.
- Possess excellent communication and interpersonal skills.

Letter with Bulleted Items in Hanging Indent Style

A variation of block format (see Resources p. R51) is the modified block format. The following paragraphs contain information about this letter style and other letter and memo features.

Modified block format. In modified block format the block format is changed. (See the first model at the left.) The date and the closing lines (complimentary close, writer's name, and writer's title) begin near the horizontal center of the page instead of at the left margin. The tab nearest to center may be used to place the date and closing lines.

The paragraphs of a letter in modified block format may be indented 0.5", or they may be blocked at the left margin.

Open or mixed punctuation. Open or mixed punctuation may be used with modified block format. You have used open punctuation, which has no punctuation mark after the salutation or complimentary close. Mixed punctuation uses a colon (:) after the salutation and a comma (,) after the complimentary close. (See models at the left.)

Form letters. A form letter is a standard message sent to more than one addressee. Form letters (or form paragraphs that can be combined to create varying letters) may be stored as macros and played back when needed. Thus, each letter is an original, though created from stored text.

Postscript. A postscript is an optional message added to a letter as the last item on the page. A postscript may be used to emphasize information in the body or to add a personal message to a business letter. Key postscripts a DS below reference initials or Attachment/ Enclosure notation if one is used. Block or indent a postscript to match paragraphs in the body. Omit the postscript abbreviation (P.S.).

Bulleted or numbered items. Block the second line (and succeeding lines) of each bulleted or numbered item under the first letter of the first word, instead of under the bullet or number. This is called hanging indent style. (See the third model at the left.)

Tables in letters or memos. Format an inserted table even with the left and right margin of the document or centered between them. Leave one blank line above the first line and below the last line of an inserted table. Gridlines may be used or omitted.

Mailing and addressee notations. Mailing notations (such as REGISTERED or SPECIAL DELIVERY) and addressee notations (such as CONFIDENTIAL and PERSONAL) may be included on a letter as well as the envelope. Key either type of notation a DS below the date; DS below the notation to key the first line of the letter address. On the envelope, key a mailing notation below the stamp, about 0.5" above the envelope address. Key an addressee notation at the left margin a DS below the return address.

Attention line. Use an attention line to specify a department or job title (Attention Human Resources Manager) when the name of a specific person is not available. Key it as the first line of the letter address; use *Ladies and Gentlemen* as the salutation.

Subject line. A subject line (optional) may be keyed in ALL CAPS between the letter address and salutation. Leave one blank line above and below a subject line.

Second-page heading. The second and subsequent pages of letters and memos are printed on plain paper. A three-line heading is keyed SS on these pages: (1) the addressee's name, (2) the word *Page* and the page number, and (3) the date. Place this heading 1" from the top edge, beginning at the left margin. (See the second model at the left.)

LESSON 119 IMPROVE KEYING TECHNIQUE

Objectives:

1. To improve keying techniques and straight-copy speed and control.

2. To improve language skills.

119A • 5' Conditioning Practice

Key each line twice; then key 30" writings on line 1; determine *gwam*.

alphabet 1 Wixie plans to study my notes just before taking the civics quiz.

figures 2 Our soccer league had 4,159 boys and 3,687 girls playing in 2001.

speed 3 The busy fieldhand kept the fox in a big pen to keep it in sight.

gwam 1' | 1 | 2 | 3 | 4 | 5 | 6 | 7 | 8 | 9 | 10 | 11 | 12 | 13 |

LANGUAGE SKILLS

119B • 5' Language Skills: Word Choice

1. Study the spelling and definitions of the words at the right.
2. Key the Learn lines, noting word choice.
3. Key the Apply lines, selecting the correct words.
4. Check the accuracy of your work with the instructor. Rekey lines that contain a word-choice error.

Save as: *CHOICE119B*

accept (vb) to receive; to give approval; to take

except (vb) to exclude

threw (vb) past tense of throw; to toss

through (prep/adj) beginning to end of; finished

Learn 1 I think they will **accept** all my revisions **except** for Unit 8.

Apply 2 Juliana works every day (accept/except) Saturday and Sunday.

Apply 3 Adolpho will attend the banquet to (accept/except) the award.

Learn 1 Greg **threw** the football perfectly **through** two quarters.

Apply 2 When they were (threw/through), I (threw/through) a party.

Apply 3 The cheer was (threw/through), so I (threw/through) the ball.

SKILL BUILDING

119C • 15' Technique: Response Patterns

1. Key one 3' writing. Determine errors and *gwam*.
2. Select a goal: **Control** (if more than six errors in Step 1)—reduce errors by one on each writing. **Speed** (if six or fewer errors in Step 1)—increase *gwam* by three on each writing.
3. Key three 3' writings; try to reach your goal on each writing.

Text	gwam 1'	3'	
The sales report for the quarter ending September 31 indicated	13	4	39
that sales for Easy-Change Ink Jet Cartridge (Stock #B193) were down	26	9	44
by 40% while sales of all other cartridges were up an average of	39	13	48
15%. To boost sales of B193 cartridges, the selling price will be	53	18	53
reduced during the next quarter from $27.50 to $20.62 per	64	21	56
cartridge (a 25% discount). Also, a four-color display board	77	26	61
emphasizing that the B193 cartridge can be used as a replacement	90	30	65
for TJK-133 and XRT-159 will be available to all salespersons in	103	34	69
the region.	105	35	70

gwam 1' | 1 | 2 | 3 | 4 | 5 | 6 | 7 | 8 | 9 | 10 | 11 | 12 | 13 |
3' | 1 | 2 | 3 | 4 |

LESSON 76 REVIEW LETTERS, MEMOS, AND E-MAIL

Objectives:

1. To review block letter format and letter parts.
2. To review memos and e-mail formats.

76A • 5' Conditioning Practice

Key each line twice; take 1' writings on lines 1 and 2 as time permits.

alphabet 1 To what extent was Kazu involved with my project before quitting?

figures 2 A van with License No. B928-754 is parked in Space 103 in Lot 16.

speed 3 To my dismay, the official kept the fox by the dog in the kennel.

gwam 1' | 1 | 2 | 3 | 4 | 5 | 6 | 7 | 8 | 9 | 10 | 11 | 12 | 13 |

76B • 45' Business Letters, Memos, and E-mail

Document 1 (Personal-Business Letter)

1. Format the text at the right as a personal-business letter in block format. Use open punctuation and Times New Roman, 14 pt. Use the current date and the return address given below. Bold the name of the program in ¶ 1.
2. Address a small envelope in USPS format. The return address is
   207 Brainard Rd.
   Hartford, CT 06114-2207

Recall: Place a copy notation (*c*) at the left margin a DS below the preceding letter part.

Save as: *LTR76B1*

Mr. Justin A. Alaron | Brighton Life Insurance Co. | I-84 & Rt. 322 | Milldale, CT 06467-9371 | Dear Mr. Alaron

As a senior at Milldale High School, I participate in the **Shadow Experience Program** (SEP). The enclosed resume indicates my career objective: to become an actuary for a large insurance company.

SEP encourages students to "shadow" a person who is working in their planned career field. I would like to shadow you to see firsthand what an actuary does. I can spend one or two days with you at your office during the coming month. Please send your written response to me so that I can present it to Ms. Michelle Kish, SEP Coordinator. Thank you.

Sincerely | Ms. Valerie E. Lopez | SEP Member | Enclosure | c Ms. Michelle Kish

Document 2 (E-mail)

Prepare the text at the right as an e-mail to your instructor. Send a copy to one classmate. (If you do not have e-mail software, prepare the text as a memo to **Carolyn V. Pucevich, Dean** from **Mary B. Tunno, President**. A copy goes to **Arlene Romeo, Vice President**. Use the current date.)

Save as: *MAIL76B2*

SUBJECT: MATHEMATICAL REASONING SKILLS TASK FORCE

A meeting to discuss the formation of a Mathematical Reasoning Skills Task Force has been arranged for Tuesday, April 21, in my office at 2:30 p.m. Vice President Arlene Romeo will join us.

Purposes of the meeting are to finalize the project description and identify faculty and advisory committee members who might join the task force.

118C • 30'
Skill Check

1. Key three 1' writings on each ¶ for speed; determine *gwam*.
2. Key two 1' writings on each ¶ for control; circle errors.
3. Key two 3' writings on both ¶s combined; determine *gwam*; circle errors.
4. Key two 5' writings on both ¶s combined. Record and retain your better 5' *gwam* and error count for use in 119D.

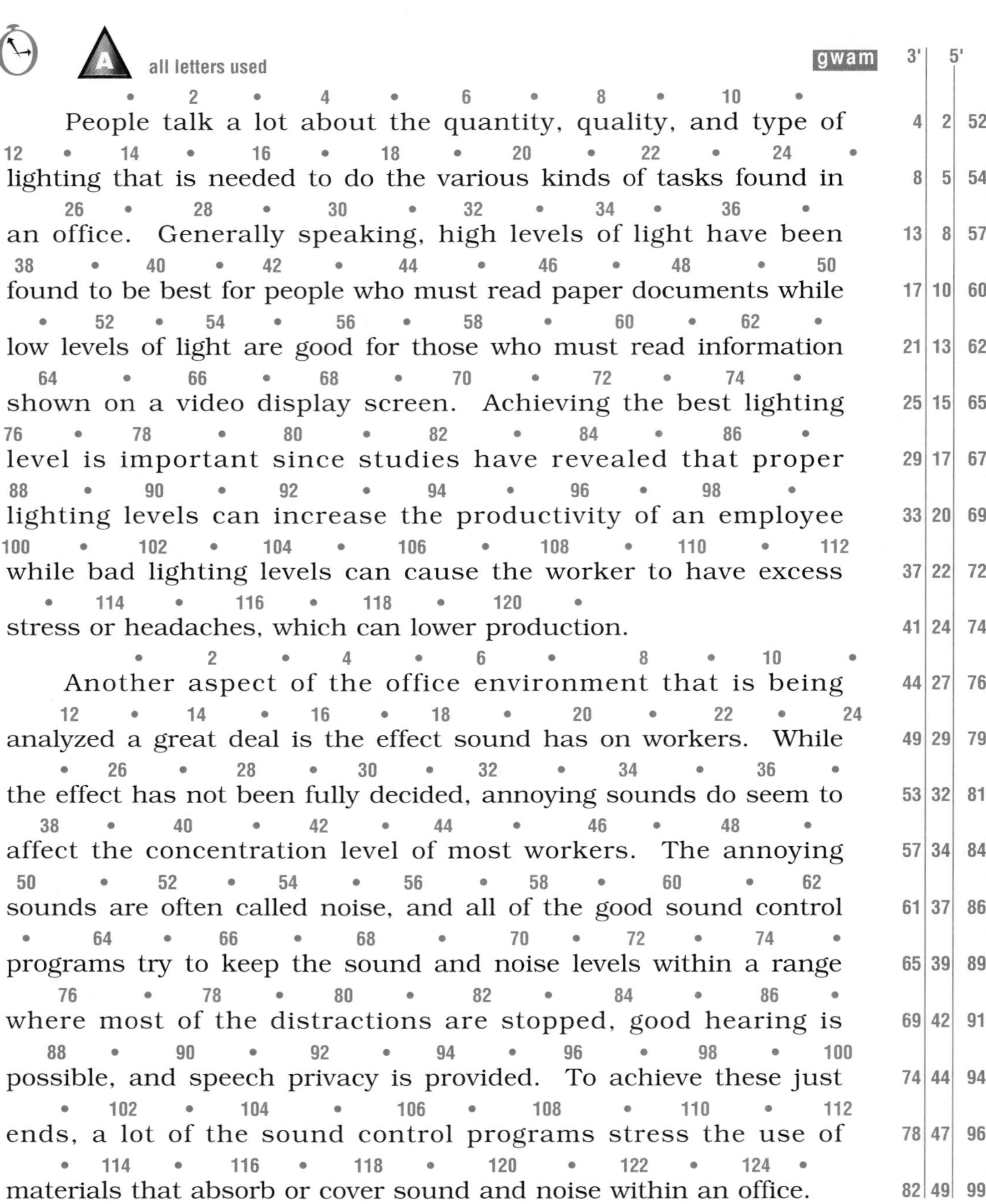

A all letters used

	gwam 3'	5'	
People talk a lot about the quantity, quality, and type of	4	2	52
lighting that is needed to do the various kinds of tasks found in	8	5	54
an office. Generally speaking, high levels of light have been	13	8	57
found to be best for people who must read paper documents while	17	10	60
low levels of light are good for those who must read information	21	13	62
shown on a video display screen. Achieving the best lighting	25	15	65
level is important since studies have revealed that proper	29	17	67
lighting levels can increase the productivity of an employee	33	20	69
while bad lighting levels can cause the worker to have excess	37	22	72
stress or headaches, which can lower production.	41	24	74
Another aspect of the office environment that is being	44	27	76
analyzed a great deal is the effect sound has on workers. While	49	29	79
the effect has not been fully decided, annoying sounds do seem to	53	32	81
affect the concentration level of most workers. The annoying	57	34	84
sounds are often called noise, and all of the good sound control	61	37	86
programs try to keep the sound and noise levels within a range	65	39	89
where most of the distractions are stopped, good hearing is	69	42	91
possible, and speech privacy is provided. To achieve these just	74	44	94
ends, a lot of the sound control programs stress the use of	78	47	96
materials that absorb or cover sound and noise within an office.	82	49	99

gwam 3' | 1 | 2 | 3 | 4
5' | 1 | 2 | 3

Document 3 (Memo)

1. Format and key the text at the right as a memo; use 14-pt. Times New Roman.
2. Proofread your copy; correct all keying and formatting errors.

 **Save as:** *MEMO76B3*

TO: Dr. Diana Patsiga, Statistics | FROM: Mary B. Tunno, President | DATE: May 25, 200- | SUBJECT: MATHEMATICAL REASONING SKILLS TASK FORCE

After discussions with members of the Presidential Planning Council, I believe that Sundy Junior College should carefully review the curriculum for developing mathematical reasoning skills.

To do so, I am establishing a task force composed of faculty from various disciplines and my planning council. Dean Carolyn Pucevich will chair the task force.

The primary charge to the task force is this: to determine what mathematical content is to be learned and applied in required general education courses, including required math courses.

If you are interested in serving on this task force, please attend an informational meeting on June 2 at 2:30 p.m. in Board Room C.

xx

Document 4 (Business Letter)

1. Format and key the text at the right as a letter in block format with open punctuation. Use a 12-pt. font. Read the Postscript information on p. 212 to complete the letter.

Recall: Key a blind copy (*bc*) notation at the left margin a DS below the preceding letter part—but not on the original letter.

2. Proofread your text; correct all keying and formatting errors.

 **Save as:** *LTR76B4*

(Insert current date) | Mr. Harry R. Dobish | Vice President of Operations | Highmark Biochemistry Laboratories, Inc. | 9180 Wayzata Blvd. | Minneapolis, MN 55440-9180 | Dear Mr. Dobish

I've met several times with the biochemistry laboratory technicians and research biochemists who work in the four Madison laboratories. We've identified the renovations needed to meet proposed safety and access regulations and the equipment that should be purchased for Highmark to maintain "world-class" facilities.

I'll have your architect prepare preliminary drawings to show proposed changes to the facilities. Also, I'll meet with a biochemistry salesperson from Hunter Science Equipment to prepare an equipment cost estimate.

When the drawings and estimate are available, I'll schedule an appointment with you.

Sincerely | Mudi A. Mutubu, Consultant | xx | bc Sandra Gimbel, Project Manager | Your staff is very receptive to change and eager to assist management with these important changes.

Document 5 (Memo)

1. Key the copy at the right as a memo to **Helen Opher** from **Joshua Franklin**. Insert the current date; use **VISITATION REQUEST** as the subject line.
2. Insert the file where indicated.
3. Proofread your copy; correct all errors.

 **Save as:** *MEMO76B5*

Students from the Pre-Engineering Club at George Westinghouse High School will be touring the plant next Friday according to this schedule.

(Insert the table in *CD-TBL76B5* here.)

Please arrange for them to see the corporate history video in Homestead Auditorium at 10:15 a.m.

Ms. Rosita Rivetti, the lead electrical engineer with the 750 CHIP TEAM, will meet you and the students at the auditorium at 11 a.m. She will speak to them briefly and then lead them on a tour of the Cyber VII assembly line.

The students plan to leave at 12:45 p.m. Will you escort them from the cafeteria to their bus? Thank you.

xx

UNIT 31

LESSONS 118–119

Building Basic Skill

LESSON 118 IMPROVE KEYING TECHNIQUE

Objectives:

1. To improve keying techniques.
2. To improve straight-copy speed and control.

118A • 5' Conditioning Practice

Key each line twice SS; then take 30" writings on line 1; determine *gwam*.

alphabet 1 Zev and Che saw pilots quickly taxi many big jets from the gates.

figures 2 She sold 105 shirts, 28 belts, 94 skirts, 36 suits, and 47 coats.

speed 3 Jen sat by the right aisle for the sorority ritual at the chapel.

gwam 1' | 1 | 2 | 3 | 4 | 5 | 6 | 7 | 8 | 9 | 10 | 11 | 12 | 13 |

SKILL BUILDING

118B • 15' Technique: Response Patterns

1. Key each line twice SS; DS between 2-line groups.
2. Take a 1' writing on each line group as time permits.

Consecutive direct reaches

1 many much loan sold vice side cent code thus fund told wide price
2 golf slow gift grow delay chance checks manual fifty cloth demand
3 forums music brown enemy hence bright signed editor specific fold

Adjacent finger

4 this time find help give plan mail into sent item high file might
5 five vote else dues which plans claim giving during thanks always
6 fine inform plant blank civil light wishes single quality furnish

Third row

7 or up it us we you pop top rut vip wit pea tea wet were quiet pit
8 pew toe tie rep per hope pour rope quip your pout tore ripe quirk
9 tip out tar war per tour keep roar fret youth pretty yuppie puppy

Home row

10 ha has kid lad led last wash lash gaff jade fads half sash haggle
11 as dad add jug leg gas lads hall lass fast deal fall leafs dashes
12 at had sad jigs lash adds gall legs fish gash lakes halls haggles

Bottom row

13 ax can bam zag sax cab mad fax vans buzz knack caves waxen banana
14 ax ban man zinc clan band calm lamb vain back amaze bronze buzzer
15 box nab and bag lot name vane clam oxen main none climb mezzanine

gwam 1' | 1 | 2 | 3 | 4 | 5 | 6 | 7 | 8 | 9 | 10 | 11 | 12 | 13 |

FORMAT MODIFIED BLOCK LETTERS

Objectives:

1. To learn modified block letter format.
2. To learn mixed punctuation.

77A • 5' Conditioning Practice

Key each line twice SS; then key a 30" writing on line 3; determine *gwam.*

alphabet 1 Jim avoids fizzling fireworks because they often explode quickly.

fig/sym 2 Runner #3019-A was first (49' 35"); runner #687-D was last (62').

speed 3 Nancy works in the big cornfield down by the lake with the docks.

gwam 1' | 1 | 2 | 3 | 4 | 5 | 6 | 7 | 8 | 9 | 10 | 11 | 12 | 13 |

FORMATTING

77B • 45' Modified Block Letters

Letters 1 and 2

Save as: *LTR77B1* and *LTR77B2*

1. Study the format guides on p. 212 and the model letter on p. 216. Note differences between the block and modified block formats.
2. **Letter 1**: Format and key the letter on p. 216 using an 11-pt. font. Use the Print View feature to check accuracy of the format.
3. **Letter 2**: Open the Letter 1 file (*LTR77B1*) and make the following changes:
   a. Font size–10 pt.
   b. Letter address–**Attention Office Manager Family Practice Associates 875 Kenilworth Ave. Indianapolis, IN 46246-0087**
   c. Salutation–**Ladies and Gentlemen**
   d. Use open punctuation.
   e. Indent the first line of each ¶ 0.5".
   f. Delete the subject line and the mailing notation.
   g. Change wording of ¶s 2 and 3 to reflect changes in punctuation style and paragraph indentations.

Letter 3

Prepare the letter at the right below, using a 12-pt. font. Indent the paragraphs. A blind copy goes to **Principal, East Tulsa High School**.

Save as: *LTR77B3*

April 15, 200- | Attention Science Department Chair | East Tulsa High School | 10916 N. Garnett Rd. | Tulsa, OK 74116-1016 | Ladies and Gentlemen: | PHYSICS LABORATORY EQUIPMENT DONATION

AnTech Laboratories has up-to-date physics laboratory furniture and equipment that it can donate to your high school. We feel certain that your physics teacher and students will derive great benefits from what we are offering.

A list of the major items we can donate is enclosed. All items will be available before the end of July so they can be delivered and installed before school starts in late August.

Please call me at (918) 138-5000, and we will arrange a meeting for your personnel to see the furniture and equipment.

Sincerely, Jose L. Domingo | Public Relations | xx | Enclosure | Our CEO, Mrs. Donna Scanlon, is a graduate of East Tulsa High (Class of 1983); and she hopes this donation will enable you to expand your science education program.

Letter 4

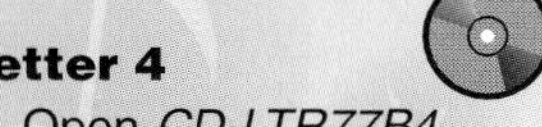

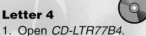

1. Open *CD-LTR77B4*.
2. Make these changes:
   a. Use mixed punctuation.
   b. Use a 13-pt. font not used previously.
   c. Change the subject line to uppercase.
   d. Insert an appropriate complimentary close.
   e. Insert the writer's (principal's) name, **Lisa A. Hammersmith, Ph.D.**
   f. Insert your initials and a copy notation for **Dr. Randy Dupont.**
   g. Prepare a large envelope with a delivery point bar code.

Save as: *LTR77B4*

ACTIVITY 2

Listening

Complete the listening activity as directed at the right.

 **Save as:** *CS12-ACT2*

1. You have answered a telephone call from Maria MacDonald, who serves as an officer in the alumni association of which your mother is president. She asks you to take the message that is recorded in the *CD-CS12LISTN* file.
2. Open *CD-CS12LISTN* and listen to the message, taking notes as needed.
3. Close the file.
4. Using your notes, key a message in sentence form for your mother.
5. Check the accuracy of your message with the instructor.

ACTIVITY 3

Write to Learn

Complete the Write-to-Learn activity as directed at the right.

 **Save as:** *CS12-ACT3*

Using word processing or speech recognition software, write a paragraph explaining the process you must use to merge information from a data file to a form file.

ACTIVITY 4

Preparing to Speak

You have accepted a nomination to run for treasurer of your district of the Future Business Leaders of America (FBLA). Now you must make a 1' to 2' speech to the voting delegates from each school in your region. Follow the steps at the right.

 **Save as:** *CS12-4OL* and *CS12-4SOUND*

1. Key an outline of the major points you want to make about yourself and your qualifications for being treasurer. Include experiences that show you to be capable, reliable, responsible, and trustworthy. Examples follow:
   - Math, accounting, and other applicable courses you have completed or are taking
   - Leadership positions you hold/held in other organizations
   - Jobs you hold/held
   - Experiences handling money (writing checks, making deposits, following a budget, investing, etc.)
2. If time and resources permit, record your speech in a sound file, with your instructor's help.
3. Submit your outline (and sound file, if made) to your instructor.

2" TM

Date — September 15, 200-

Mailing notation — REGISTERED

Letter address —
Ms. Betty Peerloff
Training and Development Department
Science Technologies
3368 Bay Path Rd.
Miami, FL 33160-3368

Salutation — Dear Ms. Peerloff:

Subject line — MODIFIED BLOCK FORMAT

Body —
This letter is arranged in modified block format. In this letter format the date and closing lines (complimentary close, name of the writer, and the writer's title) begin at or near horizontal center. In block format all letter parts begin at the left margin.

1" LM — 1" RM

Mixed punctuation (a colon after the salutation and a comma after the complimentary close) is used in this example. Open punctuation (no mark after the salutation or complimentary close) may be used with the modified block format if you prefer.

The first line of each paragraph may be blocked as shown here or indented one-half inch. If paragraphs are indented, the optional subject line may be indented or centered. If paragraphs are blocked at the left margin, the subject line is blocked, too.

A block format letter is enclosed so that you can compare the two formats. As you can see, either format presents an attractive appearance.

Complimentary close — Sincerely yours,

Writer — Derek Alan

Writer's title — Manager

Reference initials — tj

Enclosure notation — Enclosure

Copy notation — c Kimberly Rodriquez-Duarte

Letter in Modified Block Format

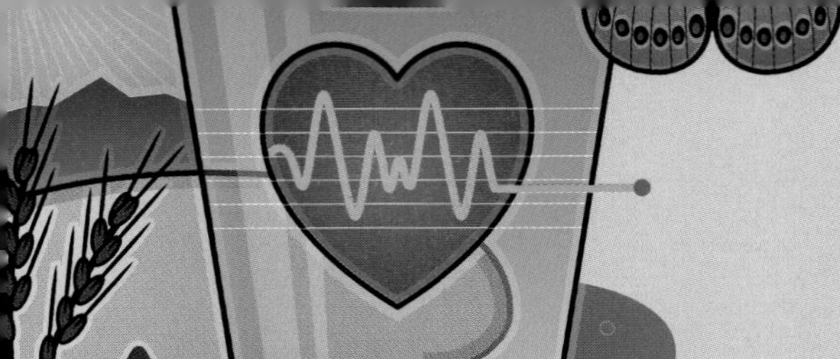

Communication Skills 12

ACTIVITY 1

Internal Punctuation: Parentheses and Dash

1. Key lines 1–10 at the right, inserting the needed parentheses and dashes.
2. Check the accuracy of your work with the instructor; correct any errors you made.
3. Note the rule number at the left of each sentence in which you made a parentheses or dash error.
4. Using the rules at the right, identify the rule(s) you need to review/practice.
5. **Read**: Study each rule.
6. **Learn**: Key the Learn line(s) beneath it, noting how the rule is applied.
7. **Apply**: Key the Apply line(s), correctly using parentheses and dashes.

 **Save as:** *CS12-ACT1*

Proofread & Correct

Rules

1 1 The appendices Exhibits A and B utilize computer graphics.
2 2 The three areas are 1 ethical, 2 moral, and 3 legal.
2 3 Emphasize: 1 writing, 2 speaking, and 3 listening.
3 4 You cited the "Liberty or Death" speech Henry, 1775 twice.
4 5 The payment terms 2/10, n/30 are clearly shown on the invoice.
4 6 The article and I know you're interested is in Newsweek.
5 7 "The finger that turns the dial rules the air." Will Durant
1 8 The contract reads: "For the sum of $600 Six Hundred Dollars."
4 9 Albert Camus, as you know a Frenchman was an existentialist.
2 10 Her talk addressed two issues: A family values and B welfare.

Internal Punctuation: Parentheses

Rule 1: Use parentheses to enclose parenthetical or explanatory matter and added information. (Commas or dashes may be used instead.)

Learn 1 Senator Dole (a Republican) ran for the presidency in 1996.
Learn 2 The contracts (Exhibits C and D) need important revisions.
Apply 3 Sean Duncan the person with highest sales is being honored.
Apply 4 The Sixth Edition 2000 copyright date has been delivered.

Rule 2: Use parentheses to enclose identifying letters or figures of lists within a sentence.

Learn 5 Check for these errors: (1) keying, (2) spelling, and (3) grammar.
Apply 6 The focus group leaders are 1 Ramos, 2 Zahn, and 3 Pyle.
Apply 7 The order of emphasis is 1 technique and 2 speed of motions.

Rule 3: Use parentheses to enclose a name and date used as a reference.

Learn 8 Thousands of us heard the "I Have a Dream" speech (King, 1963).
Apply 9 He cited "The Gettysburg Address" Lincoln, 1863 in his report.
Apply 10 We read *The Old Curiosity Shop* Dickens, 1841 in class.

Internal Punctuation: Dash

Rule 4: Use a dash (two hyphens with no space before or after) to set off clarifying or added information, especially when it interrupts the flow of the sentence.

Learn 11 The skater—in clown's disguise—dazzled with fancy footwork.
Apply 12 Our trade discounts 10%, 15%, and 20% are the best available.
Apply 13 The gown a copy of an Italian original sells for only $150.

Rule 5: Use a dash before the author's name after a poem or quotation.

Learn 14 "All the world's a stage. . . ." —William Shakespeare
Apply 15 "I have taken all knowledge to be my province." Francis Bacon

EDIT MODIFIED BLOCK LETTERS

Objectives:

1. To practice formatting modified block style letters.
2. To apply language usage skills.

78A • 5' Conditioning Practice

Key each line twice; take 1' writings on lines 1 and 2 as time permits.

alphabet	1	Pam will acquire two dozen red vinyl jackets for the big exhibit.
figures	2	The library has 95,684 books, 1,205 periodicals, and 3,457 tapes.
speed	3	They may sign the usual proxy if they make an audit of the firms.

gwam 1' | 1 | 2 | 3 | 4 | 5 | 6 | 7 | 8 | 9 | 10 | 11 | 12 | 13 |

FORMATTING

78B • 45' Editing Letters

Letter 1 (Rough Draft)

1. Format the text at the right as a modified block letter. Use a 12-pt. font; indent paragraphs; and make the marked changes.
2. Proofread and correct any errors that you find.

Save as: *LTR78B1*

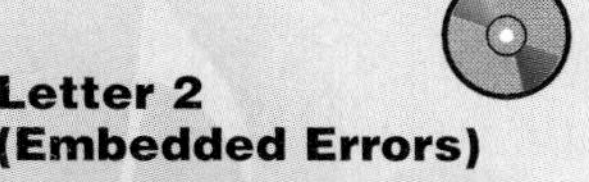

Letter 2 (Embedded Errors)

1. Open *CD-LTR78B2*.
2. Make these changes:
   a. Delete the ¶ indentions and use open punctuation.
   b. Change the complimentary close to **Sincerely yours**.
   c. Add *Gold* before *Instant Access* in ¶ 1.
   d. Change all occurrences of *automatic teller* to *ATM*.
3. Correct the 12 unmarked errors in the letter body.
4. Proofread and correct any other errors you find.

Save as: *LTR78B2*

May 25, 200- | Dr. Fouad A. Shia | 212 Seventh St. | Bangor, ME 04401-4417

Dear Dr. Shia:

Thank you for conducting the actuarial forcasts seminar four the administrative support staff at Bank Mart last week.

I have reveiwed the enclosed results of the evalaution completed by the participants. Without exception all the participants rank each of your topics as important to there needs. The topic pertainingtoprobability recieved the higher ranking.

You should also know that all most all participants rated you're style and materials as good or excellent. Most of the administrative support people involved stated they wanted you back for another seminar within the near future.

Yours sincerely, | Ms. Susan L. Delpiore | Training and Development | xx | Enclosure | c Mr. L. James Walter | Vice President, Operations

If at any time you have questions about your coverage, please call our client hotline at 1-800-555-0192.

Sincerely, | Martin D. Thomas | New Client Liaison | jd

FILL-IN INFORMATION			
Records 1-4	**Amount**	**Records 5-8**	**Amount**
Perez	$710.47	Barichal	$664.23
Brletich	$710.47	Greene	$664.23
Kamerer	$265.89	Awan	$265.89
Neumann	$265.89	Martz	$524.78

LANGUAGE SKILLS

117D • 10' Language Skills: Word Choice

1. Study the spelling and definitions of the words at the right.
2. Key the Learn lines, noting word choice.
3. Key the Apply lines, selecting the correct words.
4. Check your work with the instructor. Rekey lines that contain a word-choice error.

Save as: *CHOICE117D*

personal (adj) private; individual

personnel (n) employees

wait (vb/n) to stay in place; to pause; to serve as a waiter; act of waiting

weight (n) amount something weighs

Learn 1 The **personnel** committee took a **personal** interest in all workers.
Apply 2 Max thought the case too (personal/personnel) to discuss openly.
Apply 3 The (personal/personnel) manager will mediate the dispute.

Learn 1 Opal wants to **wait** until her **weight** loss is complete.
Apply 2 I'll gain more (wait/weight) the longer I (wait/weight).
Apply 3 He will (wait/weight) to gain (wait/weight) to wrestle heavier.

INTERNET ACTIVITY

1. Read the two ¶s at the right.
2. Perform a search on an exercise topic of your choice and then compose (either at the keyboard or using speech recognition software) two or three ¶s describing what you learned.
3. Print one or two pages from an Internet site that relate to what you wrote.

Exercise is very important to maintaining a healthy body and mind. People exercise to lose weight, get in shape and stay in shape, reduce stress, improve overall health, increase muscular strength, recover from an illness or injury, etc.

Maybe you know what you want to accomplish through exercise, but don't know where to start. This activity requires you to search the Internet to find information about a method of exercise that interests you. For example, you may want to search the broad topic "exercise" and then follow links that interest you. Or you may want to narrow your search by selecting a few exercise routines that are of particular interest to you and searching for them. Such routines include aerobics, bodybuilding, climbing, cycling, martial arts, running, swimming, walking, yoga, etc.

Letter 3 (Embedded Errors)

1. Open *CD-LTR78B3*.
2. Make these changes:
   a. Change *first* to *second* in ¶ 1.
   b. Change all occurrences of *pamphlet* to *brochure*.
   c. Change *Monday* in last line to *Friday*.
   d. Change *Public relations* in ¶ 2 to *The Public Relations Department*.
   e. Change the format to modified block.
3. Correct the 12 unmarked errors throughout the document.
4. Proofread and correct any other errors you find.

Save as: *LTR78B3*

LESSON 79 CREATE LETTERS FROM FORM PARAGRAPHS

Objectives:

1. To enhance language skills.
2. To learn how to prepare letters from form paragraphs.

79A • 5' Conditioning Practice

Key each line twice; take 15" writings on line 3 as time permits.

alphabet 1 Zac, be a good fellow and keep extra quiet to enjoy these movies.

figures 2 He arrived at 12:43 p.m. on Flight #80-7 (Gate 6) with 59 others.

speed 3 Pamela and Susi may fix the penalty box when they visit the city.

gwam 1' | 1 | 2 | 3 | 4 | 5 | 6 | 7 | 8 | 9 | 10 | 11 | 12 | 13 |

LANGUAGE SKILLS

79B • 5' Language Skills: Word Choice

1. Study the spelling and definitions of the words at the right.
2. For each set of sentences, key the Learn line, noting word choice. Then key the Apply lines, selecting the correct words.
3. Check your work with your instructor. Rekey lines that contain word-choice errors.

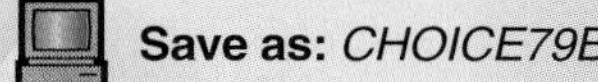

Save as: *CHOICE79B*

farther (adv) greater distance
further (adv) in greater depth; extent, or importance; additional
whose (adj) of or to whom something belongs
who's (cont) who is

Learn 1 The **farther** I drive, the **further** my mind wanders.

Apply 2 With (farther, further) effort, I ran (farther, further) ahead of the group.

Apply 3 Tom could see (farther, further) into the distance than Jane.

Apply 4 With (farther, further) practice, he threw the javelin (farther, further).

Learn 1 **Who's** to say **whose** fault it is that we scored only one touchdown?

Apply 2 (Whose, Who's) kite is it, and (whose, who's) going to fly it?

Apply 3 (Whose, Who's) going to accompany Mr. Smith to the store?

Apply 4 (Whose, Who's) knit sweater is hanging in the closet?

117B • 15' Edit Data Source File

1. Open file *CD-L117BDS*.
2. Add the records in the ADD RECORDS table at the right.
3. Add a **Company** field and a **Plan** field to each record. Then add the information in the ADD FIELDS table.

 **Save as:** *L117BDS*

ADD RECORDS			
Field Name	**Record 1**	**Record 2**	**Record 3**
Title	Mrs.	Dr.	Ms.
FirstName	LaJunta	Vijay	Rita
LastName	Greene	Awan	Martz
Address	8606 Wiley Post Ave.	1148 Hyde Park Blvd.	601 Centinela Ave.
City	Los Angeles	Inglewood	Inglewood
State	CA	CA	CA
PostalCode	90045-8600	90302-2640	90302-5519

ADD FIELDS					
Records 1-4			**Records 5-8**		
Last Name	**Company**	**Plan**	**Last Name**	**Company**	**Plan**
Perez	P & B Auto Trim	Family	Barichal	Ace Auto Parts	Husband/ Wife
Brletich	Security Auto Service	Family	Greene	Greene Auction House	Husband/ Wife
Kamerer	Bank and Trust	Individual	Awan	Inglewood Orthopedics	Individual
Neumann	Lawndale Bakery	Individual	Martz	Hercules.com	Parent/ Child

117C • 20' Personalized Form Letter

1. Use the information at the right and on the next page to create a main document file with a fill-in merge field.
2. Use block format with mixed punctuation.

 **Save as:** *L117CMD*

3. Merge main document file *L117CMD* with data source file *L117BDS*, inserting the information in the table on the next page in each letter during the merge process.

 **Save as:** *L117CLTRS*

4. Print the Perez, Neumann, and Martz letters.

September 29, 200- | <<Title>> <<FirstName>> <<LastName>> | <<Company>> | <<Address1>> | <<City>>, <<State>> <<PostalCode>> | Dear <<Title>> <<LastName>>:

This letter is to serve as acknowledgement that you have selected Asbury Health Insurance, Inc. to be the provider of your medical and dental insurance. This insurance is provided through <<Company>>.

You have been enrolled in the <<Plan>> Plan and your new coverage will become effective November 1. The premium for this plan is <<*Insert fill-in field*>> monthly. Your employer will pay 80% of this amount and you will pay 20%. It is our understanding that your 20% will be deducted from your monthly paycheck and forwarded to us by your benefits staff member.

We at Asbury Health Insurance are pleased that you have selected us to insure your health risks, and we look forward to providing you with excellent service throughout the coming years.

(Letter continued on next page)

79C • 40'
Form Paragraphs

1. Review the Macro feature (p. 159) and then record each ¶ at the right, using a 12-pt. font. Define each paragraph with a letter (A-H). Correct errors as you record.
2. Play back each macro as needed to create Letters 1–4. Use modified block format, indented paragraphs, and mixed punctuation. Insert the current date and the salutation. Add an enclosure notation if needed.

Letter 1

Ms. Tonya Meinert
12306 Hicks Rd.
Hudson, FL 34669-3708
¶s: A, E, G, and H
Major: **Biology**

 **Save as:** *LTR79C1*

Letter 2

Mr. Monte Swauger
101 La Costa St.
Melbourne Beach, FL 32951-3480
¶s: B, C, F, G, and H
Major: **Mechanical Engineering**

 **Save as:** *LTR79C2*

Letter 3

Ms. Jodie Cresmonauski
1621 Flagler Ave.
Jacksonville, FL 32207-3119
¶s: B, D, E, G, and H
Major: **Electrical Engineering**

 **Save as:** *LTR79C3*

Letter 4

Ms. Kelli Pardini
598 S. Sundance Dr.
Lake Mary, FL 32746-6355
¶s: A, C, D, F, G, and H
Major: **Mathematics**

 **Save as:** *LTR79C4*

A

Congratulations! You have been accepted into the School of Arts and Sciences at Duncan College for the semester that begins in September. Your major will be [major name].

B

Congratulations. You have been accepted conditionally into the School of Engineering at Duncan College for the semester that begins in September. Your major will be [major name].

C

You should schedule a placement examination to determine your beginning mathematics and English courses at Duncan. Choose a date and time from those listed on the enclosed card and return the card.

D

The courses you have completed, the grades you have earned, and your class rank indicate that you are eligible for a Presidential Scholarship. This is an academic scholarship awarded without regard to financial need to six outstanding freshmen. To be considered, you must schedule an interview with faculty. The interview dates and times are listed on the enclosed card. Indicate your first three choices and return the card as soon as possible.

E

To reserve your spot in the September freshman class, you need to remit a $50 deposit. This deposit will be deducted from your tuition and fees for the first semester.

F

To reserve your spot in the September freshman class and the dormitory, you need to remit a $150 deposit. This deposit will be deducted from your tuition, fees, and room and board charges for the first semester.

G

We are glad that you chose Duncan College. We are committed to offering quality education in and out of the classroom.

H

Sincerely,

Gerri D. Rhodes, President

xx

115G–116G • 20'
Personalized Form Letters and Name Badges

1. Use the information at the right to create a main document file.
2. Use modified block format, mixed punctuation, and ¶ indentations.

Save as: *L115GMD*

3. Merge main document file *L115GMD* with data source file *L115FDS*.

Save as: *L115GLTRS* (merged letters)

4. Print the Dunn and Cougar letters.
5. Create a main document for name badges. Use ALL CAPS and print the title, first and last name, company, and city.

Save as: *L115GBDGSMD*

6. Merge main document file *L115GBDGSMD* with data source file *L115FDS*.

Save as: *L115GBDGS* (name badges)

7. Print the name badges.

May 25, 200- | <<Title>> <<FirstName>> <<LastName>> | <<Company>> | <<Address1>> | <<City>>, <<State>> <<PostalCode>> | Dear <<Title>> <<LastName>>:

We know what a burden it is for small businesses like <<Company>> to offer excellent health insurance benefits to employees. That is why First Health is holding an informational session at the Hartley Hotel on Wednesday, June 10, from 4:30 p.m. to 6 p.m.

<<Title>> <<LastName>>, we invite you and another representative from <<Company>> to join us. You will learn about the major features of our medical, dental, and long-term disability coverage so that you can compare them to your present plan's features. We are convinced that you will be pleasantly surprised by what we can offer at affordable premiums.

One reason we are able to give you more for your benefit dollars is the way in which we place our small business employees in large groups to spread health risk over a large population.

Please use the enclosed card to reserve your places at the informational session. Refreshments will be served, and you will have ample time to discuss your specific needs with one of our staff members who will be attending.

Sincerely, | Robyn L. Young-Masters | Regional Marketing Manager | xx | Enclosure | <<FirstName>>, Tom Durkin has told me a great deal about the success of <<Company>>, and I am looking forward to meeting you to find out what you are doing to be so successful in such a competitive field.

LESSON 117 PREPARE PERSONALIZED FORM LETTERS WITH FILL-IN FIELD

Objectives:

1. To use Mail Merge to prepare form letters with a fill-in field.
2. To improve language skills.

117A • 5'
Conditioning Practice

Key each line twice; take 30" writings on lines 1, 2, and 3; determine *gwam*.

alphabet 1 Pamela will acquire eight dozen red vinyl jackets for an exhibit.

figures 2 The next school dances will be on 04/29 and 06/18 at 07:35-10:50.

speed 3 Their visit may end the problem of the firm and make us a profit.

gwam 1' | 1 | 2 | 3 | 4 | 5 | 6 | 7 | 8 | 9 | 10 | 11 | 12 | 13 |

LESSON 80 FORMAT TWO-PAGE LETTERS

Objectives:

1. To review second-page heading.
2. To prepare two-page letters.

80A • 5' Conditioning Practice

Key each line twice; take 15" writings on line 3 as time permits.

alphabet 1 Jay asked four zany questions before each good example was given.

figures 2 My mutual fund fell 4.87 points to 65.92 on Friday, May 30, 1998.

speed 3 The men may pay for a big emblem of the chapel with their profit.

gwam 1' | 1 | 2 | 3 | 4 | 5 | 6 | 7 | 8 | 9 | 10 | 11 | 12 | 13 |

FORMATTING

80B • 45' Business Letter and E-mail

Document 1 (Two-page Letter)

1. Read the second-page heading information on p. 212. *Reference:* Bullets feature, p. 135 Indents feature, p. 68
2. Format and key the text at the right and on the next page as a modified block letter. Use paragraph indentations, open punctuation, and Courier 12 pt.

 **Save as:** *LTR80B1*

(Current date) | Ms. Valerie E. Lopez | 207 Brainard Rd. | Hartford, CT 06114-2207 | Dear Ms. Lopez | SHADOWING AT BRIGHTON LIFE INSURANCE CO.

I'm pleased that you have chosen Brighton Life Insurance Co. as the place where you want to complete your shadow experience. I believe that you will learn a great deal about being an actuary by spending two days at Brighton with me.

To help you prepare for your visit, I have listed some of the things you should know about actuaries:

- Gather and analyze statistics to determine probabilities of death, sickness, injury, disability, unemployment, retirement, and property loss.
- Specialize in either life and health insurance or property and casualty insurance; or specialize in pension plans or employee benefits.
- Hold a bachelor's degree in mathematics or a business area, such as actuarial science, finance, or accounting.
- Possess excellent communication and interpersonal skills.

Also, I have enclosed actuarial career information published by the Society of Actuaries (life and health insurance), Casualty Actuarial

(Letter continued on next page)

115D–116D • 20'
Mail Merge

Document 1 (Mailing Labels)

1. Prepare a standard mailing label in USPS format for each record in data source file *L115CDS* that has *Garland* or *Mesquite* in the City field.
2. Print the mailing labels.

Save as: *L115D1MD* (main document) and *L115DLBLS* (merged document)

Document 2 (Envelopes)

1. Prepare a No. 6¾ envelope in USPS style for each record in data source file *L115CDS* that has *Seagoville* or *Rowlett* in the City field. Use **LTV Ecological Services, 3224 Highway 67, Mesquite, TX 75180-3224** as the return address.

Save as: *L115D2MD* (main document) and *L115DENV* (merged document)

2. Print the envelopes.

Document 3 (Name Badges)

1. Prepare a name badge for each record in data source file *L115CDS* that has *Irving* or *Mesquite* in the City field and *Ms.* in the Title field.
2. Horizontally center in ALL CAPS the fields below on two lines; DS between the lines.

   Title, First Name, Last Name
   City

3. If necessary, sort badges in alphabetical order by last name.

Save as: *L115D3MD* (main document) and *L115DBDGS* (merged document)

4. Print the name badges.

115E–116E • 15'
Edit a Data Source File

1. Delete all records in data source file *L115CDS* that have *Irving*, *Hutchins*, *Rowlett*, or *Plano* in the City field.
2. Add the records at the right to the data source file.
3. Print the edited file.

Save as: *L115EDS*

Field Name	Record 1	Record 2	Record 3
Title	Ms.	Mrs.	Ms.
FirstName	Nyla	Lori	Diana
LastName	Schnurr	O'Dea	Olech
Address	801 W. Kearney St.	350 S. Belt Line Rd.	12726 Audelia Rd.
City	Mesquite	Mesquite	Dallas
State	TX	TX	TX
PostalCode	75149-0801	75185-3150	75243-8899
Field Name	**Record 4**	**Record 5**	**Record 6**
Title	Mrs.	Mr.	Mrs.
FirstName	Tara	Dean	Sandy
LastName	Koget	Korch	Cougar
Address	2256 Arapaho Rd.	1400 W. Arapaho Rd.	1700 W. Kingsley Rd.
City	Garland	Richardson	Garland
State	TX	TX	TX
PostalCode	75044-2256	75080-5569	75041-6612

115F–116F • 5'
Edit a Data Source File

1. Open data source file *L115EDS*.
2. Delete all records that have *Dallas* or *Mesquite* in the City field.
3. Add a new field for **Company** and add the company names at the right.

Save as: *L115FDS*

Records 1-4		Records 5-8	
LastName	**Company**	**LastName**	**Company**
Dunn	Dunn Plumbing	Shultz	C & H Floors
Como	Pete's Transmissions	Koget	Koget Florist
Nguyen	Great American Savings	Korch	Database Dallas
Durkay	Super Quality Dry Cleaners	Cougar	Airco Welding

Document 1, cont.

Society (property and casualty insurance), and American Society of Pension Actuaries (pensions). These three associations offer actuaries professional certification through a series of examinations. We can discuss the societies and the importance of obtaining the professional designations they offer.

A good two-day period for you to be with me is the last Thursday and Friday of the month. My activities on those days will give you a good orientation. Can you be here from 8:30 a.m. to 5 p.m.? Casual business dress is appropriate. My office is on Floor 37 of the Brighton Building.

Please tell me if these two days are good for you. If you have e-mail, you can send your message to alaron@brighton.com.

Sincerely | Justin A. Alaron | Senior Actuary | xx | Enclosures

---

Document 2 (E-mail)
Prepare this message as e-mail to your instructor. Send a copy to a classmate. If you do not have e-mail software, prepare the message as a personal-business letter in block format. Use the current date and the same return and letter addresses as 76B, Document 1 (*LTR76B1*). Use the same font and font size also. Supply a salutation and complimentary close. The letter is from **Ms. Valerie E. Lopez, SEP Member**.

Save as: *MAIL80B2*

SUBJECT: CONFIRMATION OF DATES

Thank you for letting me shadow you at Brighton Life Insurance Co. on the last Thursday and Friday of this month. I will be at your office by 8:30 a.m. and can stay until 5 p.m. I look forward to learning from you about being an actuary.

Explore space at the National Aeronautics and Space Administration (NASA).

1. Access NASA's home page at http://www.nasa.gov.
2. In the Cool NASA Links section, click a link that interests you.
3. Explore the link you selected. Then write a letter to a friend describing what you located. Use the letter format of your choice and supply all letter parts.
4. Print one or two pages of the Web site that relate to your letter to enclose with it.
5. Explore the History link.
6. Print a Web page that provides historical information about NASA or its many operations or achievements.

115B–116B • 20' Personalized Form Letter

1. Use the information at the right to create a main document file.
2. Format the letter in block style with mixed punctuation.

Save as: *L115BMD*

3. Merge the main document file *L115BMD* with the data source file *L114BDS*.
4. Print the personalized form letters addressed to Raible and White.

Save as: *L115BLTRS*

October 5, 200- | <<Title>> <<FirstName>> <<LastName>> | <<Address1>> | <<City>>, <<State>> <<PostalCode>> | Dear <<Title>> <<LastName>>:

(¶) Thank you for attending the recent open house reception sponsored by the Dallas Area Environmental Health Association. We hope that you enjoyed meeting our expert staff of scientists, physicians, nutritionists, technicians, and others who work on your behalf to improve your quality of life.

(¶) Headaches, sinusitis, fatigue, joint aches, and asthma are some of the common ailments that are often caused by our environment. The Dallas Area Environmental Health Association is dedicated to conducting the research that documents the link between the common ailments and the environment so effective treatments can be offered.

(¶) <<Title>> <<LastName>>, now that you know more about the Association, we ask you to schedule a 20-minute consultation with one of our staff members to discuss your health concerns. This consultation is free and carries no obligation to use our services. Just call me at 972-555-0119 to schedule a mutually convenient time.

Sincerely, | Margarita L. Jiminez | Director of Services | xx

115C–116C • 10' Edit a Data Source File

Make the changes given at the right to data source file *L114BDS*.

Save as: *L115CDS*

1. Add these records:

Field Name	Record 1	Record 2	Record 3
Title	Mrs.	Ms.	Mrs.
FirstName	Judy	Janet	Clara
LastName	Nguyen	Durkay	Shultz
Address	404 S. Watson St.	800 Austin St.	475 W. Oates Rd.
City	Seagoville	Garland	Garland
State	TX	TX	TX
PostalCode	75159-9901	75040-8000	75043-4752

2. Delete the records for Mr. Daniel Raible, Ms. Stacey Bethel, and Mrs. Helen Wever.
3. Make these changes to other existing records:
   - Change Sally Lysle's last name to **Beam**.
   - Change Jack Dunn's address to **1606 School Rd., Carrolton, TX 75006-4471**.
   - Change Ms. Anne Sige's last name to **Holtus** and her address to **718 N. Bagley St., Dallas, TX 72511-0718**.

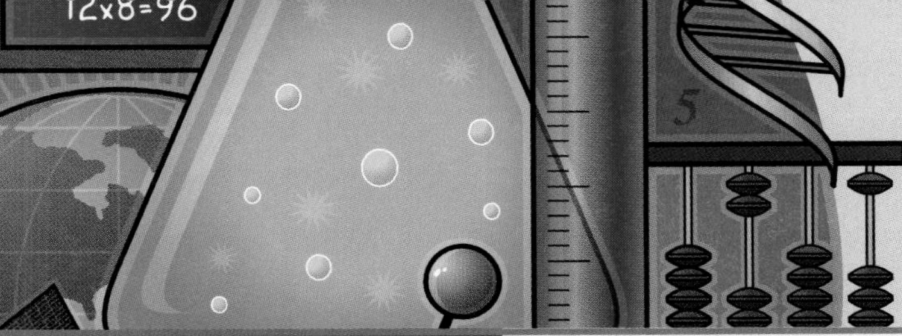

ACTIVITY 1

Internal Punctuation: Semicolon and Underline

1. Key lines 1–10 at the right, supplying the needed semicolons and underlines.
2. Check the accuracy of your work with the instructor; correct any errors you made.
3. Note the rule number at the left of each sentence in which you made a semicolon or underline error.
4. Using the rules below the sentences and on p. 223, identify the rule(s) you need to review/practice.
5. **Read**: Study each rule.
6. **Learn**: Key the Learn line(s) beneath it, noting how the rule is applied.
7. **Apply**: Key the Apply line(s), adding semicolons and underlines as needed.

 **Save as:** *CS9-ACT1*

Proofread & Correct

Rules

1 1 Ms. Barbour is a great coach she is honest and fair.
1 2 Joe Chin won a scholastic award Bill Ott, an athletic one.
1 3 Maxine works from 4 to 7 p.m. she studies after 8:30 p.m.
3 4 The cities are as follows: Ames, IA Provo, UT and Waco, TX.
2 5 The play starts at 8 therefore, you should be ready by 7:30.
3 6 They hired 11 new workers in 1997 6, in 1998 and 8, in 1999.
1,4 7 Troy said, "You can do it" Janelle said, "You're kidding."
1,4 8 Rona sang "Colors of the Wind" Cory sang "Power of the Dream."
5 9 TV Guide ranks No. 2 according to Information Please Almanac.
6 10 "Why," she asked, "can't people use affect and effect properly?"

Internal Punctuation: Semicolon

> Rule 1: Use a semicolon to separate two or more independent clauses in a compound sentence when the conjunction is omitted.

Learn 1 Ms. Willis is a superb manager; she can really motivate workers.
Apply 2 His dad is a corporate lawyer his law degree is from Columbia.
Apply 3 Orin is at the Air Force Academy Margo is at the Naval Academy.

> Rule 2: Use a semicolon to separate independent clauses when they are joined by a conjunctive adverb (*however, therefore, consequently,* etc.).

Learn 4 Patricia lives in Minneapolis; however, she works in St. Paul.
Apply 5 No discounts are available now consequently, I'll buy in July.
Apply 6 I work mornings therefore, I prefer an afternoon interview.

> Rule 3: Use a semicolon to separate a series of phrases or clauses (especially if they contain commas) that are introduced by a colon.

Learn 7 Al spoke in these cities: Denver, CO; Erie, PA; and Troy, NY.
Apply 8 Overdue accounts follow: Ayn, 30 da. Lowe, 60 da. Shu, 90 da.
Apply 9 I paid these amounts: April, $375 May, $250 and June, $195.

> Rule 4: Place the semicolon outside the closing quotation mark. (A period and a comma are placed inside the closing quotation mark.)

Learn 10 Miss Trent spoke about "leaders"; Mr. Sanyo, about "followers."
Apply 11 The coach said, "Do your very best" Paula said, "I'll try."
Apply 12 He said, "It's your own fault" she said, "With your help."

Internal Punctuation: Underline

> Rule 5: Use an underline to indicate titles of books and names of magazines and newspapers. (Titles may be keyed in ALL CAPS or *italic* without the underline.)

Learn 13 The <u>World Almanac</u> lists <u>Reader's Digest</u> as the top seller.
Apply 14 I read the review of Runaway Jury in the New York Times.
Apply 15 He quoted from an article in Newsweek or the Chicago Sun-Times.

(continued on next page)

Title	First Name	Last Name	Address1	City	State	Postal Code
Ms.	Lois	Poulos	1632 New Market Rd.	Mesquite	TX	75149-1056
Mr.	Peter	Como	701 W. State St.	Garland	TX	75040-0701
Ms.	Karen	Rolle	1026 F Ave.	Plano	TX	75074-3591
Mr.	Dale	Zeman	4412 Legacy Dr.	Plano	TX	75024-4412
Mr.	Yu	Wei	12726 Audelia Rd.	Dallas	TX	75243-7789
Ms.	Anne	Sige	532 N. Story Rd.	Irving	TX	75061-0506
Mr.	David	White	3700 Chaha Rd.	Rowlett	TX	75088-3700

114C • 8'
Mailing Labels

1. Prepare a standard mailing label for each record in the data source file *L114BDS*.

Save as: *L114CMD* (main document) and *L114CLBLS* (merged document)

2. Print the mailing labels.

114D • 7'
Envelopes

1. Prepare a No. 10 envelope for each record in the data source file *L114BDS* that has *Plano* in the City field. Use your name and address as the return address.

Save as: *L114DMD* (main document) and *L114DENV* (merged document)

2. Print the envelopes.

LESSONS 115–116
USE MAIL MERGE

Objectives:

1. To create main document files.
2. To use Mail Merge to create personalized form letters, labels, envelopes, and name badges.
3. To edit data source files.

115A–116A • 10' (5' daily)
Conditioning Practice

Key each line twice; take 30" writings on lines 1, 2, and 3; determine *gwam*.

alphabet 1 Marvin will be expected to judge the quality of the tyke's kazoo.

fig/sym 2 Stopwatch (#93-408) and pedometer (321-657) are on sale Saturday.

speed 3 Ryan and my tidy neighbor may dismantle the shanty on the island.

gwam 1' | 1 | 2 | 3 | 4 | 5 | 6 | 7 | 8 | 9 | 10 | 11 | 12 | 13 |

Rule 6: Use an underline to call attention to words or phrases (or use quotation marks). **Note:** Use a continuous underline (see line 13 under Rule 5) unless each word is to be considered separately as shown below.

Learn 16 Students often use then for than and its for it's.
Apply 17 I had to select the correct word from their, there, and they're.
Apply 18 He emphasized that we should stand up, speak up, then sit down.

ACTIVITY 2

Listening

Complete the listening activity as directed at the right.

 **Save as:** *CS9-ACT2*

1. Open *CD-CS9LISTN*. It contains three mental math problems.
2. Each problem starts with a number, followed by several addition and subtraction steps. Key or handwrite the new answer after each step, but *compute* the answer mentally.
3. Record the last answer for each problem.
4. After Problem 3, close the file.
5. Check the accuracy of your work with the instructor.
6. If you made an error, repeat the activity.

ACTIVITY 3

Write to Learn

Complete the Write-to-Learn activity as directed at the right.

 **Save as:** *CS9-ACT3*

1. Using word processing or speech recognition software, write a paragraph explaining how to insert a dot leader tab in a table of contents.
2. Write a second paragraph explaining how to add a light red shaded row in a table.

ACTIVITY 4

Composing

1. Key the paragraph at the right, correcting the punctuation and word-choice errors it contains.
2. Check the accuracy of your work with the instructor; correct any errors you made.
3. Compose/key a second paragraph, including the information below.
   - The level of your self-image: high, low, or in-between
   - Factors that make your self-esteem what it is
   - Factors you think could improve your self-esteem
   - Plans you have to raise your self-esteem

 **Save as:** *CS9-ACT4*

Narcissus, a mythical young man saw his image reflected in a pool of water fell in love with his image, and starved to death admiring himself. Unlike Narcissus, our self-esteem or self-image should come not threw mirror reflections but buy analysis of what we are—inside. Farther, it is dependent upon weather others who's opinions we value see us as strong or week, good or bad positive or negative. No one is perfect, of course; but those, who develop a positive self-image, wait the factors that affect others views of them and work to improve those factors. Its time to start.

LESSON 114 CREATE DATA SOURCE FILE AND MAIL MERGE

Objectives:

1. To create a data source file.
2. To use Mail Merge to prepare envelopes and mailing labels.

114A • 5' Conditioning Practice

Key each line twice; take 30" writings on lines 1, 2, and 3; determine *gwam*.

alphabet 1 Mack and Jebb expect high scores on every law quiz if they study.

figures 2 I wanted to have 557-4280 or 557-3196 as my new telephone number.

speed 3 The man with the rifle saw six turkeys by the dock at Lake Tibor.

gwam 1' | 1 | 2 | 3 | 4 | 5 | 6 | 7 | 8 | 9 | 10 | 11 | 12 | 13 |

114B • 30' Data Source File

1. Create a data source file using the 20 records on this and the next page.
2. Use the column headings as field names.

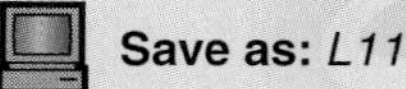

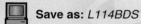

Save as: *L114BDS*

Title	First Name	Last Name	Address1	City	State	Postal Code
Mr.	Daniel	Raible	13811 Seagoville Rd.	Dallas	TX	75253-1380
Ms.	Sally	Lysle	3707 S. Peachtree Rd.	Mesquite	TX	75180-3707
Mrs.	Luz	Ruiz	13105 Timothy Ln.	Mesquite	TX	75180-1310
Mrs.	Jane	Alam	1414 Alstadt St.	Hutchins	TX	75141-3792
Mr.	Paul	Regina	11435 Ravenview Rd.	Dallas	TX	75253-1143
Mrs.	Jane	Abbott	3300 LaPrada Dr.	Mesquite	TX	75149-3300
Mr.	John	Eaton	P.O. Box 852238	Mesquite	TX	75185-8522
Ms.	Stacey	Bethel	1717 Castle Dr.	Garland	TX	75040-1717
Dr.	Jash	Sharik	2021 E. Park Blvd.	Plano	TX	75074-2021
Mr.	Jack	Dunn	4007 Latham Dr.	Plano	TX	75023-4000
Mrs.	Helen	Wever	1001 Cuero Dr.	Garland	TX	75040-1001
Ms.	Ann	Buck	1919 Senter Rd.	Irving	TX	75060-1919
Dr.	Tim	Prady	3901 Frisco Ave.	Irving	TX	75061-3900

(continued on next page)

WORD PROCESSING 10

ACTIVITY 1

Outline

1. Read the copy at the right.
2. Learn to create and organize a numbered outline in your wp software.
3. Using the Outline feature default settings, key the outline at the right, DS.

 **Save as:** *WP10ACT1A*

4. With the file open, rename it (save as) *WP10ACT1B*.
5. Make these changes:
   - Add **THE EAR** as a centered title a DS above the first outline heading.
   - Use a 2" top margin and 2" side margins.
   - In section I, switch the order of Level 2 headings so "inner ear" is A and "outer ear" is C.
   - Use a different numbering system.
   - Delete outline section III and its two subheadings.

 **Save as:** *WP10ACT1B*

Use the **Outline** feature to create and reorganize text into main points and subpoints when planning a document (report or presentation). The feature numbers each topic with the numbering system that you choose. The *alphanumeric* system—shown in the three-level outline below—is most common. It uses both numbers (Roman and Arabic) and letters (capitals and lowercase) to label points at each level. Other numbering systems are available, or can be initiated by users. Some software also has an Outline View. In this view users can move topics from one level to another and switch the order of topics at a given level.

I. PARTS OF THE EAR (Level 1 heading)
   A. The outer ear (Level 2 heading)
      1. The auricle (Level 3 heading)
      2. The external auditory canal
   B. The middle ear
      1. Auditory ossicles
      2. Malleus
      3. Hammer
   C. The inner ear
      1. The vestibule
      2. The semicircular canals
      3. The cochlea
II. HOW WE HEAR
   A. How sounds reach the inner ear
   B. The inner ear sends sounds to the brain
III. CARE OF THE EAR
   A. Preventing ear infections
   B. Preventing ear injury

ACTIVITY 2 

Header and Footer

1. Read the copy at the right.
2. Learn to insert headers and footers with your wp software.
3. Open *CD-WP10ACT2*, and insert the header and footer shown at the right.
4. View the pages together to see the header and footer.
5. Delete the header. In the footer, insert the school name at the left and center the date.

 **Save as:** *WP10ACT2*

A **header** or **footer** is text (such as a chapter title, date, filename, or name of a person or company) or graphic (a company logo, for example) printed in the top margin (header) or bottom margin (footer) of a page. Reports—especially long ones—often contain headers and/or footers. Page numbers are often included in a header or footer. The header or footer may be invisible as you key the report but will show when you use View and when you print.

1. Insert header (name ends at the right margin):

Summerville High School A History Report by Barry Gertsner

2. Insert footer on both pages (page number ends at right margin):

December 200- Page #

Document 2

1. Key the letter at the right in modified block format with mixed punctuation and ¶ indentations.
2. Use Arial font, 12 pt.

 **Save as:** *LTR113B2*

Document 3

1. Change the format of Document 2 to a two-page block letter with open punctuation.
2. Add a subject line: **TRIAL MEMBERSHIP FOR YOUR EMPLOYEES**; use Times New Roman, 16 pt.; bold the name of the fitness center in the body of the letter; and add the center's name in the closing lines.

 **Save as:** *LTR113B3*

March 5, 200- | Attention Human Resources Department | Central Life Assurance, Inc. | 1520 W. Ohio St. | Indianapolis, IN 46222-1578 | Ladies and Gentlemen

(¶) The Action Fitness and Exercise Center is offering an introductory membership to employees of area corporations. This membership is for 90 days and costs only $50, the regular monthly membership fee.

(¶) During this 90-day trial period, your employees can use the indoor running track, weight-lifting stations, and exercise equipment (including treadmills, stair climbers, and rowing machines).

(¶) Your employees can also enroll in any of the aerobics, weight-control, and healthy-eating classes that are offered on a regular basis.

(¶) To take advantage of this offer, distribute the enclosed cards to interested employees. These cards can be presented on the first visit.

Sincerely | Ned V. Mowry | President | xx | Enclosure | c Mary Parker, Club Membership Coordinator

Document 4

1. Key the letter at the right in block format with mixed punctuation.
2. Use Times New Roman, 14 pt.

 **Save as:** *LTR113B4*

Document 5

1. Change the format of Document 4 to modified block with open punctuation and ¶ indentations.
2. Use Arial, 12 pt.

 **Save as:** *LTR113B5*

May 17, 200- | REGISTERED | Susan T. Kipin, M.D. | 404 E. Washington St. | Indianapolis, IN 46204-8201 | Dear Dr. Kipin | CHANGE IN HAZARDOUS REMOVAL CONTAINERS

(¶) The waste removal containers that we have located at your office will be removed on May 30 and replaced with new containers that provide greater safety for your patients, your employees, and you. A brochure showing the container dimensions is enclosed.

(¶) Our technician will fasten a container to the wall in each room you designate. Please be certain that your office manager knows the specific locations.

(¶) Once the new containers have been installed, TRT technicians will schedule a time when the waste can be removed daily.

Sincerely | Dorothy C. McIntyre | Service Manager | xx | Enclosure | bc Harry Williams, Technician

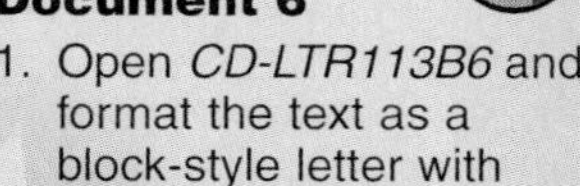

Document 6

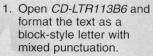

1. Open *CD-LTR113B6* and format the text as a block-style letter with mixed punctuation.
2. Key the ¶ at the right as the final ¶.

Proofreading Alert

The file contains four errors; find and correct them as you process the letter.

(¶) The association's staff thanks you for supporting this important nonprofit organization. Without contributions from citizens such as you, thousands more men and women would suffer fatal heart attacks each year.

 **Save as:** *LTR113B6*

ACTIVITY 3

Page and Paragraph Borders

1. Read the copy at the right.
2. Learn how to add borders to a paragraph, column, or page using your wp software.
3. Follow the steps at the right to add a border to a page and paragraphs.

Save as: *WP10ACT3C*

Use the **Border** feature to add a border to any or all sides of a page, paragraph, or column, as well as a table, or cell within a table. Many line styles and colors are available. In addition, page border options include small graphics (pictures). Borders not only enhance appearance; they also can make text easier to read by emphasizing certain passages. Borders are most effective when used sparingly, however.

1. Open *CD-WP10ACT3* and put borders around the third and fourth ¶s.
2. Save the file as *WP10ACT3A.*
3. Change each of the borders around ¶s 3 and 4 to a shadow border.
4. Save the file as *WP10ACT3B.*
5. Add a page border in the line style of your choice. Save the file as *WP10ACT3C.*

ACTIVITY 4

Insert Clip Art

1. Read the copy at the right.
2. Learn how to insert clip art using your software.
3. Follow the steps at the right to add clip art.

Save as: *WP10ACT4*

Using the **Clip Art** feature, you can insert drawings and photographs, even sounds and video clips into documents. You can select from a collection of clip art files provided with your wp software or from files you add to the clip art files. Most wp programs have a Search feature to help you locate the right clip art for your document.

1. Open *CD-WP10ACT4.*
2. From Clip Art, select a picture that represents a construction worker or one of the building trades named in the paragraph.
3. Insert the picture into the middle of ¶ 2, wrapping text around the picture.
4. Select a picture of a building from Clip Art.
5. Insert the picture into the middle of ¶ 3, wrapping text around the picture.

ACTIVITY 5

Apply What You Have Learned

TM 2" LM 1.5"

1. Using the text at the right, prepare an outline DS; add **COMPUTER GRAPHICS** as a centered heading.
2. Insert a footer with your name (left), your class period (centered) and the date (right).

Save as: *WP10ACT5*

I. INTRODUCTION
    A. What is a computer graphics program?
    B. Why and when should you use one?
II. GRAPHICS PROGRAMS
    A. Those that come with a software program
    B. Those that are stand-alone programs
III. COMPUTER GRAPHS
    A. Bar graph
        1. Vertical bar
        2. Horizontal bar
    B. Circle graphs
        1. Whole circle
        2. Exploded circle
        3. Segmented circle
    C. Line graphs
        1. Without shaded area
        2. With shaded area

ACTIVITY 6

Prepare a one-page announcement, using file *CD-WP10ACT6* and the information at the right.

Save as: *WP10ACT6*

1. Open the file (*CD-WP10ACT6*) and insert a page border. If possible, use an art border appropriate for a birthday party.
2. Insert one or two pictures from Clip Art that are also appropriate for a birthday party.
3. Format the page (wrap the text) as you prefer.

PREPARE LETTERS WITH SPECIAL PARTS

Objectives:

1. To review letters with special parts.
2. To review format features of two-page letters.

113A • 5' Conditioning Practice

Key each line twice; take 30" writings on lines 1, 2, and 3; determine *gwam*.

alphabet 1 To what extent was Kaz involved with my projects before quitting?

fig/sym 2 Runner #3019 was 1st (49' 35") and runner #1687 was 2d (50' 12").

speed 3 Ken and my neighbor are to visit an ancient chapel on the island.

gwam 1' | 1 | 2 | 3 | 4 | 5 | 6 | 7 | 8 | 9 | 10 | 11 | 12 | 13 |

FORMATTING

113B • 45' Two-Page Letters with Special Parts

Document 1

1. Key the letter at the right in block format with mixed punctuation.
2. Use a 14-pt font.

Save as: *LTR113B1*

Learning **C • U • E**

When a company name is used in the closing lines, key the name a DS below the complimentary close in ALL CAPS. Then QS to the writer's name.

April 3, 200- | SPECIAL DELIVERY | Mrs. Carol T. Yao | Director of Human Resources | Franklin Tool & Die Company | 600 E. Lake St. | Addison, IL 60101-3492 | Dear Mrs. Yao: | YOUR REQUEST FOR ADDITIONAL INFORMATION

(¶) Thank you for agreeing to give further consideration to making Protect III available to your employees, beginning with the open enrollment period that starts in June.

(¶) Protect III has been among the leaders in the health insurance industry for the past 15 years. Our plan is now used by hundreds of thousands of people in Illinois and is accepted by almost every physician, hospital, and pharmacy in your area.

(¶) The enclosed materials will provide you with more information about Protect III that should help you prepare the proposal for your vice president. The following materials are included:

- ❑ "Top Choice Protection" brochure that explains Protect III's key features.
- ❑ A benefit summary chart that outlines specific benefits.
- ❑ A provider directory that lists all the Illinois primary care physicians and facilities participating in Protect III.
- ❑ A pharmacy directory that lists the pharmacies your employees can use as part of the Protect III prescription plan.
- ❑ A chart of monthly fees for the various levels of coverage your employees may choose.

(¶) If you have any questions about Protect III features, the provider network, or the fees that will apply to Franklin Tool & Die Company, call me at 1-800-555-0113.

Sincerely | PROTECT III, INC. | Carlos V. Santana | Corporate Account Rep | xx | Enclosures | Carol, thank you for giving Protect III the opportunity to provide your company's health care benefits. We're looking forward to serving you and your employees.

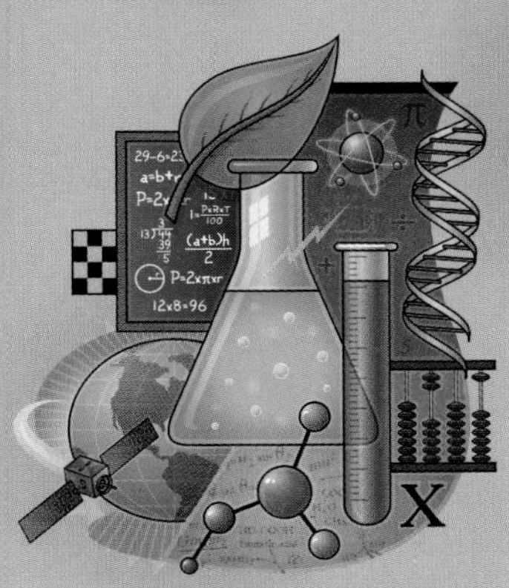

UNIT 23

LESSONS 81–86

Improving Report Formatting Skills

Format Guides: Reports

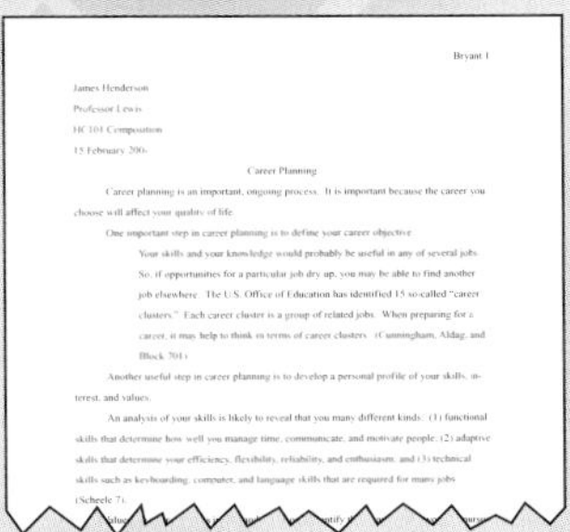

Report (p. 1) in MLA Style

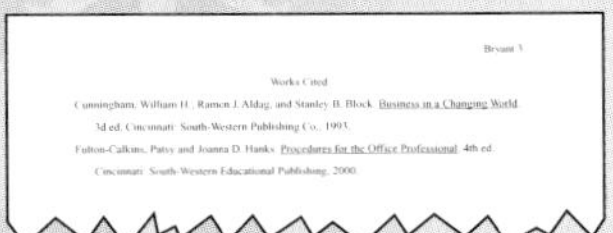

List of References (Works Cited) in MLA Style

Summary Meeting Minutes (p. 1) in Unbound Report Format

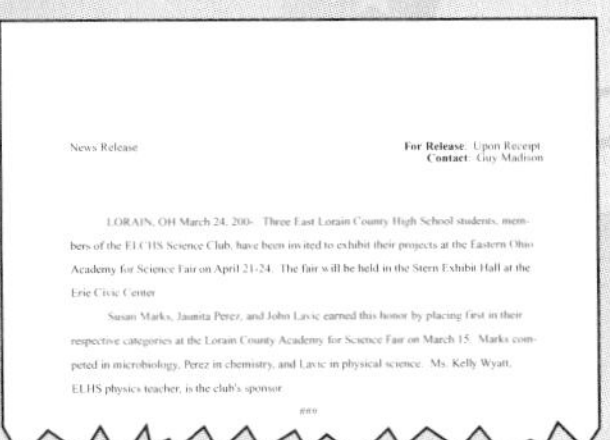

News Release in Unbound Report Format

MLA Style

The **Modern Language Association (MLA)** style is often used to document and format students' papers. The MLA documentation method, called *parenthetical reference,* is similar to the textual citation method. MLA reports have these distinctive format features:

Margins. On all pages, the top, bottom, left, and right margins are 1" (or default margins).

Header and page number. A header contains the page number; the writer's last name may be included. The header is right-aligned. Every page is numbered, including the first.

Line spacing. The entire report is double-spaced, including long quotations, bulleted and numbered items, tables, and works cited.

Report identification. The writer's name, instructor's name, course title, and date (day/month/year style) are keyed on separate lines at the left margin on p. 1.

Report title. The title is centered a DS below the date in title case. The body begins a DS below the title.

Indentations and long quotations. The first line of each paragraph is indented 0.5" (or at the first default tab setting). Long quotations (four or more lines) are indented 1" (or at the second default tab setting) from the left margin.

Inserted tables. Insert a table as near as possible to the text that it illustrates. Key a number (*Table 1*) and caption (title) above the table left-aligned in title case. DS above the table number, below the last line (or source note), and between lines within the table. Hide table gridlines. Adjust table width to fit *within* the left and right margins.

Works cited (references). Key the works cited on a separate page, using the same margins and header as the report body. Center *Works Cited* in title case at the top margin. A DS below the title, list the references in alphabetical order by authors' last names. DS the list and use hanging indent.

Binding. Staple or clip all pages of the report at the top-left corner.

Unbound and Bound Reports

Many business documents, including news (press) releases and meeting minutes, may be keyed in unbound or bound report format (not MLA style).

News release. Use format guides for unbound reports (p. 70), with these additional guides. On p. 1, key **News Release** at the top left and **For Release:** . . . at the top right margin. On the line below (SS), key **Contact:** . . . at the right margin. QS; begin the news release body. Center the symbols ### a DS below the last line.

Summary meeting minutes. Use format guides for unbound reports, but SS the body. Insert a DS above and below side headings and between paragraphs. Number each item of business summarized in the minutes.

Inserted tables. In a report or report-like document, insert a table as near as possible to the text that it illustrates. Identify the table with a centered heading above the table or in the first row. DS above the heading and below the last row. Gridlines may be shown or hidden. Center the table horizontally *within* the left and right margins.

Topic Outline

Topic outlines, useful for planning and organizing reports, occasionally appear in a finished document—so readers can see the report structure. If a system is not specified for showing different topic levels, use the familiar alphanumeric system (p. 224). Unless directed otherwise, use the default indentations (each level indented 0.5" more than the previous level). The margins and line spacing for an outline should match the report body.

Document 2 (Letter)

1. Key the business letter at the right in block format with open punctuation.
2. Use Arial font, 14 pt.

 **Save as:** *LTR112B2*

Document 3 (Letter)

1. Change the format of Document 2 to modified block with open punctuation and no ¶ indentations.
2. Use Times New Roman font, 15 pt.

 **Save as:** *LTR112B3*

(Current date) | Mr. Max R. Rice | 23 Oak St. | Schiller Park, IL 60176-6932 | Dear Mr. Rice

(¶) If the health plan you chose last year has not delivered everything you thought it would, we have some good news for you. Health Plus is now available to you during this open enrollment period.

(¶) Health Plus is the area's largest point-of-service plan that combines the managed care features of an HMO with the freedom of choice of a traditional health plan. As the enclosed directory indicates, this plan gives you access to the best doctors and medical facilities in the area.

(¶) To enroll, simply complete the enclosed application and return it to your benefits office within 30 days.

Sincerely | Ms. Peg Jerzak | Account Specialist | xx | Enclosure

---

Document 4 (Letter)

1. Key the business letter at the right in modified block format with mixed punctuation and ¶ indentations.
2. Use Century Gothic font, 12 pt.

 **Save as:** *LTR112B4*

Document 5 (Letter)

1. Change the format of Document 4 to block with mixed punctuation.
2. Use Courier New font, 12 pt.

 **Save as:** *LTR112B5*

October 2, 200- | Ms. Paula Kenney | Sterling Medical Supplies | 4259 Rosegarden Rd. | Long Beach, CA 98766-4259 | Dear Ms. Kenney

(¶) Please accept this invitation to participate in East High's Fifth Annual Health Occupations Career Fair that will be held on Thursday, November 17, from 2 to 4 p.m. at East High.

(¶) Last year's career fair attracted 26 employers and associations and more than 400 students. The employers represented hospitals, long-term health care providers, outpatient clinics, medical insurance providers, medical supply and equipment vendors, and large physician practices. In addition, several associations attended to provide students with career information related to the technical areas.

(¶) To reserve a table for your company, please fill out and return the enclosed registration form by November 1. We look forward to having you present.

Sincerely | Lawrence R. Aamont | Health Occupations | xx | Enclosure

---

Document 6 (Memo)

1. Format the copy at the right as a memo, using this information:
   DATE: April 16, 200-
   TO: Harriett Gross
   FROM: Helen Otto
   SUBJECT: BEST DENTAL CHOICE
2. Use Times New Roman font, 18 pt.

 **Save as:** *MEM112B6*

(¶) A representative from Best Dental Choice will be visiting the Benefits Office on Tuesday, April 25, to explain the advantages of that dental insurance plan.

(¶) Please arrange your schedule so you can attend the 2 p.m. meeting, during which the Best Dental Choice sales rep will outline the features of the plan and compare the benefits to our present plan.

(¶) Please bring one of your assistants who works closely with the dental plan to the meeting.

FORMAT MLA-STYLE REPORTS AND OUTLINES

Objectives:

1. To format a topic outline.
2. To format reports in MLA style.

81A • 5' Conditioning Practice

Key each line twice SS; then take 30" writings on line 2; determine *gwam*.

alphabet 1 Jake will buy very good quality zinc from experts at the auction.

fig/sym 2 Al's gas bill was $89.35 (+6%); his office bill was $40.17 (-2%).

speed 3 Nancy may go with me to visit them by the cornfield and big lake.

gwam 1' | 1 | 2 | 3 | 4 | 5 | 6 | 7 | 8 | 9 | 10 | 11 | 12 | 13 |

FORMATTING

81B • 45' Outline and MLA-Style Report

Document 1 (Outline)

1. Read the formatting guides for outlines on pp. 224 and 226.
2. Prepare the topic outline at the right DS.

Save as: *TOL81B1*

Document 2 (Revised Outline)

1. Open *TOL81B1*.
2. Make these changes:
   - Use a different numbering method.
   - Reverse the order of topics II and III.
   - Reverse the order of topics IV and V.
   - Change the title and Level 1 headings to uppercase; change the TM to 2" and line spacing to SS. QS below the title.

Save as: *TOL81B2*

Document 3 (Report)

1. Read about MLA style on p. 226; study the models on pp. 228 and 229.
2. Format and key the MLA-style report on pp. 228 and 229.

Save as: *TOL81B3*

Earth's Nearest Neighbor in Space

I. Introduction
   A. Moon's size
   B. Moon's reflection
   C. Moon's atmosphere
II. Moon's Surface
   A. Lowlands (called *maria*) and highlands
   B. Craters
      1. Ray craters
      2. Secondary craters
III. Moon's Composition
   A. Soil
      1. Color is dark gray to brownish gray
      2. Consists of ground-up rock and bits of glass
      3. Depth of soil varies
   B. Rocks
      1. Minerals in the rock
      2. Basalt and breccia rocks
IV. Moon's Orbit
   A. Time to revolve around Earth
   B. Shape of its orbit
   C. Phases of the moon
      1. New moon
      2. First quarter
      3. Full moon
      4. Last quarter
V. Eclipses
   A. Lunar eclipse
   B. Solar eclipse
VI. Tides
   A. Caused by the moon's gravity
   B. Frequency of daily high and low tides

UNIT 30

LESSONS 112–117

Processing Business Correspondence

LESSON 112 REVIEW LETTERS AND MEMOS

Objectives:

1. To review block and modified block letter and memo formats.
2. To review open and mixed punctuation and basic letter and memo parts.

112A • 5' Conditioning Practice

Key each line twice; take 30" writings on lines 1, 2, and 3; determine *gwam*.

alphabet 1 Avoid fizzling fireworks because they just might explode quickly.

figures 2 He surveyed 3,657 women, 2,980 men, and 1,400 children last June.

speed 3 It may be a big problem if both of the men bid for the dock work.

gwam 1' | 1 | 2 | 3 | 4 | 5 | 6 | 7 | 8 | 9 | 10 | 11 | 12 | 13 |

FORMATTING

112B • 45' Business Letters and Memos

Document 1 (Memo)

1. Format the text at the right as a memo, adding any memo parts that may be missing.
2. Proofread and correct all errors—those that are marked and those that are embedded.

Proofreading Alert
The revised copy contains five unmarked errors; find and correct them as you process the memo.

Save as: *MEM112B1*

TO: Olu T. Sangoeyhi, Physical Therapy

FROM: William M. Glause, Administrative Services

DATE: May 14, 200-

SUBJECT: PHYSICAL THERAPY BROCHURE [Change this and all other occurrences of "brochure" to "pamphlet."]

Here is the first draft of the physical theraphy brochure that has been ~~okayed~~ authorized for publication in this years budget. Please ~~check~~ proofread the copy ~~very~~ carefully, and make sure the pictures are correct.

The public relations staff is in the process of getting permission to use each persons picture in the brochure. All permision forms should be completed within the next 10 [sp] days. If there are ~~any~~ changes in the pictures ~~we are using~~, I will see that you get to review ~~all~~ the ~~changes before we go to printing~~ new pictures.

Please ~~make the necessary~~ mark your suggested changes ~~in the copy~~ and retun the brochure to me by next Monday.

xx

Enclosure

header

Bryant 1

1"

DS

James Henderson

Professor Lewis

HC101 Composition

15 February 200-

DS

Career Planning

DS

0.5"

DS paragraphs

Career planning is an important, ongoing process. It is important because the career you choose will affect your quality of life.

One important step in career planning is to define your career objective.

Indent long quotes 1" from left margin and DS

> Your skills and your knowledge would probably be useful in any of several jobs. So, if opportunities for a particular job dry up, you may be able to find another job elsewhere. The U.S. Office of Education has identified 15 so-called "career clusters." Each career cluster is a group of related jobs. When preparing for a career, it may help to think in terms of career clusters. (Cunningham, Aldag, and Block 701)

2 spaces

DS

1" LM

1" RM

Another useful step in career planning is to develop a personal profile of your skills, interests, and values.

0.5"

An analysis of your skills is likely to reveal that you have many different kinds: (1) functional skills that determine how well you manage time, communicate, and motivate people; (2) adaptive skills that determine your efficiency, flexibility, reliability, and enthusiasm; and (3) technical skills such as keyboarding, computer, and language skills that are required for many jobs (Scheele 7).

Values are your priorities in life, and you should identify them early so that you can pursue a career that will improve your chances to acquire them. Values include the importance you

1" bottom margin

MLA Report, page 1

ACTIVITY 6

Edit Data Source Files

1. Read the information at the right.
2. Learn how to make changes to records and fields with your wp software.
3. Open *WP12ACT2DS* and make the changes specified at the right.

 **Save as:** *WP12ACT6DS*

You can edit both **records** and **fields** in a data source file. For example, you can add records to, delete records from, or revise records in an existing data source file.

Also, you can add, delete, or revise fields in an existing data source file.

Data source files can be word processing, spreadsheet, or database files.

1. In Record 3, change Elizabeth's title to **Mrs.** and last name to **Popelas**.
2. Delete the record for Harold Dominicus and add these two records:

   Dr. Eugene Whitman, 531 Kiefer Rd., Ballwin, MO 63025-0531
   Ms. Joyce Royal, 417 Weidman Rd., Ballwin, MO 63011-0321

3. Add a field called **Company** and then insert the company name in each record as indicated below:

   Mueller—**Allmor Corporation**
   Whitman—**Whitman Family Practice**
   Popelas—**Kurtz Consumer Discount**
   Royal—**Better Delivery, Inc.**

ACTIVITY 7

Mail Merge Applications

1. Read the information at the right.
2. Learn how to use Mail Merge to prepare envelopes, mailing labels, and name badges with your wp software.
3. Follow the directions at the right.

Mail Merge can be used for many other tasks. Frequently, envelopes, mailing labels, and name badges are prepared from information in a data source file.

1. Using all fields in *WP12ACT6DS* and a main document you create, prepare a large (No. 10) envelope for each record in the data source file. Use your name and home address as the return address.

    **Save as:** *WP12ACT7MD* (main document) and *WP12ACT7ENV* (envelopes)

2. Using all fields in *WP12ACT6DS* and a main document you create, prepare a mailing label for each record in the file.

    **Save as:** *WP12ACT7LBLSMD* (main document) and *WP12ACT7LBLS* (labels)

3. Using the Title, FirstName, LastName, Company, and City fields in *WP12ACT6DS* and a main document you create, prepare a name badge (using ALL CAPS) for each record in the data source file.

    **Save as:** *WP12ACT7BDGSMD* (main document) and *WP12ACT7BDGS* (name badges)

ACTIVITY 8

Use Fill-in Fields in a Mail Merge

1. Read the information at the right.
2. Learn how to use fill-in fields in a mail merge with your wp software.
3. Follow the directions at the right.

Fill-in fields display prompts so that you can add information that is not suitable to store in a database. The fill-in prompt can be displayed each time a record is merged with the main document so unique information can be keyed in each form letter. Fill-in field codes are entered into the main document.

1. Open file *CD-WP12ACT8MD* and insert a fill-in field code at the end of the second paragraph.

    **Save as:** *WP12ACT8MD*

2. Merge *WP12ACT8MD* and *WP12ACT6DS*, using a fill-in prompt to enter the time and date of each person's appointment, given below:

   Mueller—**9 a.m. on May 5**
   Popelas—**8 a.m. on May 5**
   Whitman—**2 p.m. on May 5**
   Royal—**3 p.m. on May 6**

    **Save as:** *WP12ACT8LTRS*

header

Bryant 2

1"

place on family, security, wealth, prestige, creativity, power, and independence (Fulton-Calkins and Hanks 93).

Interests are best described as activities you like and enthusiastically pursue. By listing and analyzing your interests, you should be able to identify a desirable work environment. For example, your list is likely to reveal if you like to work with things or people, work alone or with others, lead or follow others, or be indoors or outdoors.

MLA Report, page 2

header

Bryant 3

1"

Works Cited

Cunningham, William H., Ramon J. Aldag, and Stanley B. Block. Business in a Changing World. 3d ed. Cincinnati: South-Western Publishing Co., 1993.

0.5"

Fulton-Calkins, Patsy and Joanna D. Hanks. Procedures for the Office Professional. 4th ed. Cincinnati: South-Western Educational Publishing, 2000.

all DS

Works Cited Page

ACTIVITY 3

Create a Main Document

1. Read the text at the right.
2. Learn to create a main document using your wp software.
3. Create the main document shown at the right.

Save as: *WP12ACT3MD*

The **main document** file contains the generic text and format of the document that remains constant in each letter, plus the **field codes**. The **field codes** are inserted into the main document file where the variable information from the data source is to appear. The merge process will create the **merged file**, containing a personalized letter for each recipient.

January 15, 200-

<<Title>> <<FirstName>> <<LastName>>
<<Address1>>
<<City>>, <<State>> <<PostalCode>>

Dear <<Title>> <<LastName>>:

(¶) It was a pleasure to meet you last week to discuss your long-term health care needs. As you requested, I have charted the various policy features from three leading insurance providers.

(¶) The chart will show the various options each provider extends and the cost for each option. You can select those that meet your needs the best.

(¶) I will call you in a week to arrange an appointment so we can discuss this matter thoroughly.

Sincerely,

Katherine Porter
Agent

xx

Enclosure

ACTIVITY 4

Apply What You Have Learned

1. Merge the main document file (*WP12ACT3MD*) with the data source file (*WP12ACT2DS*) to produce three personalized form letters.
2. View the letters in the merged file and print the Theilet letter.

Save as: *WP12ACT4LTRS*

ACTIVITY 5

Query Option

1. Read the text at the right.
2. Learn to use the Query Option in your wp software, and then complete the activity at the right.

After the data source file and main document file have been created, they are ready to be merged. However, if you need a personalized form letter for only some of the records in the data source file, you can use the **Query Option** to select the one(s) you want to create and print. Form letters will not be created for the records not selected.

1. Using *WP12ACT3MD* and *WP12ACT2DS* and the Query Option, create a letter for each record with *Chesterfield* in the City field.
2. Print the letters.

Save as: *WP12ACT5LTRS*

LESSON 82 FORMAT MLA-STYLE REPORT WITH TABLE

Objectives:
1. To practice MLA-style report formatting skills.
2. To insert a table in an MLA-style report.

82A • 5' Conditioning Practice

Key each line twice SS; then key 30" writings on line 3; determine *gwam*.

alphabet	1	Elvira enjoyed the amazing water tricks of six quick polar bears.
figures	2	Tom flew 2,467 miles in June, 3,158 in July, and 1,905 in August.
speed	3	The man paid a visit to the downtown firm to sign the work forms.

gwam 1' | 1 | 2 | 3 | 4 | 5 | 6 | 7 | 8 | 9 | 10 | 11 | 12 | 13 |

FORMATTING

82B • 45' MLA-Style Reports

Report 1

1. Format the report at the right and on the next page, making the changes indicated.
2. Insert a header that contains your last name and the page number.
3. Insert the following report identification:
   - Your name
   - Your instructor's name
   - The course title
   - The current date (day/month/year)
4. Prepare the Works Cited page as the last page of the report using the references below:

   Dietz, James E. and James L. Southam. Contemporary Business Mathematics for Colleges. 12th ed. Cincinnati: South-Western College Publishing, 1999.

   The World Almanac and Book of Facts, 1999. Mahwak, NJ: World Almanac Books, 1999.
5. Eliminate any widow/orphan lines, and keep side headings with the text that follows them.

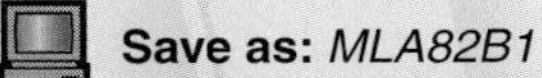

Save as: *MLA82B1*

DS

A Need To Know Metrics

Todays students need to learn two systems of measurement--the metric system, which is used throughout the world, and the English or customary system, which is the most-used system in the United States (Dietz and Southam 446).

Rationale for the Instruction

DS entire report.

Metrics instruction must be included in the curriculum of our nation's schools because all people must understand the metric system to function in today's society. Metrics is everywhere! Automobile engines; soft drink containers; nutrition information listed on food packages; jean and film sizes; and most of the nuts, bolts, and screws used to assemble products imported to the United States ~~is an~~ are example of ~~a~~ common item ~~that is~~ measured in ~~a~~ metric unit.

Students must complete a series of learning activities ~~that will enable them~~ to ~~do these activities~~:

1. Read, write, and pronounce the basic metric measures for length, weight, and capacity.

2. Add, subtract, multiply, and divide metric measurements.

3. Convert from one metric unit to another

4. Solve problems that use metric measurements.

5. Convert commonly used metric measures to English measures and vice versa.

Instructional Strategies

To accomplish the learning goals, a variety of learning aid, such as charts, oral and written exercises, and word problems, can and should be used extensively in the learning process. A chart is an excellent learning resource that can be used to accomplish many of the objectives.

Table 1 is an example of how basic metric units of length can be presented in visual form (The World Almanac 1999). A similar chart for weight and capacity could be developed.

ACTIVITY 1

Mail Merge

1. Study the text and illustration at the right.
2. Learn how to merge files using your wp software.
3. Prepare three letters by merging the files as directed at the right.

The **Mail Merge** feature is used to combine information from two files into a personalized file that is created via the merge process.

The Merge feature is often used to merge a form letter file (**main document**) with a name and address file (**data source**) to create a personalized letter (**merged file**) to each person in the data source file.

This file *merged with* this file *creates* this file.

Data Source File	Main Document File	Merged File
contains variable information	contains generic information	contains personalized (variable and generic) information

1. Open the main document file (*CD-WP12ACT1MD*) and merge it with the data source file (*CD-WP12ACT1DS*).
2. View the three letters in the merged file created by the mail merge.

Save as: *WP12ACT1LTRS*

3. Print one of the merged letters.

ACTIVITY 2

Create a Data Source File

1. Read the text at the right.
2. Learn to create a data source file using your wp software.
3. Open a new wp file.
4. Use the information in the table at the right to create a data source file with three records, each with seven fields.

Save as: *WP12ACT2DS*

Data source files contain a **record** for each name in the database. Each **record** contains **fields** of information about the person, such as her or his title, first name, last name, street address, city, state, postal code, etc.

Word processors insert **field codes** to separate and distinguish fields of information. Word processors insert **end of record codes** in the data source file to separate and distinguish each record that you key into the file.

INFORMATION FOR THE DATA SOURCE FILE			
Field Name	**Record 1**	**Record 2**	**Record 3**
Title	Mr.	Mrs.	Ms.
FirstName	Harold	Noreen	Elizabeth
LastName	Dominicus	Mueller	Theilet
Address1	14820 Conway Rd.	15037 Clayton Rd.	1843 Ross Ave.
City	Chesterfield	Chesterfield	Saint Louis
State	MO	MO	MO
PostalCode	63025-1003	63017-8734	63146-5577

(Insert the table in *CD-TBL82B* here. Then hide the gridlines.)

The table can be used several ways to accomplish the instructional objectives.

1. The first column can be used for an oral exercise in which students pronounce each unit of measurement.

2. The second column can be used to show students the abbreviations for metric units, which are always shown in lowercase letters and w/o punctuation.

3. The third column can be used to explain that the meter is the basic unit used for measuring length and that other units are parts or multiples of a meter. The table lists the units of measurement from the smallest to the largest.

4. The third column can also be used to show students how to convert from one metric unit to another. Moving the decimal point in the meter measurement to the left converts it to smaller units; moving the decimal point to the right converts it to larger units.

5. The last column of the table can be used to establish the relationship between selected metric and English measurement units.

Summary

The metric system of measurement must be taught along with the English system. Metrics can be presented in an understandable manner if the teacher establishes goals and uses good examples, illustrations, and applications. The table in this report can be used easily to enhance learning.

Report 2

1. Format the report below in MLA style, correcting the unmarked errors (about 12).
2. Insert a header that has your last name and the page number.
3. Insert the following report identification:
   - Your name
   - Your instructor's name
   - The course title
   - The current date

 **Save as:** *MLA82B2*

words

The Importance of Saving Money 6

Open savings account early, financial 14
planners say, so you get into the habit of sav- 23
ing. Later, you may chose higher-yielding and 33
higher-risk investments such as stocks and 41
bonds; but opening an savings account (in 49
your teens or earlier) is a critical first step to a 60
secure future. 63

A good financial plan is one that makes 71
you feel good now in anticipation of what your 80
will be able to do with your savings in the 89
future. 91

One of the best ways to save is to have 99
money deducted from earnings before receiv- 107
ing you're paycheck. The idea is this: You 116
wont miss what you dont receive. 123

Experts agree that saving is simpler 130
when your set financial goals. The goals may 139
relate to a major purchase like a house or car, 149
a college education for yourself or some one 158
else, or retirement. 162

By saving regularly and allowing the 170
interest to accumulate, you earn interest on 179
the original investment *and* on the interest 187
earned. This is known as *compounding* and it 196
is a important part of any savings plan. 205

Besides helping you reach goals for the 213
future, saving also helps the economy, as you 222
savings increase money flow. Thus, your sav- 231
ings may help build a house or school or office 241
building that, in turn, helps other industry's 250
prosper. 252

SKILL BUILDER 7

Technique: Keystroking Patterns
Key each line twice SS; DS between 2-line groups; key difficult lines again as time permits.

Adjacent key

1 are ire err her cash said riot lion soil join went wean news
2 pew art sort try tree post upon copy opera three maker waste
3 sat riot coil were renew forth trade power grope score owner

One hand

4 ad bar car deed ever feed hill jump look null noon poll upon
5 him joy age kiln noun loop moon bear casts deter edges facet
6 get are save taste versa wedge hilly imply phony union yummy

Balanced hand

7 go aid bid dish elan fury glen half idle jamb lend make name
8 oak pay hen quay rush such urus vial works yamen amble blame
9 cot duty goal envy focus handy ivory lapel oriel prowl queue

gwam 1' | 1 | 2 | 3 | 4 | 5 | 6 | 7 | 8 | 9 | 10 | 11 | 12 |

Timed Writings

1. Key three 1' writings on each ¶; determine *gwam*. Count errors. If errors are 2 or fewer on any writing, goal is to increase speed by 1 or 2 words on next writing. If errors on any writing are more than 2, goal is control on next writing.
2. Key two 3' writings on ¶s 1–3 combined; determine *gwam* and count errors.
3. Key a 5' writing on ¶s 1–3 combined; determine *gwam* and count errors.

A all letters used — gwam 3' | 5'

There are many opportunities for jobs in the physical fitness 4 | 2 | 42
industry. The first step for many people is to be a fitness in- 8 | 5 | 45
structor in a fitness center or program. A genuine interest in the 13 | 8 | 48
field as well as evidence of a personal commitment to good fitness 17 | 10 | 50
are frequently the major things needed to land a job as a fitness 22 | 13 | 53
instructor. 22 | 13 | 54

Another opportunity in the fitness industry is to become a 26 | 16 | 56
strength coach for an athletic team. This person works to make the 31 | 19 | 59
team members fit and strong at the same time the athletic coach 35 | 21 | 61
works to maximize their skills. A college degree in physical 39 | 24 | 64
education or a related field is usually needed for this kind of job. 44 | 26 | 66

Others in the fitness field often get a job in a big company 48 | 29 | 69
or hospital as a fitness program director. These directors run 52 | 31 | 71
programs that improve the fitness and overall health of the people 57 | 34 | 74
who work in the hospital or company. Directors usually need a 61 | 37 | 77
college degree and a lot of training in fitness skills, health 65 | 39 | 79
promotion, and business. 67 | 40 | 80

gwam 3' | 1 | 2 | 3 | 4 |
5' | 1 | 2 | 3 |

LESSON 83 PROCESS MLA REPORTS

Objectives:

1. To practice MLA-style report formatting skills.
2. To practice keying from rough-draft copy.

83A • 5' Conditioning Practice

Key each line twice SS; then take 30" writings on line 3; determine *gwam*.

alphabet	1	Fay's bright jacket has an amazing weave and exceptional quality.
fig/sym	2	The computer (786-SX) was $2,159 and printer (Elon 340) was $259.
speed	3	If they go to the social with us, they may visit the eight girls.

gwam 1' | 1 | 2 | 3 | 4 | 5 | 6 | 7 | 8 | 9 | 10 | 11 | 12 | 13 |

FORMATTING

83B • 45' MLA-Style Reports

Report 1

1. Format the report at the right and on the next page, making the changes indicated.
2. Insert a footer that has your last name, the page number, and the current date *field*.
3. Insert the following report identification:
   - Your name
   - Your instructor's name
   - The course title
4. Insert **Mathematics** as the report title.
5. Eliminate any widow or orphan lines, and keep all headings with the text that follows them.

Save as: *MLA83B1*

Note:

Review the Widow/Orphan feature on p. 67.

Most high school students study several mathematics. In college, they complete math courses, some of which prepare them to study even *more* kinds of mathematics. You may think of math as one subject; in fact, there are many mathematics. This report describes 7 kinds.

Arithmetic

Arithmetic is branch of mathematics that you study in elementary and middle school. It deals with the study of numbers and the use of the four fundamental processes:

- Addition
- Subtraction
- Multiplication
- Division

Arithmetic is every day math. You use it in your personal affairs, and it is the basis for most other mathematics.

Algebra

Algebra is used widely to solve problem in business, industry, and science s by using symbols, such as *x* & *y*, to represent unknown values. The power of algebra is that it enables us to create, write, and rewrite problem-solving formulas.

> Algebra is one of the cornerstones of today's technology boom. Without algebra there would not exist a single TV, radio, telephone, microwave oven, or other gadget that makes modern life so comfortable and interesting. Once you learn to use algebra, you will have the opportunity to help design and create the next generation of technology. (Cord Algebra 1)

(Report continued on next page)

CYCLE 4

UNITS 30-38

Computer Skills: Enhance & Create

We all have a responsibility as citizens of the world to learn about and care for the environment. "Environment" encompasses a wide range of topics including health, population, climate, pollution, recycling, forestry, food, sports, and many more. Some of you may choose environmental careers. You might work at Sea World or study oceanography. You could devote your energies to ecology or focus on forestry. You could work in the wilderness or in a corporate office. You could become a teacher or join the Peace Corps.

Whatever career you choose will require some basic job-seeking skills, including the ability to create effective business documents. Your keying skills, organizational abilities, and facility with computer software will enhance your appeal as an employee. In addition, knowledge of your chosen career field as well as knowledge of the business world will give you an edge.

In this unit you will complete activities using business documents on health and environmental subjects. You will improve your keying and computer skills while learning about such diverse topics as insurance coverage, exercise, physical therapy, environmental Web sites, and careers in sports medicine and training. You'll become a more effective communicator as you enhance documents with graphics, create a flyer, work on a newsletter, and even prepare a business plan.

Whether you decide to go into business for yourself, choose a career in an environment or health field, or take another direction, your keyboarding and software skills will serve you all of your life. As you learn about health and environment, use the skill-building lessons in this unit to help you stay in the game!

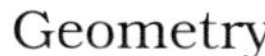

Geometry

Geometry is the branch of mathematics that deals with shapes (Gerver 9). More specifically, geometry is the study of relations, properties, and measurements of solids, surfaces, lines, and angles. It is most useful in building or measuring things. Architects, astronomers, construction engineers, navigators, and surveyors are just a few professionals who rely on geometry.

Trigonometry

Trigonometry is mathematics that deals with triangular measurements. Plane trigonometry computes the relationships between the sides of triangles on level surfaces called *planes*. Spherical trigonometry studies the triangles on the surface of a sphere.

Calculus

Calculus is high-level mathematics dealing with rates of change. It has many practical applications in engineering, physics, and other branches of science. Using calculus, we understand and explain how water flows, the sun shines, the wind blows, and the planets cycle through the heavens. Differential calculus determines the rate at which an object's speed changes. Integral calculus determines the object's speed when the rate of change is known.

Probability

Probability is the study of the likelihood of an event's occurrence (<u>Cord Algebra 1</u> A6). It is useful in predicting the outcomes of future events. Probability originated from the study of games of chance. It is now used for other purposes, including (1) to control the flow of traffic through a highway system; (2) to predict the number of accidents people of various ages will have; (3) to estimate the spread of rumors; (4) to predict the outcome of elections; and (5) to predict the rate of return in risky investments.

Statistics

Statistics is the branch of mathematics that helps mathematicians organize and find meaning in data (<u>Cord Applied Mathematics</u> 3). For example, teachers may collect students' test scores, then analyze these data (scores) to learn about a class's achievements or to compare one student's score with all others who took the same test. Coaches use statistics to describe the batting, fielding, pitching, rebounding, and scoring performance of teams and individual players. Besides describing teams and players, statistics help coaches predict each player's or team's future performance.

Works Cited

Center for Occupational Research and Development. <u>Cord Algebra 1, Mathematics in Context</u>. Cincinnati: South-Western Educational Publishing, 1998.

Center for Occupational Research and Development. <u>Cord Applied Mathematics, Unit 19 Working with Statistics</u>. Cincinnati: South-Western Educational Publishing, 1989.

Gerver, Robert, et al. <u>South-Western Geometry, An Integrated Approach</u>. Cincinnati: South-Western Educational Publishing, 1998.

Report 2

1. Open file *CD-RPT83B2* and format it as an MLA-style report.
2. Using Find and Replace, change all occurrences of *unit* to *department* and *teachers* to *instructors*.
3. The report contains about 20 errors in capitalization, grammar, punctuation, word choice, etc. Correct them.
4. Reverse the order of the Advisory Boards and Awards and Recognition sections. Use the Outline view if available, or cut and paste.

Save as: *MLA83B2*

Your Perspective

The **exchange rate** determines how much of another country's currency you can get in exchange for U.S. dollars. Exchange rates in the world today are **flexible**. This means that rates are not fixed against a standard like gold but change constantly, affected mostly by supply and demand.

EXCHANGE RATES FOR SELECTED CURRENCIES
July 16, 2000, 7:33 a.m.

Country	Exchange Rate	$200 (U.S.) in Local Currency
British pound	0.6664	
Canadian dollar	1.4847	
Euro	1.0655	
Japanese yen	107.87 (x 100)	
Swiss franc	1.6508	

Source: "Cross Currency Rates." http://www.bloomberg.com/markets/fxc.html (16 July 2000).

Global Awareness

ACTIVITIES

1. Assume you are going on a trip and taking $200 in spending money. Using the exchange rates in the table at the left, determine how much of each type of currency you can get for your $200.
2. Key and format the table at the left, completing Column C. Use the table formatting features that you have learned to arrange the information attractively on the page.
3. In a group, discuss these questions: What are some other factors that might affect how much you would get for your money in each country? What are some ways in which increases and decreases in exchange rates might affect these countries?
4. Find the exchange rates for these countries today; then compute how much of each type of currency you would get for your $200. Replace the information in the last two columns of your table with the new information.

Wherever you work, you will interact with coworkers and customers who differ from you in age, physical ability, and culture. America's workforce is becoming more diverse and its markets more global. One employee skill that employers are on the lookout for is **multicultural experience**. Companies want employees who are open to other cultures' values and who can work well with people from different cultures.

U.S. Labor Force

Group	1995	2005	2020
White, Non-Hispanic	76%	73%	68%
Women	46%	48%	50%
Hispanic	9%	11%	14%
Asian-American	4%	5%	6%

Source: *Workforce 2020,* Hudson Institute. Figures for 2005 and 2020 are estimates.

Cultural Diversity

ACTIVITIES

1. Key and format the table at the left. Use the table formatting features that you have learned to arrange the information attractively on the page.
2. In a group, discuss these questions: What are some implications of the decreasing number of white non-Hispanics in the workplace? of the increasing number of women? Can you explain the slow increase in the percentage of women in the workforce compared to the percentage of Hispanics?

PROCESS NEWS RELEASES AND SUMMARY MEETING MINUTES

Objectives:

1. To format summary meeting minutes.
2. To format a news release.

84A • 5' Conditioning Practice

Key each line twice SS; then take 30" writings on line 1; determine *gwam*.

alphabet 1 June quickly wraps the five dozen macaroons and six big cupcakes.

fig/sym 2 I got 25% off on orders over $83,900 because of contract #41-6-7.

speed 3 If I go to the city to visit them, I may go to the spa and dorms.

gwam 1' | 1 | 2 | 3 | 4 | 5 | 6 | 7 | 8 | 9 | 10 | 11 | 12 | 13 |

FORMATTING

84B • 45' Minutes and News Release

Document 1 (Minutes)

1. Read the format guides for preparing summary meeting minutes on p. 226. Study the model minutes on that page.
2. Prepare the minutes at the right.

 **Save as:** *MIN84B1*

words

WOODWARD HIGH SCHOOL BIOLOGY CLUB 7

March 2, 200- Meeting Minutes 13

Participants: All officers, committee chairs, and faculty sponsor attended. 29

Recorder of minutes: Jerry Finley, Secretary. 38

1. President Marcie Holmquist called the meeting to order at 2:45 p.m. 53
2. Written reports from the following officers and committee chairs 66
were distributed, discussed, and approved or accepted (copies are 80
retained by the secretary): 85

   Vice President/Membership Committee Chair--Accepted 96
   Treasurer--Approved 100
   Secretary--February meeting minutes were approved 110
   Fundraising--Accepted 114
   Community Service--Accepted 120

3. This unfinished business was acted upon: 129

   A. Approved candy sale to begin May 1. 137
   B. Approved that the Biology Club care for one mile of State Route 151
   163 as part of the community's Adopt-A-Highway Program. 162
   C. Tabled the recommendation that the Club help support an inter- 175
   national student, pending receipt of additional information. 188

4. This new business was discussed and acted upon: 198

   A. President Holmquist appointed nominating committee (Sissy 211
   Erwin, Roberta Shaw, and Jim Vance). 218
   B. Approved officers to attend regional leadership conference at 231
   Great Valley Resort and Conference Center on April 12. 243

5. The next meeting is April 3 at 2:45 p.m. in Room 103. The meeting 257
was adjourned at 3:35 p.m. 262

Your Perspective

I should have . . . I shouldn't have . . . Sometimes we find ourselves thinking, after we have taken an action, that we were wrong. Making good ethical decisions doesn't end with the choice itself. You need to take the time to look at your decision again later, especially if you think it was wrong.

Often, a bad choice is the result of something beyond our control. Something happened that we couldn't have expected. There was something important that we couldn't have known. But other times, the problem is that we were not careful enough in the way we made our decision. An article in *Issues in Ethics,* the online journal of the Markkula Center for Applied Ethics at Santa Clara University, identifies three things that can cause people to unintentionally take unethical actions at work.

The first factor psychologists call **scripts**. Scripts are tasks we have performed so many times that they have become automatic—we do them without thinking. An example might be braking at a stop sign. Scripts can be a problem when they cause you not to pay attention to a situation that demands it. Suppose a security guard is responsible for checking employee ID cards. She is so used to doing this that she barely glances at the forged ID of a potential thief and lets the thief into the building.

The second factor is **distractions**. Distractions take our focus from one thing to another. If you are studying hard for a very important test, a loud radio or television can be a distraction. If an employee is focusing all his attention on a project that is due, he might barely glance at a memo that points out safety flaws in a product because he sees the memo as a distraction.

The third factor is **moral exclusion**. Moral exclusion means not showing some individuals or groups the same consideration that you give everyone else. You may have come across a store clerk who is courteous and respectful to all customers except teenagers. The clerk may think that teenagers don't have much money to spend. What do you think will happen when a high school student tries to warn this clerk of a theft in progress?

When we recognize the three factors, we can find solutions. A Japanese drug company came up with a good solution to a moral exclusion problem. The company decided its employees needed a better understanding of the people who used its products. After a week of training, the company sent 100 managers to work with sick people. The program grew to include more than 1,000 employees. The company produced many new drugs as a result.

Source: Dennis J. Moberg. "When Good People Do Bad Things at Work." *Issues in Ethics* vol. 10, no. 2. http://www.scu.edu/SCU/Centers/Ethics/publications/iie/v/10n2/peopleatwork.html (16 July 2000).

Ethics: The Right Thing to Do

ACTIVITIES

1. Read the material at the left.
2. Key a list of scripts that you or others use.
3. To be sure that you understand the three factors, have a group or class discussion in which you give new examples of scripts, distractions, and moral exclusion.
4. Suppose you are planning a meeting about effective workplace decisions. You are to inform others about the three factors discussed on this page. How would you present the information? Develop and key, in correct format, a detailed agenda for the meeting.

Document 2 (Minutes)

1. Prepare the meeting minutes below. Center the page number in the footer.
2. Proofread and correct any errors.

 **Save as:** *MIN84B2*

words

SUMMARY MINUTES 3
COMPUTER SCIENCE 7
ADVISORY COMMITTEE MEETING 12

November 15, 200- 16

Committee members present: Robert Dry- 23
Kenich, Deborah Edington, Amy Lovetro, Ray 32
Meucci, Rosemary Radmanich, Kenneth 39
Ryave, Kim Van Aken, and Leo Yazzani. 47

School employees present: Mary Amaral, Drew 56
Bowen, Larry Kaufmann, Fred Niklas, Carla 64
Nilson, and Margaret Palmero. 70

Recorder of minutes: Joseph Gloss. 78

1. Amy Lovetro, committee chair, called the 87
meeting to order at 11:15 a.m. and welcomed 96
all to the meeting. Ms. Lovetro introduced Kim 105
Van Aken, Hermanie Engineering, as a new 113
member. 115

2. The minutes from the May 14 meeting were 124
read and approved. 128

3. Mr. Fred Niklas reported: 134

A. At least 125 students are presently enrolled 144
in the computer science programs. Dunlap 153
High has the most with 25 and West High has 161
the least with 7. 165

B. Of the 53 health occupation students who 174
were graduated last June, 28 are employed in 183
a computer-related field, 15 have gone on to 192
higher education, 3 entered the military, 5 are 202
employed in unrelated fields, and 2 are unem- 211
ployed. 212

4. Unfinished business included passing a 221
motion to recommend that Eastway AVTS stu- 229
dents charter a Computer Science Student 237
Organization and that Mary Amaral be 245
appointed sponsor. Each committee member 253
agreed to work closely with the students and 262
the faculty sponsor. 267

5. New business included passing motions to 276
support these three recommendations: 283

A. All committee members be invited to partic- 292
ipate in the AVTS's career fair. 299

B. Two members of the committee (Deborah 308
Edington and Kenneth Ryave) be appointed to 316
the AVTS's Strategic Planning Committee. 325

C. The advisory committee chair be appointed 334
to the AVTS's School-to-Work Transition 342
Committee. 344

6. The formal meeting was adjourned at 12:35 354
p.m., and the committee members and school 362
personnel moved to Gessey Dining Room for 371
lunch and informal conversation. 377

7. The next meeting is scheduled for May 15 at 387
11:15 a.m. 389

Document 3 (News Release)

1. Read the format guides for preparing news releases on p. 226. Study the model news release on that page.
2. Format the text at the right as a news release.
3. Proofread and correct all errors.

 **Save as:** *NEWS84B3*

words

News Release **For Release:** Upon Receipt 8
Contact: Guy Madison 12

LORAIN, OH, March 24, 200-. Three East Lorain County High 24
School students, members of the ELCHS Science Club, have been in- 37
vited to exhibit their projects at the Eastern Ohio Academy for Science 51
Fair on April 21-24. The fair will be held in the Stern Exhibit Hall at 66
the Erie Civic Center. 71

Susan Marks, Juanita Perez, and John Lavic earned this honor 83
by placing first in their respective categories at the Lorain County 97
Academy for Science Fair on March 15. Marks competed in microbiol- 110
ogy, Perez in chemistry, and Lavic in physical science. Ms. Kelly Wyatt, 125
ELCHS physics teacher, is the club's sponsor. ### 135

Document 3 (Itinerary)

Format the itinerary shown at the right. Make body rows equal in height. Select and apply an appropriate AutoFormat. Center the itinerary on the page.

Save as: *ITIN111B3*

			words
	FLIGHT ITINERARY		3
	Marilyn Marchionda		7
	Landis Engineering and Construction		14
Date	Time	Flight Information	20
August 23	9:43 a.m.	Depart Pittsburgh International Airport for Logan International (Boston) on Airtravel Flight 327.	31 / 37 / 44
August 24	7:47 a.m.	Depart Logan for Miami International on USEast Flight 758.	55 / 60
August 24	5:45 p.m.	Depart Miami for O'Hare International (Chicago) on Midwest Flight 251.	72 / 78
August 25	3:30 p.m.	Depart O'Hare for Pittsburgh on USEast Flight 972.	89 / 92

111C • 15' Timed Writing

Take two 5' writings on both ¶s at the right; determine *gwam;* count errors.

all letters used

gwam 3' | 5'

Many obvious steps should be taken when you search for a 4 2 52
job. One step that is not so obvious and often is overlooked by 8 5 55
applicants is reviewing the interview session. By taking the 12 7 57
time and effort needed to accomplish this, you might give 16 10 60
yourself the slight edge you need to convince an employer that 20 12 62
you are the one who should be hired. This critical step involves 25 15 65
reviewing and analyzing all aspects of the interview to determine 29 18 68
what went well and what did not. Your review should be completed 34 20 70
as soon as the interview is over, and it should give you all the 38 23 73
information you need when you call or write the interviewer for 42 25 75
the follow-up step. 44 26 76

Begin the survey by listing all the questions you were asked 48 29 79
during the session and then examine your answers. Were they 52 31 81
clear, complete, accurate, and to the point? Next, list your 56 34 84
best qualities for the job; and relate them to what you studied. 61 36 86
Did you stress your assets for the position? Last, try to figure 65 39 89
how you could have presented yourself in a better way. Did you 69 42 92
project interest and energy, use proper body language, and 73 44 94
respond to every question properly? Jot down what you learned 77 46 96
from the session that may help you if you are interviewed again 81 49 99
for this job or one at another company. 84 50 101

gwam 3' | 1 | 2 | 3 | 4 | 5
5' | 1 | 2 | 3

LESSONS 85-86

FORMAT UNBOUND AND BOUND REPORTS

Objectives:

1. To prepare title pages.
2. To apply report formatting skills.

85A–86A • 5' (daily) Conditioning Practice

Key each line twice SS; then key 30" writings on line 1; determine *gwam*.

alphabet 1 We moved quickly to pack an extra dozen lanyards Bif just bought.

fig/sym 2 I sold 22 at $45 less 13%, 8 at $69 less 5%, & 16 at $70 less 8%.

speed 3 Both of the men risk a big penalty if they dismantle their autos.

gwam 1' | 1 | 2 | 3 | 4 | 5 | 6 | 7 | 8 | 9 | 10 | 11 | 12 | 13 |

FORMATTING

85B–86B • 40' (daily) Bound and Unbound Reports

Document 1 (Bound Report with Textual Citations)

1. Review the format guides for bound reports on p. 137 and the model report on p. 142.
2. Format the text at the right and on the next page as a bound report, making the necessary changes.
3. You determine the font(s), font size(s), and font style(s).
4. Format the references as a separate page.
5. Proofread your work and correct all keying and formatting errors.

Save as: *RPT85B1*

THE GREAT LAKES

The five GReat Lakes are the largest group of freshwater lakes, in the world and they make up an inland waterway in North America the most important The lakes formed more than 250,000 years ago during the Ice Age.

A glacier moved south across the land of what is now the Great Lakes region. The glacier dug out deep depressions in the soft rocks of the region and picked up great amounts of earth and rocks. The glacier withdrew from 11,000 to 15,000 years ago, and the earth and rocks blocked the natural drainage of the depressions. Water from the melting glacier gradually filled in the depressions and formed the Great Lakes. (World Book Encyclopedia 1993)

Physical Features — Insert handwritten ¶ at end of report.

The Great Lakes have a combined area of 94,510 sqaure miles (244,780 square kilometers). Lake Superior, the largest of the lakes, is only slightly smaller than Maine; and Lake Ontario, the smallest of the lakes, is about the size of New Jersey.

The lakes vary quite a bit greatly in elevation. Lake Superior, the highest, lies 600 feet (183 meters) above sea level, while Lake Ontario, the lowest, lies just 245 feet meters (75 meters)) above sea level. There is a 325-foot difference in elevation between lakes Erie and Ontario. Most of the water from the lakes drains into the St. Lawrence River, which flows into the Atlantic Ocean (The World Almanac and Book of Facts 1999)

LESSON 111 ASSESS TABLE FORMATTING AND BASIC SKILLS

Objectives:

1. To assess table formatting skill.
2. To assess straight-copy skill.

111A • 5' Conditioning Practice

Key each line twice SS; then key 30" writings on line 3; determine *gwam.*

alphabet 1 Packy thought Dom's long joke about the next quiz was very funny.

figures 2 The listing on June 9, 2001, had 87 cars, 45 vans, and 36 trucks.

speed 3 Eight was the divisor for half the problems Nancy did on the bus.

gwam 1' | 1 | 2 | 3 | 4 | 5 | 6 | 7 | 8 | 9 | 10 | 11 | 12 | 13 |

111B • 30' Table, Agenda, and Itinerary

Document 1 (Table)

1. Center this table on the page. Make the amount columns equal width. Make all rows containing numbers the same height, and bottom-align those cell entries. Center all headings; left-align Column A and right-align all other columns; bold headings.
2. Shade the single-cell rows and Totals row, or apply an AutoFormat.

 **Save as:** *TBL111B1*

TOP FUNDRAISERS					words 3
Student	**March**	**April**	**May**	**Total**	9
Sophomore Class					12
Singleton Elizabeth	$525	$510	$893	$1,928	14 21
Kitterman Alexander	$475	$457	$614	$1,546	23 29
Junior Class					32
Gethsemane Constance	$513	$627	$739	$1,879	34 40
Biddlestone Christopher	$458	$761	$568	$1,787	43 50
Totals	$1,971	$2,355	$2,814	$7,140	56

Document 2 (Agenda)

Format and key this agenda.

 **Save as:** *AGNA111B2*

words

AGENDA 1

Hyattsville Zoo Support Group Meeting 9

September 23, 200- at 6:30 p.m. in Civic Center 19

1. Call to order . . . . Sam Kohl, President 26
2. Approval of June minutes . . . . Rosalita Jiminez, Secretary 37
3. Reports . . . . Treasurer and Committee Chairs 46
4. Unfinished business . . . . Sam Kohl 52
   A. Tour guide assignments . . . . Gerry Michaelson 61
   B. Fundraising . . . . Janice Sovich 66
5. New business 70
   A. Adopt-a-pet project . . . . Tom Hazel 76
   B. New directors . . . . Owen Burgman 82
6. Adjournment . . . . Sam Kohl 87

The depth of the Great Lakes varies. The deepest, Lake Superior, is 1,333 feet (406 meters) deep. Lake Erie, the shallowest, is only 210 feet (64 meters) deep (The Information Please Almanac 1994).

Connecting Waterways

Three sets of locks and canals make it possible for ships to sail from one Great Lake to another and from Lake Ontario to the Atlantic Ocean, from which they can sail to any port in the world. The canal and the bodies of water they connect are listed here.

1. Welland Canal--connects Lake Erie and Lake Ontario.

2. Soo Canal--connects Lake Superior and Lake Huron.

3. St. Lawrence Seaway--connects Lake Ontario with the ocean.

Significance of the Lakes

The five Great Lakes and the canals that link them together make up the most important inland water way in North America. They provide the inexpensive transportation system needed to make the Great Lakes region one of the most important industrial areas in the United States.

Although the Great Lakes (Lake Erie, Lake Huron, Lake Michigan, Lake Ontario, and Lake Superior) were all formed by glacial activity during the same period, they are quite different from one another. The irregular movement of the glacier created variation in the size, elevation, and depth of the lakes.

Use hanging indent style.

References

The Information Please Almanac. "Large Lakes of the World." Boston, MA: Houghton Mifflin Company, 1994.

The World Almanac and Book of Facts. "Major Natural Lakes of the World." Mahwah, NJ: World Almanac Books, 1999.

The World Book Encyclopedia. "Great Lakes." Chicago, IL: World Book, Inc., 1993.

Document 2 (Title Page)

1. Prepare a title page for the Great Lakes report.
2. Use your name, your school's name, and the current date.
3. Insert an appropriate page border. Insert clip art appropriately on the page.

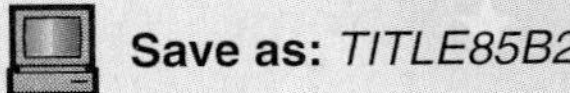

Save as: *TITLE85B2*

Learning **C · U · E**

To format a title page, center the report title in ALL CAPS on or near the 2" line. Center the writer's name on or near the 5" line, and center the writer's organization a DS below the name (both in Title Case). Center the date on or near the 9" line.

Document 3 (MLA Report)

1. Key the report at the right in MLA format. Identification information follows.

   Student's name: **Kirk Robey**

   Instructor's name: **Ms. Li Pak**

   Course: **Computer Literacy**

   Date: **25 June 200-**
2. Add this bulleted item at the end of the report:
   - **Designing and posting a Web page to provide information about yourself, your family, a club or organization, or a business.**
3. Place these works cited on a separate page:

Fulton-Calkins, Patsy. Office Technology and Procedures, 5th ed. Cincinnati: South-Western Educational Publishing, 1998.

Odgers, Pattie and B. Lewis Keeling. Administrative Office Management, 12th ed. Cincinnati: South-Western Educational Publishing, 2000.

Oliverio, Mary Ellen, William R. Pasewark, and Bonnie R. White. The Office: Procedures and Technology, 3d ed. Cincinnati: South-Western Educational Publishing, 1998.

 **Save as:** *MLA110B3*

Document 4 (Title Page)

Key a title page for Document 3. Use your school name. Add a page border and/or clip art.

 **Save as:** *TP110B4*

words

opener 11

The Internet 13

Anyone using computers for school, business, or personal use 25
knows the difficulty of keeping up with changing technology. 38
Computer users are demanding that microprocessors become faster 51
and easier to use in order to keep up with the many applications used 65
today. Just when users thought they were catching up, the Internet 78
became popular. 82

Defining the Internet 86

Networks have changed the way people communicate. Each day, 98
transactions are sent across high-speed connections to computers all 112
over the world via the Internet. A working definition of the Internet 126
follows: 128

> The Internet is an international "network of networks" comprised 141
> of government, academic, and business-related networks that 153
> allow people at diverse locations around the world to 164
> communicate through electronic mail, to transfer files back and 177
> forth, and to log on to remote computer facilities. (Odgers and 189
> Keeling 289) 192

Connecting to the Internet 198

You must have a device called a modem to link your computer to 210
other computers through telephone or cable lines. With some 223
connections, you need to have an account name and password to 235
access the Internet; with others, you may be connected directly to the 249
Internet and need only to "click" the Internet icon on your computer's 263
desktop (Fulton-Calkins 62). 269

If you are using the Internet at school or work, the organization 283
is paying a fee for use of the Internet. If you want to access the 296
Internet on your home computer, you will need to subscribe to a 309
commercial Internet service provider (often referred to as an ISP). 323
Most of these providers charge a monthly fee. 332

Using the Internet 336

Once you have access to the Internet, you will find many uses 348
for it (Oliverio, Pasewark, and White 699). You will want to establish an 363
e-mail account so you can send electronic messages to your 375
friends and relatives who are also connected to the Internet. You can 389
also use e-mail to send word processing, spreadsheet, database, and 403
presentation files, including pictures, to others. 413

In addition to e-mail, the Internet has many other useful 425
applications. Common uses include: 432

- Retrieving information by using search engines or directories 445
  that enable you to search massive databases. 454
- Using bulletin boards to read and post messages related to 466
  topics of interest to you and others. 474

additional bulleted item 499

Document 3 (News Release)

1. Format the text at the right as a news release.
2. Insert **For Release: Immediate** and **Contact: Heidi Zemack** above the body of the news release.

 **Save as:** *NEWS85B3*

CLEVELAND, OH, May 25, 200-. Science teachers from school districts in six counties are eligible for this year's Teacher Excellence awards funded by The Society for Environmental Engineers.

Nominations can be submitted through Friday, July 31, by students, parents, residents, and other educators. Nomination forms are available from the participating school districts or on the Society's Web site at http://www.tsee.org/tea.html.

An anonymous committee reviews the nominations and selects ten finalists. From that group, seven "teachers of distinction" and three award winners are selected. The top award winner receives $5,000, the second receives $2,500, and the third receives $1,500. Each teacher of distinction receives $500. The teachers of distinction and the award winners will be announced on September 5 at a dinner at the Cleveland Inn.

School districts participating in the program include those in these counties: Cuyahoga, Lorain, Medina, Summit, Lake, and Geauga.

Document 4 (Unbound Report)

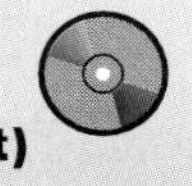

Note:
Review Endnotes on p. 135.

1. Format the copy below and on the next page as an unbound report with endnotes.
2. You determine font(s), font size(s), and font style(s); also, location and format of page numbers.
3. Insert file *CD-RPT85B4* where indicated.
4. Format the references as a separate page.

 **Save as:** *RPT85B4*

---

words

LEADERSHIP SEMINAR PROGRESS REPORT 7
Development of the leadership seminars 15
for supervisors and first-line managers is pro- 24
gressing on schedule. One seminar will be 33
conducted at each of the four Indiana plant 41
sites. The primary objective of the seminars is 51
to have the participants understand the follow- 60
ing points: 63

- The importance of having leaders at all 71
levels of the corporation. 77
- The definition of leadership. 84
- How leadership traits are developed for 92
use within the corporation and the 99
community. 101
- That various styles of leadership exist 110
and that there is no one best leader- 117
ship style. 120

Seminar Presenter 123
Three staff members observed training 131
sessions conducted by five professional training 141
and development companies before selecting 149
the firm to conduct these leadership seminars. 159
Derme & Associates, Inc., a local consulting 168
firm specializing in career enhancement semi- 177
nars, has been selected to develop and conduct 186
the four seminars. 190

words

One reason for selecting Derme & 197
Associates is that they will develop the content 206
of the seminars around Odgers and Keeling's 215
definition of leadership,[1] which we want to 224
emphasize with employees. 229

[1]Pattie Odgers and B. Lewis Keeling, 237 Administrative Office Management (Cincinnati: 246 South-Western Educational Publishing, 2000), 255 p. 419. 257

Seminar Development 261
We have had two meetings with partners 269
of Derme & Associates since the signing of the 278
agreement two weeks ago. 283
The first meeting was held so that we 291
could learn about the content of leadership 300
seminars that Derme & Associates, Inc., has 309
presented for other clients. 315
The specific content of the four seminars 323
was identified at the second meeting. Also, we 333
decided to use the prepared content for each 342
seminar except for the changes we suggest. 350
These suggestions will be based on the feed- 359
back we get from the participants at the end of 369
each seminar. 372

(Report continued on next page)

110B • 45'
Reports

Document 1 (Outline)

Format and key the outline at the right. Key first-level topics in ALL CAPS.

Save as: *TOL110B1*

words

LEADERSHIP SEMINAR PROGRESS REPORT 7

I. Introduction 10
II. Seminar presenter 15
    A. Selection--Jackson & Associates selected 23
    B. Reason--Jackson & Associates' definition of leadership 35
III. Seminar development 40
    A. Meeting #1--Review content of previous seminars 50
    B. Meeting #2--Decide content of seminars 59
IV. Seminar dates and locations 65
    A. October 15--Coultersville 71
    B. October 22--North Irwin 76
    C. October 29--Port Washington 82
    D. November 5--Portersburg 88
V. Seminar content 92
    A. Leadership characteristics 98
        1. Social and environmental responsibility 106
        2. International awareness 112
        3. Honesty and consistency 117
    B. Leadership styles--from autocratic to democratic 127

Document 2 (Minutes)

Format and key the minutes at the right.

Save as: *MIN110B2*

words

GREENWOOD HIGH SCHOOL SCIENCE CLUB 7

May 15, 200-, Meeting Minutes 13

All officers, committee heads, and 15 members were present. Sponsor 27
Terry L. Gronbacher was present. 34

1. President Dee McClinton called the meeting to order at 2:25 p.m. 47

2. Secretary Sue Smedley read the minutes, which were accepted. 60

3. Treasurer LaVerne Blatt distributed the April 30 balance sheet and 74
   income statement and reported a balance of $1,056. The 86
   treasurer's report was approved by unanimous vote. 96

4. Victor Block, fundraising committee chair, reported that $376.09 110
   was raised from the windsock sale. 117

5. Under unfinished business, President McClinton reported that the 130
   school science fair will have 150 exhibits. Awards will be given to 144
   first-, second-, and third-place winners by grade level. Engineers 158
   from Greenwood Laboratories will serve as judges and assist in 170
   presenting the awards. 175

6. Under new business, the Club approved the purchase of a 187
   microscope as the Science Club's gift to the Greenwood High 199
   School Science Department. The microscope will be presented to 212
   the Greenwood Board of Education at its June meeting. 223

7. The meeting ended at 3:35 p.m. 229

words

Seminar Dates 374
The first seminar will be on October 15 at 383
the Logansport Plant; the second will be at the 393
Muncie Plant on October 22; the third meets at 402
the Fort Wayne Plant on October 29; and the 411
fourth will be at the Evansville Plant on 419
November 5. The 85 employees who are to 427
attend will be notified of the dates and times by 437
the end of this week. Instructions will be given 447
for arranging coverage during the attendees' 456
absences. 459

Seminar Content 462
The seminars will focus on leadership 469
characteristics and styles that are applicable 479
to most work and community environments. 487

words

The following four characteristics will be 496
targeted for development: 501

- Social and environmental responsi- 508
  bility. 510
- International awareness. 516
- The importance of honesty. 522
- The consistent leader.[2] 527

[2]Patsy Fulton-Calkins and Joanna Hanks, 535
Procedures for the Office Professional, 4th ed. 545
(Cincinnati: South-Western Educational Pub- 553
lishing, 2000), p. 558. 558

(Insert file *CD-RPT85B4* here; proofread it carefully and format the text to match the text you keyed.)

Document 5 (Title Page)

Prepare a title page for the leadership report, using the information at the right.

1. Use **LEADERSHIP SEMINAR PROGRESS REPORT** as the title.
2. Use **Kimberly Jurgaitis** as the writer, **The Kemp Group** as the organization, and **August 15, 200-** as the date.
3. Insert an appropriate page border.
4. Insert clip art appropriately on the page.

Save as: *TITLE85B5*

LANGUAGE SKILLS

85C–86C • 5'
Language Skills: Word Choice

1. Study the spelling and definitions of the words at the right.
2. Key the Learn lines, noting word choice.
3. Key the Apply lines, selecting the correct word.
4. Check your work with the instructor. Rekey lines that contain a word-choice error.

Save as: *CHOICE85C*

affect (vb) to influence

effect (n) result; consequence; (vb) to cause; to accomplish

complement (n) something that completes or makes up a whole

compliment (n) an expression of praise or congratulation

Learn 1 The **effect** of the recent change will **affect** our annual profit.
Apply 2 Will cutting the staff 25 percent (affect/effect) worker morale?
Apply 3 What (affect/effect) will new equipment have on productivity?

Learn 1 Jo's **compliment** to Dan was that his tie **complemented** his suit.
Apply 2 The laser printer is a (complement/compliment) to the system.
Apply 3 Gloria accepted Kevin's (complement/compliment) with a smile.

INTERNET ACTIVITY

1. Access the National Air and Space Museum at http://www.nasm.si.edu.
2. Find answers to the questions at the right.
3. Key your answers in sentence form.

1. How long and how far did Orville Wright fly during the Kitty Hawk's first flight (12/17/1903)? How much did the Kitty Hawk weigh?
2. What were the three parts of the Apollo 11 spacecraft (first manned flight to land on the moon)? How much did Apollo 11 weigh?
3. How many miles did the Breitling Orbiter 3 Gondola fly during the first nonstop balloon flight around the world (March 1999)? How much did the gondola weigh?

Document 4 (Two-page Memo)

Format the copy at the right as a memo. Insert the *CD-109B-4* file where indicated.

Save as: *MEMO109B4*

words

TO: Dorothy A. McIlvain, Dean, Semak College of Arts and Sciences | 13
FROM: Jim R. Tedrow, Head, Faculty Committee on Freshman 25
Qualifications | DATE: June 15, 200- | SUBJECT: SCHOOL OF 36
ARTS AND SCIENCES FRESHMAN MATH SKILLS 44

(¶) At a recent meeting of the Faculty Committee on Freshman 55
Qualifications, the Enrollment Management representative reported 69
that freshmen entering the Semak College of Arts and Sciences (SCAS) 82
this year have higher average SAT math scores than the freshmen who 96
entered SCAS in each of the past five years. 105

(¶) Much discussion centered on the significance of the increase, and we 119
finally decided to compare the math placement records for these same 133
freshmen over the same time period. By doing this, the committee 146
believes it can determine if students are being placed into higher-level 160
math courses as a result of the increase in scores. 171

(¶) This study revealed the course placements (by percent and number) 184
that are reported below. ***(Insert CD-109B-4 here.)*** 189

(¶) A comparison of the course placements reveals a steady decline in 202
the percent and number of students needing to enter MATH 100 Pre- 215
college Algebra and a steady increase in the percent and number of 229
students entering MATH 180 College Algebra and MATH 250 Calculus 242
I. This finding supports the contention that as SAT math scores 254
increase, students will begin their college studies in higher-level 268
courses. 270

(¶) This comparison will be reported to Dr. Theodore R. Ostrom, head of 284
the Mathematics Department in SCAS. He and his faculty will then 297
know that more and more arts and sciences students are enrolling in 310
higher-level math courses and that the number needing MATH 100 is 324
decreasing. 326

(¶) I will e-mail the comparison to all SCAS faculty so that they, too, will 341
be aware of the increasing mathematical ability of the students entering 355
SCAS programs. 359

(¶) Perhaps you would like to share this information with the dean of 372
the School of Education since it provides further evidence of success in 386
the education reform movement. 392

LESSON 110 ASSESS REPORT FORMATTING SKILL

Objectives:

1. To assess outline and report formatting skill.
2. To assess formatting skill on minutes and news releases.

110A • 5' Conditioning Practice

Key each line twice SS; then take 30" writings on line 3; determine *gwam.*

alphabet 1 Myra's expensive black racquet is just a wrong size for children.

figures 2 Order 97-341 for 20 Series 568 storm windows was faxed on May 25.

speed 3 Claudia saw my hand signal to go right when she got to the field.

gwam 1' | 1 | 2 | 3 | 4 | 5 | 6 | 7 | 8 | 9 | 10 | 11 | 12 | 13 |

SKILL BUILDER 5

Timed Writings: Straight Copy

1. Key a 5' writing on ¶s 1–3 combined; determine *gwam* and count errors.
2. Take two 1' writings on each ¶; determine *gwam* and count errors.
3. Key another 5' writing on ¶s 1–3 combined; determine *gwam* and count errors.

Additional Skill Building

1. Key a series of 1' guided writings on each ¶. Maximum: three writings per ¶.
2. Key additional 5' writings to measure skill increases.

Quarter-Minute Checkpoints				
gwam	1/4'	1/2'	3/4'	1'
24	6	12	18	24
28	7	14	21	28
32	8	16	24	32
36	9	18	27	36
40	10	20	30	40
44	11	22	33	44
48	12	24	36	48
52	13	26	39	52
56	14	28	42	56

A all letters used

Text	gwam 3'	5'	
New office technology continues to have a major impact on the	4	2	56
way we exchange information. Until recently most of us shared	8	5	59
information with other firms by using the mail service or by using	13	8	62
the phone. Today we can still use those same media, or we can use	17	10	64
newer electronic means to communicate with others. More and more	22	13	67
people are using the newer electronic media because of the speed	26	16	70
and ease with which information can be shared.	29	17	71
Electronic mail and fax transmission are among the most	33	20	74
recent technologies that have had a great impact on the sending	37	22	76
and receiving of data and text in the office. The fax machine is	41	25	79
a machine that sends documents electronically from one place to	46	27	81
another in a matter of a few seconds. Even though this concept	50	30	84
is not a new one, its use in the office environment is relatively	54	33	87
new. Even greater usage can be expected in the future.	58	35	89
It is hard to imagine the impact that future changes in	62	37	91
technology will have on how we share data and text with others in	66	40	94
the office. If changes in the next few years are as great as	70	42	96
those we have had during the last few years, the impact will be	75	45	99
quite amazing. Microcomputers, word processing packages,	78	47	101
spreadsheets, and laser printers are all relatively new concepts	83	50	104
in business. It really has not been all that long ago that most	87	52	106
information was processed at a typewriter.	90	54	108

gwam 3' | 1 | 2 | 3 | 4
5' | 1 | 2 | 3

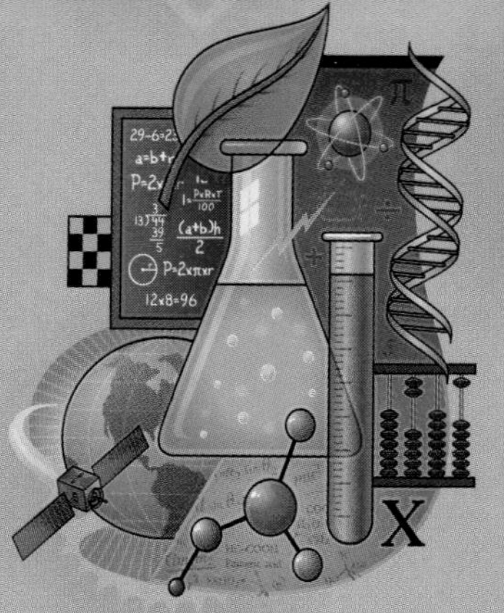

UNIT 29

LESSONS 109-111

Assessing Document Formatting Skills

LESSON 109 ASSESS CORRESPONDENCE FORMATTING SKILL

Objective:
To assess letter, memo, and e-mail formatting skills.

109A • 5' Conditioning Practice

Key each line twice SS; then key 30" writings on line 3; determine *gwam.*

alphabet 1 Jimmy wants seven pens and extra clips in a kit for the big quiz.

figures 2 I sold 56 advertisements for $6,798 between 9/14/02 and 12/25/03.

speed 3 A goal of the proficient tutor is to quantify the right problems.

gwam 1' | 1 | 2 | 3 | 4 | 5 | 6 | 7 | 8 | 9 | 10 | 11 | 12 | 13 |

109B • 45' Correspondence

Document 1 (Letter)

Prepare the letter using modified block format, open punctuation, and no ¶ indentations.

 **Save as:** *LTR109B1*

Document 2 (Letter)

1. Change Document 1 to block format with mixed punctuation.
2. Delete the subject line, copy notation, and postscript.

Save as: *LTR109B2*

Document 3 (E-mail)

With e-mail software: E-mail this message to your instructor; attach your *MLA107B3* file. Send one classmate a courtesy copy.

With wp software: Format the text as a memo to your instructor; attach file *MLA107B3*. Use the current date. Prepare a copy for a classmate.

 **Save as:** *MAIL109B3* (*MEMO109B3*)

words

June 9, 200- | Mrs. Vera L. Bowden | 3491 Rose St. | Minneapolis, MN 13
55441-5781 | Dear Mrs. Bowden | SUBJECT: YOUR DONATION 23

(¶) What a pleasant surprise it was to find your $50 donation to Beta Xi 37
in my mail this morning. I think it is great that you thought of Beta Xi 52
and decided to help members of your local chapter serve those who are 66
less fortunate. 69

(¶) Your contribution will be used to purchase food and clothing for 82
young children in our community as part of Community Day. As you 95
know, Beta Xi, Minnesota Epsilon Chapter, conducts a fall drive to 109
support this event. 113

(¶) I have heard about the success you are having in microbiology. 125
Perhaps you would return to speak to our Beta Xi members? Please 139
let me know if you can. 144

Yours truly | Miss Amelia R. Carter | Beta Xi Sponsor | xx | 154
Enclosure | c Thomas Turnball, Treasurer | A receipt is enclosed 166
since your contribution is tax deductible. 175

words

Subject: CAREER INTEREST 5

My report about health-care management--one of my career interests-- 19
is attached. I will be ready to give a two-minute presentation (with 33
three to five slides) in class next Tuesday. 42

In the meantime, I have an appointment with my vocational guidance 55
counselor, Mr. Duncan. Also, since my mother is a health-care 68
manager at Richland County Hospital, I'm going to talk with her some 82
more about her work. 86

ACTIVITY 1

Tab Stops and Indentations in Tables

1. Read the copy at the right.
2. Learn to use tab stops and indentations with your software.
3. Format and key Table 1 in a 12-pt. font, using:
   - a left tab to indent first name and initial 0.2" under last name (Column A).
   - a 0.2" first-line indentation (Column B).
   - a decimal tab near the center of Column C.
   - a right tab with dot leaders about 0.2" from the right edge of Column D.
4. Vertically center all text within the cells; horizontally center and bold the main title and column headings.
5. Center the table on the page.

 **Save as:** *WP11ACT1*

Tab stops and indentations can be set within table cells in much the same way they are set in document text. While all tab stops and indentations can be used within cells, the left tab, decimal tab, dot leader tabs, first-line indentation, and hanging indentation are used most frequently. The illustration below shows these various tab stops and indentations.

Left tab	Decimal tab	Right tab with dot leader	First line indent	Hanging indent
Lawrence Mary Sue	123.456 12.34 12345.6789	.... Lawrence .... Mary .... Sue	This is an example of first line indent.	This is an example of hanging indent.

TABLE 1 RESULTS OF MATH COMPETITION			
Name of Student	**Student's Recent Math Background**	**Answer Submitted**	**Prize**
Ankenbrandt Rebecca	Algebra I in the freshman year. Geometry in the sophomore year.	9726.35569	. . Second Place--$100
Frontier George H.	Algebra II in the sophomore year. Pre-Calculus in the junior year.	9727.34	. . . . First Place--$250
Pappalardo Brandey L.	Algebra II in the freshman year. Trigonometry in the sophomore year.	9726.3256	. . . . Third Place--$50

ACTIVITY 2

AutoFormat

1. Read the copy at the right.
2. Learn to use the AutoFormat feature in your software.
3. Follow the directions at the right using the feature.

Most wp software has many predesigned table formats from which you can select. Because these designs include alignment, borders, effects, shading, and font, they save time. These formats can be modified for specific rows or columns or the entire table.

1. Open *CD-WP11ACT2*.
2. Format the table using only horizontal lines, with or without color, and no shading.

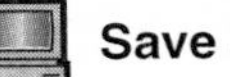 **Save as:** *WP11ACT2A*

3. Reformat the table with vertical and horizontal lines, shading, and color.

 **Save as:** *WP11ACT2B*

4. Reformat the table by choosing a format that you think is appropriate.

 **Save as:** *WP11ACT2C*

Document 3 (Itinerary)

Format the itinerary shown at the right as a three-column table. Select and apply an AutoFormat.

 **Save as:** *ITIN108B3*

TRAVEL ITINERARY **Ronald T. Melrose** **American Science Teachers Association Conference**		
Date	**Time**	**Flight Information**
August 23	2:47 p.m.	Depart Wichita on West Air (Flight 835) for Louisville, KY.
	6:14 p.m.	Arrive Louisville; take Caldwell Shuttle to Caldwell Hotel, 572 Sage Street.
August 25	2:15 p.m.	Depart hotel via Caldwell Shuttle for Louisville Airport.
	3:30 p.m.	Depart Louisville on West Air (Flight 259) for Wichita.
	4:33 p.m.	Arrive Wichita.

108C • 15' Timed Writing

Take two 5' writings on the three ¶s at the right; determine *gwam;* count errors.

  all letters used

gwam 3' | 5'

Learning to prepare a good resume is an important step in 4 2 52
the process of searching for a job. The resume given to a 8 5 54
prospective employer is critical because the average time an 12 7 57
employer takes to review a resume is about one-third of a minute, 16 10 59
studies have shown. You have only about twenty seconds, there- 20 12 62
fore, to make the impression that you have something extra to 25 15 64
offer and are worth more attention. 27 16 66

To make a good presentation, you should plan carefully what 31 19 68
you want to include in your resume. Begin by taking time to 35 21 71
prepare a list of your most important attributes. The list may 39 24 73
include many of the business courses you completed, the quality 44 26 76
point average you attained, the clubs you joined, the offices you 48 29 78
held, and the awards and honors you won. Also, be sure to 52 31 81
describe any jobs you held while attending school. 55 33 83

After you have selected the content of your resume, you 59 36 85
should format it so that your strengths are emphasized early. 63 38 88
Make a point of explaining how your strengths relate to the 67 40 90
position for which you are applying. Most students find that 72 43 92
they prefer to list their related educational experience at the 76 45 95
beginning of the resume because it is often the most valuable 80 48 97
quality being offered to the employer. 82 49 99

ACTIVITY 3

Changing Row Height and Column Width

1. Read the copy at the right.
2. Learn to use the AutoFit feature in your software.
3. Follow the directions at the right using AutoFit.

Once a table has been created, you can quickly resize the columns and rows to fit the data. You can use the **AutoFit** feature to modify each column's width so it automatically matches the column's content. You can also use AutoFit to make multiple rows or columns within a table the same size.

1. Open *CD-WP11ACT3A.* Use AutoFit to make the width of each column match the width of its contents.

 **Save as:** *WP11ACT3A*

2. Open *CD-WP11ACT3B.* Use AutoFit to make the last two columns the same width.
3. Center the column headings vertically.

 **Save as:** *WP11ACT3B*

ACTIVITY 4

Border Color and Font Color

1. Read the copy at the right. Learn to change border color and font color using your software.
2. Key the table at the right using equal columns.
3. Apply an appropriate predesigned format.
4. Make each column width match the contents of the column.
5. Change the color of all vertical borders; change the text color of headings.
6. Center the table on the page.

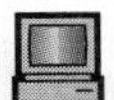 **Save as:** *WP11ACT4*

The color of table borders can be changed. One color may be used for all borders, or a different color may be used to highlight a specific cell, column, or row.

The **Font Color** feature changes text from black to many other colors. It is important to use a font color that contrasts clearly with the background (shading or paper color).

The wp features change border and font colors onscreen, but the printer must support color options for these changes to appear in printed documents.

GAME STATISTICS FOR NOEL FORD

Opponent	Tackles	For Loss	Sacks
James Madison	5	2	1
Woodward	6	2	3
Jennings	5	3	2
East Ford	5	3	1
Jones Mill	4	1	1
South Harris	7	4	3
Mapleton	6	2	2
Sussex	8	3	4
Totals	46	20	17

ACTIVITY 5

Apply What You Have Learned

1. Key the table at the right, using equal columns and a decimal tab in Column E.
2. Reformat the table by making each column width match the contents.
3. Center the table on the page and show gridlines.

 **Save as:** *WP11ACT5A*

4. Reformat the table by making the width of the last four columns equal and hiding the gridlines.

Save as: *WP11ACT5B*

CENTRAL CONFERENCE STANDINGS

Team	Won	Lost	Tied	Pct.
Harrison	24	0	0	1.000
Pikesville	20	3	1	.833
Doylestown	19	5	0	.792
Kingston	15	9	0	.625
Westerville	14	9	1	.583
Linesville	9	15	0	.375
Bedford	7	17	0	.292
Laurel Hills	5	19	0	.208
Southfield	3	20	1	.125
Creekside	2	21	1	.083

LESSON 108 PREPARE TO ASSESS TABLE PROCESSING AND BASIC SKILLS

Objectives:

1. To prepare for assessment of table processing skill.
2. To prepare for assessment of straight-copy skill.

108A • 5' Conditioning Practice

Key each line twice SS; then key 30" writings on line 3; determine *gwam.*

alphabet 1 Kay Gazbo is not exempt from equal justice if she violated a law.

figures 2 Order monitor 4103, printer 5278, and fax 3956 for the registrar.

speed 3 To their dismay, the haughty man kept the dog by the city kennel.

gwam 1' | 1 | 2 | 3 | 4 | 5 | 6 | 7 | 8 | 9 | 10 | 11 | 12 | 13 |

108B • 30' Table, Agenda, and Itinerary

Document 1 (Table)

1. Center this table on the page; make the amount columns equal width. Make all rows containing numbers the same height, and bottom-align these cell entries. Left-align Column A and center all other columns.
2. Shade the last column or apply a simple AutoFormat.

Save as: *TBL108B1*

TUITION INCOME COMPARISON BY SCHOOL				words
				7
Department	**This Year**	**Last Year**	**% Change**	15
Liberal Arts				18
English	$44,653	$43,543	2.55%	24
Social Sciences	$75,566	$72,983	3.53%	25 / 31
Natural Sciences	$55,678	$53,978	3.15%	33 / 39
Business				41
Accounting	$45,391	$42,687	6.3%	47
Computer Science	$47,814	$45,806	4.4%	49 / 54

Document 2 (Agenda)

Format and key this agenda. Refer to p. 243.

Save as: *AGNA108B2*

words

AGENDA 1

Salinas County Environmental Society 9

1. Call to order . . . . Sally Kurt, President 17
2. Approval of January minutes . . . . John Green, Secretary 27
3. Treasurer's report . . . . Mary Perez, Treasurer 36
4. Strategic planning report . . . . Debbie Turk 44
5. Education committee report . . . . Juan Quinnes 53
6. Unfinished business . . . . Sally Kurt 60
7. New Business 63
   A. Rezoning of Helton property . . . . Tom Kite, SCES 72
   B. Adopt-a-lot project . . . . Debbie Turk 79
8. Adjournment . . . . Sally Kurt 84

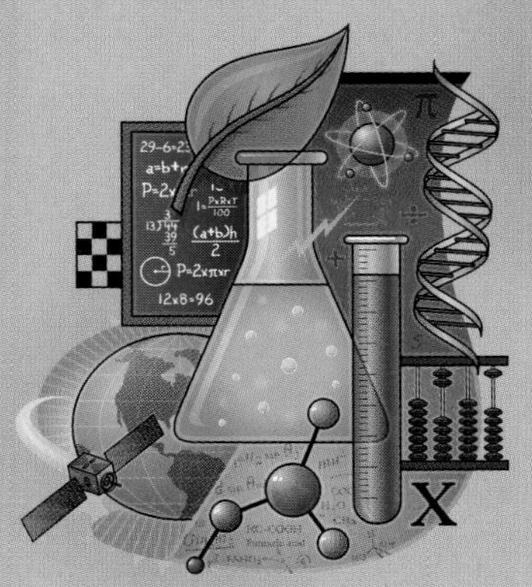

UNIT 24

LESSONS 87–92

Improving Table Formatting Skills

Format Guides: Itineraries and Agendas

Itinerary

Agenda

Formatting tables using software Table features is the focus of this unit. A document called an *itinerary*, which is keyed in a table shell, is introduced later in the unit. A document called an *agenda* is introduced in the last lesson. Though not a table, an agenda contains two columns of text, connected by dot leaders.

Itinerary

An itinerary (see illustration at the left) is an outline of a person's travel activities for a specific period of time. The information on an itinerary is attractively formatted to show at a glance the traveler's approximate location and activity at all times while away.

An itinerary can be prepared as a centered table with or without gridlines.

Agenda

An agenda (see illustration at the left) is a list of things to be done or actions to be taken, usually at a meeting. An agenda is prepared with a 2" top margin (or centered vertically),* 1" side margins, and a 1" bottom margin (approximate). The main and secondary headings are DS. A DS precedes and follows each main agenda item; other items may be SS.

Agendas are usually prepared by setting a right tab stop with dot leaders at the right margin and keying the text in the right column at this tab stop.

*If an agenda has more than one page, each page after page 1 has a 1" top margin.

LESSON 87 FORMAT TABLES WITH TAB STOPS AND INDENTATIONS

Objectives:

1. To prepare tables with tab stops in cells.
2. To prepare tables with indentations in cells.

87A • 5' Conditioning Practice

Key each line twice SS; key 30" writings on line 2; determine *gwam*.

alphabet 1 Lizzy checked the liquid oxygen just before moving down the path.

figures 2 Her fax (50-473) was $256.98 and his ink jet printer was $175.59.

speed 3 Did eight firms bid for title to the authentic map of the island?

gwam 1' | 1 | 2 | 3 | 4 | 5 | 6 | 7 | 8 | 9 | 10 | 11 | 12 | 13 |

Document 3 (MLA Report)

1. Format and key the report at the right, using MLA style.
2. Add these two groups as bulleted items at the end of the report:
   - **Medical Group Management Association, 104 Inverness Terrace E., Englewood, CO 80112-5313**
   - **American College of Health Care Administrators, P.O. Box 5890, 8120 Woodmont Ave., Ste. 200, Bethesda, MD 20814-3219**
3. Place the works cited below on a separate page at the end of the report.

Kleiman, Carol. 100 Best Job$ for the 1990s & Beyond. Chicago: Dearborn Financial Publishing, Inc., 2000.

United States Department of Labor, Bureau of Statistics. Occupational Outlook Handbook: 1998-1999 ed. http://stats.bls.gov/oco/ocos014.htm (25 January 2000).

Refer to p. 226 as needed.

Save as: *MLA107B3*

Document 4 (Title Page)

Key a title page for Document 3. Use your school name. Add clip art representing health care and/or a page border.

Save as: *TP107B4*

words

Susan LeCartia 3
Ms. Julia Betters 7
Introduction to Business 12
5 June 200- 14

Health Services Management Program 21

This report gives information about opportunities in health 33
services management, a program of study that several of my 45
classmates and I are considering upon graduation from high school. 58

Employment Opportunities 63

Opportunities for employment in health services are numerous 75
and growing "faster than the average for all occupations through the 89
year 2006 as health services continue to expand and diversify" (United 103
States Department of Labor 2000). 111

People who manage health services are needed in a wide variety 123
of work settings. The most common place of employment for these 136
individuals is hospitals, followed by the offices of physicians, dentists, 151
and other health-related practitioners (United States Department of 165
Labor 2000). 168

Careers in the health-care area are included in Kleiman's 100 180
Best Job$ for the 1990s & Beyond (197–228). Demand for health 193
services managers is expected to be strong as the country's population 207
ages and uses more health-care services. Also, demand for managers 221
will increase as the providers of health care become more oriented to 235
the bottom line because of competition and the need to cut costs. 248

Educational Opportunities 253

> In 1999, 36 colleges and universities offered bachelor's degree 266
> programs in health services administration. Seventy-seven 278
> schools had programs leading to the master's degree in health 290
> services administration. . . . (United States Department of Labor 303
> 2000) 305

Health services managers are often recruited from the college or 318
university they attend before they graduate. In larger hospitals, they 332
are often recruited to fill assistant department head positions. In 346
smaller hospitals, they may enter at the department head level. 359

Additional Information 364

The organizations listed below will be contacted to gather 375
information about academic programs and employment opportunities 388
in health services management. 395

- American College of Healthcare Executives, One N. Franklin 407
  St., Ste. 1700, Chicago, IL 60606-3421. Home page: 418
  http://www.ache.org 422
- Association of University Programs in Health Administration, 434
  1911 N. Fort Meyer Dr., Ste. 503, Arlington, VA 22209-1603. 446
  Home page: http://www.aupha.org 453

additional bulleted items 495

87B • 45'
Tables with Tab Stops and Indentations

Table 1

1. Center on page; bold and center main title and column headings; align numbers at decimal point in Column C.
2. Change height of Row 1 to 0.5"; all others to 0.3".
3. Center the title vertically.

 **Save as:** *TBL87B1*

Table 2

Center on page; bold and center main title, column headings, and fund names; center all data vertically in cells.

 **Save as:** *TBL87B2*

Table 3

1. Open Table 2 (*TBL87B2*) and make these changes:
   Column A: Add
   Philadelphia Fund
   Real Estate
   Government Bonds
   Column B: **NA**
   Column C: **$25,896**
   Column D: **Beneficiary**
2. Sort funds by Value This Year (Column C) in descending order.

 **Save as:** *TBL87B3*

Table 4

1. Set width of Columns A and B to 1.5"; Column C to 2.5".
2. Set left tab in Column A; use hanging indent in Column C.
3. Center on page; bold and center main title and column headings; bold office name; center all data vertically in cells.
4. Make the last three rows equal height.
5. Make Row 1 0.5" high.

 **Save as:** *TBL87B4*

CONVERSION FACTORS		
To Change	**To**	**Multiply By**
feet	meters	.3048
meters	feet	3.2808
gallons	liters	3.7853
liters	gallons	.2642
inches	millimeters	25.4
millimeters	inches	.0394

INVESTMENTS			
Mutual Fund	**Value Last Year**	**Value This Year**	**Destination**
Washington Fund Small Cap Growth Corporate Bonds Money Market	$162,930	$179,223	Family Trust
Iroquois Fund Large Cap Stock Balanced Stock Money Market	$53,123	$61,149	Family Trust
President's Fund Low Grade Bonds Global Bonds Foreign Stock Balanced Stock	$123,897	$133,808	Beneficiary

SELECTED EXECUTIVE BOARD OFFICERS		
Name and Office	**Primary Occupation**	**Education**
Andrea Potter **Chairperson**	Securities Analyst	B.S. degree in finance from Bastion College M.S. degree in finance from Welling College
David Gerea **President**	Actuary	B.A. and M.S. degrees in math from Reed University
Susan Flanagan **Treasurer**	Attorney	B.A. degree in history and J.D. degree from Hearth College

107B • 45'
Reports

Document 1 (Outline)

Format and key the topic outline at the right. Use a 2" top margin. Show first-level topics in ALL CAPS. Refer to p. 226 if necessary.

Save as: *TOL107B1*

words

HIRING EMPLOYEES 3

I. Establish position goals, aims, and purposes 13
  A. Consult staff members 18
  B. Determine company trends and needs 26
  C. Write position requirements 32
II. Advertise the position 37
  A. Professional journals 42
  B. Area newspapers 46
    1. Daily papers 49
    2. Sunday papers 53
  C. Personal calls 56
  D. Placement services 61
III. Hire the right person 66
  A. Evaluate applicants' resumes 72
  B. Identify top applicants 78
    1. Check references and credentials 85
    2. Rank applicants 89
  C. Interview top three applicants 96
  D. Decide top applicant 100
  E. Make offer 103

Document 2 (Minutes)

Format and key the minutes at the right. Refer to p. 226 as needed.

Save as: *MIN107B2*

words

MATH DEPARTMENT PLANNING MEETING MINUTES 8

November 12, 200- 12

Department members present: All teachers were present. 23

1. Michael Mariani called the meeting to order at 2:30 p.m. 35
2. Minutes of the October 11 meeting were approved. 46
3. Nancy Thayer explained the planning procedures to be used to 59 identify external factors that are apt to affect the school's math 72 curriculum during the next five years: 80
   A. Spend ten minutes writing the external factors on small 92 notepaper. Council members will prepare their notes 103 individually. 106
   B. Post written notes on the walls. 113
   C. Review all posted notes and group similar ones. Members will 126 not talk to each other during this time. 134
   D. Discuss the groupings and attempt to label each group. 146
   E. Make needed revisions to the factors in each group. 157
4. The planning council carried out the planning procedures and 170 generated about two dozen external factors that were grouped into 183 six categories. The factors and categories will be processed and 197 distributed to the faculty before the December 14 meeting. 209
5. The meeting was adjourned at 4:30 p.m. 217

FORMAT TABLES WITH COLUMN WIDTHS SET AUTOMATICALLY

Objectives:

1. To prepare tables with column widths set automatically to contents of columns.
2. To improve table formatting skills.

88A • 5'
Conditioning Practice

Key each line twice SS; then take 30" writings on line 2; determine *gwam*.

alphabet 1 Jacques puzzled over the large amount of worker tax paid by Ruth.

figures 2 Robert flew 3,670 miles in May, 2,980 in June, and 1,450 in July.

speed 3 Eight ensigns and the airmen got the visual signal to turn right.

gwam 1' | 1 | 2 | 3 | 4 | 5 | 6 | 7 | 8 | 9 | 10 | 11 | 12 | 13 |

88B • 45'
Tables with Automatic Column Widths

TM: 2"

Table 1

1. Format the table at the right; fit column width to the contents (AutoFit feature).
2. Add a border and/or shading as desired.

Save as: *TBL88B1*

Table 2

1. Open *TBL88B1* (Table 1).
2. Sort alphabetically by Program.

Save as: *TBL88B2*

Table 3

1. Prepare the table at the right using AutoFit.
2. Format as illustrated; show gridlines.
3. Add shading as desired.

Save as: *TBL88B3*

Table 4

1. Open *TBL88B3* (Table 3).
2. Sort by Room and Board in ascending order.
3. Change row height to 0.5" and center all text vertically in cells.

Save as: *TBL88B4*

CENTURY COLLEGE

School of Applied Sciences

Program	**Students Enrolled**			
	Last Year		**This Year**	
	Females	**Males**	**Females**	**Males**
Actuarial Science	10	14	12	11
Operations Management	33	28	37	30
Sport Management	56	54	50	62
Health Services Management	27	31	32	35
Logistics Engineering	12	10	14	14
Software Engineering	22	24	20	26
Applied Math	14	16	10	12

STUDENT CHARGES AT SELECTED COLLEGES					
College	**Tuition and Fees**				**Room and Board**
	Undergraduate		**Graduate**		
	In State	**Out of State**	**In State**	**Out of State**	
Boles	$13,800	$13,800	$14,580	$14,580	$6,508
Curtis	$18,550	$18,550	$21,355	$21,355	$6,805
Elser	$10,750	$14,375	NA	NA	$5,950
Hult	$15,400	$18,950	$17,500	$20,100	$7,100
Kerr	$11,450	$11,450	NA	NA	$6,300
Obley	$22,000	$22,000	$26,500	$26,500	$7,900
Reed	$5,500	$16,500	NA	NA	NA
Shull	$21,700	$21,700	NA	NA	$7,500
Valley	$11,200	$15,300	$15,780	$19,300	$6,435

Document 4 (Two-page Memo)

Save as:
MEMO106B4

1. Format the copy below as a memo.
2. Choose a different bullet style if you wish, but use only one bullet style for the document.
3. To review special features of two-page correspondence, refer to p. 160.

words

TO: All Department Managers | FROM: Jim 8
Nelson, Office Systems | DATE: June 3, 16
200- | SUBJECT: NEED TO IMPROVE 22
TELEPHONE SKILLS 25

Next to face-to-face communication, the 33
telephone is the most popular means of 41
exchanging information in business. It is 50
important, therefore, to review proper 57
telephone use at your next department 65
meeting. 67

The use of good telephone techniques 74
can: 76

- turn complaining callers into satisfied 84
ones; 85
- create a very good image for the business 94
with its customers, clients, and suppliers; 103
- and help us get more done each day. 111

These techniques should be used to handle 119
incoming calls efficiently and effectively: 128

Answer all incoming calls promptly. 135
Identify yourself immediately and speak in a 144
relaxed, low-pitched tone. Keep a writing pad 154
near the phone so that important parts of the 163
call can be recorded. Thank the caller at the 172
end of the conversation. 178

If the incoming call goes to voice mail, the 187
caller should hear a timely, courteous 194
message that indicates when the call will be 203
returned. Try to respond to all voice 211
messages within one hour when you are in the 220
office. If out of the office, check messages 229
twice each day and respond to the messages 238
promptly. Our goal is to return every 246
customer's call on the same day it is received. 256

Screen incoming calls by determining 263
who is calling and the purpose of the call. 272
Thus, you can decide to process the call or 281
transfer it to another person. 287

Whenever you transfer a call, be certain 295
the caller speaks to the correct person on the 305
first transfer. 308

Place calls on hold only when necessary, 316
for short periods, and in a courteous manner. 326
If calls need to be put on hold for more than a 335
minute or two, give callers the option of being 345
called back. 348

These techniques should be used to 355
improve outgoing calls: 360

- Outline the major points, and gather 367
needed materials before placing each call. 376
- Group calls and make them during set 384
times each day. 387
- Place calls in order of importance. 395
- Identify yourself as soon as your call is 404
answered. 406
- Write down the name and extension 413
number of the person with whom you are 421
speaking, for when a follow-up call must 429
be made. 431

LESSON 107 PREPARE TO ASSESS REPORT PROCESSING SKILL

Objectives:

1. To prepare for assessment of outline and report processing skill.
2. To prepare for assessment of formatting skill on minutes and news releases.

107A • 5' Conditioning Practice

Key each line twice SS; then key 30" writings on line 3; determine *gwam*.

alphabet 1 Beth Vegas excluded quick jaunts to the town zoo from many plans.

fig/sym 2 Kaitlin renewed Policies #23-4598 (truck) and #65-9107-44 (auto).

speed 3 The man is to visit the widow when he works by the mall downtown.

gwam 1' | 1 | 2 | 3 | 4 | 5 | 6 | 7 | 8 | 9 | 10 | 11 | 12 | 13 |

Table 5

1. Prepare the table at the right using AutoFit.
2. Format as illustrated.
3. Add borders and/or shading as desired.

 **Save as:** *TBL88B5*

Table 6

1. Open *TBL88B5* (Table 5); add eight rows to the bottom.
2. Complete the table by filling in the numbers needed for 9/16 through 16/16.

 **Save as:** *TBL88B6*

COMMON FRACTIONS REDUCED TO DECIMALS			
4ths	**8ths**	**16ths**	**Decimal**
		1	0.0625
	1	2	0.125
		3	0.1875
1	2	4	0.25
		5	0.3125
	3	6	0.375
		7	0.4375
2	4	8	0.5

LESSON 89 FORMAT TABLES WITH EQUAL COLUMNS

Objectives:

1. To prepare tables with multiple columns of equal width.
2. To improve table formatting skills.

89A • 5' Conditioning Practice

Key each line twice SS; then key 30" writings on line 2; determine *gwam*.

alphabet 1 Val just needs a pretty gift box for the quartz clock Mary wants.

fig/sym 2 Buy 23 monitors (#674-05-C) and 19 CPU's (#25-486-DX) at 15% off.

speed 3 The busy auditor is to handle the problem when he works downtown.

gwam 1' | 1 | 2 | 3 | 4 | 5 | 6 | 7 | 8 | 9 | 10 | 11 | 12 | 13 |

89B • 45' Tables with Equal-Width Columns

Center each table on the page. Bold and center all titles and headings horizontally and vertically. Fit column width to content and use the default row height unless directed otherwise. Apply the borders and shading you prefer if none is specified.

Table 1

1. Right-align the numbers.
2. Make the last four columns equal in width.

 **Save as:** *TBL89B1*

Table 2

1. Open *TBL89B1* (Table 1) and add a column at the right with **Total** as the heading.
2. Calculate and key monthly totals and grand total (sum of the Total column and Totals row).

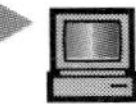 **Save as:** *TBL89B2*

ANNUAL AUTOMOBILE SALES Team Blue				
Month	**Car**	**Van**	**SUV**	**Truck**
January	6	4	7	6
February	8	4	7	5
March	9	2	4	7
April	11	5	5	2
May	9	4	2	6
June	11	2	7	4
July	8	1	6	8
August	7	3	4	4
September	12	6	5	5
October	11	3	6	6
November	12	5	9	8
December	7	1	5	7
Totals	111	40	67	68

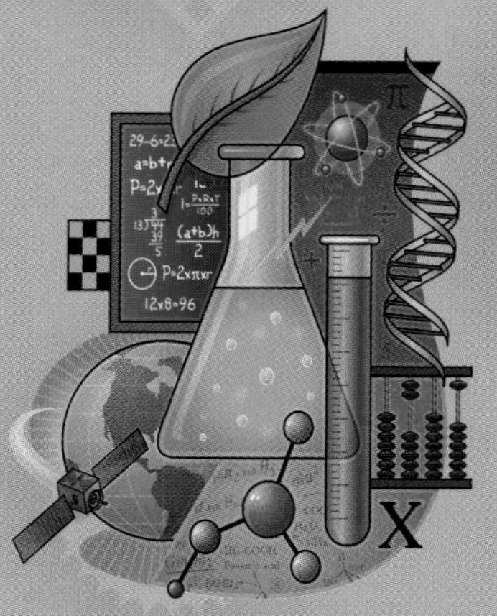

UNIT 28

LESSONS 106–108

Preparing for Assessment

LESSON 106 PREPARE TO ASSESS CORRESPONDENCE PROCESSING SKILL

Objective:
To prepare for assessment of letter, memo, and e-mail processing skill.

106A • 5' Conditioning Practice

Key each line twice SS; then take 30" writings on line 3; determine *gwam.*

alphabet 1 Sixty glazed rolls with jam were quickly baked and provided free.
figures 2 Ted was born 1/7/42, Mel was born 3/9/64, and I was born 5/18/80.
speed 3 The auditor cut by half the giant goal of the sorority endowment.

gwam 1' | 1 | 2 | 3 | 4 | 5 | 6 | 7 | 8 | 9 | 10 | 11 | 12 | 13 |

106B • 45' Correspondence

Document 1 (Letter)

Prepare the letter using modified block format, mixed punctuation, and ¶ indentations.

 **Save as:** *LTR106B1*

Document 2 (Letter)

1. Change Document 1 to block format with open punctuation.
2. Insert a subject line: **SEPTEMBER MEETING NOTICE**.

 **Save as:** *LTR106B2*

Document 3 (E-mail)

E-mail this message to your instructor; attach your resume (*MYELREZ95-4*). Send one classmate a ***Cc***; send another a ***Bcc***. (If you do not have e-mail software, format the text as a memo to your instructor [current date]. Prepare a ***c*** for a classmate and a ***bc*** for another.)

 **Save as:** *MAIL106B3* (*MEMO106B3*)

words

September 5, 200- | Dr. Louis L. Elmore | Medical Park Dr. | 11
Birmingham, AL 35213-2496 | Dear Dr. Elmore 19

(¶) The next meeting of the Longfellow Observatory Amateur 30
Astronomers Club is scheduled for 7:30 p.m. on Friday, September 23, 44
in Room 102 of the Longfellow Observatory. 53

(¶) As the enclosed agenda indicates, the primary purpose of the 65
meeting is to plan next year's schedule of events. As usual, the events 80
are likely to include a lecture series and one or two star parties. A 94
project to involve high school students in astronomy needs to be 107
planned and approved. 112

(¶) Please mark your calendar for this important meeting. If you are 125
unable to attend, please call me at 555-0151. 134

Sincerely | Richard Clavijo | Assistant Director | xx | Enclosure | I'm 147
glad that you are bringing Aaron Lee to the meeting. Perhaps he will 161
consider joining LOAAC. 165

---

words

Subject: MY ELECTRONIC RESUME 6

Here is the resume I prepared for the job opening you told me about at 20
Safeco. I will appreciate any feedback you give me for improving it. 35
I'm still working on my application letter and will send it to you when 49
I'm finished. 52

Thanks for all your help with my documents and for permission to 65
include your name on my references list. I'll definitely let you know if 80
I'm called for an interview at Safeco. 87

Table 3

1. Bold and center the entries in the last three columns.
2. Make the last three columns equal in width.
3. Add shading, color, and borders as desired.

 **Save as:** *TBL89B3*

Table 4

1. Open Table 3 (*TBL89B3*).
2. Sort the chemical elements alphabetically.
3. Change the font and font size for headings.

 **Save as:** *TBL89B4*

Table 5

1. Right-align all numbers.
2. Make the last three columns the same width.
3. Apply a box border; apply shading to each odd-numbered row.

 **Save as:** *TBL89B5*

Table 6

1. Hide the gridlines and right-align all text.
2. Underline column headings.
3. Modify column width and row height as you prefer.

 **Save as:** *TBL89B6*

Table 7

1. Reformat Table 6 (*TBL89B6*) by showing gridlines and centering all headings.
2. Change all gridlines to green; apply a wide green border to the table.

 **Save as:** *TBL89B7*

CHEMICAL ELEMENTS

1950 through 1999 Discoveries

Chemical Element	**Atomic Symbol**	**Weight**	**Year**
Californium	(Cf)	251	1950
Einsteinium	(Es)	254	1952
Fermium	(Fm)	257	1953
Mendelevium	(Md)	258	1955
Nobelium	(No)	259	1958
Lawrencium	(Lr)	260	1961
Rutherfordium	(Rf)	261	1969
Bohrium	(Bh)	264	1981
Meitnerium	(Mt)	268	1982
Hassium	(Hs)	269	1984

FIRST-QUARTER STATEMENT

Department	**Cost of Goods Sold**	**Operating Expenses**	**Operating Profits**
Automotive	$4,652	$3,987	$665
Electrical	$5,983	$4,710	$1,273
Garden	$3,756	$3,254	$502
Hardware	$2,568	$2,107	$461
Household	$2,597	$1,968	$629
Paint	$3,619	$2,754	$865
Plumbing	$3,286	$2,108	$1,178

COMPOUND INTEREST

Compounded Annually on $100 Principal

Period	**6%**	**7%**	**8%**	**9%**	**10%**
6 months	3.00	3.50	4.00	4.50	5.00
1 year	6.00	7.00	8.00	9.00	10.00
2 years	12.36	14.49	16.64	18.81	21.00
3 years	19.10	22.50	25.97	29.50	33.10
4 years	26.25	31.08	36.05	41.16	46.41
5 years	33.82	40.26	46.93	53.86	61.05
10 years	79.08	96.72	115.89	136.74	159.37
12 years	101.22	125.22	151.82	181.27	213.84
15 years	139.66	175.90	217.22	264.25	317.72
20 years	220.71	286.97	366.10	460.44	572.75

SKILL BUILDER 6

Tabulation

1. Clear tabs; set tabs 1.5", 3", and 4.5" from the left margin.
2. Key the text at the right.
3. Learn the names of the state capitals.
4. Key only the names of the states.
5. Go back and insert the names of as many of the capitals as you can below the state without looking at the book.

				words
Alabama	Alaska	Arizona	Arkansas	6
Montgomery	Juneau	Phoenix	Little Rock	14
California	Colorado	Connecticut	Delaware	22
Sacramento	Denver	Hartford	Dover	29
Florida	Georgia	Hawaii	Idaho	35
Tallahassee	Atlanta	Honolulu	Boise	42
Illinois	Indiana	Iowa	Kansas	47
Springfield	Indianapolis	Des Moines	Topeka	56

Timed Writings: Script

1. Take a 1' writing, DS.
2. Add 5 *gwam* to the rate attained in Step 1.
3. Take four 1' writings, trying to achieve the rate set in Step 2.

all letters used

A basic knowledge of parliamentary procedure is an excellent 12
skill to acquire. Those who possess this skill will be able to 25
put it to use in any organization they belong to that conducts 38
meetings based on parliamentary law. A meeting that is run by 50
this procedure will be conducted in a proper and very orderly 63
fashion. Just as important, the rights of each member of the 75
group are protected at all times. 82

Reading/Keying Response Patterns

Key each line 3 times (slowly, faster, top speed).

Goal:
To reduce time interval between keystrokes (read ahead to anticipate stroking pattern).

Emphasize curved, upright fingers; finger-action keystroking.

one-hand words
1 car no cat inn fat ink ear beg verb sea lip oil tea pull see milk
2 acre pool rest link base lily seat lion vase noun dear junk barge

Emphasize independent finger action; stationary hands.

one-hand phrases
3 at my best | in my career | best dessert | my bad debts | my exact grades
4 only rebate | in my opinion | we deserve better | minimum grade average

Emphasize continuity; finger action with fingers close to keys.

one-hand sentences
5 Ada agreed on a minimum oil target after a decrease in oil taxes.
6 In my opinion, Edward Freeberg agreed on a greater water reserve.

gwam 1' | 1 | 2 | 3 | 4 | 5 | 6 | 7 | 8 | 9 | 10 | 11 | 12 | 13 |

LESSON 90 PROCESS TABLES WITH PREDESIGNED FORMATS

Objectives:

1. To prepare tables using predesigned formats.
2. To improve table formatting skills.

90A • 5' Conditioning Practice

Key each line twice SS; then take 30" writings on line 2; determine *gwam*.

alphabet 1 Que rejects my idea of having two dozen oak trees by the complex.

figures 2 Flights leave for Chicago at 6:48 a.m., 12:09 p.m., and 5:37 p.m.

speed 3 Di and the eight sorority girls may handle half of the endowment.

gwam 1' | 1 | 2 | 3 | 4 | 5 | 6 | 7 | 8 | 9 | 10 | 11 | 12 | 13 |

90B • 45' Tables with Predesigned Formats

Table 1

1. Format the table at the right as illustrated.
2. Select and apply a predesigned table format.

Save as: *TBL90B1*

SCIENCE PROJECT TEAMS					
Team	**Members**				
Earth	Mazur Alicia	Craig Suzanne	Whitfield Victoria	Pugliano Frank	Lightfoot Dale
Mars	Weigler Pamela	Neander Stephen	Craven Felicia	VanRyn Donald	Lamison Vincent
Pluto	Lobaugh Michele	Fleming Clifford	Molanick Timothy	Coffman Mary	Hvozdik Terry
Saturn	Romesburg Lewis	Harrison Ronald	Ekholm Ashley	McClelland Clayton	Petrolio Gary
Neptune	Peterson Samuel	Stoyanoff Anna	Hoskin Bonnie	Hrinda Heather	Woodring Kimberly

Table 2

1. Prepare the table at the right, formatting cells in Rows 3 through 8 to be 1" × 1".
2. Top-align all entries in Rows 3 through 8.
3. Select and apply a predesigned table format.

Save as: *TBL90B2*

General Science--Period 5--Seating Chart				
Back of Room				
Angelo Eugene	Diangelo Janelle	Anthony Kerry	Puhala Michelle	Churning Jill
Taylor Jennifer	Wallace Beverly	Irwin Matthew	Richardson John	Tyson Nicole
Vandall Tina	Ehrenfeld William	Kieffer Emily	Richardson Jason	
Biddlestone Sharon	Mellinger Moira	Farrell Mark	Behanna Blaine	Locke Haley
	Fowler Laura	Drakulic Christopher	Sedor Carrie	Sharma Usha
Cicconi Pietro	Gasparovich Sandra		Maxwell Kenneth	Whitehouse Gary
Row A	**Row B**	**Row C**	**Row D**	**Row E**
Front of Room				

Job 14

TSEA

Prepare this announcement and then below it add the form you designed in Job 7 so it can be cut off and returned. Try to have the form begin and end with the margins for the announcement. Also, insert some appropriate clip art where you think it fits best.

YP

TSEA GOLF OUTING

Announcement and Registration Form

The TSEA 18-hole golf outing will be held on June 14 at the well-known Twin Lakes Golf Course. A shotgun start is scheduled at 11:20 a.m. Plan to be at the course no latter than 10:45 a.m. Roundtrip transportation from the Russell Hotel will be provided.

The cost for the outing is $75, and that includes green and cart fees and a cookout at 4:30 p.m. The outing will end in time for you too be at the TSEA opening general session at 7:30 p.m.

If you plan to participate complete the form below and return it by June 5 to:

Nancy Hyduk
East Lake Middle School
9600 Southern Pines Blvd.
Charlotte, NC 28273-5520

✂-----------------------✂-----------------------✂-----------------------✂

Job 15

TSEA

Prepare this letter. Please use a 14-pt. font.

YP

The Hon. James G. Able
Mayor of Charlotte
600 E. 4th St.
Charlotte, NC 28202-2870

Dear Mayor Able:

The Tri-County Science Education Association will be holding its Sixth Annual Conference at the Russell Hotel in June, and we respectfully request that you be present to give the official welcome to Charlotte at 7:30 p.m. on June 14.

Your audience would be more than three hundred science teachers from the Tri-County area. The teachers, representing elementary, middle, and high school grades, assemble once each year for this three-day conference to learn about effective instructional resources and strategies.

We look forward to your support of our dedicated teachers by having you participate in this major event. Please respond to me at (704) 555-0128 at your earliest convenience.

Table 3

1. Format the table at the right as illustrated.
2. Select and apply a predesigned table format.

 **Save as:** *TBL90B3*

Table 4

1. Key the second table at the right; you decide column width and row height.
2. Select and apply a predesigned table format.

 **Save as:** *TBL90B4*

Table 5

1. Open Table 4 (*TBL90B4*) and add rows for Sept. 1 and Oct. 2 using these numbers and directions:

	Sept	Oct
Units Bought	**275**	**290**
Units Sold	**260**	**280**
Unit Cost	**$5.30**	**$5.30**
Units on Hand	*You compute*	

2. Apply a different predesigned format.

 **Save as:** *TBL90B5*

Table 6

1. Format the table at the right with these features:
   - Use 10-pt. font for Column A, Rows 5–9 and 12–13; 12-pt. font for all others.
   - Bold text as shown.
   - Insert right tab with dot leaders for Columns B and C.
   - Hide gridlines.
   - Insert a blank line space above and below the column headings.
   - Underline the column headings.
   - Double-underline the Net Profit amounts, including the dollar signs.

 **Save as:** *TBL90B6*

REVENUE, EXPENSES, AND NET PROFIT

Month	**Revenue**	**Cost of Goods Sold**	**Operating Expenses**	**Net Profit**
January	$68,000	$35,000	$25,200	$7,800
February	63,000	33,000	29,700	300
March	75,000	40,000	27,600	7,400
April	73,000	41,000	27,500	4,500
May	78,000	44,000	26,300	7,700
June	83,000	46,000	32,900	4,100

INVENTORY RECORD				
Date	**Units Bought**	**Unit Cost**	**Units Sold**	**Units on Hand**
January 3				55
February 1	300	$5.32	162	193
March 1			183	10
April 3	315	$5.38	194	131
May 1	75	$5.37	202	4
June 1	325	$5.35	260	69
July 3	225	$5.34	265	29
August 1	250	$5.34	270	9

Jordan Florists **Comparative Income Statement** **For Last Year and This Year Ending December 31**		
	This Year	**Last Year**
Net Sales	$827,540	$815,595
Cost of Goods Sold:		
Merchandise Inventory, 01/01	55,976	70,672
Purchases	600,335	580,543
Merchandise Available for Sale	656,311	651,215
Merchandise Inventory, 12/31	40,692	60,758
Cost of Goods Sold	615,619	590,457
Gross Profit on Sales	211,921	225,138
Expenses:		
Selling	65,498	86,912
Other	42,864	46,321
Total Expenses	108,362	133,233
Net Profit	$103,559	$91,905

Registration

The conference registration form has been designed and will be included with the next TSEA newsletter that is mailed. Additionally, a separate mailing that contains conference highlights and registration procedures will be sent to all science teachers in the Tri-County area 6 by May 1. The early-bird registration fee will be offered to all who register before June 5. Efforts are underway to recruit teachers to staff the registration tables throughout the conference.

Special Events

The conference golf outing will be held on June 14 at the Twin Lakes Golf Club, prior to the first general session at 7 p.m. Up to 72 golfers can be accommodated. The customary cookout will begin at 4:30 p.m. and all Executive Board members are encouraged to attend. The cost has increased only slightly--from $73 last year to 75 this year.

Hospitality

I will be working very closely with Connie Taylor during the next week to bring her up-to-date with what Janice Pearson had arranged. With that information, Connie will be able to finalize all of the gifts and information we need to provide our conference participants.

Conclusion

The Conference Board is an excellent one. The members are very responsible, eager to work, knowledgeable, and cooperative. Their goal is to provide an excellent conference at a reasonable price and to generate income for TSEA. I will have each committee's final budget and estimated conference revenues for you to review and act upon at the next meeting.

FORMAT ITINERARIES AND TABLES

Objectives:

1. To format itineraries.
2. To improve table formatting skills.

91A • 5' Conditioning Practice

Key each line twice SS; then key 30" writings on line 2; determine *gwam*.

alphabet 1 Julie passed the extra keyboarding quiz as we got back from Vail.

fig/sym 2 Mary's house at 267 Weston Drive was appraised at $153,490 (+8%).

speed 3 Nancy may sign the usual proxy if they make an audit of the firm.

gwam 1' | 1 | 2 | 3 | 4 | 5 | 6 | 7 | 8 | 9 | 10 | 11 | 12 | 13 |

91B • 45' Itineraries and Tables

Document 1

1. Read the format guides for itineraries on p. 243.
2. Create a table; key the itinerary at the right; and format it as illustrated. Use a 10-pt. font for the entries in the last column and a 12-pt. font for all other column entries.
3. Center the itinerary on the page.

Save as: *ITIN91B1*

TRAVEL ITINERARY FOR LISA PEROTTA

MEA Convention—Anaheim, California—April 18-22, 200-

Date	Time	Activity	Comments
Tuesday April 18	6 p.m.	Depart **Pittsburgh International Airport** (PIT) for Santa Ana, CA, Airport (SNA) on **USEast Flight 146**. *Frequent flyer number has been entered. Arrival time is 8:01 p.m.*	The flight is nonstop on an Airbus A319, and you are flying coach.
	8:30 p.m.	Reservation with **Star Limousine** (714-555-0190) for transportation to **Anaheim Inn and Convention Center**, 500 Convention Way, Anaheim.	Confirmation numbers: 33-345 for limo and 632A-04/18 for hotel.
Wednesday April 19	1 p.m.	Tour of Discovery Science Center and Queen Mary. A **Five Star Tour** van is to be at hotel main entrance at 1 p.m. for 1:15 p.m. departure.	Return to hotel by 5:30 p.m.
Thursday April 20	6 p.m.	MEA evening at Universal Studios Hollywood. **Buses chartered by MEA** will transport all registered participants to and from the studios.	Check MEA message board for boarding times and registration packet for ticket.
Saturday April 22	11:15 a.m.	Reservation with **Star Limousine** for transportation from Anaheim to **USEast Airlines** at the Santa Ana Airport.	Confirmation number for limo: 33-375.
	1:25 p.m.	Depart **Santa Ana Airport** (SNA) for Pittsburgh International Airport (PIT) on **USEast Flight 148**. *Frequent flyer number has been entered. Arrival time is 8:52 p.m.*	The flight is nonstop on an Airbus A319, and you are flying coach.

members. To date, 15 papers have been received. Reviewers are deciding if the content is appropriate for conference presentation. Within the next two months, the Program Committee plans to have presenters for all concurrent and general sessions confirmed. Two publishing houses have been asked to sponsor the two general session speakers. If they agree to do this, they will pay for the speakers' travel and lodging expenses and provide a generous honorarium. In return for this contribution, each publisher will receive prominent, public recognition for their significant contribution.

Exhibitors

The Conference Board members, led by Jim Herriott, Exhibits Chair, are making a concerted effort to increase conference revenues by increasing the number of exhibits spaces sold. They are doing this in two ways:

Increase the number of exhibitors.

Increase the number of tables exhibitors buy.

The following chart indicates how revenue may be increased if we attract four new exhibitors averaging two tables each, retain all exhibitors from last year, persuade last year's exhibitor's to purchase 7 additional spaces, and there is no change in the exhibit fee per table.

REVENUE FROM EXHIBITS					
Last Year			This Year		
Vendors	Tables	Revenue	Vendors	Tables	Revenue
7	1	$1,750	4	1	$1,000
5	2	$2,250	11	2	$4,950
2	3	$1,200	3	3	$1,800
14		$5,200.00	18		$7,750.00

(continued on next page)

Document 2

1. Format the itinerary at the right using the following features:
   - Use 1.5 line spacing in Row 1.
   - Use the small caps font effect for Rows 3 and 6.
   - Use bold as shown.
   - Bottom-align all cell entries.
   - Center all lines horizontally.
   - Top margin: 2".
   - You select column width and row height.

Save as: *ITIN91B2*

FLIGHT ITINERARY FOR ROBERT HALLAS **Roundtrip Between Indianapolis, IN, and Shreveport, LA** **August 18 and August 20, 200-**			
Flight	**Departure**	**Arrival**	**Equipment**
SEGMENT ONE--AUGUST 18--INDIANAPOLIS TO SHREVEPORT			
Amerifast #1233	8:38 a.m. Indianapolis (IND)	11:04 a.m. Houston, TX (IAH)	Boeing 737-300
Amerifast #3482	1:10 p.m. Houston, TX (IAH)	2:15 p.m. Shreveport (SHV)	Aerospatiale ATR
SEGMENT TWO--AUGUST 20--SHREVEPORT TO INDIANAPOLIS			
Southern #3416	5:55 p.m. Shreveport (SHV)	7:20 p.m. Memphis, TN (MEM)	Saab- Fairchild 340
Southern #1706	8:30 p.m. Memphis, TN (MEM)	9:48 p.m. Indianapolis (IND)	McDonnell Douglas MD-80

Document 3

1. Format the table at the right, using the following features:
   - Left-align all lines except Row 2; use Justify alignment in Row 2.
   - Use bold as shown.
   - Use a 9-pt. font for Row 2.
   - Center table horizontally and vertically.

Save as: *TBL91B3*

PREFIXES

These prefixes, in combination with the basic unit names, provide the multiples in the International System of Units. For example, the unit name *meter*, with the prefix *kilo* added, produces *kilometer*, meaning "1,000 meters".

Prefix	**Symbol**	**Multiples**	**Equivalent**
deca	da	10	tenfold
hecto	h	10^2	hundredfold
kilo	k	10^3	thousandfold
mega	M	10^4	millionfold
giga	G	10^5	billionfold
tera	T	10^6	trillionfold
peta	P	10^7	quadrillionfold

Source: *The 1999 World Almanac and Book of Facts.*

Document 4

Decide all the formatting features when keying the table at the right.

Save as: *TBL91B4*

BUSINESS EXPENSE SUMMARY

Quarter	**Travel**	**Meals**	**Lodging**	**Other**
First	$5,753.59	$2,308.54	$1,987.45	$1,005.67
Second	6,453.20	2,756.08	2,451.74	678.98
Third	5,642.05	2,645.78	3,003.54	985.05
Fourth	4,984.02	1,805.45	1,954.33	1,105.94
Totals	$22,832.86	$9,515.85	$9,397.06	$3,775.64

Job 12

TSEA

Create a form with this information. It will be a one-page enclosure for a letter we will write soon.

YP

Tri-County Science Association Conference--June 14 to 16--Russell Hotel, Charlotte

Instructions: Complete and return this form by May 31.

Presenter's Name:

Presenter's School:

Check or List Audio-Visual Equipment Needed:

_______ Overhead projector with screen

_______ Slide projector with screen

_______ Computer projector with screen

_______ Computer

_______ Other (list below)

Exact title of presentation:

Brief description of presentation (for program booklet):

Date returned:

Telephone and e-mail:

Job 13

TSEA

Here's a rough draft of the progress report I have to present to the board. Please make the changes indicated and format as a report so I can review it. Correct any errors you find.

YP

16-pt. bold— SECOND TSEA CONFERENCE BOARD PROGRESS REPORT

14-pt. bold— (Yvonne Porterfield, Conference Director)

Satisfactory progress is being made in all areas as the Conference Board continue s to make ~~all the~~ arrangements for the Sixth Annual TSEA Conference, ~~that is~~ scheduled at the Russell Hotel (Charlotte) from June 14 through June 16.

Conference Board — 14-pt. bold

The Conference Board has met monthly since it was appointed shortly after last year's conference ~~ended~~. There has been one change in the makeup of the board: Connie Taylor replaced Janice Pearson, who ~~had to~~ relinquished her position as Hospitality Chair due to illness in her family.

Program

The Program Committee has designed the entire program for the 3-day conference and has mailed a Call for Papers to all TSEA

(continued on next page)

FORMAT AGENDAS

Objectives:

1. To format agendas.
2. To improve language skills.

92A • 5' Conditioning Practice

Key each line twice SS; then take 30" writings on line 2; determine *gwam*.

alphabet 1 Danny bought major equipment to vitalize work after the tax cuts.

figures 2 Call 192-7648 in 30-35 days to get the orders Sean has requested.

speed 3 The busy maid bid for the ivory soap dish and antique ivory bowl.

gwam 1' | 1 | 2 | 3 | 4 | 5 | 6 | 7 | 8 | 9 | 10 | 11 | 12 | 13 |

92B • 35' Agendas

Agenda 1

1. Read the guide for formatting agendas on p. 243 and study the model.
2. Format the agenda at the right.

Note:

To insert leaders, strike the Space Bar before striking the TAB key; strike it again before keying text in the right column.

Save as: *AGNA92B1*

AGENDA
MATHEMATICS AND SCIENCE DEPARTMENT
March 15, 200-, 2:40 p.m.
John Wilson High School—Room 218

1. Call to Order . . . . Mary Underwood, Department Head
2. Approval of February Minutes . . . . M. Underwood
3. Preliminary Fall Teaching Assignments . . . . Sam Reilly, Principal
4. Science Teacher Applications . . . . Vince Cummings, Teacher
5. Interview Dates and Itinerary . . . . M. Underwood
6. Math Teacher Applications . . . . Susan Hughes, Teacher
7. Interview Dates and Itinerary . . . . M. Underwood
8. Science Fair . . . . Janis Haverford, Teacher
9. Retirement Banquet Plans . . . . Becky Hopkins, Teacher
10. Textbook Adoptions . . . . M. Underwood
11. Other Business . . . . M. Underwood
12. Next Meeting Date and Adjournment . . . . M. Underwood

Agenda 2

1. Format the agenda at the right, centering it on the page.
2. Change the font for the ALL CAPS headings.
3. Select and apply a page border.

Save as: *AGNA92B2*

AGENDA
QUANTITATIVE REASONING SKILLS TASK FORCE
May 5, 200-, Harris Conference Room

1. Call to Order . . . . Carlos Diego, Task Force Head
2. Superintendent's Charge . . . . Kate Lewis, Superintendent
3. Task Force Discussion and Questions . . . . C. Diego/K. Lewis
4. Preliminary Research Plans . . . . C. Diego
5. Available Budget . . . . Florence Wilson, Principal
6. Consultants . . . . K. Lewis
7. Meeting Schedule and Rules . . . . C. Diego
8. Other Business . . . . Task Force Members
9. Adjournment . . . . C. Diego

Job 9

TSEA

Prepare this news release for immediate release. I am the contact person.

YP

CHARLOTTE, NC, (insert current date). The Sixth Annual Tri-County Science Education Conference will be held at Charlotte's Russell Hotel on June 14, 15, 16. Over three hundred science teachers are expected to attend to learn about the newest instructional resources and strategies for teaching science courses in elementary, middle, and high school grades.

TSEA teachers who want to serve as session chairs, session recorders, or on the registration or hospitality committees should contact Ms. Yvonne Porterfield, the Conference Director. Ms. Porterfield is a biology teacher at Madison High School and can be reached at 704-555-0128 or porterfi@madison.k12.nc.us.

###

Job 10

TSEA

Prepare this agenda for my meeting with the conference board next Tuesday.

YP

AGENDA

TSEA CONFERENCE BOARD MEETING

(Insert next Tuesday's date)

Russell Hotel, Conference Room D

1. *Call to order* . . . . *Yvonne Porterfield*
2. *Minutes from last meeting* . . . . *Jim Herriott*
3. *Committee reports*

   Program . . . . *Rodger Acosta*

   Registration . . . . *Marian Coughenour*

   Exhibits . . . . *Herriott*

   Hospitality . . . . *Connie Taylor*

   Special events . . . . *Nancy Hyduk*
4. *Unfinished business* . . . . *Porterfield*

   Registration, hospitality, session chairs, and recorders . . . . *Attendees*

   Operating funds for committees . . . . *Porterfield*

   Exhibit security . . . . *Herriott*
5. *New business* . . . . *Porterfield*

   Meal selections . . . . *Attendees*

   AV needs . . . . *Acosta*
6. *Next meeting and adjournment* . . . . *Porterfield*

Job 11

TSEA

Access one of the directories on your favorite Internet search engine. Try to find museums in the 28208 ZIP Code area. If you find some, list the names, addresses, telephone numbers, and hours; or simply print the Web pages. I need to give this information to Connie Taylor.

YP

Agenda 3

Format the agenda at the right, including these features:

- In the title, format the organization name in 14-pt. Arial, blue, bold.
- Apply shading (gray—5%) to agenda item 3, including the blank line and two items of unfinished business.

Save as: *AGNA92B3*

AGENDA

Ford County Science Society

July 31, 200-

1. Approval of April minutes . . . . J. Gusset
2. Reports
   Treasurer's . . . . T. Meliton
   Membership . . . . F. Parker
   Fundraising . . . . C. Whiteman
3. Unfinished business
   Hall of Fame inductees . . . . T. Horner
   Lowden correspondence . . . . A. Price
4. New business
   Membership drive . . . . F. Parker
   Web site proposal . . . . W. Ehlinger
5. Next meeting date and adjournment . . . . R. Holloway

LANGUAGE SKILLS

92C • 10'
Language Skills: Word Choice

1. Study the spelling and definitions of the words at the right.
2. Key the Learn lines, noting word choice.
3. Key the Apply lines, selecting the correct words.
4. Check your work with the instructor. Rekey lines that contain a word-choice error.

Save as: *CHOICE92C*

principal (n/adj) a person in authority; a capital sum; main, primary

principle (n) a rule

stationary (adj) fixed in position, course, or mode; unchanging in condition

stationery (n) paper and envelopes used for processing personal and business documents

Learn 1 The new **principal** is guided by the **principle** of fairness.
Apply 2 The (principal/principle) reason I'm here is to record the talk.
Apply 3 What (principal/principle) of law was applied in the case?

Learn 1 We store **stationery** on **stationary** shelves in the supply room.
Apply 2 Desks remain (stationary/stationery), but we'll shift the files.
Apply 3 Were you able to get a good discount on (stationary/stationery)?

INTERNET ACTIVITY

Follow the directions at the right to learn about a math or science course.

1. Search the World Wide Web, using one or more of the search engines listed below. Enter the name of a math or science course you are taking (or plan to take) as the keyword(s).
   Altavista: http://www.altavista.com
   Excite: http://www.excite.com
   Yahoo: http://www.yahoo.com
   Go: http://www.go.com
   Lycos: http://www.lycos.com
2. Find a link that interests you and go to that site.
3. Identify the link by its URL (Web address). Then key a paragraph or two describing information at the site and how you can use it.

Job 8

TSEA

Here's a rough draft of the minutes I need to take to the conference board meeting next Tuesday. Please prepare a final draft. Insert the first Tuesday of last month as the date.

YP

SS all ¶s; DS between

TSEA Conference Board

Participants: R. Acosta, M. Coughenour, J. Herriott, N. Hyduk, Y. Porterfield, C. Taylor

Recorder of minutes: J. Herriott

1. **Call to order:** Conference Director Yvonne Porterfield called the meeting to order at 4:15 p.m. at the Russell Hotel.

2. **Committee reports:** **Program.** R. Acosta reported that he has prepared the Call for Papers that will be mailed to all members within a week. In addition, he has contacted two publishing houses to sponsor key note speakers for the general sessions.

   Registration. M. Coughenour has designed the registration form, and it will be included in the next newsletter as well as the special conference mailing that will be sent. She stated she needed assistance with getting teachers to work the registration table during the conference.

   Exhibits. J. Herriott reported that he is gathering data on past exhibitors and is identifying prospective exhibitors.

   Hospitality. C. Taylor had nothing to report this time.

   Special events. N. Hyduk is planning to have the golf outing at Twin Lakes Golf Course. She hopes to have confirmation in a few matter of days.

3. **Unfinished business:** Y. Porterfield stated that she set a meeting with Russell Hotel personnel and that she and J. Herriott will meet with them soon. Other committee chairs are invited to the meeting. If they need ing specific information about hotel facilities and services are to tell Yvonne within ten days.

4. **New business:** Security for the exhibits area was discussed. and it was decided to request funding will be requested to post a security guard during all hours the exhibits are Closed not open to the conference participants.

   Committee chairs are to submit a final requests for funds that they need at the next meeting so that Yvonne can present a final budget to the TSEA Executive Board for approval.

5. Next meeting: The next meeting date was not set; but all agreed that a Tuesday would be was best. Yvonne will set the date and notify each Conference Board member.

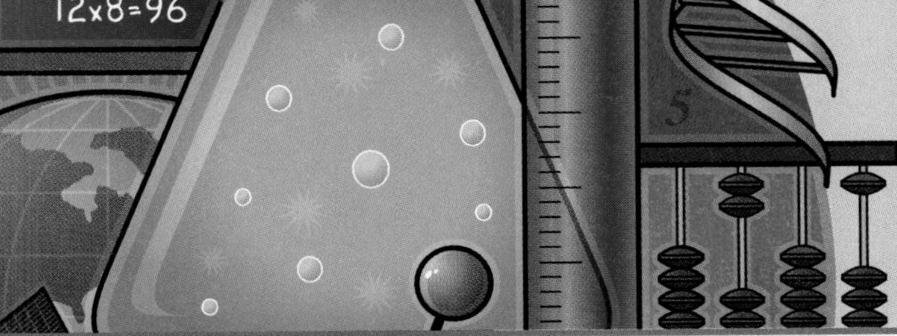

Communication Skills 

ACTIVITY 1

Internal Punctuation: Apostrophe

1. Key lines 1–10 at the right, inserting the needed apostrophes.
2. Check the accuracy of your work with the instructor; correct any errors you made.
3. Note the rule number at the left of each sentence in which you made an apostrophe error.
4. Using the rules below the sentences and on p. 255, identify the rule(s) you need to review/practice.
5. **Read**: Study each rule.
6. **Learn**: Key the Learn line(s) beneath it, noting how the rule is applied.
7. **Apply**: Key the Apply line(s), correctly using apostrophes.

 **Save as:** *CS10-ACT1*

Proofread & Correct

Rules		
1	1	Jay Corbin played 12 min. 30 sec.; Jack Odom, 26 min. 20 sec.
1	2	My desk is 3 ft. x 5 ft. 6 in.; the credenza is 2 ft. x 6 ft.
2	3	Didnt O'Brien prepare a sales comparison for 98 and 99?
3	4	Major changes in technology occurred in the 1980's and 1990s.
3	5	Dr. Knox gave mostly As and Bs, but he gave a few Cs and Ds.
2,4	6	Didnt you go to the big sale on childrens items?
5	7	Tess escort gave her a wrist corsage of exquisite violets.
6	8	The boys and girls teams appreciated Dr. Morris compliments.
6	9	Do you know whether the ladies swim coach is in her office?
2,6	10	Didnt you ask if the cast is set for Miss Winters new play?

Internal Punctuation: Apostrophe

> Rule 1: Use an apostrophe as a symbol to represent feet or minutes. (Quotation marks may be used to signify inches or seconds.)

Learn 1 Floyd bought twenty-four 2" x 4" x 12' studs for the new deck.
Learn 2 Shawnelle scored the 3-pointer with only 1' 18" left to go.
Apply 3 The new computer lab at my school is 18 ft. 6 in. x 30 ft.
Apply 4 Students were told to print 3 min. writings on 8.5 in. x 11 in. paper.

> Rule 2: Use an apostrophe as a symbol to indicate the omission of letters or figures (as in contractions).

Learn 5 Didn't you enjoy the "Spirit of '76" segment of the pageant?
Apply 6 I dont know why he doesnt take advantage of our new terms.
Apply 7 Last years reunion combined the classes of 97, 98, and 99.

> Rule 3: Use an apostrophe plus *s ('s)* to form the plural of most figures, letters, and words used as words rather than for their meaning *(6's, A's, five's)*. In stock quotations and to refer to decades or centuries, form the plural of figures by adding *s* only.

Learn 8 She studied hard and earned A's throughout the 1990s.
Learn 9 Add Century As and 4s; show the Cosco 45s in boldface.
Apply 10 Correct the outline by changing the As, Bs, and Cs to CAPS.
Apply 11 My broker urged that I buy Apache 76's in the 1980's.

(continued on next page)

Job 5

TSEA

Prepare this letter for my signature, please.

YP

Mr. Carlos Bautista, Sales Manager, Russell Hotel, 222 E 3d St., Charlotte, NC 28202-0222

This letter ~~is to~~ confirm a meeting that Mr. James Herriott and I have with you next Friday afternoon at the Russell Hotel.

The primary purpose of the meeting is to tour areas of the hotel that will be used for sessions, exhibits, dining, and registration at the ~~TSEA~~ Tri-County Science Education Conference ~~that is~~ scheduled for June 14-16, 200-.

In the session rooms, we need to see ~~different~~ various seating arrangements and determine what ~~AV~~ audio-visual and other aids speakers can use. We will need access to the ~~Web~~ Internet in at least ~~two~~ three of the rooms. Also, we need to discuss security issues relating to the exhibit area and ~~discuss~~ the electrical service to each exhibit space.

James and I will meet you in your office next Friday at 3:30 p.m.

Job 6

TSEA

Prepare this memo for me.

YP

TO: Nancy Hyduk

SUBJECT: INFO FOR THE GOLF OUTING

Harry Spahr, the golf pro at Twin Lakes Golf Course, called with the information you've been waiting for to prepare the Golf Outing Announcement and Registration Form.

TSEA can have a shotgun start at 11:20 a.m. on June 14. Up to 72 golfers can participate in the outing. The cost for each golfer is $75. The price includes the green and cart fees and a cookout (hot dogs, three cold salads, and soft drinks) at 4:30 p.m. Left- and right-handed clubs can be rented for an additional $10.

Mr. Spahr believes he has given me all the information you requested. If not, he said for you to call him at 704-555-0124, or you can e-mail him at hspahr@twinlakes.com.

Job 7

TSEA

Will you create a golf registration form with this information. Add a heading (TSEA Golf Outing) and checkboxes for answers to questions. Suggestion: Make a table and use a half page or less. N. Hyduk wants to put this in the registration packet.

YP

Name	Address	Phone	E-mail	Fax
Handicap (approx.) OR average score:				
Name of preferred playing partner:				
Need transportation? ☐ Yes ☐ No	Need to rent clubs? ☐ Right handed ☐ Left handed	How paying ($75)? ☐ With registration ☐ Separately		

Rule 4: To show possession, use an apostrophe plus *s* after (a) a singular noun and (b) a plural noun that does not end in *s*.

Learn 12 Jerrod's store had a great sale on men's and women's apparel.

Apply 13 Ritas class ring was lost under the stands in the schools gym.

Apply 14 Our back-to-school sale on childrens clothes is in progress.

Rule 5: To show possession, use an apostrophe plus *s* (*'s*) after a proper name of one syllable that ends in *s*.

Learn 15 Jon Hess's next art exhibit will be held at the Aronoff Center.

Apply 16 Rena Haas new play will premiere at the Emery Theater.

Apply 17 Jo Parks ACT scores were superb; Ed Sims SAT scores, mediocre.

Rule 6: To show possession, use only an apostrophe after (a) plural nouns ending in *s* and (b) a proper name of more than one syllable that ends in *s* or *z*.

Learn 18 The girls' new coach will visit at the Duclos' home next week.

Apply 19 The new shipment of ladies sportswear will arrive on Friday.

Apply 20 Lt. Santos plan for the officers annual ball was outstanding.

ACTIVITY 2

Composing

1. Read at the right the case of the "extra change" error.
2. After considering the comments and suggestions of your friends, what would you do in this situation?
3. Compose/key a paragraph to indicate your choice, how you made it, and why.
4. As a group, discuss the decision(s) reached by various members of the class in terms of *honesty*, *fair play*, and *caring about others*.

Save as: *CS10-ACT2*

You and your friends have arranged to go to dinner together before separating for other activities: a ball game, a movie, a "mixer." To pay for the dinner, you have collected money from each friend.

The restaurant is upscale, the food very good, and the service excellent. Your server has been friendly and has quickly met all your needs. Your server has not rushed you to finish, so you and your friends have enjoyed conversation and laughter long after the meal ended.

When it's time to go, you ask your server for the check and pay it. When you receive your change and are leaving a tip, you notice that your change is $10 more than you should have received.

A discussion takes place among the six of you about this error. Various comments and suggestions are made:

1. Keep the money; the server will never know to whom he gave the extra change.
2. Are you lucky! This never happens to me.
3. You have to return the money. If you don't, the server will have to make up the loss of money at the end of the evening.

Several thoughts go through your mind as you listen to the comments of your friends. You know it would be great to have ten extra dollars to share with your friends. What will my friends think if I return the money, or if I keep it? The server has been very pleasant and has worked hard this evening. If I keep the money, is it right to make the server pay for the error? How would I want to be treated if I made the same mistake at my job?

Job 4

TSEA

We'll use these form ¶s for letters to exhibitors. Key each of the nine ¶s as a separate macro. Use the updated exhibitors list (Job 3) to prepare three "sample" letters to:

- *a business that has never exhibited at TSEA (¶s 2, 4, 5, 8, and 9).*
- *a business that exhibited one to three years (¶s 1, 3, 5, 7, and 9).*
- *a business that exhibited four or more years (¶s 1, 3, 6, 7, and 9).*

Mr. Herriott wants to review these letters before you do the rest.

yp

---

1 The Tri-County Science Education Association's Sixth Annual Conference is scheduled for June 14, 15, and 16 at the Russell Hotel in Charlotte; and you are invited to exhibit your products and services once again.

2 Do you want to exhibit your products and services at a conference that attracts 300+ science teachers in the Charlotte area? If so, you should reserve exhibit space at the Tri-County Science Education Association's Sixth Annual Conference, scheduled for June 14, 15, and 16 at the Russell Hotel in Charlotte.

3 If you respond within 30 days, we can reserve the same space you had last year. If you prefer another location, please review the locations on the enclosed floor plan and identify your first three choices. We will assign your new location after the 30-day period.

4 To reserve a prime location in the exhibit hall, review the enclosed floor plan and select your first three choices. We will assign exhibit space in the order in which the requests are received. Past exhibitors are given preference for a 30-day period.

5 The cost of reserving one space is $250; two spaces, $450; and three spaces, $600. A $100 deposit is required when the space is reserved, and full payment must be received no later than May 15. Exhibitors not paying by May 15 run the risk of losing their space.

6 This year's cost for reserving one space is $250; two spaces, $450; and three spaces, $600. Your cost will be reduced since you have exhibited at the conference for four or more years. Your discount is $50 for one space, $75 for two spaces, and $100 for three. A $100 deposit is required when the space is reserved, and full payment must be received no later than May 15. Exhibitors not paying by May 15 run the risk of losing their space.

7 The Association hopes you will return to our conference so that 300+ science teachers in the Charlotte area can learn firsthand about your science education products and services.

8 TSEA's officers and conference leaders hope you will decide to exhibit at this conference. Over three hundred science teachers in the Charlotte area will be able to speak with your representative and learn how your products and services will help them improve learning.

9 Fill out and return the enclosed exhibitor's registration form soon so that you get the location you prefer. Thank you.

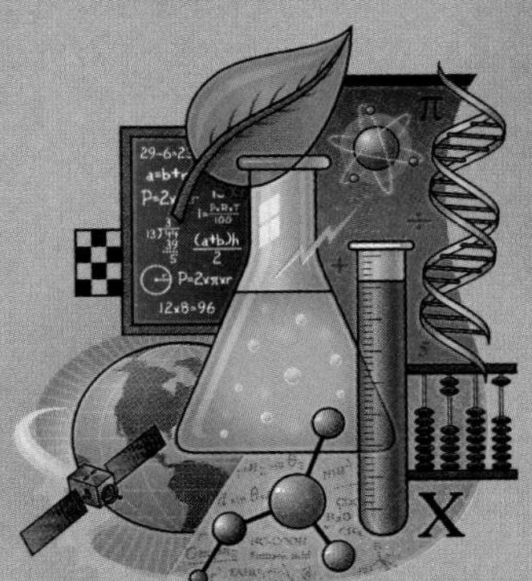

UNIT 25

LESSONS 93–94

Building Basic Skills

LESSON 93 BUILD KEYBOARDING SKILLS

Objectives:

1. To improve keyboarding techniques.
2. To improve straight-copy speed and control.

93A • 5' Conditioning Practice

Key each line twice SS; then key 30" writings on line 3; determine *gwam.*

alphabet 1 If Marjorie has extra help, jigsaw puzzles can be solved quickly.

fig/sym 2 Tom mailed checks #398 & #401 to show he paid for Model #325-769.

speed 3 The busy maid is to rush the clay to the eight girls in the dorm.

gwam 1' | 1 | 2 | 3 | 4 | 5 | 6 | 7 | 8 | 9 | 10 | 11 | 12 | 13 |

SKILL BUILDING

93B • 15' Technique: Response Patterns

1. Key each line twice SS; DS between 2-line groups.
2. Take a 1' writing on each group (lines 4 and 5, 9 and 10, and 14 and 15) as time permits.

Practice **C·U·E**

Letter response—Key these one-hand words steadily and evenly.

Word response—Key these balanced-hand words as words, not letter by letter.

Combination response—Vary your speed: Speed up for easy words; drop back for harder ones.

Letter response

1 at ad be ho we him age ill awe pop cabs hull deaf junk mill areas

2 as we up in be at pin up see him look upon were traded phony beef

3 my ink red car pink nylon sets free join union fast reader awards

4 Extra reserved seats set up in my area at noon served only a few.

5 Rebecca served a plump, sweet plum dessert on my terrace at noon.

gwam 1' | 1 | 2 | 3 | 4 | 5 | 6 | 7 | 8 | 9 | 10 | 11 | 12 | 13 |

Word response

6 by to do or it am bus key off cog cod rot hep make clap bury risk

7 of so is if me cot sit fig zoo jam yang zori thru make wick virus

8 to roam rush it six pairs sight land may mend cozy flame the fork

9 Dirk is due to dismantle the worn antique chair in the dorm hall.

10 My busy neighbor is to go downtown to the giant mall to visit me.

gwam 1' | 1 | 2 | 3 | 4 | 5 | 6 | 7 | 8 | 9 | 10 | 11 | 12 | 13 |

Combination response

11 xi mu pi nu eta chi rho tau phi psi beta zeta kappa sigma phi eta

12 see far eye him jump fast hand held save this they fish do it now

13 dials six queue up right hand look at him men and girls profit by

14 The six beggars deserved a better neighbor than the neurotic man.

15 As a visitor, you may see my hilly island area better by bicycle.

gwam 1' | 1 | 2 | 3 | 4 | 5 | 6 | 7 | 8 | 9 | 10 | 11 | 12 | 13 |

101B-105B • 45' (daily)
Work Assignments

Job 1

> **TSEA**
> *Mr. Herriott wants you to add these exhibitors to the list in CD-TSEA-1. Sort them in alpha order by company and then add five blank rows at the bottom. Print: 2 for the TSEA president and VP.*
> *YP*

Adante Technologies, Tara Olen, 8539 Monroe Rd., Charlotte 28212-7525, 704-555-0110, 1

Compulink, Anne Crevar, 5018 Sunset Rd., Charlotte 28269-2749, 704-555-0156, 1

CT Science Laboratories, Bill Hughes, 5212 W. Highway 74, Monroe 28110-8458, 704-555-0131, 1

DFA Labs, Ed White, 820 Tyvola Rd., Ste. 100, Charlotte 28217-3534, 704-555-0107, 1

MTI, Sidorn Huynh, 227 Franklin Ave., Concord 28025-4908, 704-555-0145, 1

MAR WIN School Supplies, Martha Winter, 700 Hanover Dr., Concord 28027-7827, 704-555-0121, 1

Job 2

> **TSEA**
> *Key this memo from me. Print: 2.*
> *YP*

TO: Katherine Moorcroft, TSEA President
Darrin Thiem, TSEA Vice President

SUBJECT: EXHIBITORS FOR TSEA

Enclosed is a list of the businesses that exhibited at the TSEA Conference last year. Will you review the list and add businesses that you would like Mr. Herriott to invite to this year's conference.

Return your additions to me within 10 days. I will add them to the list; then James Herriott, Exhibits Chair, will write letters to the new exhibitors as well as to those who exhibited last year.

Thank you.

Job 3

> **TSEA**
> *Add these exhibitors to the list (Job 1). None of them exhibited in the past, so enter a zero in the last column. Sort the new list by number of years exhibited (descending order), so Mr. Herriott can send an appropriate letter to each. Print: 1.*
> *YP*

CAI Books
Russ Alarmi
4002 Concord Hwy.
Monroe 28110-8233
704-555-0119

Adobe Systems
Joyce Farno
6701 Carmel Rd., Ste. 203
Charlotte 28226-0200
704-555-0149

Toor Publishers
Karen Fernandez
9812 Rockwood Rd.
Charlotte 28215-8555
704-555-0198

Liberty Press
Vera Green
3601 Rose Lake Dr.
Charlotte 28217-2813
704-555-0159

FirstPlus Experiments
Ralph McNash
5250 77 Center Dr., Ste. 150
Charlotte 28226-0705
704-555-0191

Integra Biology
John Petroni
5795 Gettysburg Dr.
Concord 28027-8855
704-555-0167

93C • 30'
Skill Check

1. Key three 1' writings on each ¶ for speed; determine *gwam*.
2. Take two 1' writings on each ¶ for control; circle errors.
3. Take two 5' writings on all ¶s combined; determine *gwam*; circle errors.
4. Record your better 5' *gwam* and error count for use in 94D.

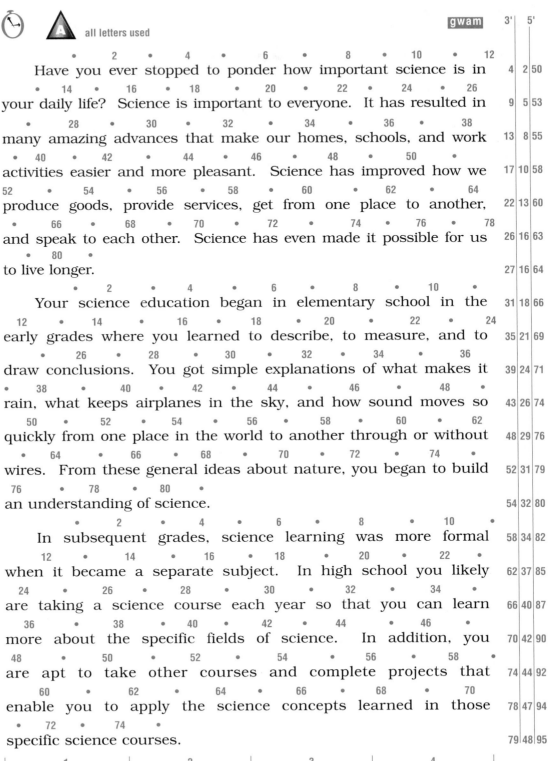

all letters used — gwam 3' | 5'

Have you ever stopped to ponder how important science is in 4 | 2 | 50
your daily life? Science is important to everyone. It has resulted in 9 | 5 | 53
many amazing advances that make our homes, schools, and work 13 | 8 | 55
activities easier and more pleasant. Science has improved how we 17 | 10 | 58
produce goods, provide services, get from one place to another, 22 | 13 | 60
and speak to each other. Science has even made it possible for us 26 | 16 | 63
to live longer. 27 | 16 | 64

Your science education began in elementary school in the 31 | 18 | 66
early grades where you learned to describe, to measure, and to 35 | 21 | 69
draw conclusions. You got simple explanations of what makes it 39 | 24 | 71
rain, what keeps airplanes in the sky, and how sound moves so 43 | 26 | 74
quickly from one place in the world to another through or without 48 | 29 | 76
wires. From these general ideas about nature, you began to build 52 | 31 | 79
an understanding of science. 54 | 32 | 80

In subsequent grades, science learning was more formal 58 | 34 | 82
when it became a separate subject. In high school you likely 62 | 37 | 85
are taking a science course each year so that you can learn 66 | 40 | 87
more about the specific fields of science. In addition, you 70 | 42 | 90
are apt to take other courses and complete projects that 74 | 44 | 92
enable you to apply the science concepts learned in those 78 | 47 | 94
specific science courses. 79 | 48 | 95

gwam 3' 5'

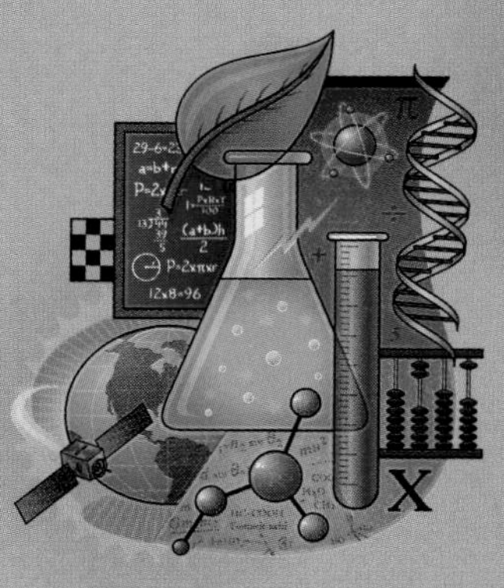

UNIT 27

LESSONS 101–105

TSEA: A Science Conference Simulation

Notes:

Software features. If you need help with software features to complete your work, refer to Software Features Index on pp. R59–R60. Use the Help features in your software, too. Using Help, you can recall or review a feature that you have forgotten. Also use it to learn any new features you may need.

Document formats. Here is a list of formats learned recently. Use the index to find format guides for documents not listed here.

Agenda, p. 243
Form paragraphs, p. 219
Meeting minutes, p. 226
News release, p. 226

Work assignment. Assume that you are participating in a school-based work program for Ms. Yvonne Porterfield, a high school biology teacher. Ms. Porterfield is serving as conference director for the Tri-County Science Education Association's Conference that will be held at the Russell Hotel in Charlotte, NC, in June.

Another teacher, Mr. James Herriott, is serving as Exhibit Chair for the conference. You will work for him as well, but Ms. Porterfield will give his work to you.

As an administrative specialist, your main duty is to process documents needed for the conference.

You completed a job orientation that focused on policies, procedures, and routines in Ms. Porterfield's office. To help you further, she wrote these guidelines for you:

Correspondence. Center all letters vertically in modified block format with mixed punctuation and paragraph indentations. I do not use *Ms.* before my name in the closing lines of letters. Use *Conference Director* as my title.

Supply an appropriate salutation and complimentary close; use your reference initials; and include enclosure and copy notations as needed.

Tables. Center tables horizontally and vertically. Choose all other formatting features to make tables easy to read and attractive.

Reports. Format reports as unbound. Begin and end tables at the margins.

Other.

- Be alert to and correct errors in capitalization, punctuation, spelling, and word usage.
- If a formatting guide or direction is not given, use your knowledge and judgment to complete the task.
- Unless otherwise directed, use the current date.
- Name all files you create with *TSEA* and the job number (*TSEA1*, *TSEA2*, etc.). If a job involves more than one document, add *A, B, C*, etc., to the filename. Existing files have *CD* as a prefix.

LESSONS 101-105 — A SCIENCE CONFERENCE SIMULATION

Objectives:

1. To demonstrate your ability to integrate your knowledge and skills.
2. To demonstrate your ability to solve problems and make correct decisions.

101A-105A • 5' (daily) Conditioning Practice

Key each line twice SS; take 1' writings on lines 1–3 as time permits.

alphabet 1 Zelda was quite naive to pack two big boxes with just fresh yams.
figures 2 Flight 4365 will leave Runway 28L at 10 p.m. with 297 passengers.
speed 3 Pamela kept the emblem and shamrock in the fir box on the mantle.

gwam 1' | 1 | 2 | 3 | 4 | 5 | 6 | 7 | 8 | 9 | 10 | 11 | 12 | 13 |

BUILD KEYBOARDING AND LANGUAGE SKILLS

Objectives:

1. To improve keyboarding techniques.
2. To improve straight-copy speed and control.

94A • 5'
Conditioning Practice

Key each line twice SS; then take 30" writings on line 3; determine *gwam.*

alphabet 1 Both weary girls were just amazed by the five quick extra points.

fig/sym 2 JR & Sons used P.O. #7082-B35 to order 154 chairs (Style LE-196).

speed 3 The antique bowl she saw at the downtown mall is authentic ivory.

gwam 1' | 1 | 2 | 3 | 4 | 5 | 6 | 7 | 8 | 9 | 10 | 11 | 12 | 13 |

LANGUAGE SKILLS

94B • 7'
Language Skills: Word Choice

1. Study the spelling and definitions of the words at the right.
2. Key the Learn lines, noting word choice.
3. Key the Apply lines, selecting the correct words.
4. Check your work with the instructor. Rekey lines that contain word-choice errors.

Save as: *CHOICE94B*

poor (adj) having little wealth or value

pore (vb/n) to study carefully; a tiny opening in a surface, such as skin

pour (vb) to make flow or stream; to rain hard

right (adj) factual; true; correct

rite (n) customary form of ceremony; ritual

write (vb) to form letters or symbols; to compose and set down in words, numbers, or symbols

Learn 1 **Pour** the fertilizer over the **poor** soil before you till it.
Learn 2 As we **pore** over these formulas, others are playing football.
Apply 3 You can (poor/pore/pour) the soup for the (poor/pore/pour) men.
Apply 4 (Poor/Pore/Pour) over the fine print before you buy the policy.

Learn 1 I may **write** a paper on the tribal **rite** of passage into manhood.
Learn 2 You have a **right** to participate in the **rite** of graduation.
Apply 3 To succeed, (right/rite/write) in the (right/rite/write) way.
Apply 4 The processional is just one (right/rite/write) in the ceremony.

SKILL BUILDING

94C • 8'
Technique: Response Patterns

1. Key each line twice SS; DS between 2-line groups. Try to increase your rate when repeating a line.
2. Take a 1' writing on each group of lines as time permits.

Technique **C • U • E**

Keep fingers curved and upright, lightly touching home-row keys. Reach with fingers; keep hands still.

One-hand words

1 are ace ill bar lip cat mom dad nil ear oil fad pop cab were upon
2 beg rag hip sat hop sew ink tag joy tea mop wax pin web noun seat
3 cab area hook beef join drab jump edge look fact moon nylon gates
4 egg rare imply saga jolly star onion tear phony weave union zebra

gwam 1' | 1 | 2 | 3 | 4 | 5 | 6 | 7 | 8 | 9 | 10 | 11 | 12 | 13 |

Balanced-hand words

5 aid bug cob cut dig elf fit got ham iris jams kept lake meld name
6 owl own pro pay quay roam sick soap than curl vial wish yang meld
7 rue also body city disk envy foam goal half idle jape kale laughs
8 oak usual mantle naught orient papaya quench enrich social theory

gwam 1' | 1 | 2 | 3 | 4 | 5 | 6 | 7 | 8 | 9 | 10 | 11 | 12 | 13 |

Internal Punctuation: Hyphen

> Rule 5: Use a hyphen to join compound numbers from twenty-one to ninety-nine that are keyed as words.

Learn 14 Sixty-seven students met in the gym; about twenty-seven wore the uniform.
Apply 15 Thirty five guests attended Anita's twenty first birthday party.
Apply 16 Thirty four delegates went to the national convention.

> Rule 6: Use a hyphen to join compound adjectives preceding a noun they modify as a unit.

Learn 17 End-of-term grades will be posted outside the classroom.
Apply 18 The most up to date fashions are featured in the store window.
Apply 19 Their new computer programs feature state of the art graphics.

ACTIVITY 2

Listening

Complete the listening activity as directed at the right.

Save as: *CS11-ACT2*

1. Open the sound file (*CD-CS11LISTN*) that contains three mental math problems.
2. Each problem starts with a number, followed by several addition, subtraction, multiplication, and division steps. Key or handwrite the new answer after each step, but *compute* the answer mentally.
3. Record the last answer for each problem.
4. After the third problem, close the file.
5. Check the accuracy of your work with the instructor.
6. Repeat the activity if you made an error.

ACTIVITY 3

Write to Learn

Complete the Write-to-Learn activity as directed at the right.

Save as: *CS11-ACT3*

1. Using word processing or speech recognition software, write a paragraph explaining how to insert clip art from a file into a word processing document.
2. Write a second paragraph explaining how to add a border to a title page.

ACTIVITY 4

Reading

1. Open the file *CD-CS11READ* and read the document carefully.
2. Close the file.
3. Key the answers to the questions at the right.
4. Check the accuracy of your work with the instructor.

Save as: *CS11-ACT4*

1. What service does WebGate provide?
2. What is the amount of the most recent acquisition?
3. Was WebGate founded more than five years ago?
4. In what states does WebGate do business?
5. In what state does the most recent acquisition do business?
6. Have all acquisitions been financed by a Charlotte bank?
7. About how many customers does WebGate serve?

94D • 30'
Skill Check

1. Key two 1' writings on each ¶ for speed; determine *gwam.*
2. Take two 1' writings on each ¶ for control; circle errors.
3. Take two 3' writings on all ¶s combined; determine *gwam;* circle errors.
4. Record your better 3' *gwam.*
5. Key one 5' writing on all ¶s combined; determine *gwam;* circle errors.
6. Compare your 5' rate to your 3' rate and to the 5' rate and error count recorded for 93C.

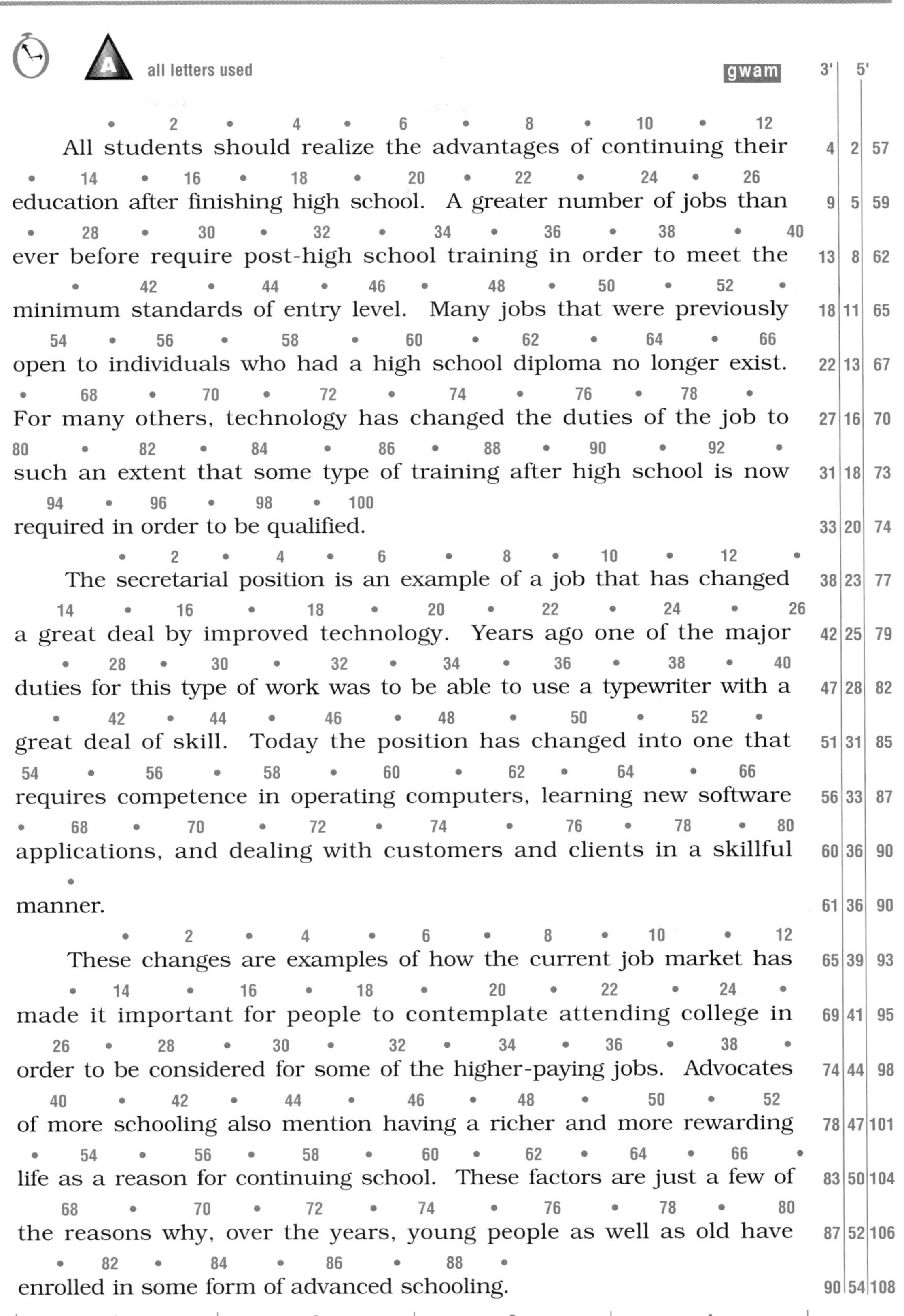

all letters used

	gwam 3'		5'
All students should realize the advantages of continuing their	4	2	57
education after finishing high school. A greater number of jobs than	9	5	59
ever before require post-high school training in order to meet the	13	8	62
minimum standards of entry level. Many jobs that were previously	18	11	65
open to individuals who had a high school diploma no longer exist.	22	13	67
For many others, technology has changed the duties of the job to	27	16	70
such an extent that some type of training after high school is now	31	18	73
required in order to be qualified.	33	20	74
The secretarial position is an example of a job that has changed	38	23	77
a great deal by improved technology. Years ago one of the major	42	25	79
duties for this type of work was to be able to use a typewriter with a	47	28	82
great deal of skill. Today the position has changed into one that	51	31	85
requires competence in operating computers, learning new software	56	33	87
applications, and dealing with customers and clients in a skillful	60	36	90
manner.	61	36	90
These changes are examples of how the current job market has	65	39	93
made it important for people to contemplate attending college in	69	41	95
order to be considered for some of the higher-paying jobs. Advocates	74	44	98
of more schooling also mention having a richer and more rewarding	78	47	101
life as a reason for continuing school. These factors are just a few of	83	50	104
the reasons why, over the years, young people as well as old have	87	52	106
enrolled in some form of advanced schooling.	90	54	108

gwam 3' | 1 | 2 | 3 | 4
5' | 1 | 2 | 3

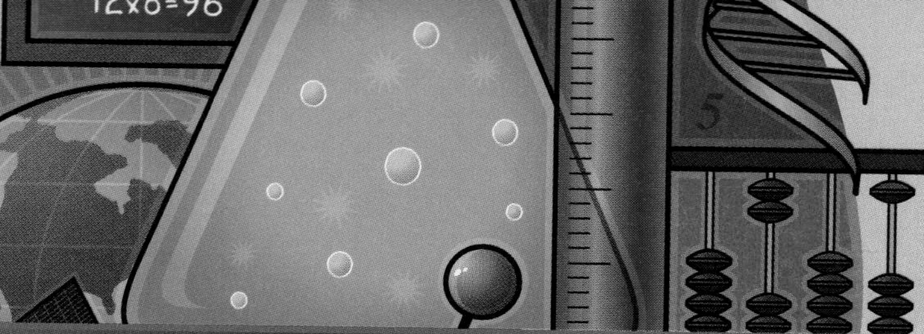

Communication Skills

11

ACTIVITY 1

Internal Punctuation: Quotation Marks and Hyphens

1. Key lines 1–10 at the right, inserting the needed single and double quotation marks and hyphens.
2. Check the accuracy of your work with the instructor; correct any errors you made.
3. Note the rule number at the left of each sentence in which you made a quotation mark or hyphen error.
4. Using the rules at right and on p. 271, identify the rule(s) you need to review/practice.
5. **Read**: Study each rule.
6. **Learn**: Key the Learn line(s) beneath it, noting how the rule is applied.
7. **Apply**: Key the Apply line(s), correctly using single and double quotation marks and hyphens.

Save as: *CS11-ACT1*

Proofread & Correct

Rules

1 1 The coach asked, How many of you practiced during the summer?

1 2 Didn't Browne say, "There is no road or ready way to virtue?"

2 3 Do you and your sister regularly watch The Nanny on TV?

2 4 My mom's column, Speak Up, appears in the local newspaper.

3 5 You have trouble deciding when to use accept and except.

1,4 6 I said, I must take, as Frost wrote, 'the road less traveled.

5 7 Jae boasted, "I'm almost twenty one; you're thirty two."

6 8 My older self confident cousin sells life insurance door to door.

6 9 The hard working outfitter readied our canoe faster than I expected.

6 10 Over the counter sales showed a great increase last month.

Internal Punctuation: Quotation Marks

Rule 1: Use quotation marks to enclose direct quotations. **Note**: When a question mark applies to the entire sentence, place it outside the quotation marks.

Learn 1 Professor Dye asked, "Are you spending the summer in Europe?"

Learn 2 Was it Emerson who said, "To have a friend is to be one"?

Apply 3 Marcella asked, May I borrow your class notes from yesterday?

Apply 4 Did John Donne say, No man is an island, entire of itself?

Rule 2: Use quotation marks to enclose titles of articles, films/movies, plays, poems, songs, television programs, and unpublished works, such as theses and dissertations.

Learn 5 Kari read aloud the poem "Fog" from Sandburg's Selected Poems.

Apply 6 The song Getting to Know You is from The King and I.

Apply 7 The title of his term paper is Computer Software for Grade 4.

Rule 3: Use quotation marks to enclose special words or phrases used for emphasis or for coined words (words not in dictionary usage).

Learn 8 My problem: I have "limited resources" and "unlimited wants."

Apply 9 His talk was filled with phrases like ah and you know.

Apply 10 She said that the words phony and braggart describe him.

Rule 4: Use a single quotation mark (the apostrophe) to indicate a quotation within a quotation (including titles and words as indicated in Rules 2 and 3, above).

Learn 11 I wrote, "We must have, as Tillich said, 'the courage to be.'"

Apply 12 I said, "As Milton wrote, he is 'sober, steadfast, and demure."

Apply 13 I say, "Don't lie, for Swift said, facts are stubborn things."

(continued on next page)

UNIT 26

LESSONS 95–100

Creating Employment Documents

Format Guides:

Resume (Data Sheet), Reference List, Application Letter, Application Form, Interview Follow-up Letter

Douglas H. Ruckert
8503 Kirby Dr.
Houston, TX 77054-8220
(713) 555-0121
dougr@suresend.com

SUMMARY

Strong communication and telephone skills; excellent keyboarding, computer, and Internet skills; and good organizational and interpersonal skills.

EDUCATION

Will be graduated from Eisenhower Technical High School in June 2002, with a high school diploma and business technology emphasis. Grade point average is 3.75.

Relevant Skills and Courses:

Proficient with most recent versions of Windows and Office, including Word, Excel, Access, PowerPoint, and FrontPage.

Excelled in the following courses: Keyboarding, Computer Applications, Business Communication, and Office Technology.

Major Accomplishments:

Future Business Leaders of America: Member for four years; vice president for one year. Won second place in Public Speaking at District Competition; competed (same event) at state level.

Varsity soccer: Lettered three years and served as captain during senior year.

Recognition: Named one of Eisenhower's Top Ten Community Service Providers at end of junior year.

WORK EXPERIENCE

Hinton's Family Restaurant, Server (2001-present): Served customers in culturally diverse area; oriented new part-time employees and resolved routine customer service problems.

Tuma's Landscape and Garden Center, Sales (2000-2001): Assisted customers with plant selection and responsible for stocking and arranging display areas.

REFERENCES

Will be furnished upon request.

Electronic Resume

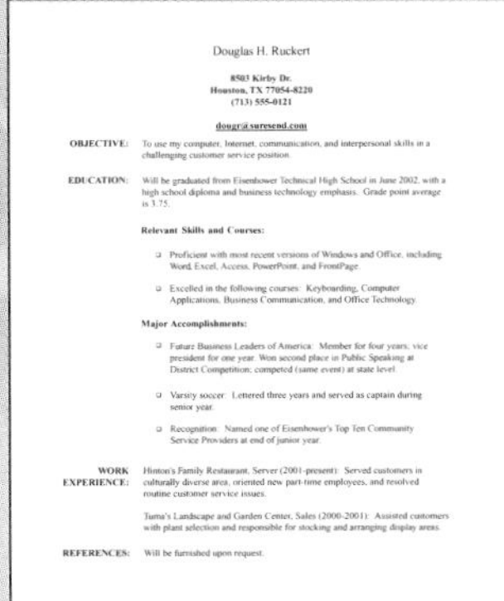

Douglas H. Ruckert

8503 Kirby Dr.
Houston, TX 77054-8220
(713) 555-0121

dougr@suresend.com

OBJECTIVE: To use my computer, Internet, communication, and interpersonal skills in a challenging customer service position.

EDUCATION: Will be graduated from Eisenhower Technical High School in June 2002, with a high school diploma and business technology emphasis. Grade point average is 3.75.

Relevant Skills and Courses:

- Proficient with most recent versions of Windows and Office, including Word, Excel, Access, PowerPoint, and FrontPage.
- Excelled in the following courses: Keyboarding, Computer Applications, Business Communication, and Office Technology.

Major Accomplishments:

- Future Business Leaders of America: Member for four years; vice president for one year. Won second place in Public Speaking at District Competition; competed (same event) at state level.
- Varsity soccer: Lettered three years and served as captain during senior year.
- Recognition: Named one of Eisenhower's Top Ten Community Service Providers at end of junior year.

WORK EXPERIENCE: Hinton's Family Restaurant, Server (2001-present): Served customers in culturally diverse area, oriented new part-time employees, and resolved routine customer service issues.

Tuma's Landscape and Garden Center, Sales (2000-2001): Assisted customers with plant selection and responsible for stocking and arranging display areas.

REFERENCES: Will be furnished upon request.

Print Resume

Employment Document Guidelines

Employment documents provide applicants an opportunity to present their best qualities to prospective employers. These qualities are represented by the content of the documents as well as by their accuracy, format, and neatness. The care with which you prepare your documents suggests to employers how carefully you would work if hired. Therefore, give special attention to preparing your employment documents.

In addition to a data sheet, or resume (pronounced REZ oo MAY), common types of employment documents are an application letter, application form, reference list, and interview follow-up letter.

Resume

In most cases, a **resume** should be limited to one page. The information presented usually covers six major areas: *personal information* (your name, home address, e-mail address, and telephone number[s]); *objective* (clear definition of position desired); *education* (courses and/or program taken, skills acquired, grade point average [and grades earned in courses directly related to job competence], and graduation date); *school and/or community activities or accomplishments* (organizations, leadership positions, and honors and awards); *work experience* (position name, name and location of employer, and brief description of responsibilities); and a notation that *references* (names of people familiar with your character, personality, and work habits) will be provided upon request.

In general, the most important information is presented first, which means that most people who have recently graduated from high school will list educational background before work experience. The reference section is usually last on the page.

Print versus electronic resumes. *Print resumes* are those printed on paper and mailed to prospective employers. *Electronic resumes* are those attached to e-mail or posted to a Web page. (See model electronic and print resumes on pp. 263 and 264, respectively.)

Resume scanning. Many companies scan both print and electronic resumes into database files and then search each file for specific information. They may search for education level, work experience, or keywords that are closely related to the position being filled.

When you believe an employer is not likely to scan your resume, your print resume may contain format features, such as indentations and columns; and text enhancements, such as bold, bullets, several font designs and sizes, and underlines. These types of features and enhancements can cause errors or disappear entirely or partially when a resume is scanned, attached to e-mail, or posted to a Web page. Therefore such features and enhancements should be omitted from an electronic resume—and from a print resume that may be scanned.

To increase the likelihood that their resume will be selected in a database search, many people replace the Objective section with a Summary section (see the electronic resume on p. 263). The summary contains keywords describing education, positions held, skills, and/or accomplishments that relate to the position being sought.

Note:
Some large organizations offer a Web page on which job applicants can post electronic resumes. Applicants also can post electronic resumes at career-oriented Internet sites, such as www.monster.com.

100C • 10'
Employment Test: Timed Writing

1. Take a 5' writing on all ¶s.
2. Determine *gwam* and number of errors.

  all letters used

	gwam 3'	5'	
Appearance, which is often defined as the outward aspect of	4	2	41
someone or something, is quite important to most of us and af-	8	5	44
fects just about every day of our lives. We like to be around	12	7	46
people whom and things that we consider attractive. Because of	16	10	49
this preference, appearance is a factor in almost every decision	21	12	52
we make.	21	13	52
Appearance often affects our selection of food, the place in	25	15	54
which we live, the clothes we purchase, the car we drive, and the	30	18	57
vacations we schedule. For example, we usually do not eat foods	34	20	60
that are not visually appealing or buy clothing that we realize	38	23	62
will be unattractive to others who are important to us.	42	25	64
Appearance is important in business. People in charge of	46	27	67
hiring almost always stress the importance of good appearance.	50	30	69
Your progress in a job or career can be affected by how others	54	33	72
judge your appearance. It is not uncommon for those who see but	59	35	74
do not know you to evaluate your abilities and character on the	63	38	77
basis of your personal appearance.	65	39	78

gwam 3' 5'

Use the Occupational Outlook Handbook to find information on jobs. Follow directions at the right.

1. Access this site: http://stats.bls.gov:80/ocohome.htm.
2. Perform a keyword search on an occupation that interests you. For example: teacher, engineer, mathematician, scientist, attorney, physician, etc.
3. Find a link you are interested in and access it.
4. Access one of these links and read the information provided: (a) Training, Other Qualifications, and Advancement; (b) Job Outlook; or (c) Earnings.
5. Use speech recognition software or your keyboard to compose one or more paragraphs describing what you learned about the occupation you chose. Save it as *U26INTACT*.
6. Print one page from the Web site that pertains to what you composed.

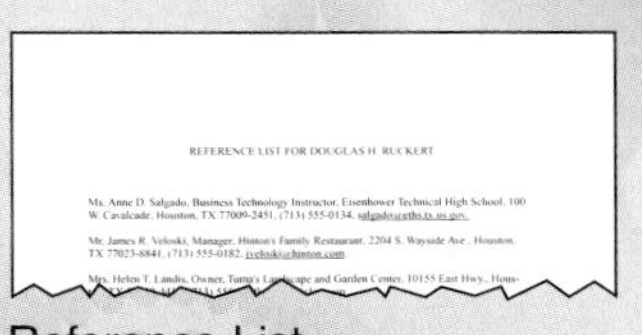

Reference List

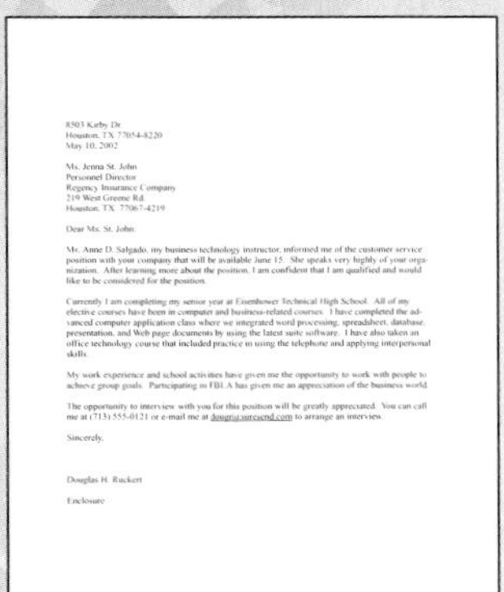

Application Letter

Application Form

Follow-up Letter

Resume do's and don'ts. Follow these guidelines when creating your resume.

- Do use a simple format. Top, bottom, and side margins of 1" are acceptable but may vary slightly depending on the amount of information presented.
- Do key your name at the top of the page on a line by itself. Key your address (standard, not USPS style) below your name, and list each telephone number on a separate line.
- Do arrange the resume parts attractively on the page. The arrangement may vary with personal preference and the purpose of the resume.
- On an electronic resume or print resume that may be scanned, don't use font effects, such as engrave and outline; apply borders or shading; or insert clip art, horizontal lines, or photographs.
- Do use a basic font, such as Times New Roman or Courier, 12 pt.
- Do use white, ivory, or light-colored (gray or tan) paper, standard size (8.5" x 11") for a print resume.

Reference List

When a resume indicates that references will be furnished upon request, you should prepare a **reference list** to take with you to employment interviews. If you prefer, references may be listed on the resume, at the end of the page.

The reference list should contain the name, address, telephone number, and e-mail address (if the person uses e-mail) of three to six people (not relatives) who know you well. Teachers, clergy, and part-time employers usually make good references.

Ask each person in advance for permission to list her or his name as a reference, and describe the job for which you are applying. Be sure all names are spelled correctly and that addresses and telephone numbers are accurate. Include each person's organization and job title.

To format a reference list, use a 2" top margin and 1" side margins. Include a centered title, such as REFERENCES FOR *(insert your name)*. QS below the title; list the references SS with a DS between them.

Application Letter

An **application letter** should always accompany a resume. This personal-business letter should be limited to one page.

The application letter should include three topics—generally in three to five paragraphs. The first topic (¶) should specify the position for which you are applying and may state how you learned of the opening and something positive about the company.

The second topic (one to three ¶s) should include evidence that you qualify for the position. This is the place to interpret information presented in your resume and to show how your qualifications relate to the job for which you are applying.

The last paragraph should request an interview and give precise information for contacting you to arrange it.

Application Form

Many companies require an applicant to complete an **application form** even though a resume and application letter have been received. Applicants often fill in forms at the company, using a pen to write on a printed form or keying information into an online form.

Sometimes applicants may take an application form home, complete it, and return it by mail or in person. In this case, the information should be keyed on the form, although hand printing is acceptable. In any case, you should strive to provide information that is accurate, complete, legible, and neat.

To lessen the chance of error on an application, make a copy of the blank form to complete as a rough draft.

Interview Follow-up Letter

The **follow-up letter** is a thank-you for the time given and courtesies extended to you during a job interview. This personal-business letter lets the interviewer know that you are still interested in the job, and it reminds him/her of your application and qualifications. This letter should be mailed within 24 hours after the interview to increase the likelihood that it is received before an applicant is selected for the job.

100B • 45' Document Processing Employment Test

Employers often require job applicants to take a test on job-related tasks. Since keyboarding and word processing skills are important to a customer service position, you are asked during your employment interview to return to complete the document processing portion of an employment test.

Document 1 (Letter)

Format the text at the right as a letter in modified block style, using mixed punctuation, ¶ indentations, and the current date.

 **Save as:** *LTR100B*

Ms. Carol Parker | Facilities Manager | **TPC**, Inc. | 8290 Rockdale Dr. | Dallas, TX 75220-0396 | Dear Ms. Parker

(¶) You have probably heard the saying **"Time is money."** If you are concerned about your company's time and money, you will be interested in hearing how the **T**elephone **P**rofessional **C**onsultants can save your company both ***time*** and ***money***.

(¶) Improved technology continues to change the way a telephone system can enhance your business operations by increasing the productivity of your employees and the satisfaction of your customers.

(¶) Please call me at (505) 555-0128 to schedule one of our **T**elephone **P**rofessional **C**onsultants for a complimentary update on new options that will improve your telephone system.

Sincerely | Jason Hawthorn | New Accounts Manager | xx

Document 2 (Table)

Format the table at the right, making these changes:

a. Make row height 0.5".
b. Place the secondary heading in a row by itself.
c. Adjust column width to fit contents.
d. Center the table on the page.

 **Save as:** *TBL100B*

HOW AIRLINES RATE **Performance for the Airlines for October**			
Airline	**% of On-Time Arrivals**	**Mishandled Bags Per 1,000 Passengers**	**Complaints Per 10,000 Passengers**
Five Star	84.7%	4.27	.75
Alpha	85.3%	3.98	.82
Airtram	75.2%	4.76	.98
GTY	86.0%	4.98	.95
Ameriway	79.2%	4.12	.96

Document 3 (Report)

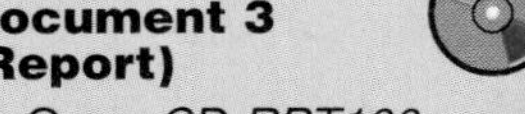

1. Open *CD-RPT100.*
2. Format the document as a bound report with textual citations, following the directions at the right.

 **Save as:** *RPT100B*

1. Bold all headings.
2. Change all occurrences of *candidates* to *applicants.*
3. Eliminate all occurrences of *prospective* before *employers.*
4. Move the section titled **Making a "Trial Run"** below the section titled **Preparing for the Interview.**
5. Add these references at the end of the report, properly formatted.

REFERENCES

Fulton-Calkins, Patsy and Joanna D. Hanks. Procedures for the Office Professional, 4th ed. Cincinnati: South-Western Educational Publishing, 2000.

"Interviewing Tips." Management Recruiters of Chanhassen. http://www.mrchan.com/interview.htm (15 January 2000).

Oliverio, Mary Ellen, William R. Pasewark, and Bonnie R. White. The Office: Procedures and Technology, 3d ed. Cincinnati: South-Western Educational Publishing, 1998.

6. Bold and italicize the last sentence of the report.
7. Prevent widow/orphan lines and keep side headings with text.
8. Number all pages except p. 1 at the top right.
9. Proofread and correct all errors. (The file does contain errors.)

LESSONS 95-96

CREATE ELECTRONIC AND PRINT RESUMES

Objectives:

1. To learn to format print and electronic resumes.
2. To learn to format reference lists.

95A-96A • 5' (daily) Conditioning Practice

Key each line twice SS; then take 30" writings on line 3; determine *gwam.*

alphabet 1 Vicki expects to query a dozen boys and girls for the major show.

figures 2 Ramon Jones & Company's fax number was changed to (835) 109-2647.

speed 3 If the tug slams the dock, it may make a big problem for the men.

gwam 1' | 1 | 2 | 3 | 4 | 5 | 6 | 7 | 8 | 9 | 10 | 11 | 12 | 13 |

FORMATTING

95B-96B • 40' Two Resume Models

Resumes 1 and 2

Save as: *ELREZ95-1, PRREZ95-2*

1. On pp. 260–261, read the entire section titled *Resume.*
2. Study the electronic resume model on p. 263.
3. Format and key the electronic resume from the model.
4. Study the print resume model on p. 264.
5. Format and key the print resume from the model.

95C-96C • 10' Reference List

Save as: *REF95-3*

1. Read the Reference List section of the Format Guides on p. 261.
2. Open the file *CD-REF95.* Insert this title and reference *above* the two references in the file, and format the list.

REFERENCE LIST FOR DOUGLAS H. RUCKERT

Ms. Anne D. Salgado, Business Technology Instructor, Eisenhower Technical High School, 100 W. Cavalcade, Houston, TX 77009-2451, (713) 555-0134, salgado@eths.tx.us.gov.

95D-96D • 45' My Resumes

My Resumes 1 and 2

Save as: *MYELREZ95-4 MYPRREZ95-5*

1. Compose a resume for yourself.
2. Edit the rough draft; then format the final draft as an electronic resume. Save and close the file.
3. Open your electronic resume. Reformat the document as a print resume.

LESSON 97

CREATE AND REVISE EMPLOYMENT APPLICATION LETTERS

Objective:

To study the content of and create and revise application letters.

97A • 5' Conditioning Practice

Key each line twice SS; then take 30" writings on line 3; determine *gwam.*

alphabet 1 Cody acquired six new blue jackets to give as prizes to freshmen.

figures 2 Lori served 439 hot dogs, 528 donuts, and 1,067 drinks yesterday.

speed 3 Turn down the lane by the lake to see them work in the cornfield.

gwam 1' | 1 | 2 | 3 | 4 | 5 | 6 | 7 | 8 | 9 | 10 | 11 | 12 | 13 |

(After completing 97A, turn to p. 265)

Application for Employment
Regency Insurance Company

An Equal Opportunity Employer

PERSONAL INFORMATION

NAME (LAST FIRST)	SOCIAL SECURITY NO.	CURRENT DATE	TELEPHONE NUMBER
Ruckert, Douglas H.	368-56-2890	5/22/02	(713) 555-0121

ADDRESS (NUMBER, STREET, CITY, STATE, ZIP CODE)	U.S. CITIZEN	DATE YOU CAN START
8503 Kirby Dr., Houston, TX 77054-8220	☒ YES ☐ NO	6/08/02

ARE YOU EMPLOYED NOW?	IF YES, MAY WE INQUIRE OF YOUR PRESENT EMPLOYER?	IF YES, GIVE NAME AND NUMBER OF PERSON TO CALL
☒ YES ☐ NO	☒ YES ☐ NO	James Veloski, Manager (713) 555-0182

POSITION DESIRED	SALARY DESIRED	STATE HOW YOU LEARNED OF POSITION
Customer Service	Open	From Ms. Anne D. Salgado, Eisenhower Business Technology Teacher

HAVE YOU EVER BEEN CONVICTED OF A FELONY?
☐ YES ☒ NO   IF YES, EXPLAIN.

EDUCATION

	NAME AND LOCATION OF SCHOOL	YEARS ATTENDED	DID YOU GRADUATE?	SUBJECTS STUDIED
COLLEGE				
HIGH SCHOOL	Eisenhower Technical High School, Houston, TX	1998 TO 2002	Will be graduated 06/02	Business Technology
GRADE SCHOOL				
OTHER				

SUBJECTS OF SPECIAL STUDY/RESEARCH WORK OR SPECIAL TRAINING/SKILLS DIRECTLY RELATED TO POSITION DESIRED

Windows and Office Suite, including Word, Excel, Access, PowerPoint, and FrontPage

Office technology course with telephone training and interpersonal skills role-playing

FORMER EMPLOYERS (LIST LAST POSITION FIRST)

FROM - TO (MTH & YEAR)	NAME AND ADDRESS	SALARY	POSITION	REASON FOR LEAVING
9/01 to present	Hinton's Family Restaurant, 2204 S. Wayside Ave., Houston, TX 77023-8841	$6.85/hr.	Server	Want full-time position in my field
6/00 to 9/01	Tuma's Landscape and Garden Center, 10155 East Hwy., Houston, TX 77029-4419	$5.75/hr.	Sales	Employed at Hinton's

REFERENCES (LIST THREE PERSONS NOT RELATED TO YOU, WHOM YOU HAVE KNOWN AT LEAST ONE YEAR)

NAME	BUSINESS ADDRESS	TELEPHONE NUMBER	TITLE	YEARS KNOWN
Ms. Anne D. Salgado	Eisenhower Technical High School, 100 W. Cavalcade, Houston, TX 77009-2451	(713) 555-0134	Business Technology Instructor	Four
Mr. James R. Veloski	Hinton's Family Restaurant, 2204 S. Wayside Ave., Houston, TX 77023-8841	(713) 555-0182	Manager	One
Mrs. Helen T. Landis	Tuma's Landscape and Garden Center, 10155 East Hwy., Houston, TX 77029-4419	(713) 555-0149	Owner	Three

I UNDERSTAND THAT I SHALL NOT BECOME AN EMPLOYEE UNTIL I HAVE SIGNED AN EMPLOYMENT AGREEMENT WITH THE FINAL APPROVAL OF THE EMPLOYER AND THAT SUCH EMPLOYMENT WILL BE SUBJECT TO VERIFICATION OF PREVIOUS EMPLOYMENT DATA PROVIDED IN THIS APPLICATION, ANY RELATED DOCUMENTS, OR DATA SHEET. I KNOW THAT A REPORT MAY BE MADE THAT WILL INCLUDE INFORMATION CONCERNING ANY FACTOR THE EMPLOYER MIGHT FIND RELEVANT TO THE POSITION FOR WHICH I AM APPLYING, AND THAT I CAN MAKE A WRITTEN REQUEST FOR ADDITIONAL INFORMATION AS TO THE NATURE AND SCOPE OF THE REPORT IF ONE IS MADE.

Douglas H. Ruckert
SIGNATURE OF APPLICANT

Employment Application Form

Douglas H. Ruckert
8503 Kirby Dr.
Houston, TX 77054-8220
(713) 555-0121
dougr@suresend.com

SUMMARY

Strong communication and telephone skills; excellent keyboarding, computer, and Internet skills; and good organizational and interpersonal skills.

EDUCATION

Will be graduated from Eisenhower Technical High School in June 2002, with a high school diploma and business technology emphasis. Grade point average is 3.75.

Relevant Skills and Courses:

Proficient with most recent versions of Windows and Office, including Word, Excel, Access, PowerPoint, and FrontPage.

Excelled in the following courses: Keyboarding, Computer Applications, Business Communication, and Office Technology.

Major Accomplishments:

Future Business Leaders of America: Member for four years; vice president for one year. Won second place in Public Speaking at District Competition; competed (same event) at state level.

Varsity soccer: Lettered three years and served as captain during senior year.

Recognition: Named one of Eisenhower's Top Ten Community Service Providers at end of junior year.

WORK EXPERIENCE

Hinton's Family Restaurant, Server (2001-present): Served customers in culturally diverse area; oriented new part-time employees and resolved routine customer service problems.

Tuma's Landscape and Garden Center, Sales (2000-2001): Assisted customers with plant selection and responsible for stocking and arranging display areas.

REFERENCES

Will be furnished upon request.

Electronic Resume (Resume 1)

LESSONS 98-99

PREPARE APPLICATION FORMS AND FOLLOW-UP LETTERS

Objectives:

1. To identify typical information on job application forms and prepare one.
2. To study content of and key follow-up letters.

98A-99A • 5' (daily) Conditioning Practice

Key each line twice SS; then take 30" writings on line 3; determine *gwam.*

alphabet 1 Jaxie amazed the partial crowd by kicking five quick field goals.

figures 2 Call 375-4698 by April 27 to set the 10 a.m. meeting with Sandra.

speed 3 Their visit may end the problems and make the firm a tidy profit.

gwam 1' | 1 | 2 | 3 | 4 | 5 | 6 | 7 | 8 | 9 | 10 | 11 | 12 | 13 |

98B-99B • 55' Employment Application Forms

Forms 1 and 2

1. Open file *CD-FORM98.* Print *two* copies of the application form; then close the file.
2. Complete one form (print neatly) using information from the model on p. 267 (Form 1).
3. Using information from your resume (*MYELREZ95-4*), complete an application form for one of the positions advertised on p. 265 (Form 2).

98C-99C • 40' Follow-up Letters

Letter 1

1. Read guides for follow-up letters on p. 261.
2. Format/key the letter at the right in block style.

Save as: *LTR98C1*

Letter 2

1. Assume you were interviewed for the position selected in 98B, Form 2.
2. Compose a follow-up letter; edit and prepare a final copy.

Save as: *LTR98C2*

8503 Kirby Dr. | Houston, TX 77054-8220 | May 25, 2002 | Ms. Jenna St. John | Personnel Director | Regency Insurance Company | 219 West Greene Rd. | Houston, TX 77067-4219 | Dear Ms. St. John:

(¶) Thank you for discussing the customer service opening at Regency Insurance Company. I have a much better understanding of the position after meeting with you and Mr. Meade.

(¶) Mr. Meade was extremely helpful in explaining the specific job responsibilities. My previous jobs and my business technology classes required me to complete many of the tasks that he mentioned. With minimal training, I believe I could be an asset to your company.

(¶) Even though I realize it will be a real challenge to replace a person like Mr. Meade, it is a challenge that I will welcome. If there is further information that would be helpful as you consider my application, please let me know.

Sincerely, | Douglas H. Ruckert

LESSON 100

TAKE A DOCUMENT PROCESSING EMPLOYMENT TEST

Objectives:

1. To identify typical tasks in a document processing employment test.
2. To take an employment test.

100A • 5' Conditioning Practice

Key each line twice SS; then key 30" writings on line 3; determine *gwam.*

alphabet 1 Quent packed an extra big jar of very zesty wild apples for them.

figures 2 I tried this equation: 7(12X + 140) + 5(X - 6) = 3(X + 50) - 98.

speed 3 The ensign works with the busy official to right the big problem.

gwam 1' | 1 | 2 | 3 | 4 | 5 | 6 | 7 | 8 | 9 | 10 | 11 | 12 | 13 |

Douglas H. Ruckert

8503 Kirby Dr.
Houston, TX 77054-8220
(713) 555-0121

dougr@suresend.com

OBJECTIVE: To use my computer, Internet, communication, and interpersonal skills in a challenging customer service position.

EDUCATION: Will be graduated from Eisenhower Technical High School in June 2002, with a high school diploma and business technology emphasis. Grade point average is 3.75.

Relevant Skills and Courses:

- Proficient with most recent versions of Windows and Office, including Word, Excel, Access, PowerPoint, and FrontPage.
- Excelled in the following courses: Keyboarding, Computer Applications, Business Communication, and Office Technology.

Major Accomplishments:

- Future Business Leaders of America: Member for four years; vice president for one year. Won second place in Public Speaking at District Competition; competed (same event) at state level.
- Varsity soccer: Lettered three years and served as captain during senior year.
- Recognition: Named one of Eisenhower's Top Ten Community Service Providers at end of junior year.

WORK EXPERIENCE: Hinton's Family Restaurant, Server (2001-present): Served customers in culturally diverse area, oriented new part-time employees, and resolved routine customer service issues.

Tuma's Landscape and Garden Center, Sales (2000-2001): Assisted customers with plant selection and responsible for stocking and arranging display areas.

REFERENCES: Will be furnished upon request.

Print Resume (Resume 2)

97B • 45'
Application Letters

Document 1

1. Read the format guides for application letters on p. 261.
2. Format and key the application letter for Douglas H. Ruckert. Format the personal-business letter in block style with mixed punctuation. Use the resume on p. 264 to find Mr. Ruckert's return address.
3. Check the content of this application letter against the guidelines on p. 261. Note the kinds of information in each paragraph.

Save as:
APPLTR97B-1

May 10, 2002 | Ms. Jenna St. John | Personnel Director | Regency Insurance Company | 219 West Greene Rd. | Houston, TX 77067-4219 | Dear Ms. St. John:

Ms. Anne D. Salgado, my business technology instructor, informed me of the customer service position with your company that will be available June 15. She speaks very highly of your organization. After learning more about the position, I am confident that I am qualified and would like to be considered for the position.

Currently I am completing my senior year at Eisenhower Technical High School. All of my elective courses have been in computer and business-related courses. I have completed the advanced computer application class where we integrated word processing, spreadsheet, database, presentation, and Web page documents by using the latest suite software. I have also taken an office technology course that included practice in using the telephone and applying interpersonal skills.

My work experience and school activities have given me the opportunity to work with people to achieve group goals. Participating in FBLA has given me an appreciation of the business world.

The opportunity to interview with you for this position will be greatly appreciated. You can call me at (713) 555-0121 or e-mail me at dougr@suresend.com to arrange an interview.

Sincerely, | Douglas H. Ruckert | Enclosure

Documents 2, 3, & 4

1. Open the application letter created as Document 1.
2. Revise the letter as necessary to apply for each position advertised at the right.

Save as:
APPLTR97B-2
APPLTR97B-3
APPLTR97B-4

CUSTOMER SERVICE

Woodlands College is seeking both full-time and part-time motivated individuals to provide customer service to the college community. Good analytical, mathematical, personal computer skills are required. Excellent communication and interpersonal skills are essential. We will provide training on our network-based system.

Woodlands College is an affirmative action, equal opportunity employer.

Please respond with letter and resume to:
J. W. Salazar
Woodlands College
1150 West Dallas St.
Conroe, TX 77301-4482
or e-mail:
resume@exchange.hr.wc.edu

CUSTOMER SERVICE REPRESENTATIVE

IHM, an international direct marketing company, is seeking candidates to work in our customer service center.

We have openings for full-time and part-time positions to handle customer inquiries for the U.S. and Canadian markets. **We have several openings for Spanish-speaking reps**.

To qualify, you must have excellent telephone and communication skills, strong keyboarding and PC skills, the ability to work in a structured environment, and the desire to learn.

Please mail or fax resume to:
Human Resources Dept-SP
IHM, 27350 Blueberry Hill Dr.
Conroe, TX 77385-3381
FAX: (713) 555-0153

CUSTOMER SERVICE OPPORTUNITY

PTI is seeking an outstanding individual for our expanding Customer Service team. Qualified candidates will demonstrate strong organizational skills, creativity, powerful problem-solving ability, and a passion for delighting customers. Strong computer skills including knowledge of suite software is essential. If you are interested in an exceptional opportunity to be part of a growing organization where you can have a real impact, please mail your resume or e-mail it to:

hr@pti.com

Precision Therapeutics, Inc.
23741 Highway 59
Suite 30
Porter, TX 77385-9963

Resources

SPREADSHEET FEATURES

DATABASE FEATURES

WEB BROWSER FEATURES

New-Key Learning

LESSONS 1-15

LESSON 1 HOME KEYS (fdsa jkl;)

Objectives:

1. To learn control of home keys (**fdsa jkl;**).
2. To learn control of **Space Bar** and **Enter** key.

1A • Work Area Arrangement

Arrange work area as shown at the right.

- alphanumeric (main) keyboard directly in front of chair; front edge of keyboard even with edge of table or desk
- monitor placed for easy viewing
- disk drives placed for easy access and disks within easy reach (unless using a network)
- book behind or at side of keyboard; top raised for easy reading

Properly arranged work area

1B • Keying Position

The features of proper position are shown at right and listed below:

- fingers curved and upright over home keys
- wrists low, but not touching keyboard
- forearms parallel to slant of keyboard
- body erect, sitting back in chair
- feet on floor for balance

Proper position at computer

Software Features Index

1C • Home-Key Position

1. Find the home keys on the chart: **f d s a** for left hand and **j k l ;** for right hand.
2. Locate and place your fingers on the home keys on your keyboard with your fingers well curved and upright (not slanting).
3. Remove your fingers from the keyboard; then place them in home-key position again, curving and holding them *lightly* on the keys.

1D • Techniques: Home Keys and Spacebar

1. Read the hints and study the illustrations at the right.
2. Place your fingers in home-key position as directed in 1C above.
3. Strike the key for each letter in the first group below the illustration.
4. After striking *;* (semi-colon), strike the *Space Bar* once.
5. Continue to key the line; strike the *Space Bar* once at the point of each arrow.
6. Review proper position (1B); then repeat Steps 3–5 above.

Technique **H · I · N · T**

Keystroking: Strike each key with a light tap with the tip of the finger, snapping the fingertip toward the palm of the hand.

Spacing: Strike the Space Bar with the right thumb; use a quick down-and-in motion (toward the palm). Avoid pauses before or after spacing.

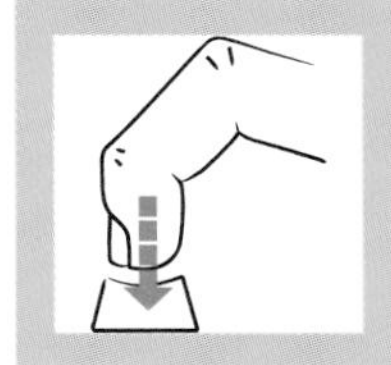

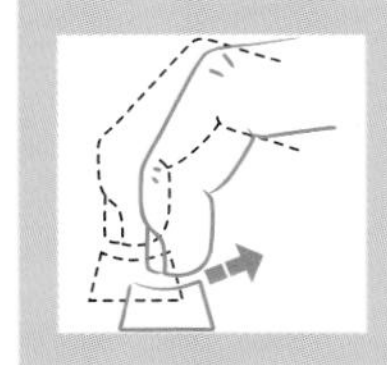

Space once.

```
fdsajkl; f d s a j k l ; ff jj dd kk ss ll aa ;;
```

1E • Technique: Hard Return at Line Endings

1. Read the information and study the illustration at the right.
2. Practice the ENTER key reach several times.

Hard Return
To return the insertion point to the left margin and move it down to the next line, strike ENTER**.**

This is called a **hard return**. Use a hard return at the end of all drill lines. Use two hard returns when directed to double-space.

Hard Return Technique
Reach the little finger of the right hand to the ENTER key, tap the key, and return the finger quickly to home-key position.

Douglas H. Ruckert
8503 Kirby Dr.
Houston, TX 77054-8220
(713) 555-0121
dougr@suresend.com

SUMMARY

Strong communication and telephone skills; excellent keyboarding, computer, and Internet skills; and good organizational and interpersonal skills.

EDUCATION

Will be graduated from Eisenhower Technical High School in June 2002, with a high school diploma and business technology emphasis. Grade point average is 3.75.

Relevant Skills and Courses:

Proficient with most recent versions of Windows and Office, including Word, Excel, Access, PowerPoint, and FrontPage.

Excelled in the following courses: Keyboarding, Computer Applications, Business Communication, and Office Technology.

Major Accomplishments:

Future Business Leaders of America: Member for four years; vice president for one year. Won second place in Public Speaking at District Competition; competed (same event) at state level.

Varsity soccer: Lettered three years and served as captain during senior year.

Recognition: Named one of Eisenhower's Top Ten Community Service Providers at end of junior year.

WORK EXPERIENCE

Hinton's Family Restaurant, Server (2001-present): Served customers in culturally diverse area; oriented new part-time employees and resolved routine customer service problems.

Tuma's Landscape and Garden Center, Sales (2000-2001): Assisted customers with plant selection and responsible for stocking and arranging display areas.

REFERENCES

Will be furnished upon request.

Electronic Resume

Douglas H. Ruckert

8503 Kirby Dr.
Houston, TX 77054-8220
(713) 555-0121

dougr@suresend.com

OBJECTIVE: To use my computer, Internet, communication, and interpersonal skills in a challenging customer service position.

EDUCATION: Will be graduated from Eisenhower Technical High School in June 2002, with a high school diploma and business technology emphasis. Grade point average is 3.75.

Relevant Skills and Courses:

- Proficient with most recent versions of Windows and Office, including Word, Excel, Access, PowerPoint, and FrontPage.
- Excelled in the following courses: Keyboarding, Computer Applications, Business Communication, and Office Technology.

Major Accomplishments:

- Future Business Leaders of America: Member for four years; vice president for one year. Won second place in Public Speaking at District Competition; competed (same event) at state level.
- Varsity soccer: Lettered three years and served as captain during senior year.
- Recognition: Named one of Eisenhower's Top Ten Community Service Providers at end of junior year.

WORK EXPERIENCE: Hinton's Family Restaurant, Server (2001-present): Served customers in culturally diverse area, oriented new part-time employees, and resolved routine customer service issues.

Tuma's Landscape and Garden Center, Sales (2000-2001): Assisted customers with plant selection and responsible for stocking and arranging display areas.

REFERENCES: Will be furnished upon request.

Print Resume

Application for Employment — **An Equal Opportunity Employer**
Regency Insurance Company

PERSONAL INFORMATION

NAME (LAST FIRST)	SOCIAL SECURITY NO.	CURRENT DATE	TELEPHONE NUMBER
Ruckert, Douglas H.	368-56-2890	5/22/02	(713) 555-0121

ADDRESS (NUMBER, STREET, CITY, STATE, ZIP CODE)	U.S. CITIZEN	DATE YOU CAN START
8503 Kirby Dr., Houston, TX 77054-8220	☒ YES ☐ NO	6/08/02

ARE YOU EMPLOYED NOW?	IF YES, MAY WE INQUIRE OF YOUR PRESENT EMPLOYER?	IF YES, GIVE NAME AND NUMBER OF PERSON TO CALL
☒ YES ☐ NO	☒ YES ☐ NO	James Veloski, Manager (713) 555-0182

POSITION DESIRED	SALARY DESIRED	STATE HOW YOU LEARNED OF POSITION
Customer Service	Open	From Ms. Anne D. Salgado, Eisenhower Business Technology Teacher

HAVE YOU EVER BEEN CONVICTED OF A FELONY? ☐ YES ☒ NO IF YES, EXPLAIN.

EDUCATION

	NAME AND LOCATION OF SCHOOL	YEARS ATTENDED	DID YOU GRADUATE?	SUBJECTS STUDIED
COLLEGE				
HIGH SCHOOL	Eisenhower Technical High School, Houston, TX	1998 TO 2002	Will be graduated 06/02	Business Technology
GRADE SCHOOL				
OTHER				

SUBJECTS OF SPECIAL STUDY/RESEARCH WORK OR SPECIAL TRAINING/SKILLS DIRECTLY RELATED TO POSITION DESIRED

Windows and Office Suite, including Word, Excel, Access, PowerPoint, and FrontPage

Office technology course with telephone training and interpersonal skills role-playing

FORMER EMPLOYERS (LIST LAST POSITION FIRST)

FROM - TO (MTH & YEAR)	NAME AND ADDRESS	SALARY	POSITION	REASON FOR LEAVING
9/01 to present	Hinton's Family Restaurant, 2204 S. Wayside Ave., Houston, TX 77023-8841	$6.85/hr.	Server	Want full-time position in my field
6/00 to 9/01	Tuma's Landscape and Garden Center, 10155 East Hwy., Houston, TX 77029-4419	$5.75/hr.	Sales	Employed at Hinton's

REFERENCES (LIST THREE PERSONS NOT RELATED TO YOU, WHOM YOU HAVE KNOWN AT LEAST ONE YEAR)

NAME	BUSINESS ADDRESS	TELEPHONE NUMBER	TITLE	YEARS KNOWN
Ms. Anne D. Salgado	Eisenhower Technical High School, 100 W. Cavalcade, Houston, TX 77009-2451	(713) 555-0134	Business Technology Instructor	Four
Mr. James R. Veloski	Hinton's Family Restaurant, 2204 S. Wayside Ave., Houston, TX 77023-8841	(713) 555-0182	Manager	One
Mrs. Helen T. Landis	Tuma's Landscape and Garden Center, 10155 East Hwy., Houston, TX 77029-4419	(713) 555-0149	Owner	Three

I UNDERSTAND THAT I SHALL NOT BECOME AN EMPLOYEE UNTIL I HAVE SIGNED AN EMPLOYMENT AGREEMENT WITH THE FINAL APPROVAL OF THE EMPLOYER AND THAT SUCH EMPLOYMENT WILL BE SUBJECT TO VERIFICATION OF PREVIOUS EMPLOYMENT DATA PROVIDED IN THIS APPLICATION, ANY RELATED DOCUMENTS, OR DATA SHEET. I KNOW THAT A REPORT MAY BE MADE THAT WILL INCLUDE INFORMATION CONCERNING ANY FACTOR THE EMPLOYER MIGHT FIND RELEVANT TO THE POSITION FOR WHICH I AM APPLYING, AND THAT I CAN MAKE A WRITTEN REQUEST FOR ADDITIONAL INFORMATION AS TO THE NATURE AND SCOPE OF THE REPORT IF ONE IS MADE.

Douglas H. Ruckert
SIGNATURE OF APPLICANT

Employment Application Form

8503 Kirby Dr.
Houston, TX 77054-8220
May 10, 2002

Ms. Jenna St. John
Personnel Director
Regency Insurance Company
219 West Greene Rd.
Houston, TX 77067-4219

Dear Ms. St. John:

Ms. Anne D. Salgado, my business technology instructor, informed me of the customer service position with your company that will be available June 15. She speaks very highly of your organization. After learning more about the position, I am confident that I am qualified and would like to be considered for the position.

Currently I am completing my senior year at Eisenhower Technical High School. All of my elective courses have been in computer and business-related courses. I have completed the advanced computer application class where we integrated word processing, spreadsheet, database, presentation, and Web page documents by using the latest suite software. I have also taken an office technology course that included practice in using the telephone and applying interpersonal skills.

My work experience and school activities have given me the opportunity to work with people to achieve group goals. Participating in FBLA has given me an appreciation of the business world.

The opportunity to interview with you for this position will be greatly appreciated. You can call me at (713) 555-0121 or e-mail me at dougr@suresend.com to arrange an interview.

Sincerely,

Douglas H. Ruckert

Enclosure

Employment Application Letter

1F • Home-Key and Spacebar Practice

1. Place your hands in home-key position (left-hand fingers on **f d s a** and right-hand fingers on **j k l ;**).
2. Key the lines once: single-spaced (SS) with a double space (DS) between 2-line groups. Do not key line numbers.

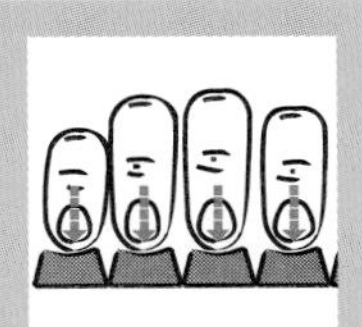

Fingers curved and upright

Down-and-in spacing motion

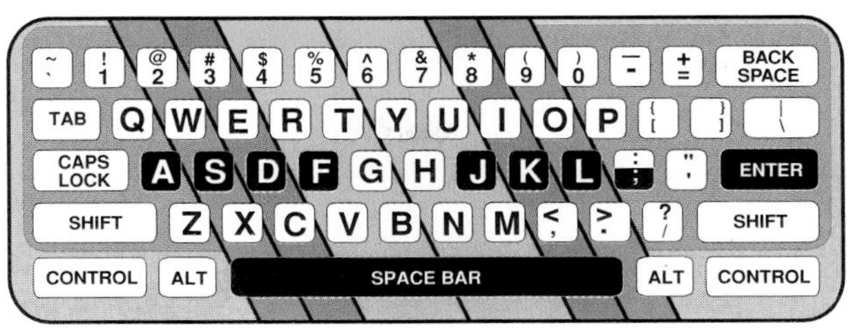

Strike Space Bar once to space.

```
1 j jj f ff k kk d dd l ll s ss ; ;; a aa jkl; fdsa
2 j jj f ff k kk d dd l ll s ss ; ;; a aa jkl; fdsa
```

Strike the ENTER key twice to double-space (DS).

```
3 a aa ; ;; s ss l ll d dd k kk f ff j jj fdsa jkl;
4 a aa ; ;; s ss l ll d dd k kk f ff j jj fdsa jkl;
```

DS

```
5 jf jf kd kd ls ls ;a ;a fj fj dk dk sl sl a; a; f
6 jf jf kd kd ls ls ;a ;a fj fj dk dk sl sl a; a; f
```

DS

```
7 a;fj a;sldkfj a;sldkfj a;sldkfj a;sldkfj a;sldkfj
8 a;fj a;sldkfj a;sldkfj a;sldkfj a;sldkfj a;sldkfj
```

Strike the ENTER key 4 times to quadruple-space (QS).

1G • Technique: Enter Key Practice

Key the lines once: single-spaced (SS) with a double space (DS) between 2-line groups. Do not key line numbers.

Spacing **C • U • E**

When lines are SS, strike ENTER twice to insert a DS between 2-line groups.

Reach with little finger; tap ENTER key quickly; return finger to home key.

```
1 a;sldkfj a;sldkfj
2 a;sldkfj a;sldkfj
```

DS

```
3 ff jj dd kk ss ll aa ;;
4 ff jj dd kk ss ll aa ;;
```

DS

```
5 fj dk sl a; a; as df ;l kj;
6 fj dk sl a; a; as df ;l kj;
```

DS

```
7 fj dk sl a; jf kd ls ;a fdsa jkl
8 fj dk sl a; jf kd ls ;a fdsa jkl
```

DS

```
9 k; fa kl ds ak dl fj s; lafj ksd; dlj
10 k; fa kl ds ak dl fj s; lafj ksd; dlj
```

DS

```
11 fa sd j; kl ak sj fl d; akdj s;lf sfk; djl
12 fa sd j; kl ak sj fl d; akdj s;lf sfk; djl
```

QS

AGENDA

FORD COUNTY SCIENCE SOCIETY

July 31, 200-

1. Approval of April minutes . . . . J. Gusset
2. Reports

   Treasurer's . . . . T. Meliton
   Membership . . . . F. Parker
   Fundraising . . . . C. Whiteman

3. Unfinished business

   Hall of Fame Inductees . . . . T. Horner
   Lowden correspondence . . . . A. Price

4. New business

   Membership drive . . . . F. Parker
   Web site proposal . . . . W. Ehlinger

5. Next meeting date and adjournment . . . . R. Holloway

Agenda

TRAVEL ITINERARY FOR LISA PEROTTA

MEA Convention—Anaheim, California—April 18-22, 200-

Date	Time	Activity	Comments
Tuesday April 18	6 p.m.	Depart **Pittsburgh International Airport** (PIT) for Santa Ana, CA, Airport (SNA) on **USEast Flight 146**. *Frequent flyer number has been entered. Arrival time is 8:01 p.m.*	The flight is nonstop on an Airbus A319, and you are flying coach.
	8:30 p.m.	Reservation with **Star Limousine** (714-555-0190) for transportation to **Anaheim Inn and Convention Center**, 500 Convention Way, Anaheim.	Confirmation numbers: 33-345 for limo and 632A-04/18 for hotel.
Wednesday April 19	1 p.m.	Tour of Discovery Science Center and Queen Mary. A **Five Star Tour** van is to be at hotel main entrance at 1 p.m. for 1:15 p.m. departure.	Return to hotel by 5:30 p.m.
Thursday April 20	6 p.m.	MEA evening at Universal Studios Hollywood. **Buses chartered by MEA** will transport all registered participants to and from the studios.	Check MEA message board for boarding times and registration packet for ticket.
Saturday April 22	11:15 a.m.	Reservation with **Star Limousine** for transportation from Anaheim to **USEast Airlines** at the Santa Ana Airport.	Confirmation number for limo: 33-375.
	1:25 p.m.	Depart **Santa Ana Airport** (SNA) for Pittsburgh International Airport (PIT) on **USEast Flight 148**. *Frequent flyer number has been entered. Arrival time is 8:52 p.m.*	The flight is nonstop on an Airbus A319, and you are flying coach.

Itinerary

SUMMARY MINUTES COMPUTER SCIENCE ADVISORY COMMITTEE MEETING

November,15, 200-

Committee members present: Robert Dry-Kenich, Deborah Edington, Amy Lovetro, Ray Meucci, Rosemary Radmanich, Kenneth Ryave, Kim Van Aken, and Leo Yazzani.

School employees present: Mary Amaral, Drew Bowen, Larry Kaufmann, Fred Niklas, Carla Nilson, and Margaret Palmero.

Recorder of minutes: Joseph Gloss.

1. Amy Lovetro, committee chair, called the meeting to order at 11:15 a.m. and welcomed all to the meeting. Ms. Lovetro introduced Kim Van Aken, Hermanie Engineering, as a new member.
2. The minutes from the May 14 meeting were read and approved.
3. Mr. Fred Niklas reported:

   A. At least 125 students are presently enrolled in the computer science programs. Dunlap High has the most with 25 and West High has the least with 7.

   B. Of the 53 health occupation students who were graduated last June, 28 are employed in a computer-related field, 15 have gone on to higher education, 3 entered the military, 5 are employed in unrelated fields, and 2 are unemployed.

4. Unfinished business included passing a motion to recommend that Eastway AVTS students charter a Computer Science Student Organization and that Mary Amaral be appointed sponsor. Each committee member agreed to work closely with the students and the faculty sponsor.
5. New business included passing motions to support these three recommendations:

   A. All committee members be invited to participate in the AVTS's career fair.

   B. Two members of the committee (Deborah Edington and Kenneth Ryave) be appointed to the AVTS's Strategic Planning Committee.

Meeting Minutes

News Release

For Release: Upon Receipt
Contact: Guy Madison

LORAIN, OH, March 24, 200-. Three East Lorain County High School students, members of the ELCHS Science Club, have been invited to exhibit their projects at the Eastern Ohio Academy for Science Fair on April 21-24. The fair will be held in the Stern Exhibit Hall at the Erie Civic Center.

Susan Marks, Jaunita Perez, and John Lavic earned this honor by placing first in their respective categories at the Lorain County Academy for Science Fair on March 15. Marks competed in microbiology, Perez in chemistry, and Lavic in physical science. Ms. Kelly Wyatt, ELCHS physics teacher, is the club's sponsor.

###

News Release

1H • Home-Key Mastery

1. Key the lines once (without the numbers); strike the ENTER key twice to double-space (DS).
2. Rekey the drill at a faster pace.

Technique **C • U • E**

Keep fingers curved and upright over home keys, right thumb just barely touching the Space Bar.

Spacing **C • U • E**

Space once after ; used as punctuation.

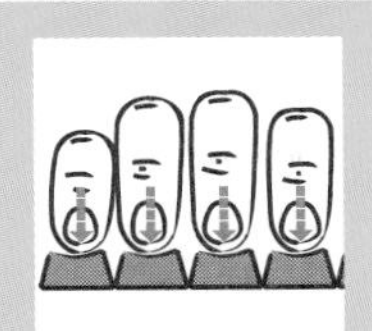

Correct finger alignment

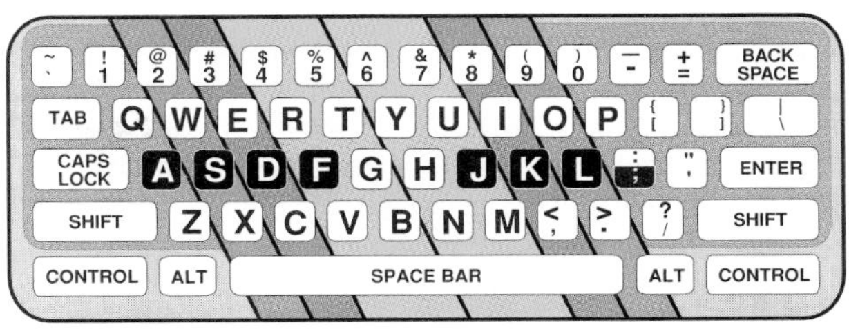

1 aa ;; ss ll dd kk ff jj a; sl dk fj jf kd ls ;a jf
DS
2 a a as as ad ad ask ask lad lad fad fad jak jak la
DS
3 all all fad fad jak jak add add ask ask ads ads as
DS
4 a lad; a jak; a lass; all ads; add all; ask a lass
DS
5 as a lad; a fall fad; ask all dads; as a fall fad;

1I • End-of-Lesson Routine

1. Exit the software.
2. Remove disk from disk drive.
3. Turn off equipment if directed to do so.
4. Store materials as the instructor directs.

Disk removal

1J • Enrichment

1. Key the drill once as shown to improve control of home keys.
2. Key the drill again to quicken your keystrokes.

Spacing **C • U • E**

To DS between single-spaced lines, strike ENTER twice.

1 ja js jd jf f; fl fk fj ka ks kd kf d; dl dk dj a;
DS
2 la ls ld lf s; sl sk sj ;a ;s ;d ;f a; al ak aj fj
DS
3 jj aa kk ss ll dd ;; ff fj dk sl a; jf kd ls ;a a;
DS
4 as as ask ask ad ad lad lad all all fall fall lass
DS
5 as a fad; as a dad; ask a lad; as a lass; all lads
DS
6 a sad dad; all lads fall; ask a lass; a jak salad;
DS
7 add a jak; a fall ad; all fall ads; ask a sad lass

REPORT DOCUMENTATION

Good report writing includes proof that the reported statements are sound. The process is called **documenting.**

Most school reports are documented in the body and in a list. A reference in the body shows the source of a quotation or paraphrase. A list shows all references alphabetically.

In the report body, references may be noted (1) in parentheses in the copy (textual citations or parenthetical documentation); (2) by a superscript in the copy, listed on a separate page (endnotes); or (3) by a superscript in the copy, listed at the bottom of the text page (footnotes). A list may contain only the sources noted in the body (REFERENCES or Works Cited) or include related materials (BIBLIOGRAPHY).

Two popular documenting styles are shown: *Century 21* and MLA (Modern Language Association).

Century 21

Examples are listed in this order: (1) textual citation, (2) endnote/footnote, and (3) References/Bibliography page.

Book, One Author

(Schaeffer, 1997, 1)

[1]Robert K. Schaeffer, Understanding Globalization, (Lanham, MD: Rowman & Littlefield Publishers, Inc., 1997), p. 1.

Schaeffer, Robert K. Understanding Globalization (Lanham, MD: Rowman & Littlefield Publishers, Inc., 1997).

Book, Two or Three Authors

(Prince and Jackson, 1997, 35)

[2]Nancy Prince and Jeanie Jackson, Exploring Theater (Minneapolis/St. Paul: West Publishing Company, 1997), p. 35.

Prince, Nancy, and Jeanie Jackson. Exploring Theater. Minneapolis/St. Paul: West Publishing Company, 1997.

Book, Four or More Authors

(Gerver, et al., 1998, 9)

[3]Robert Gerver, et al., South-Western Geometry: An Integrated Approach (Cincinnati: South-Western Educational Publishing, 1998), p. 9.

Gerver, Robert, et al. South-Western Geometry: An Integrated Approach. Cincinnati: South-Western Educational Publishing, 1998.

Encyclopedia or Reference Book

(Encyclopedia Americana, 1998, Vol. 25, p. 637)

[4]Encyclopedia Americana, Vol. 25 (Danbury, CT: Grolier Incorporated, 1998), p. 637.

Encyclopedia Americana, Vol. 25. "Statue of Liberty." Danbury, CT: Grolier Incorporated, 1998.

Journal or Magazine Article

(Harris, 1993, 755)

[5]Richard G. Harris, "Globalization, Trade, and Income," Canadian Journal of Economics, November 1993, p. 755.

Harris, Richard G. "Globalization, Trade, and Income." Canadian Journal of Economics, November 1993, 755–776.

Web Site

(Railton, 1999)

[6]Stephen Railton, "Your Mark Twain," http://www.etext.lib.virginia.edu/railton/sc_as_mt/yourmt13.html (September 24, 1999).

Railton, Stephen. "Your Mark Twain." http://www.etext.lib.virginia.edu/railton/sc_as_mt/yourmt13.html (24 September 1999).

Modern Language Association

Examples include reference (1) in parenthetical documentation and (2) on Works Cited page.

Book, One Author

(Schaeffer 1)

Schaeffer, Robert K. Understanding Globalization. Lanham, MD: Rowman & Littlefield, 1997.

Book, Two or Three Authors

(Prince and Jackson 35)

Prince, Nancy, and Jeanie Jackson. Exploring Theater. Minneapolis/St. Paul: West Publishing, 1997.

Book, Four or More Authors or Editors

(Gerver et al. 9)

Gerver, Robert, et al. South-Western Geometry: An Integrated Approach. Cincinnati: South-Western, 1998.

Encyclopedia or Reference Book

(Encyclopedia Americana 637)

Encyclopedia Americana. "Statue of Liberty." Danbury, CT: Grolier, 1998.

Journal or Magazine Article

(Harris 755)

Harris, Richard G. "Globalization, Trade, and Income," Canadian Journal of Economics. Nov. 1993: 755–776.

Web Site

(Railton)

Railton, Stephen. Your Mark Twain Page. (24 Sept. 1999) http://www.etext.lib.virginia.edu/railton/sc_as_mt/yourmt13.html.

NEW KEYS: h AND e

Objectives:

1. To learn reach technique for **h** and **e**.
2. To combine smoothly **h** and **e** with home keys.

2A • Get Ready to Key

At the beginning of each practice session, follow the *Standard Plan* given at the right to get ready to key the lesson.

Standard Plan for Getting Ready to Key

1. Arrange work area similar to the illustration on p. R2.
2. Check to see that the computer, monitor, and printer (if any) are plugged in.
3. Load the computer software specified by your instructor.
4. Align the front of the keyboard with the front edge of the desk or table.
5. Position the monitor and the textbook for easy reading.

2B • Plan for Learning New Keys

All keys except the home keys (**fdsa jkl;**) require the fingers to reach in order to strike them. Follow the *Standard Plan* given at the right to learn the proper reach for each new key.

Standard Plan for Learning New Keys

1. Find the new key on the keyboard chart given on the page where the new key is introduced.
2. Look at your own keyboard and find the new key on it.
3. Study the reach-technique picture at the left of the practice lines for the new key. (See p. R7 for illustrations.) Read the statement below the illustration.
4. Identify the finger to be used to strike the new key.
5. Curve your fingers; place them in home-key position (over **fdsa jkl;**).
6. Watch your finger as you reach it to the new key and back to home position a few times (keep it curved).
7. Refer to the set of three drill lines at the right of the reach-technique illustration. Key each line twice SS (single-spaced):
   - once slowly, to learn new reach;
   - then faster, for a quick-snap stroke. DS (double-space) between 2-line groups.

2C • Home-Key Review

Key each line twice single-spaced (SS): once slowly; again, at a faster pace; double-space (DS) between 2-line groups.

All keystrokes learned

1 a;sldkfj a; sl dk fj ff jj dd kk ss ll aa ;; fj a;

2 a a as as ask ask ad ad lad lad add add fall falls

3 as as ad ad all all jak jak fad fad fall fall lass

4 jj kk; jj kk; as jak; as jak; ask a lad; ask a lad

5 a jak; a fad; as a lad; ask dad; a lass; a fall ad

6 a sad fall; all fall ads; as a lass asks a sad lad

7 a fad; ask dad; ask a lass; add a lad; a sad lass;

Strike ENTER 4 times to quadruple-space (QS) between lesson parts.

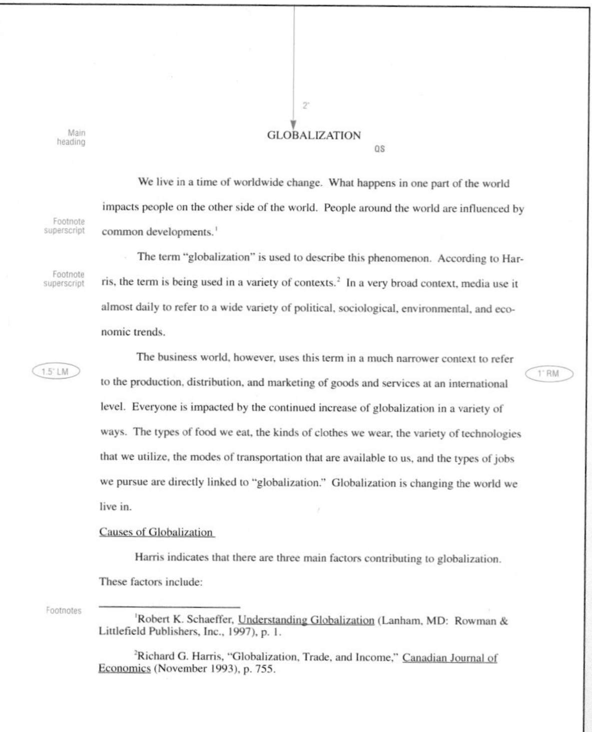

GLOBALIZATION

We live in a time of worldwide change. What happens in one part of the world impacts people on the other side of the world. People around the world are influenced by common developments.[1]

The term "globalization" is used to describe this phenomenon. According to Harris, the term is being used in a variety of contexts.[2] In a very broad context, media use it almost daily to refer to a wide variety of political, sociological, environmental, and economic trends.

The business world, however, uses this term in a much narrower context to refer to the production, distribution, and marketing of goods and services at an international level. Everyone is impacted by the continued increase of globalization in a variety of ways. The types of food we eat, the kinds of clothes we wear, the variety of technologies that we utilize, the modes of transportation that are available to us, and the types of jobs we pursue are directly linked to "globalization." Globalization is changing the world we live in.

Causes of Globalization

Harris indicates that there are three main factors contributing to globalization. These factors include:

[1]Robert K. Schaeffer, Understanding Globalization (Lanham, MD: Rowman & Littlefield Publishers, Inc., 1997), p. 1.

[2]Richard G. Harris, "Globalization, Trade, and Income," Canadian Journal of Economics (November 1993), p. 755.

Bound Report with Footnotes

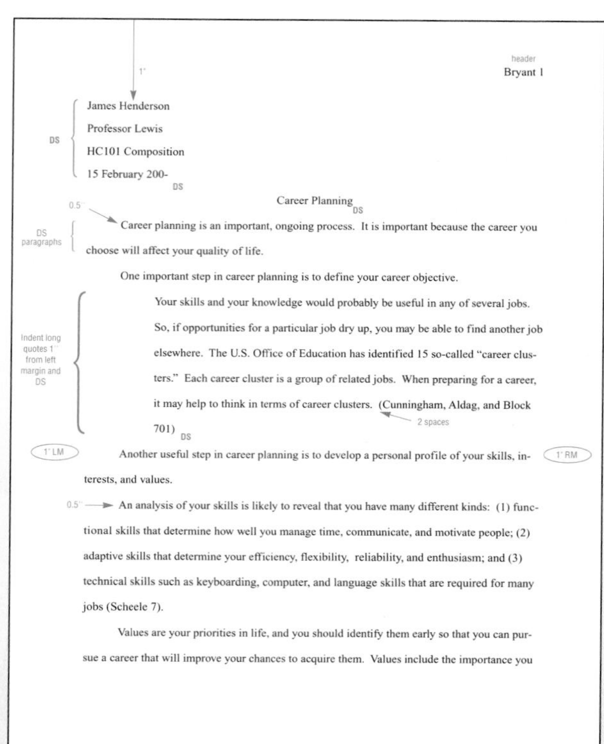

Bryant 1

James Henderson

Professor Lewis

HC101 Composition

15 February 200-

Career Planning

Career planning is an important, ongoing process. It is important because the career you choose will affect your quality of life.

One important step in career planning is to define your career objective.

> Your skills and your knowledge would probably be useful in any of several jobs. So, if opportunities for a particular job dry up, you may be able to find another job elsewhere. The U.S. Office of Education has identified 15 so-called "career clusters." Each career cluster is a group of related jobs. When preparing for a career, it may help to think in terms of career clusters. (Cunningham, Aldag, and Block 701)

Another useful step in career planning is to develop a personal profile of your skills, interests, and values.

An analysis of your skills is likely to reveal that you have many different kinds: (1) functional skills that determine how well you manage time, communicate, and motivate people; (2) adaptive skills that determine your efficiency, flexibility, reliability, and enthusiasm; and (3) technical skills such as keyboarding, computer, and language skills that are required for many jobs (Scheele 7).

Values are your priorities in life, and you should identify them early so that you can pursue a career that will improve your chances to acquire them. Values include the importance you

MLA-Style Report (p. 1)

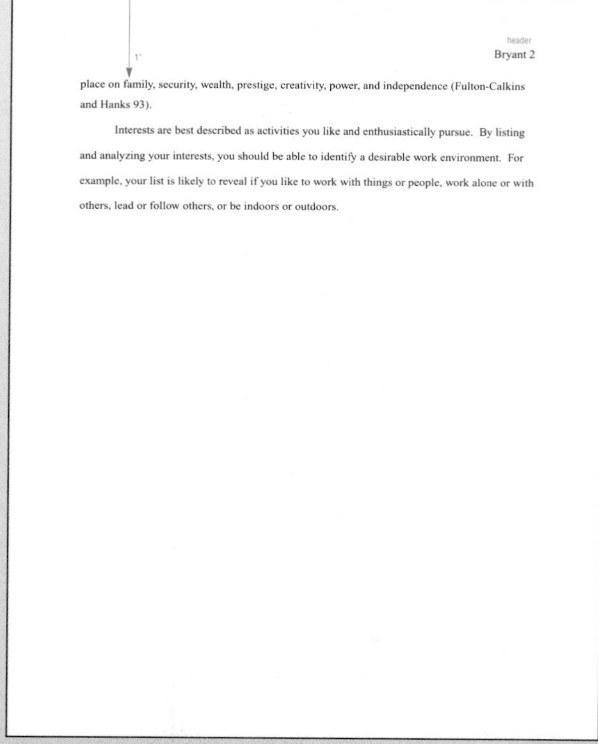

Bryant 2

place on family, security, wealth, prestige, creativity, power, and independence (Fulton-Calkins and Hanks 93).

Interests are best described as activities you like and enthusiastically pursue. By listing and analyzing your interests, you should be able to identify a desirable work environment. For example, your list is likely to reveal if you like to work with things or people, work alone or with others, lead or follow others, or be indoors or outdoors.

MLA-Style Report (p. 2)

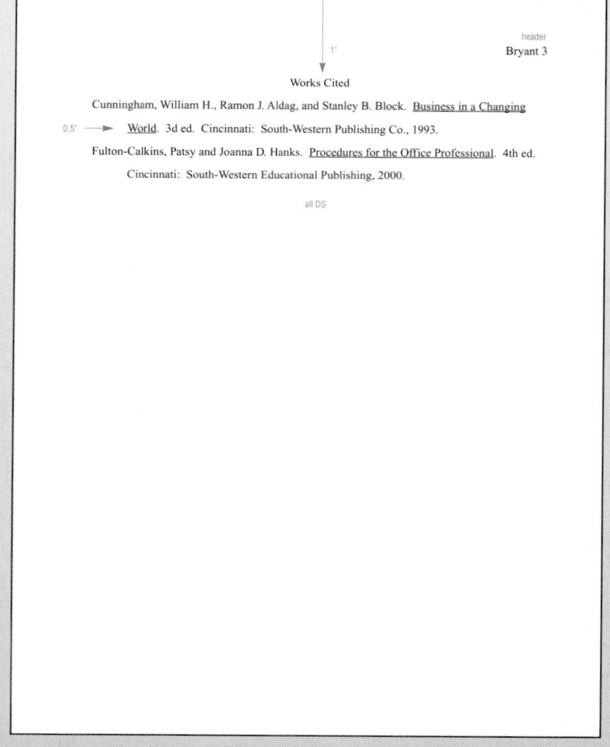

Bryant 3

Works Cited

Cunningham, William H., Ramon J. Aldag, and Stanley B. Block. Business in a Changing World. 3d ed. Cincinnati: South-Western Publishing Co., 1993.

Fulton-Calkins, Patsy and Joanna D. Hanks. Procedures for the Office Professional. 4th ed. Cincinnati: South-Western Educational Publishing, 2000.

MLA-Style Report References (Works Cited) Page

2D • New Keys: H and E

1. Use the *Standard Plan for Learning New Keys* (p. R6) for each key to be learned. Study the plan now.
2. Relate each step of the plan to the illustrations below and text at the right. Then key each line twice SS; leave a DS between 2-line groups.

h *Right index* finger

e *Left middle* finger

Do not attempt to key line numbers, the vertical lines separating word groups, or the labels (home row, h/e).

Learn h

1 j j hj hj ah ah ha ha had had has has ash ash hash
2 hj hj ha ha ah ah hah hah had had ash ash has hash
3 ah ha; had ash; has had; a hall; has a hall; ah ha

Strike ENTER twice to double-space (DS) below the set of lines.

Learn e

4 d d ed ed el el led led eel eel eke eke ed fed fed
5 ed ed el el lee lee fed fed eke eke led led ale ed
6 a lake; a leek; a jade; a desk; a jade eel; a deed

Combine h and e

7 he he he|she she she|shed shed|heed heed|held held
8 a lash; a shed; he held; she has jade; held a sash
9 has fled; he has ash; she had jade; she had a sale

Strike ENTER 4 times to quadruple-space (QS) between lesson parts.

2E • New-Key Mastery

1. Key the lines once SS with a DS between 2-line groups.
2. Key the lines again with quick, sharp strokes at a faster pace.

Spacing C·U·E

Space once after ; used as punctuation.

 **Note:**

Once the screen is filled with keyed lines, the top line disappears when a new line is added at the bottom. This is called **scrolling.**

Fingers curved

Fingers upright

home row
1 ask ask|has has|lad lad|all all|jak jak|fall falls
2 a jak; a lad; a sash; had all; has a jak; all fall

DS

h/e
3 he he|she she|led led|held held|jell jell|she shed
4 he led; she had; she fell; a jade ad; a desk shelf

DS

all keys learned
5 elf elf|all all|ask ask|led led|jak jak|hall halls
6 ask dad; he has jell; she has jade; he sells leeks

DS

all keys learned
7 he led; she has; a jak ad; a jade eel; a sled fell
8 she asked a lad; he led all fall; she has a jak ad

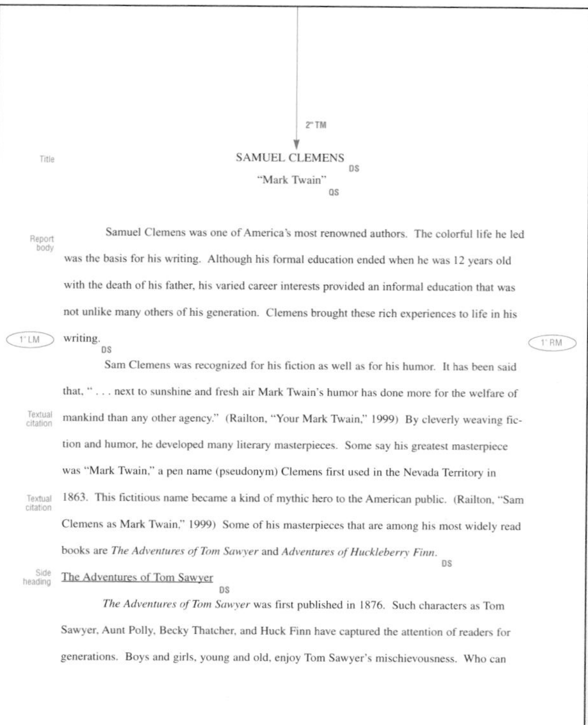

SAMUEL CLEMENS

"Mark Twain"

Samuel Clemens was one of America's most renowned authors. The colorful life he led was the basis for his writing. Although his formal education ended when he was 12 years old with the death of his father, his varied career interests provided an informal education that was not unlike many others of his generation. Clemens brought these rich experiences to life in his writing.

Sam Clemens was recognized for his fiction as well as for his humor. It has been said that, " . . . next to sunshine and fresh air Mark Twain's humor has done more for the welfare of mankind than any other agency." (Railton, "Your Mark Twain," 1999) By cleverly weaving fiction and humor, he developed many literary masterpieces. Some say his greatest masterpiece was "Mark Twain," a pen name (pseudonym) Clemens first used in the Nevada Territory in 1863. This fictitious name became a kind of mythic hero to the American public. (Railton, "Sam Clemens as Mark Twain," 1999) Some of his masterpieces that are among his most widely read books are *The Adventures of Tom Sawyer* and *Adventures of Huckleberry Finn*.

The Adventures of Tom Sawyer

The Adventures of Tom Sawyer was first published in 1876. Such characters as Tom Sawyer, Aunt Polly, Becky Thatcher, and Huck Finn have captured the attention of readers for generations. Boys and girls, young and old, enjoy Tom Sawyer's mischievousness. Who can

Unbound Report (p. 1) with Textual Citations

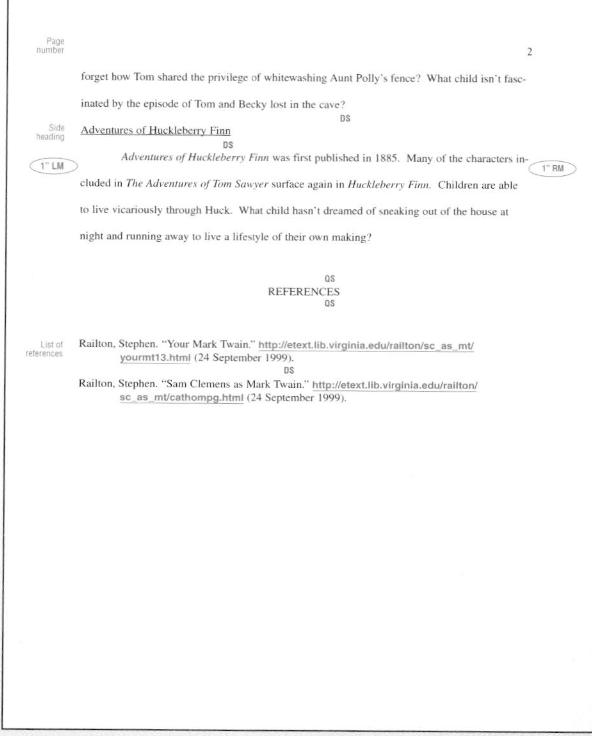

2

forget how Tom shared the privilege of whitewashing Aunt Polly's fence? What child isn't fascinated by the episode of Tom and Becky lost in the cave?

Adventures of Huckleberry Finn

Adventures of Huckleberry Finn was first published in 1885. Many of the characters included in *The Adventures of Tom Sawyer* surface again in *Huckleberry Finn*. Children are able to live vicariously through Huck. What child hasn't dreamed of sneaking out of the house at night and running away to live a lifestyle of their own making?

REFERENCES

Railton, Stephen. "Your Mark Twain." http://etext.lib.virginia.edu/railton/sc_as_mt/yourmt13.html (24 September 1999).

Railton, Stephen. "Sam Clemens as Mark Twain." http://etext.lib.virginia.edu/railton/sc_as_mt/cathompg.html (24 September 1999).

Unbound Report (p. 2) with References

Note: References are often placed on a separate page.

INFORMATION SUPERHIGHWAY

Technology has a significant impact on our lives and will have an even greater impact in the future. During the early 1990s the term "Information Highway" was starting to be used to describe the next wave of technological advancements. As always there were those who were skeptical about what impact, if any, the "Information Highway" would have on our lives.

One writer, as late as December 1993, indicated that he was not holding his breath. The information superhighway may or may not become a truly transforming technology. He felt that if it did, it may take years and compared the acceptance of the information superhighway to the acceptance of the car.

> It takes time for breakthrough technologies to make their mark. Consider the car. In 1908 Henry Ford began selling the Model T. One early effort of low-cost cars was to rid cities of horses. A picture of a New York street in 1900 shows 36 horse carriages and one car; a picture of the same street in 1924 shows 40 cars and one carriage. This was a big deal. In 1900, horses dumped 2.5 million pounds of manure onto New York streets every day. Still, the car culture's triumph was slow.[1]

Other writers during this same time period were much more optimistic about the value of the superhighway and began predicting what it would mean to all of us in the near future.

> The Information Superhighway is going to affect your life, whether you want it to or not. In the very near future you will talk to your friends and family, send letters, go shopping, get news, find answer to your questions . . . .[2]

Bound Report with Long Quotations and Endnotes

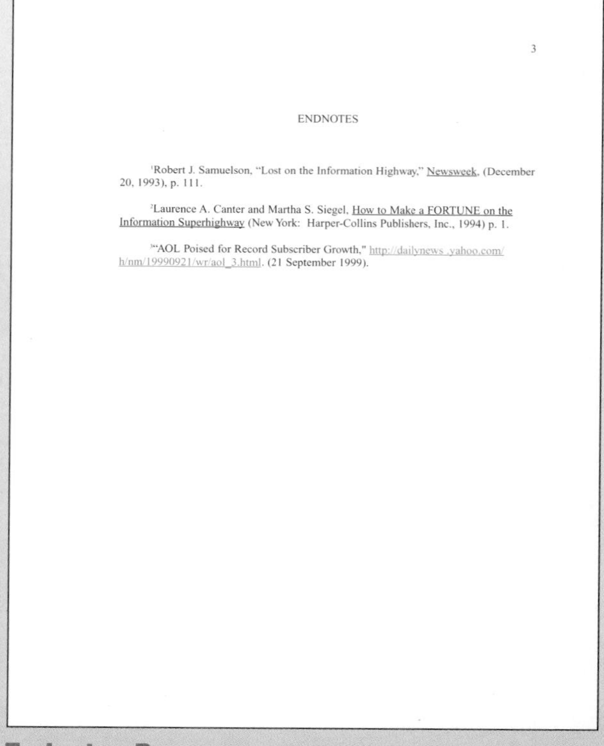

3

ENDNOTES

[1]Robert J. Samuelson, "Lost on the Information Highway," Newsweek, (December 20, 1993), p. 111.

[2]Laurence A. Canter and Martha S. Siegel, How to Make a FORTUNE on the Information Superhighway (New York: Harper-Collins Publishers, Inc., 1994) p. 1.

[3]"AOL Poised for Record Subscriber Growth," http://dailynews.yahoo.com/h/nm/19990921/wr/aol_3.html. (21 September 1999).

Endnotes Page

LESSON 3 NEW KEYS: i AND r

Objectives:

1. To learn reach technique for **i** and **r**.
2. To combine smoothly **i** and **r** with all other learned keys.

3A • 3' Get Ready to Key

Follow the steps in the *Standard Plan for Getting Ready to Key* on p. R6.

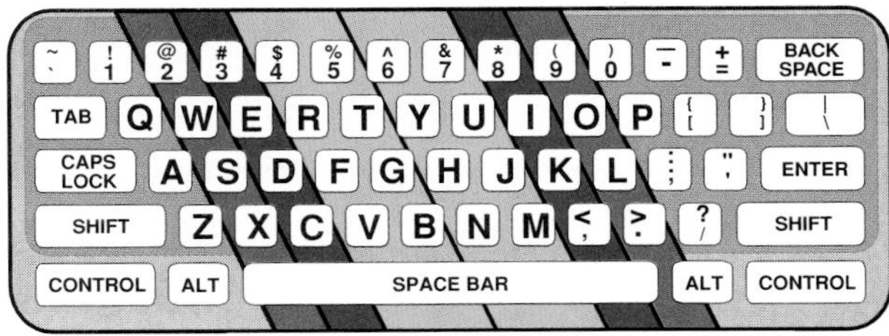

3B • 5' Conditioning Practice

Key each line twice SS; DS between 2-line groups.

Practice **C•U•E**

- Key each line at a slow, steady pace, but strike and release each key quickly.
- Key each line again at a faster pace; move from key to key quickly.

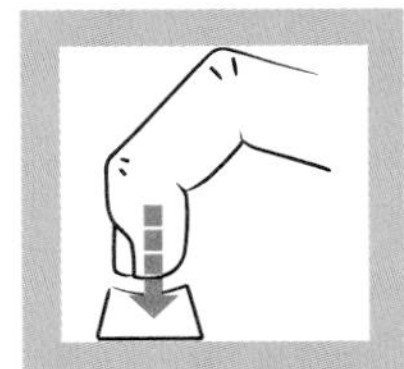

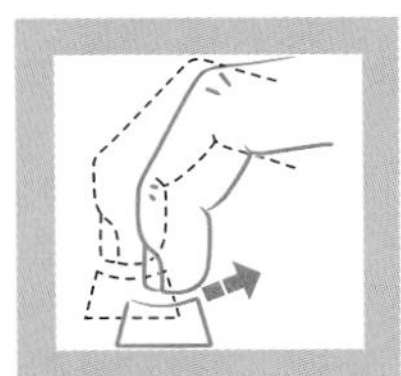

home keys 1 a;sldkfj a;sldkfj as jak ask fad all dad lads fall

Strike ENTER twice to DS.

h/e 2 hj hah has had sash hash ed led fed fled sled fell

DS

all keys learned 3 as he fled; ask a lass; she had jade; sell all jak

Strike ENTER 4 times to quadruple-space (QS) between lesson parts.

3C • 5' Speed Building

Key each line once DS.

Spacing **C•U•E**

To DS when in SS mode, strike ENTER twice at end of line.

Speed **C•U•E**

In lines 1–3, quicken the keying pace as you key each letter combination or word when it is repeated within the line.

1 hj hj | ah ah | ha ha | had had | ash ash | has has | had hash

2 ed ed | el el | ed ed | led led | eke eke | lee lee | ale kale

3 he he | she she | led led | has has | held held | sled sleds

4 he fled; she led; she had jade; he had a jell sale

5 a jak fell; she held a leek; he has had a sad fall

6 he has ash; she sells jade; as he fell; has a lake

7 she had a fall jade sale; he leads all fall sales;

8 he held a fall kale sale; she sells leeks as a fad

ENVELOPE GUIDES

Return Address

Use block style, SS, and Initial Caps or ALL CAPS. If not using the Envelopes feature, begin as near to the top and left edge of the envelope as possible—TM and LM about 0.25".

Receiver's Delivery Address

Use USPS (postal service) style: block format (SS), ALL CAPS, no punctuation. Place city name, two-letter state abbreviation, and ZIP Code +4 on last address line. One space precedes the ZIP Code.

If not using the Envelopes feature, tab over 2.5" for the small envelope and 4" for the large envelope. Insert hard returns to place the first line about 2" from the top.

Mailing Notations

Key mailing and addressee notations in ALL CAPS.

Key mailing notations, such as SPECIAL DELIVERY and REGISTERED, below the stamp and at least three lines above the envelope address.

Key addressee notations, such as HOLD FOR ARRIVAL or PERSONAL, a DS below the return address and about three spaces from the left edge of the envelope.

If an attention line is used, key it as the first line of the envelope address.

Standard Abbreviations

Use USPS standard abbreviations for states (see list below) and street suffix names, such as AVE and BLVD. Never abbreviate the name of a city or country.

International Addresses

Omit postal (ZIP) codes from the last line of addresses outside the U.S. Show only the name of the country on the last line. Examples:

```
MR HIRAM SANDERS
2121 CLEARWATER ST
OTTAWA ONKIA OB1
CANADA

MS INGE D FISCHER
HARTMANNSTRASSE 7
4209 BONN 5
FEDERAL REPUBLIC OF GERMANY
```

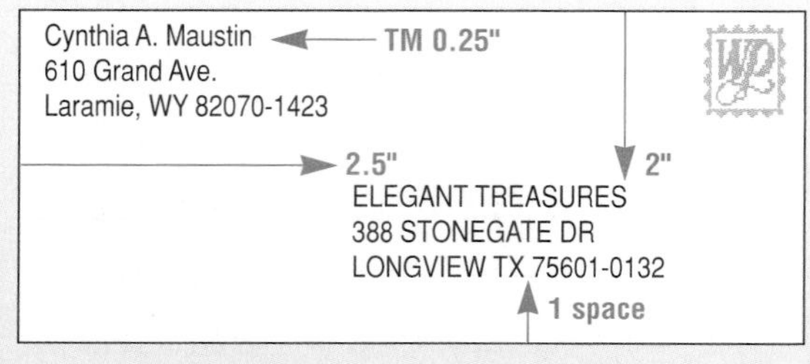

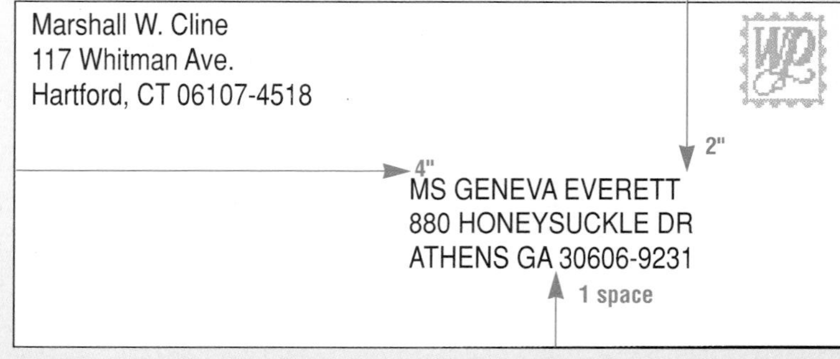

Folding Procedures

Small Envelopes (Nos. 6 3/4 , 6 1/4)

1. With page face up, fold bottom up to 0.5" from top.
2. Fold right third to left.
3. Fold left third to 0.5" from last crease.
4. Insert last creased edge first.

Large Envelopes (Nos. 10, 9, 7 3/4)

1. With page face up, fold slightly less than one-third of sheet up toward top.
2. Fold down top of sheet to within 0.5" of bottom fold.
3. Insert last creased edge first.

Window Envelopes (Letter)

1. With page face down, top toward you, fold upper third down.
2. Fold lower third up so address is showing.
3. Insert sheet into envelope with last crease at bottom.
4. Check that address shows through window.

State and Territory Abbreviations

Alabama	AL
Alaska	AK
Arizona	AZ
Arkansas	AR
California	CA
Colorado	CO
Connecticut	CT
Delaware	DE
District of Columbia	DC
Florida	FL
Georgia	GA
Guam	GU
Hawaii	HI
Idaho	ID
Illinois	IL
Indiana	IN
Iowa	IA
Kansas	KS
Kentucky	KY
Louisiana	LA
Maine	ME
Maryland	MD
Massachusetts	MA
Michigan	MI
Minnesota	MN
Mississippi	MS
Missouri	MO
Montana	MT
Nebraska	NE
Nevada	NV
New Hampshire	NH
New Jersey	NJ
New Mexico	NM
New York	NY
North Carolina	NC
North Dakota	ND
Ohio	OH
Oklahoma	OK
Oregon	OR
Pennsylvania	PA
Puerto Rico	PR
Rhode Island	RI
South Carolina	SC
South Dakota	SD
Tennessee	TN
Texas	TX
Utah	UT
Vermont	VT
Virgin Islands	VI
Virginia	VA
Washington	WA
West Virginia	WV
Wisconsin	WI
Wyoming	WY

3D • 18'
New Keys: I and R

Key each line twice SS (slowly, then faster); DS between 2-line groups; if time permits, key lines 7–9 again.

Technique Goals:

- curved, upright fingers
- finger-action keystrokes
- eyes on copy

Follow the *Standard Plan for Learning New Keys* outlined on p. R6.

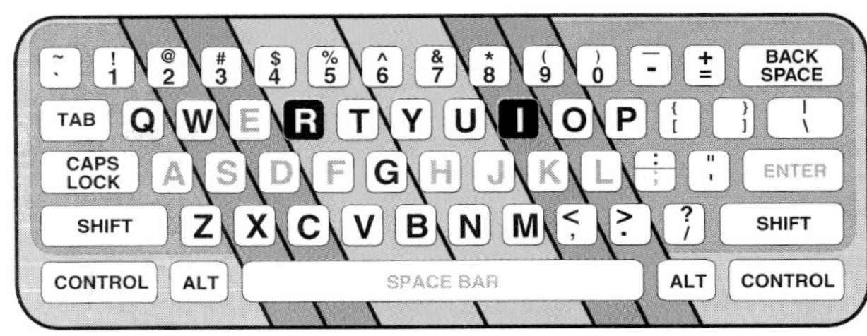

i *Right middle* finger

r *Left index* finger

Learn i

1 k k ik ik is is if if did did aid aid kid kid hail
2 ik ik if if is is kid kid his his lie lie aid aide
3 a kid; a lie; if he; he did; his aide; if a kid is

Learn r

4 f f rf rf jar jar her her are are ark ark jar jars
5 rf rf re re fr fr jar jar red red her her far fare
6 a jar; a rake; a lark; red jar; hear her; are dark

Combine i and r

7 fir fir | rid rid | sir sir | ire ire | fire fire | air airs
8 a fir; if her; a fire; is fair; his ire; if she is
9 he is; if her; is far; red jar; his heir; her aide

Quadruple-space (QS) between lesson parts.

3E • 19'
New-Key Mastery

1. Key the lines once SS with a DS between 2-line groups.
2. Key the lines again at a faster pace.

Technique Goals:

- fingers deeply curved
- wrists low, but not resting
- hands/arms steady
- eyes on copy as you key

reach review
1 hj ed ik rf hj de ik fr hj ed ik rf jh de ki fr hj
2 he he | if if | all all | fir fir | jar jar | rid rid | as ask
DS

h/e
3 she she | elf elf | her her | hah hah | eel eel | shed shelf
4 he has; had jak; her jar; had a shed; she has fled
DS

i/r
5 fir fir | rid rid | sir sir | kid kid | ire ire | fire fired
6 a fir; is rid; is red; his ire; her kid; has a fir
DS

all keys learned
7 if if | is is | he he | did did | fir fir | jak jak | all fall
8 a jak; he did; ask her; red jar; she fell; he fled
DS

all keys learned
9 if she is; he did ask; he led her; he is her aide;
10 she has had a jak sale; she said he had a red fir;

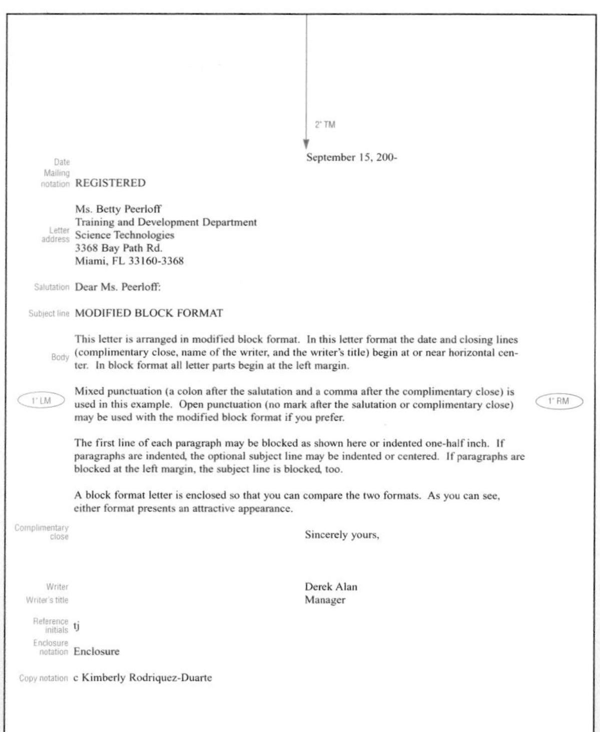

2" TM

Date September 15, 200-

Mailing notation REGISTERED

Letter address
Ms. Betty Peerloff
Training and Development Department
Science Technologies
3368 Bay Path Rd.
Miami, FL 33160-3368

Salutation Dear Ms. Peerloff:

Subject line MODIFIED BLOCK FORMAT

Body This letter is arranged in modified block format. In this letter format the date and closing lines (complimentary close, name of the writer, and the writer's title) begin at or near horizontal center. In block format all letter parts begin at the left margin.

1" LM 1" RM

Mixed punctuation (a colon after the salutation and a comma after the complimentary close) is used in this example. Open punctuation (no mark after the salutation or complimentary close) may be used with the modified block format if you prefer.

The first line of each paragraph may be blocked as shown here or indented one-half inch. If paragraphs are indented, the optional subject line may be indented or centered. If paragraphs are blocked at the left margin, the subject line is blocked, too.

A block format letter is enclosed so that you can compare the two formats. As you can see, either format presents an attractive appearance.

Complimentary close Sincerely yours,

Writer Derek Alan

Writer's title Manager

Reference initials tj

Enclosure notation Enclosure

Copy notation c Kimberly Rodriquez-Duarte

Letter in Modified Block Format without Paragraph Indentations

April 15, 200-

Attention Science Department Chair
East Tulsa High School
10916 N. Garnett Rd.
Tulsa, OK 74116-1016

Ladies and Gentlemen:

PHYSICS LABORATORY EQUIPMENT DONATION

AnTech Laboratories has up-to-date physics laboratory furniture and equipment that it can donate to your high school. We feel certain that your physics teacher and students will derive great benefits from what we are offering.

A list of the major items we can donate is enclosed. All items will be available before the end of July so they can be delivered and installed before school starts in late August.

Please call me at (918) 138-5000, and we will arrange a meeting for your personnel to see the furniture and equipment.

Sincerely,

Jose L. Domingo
Public Relations

xx

Enclosure

Our CEO, Mrs. Donna Scanlon, is a graduate of East Tulsa High (Class of 1983); and she hopes this donation will enable you to expand your science education program.

Letter in Modified Block Format with Paragraph Indentations

April 12, 200-

Ms. Valerie E Lopez
207 Brainard Rd.
Hartford, CT 06114-2207

Dear Ms. Lopez

SHADOWING AT BRIGHTON LIFE INSURANCE CO.

I'm pleased that you have chosen Brighton Life Insurance Co. as the place where you want to complete your shadow experience. I believe that you will learn a great deal about being an actuary by spending two days at Brighton with me.

To help you prepare for your visit, I have listed some of the things you should know about actuaries:

- Gather and analyze statistics to determine probabilities of death, sickness, injury, disability, unemployment, retirement, and property loss.
- Specialize in either life and health insurance or property and casualty insurance; or, specialize in pension plans or employee benefits.
- Hold a Bachelor's degree in mathematics or business area, such as actuarial science, finance, or accounting.
- Possess excellent communication and interpersonal skills.

Also, I have enclosed actuarial career information published by the Society of Actuaries (life and health insurance), Casualty Actuarial Society (property and casualty insurance), and American Society of Pension Actuaries (pensions). These three associations offer actuaries professional certification through a series of examinations. We can discuss the societies and the importance of obtaining the professional designations they offer.

A good two-day period for you to be with me is the last Thursday and Friday of the month. My activities on those days will give you a good orientation. Can you be here from 8:30 a.m. to 5 p.m. Casual business dress is appropriate. My office is on Floor 37 of the Brighton Building.

Letter in Modified Block Format with Paragraph Indentations and List

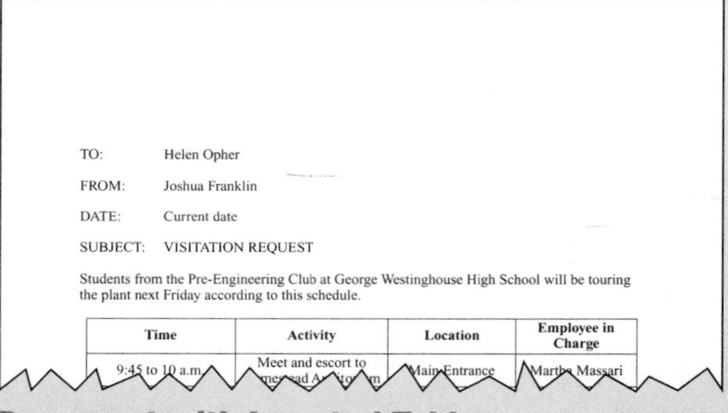

TO: Helen Opher

FROM: Joshua Franklin

DATE: Current date

SUBJECT: VISITATION REQUEST

Students from the Pre-Engineering Club at George Westinghouse High School will be touring the plant next Friday according to this schedule.

Time	Activity	Location	Employee in Charge
9:45 to 10 a.m.	Meet and escort to [illegible]	Main Entrance	Martha Massari

Document with Inserted Table

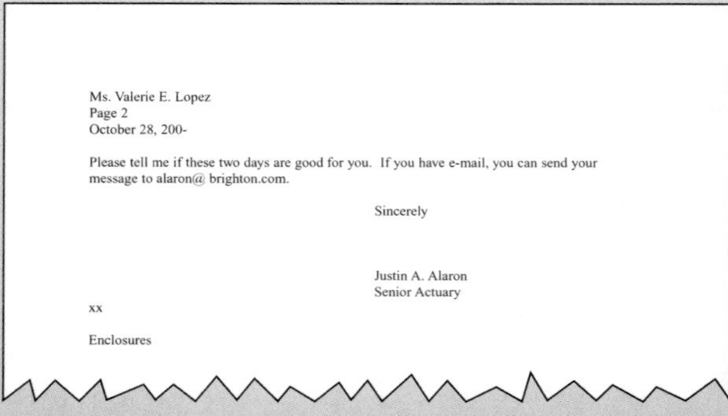

Ms. Valerie E. Lopez
Page 2
October 28, 200-

Please tell me if these two days are good for you. If you have e-mail, you can send your message to alaron@ brighton.com.

Sincerely

Justin A. Alaron
Senior Actuary

xx

Enclosures

Letter (p. 2) Showing Second-Page Heading

LESSON 4 — NEW KEYS: o AND t

Objectives:

1. To learn reach technique for **o** and **t**.
2. To combine smoothly **o** and **t** with all other learned keys.

4A • 8'
Conditioning Practice

Key each line twice SS (slowly, then faster); DS between 2-line groups.

In Lessons 4–8, the time for the *Conditioning Practice* is changed to 8'. During this time, you are to arrange your work area, prepare your equipment for keying, and practice the lines of the *Conditioning Practice* as directed.

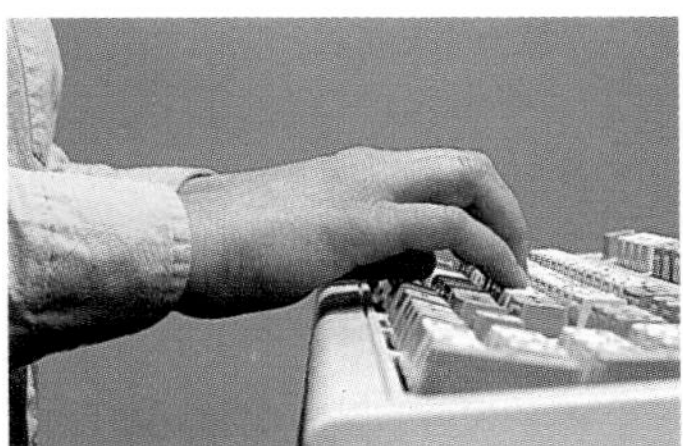

Fingers curved

Fingers upright

```
home row        1 a sad fall; had a hall; a jak falls; as a fall ad;
3d row          2 if her aid; all he sees; he irks her; a jade fish;
all keys learned 3 as he fell; he sells fir desks; she had half a jar
```

4B • 20'
New Keys: O and T

Key each line twice SS (slowly, then faster); DS between 2-line groups; if time permits, key lines 7–9 again.

o *Right ring* finger

t *Left index* finger

Follow the *Standard Plan for Learning New Keys* outlined on p. R6.

Learn o

```
1 l l ol ol do do of of so so lo lo old old for fore
2 ol ol of of or or for for oak oak off off sol sole
3 do so; a doe; of old; of oak; old foe; of old oak;
```

Learn t

```
4 f f tf tf it it at at tie tie the the fit fit lift
5 tf tf ft ft it it sit sit fit fit hit hit kit kite
6 if it; a fit; it fit; tie it; the fit; at the site
```

Combine o and t

```
7 to to|too too|toe toe|dot dot|lot lot|hot hot|tort
8 a lot; to jot; too hot; odd lot; a fort; for a lot
9 of the; to rot; dot it; the lot; for the; for this
```

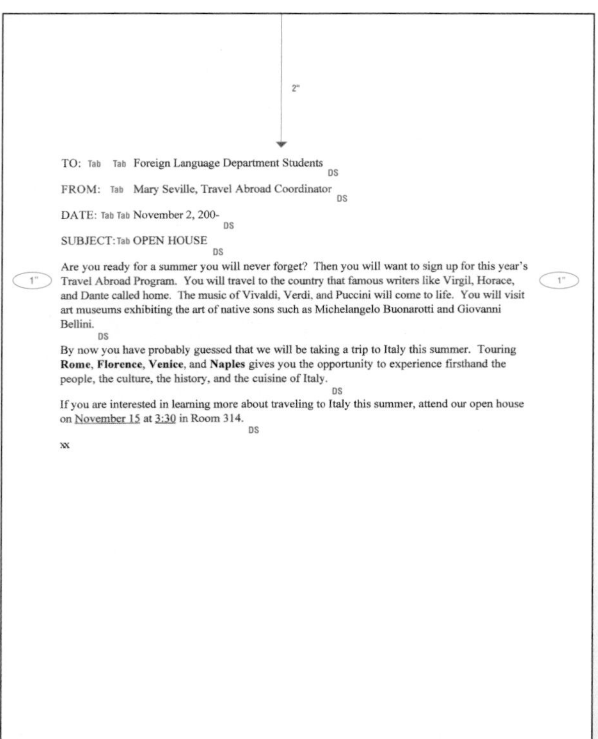

2"

TO: Tab Tab Foreign Language Department Students
DS

FROM: Tab Mary Seville, Travel Abroad Coordinator
DS

DATE: Tab Tab November 2, 200-
DS

SUBJECT: Tab OPEN HOUSE
DS

1" Are you ready for a summer you will never forget? Then you will want to sign up for this year's Travel Abroad Program. You will travel to the country that famous writers like Virgil, Horace, and Dante called home. The music of Vivaldi, Verdi, and Puccini will come to life. You will visit art museums exhibiting the art of native sons such as Michelangelo Buonarotti and Giovanni Bellini. 1"
DS

By now you have probably guessed that we will be taking a trip to Italy this summer. Touring **Rome**, **Florence**, **Venice**, and **Naples** gives you the opportunity to experience firsthand the people, the culture, the history, and the cuisine of Italy.
DS

If you are interested in learning more about traveling to Italy this summer, attend our open house on November 15 at 3:30 in Room 314.
DS

xx

Interoffice Memo

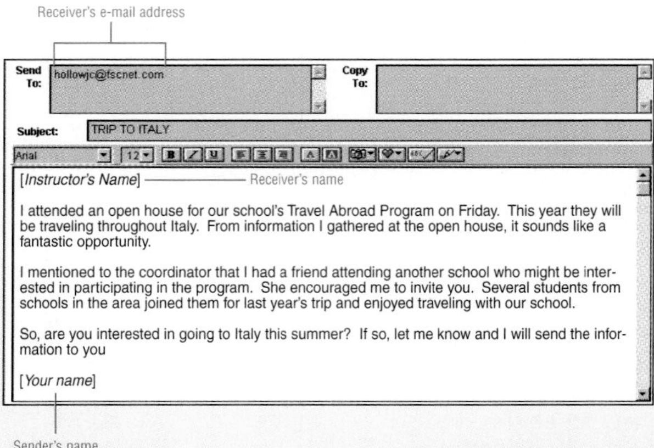

Receiver's e-mail address
Send To:
hollowjc@fscnet.com
Copy To:
Subject:
TRIP TO ITALY
Arial
12
[Instructor's Name]
Receiver's name
I attended an open house for our school's Travel Abroad Program on Friday. This year they will be traveling throughout Italy. From information I gathered at the open house, it sounds like a fantastic opportunity.
I mentioned to the coordinator that I had a friend attending another school who might be interested in participating in the program. She encouraged me to invite you. Several students from schools in the area joined them for last year's trip and enjoyed traveling with our school.
So, are you interested in going to Italy this summer? If so, let me know and I will send the information to you
[Your name]
Sender's name

E-mail Message

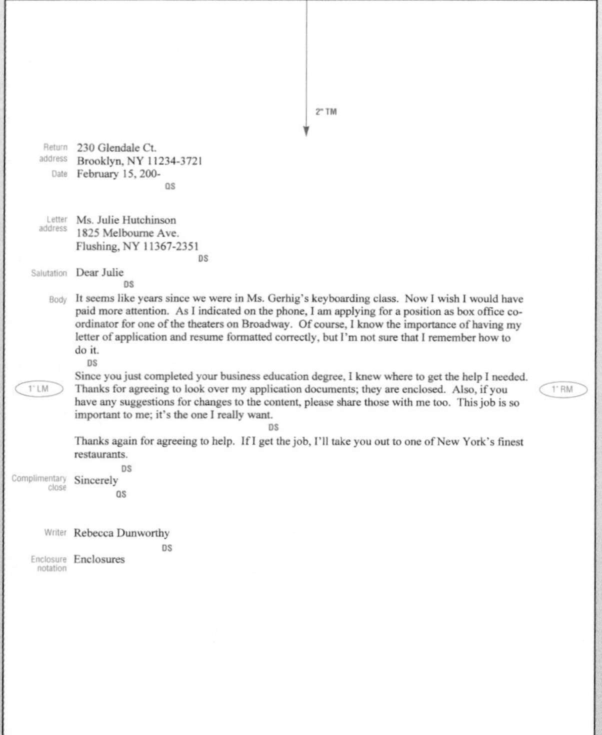

2" TM

Return address 230 Glendale Ct.
Brooklyn, NY 11234-3721
Date February 15, 200-
DS

Letter address Ms. Julie Hutchinson
1825 Melbourne Ave.
Flushing, NY 11367-2351
DS

Salutation Dear Julie
DS

Body It seems like years since we were in Ms. Gerhig's keyboarding class. Now I wish I would have paid more attention. As I indicated on the phone, I am applying for a position as box office coordinator for one of the theaters on Broadway. Of course, I know the importance of having my letter of application and resume formatted correctly, but I'm not sure that I remember how to do it.
DS

1" LM Since you just completed your business education degree, I knew where to get the help I needed. Thanks for agreeing to look over my application documents; they are enclosed. Also, if you have any suggestions for changes to the content, please share those with me too. This job is so important to me; it's the one I really want. 1" RM
DS

Thanks again for agreeing to help. If I get the job, I'll take you out to one of New York's finest restaurants.
DS

Complimentary close Sincerely
QS

Writer Rebecca Dunworthy
DS

Enclosure notation Enclosures

Personal-Business Letter

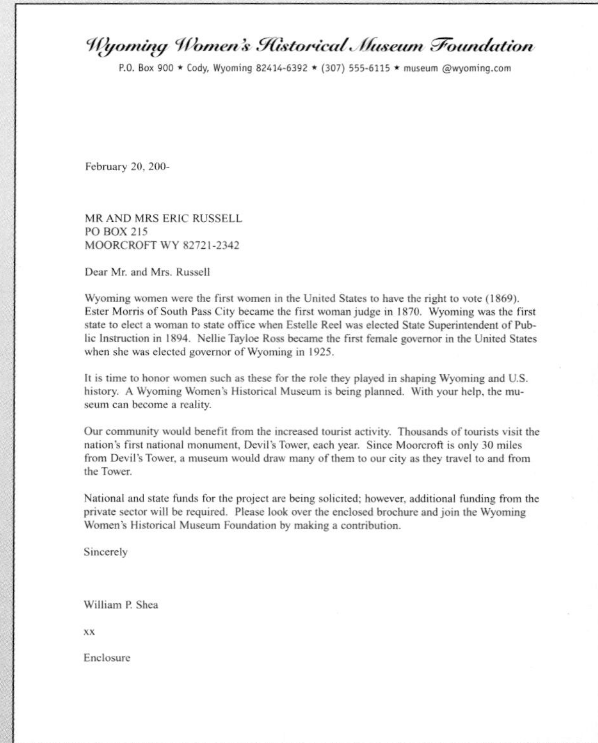

Wyoming Women's Historical Museum Foundation

P.O. Box 900 • Cody, Wyoming 82414-6392 • (307) 555-6115 • museum @wyoming.com

February 20, 200-

MR AND MRS ERIC RUSSELL
PO BOX 215
MOORCROFT WY 82721-2342

Dear Mr. and Mrs. Russell

Wyoming women were the first women in the United States to have the right to vote (1869). Ester Morris of South Pass City became the first woman judge in 1870. Wyoming was the first state to elect a woman to state office when Estelle Reel was elected State Superintendent of Public Instruction in 1894. Nellie Tayloe Ross became the first female governor in the United States when she was elected governor of Wyoming in 1925.

It is time to honor women such as these for the role they played in shaping Wyoming and U.S. history. A Wyoming Women's Historical Museum is being planned. With your help, the museum can become a reality.

Our community would benefit from the increased tourist activity. Thousands of tourists visit the nation's first national monument, Devil's Tower, each year. Since Moorcroft is only 30 miles from Devil's Tower, a museum would draw many of them to our city as they travel to and from the Tower.

National and state funds for the project are being solicited; however, additional funding from the private sector will be required. Please look over the enclosed brochure and join the Wyoming Women's Historical Museum Foundation by making a contribution.

Sincerely

William P. Shea

xx

Enclosure

Business Letter in Block Format

4C • 22'
New-Key Mastery

1. Key the lines once SS; DS between 2-line groups.
2. Key the lines again at a faster pace.

Technique Goals:

- curved, upright fingers
- wrists low, but not resting
- down-and-in spacing
- eyes on copy as you key

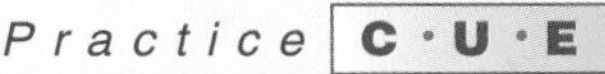

In lines of repeated words (lines 3, 5, and 7), speed up the second keying of each word.

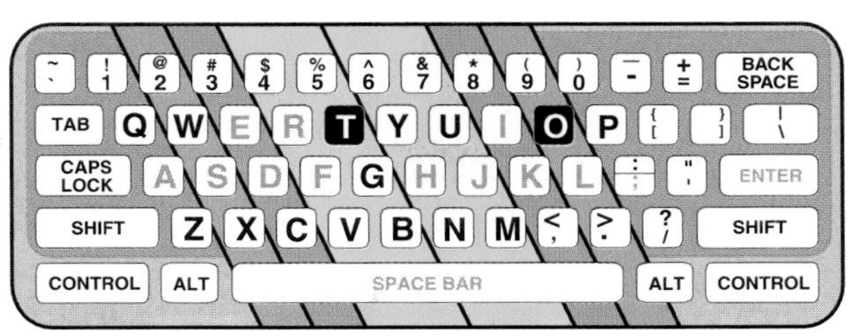


```
reach review   1 hj ed ik rf ol tf jh de ki fr lo ft hj ed ol rf tf
               2 is led fro hit old fit let kit rod kid dot jak sit

h/e            3 he he|she she|led led|had had|see see|has has|seek
               4 he led|ask her|she held|has fled|had jade|he leads

i/t            5 it it|fit fit|tie tie|sit sit|kit kit|its its|fits
               6 a kit|a fit|a tie|lit it|it fits|it sits|it is fit

o/r            7 or or|for for|ore ore|fro fro|oar oar|roe roe|rode
               8 a rod|a door|a rose|or for|her or|he rode|or a rod

space bar      9 of he or it is to if do el odd off too for she the
              10 it is|if it|do so|if he|to do|or the|she is|of all

all keys      11 if she is; ask a lad; to the lake; off the old jet
learned       12 he or she; for a fit; if she left the; a jak salad
```

4D •
Enrichment

1. Key the drill once SS at an easy pace to gain control of all your reach-stroke motions. DS between 2-line groups.
2. Key the drill again to speed up your motions and build continuity.

```
reach review   1 hj ed ik rf jhj ded kik frf a;sldkfj a;sldkfj fja;
               2 if led ski fir she ire sir jak has did jar kid rid

o/t            3 ol ol|old old|for for|oak oak|ode ode|doe doe|does
               4 tf tf|it it|to to|kit kit|the the|fit fit|sit sits

i/r            5 ik ik|if if|it it|fir fir|ski ski|did did|kid kids
               6 rf rf|or or|for for|her her|fir fir|rod rod|or for

h/e            7 hj hj|he he|ah ah|ha ha|he he|she she|ash ash|hash
               8 ed ed|el el|he he|her her|elk elk|jet jet|she|shed

all keys       9 of hot kit old sit for jet she oak jar ore lid lot
learned       10 a ski; old oak; too hot; odd jar; for the; old jet

all keys      11 she is to ski; is for the lad; ask if she has jade
learned       12 he sold leeks to her; she sells jade at their lake
```

PROOFREADERS' MARKS

Proofreaders' marks are used to mark corrections in keyed or printed text that contains problems and/or errors. As a keyboard user, you should be able to read these marks accurately when revising or editing a rough draft. You also should be able to write these symbols to correct the rough drafts that you and others key. The most-used proofreaders' marks are shown below.

||	Align copy; also, make these items parallel
¶	Begin a new paragraph
Cap ≡	Capitalize
	Close up
	Delete
<#	Delete space
No ¶	Do not begin a new paragraph
^	Insert
	Insert comma
⊙	Insert period
	Insert quotation marks
#>	Insert space
	Insert apostrophe
stet	Let it stand; ignore correction
lc	Lowercase
	Move down; lower
	Move left
	Move right
	Move up; raise
sp	Spell out
tr	Transpose
	Underline or italic

E-MAIL FORMAT AND SOFTWARE FEATURES

E-mail format varies slightly, depending on the software used to create and send it.

E-mail Heading

Most e-mail software includes these features:

Attachment: line for attaching files to an e-mail message

Bcc: line for sending copy of a message to someone without the receiver knowing

Cc: line for sending copy of a message to additional receivers

Date: month, day, and year message is sent; often includes precise time of transmittal; usually is inserted automatically

From: name and/or e-mail address of sender; usually is inserted automatically

Subject: line for very brief description of message content

To: line for name and/or e-mail address of receiver

E-mail Body

The message box on the e-mail screen may contain these elements or only the message paragraphs (SS with DS between paragraphs).

- Informal salutation and/or receiver's name (a DS above the message)
- Informal closing (e.g., "Regards," "Thanks") and/or the sender's name (a DS below the message). Additional identification (e.g., telephone number) may be included.

Special E-mail Features

Several e-mail features make communicating through e-mail fast and efficient.

Address list/book: collection of names and e-mail addresses of correspondents from which an address can be entered on the To: line by selecting it, instead of keying it.

Distribution list: series of names and/or e-mail addresses, separated by commas, on the To: line.

Forward: feature that allows an e-mail user to send a copy of a received e-mail message to others.

Recipient list (Group): feature that allows an e-mail user to send mail to a group of recipients by selecting the name of the group (e.g., All Teachers).

Reply: feature used to respond to an incoming message.

Reply all: feature used to respond to all copy recipients as well as the sender of an incoming message.

Signature: feature for storing and inserting the closing lines of messages (e.g., informal closing, sender's name, telephone number, address, fax number).

Objectives:

1. To learn reach technique for **n** and **g**.
2. To combine smoothly **n** and **g** with all other learned keys.

5A • 8' Conditioning Practice

Key each line twice SS (slowly, then faster); DS between 2-line groups.

```
home row 1 has a jak; ask a lad; a fall fad; had a jak salad;
     o/t 2 to do it; as a tot; do a lot; it is hot; to dot it
   e/i/r 3 is a kid; it is far; a red jar; her skis; her aide
```

5B • 20' New Keys: N and G

Key each line twice SS (slowly, then faster); DS between 2-line groups; if time permits, key lines 7–9 again.

n *Right index* finger

g *Left index* finger

Follow the *Standard Plan for Learning New Keys* outlined on p. R6.

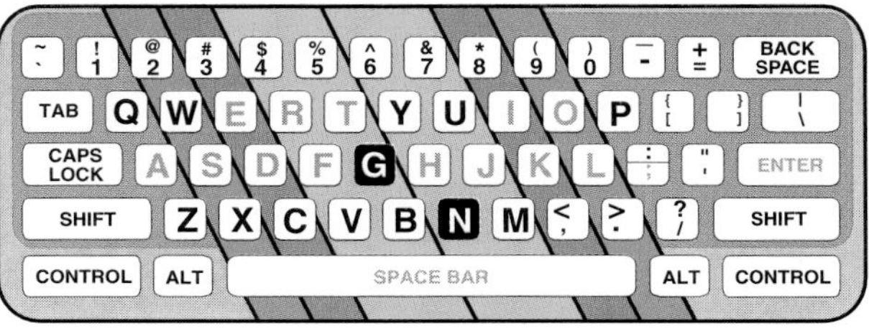

Learn n

```
1 j j nj nj an an and and end end ant ant land lands
2 nj nj an an en en in in on on end end and and hand
3 an en; an end; an ant; no end; on land; a fine end
```

Learn g

```
4 f f gf gf go go fog fog got got fig figs jogs jogs
5 gf gf go go got got dig dig jog jog logs logs golf
6 to go; he got; to jog; to jig; the fog; is to golf
```

Combine n and g

```
7 go go|no no|nag nag|ago ago|gin gin|gone gone|long
8 go on; a nag; sign in; no gain; long ago; into fog
9 a fine gig; log in soon; a good sign; lend a hand;
```

5C • 5' Technique: Enter Key

Key each line twice SS; DS between 2-line groups.

Practice **C • U • E**

Keep up your pace to the end of line, strike the ENTER key quickly, and start the new line without pause.

```
1 she is gone;
2 she got an old dog;
3 she jogs in a dense fog;
4 she and he go to golf at nine;
5 he is a hand on a rig in the north;
```

Reach out and tap ENTER.

CONFUSING WORDS

accept (vb) to receive; to approve; to take
except (prep/vb) with the exclusion of; leave out

affect (vb) to produce a change in or have an effect on
effect (n) result; something produced by an agent or a cause

buy (n/vb) to purchase; to acquire; a bargain
by (prep/adv) close to; via; according to; close at hand

choose (vb) to select; to decide
chose (vb) past tense of "choose"

cite (vb) use as support; commend; summon
sight (n/vb) ability to see; something seen; a device to improve aim
site (n) location

complement (n) something that fills, completes, or makes perfect
compliment (n/vb) a formal expression of respect or admiration; to pay respect or admiration

do (vb) to bring about; to carry out
due (adj) owed or owing as a debt; having reached the date for payment

farther (adv) greater distance
further (adv) additional; in greater depth; to greater extent

for (prep/conj) indicates purpose on behalf of; because of
four (n) two plus two in number

hear (vb) to gain knowledge of by the ear
here (adv) in or at this place; at or on this point; in this case

hole (n) opening in or through something
whole (adj/n) having all its proper parts; a complete amount

hour (n) the 24th part of a day; a particular time
our (adj) possessive form of "we"; of or relating to us

knew (vb) past tense of "know"; understood; recognized truth or nature of
new (adj) novel; fresh; existing for a short time

know (vb) to be aware of the truth or nature of; to have an understanding of
no (adv/adj/n) not in any respect or degree; not so; indicates denial or refusal

lessen (vb) to cause to decrease; to make less
lesson (n) something to be learned; period of instruction; a class period

lie (n/vb) an untrue or inaccurate statement; to tell an untrue story; to rest or recline
lye (n) a strong alkaline substance or solution

one (adj/pron) a single unit or thing
won (vb) past tense of win; gained a victory as in a game or contest; got by effort or work

passed (vb) past tense of "pass"; already occurred; moved by; gave an item to someone
past (adv/adj/prep/n) gone or elapsed; time gone by

personal (adj) of, relating to, or affecting a person; done in person
personnel (n) a staff or persons making up a workforce in an organization

plain (adj/n) with little decoration; a large flat area of land
plane (n) an airplane or hydroplane

pole (n) a long, slender, rounded piece of wood or other material
poll (n) a survey of people to analyze public opinion

principal (n/adj) a chief or leader; capital (money) amount placed at interest; of or relating to the most important thing or matter or persons
principle (n) a central rule, law, or doctrine

right (adj) factual; true; correct
rite (n) customary form of ceremony; ritual
write (v) to form letters or symbols; to compose and set down in words, numbers, or symbols

some (n/adv) unknown or unspecified unit or thing; to a degree or extent
sum (n/vb) total; to find a total; to summarize

stationary (adj) fixed in a position, course, or mode; unchanging in condition
stationery (n) paper and envelopes used for processing personal and business documents

than (conj/prep) used in comparisons to show differences between items
then (n/adv) that time; at that time; next

to (prep/adj) indicates action, relation, distance, direction
too (adv) besides; also; to excessive degree
two (n/adj) one plus one

vary (vb) change; make different; diverge
very (adv/adj) real; mere; truly; to high degree

waist (n) narrowed part of the body between chest and hips; middle of something
waste (n/vb/adj) useless things; rubbish; spend or use carelessly; nonproductive

weak (adj) lacking strength, skill, or proficiency
week (n) a series of seven days; Monday through Sunday

wear (vb/n) to bear or have on the person; diminish by use; clothing
where (adv/conj/n) at, in, or to what degree; what place, source, or cause

your (adj) of or relating to you as possessor
you're (contraction) you are

5D • 17'
New-Key Mastery

1. Key the lines once SS; DS between 2-line groups.
2. Key the lines again at a faster pace.

Technique Goals:

- curved, upright fingers
- wrists low, but not resting
- quick-snap keystrokes
- down-and-in spacing
- eyes on copy as you key

reach review

1 a;sldkfj ed ol rf hj tf nj gf lo de jh ft nj fr a;
2 he jogs; an old ski; do a log for; she left a jar;

n/g

3 an an|go go|in in|dig dig|and and|got got|end ends
4 go to; is an; log on; sign it; and golf; fine figs

space bar

5 if if|an an|go go|of of|or or|he he|it it|is is|do
6 if it is|is to go|he or she|to do this|of the sign

all keys learned

7 she had an old oak desk; a jell jar is at the side
8 he has left for the lake; she goes there at eight;

all keys learned

9 she said he did it for her; he is to take the oars
10 sign the list on the desk; go right to the old jet

5E •
Enrichment

Key each line twice SS; DS between 2-line groups; QS after lines 3, 7, and 12.

lines 1–3:

- curved, upright fingers
- steady, easy pace

lines 4–7:

- space immediately after each word
- down-and-in motion of thumb

lines 8–12:

- maintain pace to end of line
- strike ENTER key quickly
- start new line immediately

lines 13–16:

- speed up second keying of each repeated word or phrase
- think words, not each letter

Reach review

1 nj nj gf gf ol ol tf tf ik ik rf rf hj hj ed ed fj
2 go fog an and got end jog ant dog ken fig fin find
3 go an on and lag jog flag land glad lend sign hand

Space Bar

4 if an it go is of do or to as in so no off too gin
5 ah ha he or if an too for and she jog got hen then
6 he is to go|if it is so|is to do it|if he is to go
7 she is to ski on the lake; he is also at the lake;

Enter key

8 he is to go;
9 she is at an inn;
10 he goes to ski at one;
11 he is also to sign the log;
12 she left the log on the old desk

Short words and phrases

13 do do|it it|an an|is is|of of|to to|if if|or or or
14 he he|go go|in in|so so|at at|no no|as as|ha ha ha
15 to do|to do|it is|it is|of it|of it|is to|is to do
16 she is to do so; he did the sign; ski at the lake;

BASIC GRAMMAR GUIDES

Use a singular verb

1. With a singular subject.
   Dr. Cho was to give the lecture, but he is ill.
2. With indefinite pronouns (*each*, *every*, *any*, *either*, *neither*, *one*, etc.)
   Each of these girls has an important role in the class play.
   Neither of them is well enough to start the game.
3. With singular subjects linked by *or* or *nor*; but if one subject is singular and the other is plural, the verb agrees with the nearer subject.
   Neither Ms. Moss nor Mr. Katz was invited to speak.
   Either the manager or his assistants are to participate.
4. With a collective noun (*class*, *committee*, *family*, *team*, etc.) if the collective noun acts as a unit.
   The committee has completed its study and filed a report.
   The jury has returned to the courtroom to give its verdict.
5. With the pronouns *all* and *some* (as well as fractions and percentages) when used as subjects if their modifiers are singular. Use a plural verb if their modifiers are plural.
   Some of the new paint is already cracking and peeling.
   All of the workers are to be paid for the special holiday.
   Historically, about forty percent has voted.
6. When *number* is used as the subject and is preceded by *the*; use a plural verb if *number* is the subject and is preceded by *a*.
   The number of voters has increased again this year.
   A number of workers are on vacation this week.

Use a plural verb

1. With a plural subject.
   The players were all here, and they were getting restless.
2. With a compound subject joined by *and*.
   Mrs. Samoa and her son are to be on a local talk show.

Negative forms of verbs

1. Use the plural verb *do not* or *don't* with pronoun subjects *I*, *we*, *you*, and *they* as well as with plural nouns.
   I do not find this report believable; you don't either.
2. Use the singular verb *does not* or *doesn't* with pronouns *he*, *she*, and *it* as well as with singular nouns.
   Though she doesn't accept the board's offer, the board doesn't have to offer more.

Pronoun agreement with antecedents

1. A personal pronoun (*I*, *we*, *you*, *he*, *she*, *it*, *their*, etc.) agrees in person (first, second, or third) with the noun or other pronoun it represents.
   We can win the game if we all give each play our best effort.
   You may play softball after you finish your homework.
   Andrea said that she will drive her car to the shopping mall.
2. A personal pronoun agrees in gender (feminine, masculine, or neuter) with the noun or other pronoun it represents.
   Each winner will get a corsage as she receives her award.
   Mr. Kimoto will give his talk after the announcements.
   The small boat lost its way in the dense fog.
3. A personal pronoun agrees in number (singular or plural) with the noun or other pronoun it represents.
   Celine drove her new car to Del Rio, Texas, last week.
   The club officers made careful plans for their next meeting.
4. A personal pronoun that represents a collective noun (*team*, *committee*, *family*, etc.) may be singular or plural, depending on the meaning of the collective noun.
   Our women's soccer team played its fifth game today.
   The vice squad took their positions in the square.

Commonly confused pronouns

it's (contraction): it is; it has
its (pronoun): possessive form of *it*

It's good to get your e-mail; it's been a long time.
The puppy wagged its tail in welcome.

their (pronoun): possessive form of *they*
there (adverb/pronoun): at or in that place; sometimes used to introduce a sentence
they're (contraction): they are

The hikers all wore their parkas.
Will they be there during our presentation?
They're likely to be late because of rush-hour traffic.

who's (contraction): who is; who has
whose (pronoun): possessive form of *who*

Who's seen the movie? Who's going now?
I chose the one whose skills are best.

NOTE: See p. R49 for other confusing word groups.

LESSON 6 NEW KEYS: left shift AND period (.)

Objectives:

1. To learn reach technique for **left shift** and **.** (period).
2. To combine smoothly **left shift** and **.** (period) with all other learned keys.

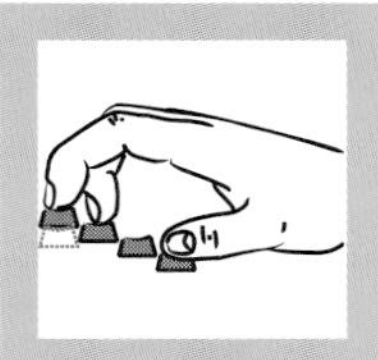

Finger-action keystrokes

Down-and-in spacing

Quick out-and-tap ENTER

6A • 8' Conditioning Practice

Key each line twice SS (slowly, then faster); DS between 2-line groups.

reach review 1 ed ik rf ol gf hj tf nj de ki fr lo fg jh ft jn a;

space bar 2 or is to if an of el so it go id he do as in at on

all letters learned 3 he is; if an; or do; to go; a jak; an oak; of all;

6B • 20' New Keys: Left [Shift] and [.]

Key each line twice SS (slowly, then faster); DS between 2-line groups; if time permits, repeat lines 7–9.

Left shift *Left little* finger

. (period) *Right ring* finger

Shifting **C • U • E**

Shift, strike key, and release both in a quick 1-2-3 count.

Learn left shift key

1 a a Ja Ja Ka Ka La La Hal Hal Kal Kal Jae Jae Lana

2 Kal rode; Kae did it; Hans has jade; Jan ate a fig

3 I see that Jake is to aid Kae at the Oak Lake sale

Learn . (period)

4 l l .l .l fl. fl. ed. ed. ft. ft. rd. rd. hr. hrs.

5 .l .l fl. fl. hr. hr. e.g. e.g. i.e. i.e. in. ins.

6 fl. ft. hr. ed. rd. rt. off. fed. ord. alt. asstd.

Combine left shift and . (period)

7 I do. Ian is. Ola did. Jan does. Kent is gone.

8 Hal did it. I shall do it. Kate left on a train.

9 J. L. Han skis on Oak Lake; Lt. Haig also does so.

Spacing **C • U • E**

Space once after . following abbreviations and initials. Do not space after . within abbreviations. Space twice after . at end of a sentence except at line endings. There, return without spacing.

PUNCTUATION GUIDES (continued)

Use an exclamation point

1. After emphatic interjections.

   Wow! Hey there! What a day!

2. After sentences that are clearly exclamatory.

   "I won't go!" she said with determination.
   How good it was to see you in New Orleans last week!

Use a hyphen

1. To join parts of compound words expressing the numbers twenty-one through ninety-nine.

   Thirty-five delegates attended the national convention.

2. To join compound adjectives preceding a noun they modify as a unit.

   End-of-term grades will be posted on the classroom door.

3. After each word or figure in a series of words or figures that modify the same noun (suspended hyphenation).

   Meeting planners made first-, second-, and third-class reservations.

4. To spell out a word.

   The sign read, "For your c-o-n-v-i-e-n-c-e." Of course, the correct word is c-o-n-v-e-n-i-e-n-c-e.

5. To form certain compound nouns.

   WGAL-TV spin-off teacher-counselor AFL-CIO

Use parentheses

1. To enclose parenthetical or explanatory matter and added information.

   Amendments to the bylaws (Exhibit A) are enclosed.

2. To enclose identifying letters or figures in a series.

   Check these factors: (1) period of time, (2) rate of pay, and (3) nature of duties.

3. To enclose figures that follow spelled-out amounts to give added clarity or emphasis.

   The total award is fifteen hundred dollars ($1,500).

Use a question mark

1. At the end of a sentence that is a direct question. But use a period after requests in the form of a question (whenever the expected answer is action, not words).

   What has been the impact of the Information Superhighway?
   Will you complete the enclosed form and return it to me.

Use quotation marks

1. To enclose direct quotations.

   Professor Dye asked, "Are you spending the summer in Europe?"
   Was it Emerson who said, "To have a friend is to be one"?

2. To enclose titles of articles, films/movies, plays, poems, songs, television programs, and unpublished works, such as theses and dissertations.

   "Matrix" with Keanu Reeves "Fog" by Sandburg
   "Survivor" in prime time "Memory" from "Cats"

3. To enclose special words or phrases or coined words (words not in dictionary usage).

   The words "phony" and "braggart" describe him, according to coworkers.
   The presenter annoyed the audience with phrases like "uh" and "you know."

Use a semicolon

1. To separate two or more independent clauses in a compound sentence when the conjunction is omitted.

   Being critical is easy; being constructive is not so easy.

2. To separate independent clauses when they are joined by a conjunctive adverb, such as *consequently* or *therefore*.

   I work mornings; therefore, I prefer an afternoon interview.

3. To separate a series of phrases or clauses (especially if they contain commas) that are introduced by a colon.

   Al spoke in these cities: Denver, CO; Erie, PA; and Troy, NY.

4. To precede an abbreviation or word that introduces an explanatory statement.

   She organized her work; for example, naming folders and files to indicate degrees or urgency.

Use an underline

1. To indicate titles of books, magazines, and newspapers. (Titles may be keyed in ALL CAPS or italic without the underline.)

   A review of <u>Runaway Jury</u> appeared in <u>The New York Times</u>.

2. To call attention to words or phrases (or use quotation marks or italic).

   Take the presenter's advice: <u>Stand</u> up, <u>speak</u> up, and then <u>sit</u> down.
   Students often confuse <u>its</u> and <u>it's</u>.

6C • 17'
New-Key Mastery

1. Key the lines once SS; DS between 2-line groups.
2. Key the lines again at a faster pace.

Technique Goals:

- curved, upright fingers
- finger-action keystrokes
- quiet hands/arms
- out-and-down shifting

Technique **C • U • E**

Eyes on copy except when you lose your place.

abbrev./initials

1 He said ft. for feet; rd. for road; fl. for floor.
2 Lt. Hahn let L. K. take the old gong to Lake Neil.

3d row emphasis

3 Lars is to ask at the old store for a kite for Jo.
4 Ike said he is to take the old road to Lake Heidi.

key words

5 a an or he to if do it of so is go for got old led
6 go the off aid dot end jar she fit oak and had rod

key phrases

7 if so|it is|to do|if it|do so|to go|he is|to do it
8 to the|and do|is the|got it|if the|for the|ask for

all letters learned

9 Ned asked her to send the log to an old ski lodge.
10 J. L. lost one of the sleds he took off the train.

6D • 5'
Technique: Spacebar and Enter

1. Key each line once SS; DS at end of line 7.
2. Key the drill again at a faster pace if time permits.

Spacing **C • U • E**

Quickly strike Space Bar *immediately* after last letter in the word.

Strike ENTER quickly and start each new line immediately.

1 Jan is to sing.
2 Karl is at the lake.
3 Lena is to send the disk.
4 Lars is to jog to the old inn.
5 Hanna took the girls to a ski lake.
6 Hal is to take the old list to his desk.
7 Lana is to take the jar to the store at nine.

6E •
Enrichment

1. Key each line once SS; DS between 3-line groups.
2. Rekey the drill at a faster pace if time permits.

Spacing/shifting **(Use down-and-in spacing; use out-and-down shifting.)**

1 K. L. Jakes is to see Lt. Hahn at Oak Lake at one.
2 Janet Harkins sent the sales sheet to Joel Hansen.
3 Karla Kent is to go to London to see Laska Jolson.

Keying easy sentences **(Keep insertion point moving steadily—no stops or pauses within the line.)**

4 Kae is to go to the lake to fish off an old skiff.
5 Joel is to ask his good friend to go to the shore.
6 Lara and her dad took eight girls for a long hike.
7 Kent said his dad is to sell the oak and ash logs.

PUNCTUATION GUIDES

Use an apostrophe

1. As a symbol for *feet* in charts, forms, and tables or as a symbol for *minutes*. (The quotation mark may be used as a symbol for *seconds* and *inches*.)

   12' x 16'   3' 54"   8' 6" x 10' 8"

2. As a symbol to indicate the omission of letters or figures (as in contractions).

   can't   do's and don'ts   Class of '02

3. To form the plural of most figures, letters, and words used as words rather than for their meaning: Add the apostrophe and *s*. In market quotations and decades, form the plural of figures by the addition of *s* only.

   7's   ten's   ABC's   Century 4s   1960s

4. To show possession: Add the apostrophe and *s* to (a) a singular noun and (b) a plural noun that does not end in *s*.

   a woman's watch   men's shoes   girl's bicycle

   Add the apostrophe and *s* to a proper name of one syllable that ends in *s*.

   Bess's Cafeteria   James's hat   Jones's bill

   Add the apostrophe only after (a) plural nouns ending in *s* and (b) a proper name of more than one syllable that ends in *s* or *z*.

   girls' camp   Adams' home   Martinez' report

   Add the apostrophe (and *s*) after the last noun in a series to indicate joint or common possession by two or more persons; however, add the possessive to each of the nouns to show separate possession by two or more persons.

   Lewis and Clark's expedition
   the secretary's and the treasurer's reports

Use a colon

1. To introduce a listing.

   These poets are my favorites: Shelley, Keats, and Frost.

2. To introduce a question or a long direct quotation.

   The question is this: Did you study for the test?

3. Between hours and minutes expressed in figures.

   10:15 a.m.   4:30 p.m.   12:00 midnight

Use a comma (or commas)

1. After (a) introductory phrases or clauses and (b) words in a series.

   When you finish keying the report, please give it to Mr. Kent.

   We will play the Mets, Expos, and Cubs in our next home stand.

2. To set off short direct quotations.

   Mrs. Ramirez replied, "No, the report is not finished."

3. Before and after (a) appositives—words that come together and refer to the same person, thing, or idea—and (b) words of direct address.

   Colette, the assistant manager, will chair the next meeting.

   Please call me, Erika, if I can be of further assistance.

4. To set off nonrestrictive clauses (not necessary to meaning of sentence), but not restrictive clauses (necessary to meaning).

   Your report, which deals with that issue, raised many questions.

   The man who organized the conference is my teacher.

5. To separate the day from the year in dates and the city from the state in addresses.

   July 4, 2002   St. Joseph, Missouri   Moose Point, AK

6. To separate two or more parallel adjectives (adjectives that modify the noun separately and that could be separated by the word *and* instead of the comma).

   The big, loud bully was ejected after he pushed the coach.

   The big, powerful car zoomed past the cheering crowd.

   Cynthia played a black lacquered grand piano at her concert.

   A small red fox squeezed through the fence to avoid the hounds.

7. To separate (a) unrelated groups of figures that occur together and (b) whole numbers into groups of three digits each. (Omit commas from years and page, policy, room, serial, and telephone numbers.)

   By the year 2001, 1,200 more local students will be enrolled.

   The supplies listed on Invoice #274068 are for Room 1953.

Use a dash

1. For emphasis.

   The skater—in a clown costume—dazzled with fancy footwork.

2. To indicate a change of thought.

   We may tour the Orient—but I'm getting ahead of my story.

3. To emphasize the name of an author when it follows a direct quotation.

   "All the world's a stage . . . ."—Shakespeare

4. To set off expressions that break off or interrupt speech.

   "Jay, don't get too close to the—." I spoke too late.

   "Today—er—uh," the anxious presenter began.

Objectives:

1. To learn reach technique for **u** and **c.**
2. To combine smoothly **u** and **c** with all other learned keys.

7A • 8'
Conditioning Practice

Key each line twice SS (slowly, then faster); DS between 2-line groups.

```
reach review  1 nj gf ol rf ik ed .l tf hj fr ki ft jn de lo fg l.
space bar     2 an do in so to go fan hen log gin tan son not sign
left shift    3 Olga has the first slot; Jena is to skate for her.
```

7B • 20'
New Keys: U and C

Key each line twice SS (slowly, then faster); DS between 2-line groups: if time permits, repeat lines 7–9.

Follow the *Standard Plan for Learning New Keys* outlined on p. R6.

u *Right index* finger

c *Left middle* finger

Learn u

```
1 j j uj uj us us us jug jug jut jut due due fur fur
2 uj uj jug jug sue sue lug lug use use lug lug dues
3 a jug; due us; the fur; use it; a fur rug; is just
```

Learn c

```
4 d d cd cd cod cod cog cog tic tic cot cot can cans
5 cd cd cod cod ice ice can can code code dock docks
6 a cod; a cog; the ice; she can; the dock; the code
```

Combine u and c

```
7 cud cud cut cuts cur curs cue cues duck ducks clue
8 a cud; a cur; to cut; the cue; the cure; for luck;
9 use a clue; a fur coat; take the cue; cut the cake
10 Jake told us there is ice on the road to the lake.
11 Jack asked us for a list of all the codes he used.
12 Louise has gone to cut the cake on the green cart.
```

Style Guide

CAPITALIZATION GUIDES

Capitalize

1. The first word of every sentence and complete quotation. Do not capitalize (a) fragments of quotations or (b) a quotation resumed within a sentence.
   Crazy Horse said, "I will return to you in stone."
   Ghandi's teaching inspired "nonviolent revolutions."
   "It is . . . fitting and proper," Lincoln said, "that we . . . do this."
2. The first word after a colon if that word begins a complete sentence.
   Remember: Keep the action in your fingers.
   These sizes were in stock: small, medium, and extra large.
3. First, last, and all other words in titles except articles, conjunctions, or prepositions of four or fewer letters.
   The Beak of the Finch
   Raleigh News and Observer
   "The Phantom of the Opera"
4. An official title when it precedes a name or when used elsewhere if it is a title of distinction.
   In what year did Juan Carlos become King of Spain?
   Masami Chou, our class president, met Senator Thurmond.
5. Personal titles and names of people and places.
   Did you see Mrs. Watts and Gloria while in Miami?
6. All proper nouns and their derivatives.
   Mexico   Mexican border   Uganda   Ugandan economy
7. Days of the week, months of the year, holidays, periods of history, and historic events.
   Friday   July   Labor Day
   Middle Ages   Vietnam War   Woodstock
8. Geographic regions, localities, and names.
   the East Coast   Upper Peninsula Michigan
   Ohio River   the Deep South
9. Street, avenue, company, etc., when used with a proper noun.
   Fifth Avenue   Wall Street   Monsanto Company
10. Names of organizations, clubs, and buildings.
    National Hockey League   Four-H Club
    Biltmore House   Omni Hotel
11. A noun preceding a figure except for common nouns, such as line, page, and sentence.
    Review Rules 1 to 18 in Chapter 5, page 149.
12. Seasons of the year only when they are personified.
    the soft kiss of Spring   the icy fingers of Winter

NUMBER EXPRESSION GUIDES

Use words for

1. Numbers from one to ten except when used with numbers above ten, which are keyed as figures. Common business practice is to use figures for all numbers except those that begin a sentence.
   Did you visit all eight Web sites, or only four?
   Buy 15 textbooks and 8 workbooks.
2. A number beginning a sentence.
   Twelve of the new shrubs have died; 48 are doing well.
3. The shorter of two numbers used together.
   fifty 33-cent stamps   150 twenty-cent stamps
4. Isolated fractions or indefinite numbers in a sentence.
   Nearly seventy members voted, which is almost one-fourth.
5. Names of small-numbered streets and avenues (ten and under).
   The theater is at the corner of Third Avenue and 54th Street.

Use figures for

1. Dates and times except in very formal writing.
   The flight will arrive at 9:48 a.m. on March 14.
   The ceremony took place the fifth of June at eleven o'clock.
2. A series of fractions and/or mixed numbers.
   Key 1/4, 1/2, 5/6, and 7 3/4.
3. Numbers following nouns.
   Case 1849 is reviewed in Volume 5, page 9.
4. Measures, weights, and dimensions.
   6 feet 9 inches   7 pounds 4 ounces
   8.5 inches by 11 inches
5. Definite numbers used with percent (%), but use words for indefinite percentages.
   The late fee is 15 percent of the overdue payment.
   The brothers put in nearly fifty percent of the start-up capital.
6. House numbers except house number *One.*
   My home is at 8 Weber Drive; my office is at One Weber Plaza.
7. Amounts of money except when spelled for emphasis (as in legal documents). Even amounts are keyed without the decimal. Large amounts (a million or more) are keyed as shown.
   $17.75   75 cents $775
   seven hundred dollars ($700)
   $7,500 $7 million $7.2 million $7 billion

7C • 17'
New-Key Mastery

1. Key the lines once SS; DS between 2-line groups.
2. Key the lines again at a faster pace.

Technique Goals:

- Reach up without moving hands away from your body.
- Reach down without moving hands toward your body.
- Use quick-snap keystrokes.

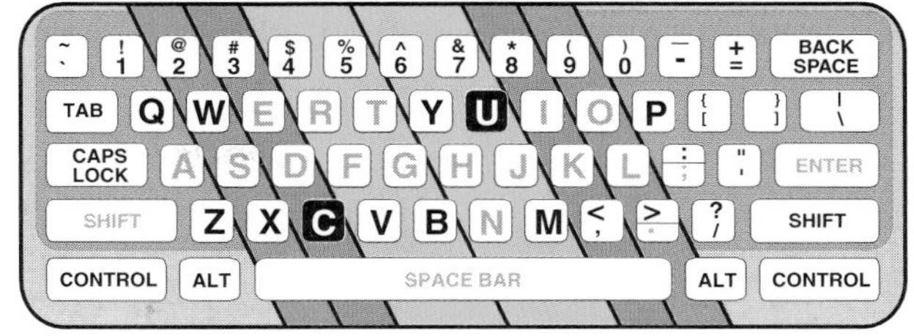

3d/1st rows

1 in cut nut ran cue can cot fun hen car urn den cog
2 Nan is cute; he is curt; turn a cog; he can use it

left shift and .

3 Kae had taken a lead. Jack then cut ahead of her.
4 I said to use Kan. for Kansas and Ore. for Oregon.

key words

5 and cue for jut end kit led old fit just golf coed
6 an due cut such fuss rich lack turn dock turf curl

key phrases

7 an urn|is due|to cut|for us|to use|cut off|such as
8 just in|code it|turn on|cure it|as such|is in luck

all keys learned

9 Nida is to get the ice; Jacki is to call for cola.
10 Ira is sure that he can go there in an hour or so.

7D • 5'
Technique: Spacebar and Left Shift

Key the lines once SS; DS between 3-line groups. Keep hand movement to a minimum.

space bar

1 Ken said he is to sign the list and take the disk.
2 It is right for her to take the lei if it is hers.
3 Jae has gone to see an old oaken desk at the sale.

left shift

4 He said to enter Oh. for Ohio and Kan. for Kansas.
5 It is said that Lt. Li has an old jet at Lake Ida.
6 L. N. is at the King Hotel; Harl is at the Leland.

7E •
Enrichment

1. Key each line once SS; DS between 2-line groups.
2. If time permits, key the lines again at a faster pace.

Practice **C • U • E**

Try to reduce hand movement and the tendency of unused fingers to fly out or follow the reaching finger.

u/c

1 uj cd uc juj dcd cud cut use cog cue urn curl luck
2 Huck can use the urn for the social at the church.

n/g

3 nj gf nj gin can jog nick sign nigh snug rung clog
4 Nan can jog to the large sign at the old lake gin.

all keys learned

5 nj gf uj cd ol tf ik rf hj ed an go or is to he l.
6 Leona has gone to ski; Jack had left here at nine.

all keys learned

7 an or is to he go cue for and jak she all use curt
8 Nick sells jade rings; Jahn got one for good luck.

Drill 5: Move Files

1. Double-click the *English* folder on the desktop to open the *English* window. Move the window, if necessary (drag it by its title bar), so you can see the *Keyboarding* folder on the desktop.
2. Drag the first file from the *English* window to the *Keyboarding* folder.
3. Double-click the *Keyboarding* folder on the desktop to open the *Keyboarding* window. You need to be able to see all of the *English* window and at least part of the *Keyboarding* window. If you cannot, move the window(s) until you can see them.
4. If the *English* window has a gray title bar, select it to make it the **active window** (the window in which you can work).
5. Select a group of files in the *English* window and move them anywhere inside the *Keyboarding* window. Continue until all the files have been moved. Do not worry if the files are not neatly arranged. You will organize them in the next drill.
6. Close the *English* window.

ARRANGING FILES AND GETTING DATA

You can arrange the icons in a window by name, type, size, or date. You can also get details about files such as the file size and the date the file was last modified. In Drill 6, you will organize the file folders in the *Keyboarding* window, then look at details of these files.

Drill 6: Arrange Files and Get Data

1. In the *Keyboarding* window, click the *View* menu, point to *Arrange Icons*, and select *by Name*.
2. With no files selected, note (between the window and the taskbar) how many files the *Keyboarding* window contains and the total file size.
3. Select one file. What does the window tell you about it? What does it tell you about a group of selected files?
4. Select *Details* from the View menu. If necessary, scroll to see the information this view provides.
5. Click the *View* menu, point to *Arrange Icons*, and choose *by Date*. When might this view be useful?

DELETING FILES AND FOLDERS

You can select and delete several files and folders at once, just as you selected several items to move or copy. If you delete a folder, you automatically delete any files and folders inside it. Here are two ways to delete a file or folder:

- In *Windows Explorer* or in a drive or folder window, select the file or folder and choose *Delete* from the File menu. Answer *Yes* to the question about sending the item to the Recycle Bin.
- Right-click the file or folder and choose *Delete*. Answer *Yes* to the question about sending the item to the Recycle Bin.

Drill 7: Delete Files

1. In the *Keyboarding* window, right-click a file, choose *Delete*, and answer *Yes* to send the file to the Recycle Bin.
2. Select several files in the *Keyboarding* window, choose *Delete* from the File menu, and answer *Yes* to send the files to the Recycle Bin.

RESTORING DELETED FILES AND FOLDERS

Assume that there was one file you didn't mean to delete from the *Keyboarding* window. When you delete a file or folder, the item goes to the Recycle Bin. You can restore files and folders from the Recycle Bin.

Drill 8: Restore a Deleted File

1. Minimize the *Keyboarding* window. Double-click the *Recycle Bin* icon on the desktop to open the Recycle Bin window.
2. Select one of the files you just deleted and click *Restore* (you may need to scroll down in the left pane to see the Restore option). Or select *Restore* from the File menu, depending on your *Windows®* operating system version.
3. Close the Recycle Bin window. Click the *Keyboarding* button on the taskbar to bring up the *Keyboarding* window. It should contain the file you just restored.
4. Close the *Keyboarding* window and delete the *Keyboarding* and *English* folders from your desktop.

Objectives:

1. To learn reach technique for **w** and **right shift**.
2. To combine smoothly **w** and **right shift** with other learned keys.

8A • 8'
Conditioning Practice

Key each line twice SS (slowly, then faster); DS between 2-line groups.

reach review	1	rf gf de ju jn ki lo cd ik rf .l ed hj tf ol gf ft
u/c	2	us cod use cut sue cot jut cog nut cue con lug ice
all letters learned	3	Hugh has just taken a lead in a race for a record.

8B • 20'
New Keys: [W] and Right [Shift]

Key each line twice SS (slowly, then faster); DS between 2-line groups; if time permits, repeat lines 7–9.

w *Left ring* finger

Right shift *Right little* finger

Shifting **C · U · E**

Shift, strike key, and release both in a quick 1-2-3 count.

Follow the *Standard Plan for Learning New Keys* outlined on p. R6.

Learn w

1 s s ws ws sow sow wow wow low low how how cow cows
2 sw sw ws ws ow ow now now row row own own tow tows
3 to sow; is how; so low; to own; too low; is to row

Learn right shift key

4 A; A; Al Al; Cal Cal; Ali or Flo; Di and Sol left.
5 Ali lost to Ron; Cal lost to Elsa; Di lost to Del.
6 Tina has left for Tucson; Dori can find her there.

Combine w and right shift

7 Dodi will ask if Willa went to Town Center at two.
8 Wilf left the show for which he won a Gower Award.
9 Walt will go to Rio on a golf tour with Wolf Lowe.
10 Wilton and Donna asked to go to the store with us.
11 Walter left us at Willow Lake with Will and Frank.
12 Ted or Walt will get us tickets for the two shows.

Drill 2: Create Folders

1. In the left pane of *Windows Explorer*, click *Desktop* (you may need to scroll up a little to find it).
2. Click the *File* menu, point to *New*, and click *Folder*. A new folder called *New Folder* will appear in both panes of the window. In the right pane, the name will be highlighted.
3. Key a name for the folder (**Century21**) and press ENTER.
4. Minimize *Windows Explorer* (click the minus sign at the upper right of the window). Right-click in a blank area of the desktop, point to *New*, and click *Folder*.
5. Key a name for the folder (**Compositions**) and press ENTER.

RENAMING FILES AND FOLDERS

You can rename a file or folder in one of these ways:

- In *Windows Explorer* or in a window opened by double-clicking a drive or folder, click the file or folder, choose *Rename* from the File menu, key the new name, and press ENTER.
- Right-click the file or folder, choose *Rename*, key the new name, and press ENTER.

In the filename *Lesson1.wpd*, the *wpd* **extension** indicates that the file is a *Corel® WordPerfect®* document. When you rename a file, be sure to include the extension that is recognized by your software program, or you may not be able to open the file.

Drill 3: Rename Folders

1. Right-click the *Century21* folder on the desktop, choose *Rename*, key **Keyboarding**, and press ENTER.
2. Click the *Exploring* button on the taskbar to bring up *Windows Explorer*. If necessary, click the *Compositions* folder. Choose *Rename* from the File menu, key **English**, and press ENTER.

MOVING AND COPYING FILES AND FOLDERS

You can move or copy files or folders in *Windows Explorer* or on the desktop.

- To move a file or folder, drag it to its new location.
- To copy a file or folder, hold down the CTRL key while dragging. The pointer icon will change to include a plus sign to indicate that you are copying.

Drag your file or folder on top of the destination drive or folder. You will know you are doing it correctly if the destination drive or folder is darkened, just as when you click it. If you are moving or copying to the open window for a drive or folder (as you will in Drill 5), drag the item anywhere inside the window.

When you are moving or copying files or folders, **selecting** (clicking) several items at once can save time.

- To select consecutive items, click the first item, hold down the SHIFT key, and click the last item.
- To select items in different places, hold down the CTRL key while you click each item.

Drill 4: Copy Files

1. In the left pane of *Windows Explorer*, locate and click the drive or folder from which you retrieve data files for this text. The files will be displayed in the right pane.
2. If necessary, scroll in the left pane until you can see the *English* folder.
3. Hold down CTRL and drag one of your data files to the *English* folder.
4. Select a block of data files to copy by selecting the first file and pressing SHIFT as you select the last file. Hold down CTRL and drag the files to the *English* folder.
5. Select several separate data files to copy from your student disk by pressing CTRL as you select each file. Hold down CTRL and drag these files to the *English* folder.
6. Close *Windows Explorer* (click the *X* at the upper right of the window).

Oops! We put keyboarding files in the *English* folder. Now we'll use the desktop to move the files to the *Keyboarding* folder.

8C • 17'
New-Key Mastery

1. Key the lines once SS; DS between 2-line groups.
2. Key the lines again at a faster pace.

Practice **C • U • E**

Key at a steady pace; space quickly after each word.

Goal: finger action reaches; quiet hands and arms

w and right shift
1 Dr. Rowe is in Tulsa now; Dr. Cowan will see Rolf.
2 Gwinn took the gown to Golda Swit on Downs Circle.

n/g
3 to go|go on|no go|an urn|dug in|and got|and a sign
4 He is to sign for the urn to go on the high chest.

key words
5 if ow us or go he an it of own did oak the cut jug
6 do all and for cog odd ant fig rug low cue row end

key phrases
7 we did|for a jar|she is due|cut the oak|he owns it
8 all of us|to own the|she is to go|when he has gone

all keys learned
9 Jan and Chris are gone; Di and Nick get here soon.
10 Doug will work for her at the new store in Newton.

8D • 5'
Technique: Spacing with Punctuation

Key each line once DS.

Spacing **C • U • E**

Do not space after an internal period in an abbreviation; space once after each period following initials.

No space
Space once.

1 Use i.e. for that is; cs. for case; ck. for check.
2 Dr. Wong said to use wt. for weight; in. for inch.
3 R. D. Roth has used ed. for editor; Rt. for Route.
4 Wes said Ed Rowan got an Ed.D. degree last winter.

8E •
Enrichment

1. Key each pair of lines once SS.
2. Key each even-numbered line again to increase speed.

Technique Goals:

- steady hands/arms
- finger-action keystrokes
- unused fingers curved, upright over home keys
- eyes on copy as you key

u/c
1 uj cd uc cut cut cue cue use use cod cod dock dock
2 Jud is to cut the corn near the dock for his aunt.

w and right shift
3 Don and Willa|Dot or Wilda|R. W. Gowan|Dr. Wilford
4 Dr. Wold will set the wrist of Sgt. Wills at noon.

left shift and .
5 Jane or Karl|Jae and Nan|L. N. Hagel|Lt. J. O. Hao
6 Lt. Hawser said that he will see us in New London.

n/g
7 nj gf ng gun gun nag nag got got nor nor sign sign
8 Angie hung a huge sign in front of the union hall.

o/t
9 ol tf to too dot dot not not toe toe got gild gild
10 Todd took the tool chest to the dock for a worker.

i/r
11 ik rf or ore fir fir sir sir ire ire ice ice irons
12 Risa fired the fir log to heat rice for the girls.

h/e
13 hj ed he the the hen hen when when then then their
14 He was with her when she chose her new snow shoes.

File Management in Windows®

Establishing a logical and easy-to-use file management system will help you organize files efficiently and find them quickly and easily. You can manage files on the desktop or in your file management program, *Windows Explorer*. This feature may be somewhat different on your computer, depending on your *Windows®* version and setup.

NAMING FILES AND FOLDERS

Good file organization begins with giving your files and folders names that are logical, relevant, and easy to understand. For example, you might create a folder for your English assignments called *English*. In this folder, you might have a journal that you add to each day (called *Journal*); monthly compositions (e.g., *Comp10-00, Comp3-01*); and occasional essays (such as *EssaySports* or *EssayEthics*). A system like this would make finding files simple.

UNDERSTANDING THE FILE SYSTEM

You can use *Windows Explorer** to see how files and folders are organized on your computer. *Windows Explorer* shows files and folders in a **hierarchical** or **tree** view. At the top is Desktop. Desktop contains all the items that appear on the desktop of your computer. The first item in Desktop, My Computer, contains the files and folders on your computer, organized by drives.

Drill 1: Navigate the File System

1. Click the *Start* button, point to *Programs* (then to *Accessories*, if you have the *Windows® 2000* operating system), and click *Windows Explorer.*
2. Click a plus sign beside a drive or folder to display below it a list of any folders that it contains. Click the minus sign to close the folder.
3. Click a folder (icon or name) in the left pane. All its contents (files and/or folders) will be displayed in the right pane.
4. Double-click a folder with a plus sign (double-click the icon or name, not the plus sign). Any folders inside the folder will be listed below, and all the contents of the folder (files and/or folders) will be displayed in the right pane.
5. Practice Steps 2–4 with other folders.

*Windows® is a registered trademark of Microsoft Corporation in the United States and/or other countries.

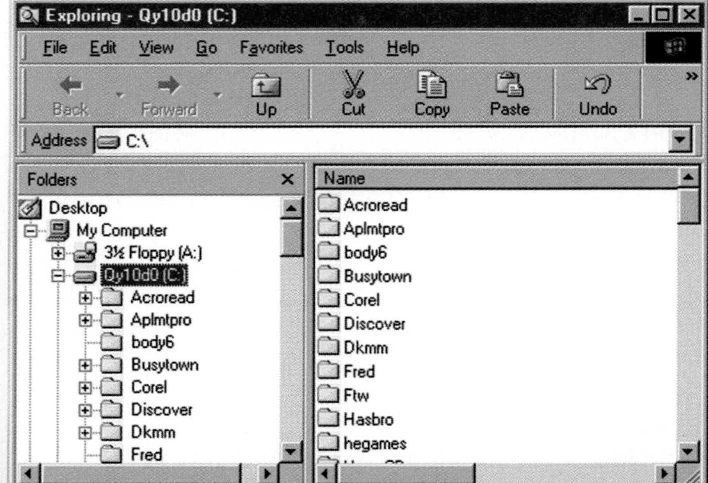

You do not have to be in *Windows Explorer* to locate a file or folder. You can use the My Computer icon on the desktop, the Find option on the Start menu, or the Address box (if available) in a drive or folder window.

CREATING FOLDERS

You will want to create folders to store files. You can do so using *Windows Explorer* or the desktop. In addition to putting files in your folders, you can create folders within folders if you need to.

- In *Windows Explorer*, click the drive or folder that will contain the new folder, click the *File* menu, point to *New*, and click *Folder*.
- On the desktop, double-click the drive or folder that will contain the new folder (if the drive or folder is not on the desktop, you can access it by double-clicking *My Computer*). In the window that opens, click the *File* menu, point to *New*, and click *Folder*. To create a folder on the desktop itself, right-click in a blank area of the desktop, point to *New*, and click *Folder*.

LESSON 9 | NEW KEYS: b AND y

Objectives:

1. To learn reach technique for **b** and **y**.
2. To combine smoothly **b** and **y** with all other learned keys.

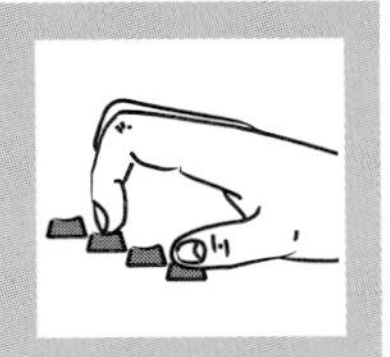

Fingers curved

Fingers upright

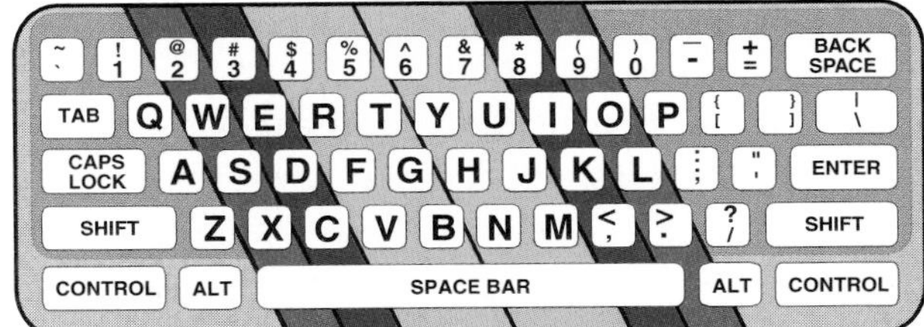

9A • 7' Conditioning Practice

Key each line twice SS (slowly, then faster); DS between 2-line groups.

reach review
1 uj ws ik rf ol cd nj ed hj tf .l gf sw ju de lo fr

c/n
2 an can and cut end cue hen cog torn dock then sick

all letters learned
3 A kid had a jug of fruit on his cart in New Delhi.

9B • 5' Technique: Spacebar

Key each line once.

Technique Goal:
Space with a down-and-in motion immediately after each word.

1 He will take an old urn to an art sale at the inn.
2 Ann has an old car she wants to sell at this sale.
3 Len is to work for us for a week at the lake dock.
4 Gwen is to sign for the auto we set aside for her.
5 Jan is in town for just one week to look for work.
6 Juan said he was in the auto when it hit the tree.

9C • 4' Technique: Enter

1. Key each line once SS; at the end of each line quickly press the ENTER key and immediately start new line.
2. On line 4, see how many words you can key in 30 seconds (30").

A **standard word** in keyboarding is five characters or any combination of five characters and spaces, as indicated by the number scale under line 4 at the right. The number of standard words keyed in 1' is called **gross words a minute** *(gwam)*.

1 Dot is to go at two.
2 He saw that it was a good law.
3 Rilla is to take the auto into the town.
4 Wilt has an old gold jug he can enter in the show.

gwam 1' | 1 | 2 | 3 | 4 | 5 | 6 | 7 | 8 | 9 | 10 |

To find 1-minute (1') *gwam*:

1. Note on the scale the figure beneath the last word you keyed. That is your 1' *gwam* if you key the line partially or only once.
2. If you completed the line once and started over, add 10 to the figure determined in Step 1. The result is your 1' *gwam*.

To find 30-second (30") *gwam*:

1. Find 1' *gwam* (total words keyed).
2. Multiply 1' *gwam* by 2. The resulting figure is your 30" *gwam*.

Welcome to MicroType Multimedia

MicroType Multimedia is the multimedia-enhanced version of *MicroType Pro.* With this full-featured software, you can use the power of your computer to learn alphabetic and numeric keyboarding and keypad operation. The Alphabetic Keyboarding and the Numeric Keyboarding modules of *MicroType* correspond to the new-key lessons in the *Century 21 Computer Applications and Keyboarding* textbook. After you complete Lesson 15 (ending on p. R33), you can use Keyboarding Skill Builder to boost your speed and accuracy.

MAIN MENU

Alphabetic Keyboarding

These 20 lessons teach the alphabetic keys, operational keys, and basic punctuation keys. Material on this disk may be used with review Lessons 1–8 (pp. 2–18), also.

Numeric Keyboarding

These 16 lessons teach/review the top-row figure keys and the more commonly used symbols. They are related to Lessons 13 and 14 (pp. 29–33) in the textbook. Activities focus on building skill as well as learning the top-row and symbol keys.

Keyboarding Skill Builder

After you learn the alphabetic keys, use these 20 lessons to boost your keyboarding speed and control. Each lesson can focus on either speed or accuracy, so you really have 40 lessons.

Numeric Keypad

You will learn numeric keypad operation by completing this module. It is related to lessons on pp. 51–54 in the textbook.

Open Screen

The Open Screen is a full-featured word processor that includes a spell checker and a built-in timer. You can practice your keyboarding skills, key letters and reports, or take a timed writing. These features can be accessed from the Menu bar, and many of them are available on the toolbar. When you take a timed writing in the Open Screen, click the Timer button and save each timing with its own name; for example, *16b-t1* would be Lesson Part 16b, timing 1.

OTHER FEATURES

Games

Each keyboarding module incorporates a game into every lesson. The games offer exciting graphics and action to help you build skill while having fun. Top-ten lists provide a way for students to compare scores.

Reports

The Lesson Report shows which lesson parts were completed as well as your speed scores and keying lines for *Build Skill* and the game. You can access performance graphs by clicking the Graph button on the Lesson Report.

In addition to the Lesson Reports, *MicroType* software provides a Summary Report, Keypad Data Sets, Top-Ten Lists, Certificate of Completion, and Performance Graphs. All of these reports, except the Lesson Report, are accessed from the Reports menu.

Diagnostic Writings

This feature checks speed and accuracy and provides simple error diagnostics. The writings are keyed from hard copy printed from the File menu in the Diagnostic Writings screen.

Quick Review

This feature of the Skill Builder module presents drill lines for practicing alphabetic and numeric reaches and operational keys. The Quick Review Report displays the average *gwam* (gross words a minute) for each section attempted.

3D Animations

This feature demonstrates proper posture and hand positioning from all angles.

Movies

This feature shows proper keystroking in action. Video clips emphasize how keyboarding is used in every profession.

9D • 19'
New Keys: B and Y

Key each line twice SS (slowly, then faster); DS between 2-line groups; if time permits, key lines 7–9 again.

Follow the *Standard Plan for Learning New Keys* outlined on p. R6.

b *Left index* finger

y *Right index* finger

Learn b

1 f f bf bf fib fib rob rob but but big big fib fibs
2 bf bf rob rob lob lob orb orb bid bid bud bud ribs
3 a rib; to fib; rub it; an orb; or rob; but she bid

Learn y

4 j j yj yj jay jay lay lay hay hay day day say says
5 yj yj jay jay eye eye dye dye yes yes yet yet jays
6 a jay; to say; an eye; he says; dye it; has an eye

Combine b and y

7 by by buy buy boy boy bye bye byte byte buoy buoys
8 by it; to buy; by you; a byte; the buoy; by and by
9 Jaye went by bus to the store to buy the big buoy.

9E • 15'
New-Key Mastery

1. Key the lines once SS; DS between 2-line groups.
2. Key the lines again at a faster pace.

Practice **C · U · E**

- Reach up without moving hands away from your body.
- Reach down without moving hands toward your body.
- Use quick-snap keystrokes.

reach review
1 fg sw ki gf bf ol ed yj ws ik rf hj cd nj tf .l uj
2 a kit low for jut led sow fob ask sun cud jet grow

3d/1st rows
3 no in bow any tub yen cut sub coy ran bin cow deck
4 Cody wants to buy this baby cub for the young boy.

key words
5 by and for the got all did but cut now say jut ask
6 work just such hand this goal boys held furl eight

key phrases
7 to do|can go|to bow|for all|did jet|ask her|to buy
8 if she|to work|and such|the goal|for this|held the

all letters learned
9 Becky has auburn hair and wide eyes of light jade.
10 Juan left Bobby at the dog show near our ice rink.

gwam 1' | 1 | 2 | 3 | 4 | 5 | 6 | 7 | 8 | 9 | 10 |

Know Your Computer

The numbered parts are found on most computers. The location of some parts will vary.

1. **CPU (Central Processing Unit):** Internal operating unit or "brain" of computer.
2. **Disk drive:** Reads data from and writes data to a disk.
3. **Monitor:** Displays text and graphics on a screen.
4. **Mouse:** Used to input commands.
5. **Keyboard:** An arrangement of letter, figure, symbol, control, function, and editing keys and a numeric keypad.

KEYBOARD ARRANGEMENT

1. **Alphanumeric keys:** Letters, numbers, and symbols.
2. **Numeric keypad:** Keys at the right side of the keyboard used to enter numeric copy and perform calculations.
3. **Function (F) keys:** Used to execute commands, sometimes with other keys. Commands vary with software.
4. **Arrow keys:** Move insertion point up, down, left, or right.
5. ESC **(Escape):** Closes a software menu or dialog box.
6. TAB: Moves the insertion point to a preset position.
7. CAPS LOCK: Used to make all capital letters.
8. SHIFT: Makes capital letters and symbols shown at tops of number keys.
9. CTRL **(Control):** With other key(s), executes commands. Commands may vary with software.
10. ALT **(Alternate):** With other key(s), executes commands. Commands may vary with software.
11. **Space Bar:** Inserts a space in text.
12. ENTER (RETURN): Moves insertion point to margin and down to next line. Also used to execute commands.
13. DELETE: Removes text to the right of insertion point.
14. NUM LOCK: Activates/deactivates numeric keypad.
15. INSERT: Activates insert or typeover.
16. BACKSPACE: Deletes text to the left of insertion point.

COMMAND **(Mac® keyboards only):** With another key, executes commands that vary with software.

LESSON 10 — NEW KEYS: m AND x

Objectives:

1. To learn reach technique for **m** and **x.**
2. To combine smoothly **m** and **x** with all other learned keys.

10A • 7'
Conditioning Practice

Key each line twice SS (slowly, then faster); DS between 2-line groups.

reach review 1 bf ol rf yj ed nj ws ik tf hj cd uj gf by us if ow

b/y 2 by bye boy buy yes fib dye bit yet but try bet you

all letters learned 3 Robby can win the gold if he just keys a new high.

10B • 20'
New Keys: [M] and [X]

Key each line twice SS (slowly, then faster); DS between 2-line groups; if time permits, key lines 7–9 again.

m *Right index* finger

x *Left ring* finger

Follow the *Standard Plan for Learning New Keys* outlined on p. R6.

Learn m

1 j j mj mj am am am me me ma ma jam jam ham ham yam

2 mj mj me me me may may yam yam dam dam men men jam

3 am to; if me; a man; a yam; a ham; he may; the hem

Learn x

4 s s xs xs ox ox ax ax six six fix fix fox fox axis

5 xs xs sx sx ox ox six six nix nix fix fix lax flax

6 a fox; an ox; fix it; by six; is lax; to fix an ax

Combine m and x

7 me ox am ax ma jam six ham mix fox men lax hem lox

8 to fix; am lax; mix it; may fix; six men; hex them

9 Mala can mix a ham salad for six; Max can fix tea.

10 Mary will bike the next day on the mountain roads.

11 Martin and Max took the six boys to the next game.

12 Marty will go with me on the next six rides today.

After you have maximized a window, the **Restore button** will replace the Maximize button. Clicking this button restores the window to its original size and location.

Clicking the **Close button** closes a window.

To move a window, drag it by the title bar. To resize a window, move the mouse pointer to a side or corner of the window. The pointer will become a double-headed arrow (↔). Drag until the window is the size you want.

When more than one window is displayed at a time, clicking a window's title bar makes it the **active window**—the one you can work in. The other window(s) will have a gray title bar to indicate that it is **inactive**.

Drill 2: Work with Windows

1. Open file *CD-TAXES*. Practice using the scroll bars to move around in this document.
2. Minimize your word processing window. Double-click the *My Computer* desktop icon. Maximize, restore, and then minimize the My Computer window.
3. Practice switching back and forth between the word processing software and the My Computer window. Close the My Computer window.
4. Maximize your word processing window, if it is not maximized already, and open a new blank document with *CD-TAXES* still open. If the new document is maximized, click the *Restore* button.
5. Drag the new document window around the screen.
6. Practice resizing the new document window and leave it on the screen for the next drill. *CD-TAXES* should still be open, but minimized or inactive.

DIALOG BOXES

A **dialog box** displays when software needs more information to carry out a task. Selecting a menu item that is followed by an ellipsis (. . .) will open a dialog box. The illustrations at the right show how to choose common dialog box options.[3] Clicking OK executes the selected option; clicking Cancel closes the dialog box.

Drill 3: Use Dialog Boxes

1. Open dialog boxes in your word processing document until you have had the chance to try three different types of dialog box options.
2. Close the document without saving, close *CD-TAXES* without saving, and exit your word processing software.

Click a tab to bring it to the front, so you can see its list of options.

Font | Character Spacing | Text Effects

Key or edit text.

File name: WindowsTutorial.doc

Click an option (you can sometimes choose more than one).

Widow/Orphan control
Keep lines together
Keep with next
Page break before

Click one radio button.

Page range
All
Current page
Pages:

(none)
(none)
First line
Hanging

Click the arrow to display a drop-down list.

Click an option in the list.

Click an arrow to increase or decrease a number.

Number of copies: 1

Click to execute a command or display another dialog box.

OK Cancel

[3]Windows® is a registered trademark of Microsoft Corporation in the United States and/or other countries.

10C • 17' New-Key Mastery

1. Key each line once SS; DS between 2-line groups.
2. Key the lines again at a faster pace.

Technique **C • U • E**

- Reach up without moving hands away from your body.
- Reach down without moving hands toward your body.
- Use quick-snap keystrokes.

Goal: finger-action keystrokes; quiet hands and arms

3d/1st rows
1 by am end fix men box hem but six now cut gem ribs
2 me ox buy den cub ran own form went oxen fine club

space bar
3 an of me do am if us or is by go ma so ah ox it ow
4 by man buy fan jam can any tan may rob ham fun guy

key words
5 if us me do an sow the cut big jam rub oak lax boy
6 curl work form born name flex just done many right

key phrases
7 or jam|if she|for me|is big|an end|or buy|is to be
8 to fix|and cut|for work|and such|big firm|the call

all keys learned
9 Jacki is now at the gym; Lex is due there by four.
10 Joni saw that she could fix my old bike for Gilda.

10D • 6' Technique: Spacing with Punctuation

Key each line once DS.

Spacing **C • U • E**

Do not space after an internal period in an abbreviation, such as Ed.D.

1 Mrs. Dixon may take her Ed.D. exam early in March.
2 Lex may send a box c.o.d. to Ms. Fox in St. Croix.
3 J. D. and Max will go by boat to St. Louis in May.
4 Owen keyed ect. for etc. and lost the match to me.

10E • Enrichment

1. Key each line twice SS (slowly, then faster); DS between 2-line groups.
2. Key each line once more at a faster pace.

Practice **C • U • E**

Keep the insertion point moving steadily across each line (no pauses).

m/x 1 Max told them that he will next fix the main axle.
b/y 2 Byron said the boy went by bus to a bayou to hunt.
w/right shift 3 Wilf and Rona work in Tucson with Rowena and Drew.
u/c 4 Lucy cut a huge cake for just the four lucky boys.
./left shift 5 Mr. and Mrs. J. L. Nance set sail for Long Island.
n/g 6 Bing may bring a young trio to sing songs at noon.
o/t 7 Lottie will tell the two little boys a good story.
i/r 8 Ria said she will first build a large fire of fir.
h/e 9 Chet was here when the eight hikers hit the trail.

START MENU

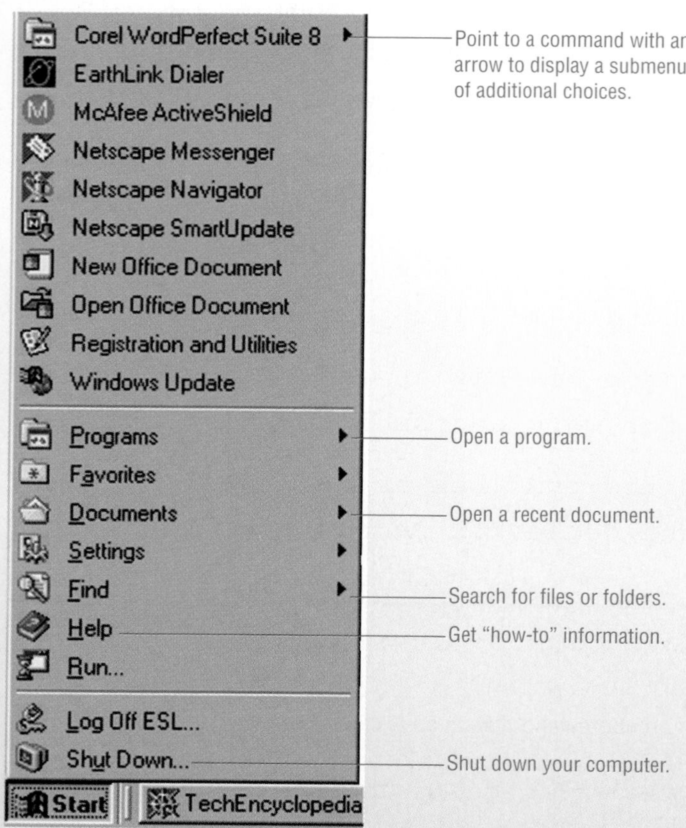

Drill 1: Open a Program from the Start Menu[2]

1. Click the *Start* button to open the Start menu. Examine the options in this menu.
2. Move your pointer to *Programs*.
3. Click the name of your word processing software to open it. Your word processing software may be inside a folder. If so, open the folder (by pointing to it) to get to the software.

BASIC FEATURES OF WINDOWS

Microsoft® Windows® displays folders, applications, and individual documents in **windows**. The basic features of all windows are the same.

The **title bar** lists the name of the window.

From the **menu bar**, you can access all the commands available in the software. Menu names are similar in

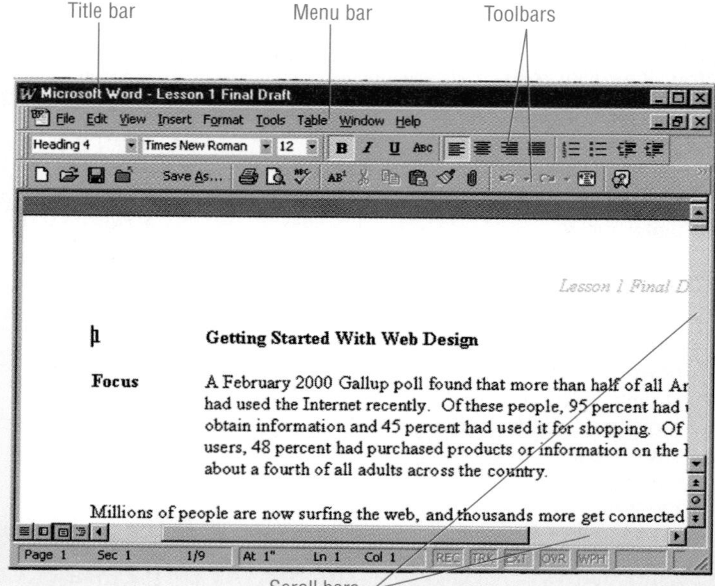

application programs that run under the *Microsoft® Windows®* operating system (as are icons and other features).

Like desktop icons, **toolbars** offer a convenient way to access frequently used commands. Application programs often have different toolbars for different tasks, like formatting text or creating tables.

If the window contains more material than you can see at once, **scroll bars** may appear at the right and/or bottom. Clicking a scroll bar arrow moves the document in small increments. Clicking a light gray area of a scroll bar moves the document in larger increments. Dragging the dark gray portion of a scroll bar moves the document exactly as much and as fast as you want.

At the right end of the title or menu bar are the Minimize, Maximize, and Close buttons. Clicking the **Minimize button** reduces a window to a button on the taskbar. This is useful when you want to **multitask** (perform more than one task at a time) and do not want to exit a program. To restore the window, click the button on the taskbar.

Clicking the **Maximize button** enlarges a window to take up almost the entire screen. Many people like to maximize application documents to have more room to work.

[2]Microsoft® and Windows® are registered trademarks of Microsoft Corporation in the United States and/or other countries.

LESSON 11 NEW KEYS: p AND v

Objectives:

1. To learn reach technique for **p** and **v**.
2. To combine smoothly **p** and **v** with all other learned keys.

Fingers upright

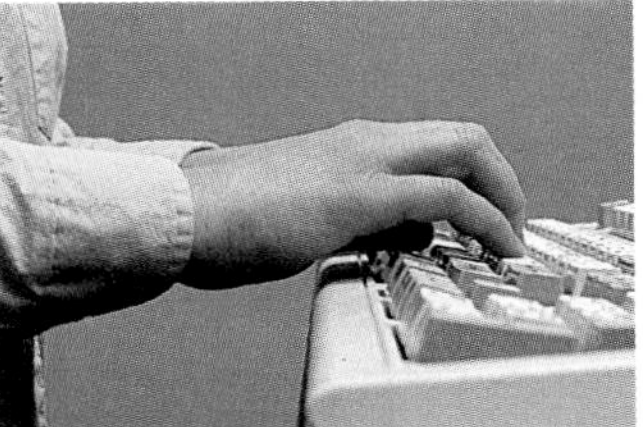
Fingers curved

Hard return

11A • 7' Conditioning Practice

Key each line twice SS (slowly, then faster); DS between 2-line groups.

one-hand words
1 in we no ax my be on ad on re hi at ho cad him bet

phrases
2 is just|of work|to sign|of lace|to flex|got a form

all letters learned
3 Jo Buck won a gold medal for her sixth show entry.

11B • 20' New Keys: P and V

Key each line twice SS; DS between 2-line groups; if time permits, key lines 7–9 again.

p *Right little* finger

v *Left index* finger

Follow the *Standard Plan for Learning New Keys* outlined on p. R6.

Learn p

1 ; ; p; p; pa pa up up apt apt pen pen lap lap kept
2 p; p; pa pa pa pan pan nap nap paw paw gap gap rap
3 a pen; a cap; apt to pay; pick it up; plan to keep

Learn v

4 f f vf vf via via vie vie have have five five live
5 vf vf vie vie vie van van view view dive dive jive
6 go via; vie for; has vim; a view; to live; or have

Combine p and v

7 up cup vie pen van cap vim rap have keep live plan
8 to vie; give up; pave it; very apt; vie for a cup;
9 Vic has a plan to have the van pick us up at five.

Windows® Tutorial

Microsoft® Windows® is an **operating system**, a program that manages all the other programs on a computer. Like other operating systems, *Windows®* provides a **graphical user interface** (**GUI**, pronounced "gooey") of **icons** (picture symbols) and **menus** (lists of commands).

This tutorial will show you how to use basic *Windows®* features. A few features may look, work, or be named slightly differently on your computer, depending on your operating system version and setup.

THE DESKTOP

After you turn on your computer and it has powered up, it will display the **desktop**, your main working area. The following illustration shows a *Windows® 98* desktop.[1] Your desktop will have many of the same features; but because the desktop is easy to customize, some items will be different.

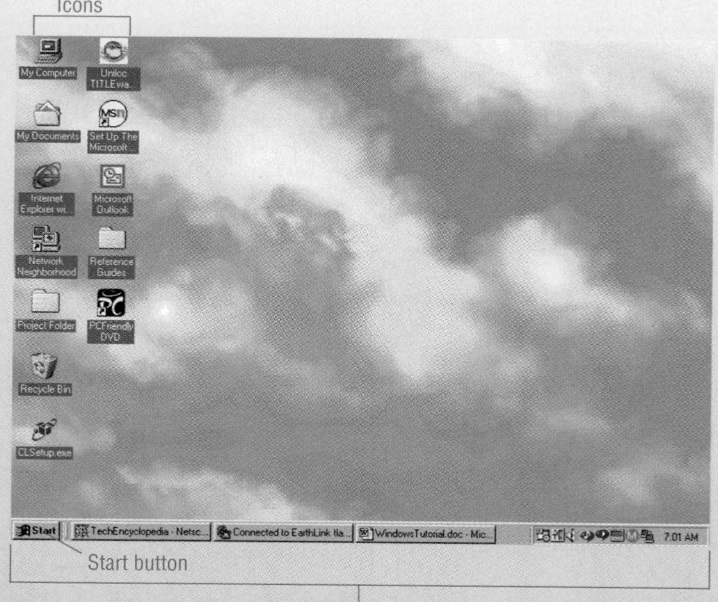

On the desktop, you will see icons and a **taskbar** (a tool for opening programs and navigating on your computer). Icons provide an easy way to access programs and documents that you use frequently. Double-click an icon to open the program, document, or **folder** (storage place for files and other folders) that it represents. (If the single-click option is selected on your computer, you will find that you can click an icon once instead of double-clicking. For more information about this option, open the Help Index—click *Help* on the Start menu—and key **single-click**.)

COMMON DESKTOP ICONS

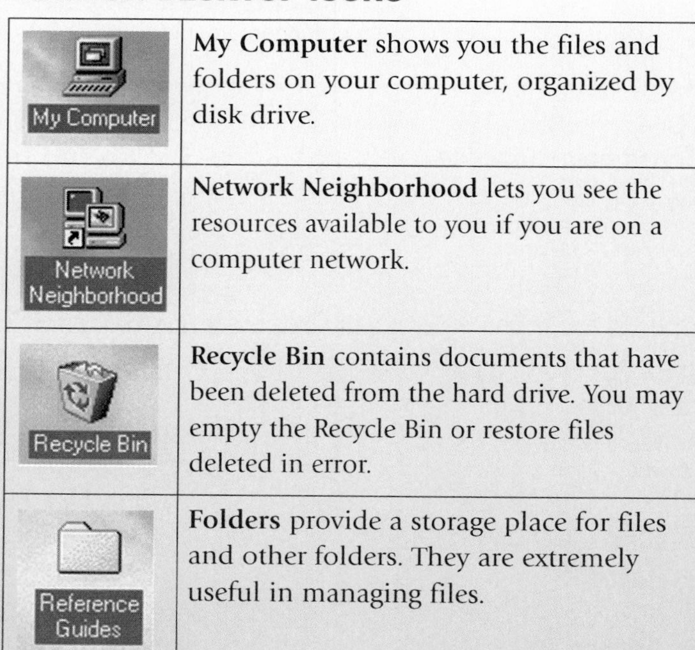

My Computer	**My Computer** shows you the files and folders on your computer, organized by disk drive.
Network Neighborhood	**Network Neighborhood** lets you see the resources available to you if you are on a computer network.
Recycle Bin	**Recycle Bin** contains documents that have been deleted from the hard drive. You may empty the Recycle Bin or restore files deleted in error.
Reference Guides	**Folders** provide a storage place for files and other folders. They are extremely useful in managing files.

The taskbar usually appears at the bottom of the screen. The standard *Windows® 98* taskbar consists of the Start button, a button for each program or document that you have open, and an icon for your computer's internal clock. Your taskbar may have additional icons.

The **Start button** opens the **Start menu**, shown on p. R38. Like a restaurant menu, a software menu offers you choices—commands you can choose. You can accomplish almost any task in *Windows®* from the Start menu.

> **Note:** The *Windows®* operating system requires a mouse or other pointing device. For help with using a mouse, see the Computer Concepts section at the front of this text.

[1]Windows® is a registered trademark of Microsoft Corporation in the United States and/or other countries.

11C • 17'
New-Key Mastery

1. Key the lines once SS; DS between 2-line groups.
2. Key the lines again at a faster pace.

Technique Goals:

- Reach up without moving hands away from your body.
- Reach down without moving hands toward your body.
- Use quick-snap keystrokes.

Goal: finger-action keystrokes; quiet hands and arms

reach review
1 vf p; xs mj ed yj ws nj rf ik tf ol cd hj gf uj bf
2 if lap jag own may she for but van cub sod six oak

3d/1st rows
3 by vie pen vim cup six but now man nor ton may pan
4 by six but now may cut sent me fine gems five reps

key words
5 with kept turn corn duty curl just have worn plans
6 name burn form when jury glad vote exit came eight

key phrases
7 if they|he kept|with us|of land|burn it|to name it
8 to plan|so sure|is glad|an exit|so much|to view it

all letters learned
9 Kevin does a top job on your flax farm with Craig.
10 Dixon flew blue jets eight times over a city park.

11D • 6'
Technique: Shift and Enter Keys

Key each 2-line sentence once SS as "Enter" is called every 30 seconds (30"). DS between sentences.

Goal:

To reach the end of each line just as the 30" guide ("Enter") is called.

The 30" *gwam scale* shows your gross words a minute if you reach the end of each line as the 30" guide is called.

Eyes on copy as you shift and as you strike ENTER key — gwam 30"

	gwam 30"
1 Marv is to choose a high goal	12
2 and to do his best to make it.	12
3 Vi said she had to key from a book	14
4 as one test she took for a top job.	14
5 Lexi knows it is good to keep your goal	16
6 in mind as you key each line of a drill.	16
7 Viv can do well many of the tasks she tries;	18
8 she sets top goals and makes them one by one.	18

11E •
Enrichment

1. Key each line once at a steady, easy pace to master reachstrokes.
2. Key each line again at a faster pace.

Technique Goals:

- Keep fingers upright.
- Keep hands/arms steady.

m/p
1 mj p; me up am pi jam apt ham pen map ape mop palm
2 Pam may pack plums and grapes for my trip to camp.

b/x
3 bf xs be ax by xi fix box but lax buy fox bit flax
4 Bix used the box of mix to fix bread for six boys.

y/v
5 yj vf buy vow boy vie soy vim very have your every
6 Vinny may have you buy very heavy silk and velvet.

FINGER GYMNASTICS

Brief daily practice of finger gymnastics will strengthen your finger muscles and increase the ease with which you key. Begin each keying period with this conditioning exercise. Choose two or more drills for this practice.

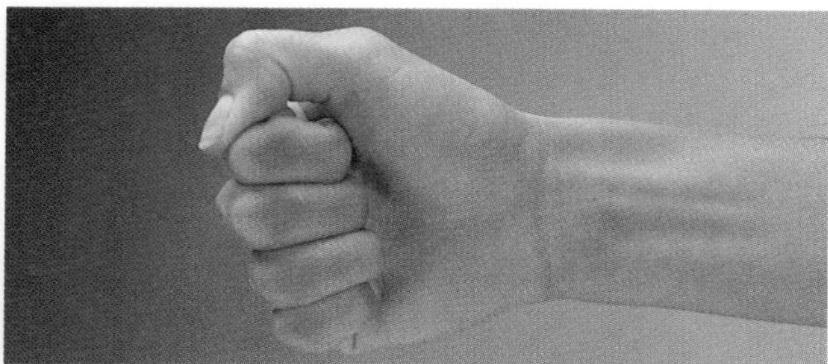

DRILL 1. Hands open, fingers wide, muscles tense. Close the fingers into a tight fist, with thumb on top. Relax the fingers as you straighten them. Repeat ten times.

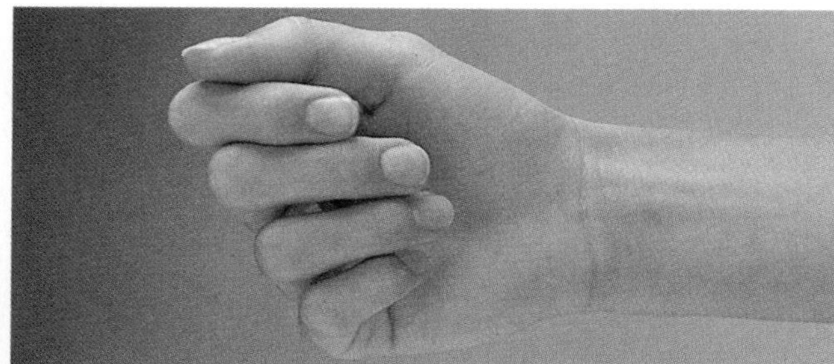

DRILL 2. Clench the fingers as shown. Hold the fingers in this position for a brief time; then extend the fingers, relaxing the muscles of fingers and hand. Repeat the movements slowly several times. Exercise both hands at the same time.

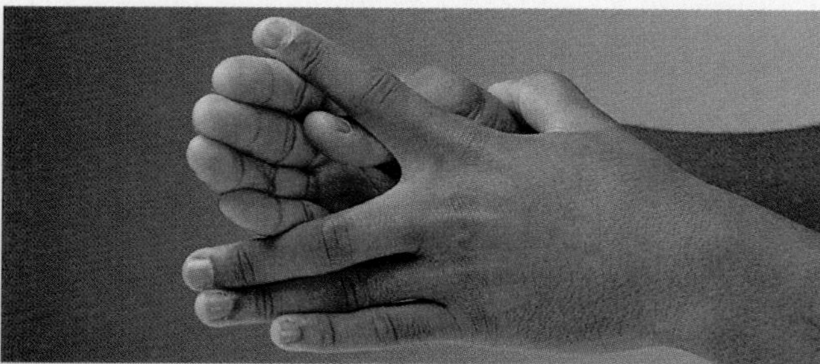

DRILL 3. Place the fingers and thumb of one hand between two fingers of the other hand, and spread the fingers as much as possible. Spread all fingers of both hands.

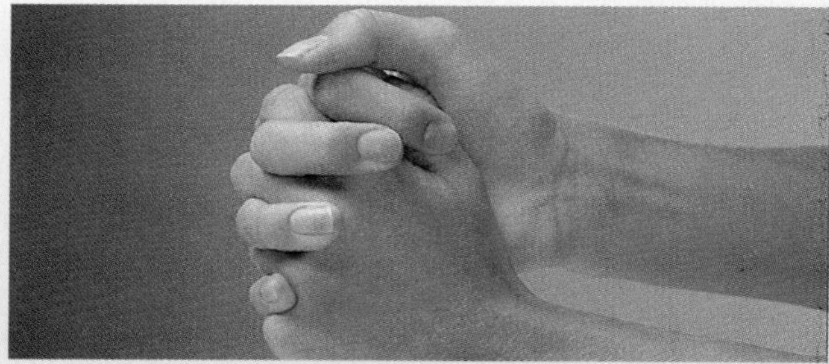

DRILL 4. Interlace the fingers of the two hands and wring the hands, rubbing the heel of each palm vigorously.

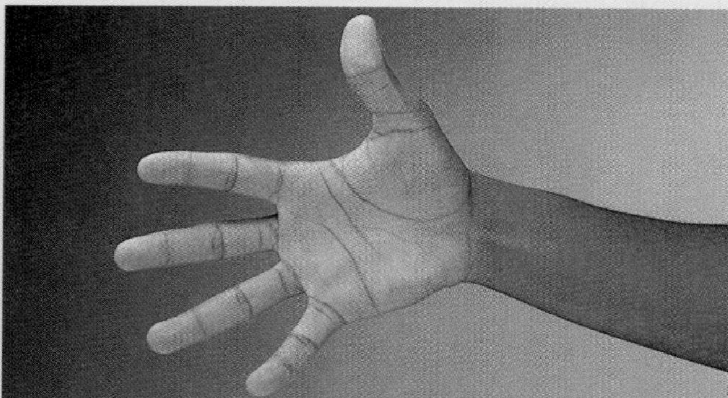

DRILL 5. Spread the fingers as much as possible, holding the position for a moment or two; then relax the fingers and lightly fold them into the palm of the hand. Repeat the movements slowly several times. Exercise both hands at the same time.

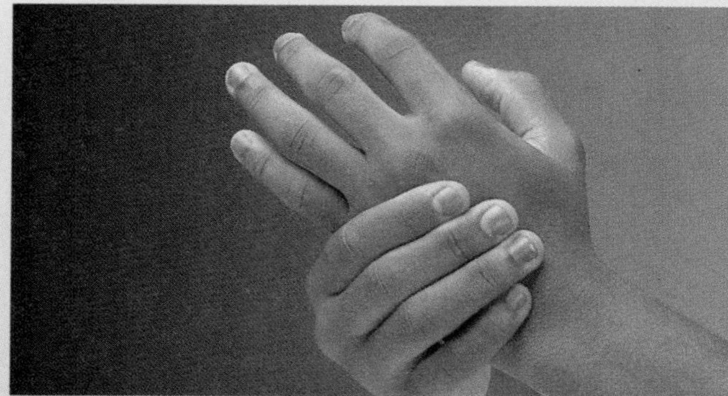

DRILL 6. Rub the hands vigorously. Let the thumb rub the palm of the hand. Rub the fingers, the back of the hand, and the wrist.

DRILL 7. Hold both hands in front of you, fingers together. Hold the last three fingers still and move the first finger as far to the side as possible. Return the first finger; then move the first and second fingers together; finally, move the little finger as far to the side as possible.

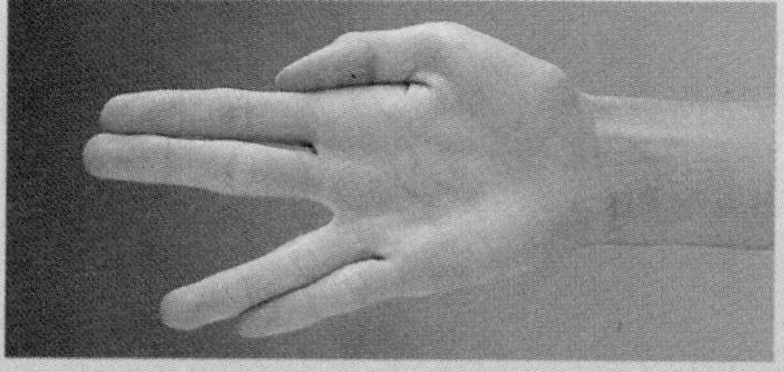

LESSON 12 — NEW KEYS: q AND comma (,)

Objectives:

1. To learn reach technique for **q** and , (comma).
2. To combine smoothly **q** and , (comma) with all other learned keys.

12A • 7'
Conditioning Practice

Key each line twice SS (slowly, then faster); DS between 2-line groups; if time permits, key the lines again.

all letters learned 1 `do fix all cut via own buy for the jam cop ask dig`

p/v 2 `a map; a van; apt to; vie for; her plan; have five`

all letters learned 3 `Beth will pack sixty pints of guava jam for David.`

12B • 20'
New Keys: [Q] and [,]

Key each line twice SS; DS between 2-line groups; if time permits, key lines 7–9 again.

q *Left little* finger

, (comma) *Right middle* finger

Spacing **C·U·E**

Space once after , used as punctuation.

Follow the *Standard Plan for Learning New Keys* outlined on p. R6.

Learn q

1 `a qa qa aq aq quo quo qt. qt. quad quad quit quits`

2 `qa quo quo qt. qt. quay quay aqua aqua quite quite`

3 `a qt.; pro quo; a quad; to quit; the quay; a squad`

Learn , (comma)

4 `k k ,k ,k kit, kit; Rick, Ike, or I will go, also.`

5 `a ski, a ski; a kit, a kit; a kite, a kite; a bike`

6 `Ike, I see, is here; Pam, I am told, will be late.`

Combine q and , (comma)

7 `Enter the words quo, quote, quit, quite, and aqua.`

8 `I have quit the squad, Quen; Raquel has quit, too.`

9 `Marquis, Quent, and Quig were quite quick to quit.`

10 `Quin, Jacqueline, and Paque quickly took the exam.`

11 `Rob quickly won my squad over quip by brainy quip.`

12 `Quit, quiet, and quaint were on the spelling exam.`

directly in front of the chair. The front edge should be even with the edge of the table or desk.

Place the monitor for easy viewing. Some experts maintain that the top of the screen should be at or slightly below eye level. Others recommend placing the monitor even lower. Set it a comfortable distance from your eyes—at least an arm's length away.

Position the monitor to avoid glare (an antiglare filter can help). Close blinds or pull shades as needed. Adjust the brightness and contrast controls, if necessary, for readability. Keep the screen clean with a soft, lint-free cloth and (unless your instructor tells you otherwise) a nonalcohol, nonabrasive cleaning solution or glass cleaner.

If you cannot adjust your equipment and the desk or table is too high, try adjusting your chair. If that does not work, you can sit on a cushion, a coat, or even a stack of books.

Use a straight-backed chair that will not yield when you lean back. The chair should support your lower back (try putting a rolled-up towel or sweater behind you if it does not). The back of your knees should not be pressed against the chair. Use a seat that allows you to keep your feet flat on the floor, or use a footrest. Even a box or a backpack will do.

Position the mouse next to and at the same height as the keyboard and as close to the body as possible. Research has not shown conclusively that one type of pointing device (mouse, trackball, touch pad, stylus, joystick, etc.) is better than another. Whatever you use, make sure your arms, hands, and fingers are relaxed. If you change to a new device, evaluate it carefully first and work up gradually to using it all the time.

Arrange your work material so you can see it easily and maintain good posture. Some experts recommend positioning whatever you look at most often (the monitor or paper material) directly in front of you so you do not have to turn your head to the side while keying.

EXERCISE AND TAKE BREAKS

Exercise your neck, shoulders, arms, wrists, and fingers before beginning to key each day and often during the workday. Finger exercises appear on the next page. Neck, shoulder, wrist, and other exercises appear at the Cornell University ergonomics Web site listed below.

Take a short break at least once an hour. Rest your eyes from time to time as you work by focusing on an object at least 20 feet away. Blink frequently.

USE GOOD POSTURE AND PROPER TECHNIQUES

Sit erect and as far back in the seat as possible. Your forearms should be parallel to the slant of the keyboard, your wrists and forearms low, but not touching or resting on any surface. Your arms should be near the side of your body in a relaxed position. Your shoulders should not be raised, but should be in a natural posture.

Keep your fingers curved and upright over the home keys. Strike each key lightly using the finger*tip*. Grasp the mouse loosely. Make a conscious effort to relax your hands and shoulders while keying.

For more information on mouse and keyboard use and CTS/RSI, visit the following Internet sites:

- http://kidshealth.org/kid/ (search for *ergonomics*)
- http://www.tifaq.org
- http://www.berkeley.edu (locate the Ergonomics Program and look for Computer Use Tips)
- http://www.office-ergo.com
- http://www.cornell.edu (search for *ergonomics*)

Ergonomic Keyboards

Ergonomic keyboards (see illustration at left) are designed to improve hand posture and make keying more comfortable. Generally they have a split design with left and right banks of keys and the ability to tilt or rotate the keyboard for comfort. More research is needed to determine just how effective ergonomic keyboards are in preventing RSI injuries and carpal tunnel syndrome.

12C • 17'
New-Key Mastery

1. Key the lines once SS; DS between 2-line groups.
2. Key the lines again at a faster pace.

Technique Goals:

- Reach up without moving hands away from your body.
- Reach down without moving hands toward your body.
- Use quick-snap keystrokes.

Goal: finger-action keystrokes; quiet hands and arms

reach review
1 qa .l ws ,k ed nj rf mj tf p; xs ol cd ik vf hj bf
2 yj gf hj quo vie pay cut now buy got mix vow forms

3d/1st rows
3 six may sun coy cue mud jar win via pick turn bike
4 to go|to win|for me|a peck|a quay|by then|the vote

key words
5 pa rub sit man for own fix jam via cod oak the got
6 by quo sub lay apt mix irk pay when rope give just

key phrases
7 an ox|of all|is to go|if he is|it is due|to pay us
8 if we pay|is of age|up to you|so we own|she saw me

all letters learned
9 Jevon will fix my pool deck if the big rain quits.
10 Verna did fly quick jets to map the six big towns.

12D • 6'
Technique: Spacing with Punctuation

Key each line once DS.

Spacing **C • U • E**

Space once after , and ; used as punctuation.

Space once.

1 Aqua means water, Quen; also, it is a unique blue.
2 Quince, enter qt. for quart; also, sq. for square.
3 Ship the desk c.o.d. to Dr. Quig at La Quinta Inn.
4 Q. J. took squid and squash; Monique, roast quail.

12E •
Enrichment

1. Key each line once at a steady, easy pace to master reachstrokes.
2. Key each line again at a faster pace.

Technique Goals:

lines 1–3:
fingers upright

lines 4–6:
hands/arms steady

lines 7–9:
two quick taps of each double letter

Adjacent keys

1 re io as lk rt jk df op ds uy ew vc mn gf hj sa ui
2 as ore ask opt buy pew say art owe try oil gas her
3 Sandy said we ought to buy gifts at her new store.

Long direct reaches

4 ce un gr mu br ny rv ym rb my ice any mug orb grow
5 nice curb must brow much fume sync many dumb curve
6 Brian must bring the ice to the curb for my uncle.

Double letters

7 all off odd too see err boo lee add call heed good
8 door meek seen huff less will soon food leek offer
9 Lee will seek help to get all food cooked by noon.

Repetitive Stress Injury

Repetitive stress injury (RSI) is a result of repeated movement of a particular part of the body. It is also known as repetitive motion injury, musculoskeletal disorder, cumulative trauma disorder, and by a host of other names. A familiar example of RSI is "tennis elbow." RSI is the number-one occupational illness, costing employers more than $40 billion a year in health-care fees and lost wages.

Of concern to keyboard and mouse users is the form of RSI called **carpal tunnel syndrome** (CTS). CTS is an inflammatory disease that develops gradually and affects the wrists, hands, and forearms. Blood vessels, tendons, and nerves pass into the hand through the carpal tunnel (see illustration below). If any of these structures enlarge, or the walls of the tunnel narrow, the median nerve is pinched and CTS symptoms may result.

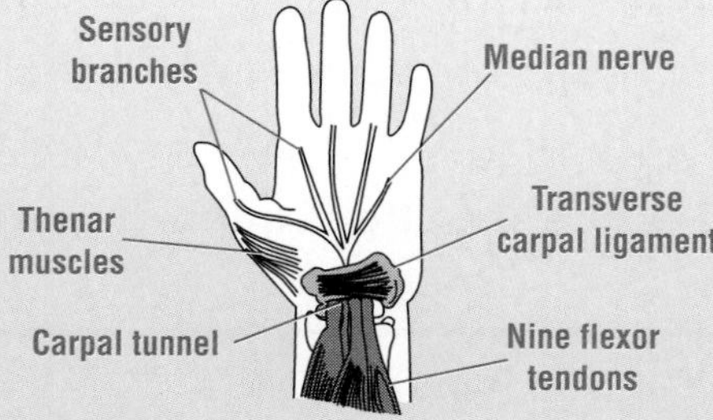

Palm view of left hand

SYMPTOMS OF RSI/CTS

CTS symptoms include numbness in the hand; tingling or burning in the hand, wrist, or elbow; severe pain in the forearm, elbow, or shoulder; and difficulty in gripping objects. Symptoms usually appear during sleeping hours, probably because many people sleep with their wrists flexed.

If not properly treated, the pressure on the median nerve, which controls the thumb, forefinger, middle finger, and half the ring finger, causes severe pain. The pain can radiate into the forearm, elbow, or shoulder. There are many kinds of treatment, ranging from simply resting to surgery. Left untreated, CTS can result in permanent damage or paralysis.

The good news is that 99 percent of people with carpal tunnel syndrome recover completely. Computer users can avoid reinjuring themselves by taking the precautions discussed later in this article.

CAUSES OF RSI/CTS

RSI/CTS often develops in workers whose physical routine is unvaried. Common occupational factors include (1) using awkward posture, (2) using poor techniques, (3) performing tasks with wrists bent (see below), (4) using improper equipment, (5) working at a rapid pace, (6) not taking rest breaks, and (7) not doing exercises that promote graceful motion and good techniques.

RSI/CTS is not limited to workers or adults. Keying school assignments, playing computer or video games, and surfing the Internet are increasing the incidence of RSI/CTS in younger people.

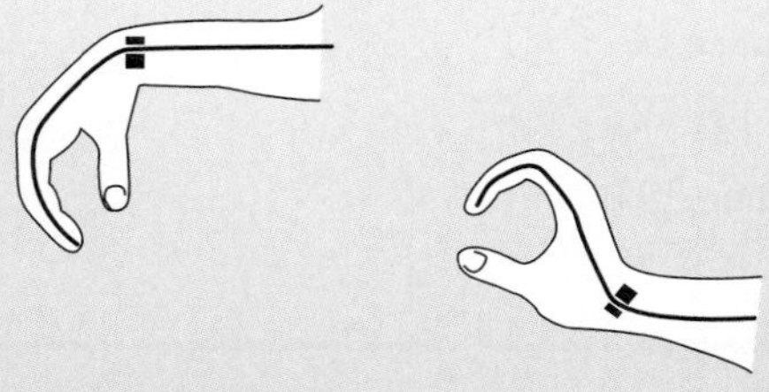

Improper wrist positions for keystroking

CTS is frequently a health concern for people who use a computer keyboard or mouse. The risk of developing CTS is less for those who use proper furniture or equipment, keyboarding techniques, posture, and/or muscle-stretching exercises than for those who do not.

REDUCING THE RISK OF RSI/CTS

By taking the following precautions, keyboard and mouse users can reduce the risk of developing RSI/CTS and can keep it from recurring. Experts stress that good computer habits like these are very important in avoiding RSI/CTS. They can also help you avoid back, neck, and shoulder pain, and eyestrain.

ARRANGE THE WORK AREA

Arrange your equipment in a way that is natural and comfortable for you. Position the keyboard at elbow height and

LESSON 13 | NEW KEYS: z AND colon (:)

Objectives:

1. To learn reach technique for **z** and **:** (colon).

2. To combine smoothly **z** and **:** (colon) with all other learned keys.

13A • 7'
Conditioning Practice

Key each line twice SS; then key a 1' writing on line 3; determine *gwam.*

all letters learned 1 Jim won the globe for six quick sky dives in Napa.

spacing 2 to own|is busy|if they|to town|by them|to the city

easy 3 She is to go to the city with us to sign the form.

gwam 1' | 1 | 2 | 3 | 4 | 5 | 6 | 7 | 8 | 9 | 10 |

13B • 18'
New Keys: Z and :

Key each line twice SS (slowly, then faster); DS between 2-line groups; if time permits, key lines 7–10 again.

z *Left little* finger

: *Left shift* and strike *:* key

Follow the *Standard Plan for Learning New Keys* outlined on p. R6.

Learn z

1 a a za za zap zap zap zoo zoo zip zip zag zag zany

2 za za zap zap zed zed oz. oz. zoo zoo zip zip maze

3 zap it, zip it, an adz, to zap, the zoo, eight oz.

Learn : (colon)

4 ; ; :; :; Date: Time: Name: Room: From: File:

5 :; :; To: File: Reply to: Dear Al: Shift for :

6 Two spaces follow a colon, thus: Try these steps:

Combine z and :

7 Zelda has an old micro with : where ; ought to be.

8 Zoe, use as headings: To: Zone: Date: Subject:

9 Liza, please key these words: zap, maze, and zoo.

10 Zane read: Shift to enter : and then space twice.

Language Skills **C • U • E**

- Space twice after : used as punctuation.
- Capitalize the first word of a complete sentence following a colon.

15D • 10'
New Key: Tab

The TAB key is used to indent the first line of ¶s. Word processing software has preset tabs called *default* tabs. Usually, the first default tab is set 0.5" to the right of the left margin and is used to indent ¶s (see copy at right).

1. Locate the TAB key on your keyboard (usually at upper left of alphabetic keyboard).
2. Reach up to the TAB key with the left little finger; strike the key firmly and release it quickly. The insertion point will move 0.5" to the right.
3. Key each ¶ once SS. DS between ¶s. As you key, strike the TAB key firmly to indent the first line of each ¶.
4. If you complete all ¶s before time is called, rekey them to master TAB key technique.

Tab key *Left little* finger

Tab → The tab key is used to indent blocks of copy such as these.

Tab → It can also be used to arrange data quickly and neatly into columns.

Tab → Learn now to use the tab key by touch; doing so will add to your keying skill.

Tab → Strike the tab key firmly and release it very quickly. Begin the line without a pause.

Tab → If you hold the tab key down, the insertion point will move from tab to tab across the line.

15E • 15'
Keyboard Reinforcement

1. Key the lines once SS; DS between 3-line groups.
2. Key lines 1–9 again at a faster pace.
3. Key a 1' writing on lines 10–12.

Reach review (Keep on home keys the fingers not used for reaching.)

1 old led kit six jay oft zap cod big laws five ribs
2 pro quo|is just|my firm|was then|may grow|must try
3 Olga sews aqua and red silk to make six big kites.

Space Bar emphasis (*Think*, *say*, and *key* the words.)

4 en am an by ham fan buy jam pay may form span corn
5 I am|a man|an elm|by any|buy ham|can plan|try them
6 I am to form a plan to buy a firm in the old town.

Shift key emphasis (Reach *up* and reach *down* without moving the hands.)

7 Jan and I are to see Ms. Han. May Lana come, too?
8 Bob Epps lives in Rome; Vic Copa is in Rome, also.
9 Oates and Co. has a branch office in Boise, Idaho.

Easy sentences (*Think*, *say*, and *key* the words at a steady pace.)

10 Eight of the girls may go to the social with them.
11 Corla is to work with us to fix the big dock sign.
12 Keith is to pay the six men for the work they did.

gwam 1' | 1 | 2 | 3 | 4 | 5 | 6 | 7 | 8 | 9 | 10 |

13C • 15'
New-Key Mastery

1. Key the lines once SS; DS between 2-line groups.
2. Key the lines again at a faster pace.

Technique Goals:

- curved, upright fingers
- quiet hands and arms
- steady keystroking pace

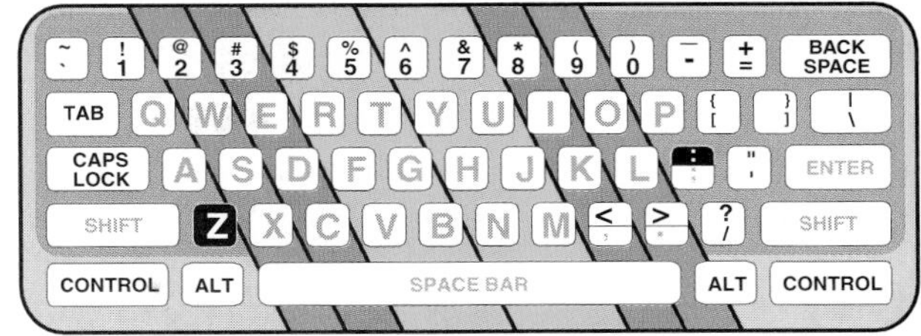

q/z
1 zoo qt. zap quo zeal quay zone quit maze quad hazy
2 Zeno amazed us all on the quiz but quit the squad.

p/x
3 apt six rip fix pens flex open flax drop next harp
4 Lex is apt to fix apple pie for the next six days.

v/m
5 vim mam van dim have move vamp more dive time five
6 Riva drove them to the mall in my vivid lemon van.

easy
7 Glen is to aid me with the work at the dog kennel.
8 Dodi is to go with the men to audit the six firms.

alphabet
9 Nigel saw a quick red fox jump over the lazy cubs.
10 Jacky can now give six big tips from the old quiz.

13D • 10'
Block Paragraphs

1. Key each paragraph (¶) once SS; DS between them; then key them again faster.
2. If your instructor directs, key a 1' writing on each ¶; determine your *gwam*.

Paragraph 1 — gwam 1'

The space bar is a vital tool, for every fifth or 10
sixth stroke is a space when you key. If you use 20
it with good form, it will aid you to build speed. 30

Paragraph 2

Just keep the thumb low over the space bar. Move 10
the thumb down and in quickly toward your palm to 20
get the prized stroke you need to build top skill. 30

gwam 1' | 1 | 2 | 3 | 4 | 5 | 6 | 7 | 8 | 9 | 10 |

13E •
Enrichment

1. Key each line once at a steady, easy pace to master reaches.
2. Key each line again at a faster pace.

Technique Goals:

- Keep fingers upright.
- Keep hands/arms steady.

x/:
1 xs :;|fix mix|Max: Use TO: and FROM: as headings.
2 Read and key: oxen, exit, axle, sixty, and sixth.

q/,
3 qa ,k|aqa k,k|quo quo,|qt. qt.,|quite quite,|squat
4 Quen, key these: quit, aqua, equal, quiet, quick.

p/z
5 p; za|;p; zaza|zap zap|zip zip|size size|lazy lazy
6 Zip put hot pepper on his pizza at the zany plaza.

m/v
7 mj vf|jmj fvf|vim vim|vow vow|menu menu move movie
8 Mavis vowed to move with a lot more vim and vigor.

LESSON 15 — NEW KEYS: tab key, apostrophe ('), hyphen (-), AND quotation mark (")

Objectives:

1. To learn reach technique for **'** (apostrophe), **-** (hyphen), and **"** (quotation mark).
2. To learn reach technique for the **tab key**.

15A • 7'
Conditioning Practice

Key each line twice SS; then take a 1' writing on line 3; determine *gwam*.

alphabet 1 Quig just fixed prize vases he won at my key club.

spacing 2 Marcia works for HMS, Inc.; Juanita, for XYZ Corp.

easy 3 Su did vow to rid the town of the giant male duck.

gwam 1' | 1 | 2 | 3 | 4 | 5 | 6 | 7 | 8 | 9 | 10 |

15B • 10'
New Keys: ', -, and "

Key each line twice SS (slowly, then faster); DS between 2-line groups.

Note:

On your screen, apostrophes and/or quotation marks may look different from those shown in these lines. Whatever their differences in appearance, the marks serve the same purpose.

Learn ' (apostrophe)

1 ;; '; '; ;' ;' I've told you it's hers, haven't I?

2 I'm sure it's Jay's. I'll return it if he's home.

3 I've been told it isn't up to us; it's up to them.

Learn - (hyphen)

4 ; - -; -; ;- ;- -; -; -;- -;- We use a 2-ply tire.

5 We have 1-, 2-, and 3-bedroom condos for purchase.

6 He rated each as a 1-star, 2-star, or 3-star film.

Learn " (quotation mark)

7 ;; "; "; ";" ";" "I believe," she said, "you won."

8 "John Adams," he said, "was the second President."

9 "James Monroe," I said, "was the fifth President."

15C • 8'
Speed Check: Sentences

1. Key a 30" writing on each line.
2. Key another 30" writing on each line. Try to increase your keying speed.

	gwam 30"
1 He bid for the rich lake land.	12
2 Suzy may fish off the dock with us.	14
3 Pay the girls for all the work they did.	16
4 Quen is due by six and may then fix the sign.	18
5 Janie is to vie with six girls for the city title.	20
6 Duane is to go to the lake to fix the auto for the man.	22

30" 2 | 4 | 6 | 8 | 10 | 12 | 14 | 16 | 18 | 20 | 22 |

Objectives:

1. To learn reach technique for **Caps Lock** and **?** (question mark).
2. To combine smoothly **Caps Lock** and **?** (question mark) with other learned keys.

14A • 7' Conditioning Practice

Key each line twice SS; then key a 1' writing on line 3; determine *gwam.*

alphabet 1 Lovak won the squad prize cup for sixty big jumps.

z/: 2 To: Ms. Mazie Pelzer; From: Dr. Eliza J. Piazzo.

easy 3 He is to go with me to the dock to do work for us.

gwam 1' | 1 | 2 | 3 | 4 | 5 | 6 | 7 | 8 | 9 | 10 |

14B • 16' New Keys: Caps Lock and ?

Key each line twice SS (slowly, then faster); DS between 2-line groups; if time permits, key lines 7–9 again.

Caps Lock
Left little finger

? (question mark)
Left shift; then *right little* finger

Depress the Caps Lock key to key a series of capital letters. To release the Caps Lock to key lowercase letters, press the Caps Lock key again.

Learn Caps Lock

1 Hal read PENTAGON and ADVISE AND CONSENT by Drury.

2 Oki joined FBLA when her sister joined PBL at OSU.

3 Zoe now belongs to AMS and DPE as well as to NBEA.

Learn ? (question mark)

Space twice.

4 ; ; ?; ?; Who? What? When? Where? Why? Is it?

5 Who is it? Is it she? Did he go? Was she there?

6 Is it up to me? When is it? Did he key the line?

Combine Caps Lock and ?

7 Did he join a CPA firm? I will stay on with NASA.

8 Is her dad still CEO at BSFA? Or was he made COB?

9 Did you read HOMEWARD? If so, try WHIRLWIND next.

10 Did Julie fly to Kansas City, MISSOURI, or KANSAS?

11 Did Dr. Sylvester pay her DPE, PBL, and NBEA dues?

12 Did you say go TWO blocks EAST or TWO blocks WEST?

14C • 18' New-Key Mastery

1. Key the lines once SS; DS between 2-line groups.
2. Key the lines again at a faster pace.
3. Key a 1' writing on line 11 and then on line 12; determine *gwam* on each writing.

Technique **C • U • E**

- Reach *up* without moving hands away from your body.
- Reach *down* without moving hands toward your body.
- Use Caps Lock to make ALL CAPS.

To determine 1' *gwam*: Add 10 for each line you completed to the scale figure beneath the point at which you stopped in a partial line.

Goal: finger-action keystrokes; quiet hands and arms

caps lock/?

1 Did she join OEA? Did she also join PSI and DECA?
2 Do you know the ARMA rules? Are they used by TVA?

z/v

3 Zahn, key these words: vim, zip, via, zoom, vote.
4 Veloz gave a zany party for Van and Roz in La Paz.

q/p

5 Paul put a quick quiz on top of the quaint podium.
6 Jacqi may pick a pink pique suit of a unique silk.

key words

7 they quiz pick code next just more bone wove flags
8 name jack flax plug quit zinc wore busy vine third

key phrases

9 to fix it|is to pay|to aid us|or to cut|apt to own
10 is on the|if we did|to be fit|to my pay|due at six

easy

11 Lock may join the squad if we have six big prizes.
12 I am apt to go to the lake dock to sign the forms.

gwam 1' | 1 | 2 | 3 | 4 | 5 | 6 | 7 | 8 | 9 | 10 |

14D • 9' Block Paragraphs

1. Key each ¶ once, using wordwrap (soft returns) if available. The lines you key will be longer than the lines shown if default side margins are used.
2. If time permits, key a 1' writing on one or two of the ¶s.

Note:

Clearing the screen from time to time between 1' writings avoids confusion when determining *gwam*. Learn how to clear the screen on your software.

Paragraph 1 gwam 1'

When you key lines of drills, strike the return or 10
enter key at the end of each line. That is, use a 20
hard return to space down for a new line. 29

Paragraph 2

When you key copy in this form, though, you do not 10
need to strike return at the end of each line if a 20
machine has wordwrap or a soft return feature. 30

Paragraph 3

But even if your machine returns at line ends for 10
you, you have to strike the return or enter key at 20
the end of a paragraph to leave a line blank. 30

Paragraph 4

Learn now when you do not need to return at ends 10
of lines and when you must do so. Doing this now 20
will assure that your copy will be in proper form. 30

gwam 1' | 1 | 2 | 3 | 4 | 5 | 6 | 7 | 8 | 9 | 10 |

Index